Modern Administration of Secondary Schools

ORGANIZATION AND ADMINISTRATION OF JUNIOR AND SENIOR HIGH SCHOOLS

SECOND EDITION

BY

HARL R. DOUGLASS, A.M., Ph.D., H.L.D.
College of Education, University of Colorado

BLAISDELL PUBLISHING COMPANY

A Division of Ginn and Company
NEW YORK · TORONTO · LONDON

Second Edition, 1963

Second Printing, 1964

Library of Congress Catalog Card Number: 63-8696

Dedication

To my wife, and to my son, Harl Gentry, and my daughter, Zanna Marian, whose lives have been a source of much pride and satisfaction to their parents, and to the memory of our Dorothy Ann.

Preface and Acknowledgments

This volume has been prepared principally for four types of use: (1) as a textbook for college and university classes in high-school administration; (2) for beginning principals and superintendents and those who are about to become administrators; (3) as a professional book for principals and superintendents in service who have not recently had a course in high-school administration; and (4) for the experienced principal who wants to check his knowledge and practices with a recent book for current changes and new and different practices in high-school administration.

The predecessors of this book have been very widely used in classes in high-school administration in hundreds of colleges and universities and have been widely used by thousands of principals and superintendents in service. It is hoped that this volume may be equally useful.

This book is more than a revision of the previous editions. It has been largely rewritten and contains subjects and topics not treated in earlier editions, such as federal subsidies, administration of six-year schools, new types of secondary-school buildings, team teaching, and small and large classes.

In the volume there is a chapter called "Assisting and Improving the Staff" and many other chapters (e.g., Chapter 4, "Staffing and School"; Chapter 5, "Arranging Staff Assignments"; Chapters 7 and 8, "Improving the Curriculum"; Chapter 9, "Problems Related to Student Learning"; and Chapter 18, "Student Accounting and Administration") have been written from the point of view of supervision as well as administration. These features, together with the many selected reading references dealing with supervision, make it practical for the book to be used as a textbook for a course on both administration and supervision of secondary schools.

In recent years the problems for and changes in high-school administration have been significant, particularly since adjustment has had to be made to such new ideas as utilization of teachers in team teaching, increased use of television and other audio-visual equipment and materials, and marked development in health and counseling services and community relationships.

In the selection and treatment of content the author has not been committed to any special school of thought; but, instead, an attempt has been made to follow the middle of the road, while pointing out current trends and the newer and more promising practices. As will be evident to those who examine the table of contents, coverage of the various topics is more comprehensive than that offered by previously published books in the field.

This volume has not been prepared with schools of any particular size especially in mind, but it perhaps applies best to schools with enrollments of from 200 to 500 students (although discussions are made of techniques for smaller and larger schools as well).

Much of the material in this book has come from the experiences of principals and superintendents who have been members of the writer's classes in high-school administration, particularly during summer school. Some of the material has been prepared from the writer's observations of schools he has visited; between 1940 and 1960 he has visited approximately 170 secondary schools in thirty-one states.

Much of the material has come from published articles and other writings. In the last eight to ten years very valuable data have been gathered from doctoral dissertations.

The author has made no attempt to write in a style indicating erudition. He has chosen to use simple language and a readable style, and to deal with practical situations in a practical way.

With a view to supplementing the materials in the text and to presenting at times a position somewhat dissimilar to that of the author, a large number of supplementary references for each chapter were carefully selected. Many of these references go into great detail about the application of various ideas to given secondary schools; enough references are provided so that the reader may be able to find at least one reference on the subject of his interest; also, a large number of references are given in order to provide the administrator in the field the opportunity to read widely on any particular topic. Listed among the references are important small publications (free or relatively inexpensive) which the principal in service may wish to send for. Also among the references are listed publications about Catholic high schools and Negro high schools.

The author is indebted to many individuals, particularly:

1. The administrators and others who are responsible for practices observed by the author or described by the administrators in the schools visited.

2. Students with administrative experience who have been in the author's graduate classes.

3. Publishers and authors of articles, books, and bulletins from which quotations have been taken, and to which acknowledgments have been made throughout this volume.

4. A number of college and university teachers, particularly those listed below, who gave criticisms or helpful suggestions:

William T. Gruhn, University of Connecticut; Edward H. LaFranchi, University of Southern California; James M. Moyer, Pennsylvania State College; Robert W. Strickler, University of Notre Dame; John Rufi, Professor of Secondary Education, University of Missouri, whose dedicated service to secondary education in general in Missouri and to his graduate students has been a source of much inspiration for many years; Harold Anderson, University of Colorado; Everett Samuelson, University of Colorado; Robert DeKieffer, University of Colorado; and Edwin H. Brown, Santa Clara University.

5. Nearly a hundred high-school principals and other officials, especially those listed below, who upon request furnished the author with data needed on various topics:

Homer S. Anderson, Ponca City, Oklahoma, High School; Herbert H. Bishop, Manhattan Senior High School, Manhattan, Kansas; I. M. Brock, Arthur Hill High School, Saginaw, Michigan; Lloyd M. Estes, Classen High School, Oklahoma City, Oklahoma; C. A. Fulmer, Wilmington, Delaware, High School; Clarence W. Johnson, Downers Grove, Illinois, Community High School; Delmas F. Miller, University High School, Morgantown, West Virginia; Ray W. Johnson, County Superintendent of Schools, Riverside, California; John J. Houghton, Ferndale, Michigan, High School; Robert G. Campbell, Edward M. Cope Junior High School, Redlands, California; Geroge W. Janke, Mitchell, South Dakota, High School; Bill Medley, Winfield, Kansas, High School; Thomas N. Keating, Hasting, Nebraska, Senior High School; Calvin E. Gross, Superintendent, Pittsburgh Public Schools; Kenneth L. Pederson, Hibbing, Minnesota, High School; Donald G. Emery, Superintendent, Shaker Heights City School District, Cleveland, Ohio; Davis W. Beggs, III, Lakeview High School, Decatur, Illinois; William H. Reed, and Christian Recht, Boulder, Colorado, Senior High School; G. H. Schoenhard, West Elementary Junior High School, and Robert L. Flemming, South High School, Youngstown, Ohio; Jerry Cantlon, Harl Douglass Junior High School, Boulder, Colorado; Glen Burnette, Supervisor, Topeka, Kansas; M. E. Herriott, Airport Junior High School, Los Angeles, California; Gene Gullette, Assistant Superintendent of Boulder, Colorado, Public Schools; John M. Houglund, Principal, Marion, Indiana, High School; Charles Welk, School Plant Consultant, Wayne County, Michigan; Harold Richards, Superintendent of Blue Island, Illinois, Community Secondary Schools; Carl L. Marburger, Director of Great Cities Program for School Improvement, Detroit, Michigan; Kenneth Lund, Superintendent of Oak Park, Illinois, Community High School; Nicholas Schreiber, Ann Arbor, Michigan, Senior High School; Charles Wells, Wayne County, Michigan, Board of Education; Roy Hinderman, Deputy Superintendent, Denver, Colorado, Public Schools; Ellsworth

Tompkins, Executive Secretary of the National Association of Secondary School Principals.

6. The following, who sent me copies of their doctoral dissertations or résumés of their findings:

Superintendent Oral L. Ballam, Logan, Utah, Public Schools; Charles W. Rutledge, Administrative Assistant, Cassopolis, Michigan, Public Schools; Robert L. Fleming, Principal, South High School, Youngstown, Ohio; Walter G. Hack, Assistant Professor of Education, Ohio State University; Harold C. Tonini, Terra Nova High School, Daly City, California; John C. Menozzi, Aurora, Colorado, Public Schools; Richard Whitmire Jarrett, Principal, John Burroughs Junior High School, Los Angeles, California; Professor Gerald Reece, University of Arizona.

7. Officials of the state departments of education, including especially H. Edgar Williams, Director of Guidance Services, and Charles L. Bostrom, Head of Title III Section of the National Defense Act, State of Colorado; J. C. Woodin, Executive Director, Kansas State Board of Vocational Education.

8. Edmund A. Ford, Sam Lambert, and Leah Ramsey, officials of the U. S. Office of Education, Research Division of the National Education Association, and Ellsworth Tompkins of the National Association of Secondary School Principals, who were so generous in sending promptly materials of various kinds upon request.

Contents

1

Human Relationships and Basic Principles

School administration and supervision is principally a matter of human relationships and group dynamics. Slowly, but definitely and certainly, principles and practices of human relationships have been changing, particularly in recent decades. Consequently, principles and practices of administration and supervision have been undergoing appropriate changes.

1. Basic Principles and Policies

It has been true in all societies that the school system and its organization and objectives have been somewhat in harmony with the nature and character of the society of which the school is a part. In totalitarian societies, such as existed in Germany, Japan, Italy, and Russia before World War II (and since that time in Russia, China, and their Communist satellites), the schools were authoritarian in nature; their curriculum and methods of teaching were chosen on the basis of their contribution to preparing young people to believe in, to be loyal to, and to participate in the achievement of the objectives of those particular societies. While, in general, this has been true in democratic societies, there have been discrepancies and the relationship has not been exceedingly close. Change in the practice in schools has lagged behind the shifts in practice and conditions in society. For example, in the United States authoritarian methods continued in the face of increasingly democratic institutions in other areas of society.

Changes in the fundamental principles and practices in several social institutions or areas of social activities are likely to result in somewhat similar changes in other social institutions and areas of social activities. It is difficult to determine whether shifts in one institution or area are the cause of shifts in other institutions or areas, or whether all the successive shifts and changes in different institutions and areas are the result of change in the basic philosophy of a people.

THE AUTHORITARIAN TRADITION. From the beginnings of modern civilization it has been characteristic of all societies that some individuals have authority over others. In some instances this authority has been accorded by common consent or by the consent of the majority of the more influential people composing the society or a given unit of the society. In some instances authority was established and maintained by the physical force of the individual leader (or leaders) and by those who cooperated with him (or them) by reason of fear, hope of gain in prestige or status, or belief in the necessity of authority. It is clear that most of the advances in social organization have been made possible only by a division of labor or responsibilities and by the selection of leaders for command and direction, as well as for the determining of policies and the deciding of disputes and other matters in which individuals composing the society might not be agreed. It has been only natural that individuals possessing authority should rationalize their possession and extension of authority; it is characteristic of human beings to rationalize about doing things which they wish to do and about situations which bring them pleasure and gratification of their desires.

AUTHORITARIANISM IN GOVERNMENT. Authority has in many ways been bolstered in the minds of men by means of attaching religion to temporal authority. Indeed, in a great many countries until recently, the belief was encouraged among the people that their rulers were chosen by divine beings and that they ruled by divine right. Under some of the Roman emperors, particularly Nero, and the Japanese emperors under the Shinto religion, people were encouraged to believe that the principal ruler was himself a god.

In totalitarian regimes there has been a carefully conducted educational campaign to cause the people to have a respect and adoration for their principal ruler amounting to little less than that accorded a divine authority. In practically all societies those in positions of authoritarian leadership have dressed themselves and appeared upon a stage so set as to give artificial strength to their position and their claims for power. They have used many devices, including special robes and crowns, scepters, resplendent chambers, palaces, and highly adorned thrones. Appropriate music to excite reverence and respect has been employed, as has the use of fire. In a great many societies the religious and civil authorities have co-operated in agreeing upon the relative areas of power and in propagandizing the people or subjecting them to the rule of authority by means of tricks and force.

AUTHORITARIANISM IN THE HOME. It is only natural that the type of social organization which supports the purposes of government and religion should also support other social institutions. For example, in very ancient times the individual of greatest physical strength naturally became the leader in the home. In most early societies the oldest male was the authority within the home; within the framework of the rules of the society, his word was law and there was no appealing from his decision. There were few personal and property rights possessed by other members of the home which the patriarchal authority had to respect.

This sort of authority has persisted almost to the present generation in American society. There are many people living today whose memory goes back to the time when the word of the father was law. In family councils there was no participation by the children and little by the wife and mother. The father sat at the head of the table; food was prepared for him and placed on the table in front of him—a rather ostentatious display of his superior position, which was further strengthened by his disposal of the food to members of the family as he saw fit. It was not until the twentieth century that women were permitted to vote; even today youth below the age of twenty-one (except in the states of Alaska, Georgia, Hawaii, and Kentucky) are not permitted to vote, although it seems very likely that the average youngster of eighteen to twenty-one today is far better informed and more intelligently trained for passing on the issues of the day than is the average individual beyond the age of twenty-one, if for no other reason than better schooling.

In religious institutions the same sort of situation has been observable. Men have monopolized the principal places of leadership and authority in the church. Ministers and priests have usually been men. The governing bodies of local churches and the hierarchy of authority in state, regional, and national churches have been confined almost completely to men. The ceremonies and worship in the church have been led by men. Although it has been somewhat modified as time has gone on, the Christian church of the earlier centuries and Middle Ages was founded very largely upon authoritarian principles.

Authoritarianism in Business. The management of business was long regarded as a matter for private control by the owner, owners, or their representatives. The owner made all the decisions. He hired and fired his help. There was little or no thought of participation in management by any but the owner or owners, except as occasionally they found it necessary to delegate authority to lower echelons because it was impossible for them to exercise all their authority. With the development and expansion of big business organizations, the delegation of power was extended; a hierarchy of authority became quite common. In these situations authority flowed from the top down to lower levels of executives and was revokable by those in the upper levels.

Authoritarianism in School Administration. It was only natural that school organization and human relationships in the school should be based upon the principles obtaining in other areas of group endeavor, such as business, government, church, and home. The teachers were invested with great authority, even being allowed to inflict corporal punishment, to say nothing of very damaging mental and emotional punishment, upon the young people entrusted to their care. As school systems became larger and it became necessary to have administrative heads for co-ordinating and advising the boards of education as to the employment, supervision, and discharge of teachers, there developed an authoritarian situation in which the superintendent of schools and the principal of the high school under him developed considerable authority.

Throughout the nineteenth century there was a steady growth in delegating powers of administration from boards of education to duly constituted authoritarian heads of schools and school systems. Probably because of the fact that the authoritarian heads of schools were new and not entirely understood or accepted by the people, the situation was conducive to the exercise of considerable power by administrators in such a way as to demonstrate the necessity for the existence of designated and well-paid leaders. The exercise of authority seemed to be desirable for the purpose of demonstrating to all concerned, including pupils, teachers, boards of education, and the public, that the individuals occupying the positions of authority were competent to exercise it. The exercise of authority also served to discourage any challenge on the part of pupils and teachers.

Following the example of big and expanded business, school administration tended to become a matter of centralized authority delegated to lower echelons. The outstanding teachers and writers on school administration in the first quarter of the twentieth century agreed upon the concept of the flow of authority from the top down; diagrams of this flow were found quite commonly in the books on school administration and administrative practice in the city school systems was in accord with the concept.

Out of the then evident necessity of giving directions to poorly trained teachers and of investing them with authority over the pupils, there were developed beliefs in principles of human relations that justified authoritarian school situations. It was believed, for example, that the most effective appeals to the students to participate in appropriate learning activities and to teachers to co-operate were made through fear and through artificial rewards. Therefore, nationally there developed a power of the executives to employ and discharge teachers almost at will, to determine the rates of pay, to inspect and rate teachers, and in other ways to exercise authority which would be respected by reason of fear or hope of reward.

Similarly, with respect to relationships between teachers and students, there developed in the school, as in the home, beliefs favorable to the authoritarian situation. Obedience was regarded as a definite virtue and as excellent mental and character training. There developed the fundamental doctrine of formal discipline as applied to human relations. Many of the practices of supervising teachers and the methods of teaching, motivating, measuring, and reporting youngsters grew out of this authoritarian concept, which has in the last half century been receding before the development of a new and democratic concept. That the shift from authoritarian to democratic concepts and practices should be slow is entirely to be expected. The pleasure that comes with enjoyment of power over other individuals naturally has caused those invested with power not only to oppose sharing it with other individuals but also to develop sincere and strong beliefs in the soundness of the authoritarian system.

2. Democratic and Co-operative Principles

NEW CONCEPTS AND PRACTICES IN HUMAN RELATIONS. It has been clearly observable that in all but totalitarian and very backward societies there has been a shift in the fundamental principles and practices of human relations which reflects less authoritarian and more democratic thinking. It is observable in almost all areas of group human relations and social activities; it has taken somewhat similar forms in various areas of group endeavor and group relations.

For example, the powers and authority of the father or the parents in the home have been gradually curtailed both by law and by common practice. The rights of children, wives, and mothers have been increasingly recognized, and the respect for all personalities in the home has increased. Not only personal lives but property rights of individuals other than the paternal authority have been recognized and protected by law as well as by popular opinion. In the field of government a similar transition has been going on for centuries. Unlimited monarchies have become in the great majority of societies a thing of the past. The efforts of highly civilized nations to support relatively totalitarian and highly authoritarian rule in "backward" countries, employing local authorities as agents for commercial exploitation, have sustained material losses. The support of nondemocratic regimes by the United States may be regarded as a temporary emergency measure designed to halt the growth and spread of Communist totalitarianism and to fill the vacuum left by the recession of Spain, Great Britain, France, Germany, and the Netherlands. As a long-term policy it is certain to be abandoned, as it cannot hope to be permanently sustained in a world of increased enlightenment, literacy, and demand for respect for the personality and lives of all individuals.

The trend away from authoritarianism has also been very noticeable in business and industry. It has been accelerated by the widespread increase of the power of labor unions, but it has also been stimulated by studies of efficiency and productivity of workmen under conditions in which the individual workman, either personally or through his representatives, participates in management and policy formulation. Studies have revealed that a worker's production is increased materially by a better understanding of the whole project of production of which he is a part and by a feeling of belonging and of security which grows out of the development of co-operation.

New Concepts and Practices in the Schools. Opportunities for the success of democratic participation and administration were definitely more limited in the days when the typical teacher was little more than a high-school graduate with a few years' teaching experience, an immature individual with very little experience in life other than as a student in school. With increased maturity, education, and experience on the part of teachers, there must be a concomitant increase in their participation in responsibility and leadership and in their growth in competence in such matters. It cannot be argued that any but a low order of participation must be postponed until teachers are obviously fully ready for participation. Growth and ability to participate effectively are a matter not only of general experience and professional study but also of experience in participation. Because of the great differences in the backgrounds of teachers, the degree of their participation must vary materially; it follows naturally that ability to participate effectively in planning and in decisions relative to administration grows out of and must be correlated with experience in such matters. Ability and experience develop concomitantly.

A good example of the fallacy of revolutionary change may be seen in the field of student government. In the early years of student government and student councils, attempts were made in many schools to transform an authoritarian situation to a somewhat democratic one overnight. Boys and girls who had spent their student life in authoritarian situations, who had little or no experience in participation in planning and management, were given the opportunity for almost complete planning, control, and management. The result was either manipulation of student government by the faculty, with the students as puppets, or a rather complete breakdown of student government by reason of the lack of experience of the youngsters in such matters.

It must also be observed that participation in planning and leadership is conditioned by the amount of time that the individuals concerned have to carry on responsibilities of leadership. This principle has been increasingly recognized in some areas. Superintendents, for example, were first relieved of much teaching, in some areas of all teaching, and indeed they were even relieved of a great deal of responsibility for supervision and other areas of leadership. Likewise, principals in larger high schools have found it impossible to perform all their duties effectively; consequently they have through the years devoted a decreasing amount of time to teaching and have also appointed assistants for some of the areas of leadership which they have no longer been able to discharge effectively.

Relations of the Staff. The trend toward democracy in staff relationships is observed in the increased tendency to employ a democratic group approach to the solving of various types of problems related to policies and procedures of administration. In an increasing number of schools, committees have been appointed for the study of problems and the recommendation of principles and procedures in administration; they have also drawn up recommendations to be passed upon by the entire high-school staff or by the administration of the school. Indeed in many schools several committees have been appointed which have administrative or management responsibilities. Good relations between the administrative and supervisory staff on the one hand and the teaching staff on the other require the efforts of both groups. Each group, while friendly and not too formal, regards and deals with the other group with respect and accordance of dignity, with an attitude of helpfulness, with honesty and reliability. The administrative and supervisory staff cultivates the habits and practices of encouragement. Many principals have developed the habit of sending brief notes of commendation to any member of the staff who has been doing something a little better than previously or doing it unusually well, or to one who has been carrying on experimentation.

DEMOCRATIC RELATIONS WITH STUDENTS. There is also observable a trend toward democratic interpersonal relationships between teachers and students. Learners are more and more encouraged and trained in planning their own learning activities, both as individuals and as groups. It is observable in an increasing number of schools that the teachers are employing methods of motivation which are more of the democratic type and less of an authoritarian nature. There is observable an increased amount of co-operation and a respect for the personality of the learner as well as for that of the teacher.

There is indeed also observable an increased tendency toward student participation in the management of the affairs of the school, particularly of those affairs which are of greater concern to the students: for example, their clubs and other extracurricular activities. As an outgrowth both of common sense based upon experience and of the democratic concept of school administration, pupils have been admitted to participation in administration and have been utilized to a greater degree in policy-making and, in an advisory capacity, in curriculum construction and the study of methods of instruction and guidance. The participation of students in government and management will be discussed in a later chapter.

Illustrative of student participation in administration is the use of students on committees on report cards, exhibits, guidance of new students, publications, discipline, commencement, and interscholastic relations. Two forms of student participation are frequently found: (1) the joint committee of students and faculty and (2) co-operating but separate student and faculty committees. Each has its advantages and disadvantages. When the single student-faculty committee is used, students are not so likely to be natural and express themselves fully because teachers tend to out-talk them. When separate committees co-operate, differences in points of view tend more to become matters of clannishness and competition. Care should be employed to avoid the dangers peculiar to whichever plan is used. Teachers should, in any instance, lean over backward in their efforts to give the students opportunity for leadership and should permit mistakes to be made rather frequently in matters not of vital concern.

DEMOCRATIC RELATIONS WITH PARENTS. There is also observable development and utilization of co-operative organizations and activities involving the school personnel and people in the community. These will be discussed in later chapters in this book. Principal types of such co-operative organization are the P.T.A., home-room parents' groups or core-block parents' groups, local advisory citizens' committees, and special parent-student-teacher committees to consider the particular problems of the schools as they arise. Such co-operation in administration was rarely used and was of limited application prior to the past two or three decades.

There have been such persistent and definite trends towards democratic and co-operative policies and practices that today the planning of all aspects of public education, and to a large extent all nonpublic education, is a partnership: (1) between the school and *society* as a whole, for which the school is educating; (2) between the school and members of the *staff,* whose understanding and co-operation are necessary not only in the development of plans and the choice of new practices but also in the important matter of putting them into effect; (3) between the school staff and the *students*, who have such a great stake in the educational program and procedures and with whom administrators and teachers must co-operate in developing desired learning; and (4) between the school and the local *community*, which contributes a large part of the support of public education as well as the boys and girls in whose education it is tremendously interested.

Laymen participate usually as members of an advisory committee and not too much time is required of any individual. Illustrative examples of their participation in some schools are as follows:

1. An advisory committee of representative citizens to make recommendations with respect to the curriculum and course of study. Often this advisory committee is divided into subcommittees for various fields such as vocational education, citizenship education, and homemaking education.
2. A joint committee of parents, students, and teachers to recommend principles and practices governing the management of student life in out-of-school hours. In some schools this committee would consider such problems as those relating to the use of cars, public or other dances, spending money, smoking, dress, and the like.
3. Joint committees of parents and teachers (and sometimes students) to concern themselves with such school problems as the amount of homework, school discipline, hazing, expenditures for extracurricular activities, opening and closing hours of the school day, and opening and closing days of the school year.

The advantages of the participation of carefully selected representatives of the community are considerable. Not only are the experience and judgment of these people made available to the school staff but also these people become much better informed concerning the philosophy, objectives, problems, and points of view of the administration and teachers. The use of laymen in these matters often leads to increased support for the school program and for improvements in the school. It affords an opportunity to bring to the attention of the staff objections of parents or others to practices in the school; it affords the school an opportunity to remedy or explain the situation before too much opposition or loss of confidence is engendered. In addition, the participation of laymen often leads to better parent education and the improvement of parent management of youngsters in out-of-school hours.

Whenever lay participation is encouraged or employed, care should be taken to select appropriate lay persons or to have the organizations appoint appropriate people, avoiding individuals of more energy than judgment and people with axes to grind. Care should be taken to have representatives of different classes of people and to obtain rotation of individuals in this service.

Basic Principles of Democratic Administration. The fundamental principles of democratic administration may be summed up as follows:

1. Democratic administration accords to a group and the individuals composing it the responsibilities for participation in the making of decisions that affect undertakings of the group and the activities and the interests of the individuals composing the group. This does not necessarily mean that each person exercises administrative responsibilities; rather, the administration provides the situation and procedure by which the individuals of various sorts of groups in the schools may co-operate in planning.
2. Democratic administration attempts to locate leadership and encourage its exercise by each person in accordance with his abilities, capacities, background, experience, interests, and needs.
3. Democratic administration provides for such flexibility of organization that adjustments may be made from time to time in the matter of human relationships, as the occasion and developments may seem to indicate.
4. Democratic administration recognizes the urge to creative activity among human beings and allows for its expression in planning and carrying out education programs and procedures.

Practices in Democratic School Administration. There are several types of plans employing democracy in the administration of secondary schools.

In New Rochelle, New York, there is a city-wide Teachers' Educational Council made up of elected representatives of teachers from elementary and high schools and one representative of the administrative and supervisory staff. The council functions as an advisory rather than as a recommending body. There is full and free discussion of problems which are to come before the superintendent and the board; every point of view has a fair hearing, but no attempt is made to make recommendations by majority vote. One year the council was principally concerned with the school calendar, the school budget, and the teachers' exchange plan, a practice of making temporary reassignments of teachers for one year only which was initiated with the general support of the council. Two all-city advisory councils of students, one representing elementary-school and the other high-school students, meet with the superintendent of schools once a month. Among matters which the councils have discussed are traffic problems in the city and around the school buildings, plans for improving the lunchrooms, improvement of the school grounds, and the qualities of an ideal teacher. Each member of the council reports back to the principal of his school and to the student council or the student body as a whole.

At Shaker Heights, Ohio, the superintendent has an advisory staff council composed of nine elected representatives chosen for two-year overlapping terms: one representative each for six levels of school from kindergarten through high school, one from the administrative personnel of several schools, one from the women's division of the nonteaching personnel, and a representative of the Shaker Heights Teachers' Association. The superintendent is chairman of the council. The council may make recommendations to the superintendent on such problems as he shall from time to time bring before it. During its existence the council has considered many subjects, particularly curriculum problems, teacher personnel, state retirement funds, budgetary problems, pupil personnel, powers of the council, publicity, the school calendar, the publication of handbooks, booklets for parents, a professional library, organization of visual-education work, and the instruction of new teachers. Of these, some have required no decision, the forum method being sufficient to clarify or to justify some policy then in effect; some have involved policy recommendations to the board; and some have involved final determinations of policy with regard to matters within the control of the staff. An enterprise growing out of the work of the council was a long-term project for rebuilding the curriculum of the entire school system. It enlisted the co-operation not only of school administrators and teachers but also of large numbers of students, parents, and other citizens.[1]

At Oak Park, Illinois, the following items are indicative of the activities of rather full participation by teachers' councils:

1. Reorganizing and building the courses of the curriculum through the work of co-operating curriculum committees.
2. Selecting textbooks.
3. Working out correlated activities between fields of instruction.
4. Assisting in the formulation of rules and regulations.

---

[1]From a letter by Superintendent Donald G. Emery.

5. Assisting in the study of salary schedules.
6. Co-operating in the development of programs of in-service training.
7. Directing activities designed to promote the welfare of the teaching staff.
8. Working toward the establishment of professional standards for teachers who are in service, at all levels of instruction.
9. The establishment and maintenance of professional morale.
10. The development and maintenance of relationships between school and home.[2]

In Denver, Colorado, there are all-city committees co-operating with the central office of administrators and supervisors as well as the administrative director and director of instruction, who work with the principal of each building and his teachers. There are two broad categories of committee work: that of the employees' council, which produces recommendations on such personal matters as salary schedules; and that of the instruction committees, which produce analyses and recommendations on content, methods, and materials of instruction. There are both building committees and all-city committees.

The all-city instruction committees, composed of school principals; co-ordinators, and teacher representatives selected by the school, meet four times a year. The building instruction committees, meeting with the co-ordinator from time to time, will discuss and formulate recommendations on such matters as scheduling of classes, procuring of instructional materials, and implementing of programs in in-service training activities and other means of improving instruction. Usually it is the building instruction committee that plans with the principal and co-ordinator the annual conference on instruction, which takes place in each building with the administrative director and deputy superintendent in charge of instructional services.[3]

In recent years the trend in Denver and Shaker Heights has been toward diverting the teachers' councils somewhat away from participation in administrative decisions and toward work on the educational program.

Organized on the principles of democratic planning is the administration of the Downers Grove, Illinois, Community High School. The organization involves co-operative endeavor on the part of the school board, administration, parents, teachers, and students. The general policies and regulations of the school are set up by the board members and the superintendent with help from an advisory committee selected by the faculty and a citizens' committee representing many areas of the community.

Seeing that these regulations and policies are administered effectively is the responsibility of the high-school administrative staff, which includes the principal, an assistant principal in charge of girls, an assistant principal in charge of instruc-

[2]From a letter by Superintendent Kenneth Lund.

[3]From a letter by Dr. Roy Hinderman, Deputy Superintendent of Schools.

tion, a dean of boys, and a director of guidance. The faculty advisory committee and department heads also work closely with this group.

To ensure a continuous evaluation of the curriculum and teaching methods, department heads meet regularly with representatives from the superintendent's office and the high-school administrative staff. This group and a research person from the guidance department serve as the curriculum council. The council reviews suggested curriculum changes and assists in formulating procedures for carrying out research projects. Many of these research studies and special projects originate within a department under the leadership of the department head. Other changes are suggested by the administration, the curriculum co-ordinator, or the student body working through counselors and the school council. At meetings scheduled periodically by the board of education, the public has an opportunity to participate in discussions of curriculum problems with members of each department. The broad membership of the curriculum council provides an effective means of communication between the administration, department heads, and teachers.

Problems of guidance are handled by a full-time director of guidance and a staff of counselors who have adequate released time for counseling individual students. Each counselor's student load is less than 250 students. To keep the guidance department informed on all aspects of the school program, class-room teachers, department heads, and school-council representatives meet frequently with the guidance department in workshops to discuss and study problems of mutual concern. Individual teacher-counselor consultations are an integral part of the guidance program.

The school council, which is made up of representatives from each home room of approximately 30 students, meets weekly to consider recommendations and questions proposed in home rooms. The council works through student committees that contact the administration and the teachers whenever they have issues that require the counsel of these persons. The school-council president meets regularly with the principal to review major problems that originate in the council meetings and to consider matters that the principal may desire the council to study. Because of its close contact with all areas of school life, the council is an important body in building and maintaining good school spirit.

There has been democratic administration under this type of organization because all concerned with the educational program are important members of the team that gives leadership in the development of the educational experiences the community desires for its youth.[4]

In the Downers Grove Community High School, democratic procedures have developed which accord responsibility not only to teachers but also to parents and to students.

3. Fundamental Principles of Organization and Administration

There are principles of organization and administration which may not be set down with complete exactness and finality but seem to be logical, which have been justified in business and personnel administration, and

[4]*A Handbook of Information,* Downers Grove Community High School (Clarence W. Johnson, Principal), Downers Grove, Illinois.

which should be kept in mind as good general rules to guide in the organization of school administration and supervision. Among these are certain clear-cut principles:

1. Priority of objectives over machinery and personal considerations.
2. Co-ordination of authority and responsibility.
3. Adaptation of responsibility to personnel.
4. Recognition of the human psychological factors.
5. Relativity of values.

PRIORITY OF OBJECTIVES OVER MACHINERY AND PERSONAL CONSIDERATIONS. There has always been a general tendency for human beings to concentrate on immediate tasks and concerns and, consequently, to lose sight of the ultimate objectives and functions of an organization or institution. Bernard Shaw many years ago defined a fanatic as "one who, having lost sight of his objectives, redoubles his efforts." Such a tendency has been observable in educational activities. Subject-matter teachers have more and more tended to consider the details of subject matter as an end in themselves rather than as the means of accomplishing pupil growth. Likewise, supervisors and administrators have become engrossed in the details of administration and have tended to lose sight of the purposes for which the administration and procedures were developed. It should be clear and always kept in mind that organization and administrative power were developed in order to achieve educational objectives; they must be so set up, operated, and changed from time to time as to make a major contribution to the educational objectives.

It is likewise true that the general character of organization and administration should be in harmony with the nature of the prevailing educational philosophy of the school. For example, if the school is dedicated to the philosophy of the all-round development of high-school youngsters, possible plans of organization and administration should be considered on the basis of which plans are most likely to be in conformity with that particular philosophy. It is difficult to maintain an authoritarian administration and at the same time urge teachers to develop democratic relationships and procedures in the classroom.

A basic principle for the formulation of procedure in any activity of life is that *objectives determine organization and procedure*. The employment of techniques whose relation to objectives is not clear or not considered is the makeshift of the novice and the practice of the incompetent. Imitation, which of course is the source of much improvement, should be guided by a consideration of objectives. Observance of the principle of objectives distinguishes blind from intelligent imitation.

CO-ORDINATION OF AUTHORITY AND RESPONSIBILITY. To the person upon whom responsibility for certain types of results is placed must be given authority and opportunity commensurate with the responsibility. This principle has been quite generally observed in successful business and industrial personnel management.

An application of the principle may be seen in the relationship of the principal to his department heads. If the department head in a given school is to be held responsible for improving the quality of instruction in his department, he should have opportunities and working conditions appropriate to the degree of his responsibility. He should be supported by the principal and superintendent in maintaining his prestige. The central office should stand ready to make unprofitable insubordination by teachers or even their passive failure to respond to the leadership of the competent department head. He should have favorable opportunity to hold a reasonable number of meetings of those giving instruction in his department. If he is competent to utilize them, *he should be given such opportunities and powers as will enable him to discharge his responsibilities to the complete satisfaction of his superior and with credit to himself.*

ADAPTATION OF RESPONSIBILITY TO THE CHARACTER OF THE PERSONNEL. It is impractical for this book to try to lay down an exact formulation of just what duties and responsibilities should be allotted to the various participants in high-school administration and supervision. Variations in size of school and amount of time free from teaching duties are factors which must be considered. *Moreover, the place of any individual in the scheme of organization for administration and supervision must be determined in part by his individual natural talents, training, and experience.* This principle has two aspects. One relates to the degree of the individual's fitness for responsibility. The other has to do with his peculiar types of talent, which should be utilized to full advantage.

Let us consider the first aspect. School boards and superintendents often promote to positions involving administrative and supervisory responsibility men and women of widely varying degrees of capacity for discharging such responsibility. The principal who has as department heads in his school individuals who have arrived at their positions by unprofessional influence or by the mechanical operation of seniority is quite likely to have department heads who are untrained in modern methods of teaching, course-of-study making, and measurement—men and women with outworn or otherwise inadequate concepts of education and its objectives. The dependence which may be safely placed on such assistants is not that which would be rightly placed on properly trained department heads. In the allotment of responsibility to the high-school principal by the superintendent, this principle must be recognized. Members of the staff who are not qualified should not be urged to become teachers of core programs or to do technical counseling.

It should be borne in mind that this principle is one governing exceptions to general practice and, for this reason, should be used with some caution.

The second phase of the principle applies to teachers or administrative assistants who possess peculiar training or natural talents for the organization and direction of some particular student activities, for educational and vocational counseling, for work with accounting problems, or for some other such specialized work. A supervisor should abandon uniformity, if necessary, to produce the most effective utilization of the special points of strength of the individual teacher.

A corollary to this principle is the principle of *continuance of participation*. Responsibility should go with probable ability to discharge responsibility, and responsibility should continue only so long as it is properly discharged.

This principle should govern the continuance of delegation of privilege, authority, or responsibility to principal or other officer, to teacher, and to pupil, even if discharge of the teacher or expulsion of the pupil is called for in extreme cases.

RECOGNITION OF PSYCHOLOGICAL FACTORS. There is a type of administrator, extremely objective and literal, who is inclined to ignore very important psychological factors and falls, therefore, into serious blunders. In all dealings with individuals where co-operation is necessary or desirable, the wishes, desires, prejudices, ambitions, and tastes of all co-workers must be taken into account. Especially is this true of situations in which the success of the plan or policy depends upon wholehearted and energetic co-operation on the part of co-workers or subordinates. In formulating an administrative policy or procedure, not only must its direct effects be considered but also its effect upon the attitudes of those concerned in its execution.

A superintendent of schools in an Indiana city of about 35,000 population persuaded his board of education to require all members of his high-school staff who had not gone to summer school for a period of three years to do so during the following summer. The end desired by the superintendent was excellent. These teachers were much in need of recent and additional professional training. The end actually achieved was not entirely to be desired. The good resulting from the measure was largely offset by the antagonistic spirit aroused in the teachers and their friends as a result of the abruptness of the demands of the board. An alternative procedure would have been to condition increase in salary above a stated level upon summer-school attendance; better still, special bonuses might have been given to those attending. A significant difference lies between the psychological effect of what seems to the teachers to be a threat or a demand and the effect of a possible reward.

The fact that the adoption of merit increases in salaries has been very effective in some schools and disastrous in others is attributable in great part to the ignoring of psychological factors in the latter group of schools. In those schools where teachers have given careful consideration to merit increases and the criteria of selecting those to whom merit increases will be given and where teachers are favorable to the idea, the plan has been very successful. Where the plan has been imposed upon teachers who are opposed to it, the plan has been definitely unsuccessful and dangerous to teacher morale.

It is desirable to encourage teachers to plan their work carefully as to objectives, content, and procedure; yet the requiring of a detailed written plan is often the cause of resentment that becomes a general unfavorable attitude toward the principal or superintendent.

When all members of the staff concerned in administration are admitted to participation in the formulation of policies and procedures, the attitude of teachers toward administrative plans and devices may be favorably predisposed in a great many instances. Teachers are much more likely to understand the reasons and theory back of administrative measures if they have had a share in determining them. The feeling that the procedures are, to some extent, of their own choice and formulation operates to give them a general concern for the success of the procedures; such a concern can hardly be expected when the plans are handed down by authority of their professional superiors. Not only is their attitude toward administration favorably affected by their participation but also the activities of participation constitute training which is of itself valuable.

The desire for expression of self is universal and strong in human beings of high intelligence and must be reckoned with in affairs of human relations. This principle should be kept in mind when considering the introduction of innovations, changes in routine, or the abolition of traditions and practices of long standing. What has been said above in respect to teachers also applies to the attitude of pupils and patrons toward the details of school administration. Changing the time of a lunch hour without consulting representative patrons or giving parents opportunity to protest may likewise cause undesirable reactions. What was originally a courtesy or gesture for psychological effect often comes to be regarded as a vested right. For this reason, care should be taken in extending participation in any instance where eventual withdrawal of the privilege may become necessary.

It is true, however, that the greater the leader the greater the extent to which he may stimulate, guide, and employ participation to advantage. It is also true that the fruits of participation are not always what might have been desired. Participation may lead to undesirable conclusions, to controversy and disagreement, making the lot of the leader difficult. The extent to which these things may be avoided depends largely upon the skill and wisdom of the leader. In general, however, a policy of participation directed with a reasonable degree of ability is likely to produce results quite superior to those typical of a completely autocratic policy.

RELATIVITY OF VALUES. It is likely that the reader, ere now, has made the observation that quite often a situation will arise in which two principles may seem to apply and to be in conflict. It would be unatural and unlike most situations in life calling for decisions if this were not so. Frequently occasions will arise when it will be desirable to abandon, apparently, the principle of co-ordination of authority and responsibility in order that the principle of psychological factors may be observed, or vice versa.

Occasionally, *not often*, a principal may have to step in and assume responsibility ordinarily belonging to a department head, teacher, or student officer in order to prevent things from "going to pot." Unfortunately, many principals constantly overestimate the necessity for such interference. At rare intervals, a principal may have to issue orders or instructions about matters which, under ordinary conditions, might have been better left to co-operative consideration or to a committee. Quite often it is desirable to dispatch small administrative matters in a manner which may imply a change or exception to general policies, without inviting participation or co-operation; an example of such a case is the excusing of students from class for reasons generally not recognized.

Perhaps, after all, the principle of the priority of objectives applies universally. That is, the compromise of one principle with another is only temporary or apparent. The true test of any policy or procedure is whether or not *in the long run* it contributes more effectively than any alternative procedure to the aims and functions of secondary education expressed in terms of child development.

Problems, Questions, and Exercises

1. Can you add anything to support or supplement in detail or to controvert the material in the first section of Chapter 1?
2. Do you think democratic philosophy and practices in other areas of American life caused the development of democracy in the schools, or vice versa? Or do you think that each influenced and reinforced the other?
3. Draw up a list of democratic practices or a plan of democratic practices in school administration, mentioning fundamental principles rather than details.
4. Can you recall any instances in which an administrator or official exercised authority not for the benefit of a school but to maintain or enhance his own prestige?
5. Give one or two illustrations of the necessity for adapting responsibility to the character of the personnel of the staff.
6. To what extent do you think the following principle should be observed by the high-school principal in his relationship with his staff:

   Each person affected by a decision or agreement upon a principle of practice should have an opportunity to participate in determining what that decision or principle should be.
7. List in the order of their importance several advantages and several dangers of democratic administration.

Selected Supplementary Readings

Amundsen, Carl L., "Today's Trend in Administration," *Bulletin of the N.A. S.S.P.* (October, 1951), Vol. 35, pp. 39-44. [Discussion of group dynamics in simple language; the results obtained when techniques are skillfully used.]

Anthony, Brother E. (F. S. C.), "Human Rights in Secondary School Administration," *Proceedings and Addresses,* 48th Annual Meeting, National Catholic Educational Association, August, 1951. [Makes a good distinction between human relations and public relations in the field of school administration.]

Bartkey, John A., *Supervision as Human Relations*, Boston, Heath, 1953. [Especially Chapter 3.]

Bent, Rudyard K., and McCann, Lloyd E., *Administration of Secondary Schools*, New York, McGraw-Hill, 1960. [Chapter 3, "Policy Guides for School Operation"; Chapter 4, "Staff Organization in the Secondary School."]

Boardman, Charles W., "What Are Good Techniques in Achieving Democratic Administration of the High School?" *Bulletin of the N.A.S.S.P.* (April, 1949), Vol. 33, pp. 206-215.

Chandler, B. J., and Petty, Paul V., *Personnel Management in School Administration,* Yonkers, New York, World Book, 1955. [Chapter 3, "Teacher Participation in Administration."]

Cory, N. Durward, "When Teachers Participate in School Administration," *Nation's Schools* (April, 1950), Vol. 45, pp. 61-62. [Values of democratic administration.]

Douglass, Harl R., "Leadership or Authority in School Administration," *Educational Administration and Supervision* (January, 1948), Vol. 34, pp. 25-28. [Analyzes the characteristics of genuine democratic leadership.]

Educational Policies Commission, *Education for All American Youth* (1952), pp. 122-123, 187-188, 212-229, and 240-242.

Farley, Genevieve J., and Santstuossi, John J., "The Effect of Authoritarianism of Organization and Administration Upon Democratic Supervision as Revealed in Periodical Literature," *Bulletin of the N.A.S.S.P.* (February, 1957), No. 226, pp. 38-46.

Fitzpatrick, E. A., "Pastor and the State Organization," *Catholic School Journal* (February, 1960), Vol. 60, pp. 67-68.

French, Will, Hull, J. Dan, and Dodds, B. L., *American High School Administration* (Revised Edition), New York, Rinehart, 1957. [Chapter 7, "The Problem of School and Staff Organization"; Chapter 8, "Staff Leadership and School Improvement."]

Grambs, Jean D., "Do Teachers Really Want Democratic Administrators?" *Education Digest* (February, 1951), Vol. 16, No. 6, pp. 40-41. [Suggests three changes which must come about before democratic faculty relations can be realized.]

Griffiths, Daniel E., *Human Relations in School Administration,* New York, Appleton-Century-Crofts, 1956. [Chapter 8, "The Structure of Groups"; Chapter 11, "Human Relations Approach to Leadership"; Chapter 15, "Organization for Human Relations"; Chapter 16, "Informal Organization."]

"Human Relations in Secondary Education," Paul Elicker, ed., *Bulletin of the N.A.S.S.P.* (March, 1955), Vol. 39, No. 209, pp. 1-108.

Innocentia, Sister Mary, "Teacher Participation in Catholic School Administration," *Catholic School Journal* (October-November, 1949), Vol. 49, pp. 261-263, 299-301.

Martin, John H., "How Can Democratic Administration Be Attained by the Principal?" *Bulletin of the N.A.S.S.P.* (March, 1950), Vol. 34, pp. 186-193. [The organization, procedures, values, and outcomes of a faculty advisory committee in a high school in New York State.]

Nadler, Maurice, "Democratic vs. Autocratic School Administration," *Bulletin of the N.A.S.S.P.* (March, 1954), No. 201, pp. 22-26.

Rounds, Lester E., "Delegating Administrative Authority," *Nation's Schools* (October, 1952), Vol. 50, pp. 57-59. [A plan whereby teachers who show special aptitude for certain administrative duties are allowed to assume them.]

Seyfert, Warren C., "Experiences in Faculty Self-Determination," *School Review* (November, 1953), Vol. 61, pp. 458-467.

Spalding, Howard G., "How May Democratic Administration Be Achieved?" *Bulletin of the N.A.S.S.P.* (May, 1952), Vol. 36, pp. 56-63. [Steps that the administrator can take to make his administration more democratic. Ten procedures and a brief discussion of each.]

Spalding, Howard G., and Guy, C. R., "How May Democratic Administration Be Achieved?" *Bulletin of the N.A.S.S.P.* (March, 1952), No. 185, pp. 56-66. [Ways to make a school administration more democratic.]

Weber, C. A., and Weber, Mary E., *Fundamentals of Educational Leadership*, New York, McGraw-Hill, 1955. [Chapter 11, "Participation in Policy Formulation."]

2

The Administrators and Their Interrelationships

1. The Outlook of the Beginning Principal

Certain developments have contributed to the evolution of a new type of administration for modern secondary schools: (1) the increased size and consequent complexity of the school and the problem of management, (2) the expansion of the scope of the program of secondary education, (3) the change in the nature of the high-school student body, (4) the increased stock of professional information and techniques of school administration, and (5) the changed attitude of the people toward specialization.

These developments have played an important part in developing the opportunity and the need for an administrative officer who is professional in occupation and training. This officer—the superintendent of schools, except in those instances where consolidation for high-school purposes only has been effected and the principal of the high school is the chief officer—has gradually taken over powers commensurate with increased responsibility and problems. The problems that relate more particularly to the high school alone he is passing on to his lieutenant in charge of that division, the principal of the high school.

Owing largely to these developments, the position of the high-school principal has undergone profound changes within the past few decades. The position of principal has come to require much technical skill and training. The principal of today must be a student of school finance, accounting, achievement and mental measurement, guidance services, extracurricular activities, supervision, curriculum construction, building and housing problems, grouping, measurement of student growth, community relations, schedule-making, and other technical activities involved in modern high-school administration. Graduate departments of schools of education are organizing the scientific knowledge relating to these activities into specialized courses to supplement the brief general courses in education which constituted the bulk of the professional training available a decade or so ago.

The high-school principalship is rapidly becoming a position demanding not only administrative personality but also specialized, intensive professional training beyond the bachelor's degree which is comparable to that of the dentist, physician, or attorney. Already in a number of states administrative certificates have been provided to furnish recognition of special training for educational administration and to ensure at least some such training on the part of those occupying administrative positions. The training required for these certificates should be thought of as constituting not the optimum or ideal amount of training but only the minimum.

A DANGEROUS PHILOSOPHY FOR THE BEGINNER. The man just entering upon his first high-school principalship should realize that, if he wishes to render the highest type of service to his school and to advance in his profession, he cannot afford to model his school administration after the administration of the school which he attended or even after that of a school in which he has taught. Such great progress has been made in the theory and practice of high-school administration that many principals lag ingloriously in the rear of the leadership of the much smaller group of men and women who have studied carefully, diligently, and systematically the objectives, principles, and techniques of the organization, administration, and supervision of secondary schools and who have been blessed with ambition, energy, and courage in such quantities as to cause them to lead in the development of new practices. The beginning principal cannot hope to solve a great many of his problems *de novo* through plain common sense, even though common sense is a very valuable asset. Many principals of the passing generation were men and women who were certificated with a minimum of professional preparation and who succeeded to high-school principalships through the quality of their personalities, their success as teachers, and their popularity in their communities. Because of superior qualities of personality, a number of them have enjoyed more than average success. Their admirable personal qualities, not their principles and practices in school administration, are the things worth imitating.

Such principals stand in the same professional position as the old family practitioner in medicine, who, while science has swept ahead of him, still has a comfortable practice and still achieves reasonable success in many types of illness and injury – a useful man in his field, but certainly no model for the young physician of today.

The young principal will find that as yet it is difficult for the public, and even for many teachers and principals not well trained in modern school administration, to distinguish between the modern, trained specialist in high-school administration and the passing type of principal. Any given public and many teachers are acquainted with but few schools and few principals and therefore have little basis for comparison. The direct contacts of the public with the school are not close and frequent. The relative effects of different types of school administration are not easy to discern and measure. The fact that the public continues to tolerate, even to approve, the methods of a passing type of administrator is no evidence that those methods constitute modern, effective administration.

The beginning principal, who in so many instances has been trained professionally only for teaching and only in an elementary way, is easily drawn into perpetuating practices which have been outgrown. He must realize that usually he should go, in a gradual way, far beyond his predecessor. To stand still is, in effect, to deteriorate as the development of administrative practices races on. Although the principal under whom he began his teaching achieved apparent success with his methods, the new principal must acquire the methods of the present and the future. He must assume new responsibilities and meet them in new ways. He must master the modern theories of organization and administration of extracurricular activities, curriculum leadership, guidance services, community relationships, building planning and supervision, and child-accounting. He faces the responsibility of assisting teachers in new methods of instruction, supervised study, problem-project methods, visual instruction, large-unit assignments, and the use and interpretation of objective and diagnostic tests.

VOCATIONAL OPPORTUNITIES. For the properly qualified individual there are excellent opportunities for employment. Not only are thousands of vacancies created annually by the resignation of high-school principals who are accepting other positions but also hundreds of new secondary schools, especially junior high schools, are established each year. With the rapidly increasing feeling that the modern principalship demands a man not only of peculiarly adapted personality and character but also of special professional training, those properly trained are discovering that they possess a vital advantage over ambitious candidates from among those trained as teachers but not as administrators in secondary education.

In addition to the principalship itself, there are many other types of positions to which the trained high-school principal may safely and properly aspire, including city superintendencies, county superintendencies, assistant superintendencies, high-school inspectorships, assistant principalships in large cities, positions on the faculties of teachers' colleges and other colleges engaged in training teachers, directorships of various bureaus, divisions, and departments, and positions with concerns furnishing textbooks, school supplies, and equipment.

PECUNIARY REWARDS. Administrative positions, of course, pay much greater salaries than teaching positions. Although these salaries are not yet equal to the salaries of business executives, there is a much greater probability of attaining a well-paid administrative position in a school than of attaining one in business, assuming an inability to make large capital investments. In 1961-1962 the salaries paid to principals of junior high schools were rarely less than $5000 and ranged up to more than $10,000; the salaries of principals of four-year and senior high schools were rarely less than $6000, ranging up to $12,500 and, in the case of superintendents of independent high-school districts, up to $22,000.

OTHER REWARDS. The high-school principal also has other rewards. More often than not, he is a leader in his community, consulted about public and community affairs of a civic and social nature. He is regarded as one of the more prominent representatives of culture and learning. Confidence in his integrity and character is accorded to him almost *ex officio*.

He cannot fail to realize that he is a leader in what is probably the most useful, important, and honorable enterprise in his community. He may justly enjoy the satisfaction that comes from the knowledge that his services and those of the persons whom he directs are almost certain to result in more permanent benefits and to be the source of more happiness to human beings than those resulting from efforts in other callings.

The opportunities for leading and directing the growth of others are great. There is splendid opportunity for initiative, originality, and self-expression, for organization, direction, and management. To any individual who demands avenues of expression for his personality and imagination and who enjoys the challenge of an important task, no other calling can offer more.

QUALITIES OF THE SUCCESSFUL HIGH-SCHOOL PRINCIPAL. There seems to be fairly common agreement among those who have made careful study of the qualities of the more successful high-school principal. The qualities most frequently mentioned by these people include the following:

1. He must possess personal qualities which make for leadership, for acceptance by teachers, pupils, and others, and for influence with them.
2. He should have competence in at least one subject-matter area of learning and be somewhat of a specialist in it.
3. He should have had several years' successful experience as a high-school teacher.
4. He should possess physical health and an abundance of energy.
5. He should have a sound, healthy personality and an understanding and practice of good mental hygiene.
6. He should be able to express himself accurately and forcefully in writing and speech.
7. He should possess a good measure of such virtues as honesty, straightforwardness, fairness, patience when dealing with other individuals, good cheer and optimism, and the ability to understand the problems of others.
8. He should possess a well-thought-through, modern, basic philosophy of education in terms of pupil growth and in terms of the needs of young people and society today and the life for which we are preparing youngsters.

9. He must possess an adequate social philosophy and an understanding of American industrial and democratic society, as well as of local communities. He must understand the relationship of the school to society and its function as a social institution.
10. He should be interested in people, particularly young people and their activities and problems.
11. He should possess an interest in ideas, not only professional ideas but also social, intellectual, and aesthetic ideas and concepts. Although not limited by books, he should be an individual who reads widely.
12. He should be a person who possesses ideals higher than those of the average individual. These include professional ideals, social ideas, and personal ideals.
13. He should possess resourcefulness, vision, and ingenuity. He should have the habit of and capacity for looking to the future; he should be able to make adjustments to new situations as they arise and to invent new ideas or modify old ones to meet changing situations.
14. He should be an individual with an open mind, capable of accepting new proposals, willing to experiment and try new methods, and willing to evaluate and accept good ideas which may come from teachers, pupils, or people of the community.

2. *Increased Complexity of Modern High-School Administration*

The Increased Size and Complexity of the School and Its Problems of Management. In contrast to the earlier secondary schools in this country, modern high schools are complex institutions with staffs ranging up to more than 200 teachers and with enrollments as high as 7500 students. Almost half of the American secondary schools now enroll more than 250 students, whereas forty years ago the median enrollment was slightly more than 100. The increase in the size of the schools has magnified their problems and their need of technical administration and supervision. In the first place, we may note the problems of co-ordinating the departments and the activities of teachers and pupils which naturally result from an increase in the size of the schools: problems of schedule-making, reports, common standards and procedures among teachers, greater burdens of routine relative to absence and tardiness, and other problems of like nature. The increased amount of labor and time involved in the selection and supervision of large numbers of teachers and in other administrative tasks formerly performed by boards of education has discouraged members of governing boards from the attempt to exercise these functions personally; the functions are now very commonly delegated to professional educators and administrators—the principal and the superintendent of schools.

Expansion of the High-School Program. The development of the elective system and the tendency to regard the function of the high school as much broader than merely the preparation of students for college and university have resulted in much wider offerings in high schools. This fact has necessitated expert administration of such problems as guidance, requirements for graduation, and the standardization, placement, and careful supervision of the newer subjects. These are matters which require more training and attention than boards of education are prepared to give them.

A second significant type of expansion of the high-school program is the rapid development of the group activities of high-school students—extracurricular, student, or collateral activities, as they are variously termed. Beginning with the more popular organized sports and the literary and debating societies, this type of educational activity has grown to include many forms of clubs, publications, and sports, as well as social, musical, dramatic, and civic organizations and activities. Such activities call for careful supervision and direction; the duties incidental to them constitute in many schools the major single responsibility of the high-school principal.

The widened scope of the curricular and extracurricular opportunities and the consequent problems arising from the fluid state of all this expansion have introduced into the administration of the upper schools very complicating factors, which call for knowledge and skills not possessed by even the more capable classroom teacher.

Changes in the Nature and Quality of the High-School Student Body. The increase of high-school enrollments, from less than 55 per cent (in 1930) of all youth from fourteen through seventeen to the present figure of more than 85 per cent, has in itself operated to bring about material changes in the average and range of the student body. The pupil personnel of today's high school includes lower economic, intellectual, and cultural levels than that of a generation ago. The presence in high school of different types of boys and girls has proved a tax upon the administrative genius of those who administer high schools. High-school students today are a less homogeneous group with respect to ability to do intellectual work, with respect to probable future occupations, and with respect to interests, outlook on life, and home training. They respresent different social groups of varying degrees of Americanization. As a result, problems of curricula, courses of study, methods of teaching, and management have grown apace. Homogeneous grouping, special and short courses, large-unit or individual-instruction plans, supervised study, and well-developed facilities for guidance are illustrative of the technical developments growing out of the need for readjustment of instruction and guidance to the student body of today.

The Increased Stock of Professional Information Relating to Principles and Techniques of School Administration. Partly because of the former relative simplicity of administrative problems or the failure to realize their significance, knowledge about the techniques of organization, administration, and supervision in the early stage of the development of high schools was meager, unorganized, and unpublished. A number of sources and influences have since contributed to the development of a vast store of information about school administration. Among these should be mentioned the development of normal schools and the subsequent development of departments of education and graduate work in education in colleges and universities, the development of professional and research organizations of schoolmen, the growth of educational research and its special techniques, the raising of professional standards for certification and employment, and the increase in the number and quality of periodicals and books on the professional aspects of education.

The last fifty years have witnessed an increase in the number of persons studying educational problems in the graduate schools of the United States from a few score to tens of thousands. Almost every year now there is more written on school administration than was published altogether prior to 1920. A student may, if he wishes, acquire in a single summer session more technical information about high-school administration than anyone possessed fifty years ago.

The increased professional knowledge of the better-informed high-school principals and superintendents of schools has gone a long way toward encouraging boards of education to relinquish the administration of the schools to their management. The modern type of administrator, whose knowledge is not confined to academic fields, discipline, and his own experience and who rivals the engineer, physician, and lawyer in his grasp and knowledge of professional problems, principles, and techniques, is winning the respect of the layman for a professional in a way that the old schoolmaster was never able to do.

Recent trends have resulted in recognition of a need for an increased and much more effective program of public relations and have definitely produced a very important effect on school organization and administration. There must be much more time and thought given to developing plans and procedures for informing the public, developing understanding of the school program, and promoting good will and friends for the public school; also much more time is needed for performing the activities growing out of the planned program and procedures. This means that administrative officers must find time for teachers, counselors, and themselves to have more contact with parents and the people of the community.

3. Relationship With Other Administrators

High-School Principal, Superintendent of Schools, and Board of Education Relationships. The principal is the lieutenant of the superintendent of schools. While he should have much authority and responsibility within his individual school, it should always be recognized that his authority has been delegated to him by the superintendent of schools. The wise superintendent will delegate sufficient authority to the principal to enable him to discharge his responsibilities in the best possible manner. In the large high school the principal will be in rather complete charge of the detailed administration of all aspects of his school, subject to advice in matters of curriculum, health, and other areas in which there are specialists in the school system who act as consultants to the principal and to whom he should turn for advice and counsel in the areas in which they are better qualified by training, interest, and experience than he is.

The superintendent of schools has the full authority to set aside decisions of the high-school principal, to veto, to revoke, to supplement, and to change procedures at any time. Actually, an intelligent superintendent of schools will exercise these powers only in matters of unusual emergency. The relationship between the principal and the superintendent should be one of co-operation and discussion; the superintendent in most instances, especially in larger schools, should defer to the judgment of the principal, who is closer to the situation, who is perhaps better qualified by training and experience to make the decisions, and whose interest in his work and prestige with his teachers and students call for a freedom of decision and action.

The principal should have his contacts with the board of education entirely through the superintendent. The wise superintendent of schools will see that the high-school principal attends some of the board meetings, particularly when matters affecting secondary education are to be discussed. He will rely upon the principal of the high school to furnish him and the board information and opinions upon these matters. Much more than before, superintendents are taking with them to board meetings various administrative, supervisory, and other special officers (including principals and committees of teachers) for the purpose of discussing with the board problems and procedures in which these people have interests, special points of view, special information, and background.

The principal and the superintendent should work closely together, be quite frank with one another, and co-operate as fully as possible. The principal should recognize that appeals can be made from his decisions by teachers or pupils in his school. The superintendent should refuse to take jurisdiction in many of these appeals, acting only in instances which he believes are of unusual importance. When he does act, the superintendent usually confers with the principal first and arrives at a mutually agreeable course of action.

THE VICE-PRINCIPAL OR ASSISTANT PRINCIPAL. In all but the smaller schools of perhaps less than 200 students, there should be at least one assistant principal or assistant to the principal, the latter title being more appropriate in schools of less than 300 or 400 students. The number and variety of the duties of a principal are so great that there is definite need for him to have at least one assistant with whom he may share his responsibilities. This is particularly true if the principal is to spend some time in the community or visiting in the classroom. Whenever the principal is not available in his office, there should be someone readily available to act as principal or as assistant principal—to meet callers, to take care of matters coming in over the telephone, to handle situations in the classrooms, and to cope with emergencies and situations in which pupils come to the office. In recent years there has been a very great increase in the number of assistant principals or vice-principals, so that in most schools there is one on full time for each 750 students enrolled. An assistant principal may in smaller schools be a classroom teacher who is spending a fraction of his time as assistant principal. Of course, in larger schools there should be two or more assistant principals who do little or no teaching.

While considerable responsibility and authority must be given to assistant principals, it must always be recognized that the principal is primarily responsible for questions of policy and decisions in critical situations. Even though certain special aspects of high-school administration and management may be farmed out to the assistant principal with very little interference from the principal, it should be recognized that the assistant principal is never completely independent of his superior officer. The principal should remember that his is the primary responsibility, especially in the event of trouble.

Quite frequently an assistant principal or vice-principal is given responsibility for a particular field of work: for example, (1) leadership for the curriculum, (2) leadership in guidance and counseling, (3) supervision of the extracurricular activity program, and (4) conferences with students who are problem cases in respect to attendance, school progress, or discipline.

In recent years there have been more women serving as assistant principals or vice-principals, particularly in cases where there is no dean of girls.

The wise principal, particularly one in a larger school, soon learns that he should delegate many of his responsibilities. Although the principal still has general supervision of these matters, the individual to whom the responsibilities are delegated must be given ample opportunity to discharge those responsibilities without too much direction.

DEPARTMENT HEADS. The duties of department heads are both supervisory and administrative, although, except in very large schools, the supervision must be carried on without benefit of classroom visitation.

The effectiveness of department heads as administrators and supervisors in secondary schools seems to vary considerably from school to school. In many schools there are people who have received the position of department head on the basis of seniority or political maneuvering.

The effectiveness of such people as department heads is usually very limited. In some schools the department heads have failed to keep up with modern movements, trends, and practices in their particular fields and in secondary education in general. Nevertheless, some department heads have proved to be very effective in performing limited administrative duties and in exercising leadership in connection with the curriculum and methods of teaching in their particular subject fields.

In those schools in which department heads are relied upon for more than nominal leadership, the principal should attempt to encourage them to keep abreast of new movements and practices in their fields and should see that they have contact with department heads in other fields and with department heads in higher or lower schools in their respective subject-matter fields. Such contact should assist in co-ordinating and articulating instruction between departments and between school levels.

Following are some important services that may be rendered by department heads:

1. Assisting teachers in developing syllabi which set forth the objectives and minimum essentials of the courses which they teach.
2. Giving assistance to new teachers in becoming oriented to the community as well as to the school, with its rules and regulations, curriculum and courses of study.
3. Bringing to the attention of teachers important current publications—books or journal articles which should be helpful to them in their field.
4. Assisting teachers in planning and carrying on educational experimentation.
5. Leading discussions and contributing ideas to teachers in the department, both individually and collectively, with respect to methods of presenting subject matter, the selection and use of audio-visual materials, and problems of discipline.
6. Assisting the principal in connection with the planning of the budget.
7. Giving leadership to teachers in the consideration of textbooks and workbooks for use in their subjects and in the recommendation of books in their field to be added to the library.
8. Assisting the principal and the superintendent in the selection of new teachers.
9. Exercising leadership in revising the course of study.
10. Participating in requisitioning, issuing, and accounting for supplies, equipment, and textbooks.
11. Assisting the principal in making departmental schedules.

In a minority of schools, department heads also prepare written reports on the work of the department, counsel students making unsatisfactory progress, and lead in making tests.

Factors in Selection of Department Heads. Criteria which are kept in mind by administrators in selecting departmental heads include especially (1) the degree of mastery of the subject matter, (2) apparent administrative ability, (3) popularity and acceptance as leaders among the staff of the department, and (4) graduate study in the subject field and in professional education.

Department heads should possess to a superior degree teaching ability, professional vigor, understanding of students, outstanding personality, disciplinary ability, ability to get results from other teachers, progressiveness in educational outlook and leadership, ability in curriculum thinking, favorable educational attitudes and a co-operative spirit, inclination to work which is comparable to knowledge and skill, disposition to grow, ability to work well with others, ability to get the vote of the school committee, and sensitivity to new trends.

4. Others Participating in Administration

Committees in Administration. Slowly but steadily the use of committees of teachers in school administration and supervision has grown in importance and has spread to an increasing number of schools. At first, committees were principally for superficial or relatively unimportant duties in the program of the school—for example, duties connected with refreshments or decorations. But the number and importance of committees have increased, as have the importance and scope of their activities, until today committees deal with such responsibilities or areas of responsibility as the following for the school as a whole:

Commencement, marking system, guidance, extracurricular activities, publications, schedule, interscholastic relations, athletics, library, salaries, promotions, public relations, curriculum, exhibits, student loans, student honors, report cards, entertainment, visual aids, discipline, student government, dramatics, home rooms, testing programs, student health, and team teaching.

In some schools a number of these committees are standing committees, which originated when a need sometime in the past seemed to indicate the desirability of a particular committee to investigate a special problem or to administer (or to advise in the administration of) a given area.

In addition, the principal may find it advantageous to appoint from time to time special temporary committees for special purposes: for example, to evaluate the P.T.A., to study the possibilities of a high-school P.T.A., to work with a student committee on a salvage campaign, to co-operate in a local celebration, to explore the idea of a credit union for teachers, or to present certain matters to the board of education.

Certain cautions should be observed in the use of committees. Teachers should not be overburdened with committee work. Most teachers have a full day's teaching load. For this reason, not too many committees should exist and committees should not be any larger than necessary. The principal or some other official should make it clear just what is expected of a committee. The principal should not dominate the committee, nor should he be too free with suggestions for its conclusions.

The principal should furnish the committee with, or aid it in locating and obtaining, publications of other schools, books, periodicals, and pamphlets in the field of its investigation or administrative responsibility. Clerical and stenographic assistance should be provided. Teachers performing a great amount of committee service should have their instructional, study-hall, or extracurricular load lightened appropriately. The results of committee investigations, the conclusions and proposals, should not be ignored. They should be reviewed by the staff and, in most instances, adopted at least upon an experimental basis, even if they are contrary to the best judgment of the principal.

In most schools, committees are appointed by the principal; in smaller schools, by principal and superintendent jointly. In some schools, however, committees are appointed by a committee on committees, which in turn is appointed by the principal.

DEANS OF GIRLS AND OF BOYS. With the development of additional knowledge and understanding of the psychology of adolescence and guidance, deans of boys and deans of girls have in many schools been replaced by counselors and new concepts of the positions have developed. Nevertheless, there still remains in a great many schools the position of dean of girls and indeed, in a considerable number, dean of boys. Perhaps as modern concepts of counseling develop and more well-trained counselors become available, these positions will disappear entirely and their administrative duties will be taken over by assistant principals, directors of student activities, and other individuals.

The dean of girls may serve as an administrative officer to advantage in many schools by assisting in the management of social activities, although in recent years there has been a tendency to have the boys' advisors and girls' advisors also act in that capacity. A dean of girls may carry on special administrative responsibilities, in addition to her advisory responsibilities in connection with special problems of girls which can be handled only by a counselor or administrator of the same sex as the student.

In the selection of a dean of girls or a dean of boys and in the assignment of duties to them, there should be borne in mind the type of office that is envisaged and the type of trained individual who will occupy it. In other words, the responsibilities and the nature of the position should be in harmony with the qualifications, training, and experience of the individual who is to occupy the position.

DIRECTORS OF GUIDANCE, CURRICULUM OR INSTRUCTION, AND CO-CURRICULAR ACTIVITIES. In a number of large schools and school systems there are directors of guidance, directors of curriculum or directors of instruction, and directors of co-curricular activities; in some schools these are given the rank of assistant principal or assistant superintendent. Directors of guidance give leadership to all counselors, including teacher counselors, and through inservice study enable all those doing counseling to avoid attempting to do counseling which is of questionable validity. The director of guidance in many schools is also the director of testing, particularly in fields other than subject-matter testing such as testing of aptitude, intelligence, and interests. In many schools he also formulates and administers programs for the gathering of counselee data such as work experience, factors in home background, and out-of-school interests.

A director of activities performs both administrative and supervisory services in that area, relieving the principal of most of his responsibility with reference to co-curricular activities and giving leadership to sponsors and coaches in better performance of their responsibilities.

The director of curriculum or instruction, operating under the direction of the principal, the superintendent of schools, or both, is responsible for giving leadership, direction, assistance, and consultation service to the teachers. His work will be discussed in later chapters.

5. Staff Organization and Relationships

TYPES OF STAFF ORGANIZATION. The organization of the staffs of secondary schools in the United States does not run true to form; moreover, not all schools have one or the other of the various types of organization. It is serviceable, however, to note the following types:

1. The functional or purpose type of staff organization, in which, under the general direction of the principal, teachers and sponsors of extracurricular activities are under the supervision and administration of various co-ordinators, such as the co-ordinator of education for vocation, the co-ordinator of education for citizenship, the co-ordinator of education for mental and physical health, the co-ordinator of education for home living and consumer education, and the co-ordinator of education for leisure and recreation. This type of organization, logical as it may seem, has not been adopted by many schools.
2. The straight-line plan of organization, which is found in most schools where each teacher is directly responsible to the principal (as is the case in most small schools) or where each teacher is responsible to a head of a department who in turn is responsible to the principal (as is the case in a great many larger schools).
3. The line and staff type of school organization, in which they are responsible to the principal, and in an advisory capacity to the teachers, various staff personnel such as the director of guidance, the director of co-curricular activities, school psychologists, social workers and home visitors, school nurses and medical personnel, and instructional consultants. These staff members perform few and minor direct administrative duties; they are largely supervisory and advisory in their special fields. They ordinarily have few responsibilities and are not active in dealing directly with students.

Acting also in an advisory capacity are various committees appointed for special purposes; these committees rarely have administrative responsibility and authority. In the larger schools, as mentioned previously in this chapter, there are assistant principals who fit in the organization in one of two types of relationship:

1. A lieutenant of the principal who functions instead of the principal in certain specified areas. Where this relationship exists, there should be a careful allocation of authority and the principal should interfere only very rarely in the administrative activities of the assistant principal, although he should in a general way supervise his activities and be in close touch with him in frequent conferences.
2. An aide who assists the principal and serves to relieve him in various duties, not in any particular homogeneous field but usually in those areas which are routine and of minor importance. Here, too, there should be careful planning of the responsibilities and relationships so that there will not be a conflict of authority and so that both teachers and pupils may understand clearly to whom they should go with the various types of problems which they might wish to carry to the administration.

In many of the larger schools various officials rank above the teachers and counselors; for example, the director of guidance, the director of activities, the dean of boys, and the director of curriculum or instruction may perform somewhat as does a cabinet, not only discharging special responsibilities but also meeting, conferring, and acting (usually in an advisory capacity) with the principal in the formation of policies and the consideration of important basic decisions.

Problems, Questions, and Exercises

1. Make a list of the most important points you would cover in a talk to a prospective or beginning high-school principal or to a group of them.
2. Be able to state in class the principal duties or area of duties of a high-school principal; for each one be able to make at least one statement of the changing nature of the responsibility of the high-school principal in the last few decades.
3. Be able to discuss in class the relationship between the high-school principal and the superintendent of schools and the division of duties between them.
4. Be able to discuss the place of the department head and his duties in administration and supervision in a high school of 250 or more students.
5. Discuss the division and allocation of responsibilities between the principal and one or more assistant principals.
6. Write a paper or be prepared to discuss in class the participation of committees of the staff in the administration and management of the high school.
7. If the functional or purpose organization of administration and supervision were to be employed, tell what you think would have to be done to cause it to succeed.
8. Be able to discuss in class the relation of the principal to the boys' counselor.
9. Review, comment upon, and supplement, if possible, the various items of good staff relationships.

Selected Supplementary Readings

"Administrative Officers of Catholic Educational Institutions," *Catholic School* Journal (September, 1953), Vol. 53, pp. 210-211.

Brandes, Louis Grant, "The Position of the Subordinate Administrator in the Secondary School," *Bulletin of the N.A.S.S.P.* (May, 1956), No. 220, pp-46-52.

Briner, Conrad, "Unhinging the High School Principalship," *School Review* (Autumn, 1960), Vol. 68, pp. 318-328. ,New ideas about the three-fold responsibilities of the high-school principal.]

Claypool. V. B., Slagle, E. R., Wright, C. P., "What Are Some New Developments in Providing Adequate Salaries for Principals?" *Bulletin of the N.A.S.S.P.* (April, 1960), No. 255, pp. 195-197.

Council for Administrative Leadership, *Administrative Organization of the Modern Junior High School,* New York, New York State Teachers Association, 1960.

Culbertson, Jack, "The School Administrator and Policy Making Functions," *School Review* (Spring, 1961), Vol. 69, pp. 98-112.

De Zafra, Carolos, "What a High School Teacher Looks for in Principals," *Clearing House* (October, 1951), Vol. 26, pp. 87-91. [Ten characteristics which a principal should have. Ten characteristics that principals believe teachers should have.]

Edmonson, J. B., "Professional Strategy for the School Administrator," *Bulletin of the N.A.S.S.P.* (March, 1954), No. 201, pp. 34-38.

Faunce, Roland C., *Secondary School Administration,* New York, Harper, 1955. [Chapter 15, "The Board of Education, the Superintendent, and the Principal."]

Fitch, George E., "Practices That Increase Administrative Efficiency," *Nation's Schools* (January, 1955), Vol. 55, pp. 50-52. [The author lists thirty-one administrative techniques used by high-school principals in Pennsylvania.]

Goebel, E. J., "Pastor As the Principal," *Catholic School Journal* (December, 1957), Vol. 57, pp. 59-61.

Harlow, James G., "Building the Principal's Team," *Bulletin of the N.A.S.S.P.* (February, 1957), No. 226, pp. 47-54. [Describes various kinds of assistants for modern large schools.]

High School in a Changing World, Thirty-sixth Yearbook, American Association of School Administration, 1958, pp. 297-332. [Chapter XI, "Leadership and the Administrator."]

Innocentia, Sister Mary, "Teacher Participation in Catholic School Administration," *Catholic School Journal* (October, 1949), Vol. 49, p. 12. [A general summary of the topic, based upon a master's thesis study.]

Jarrett, Richard W., "The Activities of the Assistant Principal in Secondary Schools," *Bulletin of the N.A.S.S.P.* (September, 1958), No. 239, pp. 28-32.

Laughery, Wayne W., "Experience or Vision in the Assignment of Assistant Principal's Duties," *Bulletin of the N.A.S.S.P.* (September, 1959), No. 248, pp. 112-114.

Levy, Ronald, "Once There Was a Principal," *School Executive* (May, 1955), Vol. 74, pp. 64-65.

Long, Charles M., "Duties of Secondary School Vice-Principals," *Bulletin of the N.A.S.S.P.* (February, 1957), No. 226, pp. 26-37. [A survey of status in New York State.]

Pehrson, B. L., "Principals Discuss Their Problems with Their Superintendents," *Bulletin of the N.A.S.S.P.* (April, 1950), No. 170, pp. 82-91. [Principles which are basic in the proper delegation of administrative functions between the superintendent and the principal.]

Rounds, Lester E., "Delegating Administrative Authority," *Nation's Schools* (October, 1952), Vol. 50, pp. 57-59.

Saunders, Juliet, "Job Analysis—Junior High School Principals," *Bulletin of the N.A.S.S.P.* (December, 1959), No. 251, pp. 46-51.

Tompkins, Ellsworth, "What Would You Demand of a High School Principal?" *School Management* (September, 1950), Vol. 4, No. 3, pp. 34-37, 84-86.

Weber, C. A., and Weber, Mary E., *Fundamentals of Education and Leadership,* New York, McGraw-Hill, 1955. [Chapter 4, "The Situational Theory of Leadership."]

Weiss, G. A. W., "The Duties of the Secondary School Vice-Principal," *Bulletin of the N.A.S.S.P.* (December, 1953), No. 198, p. 109.

Young, Christine, and Loretan, J. O., "What Critical Problems Face the Junior High School Principal?" *Bulletin of the N.A.S.S.P.* (April, 1960), No. 255, pp. 79-81, 82-84.

Zweibach, S. I., "Problems of New High School Principals," *Bulletin of the N.A.S.S.P.* (October, 1951), No. 180, pp. 69-85.

3

The Preparation, Growth, and Certification of the Principal

1. Professional Growth and Certification

Degrees Held by the Modern High-School Principal. It seems most probable that the high-school principalship of the near future, along with the school superintendency, will constitute a truly professional calling, which will require not only distinctly superior mental and personal characteristics but also continued technical and professional training and which will afford responsibility and prestige on a par with those of the more generally recognized professions of medicine, law, and architecture.

The time is close at hand when principals of all but the very small high schools will have the equivalent of a year or more of graduate professional training. There is a rather large and growing number of principals who have two years of graduate work; indeed, there is a considerable and growing number that have a doctor's degree.

Graduate Professional Education. The steady increase in the number of universities making provision for the degree of doctor of education (Ed.D.), a degree comparable to that of M.D. for the physician, suggests that three years of graduate professional training will be sought by many principals and superintendents who are desirous of becoming experts in school administration. Also, in an increasing number of universities a professional certificate in school administration is offered to those completing a year of prescribed professional training beyond the master's degree. The typical high-school principal has approximately thirty semester hours of professional graduate credit.

Perhaps in no other profession is there greater need for continued professional study and growth than in school administration. This statement is probable true in spite of the fact that those engaged in other callings find it necessary or desirable to continue study. While it is better for professional training in administration to be completed after several years of experience in teaching, it is definitely essential that at least a year of graduate training for administration be completed before entering administrative work and that a second year, or its equivalent, in systematic noninstitutional professional study be completed soon after.

The high-school principal should not consider himself properly trained for his work until he has familiarized himself with a very large number of the important problems and practices of high-school organization, administration, and supervision, including those discussed in this volume. Such study may be of the nature of experience with immediate practical problems; it may involve informal study of books, articles, and other published material or of talks made at various meetings; or it may be done in regular professional courses at teacher-training institutions.

Experience as a Method of Study. Experience in administrative work constitutes a very desirable type of stimulus to professional growth. It is an indispensable supplement to any other type of professional preparation or study, regardless of how complete or efficient the latter may be. Formal professional training will be complete only when it has been related in practice to the problems which arise in actual administrative experience.

However, experience alone as a means of professional growth leaves much to be desired. It is a slow, uneconomical method of growth. Just as children need an artificial institution—the school—to short-cut natural experience, so the administrator should not depend upon administrative experience alone for his professional growth. The experience of any one person is not sufficiently varied. There are many good plans, methods, principles, and schemes which are the result of the experiences of many people through many years. For one to neglect to study these in the hope that his own experience will lead him to discover them is impractical and unwise.

It is also true that experience will be most useful if it parallels the study of others' experience and research and is enriched by the testing of many of their ideas and plans. Experience not so stimulated is likely to lead to crystallization of practice and to the early termination of professional growth.

General Professional Preparation and Certification. General professional preparation should include work in various areas:

1. *Methods of Teaching.* Including work in methods of teaching in the secondary schools, visual aids in education, and individualizing instruction.
2. *Educational Psychology.* Including work from such subdivisions as psychology of learning, understanding the needs of youth, human growth and development, adolescent psychology, educational measurements, and mental hygiene.
3. *Curriculum.* Including work from such subdivisions as principles of curriculum construction, the high-school curriculum, study of the curriculum in one specific field, and extracurricular activities.

4. *Foundations of Education.* Including work from such subdivisions as history of education, principles of education, philosophy of education, comparative education, and educational sociology.
5. *Guidance.* Including work from such subdivisions as principles of guidance, counseling, vocational guidance, educational guidance, research in guidance, and student personnel problems.
6. *Specialization in One or More Fields of Subject Matter Taught in Secondary Schools.*

TYPES OF IN-SERVICE GROWTH. As suggested by the Eikenberry committee, the following means of in-service education of a high-school principal can be recommended:

1. The use of facilities of educational institutions, including attendance at regular school or summer school, extension-division courses, correspondence courses, special conferences, lectures, and workshops sponsored by educational institutions.
2. Activity in professional associations, involving participation in programs and meetings, writing for publication in the journals, and serving on committees of the associations.
3. Travel, not only abroad but also in his native land, which may result in broadening and educational experiences.
4. Participation in community activities which will give him opportunities to understand better his community and its educational needs, including experiences in service clubs, organizations for cultural and education development, churches, and civic organizations. The committee points out the danger, however, of spending too much time in out-of-school activities.
5. Research in education, involving careful investigation of problems of his particular school, evaluation of practices and experiments, and studies of the causes of problem situations, including disciplinary cases which involve youngsters in schools. Co-operative research stimulated by the principal is especially recommended.
6. Participation in workships or educational conferences conducted by educational institutions, professional associations, state departments of education, and other groups. In these workshops attention is most commonly given to problems faced by principals.
7. Reading, radio, television, and lectures. Stress is placed upon good professional books and journals, good fiction and nonfiction books read for their cultural value, and the programs of radio and television which have cultural value or throw light on educational problems.[1]

EXTRA-INSTITUTIONAL STUDY. The mistake should not be made of thinking that continued study can be carried on only in courses in an educational institution. The same books, articles, and other material may be read and studied independently of any institution. Set problems or exercises may be adapted to fit in with problems faced in the daily work of the principal. For many administrators, study beyond the first graduate

[1] "Training and Experience Standards for Principals of Secondary Schools," D. H. Eikenberry, Chairman, *Bulletin of the N.A.S.S.P.* (November, 1951), No. 181, p. 562.

year may have to be postponed indefinitely, if not forever. For such individuals, continued and constant informal reading and study are most essential.

Though graduate professional training is highly desirable, it by no means eliminates the necessity of continued study of the new developments reported in current books and periodical literature. Indeed, it is very likely that those with a year or more of graduate training do more professional reading from year to year than those with less training.

PROFESSIONAL READING. Among types of professional growth experiences commonly employed are summer conferences of a week or two, school-year conferences in the immediate region, local school-improvement projects, and various kinds of workshops. The high-school principal should invest at least $150 a year in professional books, journals, and organizations. Such an expenditure may be safely regarded as an investment which in the long run, for individuals fitted by personality to administrative work, will prove many times more profitable than any other investment of a corresponding amount. In later paragraphs some suggestions will be made as to the more useful types of books and journals.

In the main, the recommendations are centered upon the improvement of the individual as an administrator of secondary schools; but since he must always look upon himself as a possible city superintendent of schools, that possibility has been kept in mind.

DANGERS OF PROFESSIONAL ATROPHY. The high-school principal is especially susceptible to professional stagnation and atrophy. He is in constant danger of being so drawn into the details of his daily routine that he will fail to see beyond his immediate tasks and the local community. He has few fellows who stimulate him to continued growth. In the majority of cases the nearest principal is in the next town.

In some cases early successes serve to turn his head and to lead him to underestimate the need for increasing his professional knowledge and improving his professional skills and techniques. The ignorance of his constituency about technical phases of administration makes it easy for the principal to procrastinate and to let well enough suffice. The importance of making friends in the community leads some to put all reliance in this mode of getting on. The younger principal, flattered by the opportunities offered to him to assume leadership in many community enterprises or organizations, is prone to fill his leisure hours with activities which, while valuable to his community, contribute little to increasing his premanent professional efficiency.

Each year there may be found coming as students into summer sessions of the universities older administrators of small schools who have decided, after years of professional stagnation and neglect, to make an effort to regain the ground lost in ten, fifteen, or twenty years. They are waging an uphill battle. Their records are against them; employing bodies and individuals are prone to be suspicious, feeling that their lack of progress indicates lack of ability.

It is needless to point out here that the whole field of education is in flux and that secondary education is undergoing a rapid and thorough transformation. Organization, curriculum, methods of teaching, extra-curricular services, guidance programs, and methods of administration and supervision—all are in the process of becoming quite different from what they were a few years ago. A great deal of specific training received twenty years ago in education is already out of date. Research bureaus, subsidized investigations, and the research of professors, graduate students, superintendents, principals, and teachers are daily producing new information, new techniques, and new materials with which the principal must keep abreast.

Experimentation in the classroom is overturning old ideas and presenting new procedures to be mastered. The application to education of the psychology of learning and the principles of business administration, public finance, publicity, public health, and other fields has served to develop whole new structures of procedures which make uncomfortable the old *laissez-faire* administrator, who is content to trust to his own common sense, the ignorance of his patrons, and good luck to maintain himself and his school.

PROFESSIONAL ORGANIZATIONS AND MEETINGS. The secondary-school principal who wishes to do a first-class job and to advance professionally should belong to several professional organizations, including the National Association of Secondary School Principals and its state branch, the National Education Association, the state education association, and the Association for Supervision and Curriculum Developments. Also, he should belong to at least one special subject-matter organization—for example, the National Council of Teachers of Mathematics. Other helpful organizations are the John Dewey Society, the Association for Audio-Visual Education, the American Personnel and Guidance Association, the National Society for the Study of Education, and the Department of Audio-Visual Instruction. Of course, he should be a member of the national and state P.T.A. as well as of the local chapter.

In addition to the *Bulletin*, the National Association of Secondary School Principals publishes *News Letter, Spotlight,* and *Highlights. Student Life*, also published by the Association, is obtainable for $1 a year if three or more copies are sent to one address.

The Association carries on research studies in such fields as science, mathematics, and foreign languages in the high school, consumer education, experimental staff utilization, interscholastic athletics in junior high schools, external testing programs, junior high school grades in the six-year high school, and English language arts in the high schools.

The Association sponsors the 8800 chapters of the National Honor Society and the 1700 chapters of the National Junior Honor Society. It also has organized and sponsors the National Association of Student Councils with 8500 membership schools.

As will be discussed in a later chapter, the Association publishes at very reasonable prices various types of forms for secondary-school records. It also has available at very reasonable prices a considerable number of tape recordings to be used as teaching aids. From time to time it issues a commencement manual, which indicates new trends in commencement programs and practices, including skits and descriptions of skits. It also publishes a kit of materials and forms designed to help student officers do their work more efficiently. It publishes from time to time a handbook for the National Honor Society and one for the Junior Honor Society.[2]

The Association holds annual meetings of several days, usually in February in places alternating among the various sections of the country. An increasing majority of the boards of education pay at least part of the expenses of the principals attending these annual meetings; most boards of education pay all expenses when a meeting is held in their section of the country.

There exists in each of the states a state Association of Secondary School Principals which is associated with the national Association.

Many principals attend, at least occasionally, the meetings of the Association for Supervision and Curriculum Development, especially when they are held in their section of the country.

2. *The Reading of the High-School Principal*

BULLETINS AND CIRCULARS. Some of the most useful and practical educational literature appears in the various series of educational bulletins and circulars. Perhaps most prominent is the series of the Office of Education of the Department of Health, Education and Welfare, Washington, D.C. Single copies of current numbers may be obtained free. Every principal should request that his name be placed on the mailing list for this series of bulletins. Copies of certain back numbers may be obtained at small cost from the Superintendent of Documents, Washington, D.C. A list of all the available publications of the office may be obtained for the asking.

Among the various series issued by the institutions of higher education are those of their bureaus of educational research.

JOURNALS. The more detailed and fresher professional literature is to be found in current professional journals. Among the journals likely to be

[2]The principal should obtain the current issue of the free pamphlet describing the work, activities, and publications of the N.A.S.S.P.

of most value to those interested in secondary-school administration are the following:

SECONDARY EDUCATION IN GENERAL

The Bulletin of the National Association of Secondary School Principals. Published nine times a year by the National Association of Secondary School Principals, Washington 6, D.C. $8 a year. [A fairly large number of articles, chiefly concerning practical problems of all aspects of secondary education. Rather complete lists of new books of interest in secondary education.]

The Clearing House. Published monthly, September to May inclusive, by the Fairleigh Dickinson University Press, Teaneck, New Jersey. $4.50 a year. [Shorter, more vitalized articles, usually of a progressive or controversial nature. Good reviews and news notes.]

The School Review. Published quarterly by the Department of Education of the University of Chicago, Chicago 37, Illinois. $4.50 a year. [Contributions of general or special significance to secondary education, including a large number of scientific or semiscientific articles written to be understood by the large majority of principals. Excellent book reviews and editorial news.]

In addition to these journals, there are several which circulate largely in limited areas:

California Journal of Secondary Education. Published eight times a year by the California Association of Secondary-School Administrators, 1705 Murchison Drive, Burlingame, California. $4 a year. [Articles and committee reports relating to organization, administration, and teaching.]

High Points in the Work of the High Schools of New York City. Published by the High Schools of New York City, Far Rockaway High School, Far Rockaway 91, New York. Issued each month of the school year to all teachers in the high schools of the city of New York. $1 a year. [Articles by teachers and officials in New York City high schools, largely pertaining to work done in their schools.]

The High School Journal. Published eight times a year by the School of Education of the University of North Carolina, Chapel Hill, North Carolina. $2 a year.

The North Central Association Quarterly. Published quarterly by the North Central Association of Secondary Schools and Colleges, 4012 University High School Building, Ann Arbor, Michigan. $4 a year. [Reports and papers read at meetings and reports of committees appointed for investigations by the association.]

EMPHASIZING ADMINISTRATION

The American School Board Journal. Published monthly by the Bruce Publishing Company, Milwaukee, Wisconsin. $4.50 a year. Articles on all phases of school administration and supervision, specializing in those relating to buildings and equipment and to the financial and legal phases of administration. News notes of what other schools are doing. Advertising material showing developments in school equipment.

The Nation's Schools. Published monthly by the Modern Hospital Publishing Company, 919 North Michigan Avenue, Chicago 11, Illinois. $4 a year. Similar to *The American School Board Journal*, though specializing a little less in building and equipment and somewhat more in the educational phases of administration. Superior articles of the latter type.

Overview (replacing *The School Executive*). Published monthly by Buttenheim Publishing Corporation, New York, New York. $5 a year.

School Management. Published monthly by School Management Magazines, Greenwich, Connecticut. $8 a year. [Similar to *Nation's Schools.*]

OTHERS

Educational Leadership. Published monthly, October through May, by the Association for Supervision and Curriculum Development, National Education Association, 1201 Sixteenth Street, N.W., Washington 6, D.C. $4.50 a year. [Principally given to short articles on modern democratic approaches to improvement of education.]

The Journal of Educational Research, Published monthly except June, July, and August, Dembar Publications, Madison, Wisconsin. New, $6 a year; renewal, $5 a year. [Articles of a definite research nature, relating to all fields of education. Book reviews, news notes, and abstracts of research articles in other periodicals.]

Personnel and Guidance Journal. American Personnel and Guidance Association, 1605 New Hampshire Avenue, N.W., Washington 9, D.C. $9 a year. [All phases of guidance principles and practices, with special emphasis upon educational services.]

School Activities. Published monthly, September through May, by the School Activities Publishing Company, 1041 New Hampshire Street, Lawrence, Kansas. $4 a year.

SUGGESTED PROFESSIONAL BOOKS FOR THE HIGH-SCHOOL PRINCIPAL. In selecting professional books it is desirable to have all the major fields represented. Below are given a few of the better books in a number of fields.

GENERAL SECONDARY EDUCATION

Alexander, William M., and Saylor, J. Glenn, *Secondary Education,* Rinehart.

Anderson, Vernon, and Gruhn, William, *Principles and Practices of Secondary Education,* Ronald.

Bent, Rudyard K., and Kronenberg, Henry H., *Principles of Secondary Education,* McGraw-Hill.

Bossing, Nelson, *Principles of Secondary Education,* Prentice-Hall.

Briggs, Thomas H., Leonard, J. P. and Justman, Joseph, *Secondary Education,* Macmillan.

Chisholm, Leslie L., *The Work of the Modern High School,* Macmillan.

Douglass, Harl R., *Secondary Education,* Ronald.

Gilchrist, Robert S., Dutton, Wilbur H., and Wrinkle, William L., *Secondary Education for American Democracy,* Rinehart.

GUIDANCE

Arbuckle, Dugall S., *Guidance and Counselling in the Classroom,* Allyn and Bacon.

Foster, Charles R., *Guidance Services for Today's Schools,* Ginn.

Froelich, Clifford P., *Guidance Services in Schools,* McGraw-Hill.

Jones, Arthur, *Principles of Guidance* (Revised Edition), McGraw-Hill.

Lefever, D. Welty, Turrell, Archie M., and Weitzel, Henry I., *Principles and Techniques of Guidance* (Revised Edition), Ronald.

McKown, H. C., *Homeroom Guidance,* McGraw-Hill.

Saalfeld, Lawrence J., *Guidance and Counselling for Catholic Schools,* Loyola University Press.

Stoops, Emery, and others, *Guidance Services, Organization and Administration,* McGraw-Hill.

Warters, Jane, *High School Personnel Work Today,* McGraw-Hill.

SUPERVISION

Alberty. H. B., and Thayer, V. T., *Supervision in the Secondary School,* Heath.

Briggs, Thomas H., and Justman, Joseph, *Improving Instruction through Supervision,* Macmillan.

Douglass, Harl R., Bent, R. K., and Boardman, Charles W., *Democratic Supervision in Secondary Schools,* Houghton Mifflin.

Hammock, Robert C., and Owings, Ralph S., *Supervising Instruction in Secondary Schools,* McGraw-Hill.

CURRICULUM

Alberty, Harold, *Reorganizing the High School Curriculum,* Harper.

Douglass, Harl R., and others, *The High School Curriculum,* Ronald.

Gruhn, William T., and Douglass, Harl R., *The Modern Junior High School,* Ronald.

Krug, Edward A., *The Secondary School Curriculum,* Harper.

Leonard, J. P., *Developing a Secondary School Curriculum,* Rinehart.

Romine, Stephen, *Building the Secondary School Curriculum,* Ronald.

EXTRACURRICULAR ACTIVITIES

Frederick, Robert W., *The Third Curriculum,* Appleton-Century-Crofts.

Gruber, Frederick C., *Secondary School Activities,* McGraw-Hill.

Johnston, Edgar, and Faunce, Roland, *Extra-Curricular Activities in the High School,* Ronald.

Kilzer, L. R., Stephenson, Harold H., and Norberg, H. Orville, *Allied Activities in the Secondary School,* Harper.

McKown, Harry C., *Extra-Curricular Activities,* Macmillan.

Miller, Franklin, James H. Mayer, and Robert B. Patrick, *Planning Student Activities,* Prentice-Hall, Inc.

METHODS OF TEACHING

Alexander, William M., and Halverson, Paul M., *Effective Teaching in Secondary Schools,* Rinehart.

Bossing, Nelson Louis, *Teaching in Secondary Schools,* Houghton Mifflin.

Grambs, Jean D., and Iverson, William J., *Modern Methods in Secondary Education,* Sloane.

Klausmeier, Herbert J., *Principles and Practices of Secondary School Teaching,* Harper.

Mills, H. H., and Douglass, Harl R., *Teaching in the High School,* Ronald.

Stiles, Lindley J., and Dorsey, Mattie F., *Democratic Teaching in Secondary Schools,* Lippincott.

Rivlin, Harry N., *Teaching Adolescents,* Appleton-Century Crofts.

MEASUREMENT AND EVALUATION

Adams, Georgia S., and Forgerson, Thomas L., *Measurement and Evaluation for the Secondary School Teacher,* Dryden Press.

Schwartz, Alfred, and Tiedeman, F. C., *Evaluating Student Progress in the Secondary School,* Longmans, Green.
Super, Donald E., *Appraising Vocational Fitness by Means of Psychological Tests,* Harper.
Thorndike, Robert L., and Hagen, Elizabeth, *Measurement and Evaluation in Psychology and Education,* Wiley.

GENERAL SCHOOL ADMINISTRATION

Grieder, Calvin, Pierce, Truman, and Rosenstengel, Everett, *Modern School Administration,* Ronald.
Hagman, Harlan L., *The Administration of American Public Schools,* McGraw-Hill.
Reeder, Ward G., *The Business Administration of a School System,* Ginn.
Reeder, Ward G., *Fundamentals of School Administration* (Revised Edition), Macmillan.

PSYCHOLOGY OF SECONDARY EDUCATION

Cole, Luella, *Psychology of Adolescence,* Rinehart.
Garrison, Karl C., *Psychology of Adolescence,* Prentice-Hall.
Hollingshead, A. B., *Elmtown's Youth,* Wiley.
Hurloch, Elizabeth B., *Adolescent Development,* McGraw-Hill.
Jersild, Arthur, *The Psychology of Adolescence,* Macmillan.
Johnson, Eric W., *How to Live Through Junior High School,* Lippincott.
Josselyn, Irene M., *The Adolescent and His World,* Family Service Association of America.
Landis, Paul H., *Adolescence and Youth,* McGraw-Hill.
Moore, Glyn, *The High School Principal and Staff Study Youth,* Teachers College.

General Education of the Principal. In recent years there has been much attention given to general education in high school and college. Recognizing that special education has been emphasized to the neglect of general education, many have tried to correct this emphasis for the benefit of specialists as well as those seeking an all-round education. In a great many colleges and universities very carefully planned programs of general education have been developed and more general education has been required and encouraged.

This trend has been going on in teachers' colleges and in departments, schools, and colleges of education with respect to the preparation of teachers. In recent years much more attention has been given to the general education of administrators as well.

General education includes study of good literature, study of the history of this country and of other parts of the world, study of the social sciences (including economics, political science, sociology, and geography), and study of the natural sciences (including physics, chemistry, geology, the earth sciences, and biology); it should develop an understanding of the world in which we live—the American way of life, the factors of international relations, and the general culture of the times, its trends and problems.

General education should develop, among other things, the following:

1. Habits and skills in clear and objective thinking and in the scientific approach to problems.
2. A high degree of competence in oral and written communication.
3. A basic philosophy of life and of human relations.
4. An interest in and understanding of the various peoples of the world with their different economic, social, and cultural backgrounds.
5. Understanding of the psychology of individual human beings, both others and oneself, and the ability to develop habits and attitudes leading to mental hygiene and health.
6. The conscious capacity for effective and amiable human relations in personal and group experiences.
7. The skills and attitudes involved in leadership of other human beings, in both professional and nonprofessional relationships.

THE PRINCIPAL AND HIS GENERAL READING. The schoolman has a special responsibility for keeping informed about what is going on in the world—about the trends in all phases of life with which the average citizen is likely to be concerned and about the problems which the generation of pupils now in school will most probably face in future years. His responsibility is much greater in this respect than that of the physician, the lawyer, and the businessman, who are more specialized in their work and interest and whose work is more concerned with the present and the immediate future. The profession of school administrators has marched far beyond that of schoolmasters. Since the administrator of today must lead in curriculum revision and organization, he must be oriented in all phases of current life. He must keep oriented with respect to trends and shifting problems in this country and in the world. Secondary education is concerned very much with the preparation of young people to live not only in this country but also in the world.

Unfortunately, conditions exist which tend to prevent the schoolman from fulfilling his obligation. In the first place, the majority of schoolmen are not broadly educated, being either graduates of teachers' colleges, with much work in education, or graduates of colleges and universities, with much specialization in some teaching field like chemistry or physical education. To make matters worse, in his postcollege professional life, the school man tends to be concerned altogether too exclusively with the details of his job: public relations, finances, teachers' and pupils' troubles, correspondence, and extracurricular activities.

Under these conditions, he tends to become a headline-reader. Too often, in his early and formative professional years in small school systems, he tends to become a small-town mind along with the hardware merchant, druggist, garage man, and banker. He talks boldly about matters concerning which he has had no experience and reads very little reliable material. He gives voice to opinions which are no more than reflections of his newspaper and the uninformed opinions of the leaders in his little community.

There are, however, many well-informed men among secondary-school administrators. Here is a typical reading program of such a principal:

1. One high-grade, relatively reliable daily newspaper.
2. At least one weekly or monthly periodical in each of three classes:
a. Conservative, such as:
The National Observer *Time* *Newsweek* *Reader's Digest*
b. Liberal or progressive, such as:
The Progressive *The New Republic* *The Nation* *The Reporter*
c. Middle-of-the-road, or neutral, such as:
The Atlantic Monthly *Harper's Magazine*

This type of school administrator finds that there are many excellent small books and pamphlets, such as:

The Headline Foreign Policy Books. Foreign Policy Association, New York.
The Public Affairs Pamphlets. Public Affairs Committee, New York.
The Permabooks. Garden City Books, New York.
Home Library Books. Home University Library, Oxford University Press, New York.

He also reads each year at least one of the classics such as:

The Bible.
Plato, *The Republic*
Aristotle, *Politics* and *Ethics.*
Emerson, Ralph Waldo, *Essays.*
Bacon, Francis, *Essays.*
Cervantes, Miguel, *Don Quixote.*
The Koran.
Shakespeare, William, *Plays.*
Tolstoy, Leo, *War and Peace.*
Rousseau, J. J., *Émile.*
Hugo, Victor, *Les Misérables.*
Ibsen, Henrik, *Plays.*
Shaw, George Bernard, *Plays.*
Undset, Sigrid, *Kristin Lavransdatter.*
Franklin, Benjamin, *Autobiography.*
Gibbon, Edward, *The Decline and Fall of the Roman Empire.*
Twain, Mark, *Huckleberry Finn.*
Whitman, Walt, *Leaves of Grass.*
Darwin, Charles, *The Origin of Species.*
Dostoevski, Feodor, *Crime and Punishment.*
Steffens, Lincoln, *Autobiography.*
Adams, Henry, *The Education of Henry Adams.*
Dreiser, Theodore, *An American Tragedy.*
Sandburg, Carl, *Abraham Lincoln, The Prairie Years.*
Lewis, Sinclair, *Babbitt* or *Main Street.*

This type of administrator is not content with keeping abreast of the best current thought in the field of letters and public affairs. He tries to hear some good music and to see some good art, a few plays, and a few of the best movies. In short, he spends much time, for the most part very enjoyably, in continuing to grow intellectually and emotionally and in avoiding the mental and cultural stagnation and degeneration that afflict many of the men with whom he comes in contact in his community. He works at the job of being an educator rather than a pedagogue, a leader rather than a community hired man or politician. He soon learns to command the respect of his fellow townsmen rather than to enjoy their patronizing indulgence. He learns to be patient with provincialism and lack of culture. He learns to enjoy his superior knowledge without unduly pressing his fellow men to follow his ideas; he learns to lead, not to push. He believes that it is worth while to be the intelligent leader of the most important institution in the community, the school.

The high-grade educator reads at least a few current books each year, books of the type of the following:[3]

Ashley-Montagu, Montague, F., *Statement on Race,* Henry Schuman. [An extended discussion of the UNESCO statement, presented simply and clearly by experts on race problems.]

Barth, Alan, *Loyalty of Free Men,* Viking. [A study of the relationship between individual liberty and national security; an important addition to an expanding literature on a vital question.]

Bernstein, Leonard, *Joy of Music,* Simon and Schuster. [Highly readable, well-illustrated conversations about music, ranging from early to modern music and from opera to jazz.]

Bowen, Catherine Drinker, *Adventures of a Biographer,* Little, Brown. [An autobiography exciting for readers of biographies, particularly those of Mrs. Bowen. A charming discussion of the time and effort involved in collecting the biographical documentation and other evidence used in recreating the lives of many famous men.]

Castro, Josué de, *The Geography of Hunger,* Little, Brown. [A study of world starvation and its cure.]

Ceram, C. (pseud.), *Gods, Graves and Scholars: The Story of Archaeology,* Knopf. [Dramatic stories of archaeological discoveries, authentically presented.]

Chapmen, Sidney, *IGY: Year of Discovery: The Story of the International Geophysical Year,* University of Michigan Press. [An extremely well-illustrated popular account of some of the scientific reports made in IGY; understandable and enlightening reading.]

Commager, Henry S. (Editor), *Living Ideas in America,* Harper. [The heritage of the United States set forth in an anthology of excerpts from American writers, past and present.]

Conant, James B., *Science and Common Sense,* Yale University Press. [Selected case histories used in explaining the methods of science for the layman.]

Cousins, Norman, *Doctor Schweitzer of Lambarene,* Harper. [An appraisal, by the editor of the *Saturday Review,* of the jungle doctor, the philosopher, the opponent of nuclear testing; a study based on the editor's visits to Lambarene.]

[3]For help in compiling this list the author is indebted to Dr. Eugene Wilson, former Director of Libraries, University of Colorado, and Miss Mary Louise Lyda, Head of Education Library, University of Colorado.

Davidson, Marshall B., *Life in America,* Houghton Mifflin. [An outstanding pictorial pageant of America's social, cultural, and enonomic history.]

Douglas, William O., *Strange Lands and Friendly People,* Harper. [The kaleidoscope of the Near East and India seen through the eyes of a distinguished jurist and liberal spokesman for democracy.]

Drury, Allen, *Advise and Consent,* Doubleday. [An interesting novel concerned with the operation of the legislative branch of our government.]

Frankfurter, Felix, *Felix Frankfurter Reminisces,* Reynal. [Lively anecdotes and candid critical opinion from the reminiscences of Justice Frankfurter.]

Heilbronner, Robert L., *The Future as History,* Harper. [A discussion of the scientific, democratic, and economic revolutions of today and the revolution of expectations among peoples of the world; a study of the course the world is following in the survival of liberal civilization—a perilous course but not a hopeless one.]

Hersey, John Richard, *Hiroshima,* Knopf. [A very interesting and well-written account of what happened at Hiroshima after the atomic explosion.]

Johnson, Gerald W., *This American People,* Harper. [Sensible and thought-provoking essays on the fundamentals of our American democracy.]

Johnson, Walter, *1600 Pennsylvania,* Little, Brown. [A study which shows the changes in the American Presidency in the past thirty years by examining the four men living in the White House during that time.]

Kennan, George F., *American Diplomacy, 1900-1950,* University of Chicago. An expert commentary on the course of American foreign policy.]

Lorant, Stefan, *The Presidency; a Pictorial History of Presidential Elections,* Macmillan. [A graphic history of political life in America, presented through well-chosen photographs and cartoons.]

Michener, James, *Hawaii,* Random House. [A social history of our newest state, written as a novel and usually enjoyable reading.]

Mumford, Lewis, *The Conduct of Life,* Harcourt, Brace. [A penetrating study of man's nature in which a learned humanist proposes ways to counteract the disastrous tendencies of our times.]

Salinger, J. D., *The Catcher in the Rye,* Little, Brown. [An examination of the dilemma of modern youth in a world of rapidly changing mores; a searching psychological study of a sixteen-year-old.]

Wolfert, Ira, *An Epidemic of Genius,* Simon and Schuster. [A record of the excitement of our mechanistic age, faithful to fact but emphasizing exciting influences of science such as, for example, electronic aids which allow men to pass among icebergs, factory automation, improved mining methods, and other developments which affect the daily employment of people in industry, labor, and the professions.]

3. Certification, Age, and Experience

In recent years many states have provided, through the state department of education or the office of the commissioner of education, at least one certificate for secondary-school principals. Usually, there are two types of certificates: the provisional certificate, which is good for a limited number of years and has lower standards than the permanent certificate; and the permanent certificate, which in a few states is beginning to be required of all principals. By 1961 all but five states—Alaska, Arkansas, Colorado, Hawaii, and North Dakota—required at least a provisional certificate; in four of these five states movements were under way to require a certificate and in three of the states relevant legislation had been introduced.

In all states having certificates, teaching experience is required. In thirty of the states three years of teaching experience are required; in seven states only two years of experience are required; and in eight states four or five years of experience are required. In thirty-seven of the states a master's degree is required; in a majority of these states the master's degree must be in the field of education, if not indeed in the field of secondary-school education or school administration. In six of the states the requirement includes professional training in addition to the master's degree. In twelve of the states requiring only the bachelor's degree, from three to thirty hours of work (usually including twelve to eighteen hours of courses in administration and supervision) are required.

In all but a few of the states which have the provisional certificate, it is not renewable; if the certificate is renewable, it can be renewed only upon substantial progress toward the master's degree, including appropriate courses in secondary education, supervision, and administration. In 1961 the standard certificate in twelve states was a permanent or life certificate; in other states a certificate might be renewed once or any number of times. Although usually for a period of five years, a renewal in three states was for ten years, in one state for seven years, and in three states for four years. In a few states the standard certificate was renewable only if a few hours of education courses had been completed, usually four, five, or six semester hours. It is evident that the trend is toward raising the requirements.

Although there has been much discussion, no state has developed separate certificates for junior high school principals and other secondary-school principals.

At present, the principal of a secondary school which is accredited by the various national associations must have a year's work beyond the bachelor's degree, but there is a strong movement towards requiring the principal of an accredited school, also to hold at least a provisional certificate and to be making progress toward the standard certificate. Before applying for or accepting a principalship, one should ascertain whether he is able to obtain a principal's certificate in the state in which the school is located.

Problems, Questions, and Exercises

1. If you were planning an ideal training for a high-school principal of not more than one year's work beyond the bachelor's degree, what would it include? Do you believe that the requirement of some sort of master's degree is a good requirement?

2. What do you think the high-school principal should do in order to keep up with developments in his field? Include in your thinking about this question attendance at summer school, workshops, and one-week or two-week conferences.
3. What does general education include and to what extent is it important for the high-school principal in either his preservice education or his in-service growth?
4. From the lists of professional books mentioned in this chapter, select what you think are the best one or two and the least valuable one or two under each division; give some reason for your choice.
5. Why is the general education of the modern high-school principal a matter of importance?
6. What books and journals, in addition to those mentioned in this chapter, would you recommend for the general education of the secondary-school principal? Would you distinguish between those for a junior high school principal and those for a senior high school principal?
7. With how many of the nonprofessional books listed in this chapter are you familiar? If familiar with only a small number, how do you account for that fact?
8. Do you believe in having a professional certificate for high-school principals? Do you think it should be required by schools? Schools of what size? If such a certificate is to be required, what would be a prerequisite for it?
9. Outline a plan of in-service growth for a principal during his first ten years of service as a principal.
10. In what areas should a principal have professional training?
11. For junior high school principals should anything special be required?

Selected Supplementary Readings

Eikenberry, D. H., "Training and Experience Standards for Principals of Secondary Schools," *Bulletin of the N.A.S.S.P.* (November, 1951), Vol. 35, No. 181, pp. 5-62. [The status of requirements for certification of secondary-school principals.]

Farmer, F. M., "The High School Principalship," *Bulletin of the N.A.S.S.P.* (April, 1948), Vol. 32, pp. 82-91. [The results of a questionnaire sent to principals by the U.S. Office of Education showing that the principalship is rapidly growing in professional status.]

Faunce, Roland C., *Secondary School Administration,* New York, Harper, 1955. [Chapter 16, "Appraising the Principal's Growth."]

French, Will, Hull, J. Dan, and Dodds, B. L., *American High School Administration,* New York, Rinehard, 1957. [Chapter 6, "The High School Principalship."]

Gorman, Burton W., "Some Characteristics of a Successful High School Principal," *American School Board Journal* (June, 1949), Vol. 118, p. 28. [Six common traits of a successful high-school principal, based on the writer's own experience.]

Hoshall, C. Earle, "In-Service Education of Principals," *Clearing House* (January, 1951), Vol. 25, No. 5, pp. 271-274. [Survey of frequency with which principals participate in or use eighteen different techniques for their own in-service education; also their opinions of the relative values.]

Jensen, Lisbeth J., "I Remember 8 Principals," *Clearing House* (September, 1948), Vol. 23, pp. 34-37. [A Minneapolis teacher describes eight principals and finds a lack of courage in six of them. Gives her idea of the perfect principal.]

McKeough, Reverend Michael, "Adequate Administration of the High School through Adequate Preparation," *Catholic Educational Review* (October, 1947), Vol. 45, pp. 467-474. [Sums up the duties, preparation, training, experience, and personal qualities of a good Catholic administrator.] "Training and Experience Standards for Principals of Secondary Schools," *Bulletin of the N.A.S.S.P.* (November, 1951), No. 181, p. 562.

4

Staffing the School

1. Determining Staff Needs

Each year it is necessary to determine the staff needs of the school, particularly with respect to the teaching members of the staff. It is necessary to know how many teachers of which subjects will be needed to implement the curriculum of the school in the light of the selections of subjects by the students. It is necessary first to estimate the number of sections in each of the subjects to be offered for which teachers must be obtained and then to determine the standards of teaching load that will be observed in assigning teachers.

The means of estimating the number of sections which are likely to be required to provide for the pupils registered in the various subjects are quite different in a school that is already in operation and in a new school that is just being established. In the former situation, if a spring preregistration is provided for early enough in the season, it is possible to obtain fairly reliable data from this registration of students for the various subjects. These figures being known, it is only necessary to decide upon the size of sections in order to determine the probable number of sections that will be required.

If no preregistration is employed, or if the spring preregistration for the following semester is not taken sufficiently early, the probable numbers in the various subjects may be estimated from registrations of previous years, modified according to certain facts or very probable influences. For example, from the enrollment in first-year French, Latin, typewriting, algebra, or homemaking, the probable enrollment of the second year in any of the subjects may be determined fairly closely by taking into consideration the relative registrations in second-year and first-year classes in these fields during previous years.

The basis for further refinements of estimates may be furnished by changes in requirements for graduation or in constants in various curriculums and by reports from instructors as to whether the percentage of students going on will be normal, less than normal, or greater than normal. In small schools, a change in the personnel of the teaching staff may influence enrollments. Sometimes, especially in small schools, the purchase of new equipment or the requirements of a course will influence enrollments. The introduction of new subjects or elimination of old ones, changes in year-placement of subjects, and unusual proportions of the sexes in one or more classes also may usually be counted on to influence registrations.

On the basis of estimated enrollments, the number of sections which should be offered in each subject can be ascertained. From the required number of sections should then be deducted the sections to be taught by the teachers who are remaining for the following year, care being taken to assign sections only to teachers with appropriate subject-matter education. The difference between the total number of sections and the number of sections to be taken by teachers already on the staff represents the number of sections for which new teachers must be obtained.

In schools which are just being established, very close estimates can be made, though with somewhat less accuracy. One source of data is the enrollment in the various subjects in neighboring schools of about the same size which offer about the same program of studies. In connection with such data, influences peculiar to the particular district should be taken into consideration. One such influence is the estimated greater or less percentage of college-preparatory or vocational students in the particular district. In some instances tentative registration of prospective students in feeder schools may be obtained.

The number of teachers employed should be such that the ratio of pupils to full-time members of the staff, including the teachers, does not exceed 25 to 1 and is nearer to 20 to 1.[1] Should the ratio run much below 20 pupils to each teacher, an abnormally high cost per pupil is certain to result, unless cheap teachers are employed. A careful survey should be made to ascertain the causes of a low ratio. Among the most likely causes are the development of a program of studies too ambitious for the size of the school and the offering of subjects with very small enrollments.

In schools already established, after the members of the staff who will remain for the coming year have been assigned to sections, a tentative assignment of sections and activities should be worked out for the positions to be filled, as an aid in selecting the best-qualified teachers. Assignments of duties to positions should be tentative so that other combinations of duties may be made if desirable candidates are found who do not fit into the tentative assignments. However, care should be exercised to see that the positions that are to be filled last do not involve combinations for which it is difficult to find qualified candidates—for example, manual training, English, and supervision of glee clubs; or physics, French, and supervision of journalistic activities. In schools following the Trump or a similar plan for team teaching, it will be necessary to determine the number of master teachers needed to lecture to the large classes and to act as chairmen of the teams. The desired number of clerks and aides to teachers should also be determined.

[1]In 1961 the average pupil-teacher ratio was approximately 21 to 1 in senior high schools and 23 to 1 in junior high schools.

Extra-Class Needs. After an appraisal of the needs in the teaching staff, a careful study must be made to see what the needs will be during the coming year for teachers qualified to act as sponsors and coaches of the various units of the extracurricular program.

Furthermore, careful assessment must be made of the needed counselors, school nurses, librarians, and other professional members of the staff.

The Administrative and Supervisory Staff. The administrative and supervisory staffs of secondary schools vary from a principal, in a small school, who teaches a full day and spends only a few hours weekly in administrative and supervisory duties to quite elaborate staffs, including various combinations of vice-principals, heads of departments, directors of athletics, directors of activities, psychologists, vocational counselors, registrars, deans of girls, deans of boys, and others who give part or full time to their special duties. Without doubt, most schools need more members of the staff who give part or full time to the duties of these positions. The employment of such staff members is a wise investment, but the practice is new and boards of education are generally conservative and sensitive to the criticisms of their constituency. In most districts a fallacious idea of what constitutes economy is a powerful influence in setting the limits to expenditures of public funds for education.

It is somewhat presumptuous and rather dogmatic to prescribe what should constitute the administrative and supervisory staff of a school of a given size. However, although many varying factors operate to prevent uniformity, reasonable standards can be set for a well-balanced and well-supported school. What may be regarded as adequate staffs for the modern administration and supervision of high schools of different sizes are shown in Table 1. Staffs of few schools of these sizes are as comprehensive as the recommendations shown there. The lack of a more complete development of the staff may be attributed very largely to the following factors:

1. The comparatively recent development of very large high schools.
2. The comparatively short time that extracurricular activities have occupied a prominent place in education theory and procedure.
3. The comparatively short time that educational and vocational guidance has occupied a prominent place in educational theory and procedure.
4. The recency of the development of the concept of increased responsibility of the school for the nonintellectual development of boys and girls, including health and moral education.
5. The rapid development within a few years of the possibilities of usefulness of a school psychologist.
6. The great influx into high school of boys and girls who constitute teaching, disciplinary, and other types of problems—children from homes of low social or moral status who a few years ago would have dropped out at the age of 15 or 16.
7. The recent rapid increase of scientific and technical knowledge concerning the duties which attach to the various newly developed functions of the high school.

Since all these developments are largely contributions of the last quarter of a century, they have yet to establish themselves in school organization and administration. Some administrators are skeptical, a few are relatively professionally ignorant, some are willing to let well enough alone, many others are unable to convince boards of education that money should be provided for the proper performance of these functions, and still others are making headway, gradually but surely, toward a more complete staff.

TABLE 1. *Suggested Staffing of High Schools*[2]

POSITION	SCHOOLS OF 1500 TO 3000	SCHOOLS OF 800 TO 1500	SCHOOLS OF 300 TO 800	SCHOOLS OF 100 TO 300	SCHOOLS OF LESS THAN 100
Principal	1	1	1/2–1	1/3–2/3	—
Vice-principal or co-ordinator of instruction	1	1/2–3/4	1/3–1/2	—	—
Vice-principal or director of activities	1	1/2–3/4	1/3–1/2	—	—
Vice-principal or director of guidance	1	1/2–2/3	1/6–1/3	—	—
Psychologist	1/2–1	1/3–1/2	1/6–1/3	—	—
Counselors	6–10	3–6	1–3	1/3–1	—
Director of health and physical education	1/2–1	1/4–1/2	1/6–1/3	—	—
Librarian	2–4	1–2	1/2–1	1/3–1/2	1/6
Director of athletics	1/2–1	1/3–1/2	1/6–1/3	1/6	—
Heads of departments or special supervisors	4–6	2–3	1–2	1/2–1	—
Attendance supervisor	1–2	2/5–4/5	1/5	—	—
Physician	1	1/2–1	1/6–1/2	—	—
Nurses	2–5	1–2	2/5–1	1/5–2/5	—
Dentist	1–2	1/2–1	1/6–1/2	—	—
Director of testing and research	1	1/3–1/2	1/6–1/3	—	—
Office secretary and clerks	5–8	3–5	1–3	1/2–1	—
Director of cafeteria	1	1	1/2–1	1/3–1/2	—

It is evident that the number and the nature of the administrative and supervisory personnel of high schools will vary with the extent to which communities have been educated to provide for improved specialized types of service. The number and the nature of such agents will also vary, as they should, with the size of the school. As the school becomes larger, the number may be increased; greater specialization may be effected with less and less per-pupil cost. In the smaller schools two or even more

[2]Entries denote the proportion of the time of a full-time official which should be available for the position in question, In schools of small or medium size various combinations of duties may be centered in one individual—for example, psychologist and director of guidance; director of athletics and director of health and physical education.

types of specialized service must, for reasons of economy, be performed by one person. In the smallest schools these specialized activities will be performed by the high-school principal or by members of the teaching staff as part-time responsibilities.

Before entering into a discussion of the sources of prospective teachers or of the techniques of gathering data regarding their qualifications and selection, there should be a consideration of the standards which should be entertained in judging the fitness of candidates for different types of positions.

2. *Standards for the Selection of Secondary-School Teachers*

STANDARDS FOR JUNIOR HIGH SCHOOLS.

1. Academic Preparation. Not less than four years of college training should be required of those who teach in a junior high school. Adequate academic preparation in the field to be taught must be insisted upon. Teachers of history should have had college courses in American history, world history, political science, economics, and sociology. Teachers of English should have had courses in written and oral English and in English, American, and world literature. Teachers of general science should have had courses in biology, physics, and chemistry, either in high school or in college, preferably in addition to a course in geology or physiography. Teachers of geography should have had courses above a high-school grade in geography and some training in economics. Teachers of social studies should have had a minimum of twenty semester hours of courses in political science, economics, and sociology. Teachers of foreign languages should have had the equivalent of at least twenty-four semester hours of college instruction in the language taught; they should be able to speak the language taught with accuracy of pronunciation and considerable fluency. Teachers of mathematics should have had intermediate courses in algebra and trigonometry. Similar standards should be observed in selecting teachers of art, music, physical education, household arts, and shop.

2. Professional Training. It is not too much to insist upon a minimum of twenty-four semester hours of work in education and educational psychology (not including general psychology), including psychology of learning, secondary education, introduction to education, evaluation and measurement, theory and practice of the junior high school, general methods of teaching, practice teaching, and methods of teaching some particular subject field. Teachers who have had courses in educational and vocational guidance, curriculum construction, mental hygiene, child growth and development, and the theory and management of extra-curricular activities should be readily preferred.

It is not argued that teachers may not be successful with less than the minimum outlined above; but it is certain that a staff composed largely of teachers with less preparation is more than likely, on the whole, to do an inferior or medium order of teaching and that, other things being equal, teachers possessing this training will be superior to those who do not possess it. The fact that the junior high school is a comparatively recent development, with new aims, functions, and practices, demands that the staff be selected with much attention to professional preparation. It is quite probable that the relative failure of many junior high schools to measure up to expectations may be traced to the lack of mastery of the theory and practices of the new institution on the part of principal and teaching staff.

3. Experience. Unfortunate practices have operated to bring into the junior high school, in larger numbers than is desirable, teachers of two types of experience: younger teachers gaining the experience which is supposed to qualify them for positions in the senior high school; mature men and women of long elementary-school experience who are being "promoted" to better positions, even though they have inadequate subject-matter preparation and no course on junior high school education. Teachers with successful experience in grades 7 and 8 and sufficient subject-matter education usually make good junior high school teachers, as do those with experience in four-year high schools, a course in junior high school education, and a personality and philosophy of education suited to junior high school students.

4. Personality. One of the most potent qualifications making for success in junior high school teaching is the possession of traits of personality and abilities which adapt their owner to work with boys and girls between twelve and sixteen. Among these (very desirable in junior high school teachers, yet very difficult to measure or to recognize except in teachers in service) are patience with immaturity in scholarship, the love of young people of the ages concerned, masterfulness in management, and a sense of human values (as differentiated from subject-matter values).

STANDARDS FOR SENIOR OR FOUR-YEAR HIGH SCHOOLS.

1. Academic Preparation. It is becoming evident that five years of college or university study are needed for the complete preparation of teachers for secondary schools. As rapidly as possible, those having to do with the selection of teachers should come to require at least one year of work beyond the four-year course leading to the bachelor's degree. Already, many city school districts are requiring the fifth year; in New York, California, Oregon, and the District of Columbia (and probably in other states in the very near future) five years of college work are required for the standard certificate. In 1961 slightly more than half of the secondary-school teachers in senior and four-year high schools had at least a master's degree. In addition to bringing about more effective preparation of teachers, such a requirement will operate to reduce materially the large number of men and women who enter teaching only temporarily, are not professionally interested in their calling, and cannot be counted upon to continue their professional growth. Instructors in European secondary schools generally have the equivalent of from two to four years of training beyond the equivalent of our B.A. or B.S. degree. High-school teaching in this country can never hope to attain a truly professional status until at least some training beyond the bachelor's degree is demanded and the door is thereby closed to the great army of transients who now occupy teaching positions in high schools.

Teachers should be selected who not only possess adequate margins of scholarship in the fields in which they will teach but also have studied an appropriate pattern of subjects in those fields. For example, one who is to teach English should have had from forty to fifty semester hours in the field and the courses taken should have included courses in dramatics and public speaking, several courses in English and American literature (including some study of Shakespeare), a course in modern literature, and several courses in English language and composition. A teacher of the social studies should have had at least forty semester hours of college study in government, economics, sociology, geography, American history, and the history of the ancient, medieval, and modern world, with emphasis upon modern world history.

In the State of New York the Board of Regents has set up the minimum subject-matter requirement for high-school teachers of academic subjects as follows: English, thirty-six semester hours; foreign language, twenty-four semester hours; mathematics, eighteen semester hours; science, forty-two semester hours; social studies, thirty-six semester hours. In New York, a teacher may obtain a provisional certificate which will enable him to teach for not more than five years, during which time a fifth year of advanced study must be completed for the permanent certificate.

2. *Professional Training.* The need for special professional education is possibly not quite so great as it is in the case of junior high school teachers, but the amount which may be considered a reasonable minimum is greater than that possessed by the majority of high-school teachers throughout the United States today. At least twenty semester hours of courses, including courses in adolescent psychology, methods of student-teaching, guidance, and course of study construction, would constitute a reasonable requirement.

STANDARDS FOR ALL SECONDARY-SCHOOL POSITIONS.

1. *Personality.* In selecting secondary-school teachers as well as teachers for other units of the school system, preference must be given to those whose traits of personality are such as to make for their success in the positions. Prominent among such traits are poise and emotional balance, patience, cheerfulness, energy, enthusiasm, willingness to co-

operate, ability to get on with other people (pupils, patrons, colleagues, and professional superiors), moral stability, ideals of fairness, good personal appearance, manners, and voice, and general intelligence. The last-named trait enters into a number of the others.

2. *General Culture.* In addition to special academic and professional education, the high-school teacher should possess intellectual, cultural, and social interests and enthusiasms. He should be interested and informed in current history—political, economic, and social—and in recent developments in industry and science. He should be a well-read individual who follows the affairs of the world, not merely a purveyor of specialized subject matter who, because of the narrowness of his academic interests and experience, is unable to relate his subject to life conditions and problems.

3. *Sex.* Foreign observers of American secondary education almost invariable comment on the large number of women teachers in secondary schools. Secondary-school staffs in leading foreign countries are composed almost entirely of men. It is asserted that men are by nature and experience better qualified to teach courses in industrial arts and social studies, that they are equally qualified to teach English, foreign languages, and mathematics, and that their influence in the development of desirable traits of character and personality (particularly in boys) is needed in secondary schools. Many also maintain that men are much more interested in their work as a profession and permit outside interests to interfere much less in the discharge of their duties and in their professional advancement. With these things in mind, the better high schools throughout the country are attempting to keep on their staffs a minimum of 50 per cent of male teachers.[3] In the fall of 1960, for the first time the number of male secondary-school teachers exceeded that of female secondary-school teachers.

4. *Age.* It is best that a teaching staff not be composed in large part of very young teachers, superannuated teachers, or a combination of both. In about one district in five, usually in larger city districts, an age limit is set for appointments to the teaching staff. Forty-five years is the most common maximum age set.

5. *Experience.* In some large high schools, candidates for positions are required to have had two years of experience; in recent years, as a result of the teacher shortage, the number of schools with this requirement has decreased very materially. If salaries are distinctly above the average, this requirement is probably justified from the point of view of the interests of the local school, even though it is desirable for beginning teachers to get their first two or three years of experience in larger

[3]Herda discovered that, as far as results of the Minnesota state board examinations are concerned, what differences there are between men and women in teaching effectiveness are at least as often in favor of the women as of the men. See F. J. Herda, "Relative Instructional Efficiency of Men and Women Teachers," *Journal of Educational Research,* Vol. 29, pp. 196-203.

schools, where better supervision is usually to be had and where a more complete departmentalization exists. If salaries are not sufficient to attract the better type of experienced teacher, such a standard operates to bar the more promising novice in favor of a mediocre or inferior experienced teacher.

6. *Marital Status.* Discussions of the relative merits of married and unmarried teachers have been endless and usually decisionless. From the point of view of general social considerations, there is something to be said against taking married women away from their homes and children and putting them into competition with breadwinners. From the point of view of teaching effectiveness, test scores of pupils and opinions of supervisors do not settle the question. Married women, on the whole, seem to understand children a little better. They seem, on the whole, a little better balanced emotionally. However, they are usually not so professional in their interests and are not keenly interested in attending committee meetings, teachers' meetings, or other activities of professional growth; they usually belong to cliques, factions, or other groups along with their husbands; and they are very difficult to discharge when incompetent or unco-operative.

Studies furnish no basis for believing that married teachers are either inferior or superior on the whole. A practice which is rarely, though increasingly, being utilized is the practice of employing married women for half-days only. At present, in more than 90 per cent of the school districts maintaining high schools, married women may be given appointments as regular teachers.

7. *Health and Physical Handicaps.* In recent years increasing numbers of schools have required new teachers to submit evidence of being in good physical health (at least as far as contagious diseases are concerned) before final contracts are signed. In some districts a physical examination is required every two or three years.

In recent years less emphasis has been placed upon physical handicaps; it has been discovered that, except in rare cases, teachers with handicaps usually succeed as well in teaching as those without them.

8. *Home-Town Teachers.* Another perennial question is that of the relative desirability of the teacher whose parents live in the community—the home-talent teacher. In regard to teaching efficiency, there is in all probability little difference whether a given teacher teaches in his home town or elsewhere. There are in villages and in smaller cities, however, objections on other scores: (1) home-town teachers of poor ability can bring pressure to bear upon local boards and thus secure employment which they could not otherwise secure; (2) they are hard to deal with when they fall short in competence, co-operation, or professional growth and when they develop differences with their colleagues; and (3) they are subject to all the antagonisms which the family has developed in the community and are thus often handicapped in pupil and parent relationships.

3. *Selecting the Staff: Procedure and Machinery*

WHO SHALL SELECT HIGH-SCHOOL TEACHERS? Within recent years superintendents of schools have been engaged in educating local boards of education to the point of view that all teachers should be selected by the professional head of the schools and not by lay boards, on the grounds that he is more competent to discharge that responsibility and that his authority should parallel his responsibility. If he is to be held responsible for the results obtained by his teachers, he should have a free hand in selecting them.

In all but the smaller schools the same arguments apply to some extent to the proposal that the high-school principal should participate in the selection of instructors and heads of department for his school and should in turn consult with his department heads and the directors of the fields concerned. Except in the very large school systems where teachers are employed by the dozen for various departments and in small districts where the superintendent is in reality also the high-school principal, there is very little to be said for the practice of retaining the selection of high-school teachers completely in the hands of the superintendent of schools. The principal and the department heads are much more closely in touch with the needs of the school and are better able to decide just what training and type of personality are most desirable for a given vacancy; also it is sound business policy to co-ordinate authority with responsibility.

CO-OPERATIVE PROCEDURE. In an increasing number of schools of medium size, committees of teachers assist the principal, superintendent, or director of personnel in selecting new teachers. This type of procedure is likely to result not only in better teachers being obtained but also in professional growth on the part of the teachers participating and in good relationships between them and the teachers selected.

INDUCEMENTS TO CANDIDATES. In recent years there has been a very great shortage of qualified high-school teachers, particularly in the fields of mathematics and science. To get the best teachers for the money available, the vacant positions must be made attractive and sold to the prospective candidate. Teachers prefer to work in schools in which they find: (1) security in position; (2) superior opportunities for a well-rounded social life; (3) high morale and good feeling between the teachers, the supervisor, and administrative personnel; (4) a teaching load that is not excessive; (5) attractive and not overcrowded buildings, as well as instructional equipment; (6) a salary scale with automatic increases and a high maximum salary; and (7) a reasonably good situation with respect to student behavior. If there are opportunities for advancement for a particular candidate, opportunities for extra pay for extra services, or extra raises for demonstrated merit and value as a teacher, these may be mentioned as further inducements.

A number of schools are preparing small pamphlets to be used in describing to prospective candidates the schools and the cities in which they are located. Such a pamphlet might well give information concerning scale, the teaching load, special features in the life of the teachers of the school that might be of interest, and considerable information about the city and its attractiveness as a place in which to live.

A development which has done much to make positions more attractive to teachers is the trend, particularly strong in recent years, toward permanent tenure or continuing contracts. A continuing contract usually provides that a teacher, even at the end of the first year of teaching, is to be retained the following year unless notice has been given the teacher several months before the end of the school term, usually in April. In many places the continuing-contract plan also provides that a notice of failure to renew the contract must be approved by a majority of the board members, not just a majority of those attending any particular meeting.

TRANSFERS AND DISMISSALS. In spite of the fact that a very large majority of districts provide tenure for teachers (in many instances only after a probationary period of two or three years), it becomes necessary to dismiss some teachers and transfer others to a different type of position or a different school. Unfortunately, a somewhat unethical practice is followed in some schools relative to the attainment of tenure: employing officers in some schools do not select their teachers as carefully as they should and, as a result, a fairly high percentage of teachers in those schools do not obtain tenure after their probationary period. Because a teacher leaves a situation like this with a very black mark on his record, such cases should be held to a low minimum.

When it seems necessary to dismiss a teacher from a school system, the teacher should have ample warning, at least several months before the time for reissuing of contracts and selection of new teachers, that his work is not satisfactory and that unless marked improvement is made he will not be re-employed for the next year. In cases where dismissal is necessary, there should be a written notice of dismissal at least two months before the end of the school term. In many districts a teacher may not be dismissed without being given the opportunity of a hearing before the board of education. In practice a very large majority of the teachers who are given notices of dismissal do not request a hearing.

PROCEDURE. The matter of selecting the staff should not be left until late spring. The principal should be ready early in March with recommendations regarding the present staff. At this time, or even earlier if necessary because of earlier dates for formulating the budget for the coming year, he should have thought through the personnel needs for the coming year and have organized his data and arguments for contemplated additions to the staff. Instructors who are to be retained should be informed not later than April 1. By April 15, or soon thereafter, the principal should have a fairly accurate idea as to which of the present staff may be counted on for the coming year. If the advance registration is taken about this time and the need for new teachers fairly closely estimated, the principal and superintendent can begin the search for good prospects.

Although as a matter of organization it is probably desirable that all applications pass through the office of the superintendent, there is no reason why the principal should not exercise initiative in looking for superior candidates and encouraging them to make application. Those making personal application should be referred to the principal for interviews and their papers referred to him for evaluation. In fairness to candidates those not likely to be employed should be advised to continue their efforts to find satisfactory positions elsewhere. The contents of a confidential recommendation, favorable or unfavorable, should not be revealed or hinted at.

SOURCES OF APPLICATIONS. There may be distinguished the following means of getting in touch with interested prospective teachers:

1. Visitation of other schools.
2. Inquiries made of teachers and school people.
3. Placement bureaus of educational institutions.
4. Placement bureaus of state departments of education and state teachers' associations.
5. Voluntary applications.
6. Teachers' agencies charging commissions.
7. Candidates suggested by local friends of candidates.

Though good teachers may be obtained from each of these sources, the chances of obtaining good teachers are not equally good for all sources.

1. Recommendations by Local Friends. Names of teachers are suggested by their local friends almost invariably in the interest of the candidates, with little regard for the welfare of the school. A local friend is ordinarily not professionally competent to judge teachers and is almost always biased in favor of the candidate suggested; even if he is a competent judge, he will not hesitate to overrate the qualifications of the candidate. There is danger in employing teachers whose dismissal, in case of failure, may make influential enemies for the administration; also the promotion of such teachers will always be of interest to their local friends. The practice of following up local recommendations will eventually lead to the disappointment of local residents that recommend unqualified candidates, whose failure to be elected or re-elected will often be taken as a reflection upon the personal prestige and influence of the individuals making the recommendations.

2. Teachers' Agencies Charging Commissions. A wide variation exists in the quality of service and reliability of teachers' agencies. One objection, however, applies to them as a class: namely, they serve to reduce the net salary paid to teachers, usually by 5 per cent. Teachers' salaries are at best too low and the interposition of a middleman, even at the small commission of 5 per cent, is not to be desired if equally satisfactory teacher placement may be obtained by other means. The fact that many teachers may obtain through agencies positions which net a higher salary than they could obtain for themselves does not affect the situation as far as teachers as a class are concerned. From the standpoint of the economy of the school funds, it means that the purchasing power of the money available for salaries is decreased by the amount paid by teachers in agency commissions. The policy of some agencies of assisting superintendents who patronize them to obtain better positions for themselves has not operated to increase confidence in the agency as a means of teacher placement.

Judging by the requests sent out by many agencies to school officials who have been given as references by teachers, the agencies collect only scanty information concerning teachers, their fitness for the subjects they are willing to teach, and their moral character and personal qualities. Such a lack of thoroughness does not develop confidence in the recommendations of such agencies.

On the other hand, many superintendents and principals can recall having obtained excellent teachers through teachers' agencies. Also quite often savings may be effected in some districts by getting in touch with teachers' agencies in sections of the country where an oversupply of teachers has reduced the minimum for which they are willing to contract.

3. Voluntary Applications. Voluntary applications may bring to the attention of the employing official high-school teachers of excellent training and ability as well as a larger number of teachers who are more energetic in seeking positions than in giving service. When the candidate is teaching in a school nearby or in a school whose principal can be relied upon to recommend the candidate according to his merits, the uninvited application may prove a fruitful lead.

4. State Agencies. In a number of states, the department of public instruction or the state teachers' association furnishes teacher-placement services. Usually a very small fee or commission is charged. While these bureaus may be relied upon as fair and honest, by their very nature they are quite conservative in distinguishing between superior and inferior teachers; also, unlike the placement service of the educational institution, in few instances are they able to speak from close personal acquaintance with their candidates.

5. College Placement Bureaus. A weakness of the college placement bureau is its reliance on letters of recommendation written by professors of academic subjects who are better judges of scholastic ability than of the candidate's prospects as a classroom instructor. Yet these bureaus have decided advantages. Ordinarily, they take greater care than do teachers' agencies to investigate the preparation of the candidate in the different subjects to be taught. Academic records of teachers which indicate both their amount of training and their quality of scholarship are readily available to such bureaus. Usually, too, recommendations based on practice teaching are available; these are more likely to be frank and based upon much supervision than are other types of letters of recommendation.

6. *Professional Acquaintances.* A very fruitful source of useful information is an active inquiry made of teachers and other school officials, such as county and city superintendents and principals, about good prospects. Their recommendations, likely to be honest and frank, lead quite often to investigations which result in the employment of superior teachers.

Modern Recruitment Practices. By far the most common sources of data relative to prospective teachers are the placement bureaus of institutions of teacher education. Also, except in very rare cases, personal interviews are required. In the very great majority of cities, formal application forms are employed and information is collected from references given. The great majority of the schools require applicants to submit transcripts of their college work. Proof is required of the possession of the legal certificates. Experience records given by the candidate are verified by correspondence.

It is rather generally agreed that it is better policy to seek good teachers for positions than to confine the selection to those who apply. Many excellent teachers do not apply for positions. Those applying for positions in a large number of schools are more than likely to include a disproportionate percentage of mediocre or inferior candidates who are not valued in the schools in which they teach. The wide-awake principal or superintendent will be constantly on the lookout for superior teachers – making inquiries, noting contributions and papers of progressive teachers in local and state associations and in educational journals, and visiting other schools and the appointment bureaus of institutions which train secondary-school teachers.

Perhaps the most reliable means of uncovering a small number of excellent prospects is to inspect better teachers in other schools. However, the lack of time and funds to carry on this search, combined with the reluctance of some school officials to encourage representatives of other schools to visit their schools with a view to employing their better teachers, operates to restrict the employment of this otherwise useful method. Nevertheless, there should be no question about the propriety of visiting the classrooms of teachers who have made application, assuming, of course, that the consent of the teacher visited and the local administrator have been obtained.

In observing teachers, many things should be looked for, including particularly the following: the degree to which the teacher explains clearly, uses good examples in teaching, is cheerful and good-natured, is friendly to the pupils and has a sense of humor, is apparently interested in the work, seems to understand pupils, keeps the youngsters' minds active throughout the period, provides opportunities for the youngsters to participate, is apparently well-liked and accepted by the students, and uses visual aids in teaching.

4. Collecting Data Concerning Applicants

DATA DESIRED ABOUT PROSPECTIVE TEACHERS. The most frequently desired and most useful information regarding prospective candidates may be summarized as follows:

1. Education: amount, subjects of specialization, professional certificate, participation in extracurricular activities.
2. Experience: amount, nature, character of success, dates and places, supervision or coaching of "activities."
3. Scholarship.
4. Ability to maintain orderly classroom conditions.
5. Teaching ability.
6. Tact and ability to get along with pupils and parents.
7. Special weaknesses likely to affect teaching efficiency.
8. Enthusiasm and interest in work.
9. Character.
10. Personal appearance.
11. General success in school and community.
12. Co-operation and loyalty.
13. Social qualities.
14. Probability of professional growth.
15. General culture, including reading tastes and habits.
16. Age.
17. Health and freedom from physical defects.
18. Marital status.
19. Height and weight.
20. Salary desired.
21. Intelligence.

Some of these items merit special consideration in the selection of teachers with superior qualifications.

SOURCES OF DATA. The most commonly employed sources of information concerning prospective teachers are listed below.

Application Blanks: education, experience, age, health, marital status, height and weight, salary desired, subjects of specialization, teaching and other vocational experience, activity experience, appearance (photographs), certificate.

References: (1) previous instructors: scholarship, character, personal appearance, personality traits, social qualities, intelligence; (2) school officials: experience, ability to maintain order, teaching ability, character, personal appearance, co-operation and loyalty, health, traits of personality, defects, social qualities, probability of professional growth, enthusiasm, interest in work.

Interviews: personality, appearance, salary desired, health, physical defects, general culture.

Classroom Visitation: scholarship, ability to maintain order, teaching ability, teaching personality, enthusiasm, interest in work.

Credentials of Agencies and Bureaus: items listed under application blanks and references.

Transcripts of Credits: indication of pattern of preparation in some detail and also of quality of scholarship (occasionally candidates have been known to misrepresent the courses taken and the grades received).

NATIONAL TEACHERS' EXAMINATION. In recent years the Educational Testing Service of Princeton, New Jersey, has been preparing and giving in a large number of cities throughout the country a group of tests to measure educational preparation most likely to contribute to the success of teachers. The tests, revised annually, cover these fields:

1. Professional information in the areas of guidance, methods, curriculum, community relationships, and psychology of learning.
2. General culture, including knowledge of contemporary events and developments.
3. English expression.
4. Nonverbal reasoning.
5. Knowledge in one or two of the thirteen teaching fields in which there are examinations.

Upon payment of a small fee, the teacher or prospective teacher may take as many of these examinations as he wishes and have the papers scored, recorded, and sent to any designated administrator or board of education. There is no failing or passing mark. The score and its percentile rank among the scores of all taking the particular examination are recorded and forwarded to the employing person or board designated by the teacher. The employing agency may evaluate the score in any manner it chooses.

The National Teachers' Examinations are usually given in the second week in February. Applications must be received and approved by an announced date, usually before the end of the second week in January.[4]

PHOTOGRAPHS. Photographs are of very little value in predicting success except as they may serve to weed out what appear to be impossible candidates; even in those instances, if information from all other sources is favorable, they should not be taken too seriously. A negligible degree of correlation has been found between ratings based on photographs and the ratings of supervisors, principals, and assistant superintendents as to teaching success.

HEALTH DATA. Because of the continued close contact of pupil and teacher in the classroom, there is need for assurance that the teacher is

[4]The bulletin of information may be obtained from National Teachers' Examinations, Educational Testing Service, 20 Nassau Street, Princeton, New Jersey.

free from pulmonary and other contagious diseases. In the interests of efficiency it is also desirable to be assured that the vigor of the teacher is not impaired by constitutional physical weakness. In many schools the required health information consists only of a report on the results of a chest X-ray and a statement from a physician about the teacher's freedom from communicable diseases.

PERSONAL INTERVIEWS. Even the personal interview taken alone is not very reliable, as everyone knows who has had experience as director of a university or college placement bureau. Very often, excellent teachers do not "sell themselves" well; those who appear best at first meeting frequently lack qualities necessary for teaching success, prove to be hard to supervise, are not interested professionally, or are otherwise not suited for high-grade service.

One of the principal attainable objectives of a personal interview is to discover the fundamental educational philosophy of the person being interviewed, in order to employ for the school teachers whose philosophy of education is in harmony with that of the school and its program. Progressive, child-growth-centered teachers are very much to be desired in some schools; subject-matter-centered teachers are preferable in others. Also, in a personal interview teachers' attitudes toward working with extracurricular activities, counseling conferences, or public-relations activities may be explored.

Of course, a personal interview gives some knowledge relative to personal appearance and the correctness and forcefulness of the applicant's English expression.

In a majority of schools, including practically all of the smaller schools, applicants are interviewed by the superintendent of schools; in the larger schools the applicant is interviewed by the principal and in many instances by both the principal and the superintendent. In a small but substantial minority of schools applicants are also interviewed by one or more members of the board of education; in some schools applicants are interviewed by appropriate heads of departments.

In many instances, particularly in the case of a beginning teacher, the interview takes place at the college where the prospective teacher is about to be graduated.

MENTAL HEALTH. In recent years much more attention has been given to the mental health of teachers. There is a growing conviction that mental health is more important than physical health and that teachers who are subject especially to certain kinds of mental and emotional handicaps should be directed into kinds of occupations which do not call for working with young people and which do not involve tensions like those in the classroom. Persons who are unusually introverted, especially self-conscious, inclined to be excitable and irritable, inclined to feel that they are underestimated and that people are against them, or inclined to be morbid and pessimistic are not to be preferred as teachers.

There are certain types of tests that are available for measuring personality traits and, of course, the reports from previous principals and superintendents should throw some light on the matter of applicants' mental health. To a slight extent reliance may be placed upon personal interviews.

Certification Data. In considering possible candidates for positions, it should be determined quite early whether each applicant who is being favorably considered has or will be able to obtain a certificate valid for the position for which he is being considered. Most state departments of public instruction prepare and distribute bulletins of information regarding certification. The new principal should acquaint himself with the requirements as stated in the school law and in the regulations of the state department of instruction. The candidate's qualifications should be checked against these requirements. It is not safe to take the candidate's word or judgment on this point, especially if he comes from outside the state.

Letters from the Applicant and His References. Considerable reliance may usually be placed on the statements of the candidate as to the amount and nature (not quality) of his experience, his approximate height and weight, his marital status, his age, and the amount of his specific preparation for the teaching of any particular subject or subjects. In determining the quality and relative teaching success of candidates, no consideration should be given to general letters of recommendation furnished by them. Only fair confidence should be placed in direct letters of recommendation, even though the candidate is not aware of their contents. Various motives actuate those who write such letters and the range of their accuracy and frankness is as wide as the scale of such values. In most instances, in addition to the letters given by the candidate as references, a letter of inquiry should be sent to at least one individual who is in a position to speak of the candidate's success or probable success, particularly if there is one such individual among the friends or professional acquaintances of the selecting officer. Such inquiry should be made only if it is certain not to embarrass the candidate in his present position. If there is any doubt in this matter, permission to write a letter of inquiry should first be obtained from the candidate.

Application Forms. Though it is apparent that certain items are essential in application forms, it is difficult to say exactly what should be included in such forms. The best forms include the items listed below:

Personal: age, sex, race or nationality, state of health, sight and hearing, weight and height, bodily infirmities, marital state, photograph.

Experience: schools, subjects taught, dates, references.

Education: schools, dates, degrees, number of semester credits in major subjects and in other subjects which might be considered as preparation for teaching the subjects the candidate wishes to teach, number of semester hours in education, names of courses.

Extracurricular activities: experience or preparation, nature, schools, date.

REFERENCE FORMS. Some school officials charged with the responsibility of selecting teachers do not employ reference forms; they merely request a statement from the person given as reference regarding the probable fitness of the candidate for the type of position for which he is applying and which is described in the request. This plan has the advantage of stimulating the reference to give information concerning points which are of such a variety of types that it is practically impossible to include provision for all of them in a form. The plan also operates in many cases to inspire a feeling of responsibility for the exercise of good faith in revealing all pertinent information. On the other hand, the form saves time and the mental effort of deciding what to mention, is much more easily interpreted when filed, and is likely to call forth useful information that would otherwise be omitted, intentionally or unintentionally. The best forms sent to principals, supervisors, or others who have seen the candidate teach ask for comment on such items as the candidate's general success in teaching, ability to maintain orderly classroom procedure, suitability for various subjects or grades, co-operative spirit, capacity for growth, general intelligence, appearance, reason for leaving position, and any weak points. These forms also ask, "Would you be willing to employ this candidate?"

In order to save the person of whom information is asked from writing, many employing officials have prepared a rating device to be used in connection with appropriate points. Two devices commonly used are the best-answer underscoring device and the graphic rating scheme.

The graphic device possesses the advantage of permitting the rater to make finer distinctions, if he wishes to make them, by placing a check or cross on the line at any point which he believes appropriate, though he is under no obligation to employ intermediate points. In many of these blanks, confusion is caused by the employment of words which do not uniformly express the same degree of difference. For example, some blanks employ both "excellent" and "superior"; some of these designate the highest quality by "superior" and some designate it by "excellent." Ordinarily, it is not worth while to distinguish between more than five degrees of quality. Space should always be provided for additional comments, which should be encouraged.

THE FILING OF DATA CONCERNING THE TEACHERS ELECTED. Although it is a conventional courtesy to return to agencies and bureaus the photographs, credentials, and other papers submitted by them and to return photographs and copies of letters of reference to unsuccessful candidates as soon as it is evident that they will not be appointed, it is good policy to retain all information and all correspondence relating to a successful candidate. This material will be useful in several types of situations, including: (1) the assignment of the candidate's responsibilities in the school, (2) any misunderstanding between the candidate and the principal as to the types of work which the candidate professed to be able to do, and (3) the publication of news stories in regard to additions to the faculty or in regard to the particular candidate.

OBTAINING AN UNDERSTANDING CONCERNING THE DUTIES OF NEW TEACHERS. At the time of appointment the newly selected teacher should be informed, insofar as possible, about what his duties will be. This will enable him to make whatever preparation he may feel desirable for his new work. It also reduces the possibility of misunderstanding which may arise when he is given his assignment in the school. The teacher should receive data relative to his probable teaching load and to his extracurricular or other special responsibilities. If the details of the assignment may depend somewhat upon developments at the time of making the schedule, this possibility should be made clear to the teacher. It is wise to give any information in writing and to preserve a copy for future reference.

The assignment of teachers to their duties, which involves the measurement and size of teaching loads and the most effective allocation of duties, is in itself a very important responsibility. Chapter 5 will be devoted to this and related problems.

CONTRACTS AND TENURE OF TEACHERS. In approximately 70 per cent of the districts maintaining high schools, teachers are given, usually after a probationary period of two or three years, a protective continuing contract or assurance of permanent tenure. In some states this assurance of tenure is required. In about half of the districts granting tenure, each teacher signs a contract each year; however, in a considerable number of districts teachers sign only on a first appointment and then when first placed on continuing contract or tenure. In a very large majority of the districts maintaining high schools, there exists a salary schedule which is not legally binding upon the board of education but is maintained by it with very few exceptions and with occasional adjustments up or down to meet the rise or fall of living expenses. In a small but increasing number of districts there is provision for rapid progress to the maximum salary, and beyond, by outstanding teachers who are given merit ratings. The merit rating and related salary adjustments are still a matter of much controversy, but gradually an increasing number of districts are employing them in some form.

Problems, Questions, and Exercises

1. From a state high-school directory giving data concerning size of staff and number of pupils, determine which high schools you think are possibly understaffed and which, if any, are overstaffed.

2. What nonteaching staff should be employed for a high school of 100 students? Of 300 students? Of 700 students?
3. Draw up a list of *(a)* the minimum requirements, *(b)* the desirable requirements, and *(c)* other data that you would keep in mind when selecting the teaching staff for:
   (1) A junior high school;
   (2) A senior high school;
   (3) A junior college.
4. Discuss the relative advantages and disadvantages of "promoting" teachers from elementary school to secondary school, or from junior high school to senior high school.
5. Draw up a statement of how a high-school principal might proceed in the selection of teachers to fill vacancies for the coming year.
6. Evaluate the various sources of prospective teachers.
7. What are the most useful types of data concerning prospective teachers?

Selected Supplementary Readings

Andre, Robert G., Buran, R. C., and Salyer, Guy, "Under What Conditions Does Merit Rating Succeed or Fail?" *Bulletin of the N.A.S.S.P.* (April, 1961), No. 264, pp. 23-28.

Barr, A. S., "The Assessment of the Teacher's Personality," *School Review* (Winter, 1960), Vol. 68, No. 4, pp. 400-408.

Berry, A. L., "The Art of Interviewing Teachers," *Nation's Schools* (June, 1955), Vol. 55, No. 6, pp. 63-66. [Suggested techniques for interviewing applicants.]

Carlo, Joseph P., "Teacher Selection," *Bulletin of the N.A.S.S.P.* (September, 1959), No. 248, pp. 183-188. [A practical discussion of the procedures and criteria for the selection of high-school teachers.]

Cassel, R. N., and Johns, W. L., "The Critical Characteristics of an Effective Teacher," *Bulletin of the N.A.S.S.P.* (November, 1960), No. 259, pp. 119-124.

Gladstone, Roy, "A Note on Certain Test Score Relationships and Their Applications for Research in Teacher Selection," *Journal of Educational Psychology* (February, 1952), Vol. 33, pp. 116-118. [Since practical judgment, diagnostic skills, and prescription skills are a part of the complex which makes a good teacher, tests may be useful in choosing teachers.]

Gowan, John Curtis, "Self-report Tests in the Prediction of Teaching Effectiveness," *School Review* (Winter, 1960), Vol. 68, pp. 409-419.

Hilifer, L. R., "How to Hire a Teacher," *School Executive* (February, 1955), Vol. 74, No. 2, pp. 50-51. [A young teacher tells administrators how to hire teachers.]

Janet, Sister Mary, *Catholic Secondary Education,* National Catholic Welfare Conference, 1949 [Chapter 4.]

McKeough, Reverend Michael, *The Administration of the Catholic Secondary School,* Washington, D. C., Catholic University of America Press, 1948. [Chapter 6.]

Maul, Ray C., "What Is the Principal's Role in the Recruitment and Training of Future Teachers?" *Bulletin of the N.A.S.S.P.* (March, 1951), No. 177, pp. 77-81.

"Merit Rating and Pay," *Phi Delta Kappan* (January, 1961), Vol. 43, pp. 137-163. [Seven articles; arguments for and against; plans for its use.]

Michael, R. E., "What Is the Principal's Role in the Recruitment and Training of Future Teachers?" *Bulletin of the N.A.S.S.P.* (March, 1951,), No. 177, pp. 63-69.

Miller, V., and Spalding, Willard B., *The Public Administration of American Schools,* New York, World Book, 1952, pp. 315-354. [The use of parents, principal, and staff in the selection of teachers; items to consider in selection of teachers or retention of good teachers; the problem of teacher dismissal; brief summary on selection, retention, and dismissal of the nonacademic staff.]

Perry, Paul A., *Contract Correcting,* Harvard University, 1962, 49 pp. [How to go about employing lay readers to assist teachers of English.]

Pigott, Lee D., "What is the Principal's Role in the Recruitment and Training of Future Teachers?" *Bulletin of the N.A.S.S.P.* (March, 1951), No. 177, pp. 69-77.

Stoops, Emory and Rafferty, M. L., Jr., *Practices and Trends in School Administration,* Ginn and Company, 1961. [Chapter 20. Selection and Induction of Teachers]

Tait, Frank M., "Objective Teacher Selection without Examinations," *American School Board Journal* (May, 1952), Vol. 124, pp. 39-40. [Description of how a large city goes about evaluating candidates for teaching positions. Explanation of a scale used for rating applicants.]

Tyler, Fred T., "Teacher's Personalities and Teaching Competencies," *School Review* (Winter, 1960). No. 4, pp. 429-449.

Washburne, Carleton, and Heil, Louis M., "What Characteristics of Teachers Affect Children's Growth?" *School Review* (Winter, 1960), Vol. 68, pp. 420-428.

5

Arranging Staff Assignments

1. The Teacher's Load or Assignment

Departmental Assignment. Secondary education in the United States has traditionally been committed to assignment of teachers to subjects on the departmental basis. In a great many schools, however, some, if not indeed a majority, of the teachers are given assignments which are in several subject fields, in some instances unrelated subject fields. This has been the result of three causes: (1) the employment of the core plan of curricular organization, in which the core teachers use learning materials from two or more subject fields; (2) the impossibility of observing departmental assignments in small schools; and (3) the tendency to permit teachers remaining from previous years to select the subjects which they will teach without reference to the consequent assortment of subjects which will make up the assignment of new teachers. In very small schools it is impossible to assign teachers strictly on a departmental basis, but even in these schools pains should be taken to see that teachers are not assigned to teach any subject for which they are not reasonably well prepared. Teachers should be employed in accord with this important objective.

It is the practice in some schools to permit the teachers who are staying on to select the subjects they will teach, with the result that the remaining subjects for which new teachers have to be employed are often such that it is impossible to employ teachers on a departmental basis or even to get teachers who are prepared in the subjects which they will have to teach. This result, needless to say, is unfortunate and should be avoided. In small schools, where the practice is most frequent, the incoming teacher is very likely to be less able to do creditable work under adverse conditions than is the more experienced teacher. The welfare of the school should take precedence over the preference of the older instructor. A compromise between the two factors should be the limit to which priority is accorded to experience in the school.

In the junior high school, departmental assignments may well be modified in the interest of achieving a gradual transition from the room-teacher plan of the elementary school to the complete departmentalization of the senior high school. In many junior high schools it is the practice to assign pupils in the seventh grade to two or even three subjects with a teacher who is also their counselor or home-room adviser. In general, such assignments should be given to teachers with experience in the upper elementary-school grades. The subjects so combined depend more upon the preparation and interests of the teacher than upon the relationships between the subjects themselves.

Duplicate Preparations. It is impossible to state with any confidence a general rule for assigning sections requiring duplicate preparations. Many teachers would rather teach five sections with three or four preparations than five similar sections. It is possible, however, that what teachers prefer may not be to the best interests of the pupils. Jung found that high-school teachers spend on the average nine-tenths as much time per section when teaching duplicate sections as when teaching nonduplicate or original sections.[1] While it is certain that little or none of the time spent in marking papers and doing other clerical work is saved by assigning duplicate sections, it is clear that some of the time spent in preparation is saved by so doing. Furthermore, it seems reasonable to assume that more thorough preparation will be realized if, whenever possible, teachers are assigned classes requiring not more than three different preparations.

Number of Classes Daily. In the interest of effective teaching, care should be taken that the instructor is not asked to meet an excessive number of classes daily. The teaching load in the secondary schools of the United States has been uniformly too great. During the past quarter of a century the average teaching load in the high school, measured in terms of sections taught, has diminished from approximately six to approximately five daily. Yet this reduction has been accompanied by an increased responsibility for the extracurricular program of the school, by the need of more careful attention to greater individual differences in high-school pupils, and by the greater size of sections (which results from the increased size of high schools and the growing conviction that larger classes may be taught as effectively as smaller ones.) In England, France, and Germany the secondary-school teacher is rarely responsible for more than four class periods daily, even though the extracurricular activities in these countries require less of the instructor's time and the traditional subject matter is well crystalized and requires very little reorganization.

In schools with class periods of 55 minutes or more, a maximum assignment should include five sections daily, or four periods and substantial extra-class duties; in schools with periods of 45 minutes or less, five sections daily, plus a few hours a week in extra-class duties, should be regarded as a maximum load.

[1]Christian A. Jung, *Revision of the Douglass Teaching-Load Formula,* Ed. D. Dissertation, University of Colorado, 1950. Also Harl R. Douglass, "1950 Revision of the High-School Teaching Load Formula," *Bulletin of the N.A.S.S.P.* (May, 1951), No. 179, p. 20.

For teachers of subjects requiring double periods one or more days a week, the load should obviously be less. If an assignment of five classes a day required 270 minutes gross for class meetings, there would be left, out of an eight-hour day, 210 minutes for marking papers, conferences with pupils, teachers' meetings, various other routine and occasional duties, and preparation. Deducting 90 minutes daily for marking papers, conferences with pupils, parents, and colleagues, and other duties related to instruction, there would not be more than 120 minutes left for the preparation and planning of instruction—less than 25 minutes per class. This seems certainly an irreducible minimum if anything of a higher order than the textbook and recitation type of teaching is expected. If time for study halls or extracurricular activities must be deducted from these 120 minutes, the result is either a low grade of teaching or a longer work day. In view of the wearing nature of teaching, a work day of more than eight hours is consistent neither with teachers' health nor with fair working requirements. Where class periods are longer, as in the 55-minute to 70-minute supervised study periods, the load in terms of sections taught should be less than indicated above, depending on the length of the class periods. It is, for example, wise and fair to consider five sections of 45 minutes each as the equivalent of four and a half sections of 60 minutes each.

NUMBER OF PUPILS TAUGHT DAILY. In the foregoing paragraphs class sections have been thought of as medium-sized, averaging about 25 students. If the number of students taught daily is much greater or less than 25, the number of daily sections assigned should be correspondingly decreased or increased. Just what ratio between the number of students and the number of sections should be observed cannot be stated with any great degree of precision. A discussion of this ratio will be found in a later section of this chapter.

In 1956 the median class size in grades 9 through 12 was found by the Research Division of the National Education Association to be 26.9 students; the median class size was smaller in rural high schools (21.0 students) and somewhat greater in larger schools (28.8 students).[2]

LOAD OF THE BEGINNING TEACHER. Some principals assign a slightly lighter load to the beginning teacher than to the experienced teacher, but this practice is not uniform. In fact, it is more than offset on the whole by the tendency to assign to beginning teachers a wider range of subjects to be taught. The data of several investigations show that the beginning high-school teacher is assigned classes in two or three different fields more often than in one field and that it is not rare for the assignment to involve four fields, although this is obviously unwise.

[2]"The Status of the American Public School Teacher," *Research Bulletin of the National Education Association* (February, 1957), Vol. 35, No. 1, p. 29.

There is little cause for wonder that the beginning teacher does not organize or plan his instruction properly but teaches in a more or less impromptu, lesson-hearing manner; in an altogether too large percentage of instances, he becomes habituated to this procedure, never reaching a much higher level.

It would be fortunate and wise, indeed, if beginning teachers were required to teach not more than three classes daily, the load being gradually increased with experience. However, such assignments for beginning teachers would not be practical from the point of view of the local district unless salaries were adjusted proportionally. Since such an adjustment would reduce the salaries of beginning teachers, few beginning teachers would be interested in teaching positions except in districts paying relatively very high salaries. It is, however, practical in those districts which do pay relatively high salaries to employ a few such "apprentice teachers" each year, selecting promising candidates and assigning to them reduced teaching loads with salaries which approximate those paid in smaller districts.

Administrative Responsibility for Teacher Assignments. The problem of deciding who should arrange the assignments of teachers will naturally depend upon the size of the particular school. In the smaller schools it should be a co-operative affair in which the superintendent, principal, other teachers directly concerned, and the teacher in question should all be consulted. If the school is very small, having fewer than six or eight teachers and a superintendent who is virtually the high-school principal as well, the superintendent should take the initiative. In larger districts, particularly those in which the schedule is made by the high-school principal, the initiative in teacher assignment should rest in the principal's hands. In schools with enrollments of from 1800 to 2000 or more, the assignments of teachers may well be left almost entirely to the respective department heads, subject, of course, to the general principles and final approval of the principal. In schools of smaller size where department heads are designated, they should be consulted at least concerning assignments of teachers in their departments; their recommendations should be given consideration insofar as they approach the problem impartially and in accordance with modern theories and facts of school administration.

2. *Measuring the Teacher's Load*

Factors in the Teaching Load. The units most commonly employed in measuring teaching loads are, in the order of their importance: (1) the number of sections, (2) the number of pupils, and (3) the number of free periods. It should be obvious that none of these units taken separately is a satisfactory measure of the time required of instructors or of their teaching loads.

Since schools differ materially in the length of the class periods and in the length of the school day, the number of free periods in itself is clearly not a reliable measure of the teaching load. It is obvious that many factors affect the teaching load, the principal factors being:

1. The number of sections taught daily (or weekly).
2. The number of pupils taught.
3. The number of different preparations required.
4. The amount of time required for co-operations: study halls, activities, etc.
5. The length of the class period.
6. The nature of the subject taught and the consequent amount of time required for preparation, for marking papers and notebooks, and for arranging equipment, apparatus, and materials.
7. The personnel of the pupils taught: tractability and range of individual differences in ability (factors very difficult to measure).
8. The age and maturity of the pupils taught and the consequent character of the subject matter.

Any accurate means of measuring the teaching load should take into consideration at least several of these factors, if not all of them.

A FORMULA FOR MEASURING THE TEACHING LOAD. The formula given below for measuring the teaching load of teachers in the junior and senior high schools takes into consideration the more important factors in the teaching load.

$$TL = SGC\left[CP - \frac{Dup}{10} + \frac{NP - 25CP}{100}\right]\left[\frac{PL + 50}{100}\right] + .6PC\left[\frac{PL + 50}{100}\right]$$

TL = units of teaching load per week.
SGC = subject coefficient used for giving relative weights to classes in different subject fields. (see Table 2.)
CP = number of class periods spent in classroom per week.
Dup = number of class periods spent per week in classroom teaching on the basis of preparation which is very similar to that for some other section (not including the original section).
NP = number of pupils in classes per week.
PC = number of class periods spent per week in supervision of the study hall, student activities, teachers' meetings, committee work, administrative or supervisory work, or other co-operations.
PL = gross length of class periods, in minutes.

The subject-matter coefficients, as shown in Table 2, were determined from the data gathered by Professor Christian Jung of Indiana University in his doctoral dissertation. With the exception of those for English, the coefficients are in proportion to the number of minutes required to teach the subject involved. The data were gathered from reports of 5643 teachers, representing 26,104 classes in schools of all sizes in all sections of the United States. Because of the increased emphasis in recent years on the writing of papers by students and the consequent increased amount of time given by English teachers to reading student papers, the coefficients for classes in English have been slightly increased, as compared to those developed in the Jung investigation.

APPLICATION TO SPECIAL TYPES OF CLASSES. In applying the formula to classes requiring no reading and no marking of written work (for example, physical education or music), the term pertaining to the number of pupils should either be divided by 2 or, better still, be omitted entirely.

In applying the formula to double-period classes in science laboratory, household arts, typewriting, and art or shop of various types, the following procedure should be employed:

1. Count each double period as two periods (*CP*).
2. Count each double period as one unit of duplicate preparation over and above any other allowance made for duplicate preparation.
3. Count the number of pupils for each half of a double period.

TABLE 2. *Subject-Grade Coefficients for Use in the Teaching-Load Formula*

GRADE LEVEL	7-8	9	10-11-12
English	1.1	1.2	1.2
Art	1.0	1.0	1.0
Home Economics	1.0	1.0	1.1
Music	.9	1.0	1.0
Mathematics	1.0	1.0	1.0
Agriculture	—	—	1.3
Industrial Arts	.9	.9	1.0
Physical Education	.8	.9	.9
Health	.9	1.1	1.2
Business Subjects	1.0	1.0	1.0
Social Studies	1.0	1.1	1.1
Foreign Language	1.0	1.0	1.0
Science	1.0	1.1	1.1

For example, for an instructor who teaches four classes of 26 pupils each in physics, meeting three times a week for one period and twice a week for 90-minute laboratory periods, the first three terms in the formula are evaluated as shown:

$$TL = 1.1 \quad 28 - \frac{21+8}{10} + \frac{(4\times182)-(28\times25)}{100} \quad \text{or } 27.9 \text{ units.}$$

The 21 represents the twenty-one periods given to classes which are duplicates of the first class; the 8 represents the eight double periods, in accordance with the second of the three instructions above.

The time spent in co-operations, such as conducting home rooms and supervising or coaching extracurricular activities, should be studied in each individual school and evaluated in terms of load units. To do so will preclude the possibility of the calculated teaching loads being higher than they should be because of inordinate amounts of time being spent upon activities or because of individual teachers' faulty estimates of the time spent on activities.

ASSUMPTIONS AND UNITS INVOLVED IN THE FORMULA. In the formula as given, the teaching load *(TL)* is furnished in units, each of which is theoretically equivalent to teaching for one period a class which requires preparation, in which there are 25 pupils, and which meets for 50 minutes. The assumptions underlying the formula are as follows:

1. In teaching two sections requiring practically identical preparation, the total amount of work for the duplicate section, in class and out, is reduced approximately 10 per cent if the quality of preparation is held constant.

   While, in general, teaching a duplicate section involves, on the average for all subject fields, nine-tenths as much work as teaching an original section, this varies somewhat from field to field. A duplicate section in social studies, science, or music involves .85 of the time for the original section; in English, mathematics, industrial arts, or agriculture a duplicate section involves .95 of the time for an original section. The distinctions become pretty fine and the computations complicated. Except for situations where great precision is desired, it is recommended that all duplicate sections be regarded as requiring .9 as much time as the original section.[3]
2. The weightings assigned for different subject and grade fields are also based upon the time-study investigation by Jung. They represent ratios of the average amounts of time spent by a considerable number of teachers of particular subjects and levels to the average amount of time spent by all teachers of all high-school subjects on all levels, as indicated in the time analysis of the several thousand teachers included in the Jung study. Jung found that the average amount of time spent per daily class in grades 9-12 was as follows for the different subject fields: English, 95 minutes; history and social studies, 93 minutes; science, 92 minutes; foreign languages, 84 minutes; mathematics, 83 minutes; commercial subjects, 81 minutes; home economics, 83 minutes; industrial arts, 80 minutes; music, 82 minutes; physical education, 76 minutes; art, 82 minutes.
3. The additional teaching load resulting from large sections may be expressed in terms of the teaching load incidental to one section of average size by counting each 100 pupils met daily in excess of an average load of 25 pupils per section as equal to the load resulting from teaching one section of average size. For example, of two instructors, one teaching five sections a day averaging 42 pupils each and the other teaching five sections averaging 22 pupils each, the former is assigned a load that is greater than that of the latter by one daily section requiring preparation:

$$\frac{1050-500}{100} - \frac{550-500}{100} = 5 \text{ class periods a week.}$$

[3]For further discussion and additional data concerning difference in reduction of load incident to duplication of section and other elements of the formula, see Harl R. Douglass, "1950 Revision of the High-School Teaching Load Formula," *Bulletin of the N.A.S.S.P.* (May, 1951), No. 179, pp. 18-20; or better still, Christian A. Jung, *Revision of Douglass Teaching Load Formula*, Ed. D. Dissertation, University of Colorado, 1950.

4. One class period spent in co-operative activities is equivalent to six tenths of the load incident to teaching for one day one section of 25 students requiring average preparation.
5. Increasing the length of the class period by 5 minutes is equivalent to increasing the teaching load by one twentieth of a normal class with preparation for each period taught daily; for example, 10 minutes added to the length of the class period would add to the load involved in teaching five sections daily an amount approximately equivalent to half that for one section.

The third assumption is made on the basis of opinions of a very large number of teachers and administrators who have been graduate students in the author's classes. The first, second, fourth, and fifth assumptions are based upon the time-study data of Jung's investigation previously referred to.

EXAMPLES OF COMPUTATION OF TEACHING LOAD. Following are the computations for a teacher of mathematics and biology whose load is as follows in a school with 55-minute periods:

a. Two sections of biology of 24 and 28 tenth-graders respectively, meeting five periods a week.
b. Two sections of ninth-grade algebra of 26 and 29 pupils, meeting five periods a week.
c. One section of twelfth-grade chemistry of 21 pupils, meeting seven periods a week, including two double periods.
d. A chemistry club averaging 60 minutes a week; service on committees averaging 48 minutes a week; P.T.A. and other miscellaneous duties averaging 20 minutes a week—total 128 minutes.

$$TL = SGC\left[CP - \frac{Dup.}{10} + \frac{(NP-25CP)}{100}\right]\left[\frac{PL+50}{100}\right] + \left[.6PC\right]\left[\frac{PL+50}{100}\right]$$

For the biology classes:

$$1.1\left[10 - \frac{5}{10} + \frac{260-250}{100}\right]\left[\frac{55+50}{100}\right] =$$

$$1.1\ (10 - .5 + .1)\ (1.05) = 11.09$$

For the algebra classes:

$$1.0\left[10 - \frac{5}{10} + \frac{275-250}{100}\right]\left[\frac{55+50}{100}\right] =$$

$$1\ (10 - .5 + .25)\ (1.05) = 10.24$$

For the chemistry class:

$$1.1\left[7 - \frac{2}{10} + \frac{147-175}{100}\right]\left[\frac{55+50}{100}\right] =$$

$$1.1\ (7 - .2 - .28)\ (1.05) = 7.53$$

For the co-operative or extra-teaching duties:

$$6\left[\frac{60 + 48 + 20}{55}\right]\left[\frac{55 + 50}{100}\right] = .6 \times 2.33 \times 1.05 = 1.47$$

For the entire load:

$$11.09 + 10.24 + 7.53 + 1.47 = 30.33 \text{ units}$$

Following are the computations for a teacher of physics and algebra whose load is as follows:

a. Two sections of first-semester physics (with two double periods) with 24 and 26 eleventh-grade students.

b. Three classes in first-semester algebra, with 26, 24, and 28 ninth-grade students.

c. Three hours (four class periods) a week on the average throughout the semester spent in co-operations.

$PL = 45$ minutes.

For the physics classes:

$$1.1\left[14 - \frac{11}{10} + \frac{350 - 350}{100}\right]\left[\frac{45 + 50}{100}\right] = 1.1(14 - 1.1 + 0)\,(.95) = 13.48$$

For the algebra classes:

$$1.0\left[15 - \frac{10}{10} + \frac{390 - 375}{100}\right]\left[\frac{45 + 50}{100}\right] = 1(15 - 1 + .15)\,(.95) = 13.44$$

For co-operations:

$$.6 \times 4\left[\frac{45 + 50}{100}\right] = .6 \times 4 \times .95 = 2.28$$

For the entire load:

$$13.48 + 13.44 + 2.28 = 29.20 \text{ units}$$

MEASURING THE LOAD IN THE JUNIOR COLLEGE. For comparing teaching loads in the high school and junior college, the formulas described above may be used.

It should be obvious that units of load as measured by the formula in the junior college will not be comparable to units of load in the high school. Either different standards for the different levels must be kept in mind, or some other allowance must be made for the greater amount of time spent in preparation, conferences, and other extra-class activities in the junior college. No one knows exactly what allowance should be made. It is suggested that loads of junior-college instructors be computed by the formula, using senior high school coefficients, and the result multiplied by 1.2.

THE LOAD FOR CORE CLASSES. The formula does not apply specifically to core classes; some adjustment must be made for the teacher whose assignment includes one or more core classes. Assuming that the core class meets for a double period, that there are at least two subject-matter fields involved (for example, English and social studies), that there is considerable reorganization of subject matter to be done, that the core teacher has considerable knowledge about each of the students in his core class, that he carries on more guidance than the average classroom teacher, and that he probably does more visitation than the average classroom teacher, it would seem that the core class should be counted as two classes and given a subject-matter coefficient of 1.25. If the core teacher performs no unusual guidance services or home-visitation duties, a coefficient of 1.15 or 1.20 might be adequate.

NORMS FOR FOUR-YEAR HIGH SCHOOL TEACHING LOAD. In 1954, by employing the Douglass Teaching-Load Formula, norms were determined for a four-year high school teaching load in a study of 1545 teachers in eighty-three schools in twenty-eight states, as shown in Table 3.

TABLE 3. *Revised Norms of Teaching Load by Subject Field in High Schools in Teaching-Load Units per Week.*[4]

SUBJECT FIELD	LOWER QUARTILE	MEDIAN	UPPER QUARTILE
English	27.5	30.7	36.8
Social Studies	26.7	30.3	33.8
Mathematics	25.4	29.6	34.1
Commercial	25.5	28.3	31.3
Science	25.4	30.4	34.0
Home Economics	26.5	29.4	32.2
Industrial Arts	25.4	28.2	31.4
Vocational Ag	30.8	33.6	36.6
Foreign Language	26.4	28.3	30.2
Physical Education	27.6	30.3	35.0
Music	26.7	29.6	31.2
Art	25.4	29.3	32.5
Mixed Load	29.1	31.3	33.7
All Subjects	27.3	29.9	32.9

NORMS FOR JUNIOR HIGH SCHOOL TEACHING LOAD. In 1955 norms were determined from data based on reports from 2656 teachers representing ninety-six junior high schools of grades 7, 8, and 9, as shown in Table 4.

[4]Harl R. Douglass and Kenneth L. Noble, "Revised Norms for High School Teaching Load," *Bulletin of the N.A.S.S.P.* (December, 1954), No. 206, pp. 97-98.

3. *Equalizing and Reducing the Load*

EQUALIZING THE LOAD. In the interests of fairness, the good will of the teaching staff, and the working efficiency of the school, the principal should exercise considerable care to make his assignments in such a way that the load will be equally divided among the members of the staff; he should also be constantly alive to every opportunity to reduce the demands made upon their time and their physical and mental energy. By the use of the formula described above, or by some other reasonable method, he should keep check on the load carried by every member of his staff. It is not unlikely that it will soon become conventional to ask each instructor to file at periodic intervals estimates of time spent in various

TABLE 4. *Tentative Norms of Teaching Load by Subject Field in the Junior High School*[5]

SUBJECT FIELD	LOWER QUARTILE	MEDIAN	UPPER QUARTILE
English	27.43	29.18	30.97
Art	25.39	27.37	30.08
Home Economics	25.60	27.33	29.26
Music	24.67	27.46	30.21
Mathematics	27.00	28.66	30.68
Industrial Arts	23.79	25.74	27.91
Physical Education	23.49	25.67	28.19
Commercial	26.64	28.97	30.55
Social Studies	27.37	29.31	31.18
Foreign Language	26.67	28.34	30.30
Science	27.74	29.50	31.54
Core Curriculum	27.00	29.28	31.54
Mixed Load	25.77	26.65	30.14
All Subjects	26.19	28.38	30.50

types of co-operations, so that the principal's check may be fairly complete. Such estimates are already being filed in the majority of larger universities and colleges in the form of term work sheets. The shortcoming of these work sheets lies in the inaccuracy resulting from the large interval of time covered by each report. Checking on summaries of such reports will enable the principal to see what demands are made on the time of various members of his staff by various co-operations, to judge whether an activity is worthy of the teacher time required, and to consider the pos-

[5]Harl R. Douglass and Jack L. Rowe, "Median Teacher Loads for Junior High Schools Based Upon the Revised Douglass Teaching Load Formula," *Bulletin of the N.A.S.S.P.* (November, 1955), No. 214, pp. 34-37.

sibility of adjusting the management of those activities making excessive demands. Equalization of load may be developed by adjusting study-hall assignments and by asking the underloaded to assist with more cooperative work of one type or another.

NUMBER OF SECTIONS VERSUS SIZE. Among the most fruitful opportunities for reducing the teaching load lies in the reduction of the number of sections to be taught daily. This reduction may be brought about without increasing the size of the staff by increasing the size of the sections eliminating small sections.

The traditional belief that the results obtained in small sections are much better than those obtained in large ones has not been verified by the many studies of the influence of class size upon scores made on standard achievement tests. Whatever may be said of the possibilities afforded in small sections for instruction better adapted to individual needs and abilities, the general trend of conclusions from experimental studies is clear and marked: as measured by teachers' marks or objective tests, the results obtained in small sections are on the whole very little, if any, better than those obtained in larger sections. By no freak of chance could the results so uniformly fail to favor small sections if smaller sections were actually superior in proportion to the increased cost of instruction and increased teaching load that are necessary to make small sections possible. There are many, however, who are quite positive in their claims that, with respect to several very important types of outcomes not measured by paper-and-pencil tests, better results can be obtained in smaller classes; they also claim that pupil attitudes are better in small classes. It is very probable that in smaller classes teachers come to know more about each pupil and consequently are able to provide better guidance and counseling and better adaptation of instruction to the individual pupil.

The regional accrediting associations for years set 25 pupils as a norm for the size of sections, but within recent years they have employed no standard or maximum as to class size. Many instructors in homemaking and shop subjects believe that not more than 16 or 20 pupils can be taught effectively in one section, but they have only to visit schools in neighboring cities to find sections of 24 or more making equally desirable progress. It would seem obvious that for most teachers four sections averaging 30 pupils each is definitely a lighter load than five sections averaging 24 pupils each or six sections averaging 20 pupils each, though the pupil load is exactly 120 pupils in each instance.

In a small but increasing number of four-year senior high schools, classes which have traditionally met five times a week are now scheduled only four periods a week and the teachers are assigned six classes rather than five classes. There is much in favor of this practice, under which the student load per class is reduced and the average student is enabled to carry five "solid" subjects, in addition to physical education and another subject meeting no more than three times a week with out-of-class preparation.

ELIMINATION OF SMALL SECTIONS. There may be found in many high school sections in foreign languages, mathematics, physics, chemistry, and other subjects enrolling an extravagantly small number, often as few as 5 or 6 pupils. In the interests of effective teaching as well as of economy, the principal should exert his influence to eliminate small sections. By his so doing, the teaching load may often be materially reduced with no extra cost to the district. The principal should not be led into the fallacy in reasoning which traps many conscientious teachers in smaller schools; he should not permit a teacher to teach the small section as a labor of love in addition to a full teaching schedule. As often as not, the extra section does influence the teacher's "regular" load, smaller classes being assigned to the teacher or the extra class being made the excuse for not assisting in co-operations. Even were this not so, the other sections taught by the teacher are deprived of extra hours of his time—time, otherwise available for preparation and planning or for professional reading, which now must be given to instructing the extra class. This is an instance in which the teacher's level of effectiveness and the welfare of the students must be protected against the teacher's zeal for his favorite subject.

ASSIGNMENT IN RELATION TO SPECIAL FITNESS. Maximum effectiveness of the teaching staff may be realized only when each teacher is, as nearly as possible, given the work to do which he can do best. Results of a very large number of investigations show that teachers in large numbers are assigned subjects which they are poorly or only fairly well prepared to teach. As a measure of his preparation for teaching in a given field, the fact that the teacher had a major in the given field is inadequate. The requirements for a major in various colleges and universities differ greatly, not only in the number of semester or quarter hours but also in the pattern of subjects taken. It is desirable to know what phases of history or English he is especially interested in and qualified to teach. It is desirable to know what experience and success he has had in various subjects and in participating in, coaching, directing, or supervising extracurricular activities. Because these data are useful in making the wisest assignments, the application blank, credentials, and letters of recommendation—the entire file accumulated when the teacher was a candidate for a position—should be placed in the hands of the principal. In smaller schools interviews with new teachers may serve to furnish information on their special lines of ability.

In six-year secondary schools it is well worth while to consider whether the candidate's experience, preparation, personality, and interests better fit him for younger or for older pupils. In a number of instances the usefulness of a teacher has been materially increased by changing his teaching assignment to lower or upper grades of pupils or by changing his teaching field from what appeared first to be his strongest subject to one in which he was reasonably adequately prepared and which he was much better adapted to teach. Examples that occur to the author are the following: an English teacher who had an academic major in English but whose personality made her a much better drill master in algebra than an interpreter of literature; a teacher of junior high school history who could not manage younger children, largely because she did not understand them, but who succeeded rather well in senior high school history; and a history teacher who by nature was not interested in political and economic problems, in spite of her many college courses in history in which she received high marks, and who made a much happier and much more effective teacher of typewriting, in which she had adequate training.

A few hours spent in careful study of all available relevant data will often yield big dividends—results much greater than the results of the same number of hours spent in trying to make teachers more effective. Teachers cannot be relied upon entirely to know just what they can do best for the school. In a high school in which the author was principal, he finally withdrew the supervision of dramatics from a teacher who believed that she was outstandingly successful in that field; her work in another field, work for which she was much better adapted, had suffered from the diversion of her time and attention to dramatics, in which she made only a very mediocre showing. Teachers sometimes insist that, of the several lines they have reasonable hope to succeed in, they are best prepared to teach that which seems the best lead to greater financial returns. This is a problem which is frequently given slight attention, only gross and obvious data being considered. The results of such inattention are rarely attached to the proper causes. Since decisions bind all parties for at least a semester, they should be made with unusual care.

A wise procedure followed by many principals is to examine the transcripts of credits earned in college to see that teachers are assigned to subjects in which they are well prepared.

LIGHTENING THE TEACHER'S LOAD. Among the ways in which the loads of teachers may be reduced, the following are most likely to be useful:

1. Providing substitutes promptly, rather than allowing the teachers or the principal to assume the work of an absent teacher.
2. Providing facilities for mimeographing material needed for instructional purposes.
3. Avoiding long, tedious, uninteresting teachers' meetings at the close of a full day of regular work.
4. Preventing or reducing to a minimum the interferences with the usual routine of the daily schedule: that is, special assemblies, interruptions by visitors or by the central sound system, etc.

5. Allowing teachers to use the clerical help of the school for letters relating to school organizations or school business.
6. Providing simplified forms for all regular school reports, notices, and other clerical routine.
7. Ensuring that new teachers obtain wholesome and pleasant places to room and board and assisting them to develop something like normal social life.
8. Securing instructional supplies in advance of the date of actual use.
9. Assisting teachers to "discover" and use methods involving less tension, such as the laboratory method and recitation method.
10. Providing lay aides and student assistants in laboratory work, library work, mimeographing, reading of papers, and the like.
11. Reducing the number of different daily subject preparations per teacher and the number of fields taught.
12. Helping teachers to discover time-saving methods for conducting written quizzes and for testing daily preparations.
13. Helping teachers to discover other ways of solving disciplinary problems than that of keeping pupils after school.
14. Reducing fear and insecurity; conducting supervision in such a way as to eliminate fear.
15. Making adequate allowance for such co-operative activities as assisting with clubs, assemblies, teams, plays, musical activities, and school social affairs.
16. Keeping to an almost negligible minimum the time requirement of teachers in connection with drives, campaigns, and the like.
17. Employing specialists to conduct study halls; in small schools, combining study-hall supervision with library management.
18. Keeping down class size, preferably to not more than 25 pupils to a class.
19. Providing office space for teachers to work free from interruption when not teaching.
20. Eliminating or reducing to a minimum time spent by teachers in hall supervision.
21. Developing a considerate and co-operative attitude in working with teachers; letting them have, individually and collectively, a voice in matters concerning their work; giving them encouragement, inspiration, and constructive advice.
22. Developing throughout the school a friendly, cheerful atmosphere and cordial relations between students, teachers, and other personnel.
23. Providing specialists to take over recreational activities, possibly along with some teaching duties, to relieve teachers of responsibility for supervising playgrounds, dances, parties, noon-hour recreational activities, and the like.
24. Making available appropriate mechanical aids.

EXTRA PAY FOR EXTRA DUTIES. It has become fairly common in secondary schools to pay higher salaries or to have supplemental pay granted for "extra" work, particularly in connection with extracurricular activities. As reported by the Science Research Associations in *Guidance Newsletter* of December, 1956, more and more teachers are resisting extra-class activities for which they are not given extra pay, pointing out that a full teaching load plus test papers and assignments to be graded at night, in addition to professional meetings and the paper work which is part of any teacher's load, usually add up to more than a forty-hour week. In a survey conducted by *Nation's Schools* in the summer of 1956, 80 per cent of the superintendents queried thought that teachers should receive extra pay for responsibilities beyond the regular hours of classroom teaching. Although recent statistics are not available, extra pay is known to be given in a great majority of schools to athletic coaches, in a majority to leaders of band and choral music, and in a very substantial minority to coaches of dramatics and to sponsors of school papers and yearbooks.[6]

While there is much to be said against this practice of giving some teachers an overload which is likely to interfere with their giving their best efforts to their normal load, schools have had to resort to this practice of offering extra pay for extra duties in order to: (1) meet the competition in getting good leaders for athletics, band, and choral work; and (2) raise the salaries of male teachers, in cities where the single salary schedule exists, to the point where they are able to attract and keep good men. It seems certain that it is better for teachers to have an overload and to be given extra pay for it than it is for them to be employed in a second job in addition to their school work.

TEAM-TEACHING LOAD. In schools which employ the Trump plan or other plans of team teaching, special problems exist in the assignment of teachers. A teacher who gives the carefully prepared lectures and a teacher who is the chairman of a group will naturally have to be assigned a smaller number of class periods a week, perhaps a much smaller number. Teachers who have aides or clerks may be given somewhat larger teaching loads than those who do not have them.

In the Lakeview High School of Decatur, Illinois, the staff organization and respective duties are as follows:

Teacher Presenter*
- Function and Role: Directs program; plans methods of instruction; gives large groups instruction; supervises evaluation.
- Training: Master's degree (certified teacher).
- Fields of Use: Business Education, Driver Education, English, Foreign Language, Mathematics, Health (P.E.), Science, Social Studies.
- Distribution of Time: Fifteen hours of student contact; twenty-five hours of planning, preparing, and supervising.

Teacher Instructor*
- Function and Role: Works with small group instruction; assists with general instruction; works on student projects and individual learning problems.

---

*The Teacher Presenter and the Teacher Instructor are both of the same rank; their difference is only in function. Thus teachers are able to specialize in one phase of instruction.

[6]The number of schools giving extra day for various types of positions and the amount of pay given during 1959-1960 in cities of more than 30,000 population are shown in the National Education Association's *Educational Research Service Circular* for May, 1960.

Training: Bachelor's or Master's degree (certified teacher).
Fields of Use: Art, Business Education, English, Industrial Arts, Foreign Language, Homemaking, Mathematics, Music, P.E., Science, Social Studies.
Distribution of Time: Thirty-six hours of student contact; four hours of preparation.

Instructional Aide
Function and Role: Responsible for paper correcting; helps draft outside-of-class learning instruments.
Training: Bachelor's degree (may or may not be certified).
Fields of Use: English, Social Studies, Foreign Language, Science.
Distribution of Time: Forty hours of work.

Clerk
Function and Role: Types; duplicates materials; prepares reports; takes attendance; performs clerical chores, etc.
Training: High-school graduate in Business Education (not certified).
Fields of Use: Business Education, Driver Education, English, Foreign Language, Library, Mathematics, Social Studies.
Distribution of Time: Forty hours of activity.

General Aide
Function and Role: Responsible for student control in halls; co-curricular activities.
Training: High-school graduate (not certified).
Fields of Use: Study hall; co-curricular activities.
Distribution of Time: Forty hours of work.[7]

In varying degree, the following kinds of aides are employed in many secondary schools.

a. Student teachers from teacher-training programs
b. College students (non teacher-trainees)
c. Clerical workers
d. College trained adults from the community
e. Other adults (not college trained or clerks)

These aides function as:

a. Laboratory supervisors
b. Lay readers of some written work
c. Objective test graders
d. Teachers for make-up or remedial work by individuals or small groups
e. Hall or playground supervisors
f. Study hall supervisors
g. Library assistants
h. Shop supervisors
i. Clerks
j. Field trip assistants[8]

---

[7] *The Road to Progress*, Decatur, Illinois, Public Schools, 1960. [The Decatur-Lakeview Plan of using noncertified personnel to assist teachers.]

[8] Singer, Ira J. "Survey of Staff Utilization Practices in Six States," *Bulletin of the N.A.S.S.P.* (January, 1962), No. 270, p. 8.

At the Francis D. Raub Junior High School at Allentown, Pennsylvania, four sections of students, all of whom are registered in four different subjects in the same grade, may be scheduled at the same period, thus making it possible for all four sections to meet together for a large-group lecture.

Team teaching may be done with many variations. In each school where it is to be introduced, it should be preplanned very carefully and adapted to the local staff and housing. Teachers giving the large-group lectures must receive material reductions in the number of class periods that they teach. All teachers involved should be given some reduction of their teaching loads to compensate for the time spent in planning conferences.

Problems, Questions, and Exercises

1. To what extent should there be departmental assignment of teachers in grades 7 through 12?
2. Mention in order of importance the seven most important factors in a teacher's load. How can you measure each of them?
3. Be able to explain clearly the meaning and basis of each term in the formula for measuring the teaching load.
4. How do you account for the differences in subject-grade coefficients given in the chapter?
5. What factors in the teaching load are not taken into consideration in the teaching-load formula?
6. In the suggestions for lightening the teacher's load, pick out about half a dozen which you think are the most important and a few that you think are not as important as the others.
7. What do you think is the effect of class size upon the quality of learning experiences of youngsters in high school? Do you think it would be better for the teacher to have four classes of 35 students each or five classes of 28 students each? Which would be the greater load for the teacher? Which, do you think, would be better for the students? Be able to give reasons to support your answers.
8. Be able to tell how a principal might proceed to insure an equalized load among members of his staff.
9. To the suggestions for lightening the teacher's load, add two more.
10. Of the suggestions for lightening the teaching load, select the ten most important and arrange them in the approximate order of their importance.

Selected Supplementary Readings

Ashby, Lloyd W., "The Issue of Added Compensation for Extra Responsibility or Extra Work," *Bulletin of the N.A.S.S.P.* (March, 1951), Vol. 35, pp. 167-172.

Babcock, Chester D., "Who's the Goat? The New Teacher, Of Course," *Clearing House* (May, 1950), Vol. 24, pp. 547-549.

Bookhout, Hamilton, "Teacher Aids for Lunch-Hour Activities," *School Executive* (February, 1959), Vol. 78, pp. 136-140. [An hour of freedom for teachers.]

Christophe, Leroy M., "The Assignment and Induction of New Teachers," *Bulletin of the N.A.S.S.P.* (May, 1956), No. 220, pp. 98-103.

Douglass, Harl R., "Teaching Load Crisis in Secondary Schools," *California Journal of Secondary Education* (May, 1957), Vol. 32, No. 5, pp. 295-299.

Douglass, Harl R., and Noble, Kenneth L., "Revised Norms for High School Teaching Load," *Bulletin of the N.A.S.S.P.* (December, 1954), No. 206, pp. 97-98.

Douglass, Harl R., and Rowe, Jack L., "Median Teacher Loads for Junior High Schools Based Upon the Revised Douglass Teaching Load Formula," *Bulletin of the N.A.S.S.P.* (November, 1955), No. 214, pp. 34-37.

"Extra Pay for Extra Work," *National Education Association Research Bulletin* (April, 1952), Vol. 30, No. 2.

Extra Pay Provisions in 1959-60 Salary Schedules, Washington, D.C., National Education Association, 1960.

Garland, Philip L., "The Extra-Curriculum and the Teacher's Load," *Clearing House* (October, 1944), Vol. 19, pp. 82-84 ff. [The methods used by a principal in a Massachusetts high school to straighten out inequalities which he discovered in the extra-curriculum loads of his teachers.]

Heggerston, A. I., "Extra Pay for Extra Work," *Bulletin of the N.A.S.S.P.* (November, 1948), Vol. 32, No. 157, pp. 146-155. [Discusses methods for assignment of teachers to extra duty and factors entering into determining teaching loads; outlines the plan for extra duty compensation used in Minneapolis.]

Hinchey, C. E., "The Issue of Added Compensation for Extra Responsibility or Extra Work," *Bulletin of the N.A.S.S.P.* (March, 1951), Vol. 35, No. 177, pp. 173-178. [Presents the major points of view regarding extra pay for extra work, cites three studies of present practices, and then gives seven approaches to a solution of the problem.]

Holmgrain, F. H., Jr., "Considering Teacher Load in Large Nebraska High Schools," *Bulletin of the N.A.S.S.P.* (February, 1961), No. 262, pp. 88-90.

Howe, Harold, II, "The High School Principal in Newton, Massachusetts, Reacts to Re-deployment," *Bulletin of the N.A.S.S.P.* (January, 1960), Vol. 44, pp. 122-138.

Howe, Harold, II, and Umstattd, J. G., "How Can a School Get Started on a Staff Utilization Improvement Project?" *Bulletin of the N.A.S.S.P.* (April, 1960), No. 255, pp. 200-202, 203-204.

Jewett, Robert E., "Why the Able Public-School Teacher is Dissatisfied," *Educational Research Bulletin* (October 9, 1957), pp. 223-244. [Discusses dissatisfaction with teaching load.]

Johnson, Curtis, and VanderHorck, Karl, "Non-Certificated Laboratory Assistants Are Used to Extend Science Opportunities for Pupils at the Alexander Ramsey High School, Roseville, Minnesota, Second Year," *Bulletin of the N.A.S.S.P.* (January, 1959), No. 243, pp. 13-48.

Jung, Christian A., *Revision of the Douglass Teaching-Load Formula,* Ed.D. Dissertation, University of Colorado, 1950.

Kern, Willis P., "Teachers Need Not Be Clerks," *School Management* (May, 1960), Vol. 4, No. 5, pp. 76-84. [Use of data-processing machine.]

Lobb, M. D., Noall, M. F., and Slichenmyer, H. L., "What Are Some Promising

Practices in Team Teaching?" *Bulletin of the N.A.S.S.P.* (April, 1960), No. 255, pp. 2-6.

Michael, Lloyd S., and others, "Progressing Toward Better Schools," *Bulletin of the N.A.S.S.P.* (January, 1960), No. 252, pp. 7-346. [Third report on staff utilization studies. Experiments with team teaching and large classes.]

Nelson, Thomas L., "An Analysis of the Teacher Load Problem," *California Journal of Secondary Education* (May, 1945), Vol. 20, pp. 281-285. [Considers thirteen important factors involved in any study of teacher-load allowances, most of which have been worked out in the Douglass formula.]

Noall, Matthew F., and Rose, Gale, "Team Teaching at the Wahlquist Junior High School, Weber County, Utah," *Bulletin of the N.A.S.S.P.* (January, 1960), Vol. 44, pp. 164-171.

Petrich, Paul, "The English Lay Reader Program at Hanover High School," *Bulletin of the N.A.S.S.P.* (October, 1960), No. 258, pp. 113-119. [Assistants for helping teachers of English.]

Redefer, Frederick L., "Teacher Morale and Quality of Education," *Nation's Schools* (February, 1957), Vol. 59, No. 2, pp. 53-55. [Relationship of load to morale and quality of education.]

Ryan, L. V., "Teachers and Administrators of Our Central Catholic High Schools," Catholic School Journal (November, 1958), Vol. 58, pp. 21-22.

"Status of the American Public School Teacher," *Research Bulletin of the National Education Association* (February, 1957), Vol. 35, No. 1, p. 29.

Trump, J. Lloyd, *Images of the Future: A New Approach to the Secondary School,* Urbana, Illinois, Commission on the Experimental Study of the Utilization of the Staff in the Secondary School, 1960.

Trump, J. Lloyd, *New Directions to Quality Education: The Secondary School Tomorrow,* Washington, D. C., National Association of Secondary School Principals, Commission on the Experimental Study of the Utilization of the Staff in the Secondary School, 1960.

Trump, J. Lloyd, *New Horizons for Secondary School Teachers,* Urbana, Illinois, Commission on the Experimental Study of the Utilization of the Staff in the Secondary School, 1957.

"What Teachers Say About the Use of Their Time, *School Management* (May, 1960), Vol. 4, No. 5, pp. 63-66. [Reaction to Trump plan of team teaching.]

6

Assisting and Improving the Staff

1. Modern Ideas About Supervision[1]

INADEQUATE PRESERVICE EDUCATION OF TEACHERS. An examination of preservice training programs in institutions of higher education reveals that high-school teachers are given meager, spotty, and superficial preparation for the work they are expected to do as high-school teachers. The courses provided give a very inadequate understanding of the development of personality and character, of emotional and social adjustment, and of other very important aspects of human growth.

Prospective high-school teachers are usually given little or no actual training in the preparation of courses of study, other than some lesson-planning in connection with their student teaching. Few have had adequate preservice preparation for sponsorship and supervision of extra-curricular activities and many have had no previous experience in dealing with youngsters in that type of situation. With respect to guidance and counseling, the typical high-school teacher-training situation involves little more than a brief statement that there is such a thing as guidance and that guidance counseling in the schools has developed greatly in recent years in such areas as educational and vocational guidance. Little or no training is given in the matter of dealing with the public or in other aspects of public relations. Usually a very superficial introduction is given to the measurement of pupil growth, the introduction often consisting of a brief mention of standard and objective tests in a course in methods of teaching in high school. For these reasons, much of the training of the teacher for high-grade service on the job must often be gotten in service.

AREAS AND TYPES OF GROWTH OF TEACHERS IN SERVICE. Those who would assist high-school teachers to improve in service must keep in mind types of teaching growth, including the following:

[1]In this chapter only the more important principles and practices will be briefly described. For a more complete discussion, see some such book as Harl R. Douglass, Rudyard K. Bent, and Charles Boardman, *Democratic Supervision in Secondary Schools;* or Robert C. Hammock and Ralph S. Owings, *Supervising Instruction in Secondary Schools.*

1. Increased knowledge of methods of study of the nature of adolescents: their desires, problems, attitudes, and interests; their emotional, social, physical, and intellectual growth.
2. Increased knowledge of skills and techniques in directing and improving the emotional, social, physical, and intellectual growth of adolescents.
3. Increased understanding of American society—its philosophy, principal features, trends, and problems—and its implications for education.
4. Increased knowledge and understanding of life in the United States today in the home and in leisure time, and of people as citizens, workers, and parents; increased capacity on the part of teachers to adapt learning activities appropriately.
5. Increased knowledge and skill in the planning and adaptation of learning materials and activities to the individual, with his abilities, capacities, previous preparation, interests, and present and future out-of-school needs.
6. Development of a modern functional concept of what education is and of its relationship to human growth, the environment, and the needs of adolescent learners.
7. Acquisition of modern knowledge in their special subject fields.
8. Understanding and use of newer classroom procedures, which involve such things as group dynamics, audio-visual aids, team teaching, large units of learning activities and materials, and student participation in planning.
9. Understanding of modern concepts dealing with problems of discipline which are related to mental hygiene, character education, and personality development.
10. Ability to interrelate various high-school subjects and deal with such matters as unified studies, core program, integrated curriculum, and correlated curriculum.
11. Development of better methods for measuring and recording pupil growth.
12. Development of understandings and abilities in planning and sponsoring various types of clubs and extracurricular activities.
13. Development of understanding and skill in counseling young people and in refraining from giving unsound advice and counsel.
14. Ability to relate a course of study and learning activities to community life, problems, and needs.
15. Development of understanding and appreciation of parents and the public in general; development of techniques and skills for dealing with them.
16. Increased amount and better patterns of general education.

The last-mentioned objective invites especial attention. More neglected than professional or subject-matter education in preservice education programs, general education should receive especial attention by the teacher in service. The administration and supervision should encourage general-education activities by the following means:

1. Forming book clubs among teachers, whereby groups of teachers may purchase books and circulate them among themselves.
2. Obtaining the assistance of librarians in preparing brief descriptions of outstanding current books for distribution to the staff.
3. Purchasing with school funds general-education books and periodicals which are to be made a part of the professional library of the school.

4. Encouraging teachers to attend concerts, lectures, appropriate general-education courses in summer school, and community discussions and to take part in the civic and intellectual life of the community; encouraging intellectual interstimulation among the teachers.

CHANGING IDEAS ABOUT SUPERVISION. In the first stages of development, supervision in the schools of the United States was based squarely and rather completely upon authoritarian philosophy and assumptions. In fact, in most cities as late as the first decade or two of the present century, principals and superintendents seemed to feel the need for impressing teachers, pupils, and parents with the superior knowledge, insights, and skills of the tutor, principal, and other advisors. It seemed to be a fundamental principle that new ideas must originate with the superior officers and be handed out to the classroom teachers. Originality was discouraged. Too much creative thinking of the part of a teacher was regarded either as a lack of respect for his supervisory leaders or as evidence of freakishness. There are still some supervisors and administrators who cling to this authoritarian concept.

Classroom visits were largely of an inspectional nature. Typically, the teacher visited felt that the supervisor was there for the purpose of discovering weaknesses and that inspection, especially visitation, was closely related to teacher rating. Such a philosophy and practice of supervision caused supervision to be regarded with fear, distaste, and opposition on the part of those visited and supervised. Beginning slowly in the twenties and developing rapidly in the thirties and forties was the concept of co-operative supervision and democratic leadership, the supervisor being regarded as an individual who served to assist the staff as consultant and friend rather than as inspector and critic. As has been pointed out by a number of authors, democratic supervision demands respect for personality. It makes ample provision for self-direction on the part of teachers, who participate to a great degree in the planning of their own classroom activities and in-service growth.

DEMOCRATIC LEADERSHIP, NOT LAISSEZ FAIRE. Democratic administration should not be, although sometimes it unfortunately is, confused with *laissez faire*. The modern concept of supervision has been misinterpreted, abused, and misapplied by some principals and superintendents. To them, democracy in supervision means keeping "hands off," praising teachers indiscriminately and insincerely, and refraining from any real attempt to assist them to grow. Actually, democratic leadership involves definite activity on the part of supervisors and administrators which is aimed at increasing the effectiveness and improvement of the staff in various ways. Democratic leadership means leadership of a type which develops the morale of the staff and their desire to improve the effectiveness of the school, as well as good human relations with supervisors and administrators.

2. *Leadership Programs and Techniques*

KINDS OF SUPERVISION DESIRED. It has in recent years become increasingly clear (1) that teachers desire supervisory assistance and (2) that supervision of the right sort is not at all inconsistent with democracy and modern concepts of human interrelationships. It is apparent that the great majority of teachers welcome visitation and criticism that are friendly and constructive if the supervisor is well qualified.

Areas in which teachers want help include the following:

1. Improving teaching methods and techniques.
2. Utilizing some of the newly discovered principles of group dynamics.
3. Locating and utilizing community resources.
4. Providing for individual differences—teaching the bright and teaching the slow.
5. Dealing with pupil behavior and discipline cases.
6. Caring for the needs of the emotionally and socially maladjusted.
7. Evaluating their own teaching.
8. Making better use of visual aids, especially television and projectors, and of teaching machines.
9. Locating and making available expert resource personnel, as special problems arise.
10. Making greater contributions towards moral and spiritual education.
11. Developing the possibilities of team teaching.
12. Constructing and building teaching units on problems and topics not found in basic textbooks; for example, use of leisure time, consumer education, understanding oneself and others, the United Nations, conservation, and the making, choosing, and holding of friends.
13. Keeping oriented with respect to new curriculum and instructional principles and practices.

TYPES OF IN-SERVICE GROWTH ACTIVITIES. Those who would assist teachers in the matter of in-service growth must realize that there is a wide variety of possible approaches and techniques, including, for example, local workshops, various types of group conferences and teachers' meetings, use of consultants, intervisitation within the school and between schools, preschool institutes and workshops, demonstration of teaching activities by teachers, supervisors, and principals, supervisory bulletins from principal or other supervisor to the teachers, development of professional libraries, research and investigation, self-rating and analysis, and conference with individual teachers.

The leader who would become familiar with the principles, considerations, and practices related to these avenues of in-service growth should read carefully two or three books such as those mentioned in Chapter 3.[2]

[2]See *In-Service Education of Teachers,* Washington, D.C., Research Division of the National Education Association, August, 1960, for a brief modern discussion of the procedures for carrying on types of in-service activities, with lists of some new developments and discussions of practices in certain cities and states.

3. Personnel Organization for Supervision

RELATIONSHIP OF PRINCIPALS TO OTHER OFFICIALS. The high-school principal shares with others his responsibility for assisting the staff. In smaller school systems both the principal and the superintendent participate in supervision. In many high schools the department heads play some part in supervision. In larger school systems there are various types of special supervisory positions, including, for example, the following:

1. Supervisor of secondary education.
2. Director of curriculum.
3. Director of instruction.
4. Various supervisors of special fields: for example, of art, English, and physical education.
5. Director of research and measurement.
6. Director of guidance.
7. Co-ordinator of instruction in the individual school.

Such supervisors may operate on a city-wide basis or just with the staff members of an individual school. In some instances one or more of the fields of activity may be assigned to one or more assistant principals.

No definite pattern of division of authority and responsibility between the principal and others may be laid down for all schools. For that matter, it may not even be laid down for all schools of a given size, because of such facts as:

1. The existence or nonexistence of supervisory specialists of the types mentioned above.
2. The amount of time available to the principals who supervise.
3. The nature of the philosophy of the school and the programs being undertaken to improve learning and teachers in service.
4. The financial condition of the district as it affects the above and other factors of supervisory assistance.

THE PRINCIPAL AND THE "OUT-OF-BUILDING" SUPERVISOR. There has been a growing development of a new type of relationship between the modern secondary-school principal and the supervisor or leader who operates in more than one building. The principal has become busy with administrative and management duties, such as working with student groups, with extracurricular activities, and with parents. He is forced to recognize that at least in certain areas there are individuals specialized in their training and interests who have contributions to make beyond that which can be made by the principal. There should be and usually is no jealousy on his part. The professional supervisor or leader of teachers enters his building with his blessing and his backing. The principal keeps informed as to the type of assistance that is given to his teachers so that he may be well oriented in the developments that are going on relative to curriculum, instruction, and guidance.

The supervisor from outside realizes that the principal is the executive head of the building. He has responsibility for keeping the principal informed of his activities and programs in the building, the ideas he has presented to the teachers, and projects and developments which are the products of his inspiration and planning. He observes all the rules for administration and management of the building. He consistently encourages the teachers to respect the principal as a leader. Often he discusses in advance with the principal the ideas, plans, and projects which he is thinking of presenting to the teachers.

THE DEPARTMENT HEAD AS SUPERVISOR. In many schools the principal still relies to some extent on department heads for teacher leadership within his school. In a considerable number of instances, his reliance is not well founded. The department heads, in many cases, lack training, modern fundamental philosophy, time, or ingenuity for instructional leadership. Their principal contribution in many instances must be limited to managerial activities and to assisting the especially trained supervisor in working with the teachers in his particular department. Quite frequently the supervisor and the inservice projects of the curriculum improvement and teacher development cut across departments. Here the principal has the responsibility for bringing together department heads and teachers of different departments and contributing to interdepartmental co-operation in such matters.

OTHER SUPERVISORS IN THE BUILDING. In some schools—and the number is increasing—there are individuals who have full-time or part-time special supervisory responsibilities. They include such individuals as director or chairman of the committee on guidance, director or chairman of the committee on extracurricular activities, director or chairman of the committee on curriculum, director or chairman of the committee on home rooms, director or chairman of the committee on core program, and director or chairman of the committee on audio-visual aids.

In a small but increasing number of schools the principal selects a building co-ordinator of instruction or vice-principal in charge of instruction, who relieves the principal of the details of supervision and leadership in instruction. This person acts as liaison between the teachers in the building and outside supervisors, following up the visits of outside supervisors and assisting teachers to implement the procedures and curriculum revision stimulated by the outside supervisors.

There has in recent years been developing a practice of allocating classroom teachers who possess the desire, ingenuity, and other background for leadership to various types of projects intended to improve the curriculum or other aspects of the program of the school. Principals, department heads, and supervisors in many schools have seen the wisdom of providing a reduction of teaching load and other favorable conditions for these individuals who assume leadership and make greater contributions than the average teacher to various in-service projects. These positions of leadership by key teachers are not permanent; from time to time different teachers may be employed in this manner.

4. Types of In-Service Activities for Teacher Improvement

In the next few pages will be found a brief discussion of the more important techniques of stimulating in-service growth of teachers, techniques that could be used by the principal or other supervisor of a high school in planning a leadership program.

GOOD IN-SERVICE EDUCATION PROGRAMS. Some elements important in a good in-service education program may be listed as follows:

1. Teachers have an integral part in the planning and administering of the program.
2. Curriculum planning is carried on co-operatively by teachers, administrators, and supervisors.
3. Research and experimentation by teachers and teachers' groups are encouraged.
4. New teachers are well oriented to their positions.
5. There is teacher-parent-community co-operation.
6. Sufficient time is available to carry on group activities without injury to the teacher's health and morale.
7. The administration is fair and open-minded. Suggestions of teachers carry weight and are given careful consideration.
8. All activities are carried on by administrators, supervisors, and teachers working as a team toward their fulfillment.[3]

Among the types of teachers' in-service education activities which have been found most useful in schools are the following:

1. Participating in curriculum planning.
2. Doing professional reading, writing, and speaking.
3. Planning and carrying out a series of faculty meetings dealing with the improvement of the instructional program.
4. Assuming responsibilities in professional education organizations.
5. Visiting schools to observe other members of the profession at work.
6. Continuing with an advanced-degree program.
7. Participating in institutes, workshops, and conferences in terms of special interests and needs.
8. Traveling for specific purposes.
9. Serving as an exchange teacher.
10. Participating in civic activities in the community.
11. Conducting research and applying research findings to local situations.[4]

---

[3] *In-Service Education of Teachers,* p. 3.
[4] *Ibid.,* p. 5.

WORKSHOPS. The most interesting development of recent years in in-service growth of teachers has been that of the workshop program. The name is somewhat misleading; nevertheless, the program has at least some of the characteristics of a workshop in that it is built upon the principle that the teachers gather as individuals, small groups, or large groups to work upon some problem of improving the local educational program. It is neither a course of instruction nor a series of lectures. It is an opportunity to work on a specific problem in which the teacher or another individual of the school is interested. Frequently, the co-operative approach is used by several teachers planning together and assisting each other. Workshops are conducted in the local communities and on campuses of teacher-education institutions. In a large and increasing number of school districts, teachers' contracts call for them to be on duty 196 or more days, instead of only 180 days; it is thus possible for workshops to be held before school opens, after the term ends, or at both times.

In local workshops specialists from institutions of teacher education and from other school systems are often employed as consultants. These consultants are selected with a view to the possibility of their assisting the teachers along the lines in which they are to be engaged. Some of the consultants are employed for a long period of time, a semester, a year, or several years, and make several visits to the school system each year. Others come and work intensively for a short period of time, a few days or a few weeks.

Local workshops should ordinarily be planned co-operatively by the superintendent of schools, the supervisors and directors of special aspects of the educational program, and the high-school principals, head of departments, and teachers, or by whichever of these may be interested in the particular kind of workshop being contemplated.

The essential characteristics of an effective teacher workshop may be stated as follows:

1. The teacher participant is provided with an opportunity to make a careful study of an interest or problem which has arisen out of his experience as a teacher.
2. Each participant shares in planning programs of individual and group activities designed to meet his needs and those of his fellow workers.
3. The participant is provided with easy access to the services of various staff members representing a variety of kinds of assistance.
4. Each participant assists and receives assistance from other participants in the workshop in the solution of individual problems.

SALARY POLICIES AND CONTINUED PROFESSIONAL TRAINING. All but a small fraction of school systems have salary schedules which provide higher salaries for teachers with higher levels of preparation; for example, a five-year or master's degree or additional training beyond the master's degree usually means $200 or $300 in additional salary. This feature of the salary schedule was found more in larger districts than in smaller ones.

In about half of the school districts of the United States, teachers are required to submit every few years evidence of professional growth in order to earn annual increments; in about one fourth of the districts salary schedules recognized small blocks of credit so that enough credits could be earned in one or two summer sessions to result in permanent salary increase; in a few districts teachers who attended summer school were given a cash bonus for that year only.

As fulfillment of professional growth requirements, educative travel was accepted in the majority of the districts; committee work or special school assignments other than regular teaching duties were accepted in about one district in four; and publication of professional articles or books was accepted in about one district in five. Committees including classroom teachers were appointed in about one district in three to evaluate evidence of professional growth. These committees were appointed by the school administration in a few districts, but more often they were appointed by local educational associations or by the administration and the associations.

Teachers' Meetings. One of the earliest devices for promoting the in-service growth of teachers, as well as for expediting administrative matters, has been the teachers' meeting: the departmental meeting, the all-teacher meeting, the all-school meeting, or the all-city meeting. In general, the all-school or all-city meeting has been somewhat in disrepute. The types of teachers' meetings which are not popular are those which come at the end of a school teaching day, those in which the time is occupied with reading of notices and bulletins which could be sent to the teachers in the schools and read by them there, and those in which inadequate provision is made for participation by teachers themselves.

Among the suggestions for teachers' meetings which have proved to be sound are the following:

1. They may be held in school time as a part of the regular daily load of the teacher.
2. There should be opportunity for and encouragement of teacher participation.
3. There should be development of the social aspect of the meeting by devoting a part of the hour to refreshments and visiting among the teachers, preferably before the beginning of the professional period.
4. There should be employed committees to make investigations and to report recommendations at the meetings.
5. There should be a recognition on the part of the principal that he need not be the center of the only activity of the meeting and that much of the time might well be given over to reports of the teachers and committees.
6. There may be a series of meetings emphasizing a single theme through the semester, some new plan or field of interest in which the entire school is

interested: for example, the home rooms, evaluation of pupil growth, community relations, or audio-visual aids.
7. Mimeographed outlines and summaries may be distributed a few days after the meeting to assist in getting a clear picture and to serve as reminders and permanent records.
8. In small schools more time may well be spent in discussion among the teachers, but care must be taken to avoid such developments as the following:
   a. Monopoly of discussion by a few teachers.
   b. Tendency to digress or scatter too widely.
   c. Sales talks about the relative merits of subjects.
   d. Discussion of matters which should be handled by small committees.

There are other types of group conferences, of course: committee groups and groups that may be organized not as committees but as representatives of various committees or departments which have gathered to discuss and consult on particular problems or issues.

5. Aids to Supervision

USE OF CONSULTANTS. Increasingly, school administrators and boards of education make a budgetary provision for the use of consultants during the school year. Consultants are brought in principally from the following groups:

1. Teachers in colleges and universities engaged in the education of teachers.
2. Representatives from the state department of education in such fields as high-school curriculum, guidance, and physical health and education.
3. Local leaders in business, industry, labor, government, and social work.

Consultants should be chosen carefully so as to provide for information and ideas, as well as for discussion and criticisms, in the area of the problems of which the teachers have become conscious.

A good consultant will exercise leadership, but he will limit his services principally to giving aid when it is requested; he may be asked to visit classrooms, to examine printed and mimeographed materials relative to the program and activities of the school, and to offer his criticisms and suggestions for improvement.

In brief, the role of the consultant is:

1. To help groups formulate their problems and projects.
2. To help plan the approach to their solution and completion.
3. To provide special knowledge, understanding, and foresight.
4. To assist in bringing the project to a definite conclusion.
5. To avoid authoritative and excessive influence.

HOW TO USE CONSULTANTS. Consultants are often chosen to serve for a year or a period of years. Their activities include talking to teachers, conferring with small groups of teachers, carrying on contacts by correspondence, visiting classes, holding discussions with groups of parents and with boards of education, and other duties calculated to stimulate, direct, and promote growth activities of the staff or parts of it.

A consultant can be used to advantage:

1. When there is a need to evaluate a program to determine what the real problems are.
2. When the group wishes help in defining and limiting the problem.
3. When a problem might be better introduced by someone from outside.
4. When the group has exhausted its own resources.
5. When there is a need for progress evaluation.
6. When the group finds a need for specific or technical information.
7. When the group needs a "shot-in-the-arm" to maintain confidence in the value of further efforts.
8. When the group needs assistance in summing up and evaluating the work that has been accomplished.
9. When there is a need for assistance in determining the next steps or follow-up.

The author of this book has been a consultant in nearly a hundred districts and has found that a consultant's services can be used more effectively if:

1. There is a definite understanding and agreement by the group that a consultant is needed.
2. There is a definite understanding and agreement by the group as to why they need a consultant.
3. There is a definite recognition and statement of what is wanted.
4. There is agreement as to the framework and limitations within which the group must work.
5. There is agreement by the group as to the criteria for the selection of a consultant.
6. There has been proper clearance with all who may be concerned.
7. There is a résumé prepared of all that has transpired to date.
8. There have been some suggested procedures developed for consideration.
9. The consultant is given suggestions as to how the group feels he might function most effectively.
10. The consultant is given a complete review of the agreement of the group as to the origin of the problem, the composition of the group, progress to date, limitations or framework within which the group must work, and needs of the group as members have defined them.
11. The consultant is provided with an orientation by such data as the name and location of the school in which the group functions; type of school organization; size of school enrollment; description of the community; statement of the philosophy of the school; handbooks, etc.; statement of the outstanding problems of the school; and statement of any policies which might need to be considered in dealing with the problem.
12. The consultant is provided with some suggestions as to a tentative schedule of meetings.

VISITATION. The following is a summary of the more important considerations in regard to classroom visitation:

1. The principal should find time to visit some classes every week in order to *(a)* keep himself oriented to the problems of the school, *(b)* keep in touch with the pupils of his school and know how they are reacting to the educational program, and *(c)* be better able to assist his teachers.
2. Visitation should be planned by the principal to allow for the visitation of new teachers early in the fall and to make certain that his visitation is spread properly throughout the year.
3. Advance notice of visitation should ordinarily be given to teachers in whom the principal has not yet been able to establish the feeling that he is friendly and is visiting in a spirit of helpfulness.
4. The principal should make careful notes of every visit for a permanent record. These should be taken and used as inconspicuously as possible.
5. The principal should very rarely take over a class to demonstrate a method of teaching unless he does so at the beginning of the hour.
6. As soon as possible, the principal should discuss the visit, letting the teacher do most of the talking and giving him assurance at the beginning of the conference that he appreciates the good things he saw and heard.

The principal who wishes to become an effective supervisor should study carefully some book containing thorough discussions of the techniques of visitation and other supervisory procedures and should attempt to incorporate an increasing number of the recommendations in his daily practice.[5]

INTERVISITATION. The desire for intervisitation is usually of two types: (1) curiosity to see whether other teachers have the same problems that the visiting teacher has and (2) the desire to see a teacher in the classroom who is reputed to be doing an unusually successful quality of work or who is carrying on some sort of experiment. The principal or other supervisor should develop some plans for permitting intervisitation and for protecting it from abuse by overcurious teachers and those who wish merely to be relieved of their classroom activities for a half-day or more. Intervisitation should probably be followed by a report to some group of teachers of the same interests. Substitute teachers should be made available for teachers who can give good reasons for visiting other teachers in other classrooms, other buildings, or other cities. Teachers of academic subjects may with profit visit classes of laboratory subjects, where they may observe the increased interest of learners in "doing" types of learning activities.

INDIVIDUAL CONFERENCES. Some principals schedule each teacher for an individual conference at least once in the year and in small schools

[5]For example, Harl R. Douglass, Rudyard K. Bent, and Charles W. Boardman, *Democratic Supervision in Secondary Schools.*

several times in the year. At these conferences teachers may be more at ease since the conferences are not related to supervisory visits.

The more important changes in the philosophy of supervision have taken place in the nature of the supervisory conference between the principal or other supervisor and the individual teacher. Formerly, the principal or supervisor commonly confronted the teacher with criticisms and merely made suggestions relative to ways in which the teacher or the instruction might be improved.

Unless the postvisitation conference is expertly conducted, teachers are likely to assume a defensive attitude, to be somewhat nervous and sensitive, and to invent excuses and reasons rather than approach the analysis objectively and calmly with a view to assessment and improvement. Because of this situation, not only have supervisors and principals attempted to establish good and friendly relationships with the teacher before visitation but also they have conducted conferences in a friendly manner, concentrating largely upon good points and mentioning them first, before discussing weaknesses. The discussion of weaknesses should center around situations which involve pupils and other persons as well as the teachers themselves.

In the postvisitation conference, the approach to the improvement of teachers should be a co-operative one in which the teacher is permitted to play a leading part, with the help and the assistance of the supervisor. In other words, as in guidance and counseling generally, the teacher is encouraged to think through his own answers and solutions. A supervisor or principal may suggest alternatives or reading materials which bear upon the particular problem.

KEEPING RECORDS OF CLASSROOM VISITS. Whether or not supervisors should take notes while observing and keep records of supervisory visits has been a matter of spirited controversy in recent years. It would seem that here again the matter should turn upon the nature of the relationship between the supervisor and the supervised. If the teacher realizes that good points are noted and that the supervisor will use notes in a helpful manner, he is less likely to be confused or irritated.

PROFESSIONAL LIBRARIES. A development of the past few decades has been the growth of professional libraries in which there are not only copies of the professional journals applying to secondary education but also books, pamphlets, and bulletins issued by commercial publishing companies and publications collected from other school systems. The weakness of the professional library is that usually there is only one copy of each of the items in it; it is frequently desirable to have a considerable number of copies so that all the teachers of the school or of a department may be reading the same materials at somewhat the same time as a basis for discussions in an even-front approach to a problem. Because this is true, many schools have been taking advantage of discount rates to buy less-expensive bulletins in quantity.

PROFESSIONAL FILMS. In recent years there has been an increased use of professional films in connection with activities aimed at staff improvement. Several companies have been engaged in the producing of films that may be used for professional improvement; from these companies the films may be obtained either on a rental or on a purchase basis. Furthermore, many institutions of teacher education have provided, through their department of audio-visual education, films of this type. Usually they are films with sound tracks.

Examples of available films which are useful at the high-school level are the following:

1. *Counseling, Its Tools and Techniques,* 22 minutes.
2. *Audio-Visual Aids to Learning,* 11 minutes.
3. *Bulletin Boards Affecting Teaching Advice,* 11 minutes (in color).
4. *Problem Method I—Defining the Problem and Getting Information,* 18 minutes (high-school social studies).
5. *Problem Method II—Using Information to Solve the Problem,* 16 minutes.
6. *Problem of Pupil Adjustment I—The Drop-Out,* 20 minutes.
7. *Problem of Pupil Adjustment II—The Stay-In,* 19 minutes.
8. *We Plan Together,* 20 minutes (eleventh-grade core-group planning).

These are listed for lending by the Bureau of Audio-Visual Instruction, University of Colorado, Boulder, Colorado. A large number of useful sound track films are available from the Coronet Instructional Films, 65 East South Water Street, Chicago 1, Illinois.

EDUCATIONAL TAPES. In recent years many thousands of educational tapes have been prepared for use in all grades and in all subjects. The Kent State University at Kent, Ohio, has been one of the leaders in this movement and at low cost a wide variety of tapes are available for purchase there. In addition, many of the teacher-education institutions, through their bureaus of audio-visual instruction and extension divisions, have made or obtained educational tapes which may be borrowed at very low cost. Principals should get lists of available tapes and the conditions under which they may be obtained and see that their teachers are aware of the available helps of this nature.

SICK-LEAVE AND TRAVEL-LEAVE PROVISIONS.[6] In an increasing number of schools definite provision is made for a specific number of days each year for sick leave with full pay during absence, part pay for a stated number of days and part pay for an additional number of days, or part pay for a prescribed number of days. In some districts unused portions of sick leave may be accumulated from year to year. It is probable that the program of part pay for a prescribed number of days is best, in that it tends to discourage teachers from remaining away from school with minor ill-

[6]*Administering a Sick Leave Program for School Personnel,* Washington, D.C., American Association of School Administrators, September, 1954.

ness and from taking other advantage of the program; at the same time, of course, it tends to encourage teachers to attend school when they are mildly ill and thus to risk possible communication of a contagious disease to others or the development of serious illness. At any rate, having a definite sick-leave plan relieves teachers of financial worry in regard to illness.

In a considerable and increasing number of schools, the teachers may take a year of leave for educational purposes or travel.[7] In the great majority of districts the leave is taken without pay; in a small but increasing number of districts the leave is granted for continuation of study on part pay. Such leave is usually given with the provision that the teacher return to the school system for at least one year's service. In a few instances leave with part pay is provided for educational travel. Provisions for leaves operate to encourage and promote educational growth.

THE TEACHER'S HANDBOOK. In a great many schools the high-school principal has developed a handbook of information concerning the principles and practices of the administration and management of the high school. This book is distributed to teachers, thereby enabling them to cooperate in the management of the school and to consider recommendations for the improvement of the management and administration of the school.

Included in school handbooks are such matters as the following: statement of the philosophy of the school and its educational objectives; duties of the various officers of the school, including such specialized officers as the registrar and counselor; departmental organizations; administrative participation by students and teachers through committees; use of printed forms; necessary reports; administrative details, such as bell schedules, bulletins, handling of supplies, keys, study halls and library, fire drills, and accident reports; details that have to do with instruction, such as student programs, marking system, handling of failures, and the issuing of reports; duties of home-room teachers and home-room activities; procedure for sponsoring clubs and other student organizations; responsibility of the home-room teachers (or others) for checking pupils' programs with reference to the course of study, graduation, and college entrance; extracurricular activities and regulations governing participation in them; the guidance program and services; social policy of the school; student organizations, such as those dealing with student business affairs, the scholarship society, the honor society, girls' and boys' leagues, groups for welfare work, and clubs; the ideals and traditions of the school; building traffic; mimeographing system; parking of cars; teacher personnel policies relative to absence, continuing contracts, and substitute teachers; code of ethics; teaching aids; what to do in case

[7] *Teacher Personnel Practices, Urban School Districts, 1955-56,* Research Division of the National Education Association, June, 1956, Table 41.

of accidents; matters of discipline; management of free textbooks; assemblies; health activities; use of library; homework; telephone calls; smoking; calendar for the year; faculty directory; and requests for special rooms, equipment, and help.

Considerable experience seems to indicate the loose-leaf type of manual in a fairly permanent, dignified cover as the most satisfactory. The information should be printed on a good quality of paper. If the contents have been carefully organized, it will be no great task to reprint an occasional page as the information which it contains becomes obsolete. Space should be left on each page, either in the printed matter itself or in a wide margin, so that annotations may be made as changes of a minor sort become necessary. Pages should be numbered and, needless to say, an index is essential.

Plans must be made to keep the contents up to date continually. The contents must be supplemented by occasional bulletins. Loose-leaf binders are preferred for this reason. In some handbooks are included such things as a copy of the printed or mimeographed rules of the board of education, the students' handbook, copies of at least the principal forms used in the school by teachers with explanations for their use, pictures, and diagrams.

THE SUPERVISORY BULLETIN. In a considerable number of schools bulletins are issued to teachers both for supervisory and administrative purposes. These bulletins are usually mimeographed in the smaller schools and printed in the larger schools. In the very small schools typed copies are posted on the teachers' bulletin board. These bulletins contain such matters as the following:

1. The results of recent teachers' meetings.
2. Brief extracts of outstanding articles.
3. Book reviews of outstanding recent professional publications.
4. Reports of interesting projects and developments by various teachers, departments, or schools.
5. News stories about individuals on the staff, the personnel of the school.
6. Statistical data concerning results of tests, school attendance, and the like.

SUMMER-SCHOOL ATTENDANCE AND EXTENSION COURSES. Several trends in the area of continued college education are definitely noteworthy. The taking of correspondence or other extension courses during the school year is being increasingly discouraged. The time is needed for a richer social life, more independent reading, and a variety of leisure interests, to say nothing of the increased demands upon teachers' time for course-of-study planning, counseling, home and parent conferences, and work with student activities. Study during the school year should either be informal general education or definitely related to current in-service projects of the particular school. Increasingly, boards of education are subsidizing summer-school attendance for teachers, who attend summer-schools and take work as directed by their principals and their superintendents of schools.

RESEARCH IN SUPERVISORY TECHNIQUES. There is a great volume of research data being poured forth each year by candidates for graduate degrees in education and by committees and individuals who work in specific school systems. It is unfortunate that the results of these investigations are not available to teachers in general, being frequently buried on shelves along with theses and mimeographed reports. In a considerable number of school systems, committees have been charged with the responsibility for pulling together the research findings on particular problems or on particular areas, interpreting the findings, and reporting them to other teachers in the school system.

There is published annually by Phi Delta Kappa, Bloomington, Indiana, a list, prepared by Miss Mary Louise Lyda, Educational Librarian at the University of Colorado, and others, of completed doctoral dissertations in education and those in process of completion. Most of these theses may either be borrowed from the interloan department of the university where the thesis was done or be purchased in microfilm at a relatively small amount, ordinarily not more than $5.

In an increasing number of school systems, investigations are being carried on by teachers and others either independently or under the direction of the bureau of research or director of research. A wide variety of types of investigation of different problems seems necessary and desirable and may be carried on advantageously through local personnel in local situations. Funds, of course, must be provided for the gathering of data and their tabulation and treatment; also some reduction of the teaching load of those engaged in the study is necessary.

TEACHER RATING. Like many other relatively objective approaches to education, teacher rating went through a very rapid development which was followed by general opposition. In this instance, opposition grew out of the tension and insecurity created by the rating procedures. In recent years, especially as a result of the growth of the practice of merit ratings for special salary increases, there has been an increased use of methods of evaluation and diagnosis of learning situations and teaching activities. Also in recent years emphasis has been upon training the teacher for self-rating and upon co-operative rating by teachers and pupils, by teachers and supervisors, or by all three groups. The supervisor who would discharge his responsiblity for rating effectively should do a considerable amount of reading and give much attention and study to the problem of instruments and procedures. Teacher rating is fraught with dangers and must be approached cautiously and with very careful planning. At the end of this chapter are given several references on teacher rating which may be recommended; some of these include good scales and devices for rating and self-rating.

As reported by the Research Division of the National Education Associztion[8], in 1958-1959, 11.2 per cent of the school districts with more than 2500 people provided a salary reward for good quality service; 12.6 per cent provided a penalty for poor quality service; and 7.2 per cent provided both. In many cities where the matter has come up for consideration, the majority of teachers have opposed merit-rating salary provisions, sometimes very vigorously. The chief objections to merit rating are:

1. It leads to division among teachers and the lowering of the feeling of unity and good will.
2. Merit rating cannot be objectively done and it is very likely to lead to favoritism, injustice, or both.

In approximately 50 per cent of the districts in which merit-rating salary provisions are found, a committee or some other group of teachers helps to develop the provisions.

Among the types of evaluative methods employed, either alone or in combination, are the following, as reported by the Research Division of the National Education Association.[9]

	Per cent
Informal evaluation based on opinion of evaluator(s)	73.7
Rating scales	45.9
Interview	32.9
Check list	26.8
Teacher-to-teacher comparison	19.0
Ranking in order of merit	6.2

In 38 per cent of the schools, only one of the above methods was employed, usually the informal evaluation based upon opinion. However, in 62 per cent of the schools, two or more methods were employed: in 51.5 per cent of the schools, informal evaluation based upon opinion was one of the methods employed; rating scales were used in 35 per cent; interviews were used in 31 per cent; check lists were used in 25 per cent; and teacher-to-teacher comparisons were used in 18 per cent.

In 43 per cent of the urban schools studied, evaluation was held once a year; in 16.5 per cent it was held twice a year; in 14 per cent it was held more than twice a year; and in 21 per cent it was held at irregular times.

In 52 per cent of the schools, results of the evaluation were discussed with all teachers and in 33 per cent they were discussed only with unsatisfactory teachers. In 12 per cent of the schools, teachers were rated only by the superintendent; in 16 per cent of the schools, they were rated only by the principal; and in 77 per cent of the schools, two or more

[8] *Quality of Service Provision in Salary Schedules, 1958-59,* Washington, D.C., Research Division of the National Education Association, December, 1959.

[9] *Ibid.*, p. 22.

evaluators were employed, including the superintendent in 66 per cent of the schools, the principal in 75 per cent of the schools, the supervisor in 36 per cent of the schools, the departmental chairman in 21 per cent of the schools, and a committee of teachers co-operating in 3 per cent of the schools.

With respect to the effect of merit rating on teacher morale, much is yet to be determined and the practice hangs in the balance. As reported by the Research Division of the National Education Association, superintendents in 38.2 per cent of the schools report a good effect for most teachers; those in 29.6 per cent of the schools report good effects for some and poor effects for others; those in 28.1 per cent of the schools report little noticeable effect; and those in 4.1 per cent of the schools report bad effect.

With respect to the effect on level of performance, in 46.2 per cent of the schools superintendents reported good effect for most teachers; in 21.2 per cent they reported good effect for some and poor for others; and in 32.6 per cent they reported little noticeable effect. The principal should follow carefully the literature reporting results and procedures in merit rating and related rewards.

Every supervisor should prepare himself for evaluating and rating the teachers and the teachers' work before any visitation is made or any teacher evaluated. If he has not had a course in supervision in which he has gone through this matter very carefully, he should obtain a recent book on supervision in secondary schools and prepare on paper, as well as in his mind, a check list of things to look for in visitation and things to consider in visitation and possibly in conferences.

THE INSTRUCTIONAL-MATERIALS COLLECTION. In recent years there has been greatly increased emphasis upon providing and making available to teachers an abundant and varied supply of materials that may be of assistance in planning instructional materials and activities. Among such materials are included: films, slides, tapes, textbooks, courses of study, pamphlets, and bulletins obtained from other schools, state teacher-training institutions, state departments of education, the U. S. Office of Education, various divisions of the National Education Association, and commercial companies. There should also be provided catalogues of various types of equipment and materials from various commercial companies, a collection of professional books and magazines, and a card file of films, slides, and tapes which are available from commercial institutions and teacher-training institutions. This file should be organized in an alphabetical listing under the various subject-matter headings. There should also be made available lists of free and inexpensive learning materials, such as the list published by the Division of Survey and Field Service of the George Peabody College for Teachers, Nashville, Tennessee, and that published each year by the Educators Progress Service of Randolph, Wisconsin.

This collection of instructional materials requires adequate housing and equipment; also, there should be someone to assist the principal in collecting the material and arranging it for the use of the teachers. In an increasing number of schools the instructional-materials center includes all the audio-visual equipment and films and, in some schools, the library as well. A discussion of the housing and equipment of an instructional-materials center will be found in Chapter 22, "High-School Housing and Its Care."[10].

6. *Helping Special Types of Teachers*

DIFFERENCES IN NEED FOR HELP. All teachers need to have a thorough understanding of the immediate and ultimate aims and objectives of secondary education, of the principles and practices in curriculum construction and assignments, of the methods of modifying and directing student learning, of the ways to assist students in their extracurricular-activity organization and participation, of the ways to render counseling service appropriate for classroom teachers, and of the importance and techniques of the field of public relations. Teachers will be found to vary significantly with respect to their background, understanding, and skills in these various fields; each teacher will need help in some areas more than in others.

THE BEGINNING TEACHER. It has been increasingly recognized in recent years that the beginning teacher, compared to the more experienced teacher, needs more help and a different kind of help. Recalling that the preservice education of the teacher is definitely inadequate and very limited, supervisors have in a considerable number of schools made very special provision for the "breaking-in" and in-service growth of the beginning teacher.

In different school systems the following devices are employed for assisting the beginning teacher:

1. Decreased teaching load.
2. One period a day for visitation, conference, and planning preparation.
3. A handbook of complete information about the school.
4. The association of the beginning teacher with one outstanding teacher as a sponsor and guide.
5. A provision for a director of beginning teachers, who is responsible for directing their in-service growth in the first year and who employs various other teachers and supervisors in assisting the beginning teacher.
6. An institute held about a day or two before the beginning of school, a series of meetings held very soon after the beginning of school, or, preferably, both.

---

[10]See description of the instructional materials center's equipment and supplies by P.O. Johnson, W. O. Nesbitt, and Dell Felder, *Bulletin of the N.A.S.S.P.* (June, 1959), No. 243, pp. 146-149.

While the beginning teacher experiences most of the same problems as does the experienced teacher, areas in which he is likely to need special help include the following:

1. The matter of developing interest on the part of the student and the related matters of student control.
2. The adaptation of teaching to the individual pupil.
3. The organizing of learning activities in such a manner as to relate them to their application in everyday life.

THE TEACHER NEW TO THE SCHOOL. In a considerable number of schools where rather advanced progress has been made in curriculum revision (where, for example, the core curriculum has been employed or home rooms have been introduced after a period of in-service training and growth in the teachers), it has been discovered after a few years that the program was adversely affected by the fact that the incoming new teachers, experienced but new to the school and lacking the training and orientation that the teachers had at the beginning of the program, were not making a success of the work and, in many instances, were critical of the program and desirous of bringing the experiment to an end. For this reason, in an increasing number of schools, teachers new to the school system are being given special in-service training in various forms, including special preschool institutes for new teachers in which a thorough orientation to the program of the school and the community is emphasized.

New teachers, like beginning teachers, may well profit from a preschool institute or a series of meetings early in the year. The new teacher needs especially to feel that he belongs to the school group.

Like the beginning teacher, the new teacher of experience should be informed during the summer of his assignment, the tests used, outlines of the courses, and the use of newer methods of teaching. In addition to the handbook, information of the following type should be provided to the teacher new to the school:

1. Information concerning living quarters.
2. Information concerning community resources of educational material: public or other libraries; historical, scientific, or other museums; art galleries; botanical or zoological gardens; manufacturing or industrial plants; commercial houses; banks; printing establishments; public utilities; governmental agencies; and other types of institutions of use in various ways in education.
3. Information concerning the pertinent or unique characteristics of the school community.

Where handbooks are not issued to the teachers, comparable information should be given to them early in the school year, if not before its beginning, either in the form of mimeographed materials or oral explanations, preferably the former.

In the very great majority of schools in districts of more than 2500 population, specific help is given to new teachers in locating living quarters; conferences with new teachers are held soon after school opens, at which time their problems are discussed; and new teachers are provided with a personal copy of rules and regulations governing the school system. In an increasing number of schools, probably about half of those districts containing more than 2500 people, an experienced teacher is assigned to give counsel to each new teacher; in the selection of such a counselor, care must be taken to select an individual with an appropriate personality and the tact and diplomacy to be really effective. In about one third of the schools, new teachers are required to report several days earlier than other teachers for special meetings and discussions.

The teachers new to the school have special need for assistance in meeting people, not only other teachers and members of the clerical, custodial, and supervisory staffs of the local school but also those with whom they will have contact in the central office and people in the community, particularly those who will be likely to entertain one or more of the new teachers. The problem of an adequate social life for new teachers, especially unmarried ones, is a serious one. In most communities local civic groups hold social gatherings for new teachers.

THE OLD-FASHIONED TEACHER. In many schools the mistake has been made by principals and supervisors of attempting to prod old-fashioned, skeptical teachers into more modern methods. It has been increasingly recognized in recent years that the more aggressive approach to the old-fashioned teacher is not likely to improve his attitudes toward or abilities in newer procedures; it is likely to cause him to feel insecure and antagonistic and therefore do more harm than good.

It has also been discovered that it is not necessary for all teachers in the same school to move along at the same rate or teach in the same way. Side by side with teachers who employ one philosophy of education and appropriate course-of-study materials and teaching activities, there can be other teachers who have a completely different philosophy of education and different learning materials and activities. It has also been discovered in many instances that, if the contrast between these two groups of individuals has not been made too obvious and if invidious comparisons have not been made, many of the old-fashioned teachers after a period of a few years will slowly and gradually, and in a face-saving sort of manner, begin to take on some of the philosophy and teaching activities of the more modern and progressive group. Indeed, in a few instances it has been noted that the teachers most recently converted to modern methods are less moderate toward old-fashioned teachers and conservative methods than the earlier protagonists of modern procedures.

STUDYING THE INDIVIDUAL TEACHER. One of the newer approaches to the study of teacher efficiency has been the study of teacher personality and mental hygiene as applied to individual teachers. It has been discovered that in a considerable number of instances teachers who are least effective and least happy in their work have an inadequate and unsatisfying recreational and social life. It is difficult to apply general standards to a particular teacher in a given community; whether a teacher is well adjusted in social life is a matter that has been studied somewhat by supervisors and administrators in terms of individual cases.

Principals should gather as much data as possible about each new teacher in the school and keep up the records of the older teachers. The type of data which is of use pertains to each teacher's pattern of preparation, previous experience, special strong points, special weaknesses, hobbies and social interests, general philosophy of education, physical health defects, and relative desire for and participation in social life; such data may enable a principal to exploit the teacher's strong points, to realize his weak points, and to encourage him to participate in school life according to his interests and needs.

THE SUBSTITUTE TEACHER. The principal of the small high school should, before the beginning of each school year or very shortly after it, locate at least one individual in the community who is prepared by reason of training and experience to be a substitute for each of the teachers on his staff. The principal of a large school should have a list, with addresses, of several individuals for each department of instruction who may be called upon to teach in case it is necessary for one or more teachers in a department to be absent from the school a half-day or more.

It is very desirable for the substitute teachers to be familiar with all the rules and procedures of the school. These teachers should be given copies of the teacher's handbook and should be called together for a meeting at some time quite early in the school year and briefed with respect to the things that might be useful for them to know in order to co-operate fully in the management of the students in their classes. Such things involve the schedule, the meaning and time of the bells, the handling of reports, admissions in connection with absence, the management of pupils late to class and of excuses for pupils to leave the class, reports to be filed, information concerning fire alarms and bells and emergencies which would necessitate evacuating the building, conventional or typical handling of the more common types of disciplinary cases, and other information likely to be of use to a new teacher.

As far in advance as possible, the substitute teacher should be given information of the nature of his responsibilities, as indicated by the following form used by the Arthur Hill High School of Saginaw, Michigan. In many schools small pamphlets of special information for substitute teachers are prepared, such as the *Information for Substitute Teachers* by the Elizabeth, New Jersey, Schools. The substitute teacher should be furnished with a form for report to the regular teacher, including work covered, assignments made, and other useful information.

Attention of ____. We
(substitute teacher)
are pleased to have you here at Arthur Hill as one of our staff. You are substituting for ________ ____. Floor ____________. Room ____________. Your class schedule for the day is

	1	2	3	4	5	6	7
8:30 8:45	8:50 9:40	9:45 10:35	10:40 11:30	11:35 12:30	12:10 1:05	1:10 2:05	2:10 3:05

LUNCH	Your lunch period is 11:30-12:10, or 12:30-1:10. The cafeteria is on the third floor. Teachers are served in the kitchen. The faculty dining room is adjacent.
BELLS	A room chime and a hall bell sound at the beginning of each class period – the chime only at the close. There are no warning signals. The closing chime does not automatically dismiss classes, although you will naturally not keep students more than a few seconds overtime.
ATTENDANCE	"Absence excuses" (white or blue, Form 161) are issued by the adviser during advisory period only. Do not allow students to enter your classes late. Send them to the office for entrance permits. List names of absent students on daily absence report, Form 107a, showing the periods absent. These reports will be collected during first hour and at the beginning of seventh hour.
DEPARTMENT HEAD	Your department head ______________________________. name room floor phone no. will be pleased to assist you at any time.
CLASS CHAIRMEN	Each class has a permanent student chairman who is ready to assist you with class procedures, lesson assignments, and materials.
SEATING CHARTS, LESSON PLANS	In the shallow middle drawer of your desk there are seating charts and lesson plans with class chairmen indicated.
TOMORROW'S ASSIGNMENTS	Your assignments for tomorrow should be clearly outlined and given with the assurance that the regular teacher will recognize them.
DISCIPLINE	We have tried to establish a feeling upon the part of our students that substitute teachers are to be accorded the same respect as regular teachers. You are requested to send to the office any student who might refuse to observe this standard of conduct.
LOUNGE ROOMS	The women's room, #230, is on the second floor at the back of the building, south end (toward the city). The men's room, #221, is at the opposite end of the hall on the same floor.
SHADES, LIGHTS, LOCKS, KEYS	Shades should be adjusted during the day so as to provide the best possible light. At the close of the day, windows should be left entirely exposed excepting on Fridays when the shades should be adjusted so as to cover the upper half of each window. Turn off light switches, lock the door, and leave keys in the office at the close of the day.
MAKING YOUR REPORT	Please fill in the back of this sheet and leave your report in the office. Inquire whether or not you should return the following day. If you are to be here for a period of several days, you may combine as many as five days' reports in one if you care to do so.
OFFICE PHONES	Outer office – 13; Mr. Morrow – 12; Miss Peterson – 11; Mr. Brock – 10.

It is desirable to have the substitute teachers attend some of the teachers' meetings during the year, particularly when new plans and procedures are being discussed and reports are being made by committees of teachers with reference to such matters as course-of-study revision, home rooms, guidance, and other matters of interest to every classroom teacher.

Each teacher should know who his probable substitutes are and their phone numbers and local addresses. Having this information, the teacher who will not be present on certain days may notify his substitute and be able to discuss with him the procedures that might be followed in the classes during the period of absence of the teacher. The principal should keep on file in his office the names of all substitutes, for two reasons: (1) in case the absent teacher is too seriously injured to notify a substitute, the principal has to obtain a substitute and give him as much help as possible in dealing with the classes; and (2) the principal needs to know what substitute teachers are in the building at any given time. It should be made clear, too, that the teacher who is unable to be present for his classes should report his absence to the principal as well as contacting his substitute. Some principals require teachers to make out class lists or, better still, seating diagrams and to file them in the principal's office, where they may be picked up by the substitute teacher.

In cases where it has been impossible to obtain a substitute, some principals have found it effective for the principal, assistant principal, or clerk of the school to meet the class briefly at the beginning of the hour and ask the class to designate a chairman to preside over a discussion or a study period during the absence of the teacher.

THE WEAK OR FAILING TEACHER. The especially weak teacher should be identified early in the first year of his teaching and given special help and assistance. In the case of an extremely weak teacher, the supervisor must before the spring of the year carefully consider and make a decision as to whether he will want to recommend that the teacher (1) be transferred to another position, maybe in another school, (2) not be employed for another year, or (3) be given a warning that unless the quality of teaching is improved his contract will not be renewed at the end of the next year. For the especially weak teacher, a guided intervisitation very frequently turns out to be a useful procedure. Often, close association with an especially strong teacher will be instrumental in bringing about improvement.

Weak teachers frequently have defects of the following types:

1. Defects in voice and speech: indistinct, scolding, whining, or condescending tone and inflection; lack of energy and color; too rapid speech; lack of evidence of a sense of humor.
2. Defects in appearance and care of person: flashy or gaudy dress; untidiness of dress or person; unchanging facial expression; lack of or excessive vivaciousness; body odors.

3. Defects in character or personality: irritability; ultraseriousness; insincerity; supersensitiveness; lack of confidence; drabness; lack of understanding of youthful points of view; abnormal anxiety; emotional instability.

The help given to the weak teacher along the lines of the first two general types of defect is often effective, particularly when diplomatically handled. Assistance to the teacher with the third type of defect is less likely to be effective.

A direct comparison with other teachers is usually not effective in helping a weak teacher, although unstructured intervisitation may produce good results. Sometimes, some demonstration teaching may make the teacher conscious of his faults and the need for improvement. In many cases it is necessary for the supervisor and the teacher to have a frank discussion of the teacher's defects, although such a discussion may be painful to both parties at the moment. It is needless to say that this conference should be held in the most friendly manner. The supervisor should not bring the teacher's defects to his attention directly unless they are real and important. Tape recordings are frequently useful to "see ourselves as others see us." The supervisor may suggest to the teacher that he tape a recording and that the supervisor and the teacher hear it together.

It is unfortunate that some teachers have a great degree of emotional instability and, occasionally, definite mental illness. Although he must be careful with respect to assisting teachers with psychological problems, the supervisor must make some effort to help and must, in some aggravated cases, advise a teacher to consult a doctor to see whether or not psychiatric help is needed.[11]

Problems, Questions, and Exercises

1. What are the typical teacher's attitudes toward supervision? What are the various types of supervision that teachers object to?
2. What does democratic leadership in supervision mean to you? Give some illustrations as to how it might be carried into effect.
3. What are the ten most important areas and types of growth of teachers in service? Arrange them in the order of their importance.
4. Select a high school of a given size, say 250 students, and suggest an organization which would indicate appropriate personnel for assisting teachers in a school of that size.
5. Be able to discuss the department headship in the program of supervision—its limitations and its areas of possible good service.
6. Be able to discuss classroom visitation by supervisors. What are its dangers, advantages, and limitations and the general conditions under which it should be done?

[11]For more complete discussion of the problems of dealing with these specific types of teachers and for discussion on methods of dealing with other types of teachers, see Harl R. Douglass, R. K. Bent, and Charles W. Boardman, *Democratic Supervision in Secondary Schools.*

7. Be able to discuss teacher rating and give reasons for mentioning its limitations and its advantages. Tell how you believe teacher rating should be used in the high school today.
8. Be able to discuss the activities of the out-of-building supervisor and his relationship with the principal and his staff.
9. List suggestions as to how to carry on interviews with teachers about their work, especially interviews based upon observation of the teachers at work in the classroom.
10. In addition to the suggestions given in the book, make at least one suggestion, preferably two or three, dealing with each of the following types of teachers:
    a. The beginning teacher.
    b. The teacher new to the school.
    c. The old-fashioned teacher.
    d. The teacher who continually has discipline trouble.
11. Mention a number of types of problems or areas in which some teachers need more help than others in order that they may improve their teaching and get more satisfaction out of it.
12. How can a supervisor best evaluate the work of the members of his staff?

Selected Supplementary Readings

Administering a Sick Leave Program for School Personnel, Washington, D.C., American Association of School Administrators, 1954.

Andre, Robert G., Buran, R. C., and Salyer, Guy, "Under What Conditions Does Merit Rating Succeed or Fail?" *Bulletin of the N.A.S.S.P.* (April, 1961), No. 264, pp. 23-28.

Antell, Henry, "Junior High Supervisors Can Make the Time!" *Bulletin of the N.A.S.S.P.* (December, 1959), No. 251, pp. 9-12.

Barnes, John B., *Educational Research for Classroom Teachers,* New York, Putnam, 1960.

Bear, Willard, "The Role of the Principal in Developing a School Philosophy," *Bulletin of the N.A.S.S.P.* (December, 1959), No. 251, pp. 64-69.

Beringause, A. F., "Aids for the Supervisor," *Bulletin of the N.A.S.S.P.* (December, 1959), No. 251, pp. 18-22.

Bruce, William F., and Holden, A. John, *The Teacher's Personality Development,* New York, Holt, 1957. [A good reference for the professional library.]

Bush, William T., "What Administrators Do to Improve Instruction," *Phi Delta Kappan* (November, 1957), Vol. 41, No. 2, p. 64. [List of thirty-four practices from a survey of 708 selected administrators in the U.S.]

Davis, H., "Facts and Issues in Merit Salary Schedules," *Journal of Teacher Education* (June, 1957), Vol. 8, pp. 127-135.

Dennaire, B., "Preparing for the Substitute Teacher," *Bulletin of the N.A.S.S.P.* (February, 1953), No. 192, pp. 45-47.

Doggett, Frank A., "An Inservice Training Program," *Bulletin of the N.A.S.S.P.* (February, 1960), No. 253, pp. 118-122.

Draper, Edgar M., Meyer, George, and Unruh, Adolph, "How Develop an Inservice Education Program?" *Bulletin of the N.A.S.S.P.* (April, 1961), No. 264, pp. 199-204.

Eye, Glen G., and Laine, Willard R., *The New Teacher Comes to School,* New York, Harper, 1956.

Francis, Sister Mary Teresa (B.V.M.), "Practical Helps for Supervision." *Proceedings and Addresses,* 49th Annual Meeting, National Catholic Educational Association, August, 1952. [Suggestions of a practical nature on improvement of teachers' meetings, classroom visits, etc.]

Fraser, Stewart, and Romine, Stephen, *Merit Rating,* Bureau of Educational Research and Service, School of Education, University of Colorado, Fall, 1960. [A brief, selected, and annotated bibliography of recent articles dealing with pros and cons, theories and practices.]

Grim, Paul R., and Hoyt, Cyril J., "Appraisal of Teaching Competency," *Educational Research Bulletin* (April, 1952), Vol. 31, No. 4, pp. 85-91. [Report of a study centering around the development of two new instruments for evaluating teaching competencies: a Student Reaction Inventory, and the Teacher Characteristic List.]

Harnley, Paul W. (Chairman), and others, "Incentives Used in Motivating Professional Growth of Teachers," *North Central Association Quarterly* (April, 1953), Vol. 27, pp. 389-409.

Horrocks, John E., and Schoonover, Thelma I., "Self-Evaluation as a Means of Growth for Teachers in Service: Use of a Self-Analysis Questionnaire," *Educational Administration and Supervision* (February, 1950), Vol. 36, No. 2, pp. 83-90. [A good over-all discussion of the problem of teacher evaluation. Reference is made to the Lincoln, Nebraska, schools, which developed a co-operative survey form.]

"How to Help Your Inexperienced Teacher Do a Better Job," *School Management* (December, 1959), Vol. 22, No. 6, pp. 47-51. [Instructional-materials center discussed.]

In-Service Education of Teachers, Washington, D. C., Research Division of the National Education Association, 1960.

Jones, Robert E., "The Teacher's Handbook," *Bulletin of the N.A.S.S.P.* (September, 1959), No. 248, pp. 196-198.

Kennedy, E. D., "Advantages and Disadvantages of Teacher Merit-Rating Plans," *Bulletin of the N.A.S.S.P.* (September, 1958), No. 239, pp. 38-40.

Kottmeyer, William, "Supervision: A Contribution to Excellence," *National Catholic Educational Association Bulletin* (August, 1960), Vol. 58, pp. 351-357.

Lawrence, Noel, "In-Service Programs for High School Teachers," *Educational Leadership* (March, 1960), Vol. 17, pp. 344-346.

McCall, W. A., and Krause, G. R., "Measurement of Teacher Merit for Salary Purposes," *Journal of Educational Research* (October, 1959), Vol. 53, pp. 73-75.

"Merit Rating and Pay," *Phi Delta Kappan* (January, 1961), Vol. 42, pp. 137-163. [Seven articles by teachers, professor of education, secretary of Florida Education Association, president of American Federation of Teachers, business man; pro and con.]

Metcalf, Harold H., and Pate, W. E., "How Can Faculty Meetings Stimulate Professional Growth?" *Bulletin of the N.A.S.S.P.* (April, 1960), No. 255, pp. 75-79.

Michael, Lloyd S., "Orienting New Teachers," *Bulletin of the N.A.S.S.P.* (December, 1950), No. 174, pp. 72-78.

O'Neill, John J., "Initiating the New Teacher," *Catholic School Journal* (September, 1951), Vol. 51, No. 7. [Summarizes what the new teacher needs in the way of help as he enters a new school position.]

Philpot, Frank N., "What Are Some New Developments in In-Service Education for the Principal and His Staff," *Bulletin of the N.A.S.S.P.* (April, 1960), No. 255, pp. 163-165.

Professional Growth Requirements and Equivalents, 1958-59, Washington, D. C., Research Division of the National Education Association, December, 1958. [Data relative to practices in very large districts.]

The Pupil and the Law, Washington, D. C., National Education Association, 1959.

Quality-of-Service Provisions in Salary Schedules, 1958-59, Washington, D. C., Research Division of the National Education Association, December, 1959.

Reavis, W. C., and Cooper, D. H., *Evaluation of Teacher Merit in City School Systems,* University of Chicago Press, 1945. [The importance, functions, and current procedures of various methods of evaluating teacher merit. Several samples of rating scales used by various cities are reproduced.]

Ringkamp, Brother Henry S. (S.M.), "The Principal Looks at Supervision," *Catholic School Journal* (January, 1950), Vol. 50, No. 1. [Offers practical suggestions as to how a busy principal can get the job done.]

Ryan, L. V., "Teachers and Administrators of Our Central Catholic High Schools," *Catholic Journal of Education* (November, 1958), Vol. 58, pp. 21-22.

Stoops, Emory, and Rafferty, M. L., Jr., *Practices and Trends in School Administration,* Ginn and Co., 1961, Chapter 21 "Salaries and Salary Scheduling," Chapter 22, "Tenure, Leaves of Absence, and Work Load".

Tanner, H. Jeanne, "The High School Teacher Looks to the Principal, *School Review* (February, 1955), Vol. 63, pp. 96-97.

The Teacher and the Law, Washington, D. C., National Education Association, 1959. [Also issued annually, *The Teacher's Day in Court* and *The Pupil's Day in Court,* reviews of court decisions of the previous year.]

Teacher Personnel Practices, Urban School Districts, 1955-56, Washington, D. C., Research Division of the National Education Association, June, 1956.

Thiesen, W. W., "How to Help New Teachers Adjust to the Community," *Nation's Schools* (August, 1960), Vol. 66, No. 2, pp. 52-55.

Tompkins, Ellsworth, and Roe, Virginia, "The Case for and Against Merit Rating," *Bulletin of the N.A.S.S.P.* (October, 1956), No. 222, pp. 5-21.

Wessel, H. M., and Miller, B. R., "What Are the Pros and Cons of Teacher Merit Rating Plans?" *Bulletin of the N.A.S.S.P.* (April, 1959), No. 246, pp. 149-153.

Willink, Ross J., "In-Service Training of Junior High School Teachers," *Bulletin of the N.A.S.S.P.* (December, 1959), No. 251, pp. 13-17.

Wynn, Richard, "Teachers Are Entitled to Job Satisfaction," *Nation's Schools* (May, 1955), Vol. 55, No. 5, pp. 43-45.

7

Organizing The Curriculum

1. Increased Need for Curriculum Improvement

VIGOROUS CRITICISM. Although the curriculum of the secondary schools in the United States has always been undergoing change and evolution, in recent years for several reasons the rate of change has been increased and curriculum problems have acquired greatly heightened importance.

Criticisms have always been made of the secondary-school curriculum; but, particularly since about 1950, there has been an increased amount of criticism coming with increased vigor from a wider variety of sources. This criticism has stirred boards of education, superintendents, principals, and teachers to examine the curriculum carefully with a view to its appropriateness for a variety of students.

Immediately after the orbiting of Sputnik I and Sputnik II in October 1957, there was a hysterical demand that much more attention be given to education in the fields of science and that many more youngsters should study science of a type that would enable the United States to "catch up" with Russia in the field of space travel and space missiles. Understanding educators such as James Killian (president of the Massachusetts Institute of Technology and at that time President Eisenhower's principal advisor on science education), Nathan Pusey (president of Harvard), and James B. Conant (former president of Harvard and a close student of secondary education) attempted to calm the hysteria by pointing out that in facing its problems the nation needed a balanced education, in which fields other than science were also important.

In the past few years there has been criticism that American children are not as far advanced, particularly in the fields of science and mathematics, as children of the same age in Russian schools. It has been pointed out that in the Russian schools those who are selected to go ahead with secondary education pursue studies in science and mathematics that are ordinarily not taught in the American school system until the junior or lower college years. Although it has been repeatedly pointed out that in the United States children start school at an earlier age and that a much larger proportion go on through junior or lower college mathematics and science (though at a later age), the criticism still is heard that Russian children are prepared at an earlier age for vocational pursuits which call for knowledge of science and mathematics. The fact that the Russians have changed the curriculum in their secondary schools in recent years to include much more education for manual work has not diminished greatly the attempts to draw unfavorable comparisons between American schools and Russian schools.

THE GREAT CHALLENGE TO SECONDARY EDUCATION. Developments in the field of international relations constitute a very serious challenge to American public education in general, particularly secondary education. The division of the world into two hostile camps, the Communist and the anti-Communist, means that Americans must be prepared to follow leaders who use their understanding of the situation in proposing sound measures for the preservation of democracy and capitalism without war, which is generally recognized today as being at most a very serious threat to life on this planet and at least a threat to many millions of American lives. As Sir Charles Snow, eminent scientist and novelist, put it:

> We know, with the certainty of statistical truth, that if enough of these [nuclear] weapons are made by enough different states, some of them are going to blow up, through accident, folly, or madness, but the motives don't matter.
>
> If the world fails to reach an accord on banning nuclear weapons, the arms race not only will continue, but will accelerate and spread to many other nations. We have perhaps six years to reach agreement.
>
> On the one side we have a finite risk. On the other we have a certainty of disaster. Between a risk and a certainty, a sane man does not hesitate.[1]

The growing international significance of Asiatic nations (particularly China, Japan, India, Indonesia, and others of Southeast Asia) calls for a much greater knowledge of the Asian peoples and conditions than Americans now have; furthermore, the developments among the many nations in Africa which have become independent require that Americans learn more about the peoples of that part of the world.

At home our economic situation is threatened by serious inflation, which may become uncontrollable and result in general financial collapse and chaos. There is also a great threat involved in the great and increasing amount of unemployment. These conditions and dangers necessitate education of the great majority of voters, as well as of their leaders, relative to the basic principles of national economics and politics, if our democratic form of government is to survive the totalitarian promises of economic security.

The formulation of the senior high school curriculum is further complicated by the greatly increased percentage of boys and girls in high school who have definitely less academic ability and undoubtedly fewer academic interests.

[1]*Phi Delta Kappan* (February, 1961) p. 61.

Other Changes in American Life. Among the changes in American life which are most significant for education are the following. The implications of these changes should occur rather readily to the reader.

1. The advance of technology, by which machine processes replace human mechanical skill and strength and by which the potential rate of production of goods and gadgets is enormously increased.
2. The exploitation of physical and psychological science for propaganda purposes, which makes individualism in many respects very difficult to achieve or maintain and which tends to standardize men's beliefs and practices at a low level.
3. The control of many so-called private enterprises by local, state, and national governments because they "affect the public interest."
4. The disintegration of the family as a work unit, a social unit, and a religious unit.
5. The decline in the influence of religion as expressed in the forms and teachings of the Bible and the Church.
6. The greatly increased reliance upon commercialized and sedentary amusements and recreations, with increased emphasis upon sex, violence, and materialism.
7. The development of economic devices which spend the income of the worker before he earns or receives it and financial devices by which he borrows money at usurious rates, both types of devices materially reducing his purchasing power.
8. The development of radio and television and the consequently increased reliance upon the spoken word and decreased reliance upon the printed word, resulting in less reading on the part of the public.
9. The increased inability of the states acting separately to solve many financial problems and problems of regulation in such areas as interstate commerce and communications.
10. The gigantic developments in the field of electronics and its applications.
11. Great breakthroughs in the fields of propulsion and space travel, with most significant opportunities for developments in the fields of military missiles, space exploration, and scientific research in such areas as meteorology and astronomy.
12. The development of the automobile, which provides: (1) a means of quick escape for criminals from the scene of the crime; (2) a temptation to sacrifice resources which might be better spent for health, food, insurance, shelter, and home furnishings; (3) more time on the road and less with books; and (4) a convenient, private sitting room for questionable and immoral practices.
13. The increased membership and importance of labor unions, with the consequent necessity of training future members and employers with respect to purposes, responsibility, and understanding of economics.
14. Increased effectiveness of commercial propaganda in misleading the consumer.
15. The increasing difficulty of providing employment for all who desire it, there having been in recent years from three to five million people unemployed.

It should be obvious that these trends and changes call for increased emphasis upon certain educational objectives and certain educational experiences; they also make necessary instructional materials that will help the learner adjust to a changing world. Especially emphasized by national leaders in 1961 and 1962 was the need for a required year of instruction in economics in the senior high school.

These trends and changes tend to fall into a few broad categories, including the following:

1. Those which call for additional attention to certain kinds of instruction in the curriculum, e.g., the increased importance of relationships with other nations, the decreased opportunity of youth for work experience.
2. Those which suggest less attention for certain kinds of instruction in the curriculum, e.g., the lessened variety of skills and knowledge required by the typical vocation of today.
3. Those which call for a change in the nature of the instruction required, e.g., lessened production of foods and clothing in the home and greater dependence upon purchasing.

The need for changes in the content of courses of study taught in American secondary schools has been most prominent in the fields of science, mathematics, and the social studies. Throughout the United States today, specialists in these fields and others concerned with the curriculum are giving serious thought and spending considerable amounts of time in attempting to come up with practical and sound suggestions for new courses of study in these fields.

Those who have responsibility for leadership of teachers in improving courses of study should acquaint themselves with what is going on throughout the nation with respect to course-of-study improvement; they should organize and stimulate various groups of teachers to study carefully not only the general needs of the times but also the specific course-of-study changes that have been developed in other schools and by state and national committees.

CURRICULUM TERMINOLOGY. Before taking up the discussion of curriculum organization, it will be useful to assign definite meanings to certain terms to be employed. Confusion has resulted in discussions of curriculum because of the looseness with which the terms have been used.

Program of Studies. The list by years of all high-school courses of instruction (for example, physics and algebra) offered for study in a given school, without reference to grouping into curricula.

Curriculum. A systematic arrangement of a number of courses into a unit group for a particular group of pupils—for example, the college-preparatory or the stenographic curriculum; a term also used by many to include all the provisions for learning activities—guidance, student activities, courses of instruction.

Course of Study. The arrangement of the detailed materials of instruction within a given unit of a subject—for example, the course of study in first-semester or in first-year algebra.

Schedule of Classes. A time schedule of all sections of pupils organized as units of instruction, showing the days, hours, and places of meeting and usually the names of the instructors.

Constant or Required. A course which is required of all pupils no matter what curriculum is selected.

Variable or Curriculum Prescription. A course which is not required of all pupils in the school, but required of all pupils in a given curriculum—for example, algebra in the college-preparatory curriculum.

Limited Elective. Any one of two or more subjects, not all of which are required of all pupils of the school or of a given curriculum, but one of which must be elected by the pupil.

Free Elective. A subject not required of a pupil in the curriculum which he is following.

School Subject. Any one of the organized bodies of subject matter for instruction—for example, history, typewriting.

Class Period. The time spent in one meeting of a class section for instruction—for example, a 45-minute period.

Subject Class or Section. A group of pupils meeting regularly as a unit for instruction.

School Class or Grade. The pupils of a given stage of advancement toward graduation—for example, the senior class, the 10A class, or the low-ninth group.

Mark (not grade). The teacher's estimate of the progress or quality of the work of the pupil.

Year Unit of Credit. The credit allowed toward graduation for the successful completion of the course of study for a subject in which the section meets throughout the school year five periods a week from 40 to 60 minutes, with outside preparation.

Integrated Curriculum. A curriculum in which several fields—for example, English, history, art, science, and mathematics—are organized around topics, areas, or problems which involve all the subjects.

Core Curriculum. That part of the required curriculum consisting of integrated or closely correlated materials, from two or more subject fields, which are organized around life problems.

Broad-Fields Curriculum. A curriculum in which various relatively homogeneous subject are fused—for example, the social studies.

Unified Studies. The fused combination of materials from two subjects—for example, world history and tenth-grade English; variation of the core curriculum.

When these terms are used as above, confusion in thinking and speaking of curriculum and course-of-study problems will be avoided.

As an introduction to the discussion of the administrative aspects of curriculum organization, the following brief summary of the place of subject matter in learning and teaching is offered.

INSTRUCTIONAL MATERIALS OR ACTIVITIES IN THE SCHEME OF EDUCATION. Anything that will cause an individual to act, think, or feel in any way likely to stimulate or control future thought or action in a desirable way should be considered as possible material for education. Included are not books but also pictures, objects, the words of teachers and classmates, magazines, laboratory materials and exercises, animals, machines, newspapers, things seen, felt, smelled, or heard on field trips, journeys, or excursions, and many other types of stimuli.

The school does not exist for the purpose of teaching certain organized fields of knowledge, such as algebra, history, or biology. Subjects belong in the school curriculum only by virtue of their usefulness in contributing to desired changes in present and future behavior of the learner. It happens that the organized bodies of knowledge have been employed as school subjects and that they have rendered service as such.

General and Specialized Education. One of the basic curriculum problems is that of deciding what should constitute general education (the education which all young people should receive) and what should constitute specialized education (education along the lines of the special talents, interests, and probable specific future needs of boys and girls). This problem will be discussed later in this chapter and in the following chapter. It will suffice to say at this point that general education should encompass acquisition of knowledge and intellectual, social, and physical skills, habits, ideals, and interests which will enable young people to participate more effectively in those areas of life in which they are all practically certain to participate: namely, in their life as citizens, in their life in the home, in their leisure activities, and in their maintenance of mental, emotional, and physical health.

Specialized education is acquisition of knowledge and intellectual, social, and physical skills, habits, ideals, and interests which will enable the products of secondary school to develop specialized talents, to develop specialized leisure interests and activities (for example, in the fields of music and art), and to participate in a successful vocational life. Specialized education should also include preparation for homemaking and child-rearing activities.

Four Aspects of Curriculum Construction and Organization. There are four rather distinct areas of the task of selecting and arranging materials of instruction: (1) the determining of what subject to offer; (2) the arrangement of subjects within curricula; (3) the determining of which subjects shall be required for graduation and high-school diploma; and (4) the selection and arrangement of materials within the course of study of a subject.

2. *The Principal's Curriculum Responsibilities*

Determining Offerings. In all but the very small schools where the superintendent serves as the high-school principal, the principal is the leader in determining what subjects shall be offered in his school, their grade placement, and what subjects shall be required for graduation. He must, however, submit to the superintendent, for approval by the board of education, his recommendations with respect to these matters. He naturally discusses in advance with the superintendent of schools his proposed recommendations. Of course, even before that, he discusses these matters with the heads of various departments in his school, if there are such heads, and with the teaching staff or their representatives.

Many principals also get sample reactions from students, both former and present, concerning the offerings, their grade placement, and the requirements for graduation. Student opinions are, of course, merely advisory in nature and students should not be encouraged to believe that their opinions will necessarily be adopted. Likewise, many principals discuss the present offerings and graduation requirements with community representatives, particularly at meetings of the P.T.A.

In schools with assistant principals, these matters are discussed with them and considerable weight is attached to their opinions. In those schools in which there are directors of curriculum or directors of instruction, much of the responsibility for leadership in these matters is left to them; their recommendations are submitted to the principal for his approval or modification and transmitted to the superintendent and the board of education.

CURRICULUM ORGANIZATION. The principal also must exercise leadership in the setting up of curriculum organization. This is particularly true in those schools in which two or more curricula are offered: for example, an agricultural curriculum, a college-preparatory curriculum, and a secretarial curriculum. Relying greatly for advice upon those especially interested and especially qualified (for example, teachers of business subjects in connection with the secretarial curriculum), the principal, with the assistant principal, the director of curriculum, or both (if there are such individuals in his school) makes recommendations to the superintendent of schools, who in turn transmits them to the board of education.

CURRICULUM CONTENT. The principal must also exercise definite leadership with instructors and others in determining what in general shall be the content of each subject taught. The areas, principles, and practices of the principal's leadership (as well as that of any assistant principal or director of curriculum) with respect to determining the content of subjects offered will be discussed in the next chapter, as will the place of the principal as a leader in the textbook selection.

In connection with the principal's activities and responsibilities in matters of curriculum, there should be worked out with the superintendent of schools and all others involved an understanding of the representative responsibilities and relationships of the principal, assistant principal, director of curriculum within the school, curriculum specialists for the school system as a whole (who act as advisory leaders and principal's staff), heads of departments, and teachers. The problem of co-operation between the principal and the specialists in curriculum from the central administrative and advisory authorities is one of unusual importance, especially in those cities where the position of curriculum specialist in the central office has been recently created.

3. The Program of Offerings

In determining what the offering of a given school should be, several considerations must be carefully examined in their relation to local curriculum problems. Among these considerations are the following, each of which will be briefly considered in turn:

1. The relation of the program of studies to the aims of secondary education.
2. The peculiar needs and interests of the students and of the local community.
3. The requirements for entrance to institutions of higher education to which graduates of the local high school go.
4. The limitations imposed by superior authority—by state laws and by state departments of public instruction.
5. The relation of the program of studies to the size of the school and the cost of instruction.
6. The available housing and equipment.
7. The pressure of special groups of citizens and lay groups.
8. The professional ambitions of the local teaching staff.
9. The practices and trends of practice in other schools.

RELATION TO OBJECTIVES OF SECONDARY EDUCATION. Every program of studies should provide opportunities for a definite and large contribution in the direction of each major objective of secondary education: health, vocational efficiency, good citizenship, worthy home membership, and wholesome enjoyment of leisure. Opportunity for exploration of interests and aptitudes should be provided. Briefly, this means that instruction should be offered in at least the following: written and oral English, literature, American history, American government and citizenship, world history, physical education, general science, biology, physics, chemistry, art, music, household arts, elementary mathematics (beyond arithmetic), a foreign language, and industrial and commercial subjects as warranted by the size of the school.

The curriculum of every school should contribute to the well-being of the nation and of the whole society in which the school exists, as well as to the individual interests of those who compose that society. In general, the interests of society and of individuals are to a great extent the same, but there are important types of educational objectives which are social rather than individual in their nature.

THE NEEDS OF THE LOCAL STUDENTS AND COMMUNITY. The program of studies is likely to vary somewhat with the student constituencies of different schools and with the nature of the communities in which the schools exist. While it is easy to overestimate the extent to which communities of the same size differ in such a manner and degree as to call for different programs of studies, one must not neglect that factor entirely. Courses in agriculture meet the needs of pupils in rural high schools and stimulate interest in scientific farming even among the adults of the community. In districts in which a large part of the population is made up of workers in factories, mills, or shops, commercial and industrial courses should be offered, even in the smaller schools, to meet the needs of the many boys and girls not going to college. In such communities there is less need for foreign languages and higher mathematics and greater need for courses in homemaking and shop work.

In some communities the student body is made up very largely of youngsters of superior academic and intellectual ability of youngsters of whom an unusually large percentage will go on to college. This is true of many suburban communities which are populated largely by families of professional men and businessmen. Similarly, there are communities in which the very large proportion of the youngsters are of less than average academic and intellectual ability and interests; a definitely smaller percentage of these youngsters will go on to college. Naturally, not only the offerings but also the graduation requirements and curriculum organization will be adapted to the special nature of the student body in these communities; the content of the subjects should also be appropriate for the youngsters of the prevailing interests and academic intellectual ability.

College Entrance Requirements. It is desirable to offer in every senior high school or traditional four-year high school such studies as will enable pupils to select their subjects of study with a view to entering any one of the institutions of higher education to which a considerable percentage of the high-school graduates are likely to go. A study should be made that will show which institutions these are and statements of entrance requirements should be obtained from them and examined carefully. The requirements of some colleges are so detailed that the smaller schools can offer all the subjects required only by providing instruction for very small sections. For small schools to attempt to cater to the peculiarities of these institutions at a great increase in the cost of instruction per capita is of course not reasonable or sound policy.

The Limitations Imposed by and the Influence of Superior Authority. Unless he is already familiar with them, the principal or superintendent responsible for the program of studies should acquaint himself with the types of information indicated by the following questions:

1. What subjects of instruction are required by state law to be offered by all public high schools of the class in which the school concerned falls?
2. What subjects are required by the state department of education to be offered (1) as a condition to accrediting the school and (2) for desired state aid?
3. What limitations, if any, are imposed by state law or by the state department of public instruction upon the range, or variety, of subjects which may be offered?
4. What limitations, if any, are imposed or what subjects are required by the regional accrediting association?

Ordinarily such information may be readily obtained. In every state, law affecting public schools are collected and published, usually by the state department of public instruction. In most states, the state commissioner or superintendent of public instruction issues some sort of curriculum guide, in which are stated the requirements of the state department for approval or for financial aid. These publications are obtainable upon request. In many states, suggested programs of studies are given in such publications. As a means of facilitating administrative convenience and preventing confusion and waste to pupils transferring from one high school to another in a state, it is wise for smaller schools to follow the programs and curricula suggested in the state courses of study, except in those instances where it is clearly desirable to depart from such suggestions. It should be one of the first acts of a newly elected principal or superintendent, unless he is fully familiar with these things, to write to the state office requesting whatever information of this nature may be available in printed or mimeographed form and to study this material carefully in its relation to the local school and curriculum problems.

RELATION TO SIZE OF SCHOOL AND COST OF INSTRUCTION. Two important items of the cost of high-school facilities, amounting to approximately 90 per cent of the total cost, are teachers' salaries and housing. The number of teachers and the number of rooms required are in direct proportion to the number of sections organized for instruction. A small section contributes approximately as much to costs as a section containing several times as many pupils. In small schools teachers' salaries are low, teaching loads are heavy, and the cost of instruction per pupil is high, partly because of the large number of small, uneconomical sections existing in small schools.

It should be recognized that the small high school is a compromise between effective organization and conditions which make larger schools impossible and that small schools should not attempt to duplicate the varied program of larger schools. In schools of less than 100 or 125 students, for example, no more than two years of one foreign language should be offered; in typical schools of less than 75 students, no foreign language should be offered. In small schools, courses in physics, in chemistry, and in mathematics beyond plane geometry should be offered only in alternate years. Sections in which no more than 5 or 6 pupils enroll should ordinarily be canceled.

A student who very much needs subjects that are not offered is usually able to obtain them by correspondence from one or more of the colleges in the state in which his school is located.

THE LIMITATIONS IMPOSED BY LOCAL LAY OPINION. When changes are to be introduced in the program of studies, the probable reaction of the patrons of the school should be forecast as accurately as possible.

Those changes which are not likely to be well understood or which are likely to evoke widespread or spirited protest should be introduced carefully and only after some progress has been made in bringing about an appreciation of the proposed changes. The principal must work with his community, not against it. Nothing in this caution, however, should warrant the *laissez-faire,* or "let well enough alone," policy which characterizes the timid or unprogressive administration.

While the high-school administrator should be careful not to antagonize patrons unduly, he should resist the efforts of groups representing special interests to introduce into the local school studies for which there is not a real need.

In recent years an increasing number of secondary schools have made formal investigations of the opinions of former students relative to the value and quality of the courses they took. In Chapter 24 of this volume there is described a form for obtaining opinions of former students.

Nothing in the foregoing paragraphs should be interpreted to indicate a lack of belief in the value of the utilization of lay advisory committees or other participation by men and women in the community in planning improvement of the school program.

THE LOCAL TEACHING STAFF. The administrator must be on his guard to handle diplomatically but firmly the natural, but sometimes unwise, ambitions of department heads and teachers to expand their departments. Naturally, but sometimes unfortunately, the most capable teacher or department head is also most persuasive, insistent, and devoted to the development of his department to what seem to him adequate dimensions. Keen interest on the part of teachers and department heads is commendable, but the program-maker must not lose sight of the needs of the school as a whole.

NEW SUBJECTS. Among the offerings added to the curriculum in many schools in recent years to which careful consideration should be given are the following:

1. General mathematics: a second year course in this field.
2. Home living: comprehensive course for seniors involving some of the following areas—attractive homes and home life, consumer education, marriage relations, child rearing.
3. Core and other fused large block programs.
4. Work-experience programs: *(a)* diversified-occupations, distributive-education, and other work-for-pay plans; *(b)* civic service, school service, and no-pay plan.
5. General arts and crafts, including a variety of industrial and ceramic arts, photography, painting, etc.
6. Social geography; the study in upper high-school years of the peoples of other nations.

7. A twelfth-grade course in "occupations."
8. Advanced placement courses for bright seniors.
9. Russian.
10. Spanish.
11. Economics.

In some of the larger high schools there have been added special types of intensive vocational courses, such as: (1) restaurant training, grades 11 and 12, one unit each semester; (2) training in dressmaking, one year, grade 11 or grade 12; (3) cosmetology, two years, grade 11 and grade 12; (4) business machines, one semester, grade 12. These courses usually offer two units each semester and the classes usually meet for a period of three hours either in the morning or in the afternoon. In a few schools similar courses are being offered to seniors in mechanics of electronics, either on a similar basis or on the basis of two units for two semesters.

DRIVER EDUCATION. In an increasing majority of secondary schools, a course in driver education is offered; in 1958-1959, 72 per cent of the districts of more than 2500 population offered such a course. The question of including driver education in secondary schools has been a matter of some controversy in recent years, but a great majority of the officials and organizations interested in safety in automobile driving have strongly advocated that a course be offered in the high schools whenever possible. In order to have a course in driver education, a school must have several cars available. In many districts the local automobile dealers have been willing to lend cars or to rent them at very low rates. There must also be available someone to give the course who is fully qualified not only in driving but in teaching driver education. In some schools the school bus drivers have been employed as assistants in driver education.

In most secondary schools, courses in driver education are given for credit, although no credit is given in some. Usually, the amount of credit given is one unit. Not less than ten hours of actual experience in cars is recommended by authorities in the driver-education field. In a few schools the course in driver education is offered in the summer. It is usually offered only to students who are old enough to receive a driver's license.

Policies and Practices for Safety Education, published by the National Commission on Safety Education, is a report of the Third National Conference on Driver Education, which was held at Purdue University to review current practices and problems in driver education and to recommend action needed to strengthen present programs and to guide new efforts. This report presents in detail the thinking of the Conference on planning and evaluating instruction, preparing teachers, and administering programs; on the role of state education departments; and on research needed for the sound growth of driver education. Copies of this report may be secured from the National Education Association, 1201 Sixteenth Street, N.W., Washington 6, D.C., at $1 per copy.

WORK-EXPERIENCE PROGRAMS. Each year more and more school systems establish and offer one or more types of work-experience programs. They are of four different types:

1. *The Diversified-Occupations Type.* Under the supervision of a school coordinator and under contract with employers, high-school students spend fifteen to twenty hours a week, with pay and with credit toward graduation, in some sort of occupation. In view of the facts that (1) training in any one of a large variety of occupations may be thus obtained and (2) high schools can offer training for only a few of the hundreds of occupations in most communities, the plan is an excellent opportunity for vocational education, to say nothing of its contributions to developing maturity, responsibility, character, understanding of adults and adult ways of thinking and behaving, and the opportunity for earning money. Altogether, the plan produces a most desirable situation for boys and girls, especially those of the lower economic levels.

In secondary schools of the United States more than two hundred different occupations are represented in programs of the diversified-occupations type, including the following: retail selling, auto mechanics, radio repairing, electrical work, printing, general office work, secretarial work, stenographic work, bookkeeping, grocery work, practical nursing, beauty culture, machining, service-station operation, undertaking and embalming, work with textiles, dentistry, meat-cutting, automobile-body repairing, pharmacy, department-store work, banking, carpentry, dry cleaning, theater work, dry-goods dealing, cabinetmaking, motion-picture projection, library work, plumbing, mechanical welding, window decorating, hardware work, stock work, general newspaper work, wholesale dealing, shoe repair, men's clothing sales, variety-store operation, baking, drafting, photography, refrigerator dealing, news reporting, shipping clerking, auto-accessories dealing, sheet-metal work, show-card making, florist work, telephone operating, restaurant work, radio broadcasting, radio-station technician, architectural drafting, ladies' ready-to-wear sales, and insurance sales.

Grouped into broad classifications, these occupations fall largely into the following types:

a. Retail selling.
b. Mechanical, building, and electrical trades.
c. Industrial work.
d. Assisting in personal service—nursing, beauty culture, etc.
e. Work in wholesale businesses.
f. Bookkeeping, typing, secretarial work in stores, banks, etc.
g. Assisting professional men—doctors, dentists, etc.
h. Printing and newspaper work.

2. *The Distributive-Occupations Type.* This type is very similar to the diversified-occupations type—both are Federally and state subsidized—except that in this plan the fields of training are limited to the selling occupations.

3. *Civic Work Experience.* This is carried out in the community, in connection with drives, campaigns, community surveys, community beautification and improvement, hospitals, and so on. It is almost always without pay or credit, except as it may be part of the work of a course for which credit is given.

4. *School Work Experience.* Under plans of this type students volunteer service for the benefit of the school: assisting in drives, campaigns, and school beautification; helping in the library, in duplicating and other clerical work, or in the cafeteria; assisting teachers with papers and in laboratories and shops. This type

of plan is spreading, though slowly, in secondary schools in the United States. Students are often paid at least token wages and usually more for work requiring considerable time, such as clerical work or work in the library or cafeteria.[2]

Establishment of work-study programs has contributed greatly to increasing the percentage of students staying in the Wilmington, Delaware, High School from 50 per cent to 80 per cent.[3]

The establishment and successful operation of diversified-occupation or distributive-occupation programs involve problems of organization, administration, and supervision. These problems center around the following:

1. Creation and utilization of the services of a representative advisory committee.
2. Determination of training opportunities in the community and selection of trades or occupations which should be included in the program.
3. Determination and selection of industrial and business establishments in which to place students for training.
4. Selection of qualified students for enrollment in the program.
5. Development, from trade or occupational analysis, of schedules of processes to be learned on the job by the student.
6. Preparation of outlines of related and technical subjects, correlated with work experience.
7. Placement of students for work experience in accordance with Federal, state, and local employment regulations.
8. Issuance of needed employment certificates.
9. Preparation of reasonably rigid schedules for school classes.
10. Records of attendance at school and work.
11. Consent of parents and reports on pupil progress.
12. School credit for work.
13. Issuance of certificates of credit.

It is rather generally recommended that the amount of school credit for supervised work experience should be approximately one year unit for four hundred clock hours of work.

FEDERALLY SUBSIDIZED VOCATIONAL EDUCATION. Many administrators are able to improve their curriculum in the field of vocational education by applying and qualifying for Federal subsidies through the state department of education or state department of vocational education. The funds provided by the Federal government are administered through the state according to a five-year program which has been submitted to the state by the Federal government and approved by the state. In each state the state department of education publishes bulletins in which is described its plans for vocational education and for guidance, counseling, and testing.

---

[2]See Wilson Ivins and William B. Runge, *Work Experience in the Schools;* or Ivins, "Work Experience in the Life Adjustment Program," Chapter 15 in *Education for Life Adjustment.*

[3]Letter from C. A. Fulmer, Principal.

Each plan includes minimum requirements for buildings, rooms, and equipment for each subject approved, minimum curriculum offerings for each of the subjects, and minimum requirements for teachers of each of the subjects. The principal, superintendent, or both should, if possible, have a personal conference with the state representatives and discuss with them how to prepare a proposal for state approval and Federal aid.

The fields in which Federal aid may be obtained are vocational agriculture, home economics, distributive education, trades and industries, and diversified occupations. The vocational-agriculture course must include provision for some type of home farming project by each student, his father, and the teacher of vocational agriculture. While vocational home-economics courses were originally expected to prepare students to make their living in some aspect of home economics, the courses may now have the objective of making girls competent and happy wives, mothers, and homemakers. The major emphasis is on courses in clothing, food preparation, child care, and home management. Courses in trades and industries include vocational preparation for a wide variety of crafts and occupations, including auto mechanics, carpentry, electronics, welding, and machine work.

Distributive education involves preparation for retail selling and merchandising. Diversified occupations is a type of experience which includes work experience on the job, as described earlier in this chapter.

Such courses in vocational education should be placed in the last two years of the high-school curriculum. Students at schools providing earlier vocational education who withdraw from school before reaching the eleventh grade find it exceedingly difficult today to obtain positions for which the vocational curriculum has prepared them. In an increasing number of districts, students postpone taking vocational courses until the junior-college years, devoting the high-school years completely to nonprofessional courses.

4. Principles of Curriculum Organization

FUNDAMENTAL PRINCIPLES OF CURRICULUM ORGANIZATION. There are certain principles which appear to underlie the organization of high-school curricula and with which the principal or the superintendent should be familiar. These principles will be considered here.

1. *Each curriculum should provide abundantly for learning activities calculated to contribute to each of the general ultimate aims of secondary education—mental and physical health, citizenship, vocation, leisure life, and home life.* This should be true even of the college-preparatory curriculum, since there is no assurance that all those who elect that curriculum will go to college or that those who do go will pursue studies which will round out the accomplishment of the several aims. Every curriculum should provide instruction contributory to the development of

information, habits, and ideals which make for health; to the development of information, habits, skills, attitudes, and tastes which make for social co-operation and good will in politics, business, and social life; to the development of information, abilities, and attitudes which make for a fortunate vocational choice and for vocational success; to the development of satisfying and wholesome avocational interests, ideals, and tastes; and to the development of information, habits, ideals, and tastes which make for effective participation in home-life activities.

2. *Each curriculum should provide opportunities for exploration, through material also worth while for other purposes, of the possible interests and capacities of each pupil.* For all but those of least ability and promise for completing high school, a curriculum should provide some instruction in and introduction to the major fields of learning, even to the fields of foreign languages and mathematics beyond arithmetic. It should also provide for the termination of any study after the first year, in any field not necessary for other purposes, by any student whose interests and abilities do not seem to warrant continued pursuance of that study; such a provision would apply, for example, to mathematics, foreign language, any vocational field, music, and art.

3. *Each curriculum should make a definite contribution to the integrative function of secondary education.* Required study of certain subjects, such as American history, literature, and civics, will operate to give the next generation a feeling of unity and cultural kinship, a realization of common ideals and interests, and an understanding of the American way of life—bonds that will develop a group consciousness in the generation and render it a sufficiently homogeneous and like-minded group to guarantee social solidarity.

4. *Each curriculum should be so organized that the portion completed by any student withdrawing from school will not be dependent in any large way for realization of its values upon the study of that portion of the curriculum to which he is not likely to be exposed.* In the accomplishment of this objective it seems desirable in the larger schools, in which provision will be made for the proper differentiation of students, to provide special curricula for students who in all probability, as judged by age, economic status of family, previous school marks and record, and intelligence, will not remain to graduate. Among the courses in such curricula should be those in general shop, general business, remedial reading and language, homemaking, and consumer education. On the other hand, nothing in the application of this principle is intended to discourage the requiring of students to pursue at least one or two fields of learning for two or three years in sequence. There is often considerable value in studying for a second year a subject for which the background has been laid by study in the previous year. This is to say nothing of the impossibility of mastering some subjects in less than three or more years, as in the case of a foreign language.

5. *The placement of courses in curricula should also be guided by the maturity of the pupils.* This principle must be taken into consideration along with the one just preceding. Though the preceding principle is highly important, it should, of course, not be carried to such extreme application as the introduction of courses before the maturity of the pupils will permit of any reasonable understanding. To be practical, subject matter must be so adapted to the age, interests, vocabulary, background, and ability of the students for whom it is intended that it will actually stimulate the anticipated reaction. Pupil experiences resulting from contact with subject matter vary with two important factors: the nature of the subject matter and the nature of the individual. The same subject matter will not only produce different reactions in different pupils but also will product different reactions in the same pupil at different ages.

6. *Courses should be assigned year placement in the curricula in relation to the needs which they are intended to serve.* Courses which are especially calculated to serve needs that will not be experienced for some years to come should not be placed early in high-school curricula.

Distinctly college-preparatory courses will serve their purposes if they are placed in the last two or three years of high school. Foreign languages and mathematics, taken only to meet college-entrance requirements, are not only certain to be less well learned in the ninth or tenth grade than in the eleventh or twelfth grade but also will be forgotten in large part before the pupil has need for the outcomes of such instruction. By postponing instruction in these subjects it will be possible to offer more extensive courses; the work completed will be almost certainly of a higher order and will be retained to a greater degree until the time of need; and the enrollment in such courses will inevitably be more completely restricted to those going on to college.

Certain other advantages of this plan may be noted here. Pupils preparing for college could carry English, science, history, and social studies through grade 10. Also, a smaller percentage of pupils would be retarded or eliminated in grades 9 and 10, the years in which the percentage of failures in mathematics and foreign languages is highest in most schools.

7. *Constants should be confined to and should include all subjects for which a certain and important need may be predicted for all pupils or which may be very desirable training for all citizens.* The subjects which are recognized as falling in this category are English speech, composition, and literature through the eleventh or the twelfth grade; American history; and elementary social science, such as community civics and geography. Other subjects which should be seriously considered for classification as constants are two more years of science, at least one year of mathematics, and one year of study of home-living problems beyond the eighth grade.

8. *The ratio of constants to variables or electives should decrease slowly from the seventh grade through the twelfth.* Beginning in the seventh grade with the introduction of limited electives, the number of

subjects required for graduation should decrease gradually to not more than one half of the subjects in the eleventh and twelfth grades.

9. *Requirements in each curriculum should be sufficiently flexible to provide for differences in interests between pupils, permitting them to carry forward some fields not necessarily germane to the chief special objective of the particular curriculum.* No curriculum should demand the entire time of pupils for the study of constants and curriculum prescriptions. For example, sufficient electives should be provided in a vocational course to permit students to continue the exploration or study of a field of special interest, such as foreign languages, music, art, mathematics, or social science. In other words, with the possible exception of the seventh and eighth grades, in every year of every curriculum there should be some provision for free electives, for perhaps not less than six or eight hours a week.

10. *The curricula of the various units of secondary education should be articulated with each other and with that of the elementary school.* Care should be taken that overlapping and duplication are reduced to a minimum, an amount which is held to be desirable for necessary review, emphasis, or a different approach or point of view. This phase of the principle should be applied particularly to courses in American history in the junior and senior high schools, to general science and later science courses, and to literature in grades 7 and 8 and in grades 9 through 12 inclusive.

THE APPLICATION OF UNDERLYING PRINCIPLES. No single set program of studies or curriculum organization can be safely set up for all schools of any given class or size. Variations in minor details at least, if not great differences, should be expected from school to school. Yet, if based on adequate understanding and application of fundamental principles, curricular organizations for schools of similar size and conditions will be very similar.

A large part of curriculum maladjustment in schools may be traced to violations of one or more of these principles. The principal who undertakes the task of curriculum organization with little or no regard to such fundamental considerations is more confident than wise. More likely than not his work will appear very simple and will consist largely of pencil-and-paper shuffling of subjects with a view to producing a combination that will be expedient and that will represent prevailing practice. If he is not familiar with such principles and the underlying considerations, he will not realize how futile and amateurish his efforts have been.

In general, courses should be allocated to a certain grade in the curriculum, such as the eighth grade, tenth grade, or twelfth grade. Students in each grade should, in general, be permitted to take only the courses offered for their grade. Nevertheless, there is much to be said for the practice which exists in many schools of permitting brighter students to take courses scheduled for grades above those in which they are placed and slower students to take courses scheduled for grades lower than those in which they are placed.

5. Types of Curriculum Organization

STEM ELECTIVES AND MULTIPLE CURRICULA. The two principal types of curriculum organization are the "stem elective" and the "multiple" types. The former plan provides for a core of constants to be supplemented to the extent of a full program with electives chosen by the student under the supervision of his adviser; the latter plan involves more than one curriculum, each possessing its own core of constants and curriculum prescriptions and, in addition, possible electives. In the multiple-curricula plan the core of constants includes the constants for all curricula (for example, English and physical education) and, in addition, subjects required in a particular curriculum.

There has been a growing belief that the elective system has not worked out too well and that many students have employed it to avoid training in fields in which all high-school students should have training. There has been an increasing tendency to step up the number of required units in social studies and in science and to encourage strongly, if not actually to require, two years of either general (or basic) mathematics or a pre-engineering type of mathematics. For one reason or another, some students have been carrying more units than are required. In fact, in a large and increasing number of schools approximately half of the students are carrying what are thought of as five solid subjects, plus one or more classes which require little or no preparation and meet only two or three times a week. In many of these schools, classes conventionally meeting five times a week meet only four times a week, thus reducing the recitation load and scheduling problems of the student and the teaching load of the teacher.

PLANS FOR DIFFERENTIATING MULTIPLE CURRICULA. Three plans for differentiating the curricula which make up a multiple-curricular organization have been commonly employed. These may be designated as the "subject-matter" or "major" plan, the "occupational" or "objective" plan, and the combination plan, which is a mixture of the other two plans.

The first plan may be illustrated by the following curricula in the course of study for a certain city high school: English, mathematics, science, foreign-language, household-arts, and industrial-arts curricula. The second plan is followed in a city high school of approximately 1200 pupils in the Middle West which offers college-preparatory, general, household-arts, business, stenographic, accounting, plumbing, and industrial-arts curricula. Illustrative of the combination plan are the following curricula offered in another high school: scientific, classical, general, secretarial, commercial, industrial, fine-arts, and household-arts curricula.

The best grouping of subjects is on the basis of the future plans of the students rather than on the basis of the divisions of subject matter—that is, on the basis of objectives rather than on the basis of means. There seems to be no good reason why students of high-school age should be encouraged, much less compelled, to specialize in one of the logical divisions of learning, when they may profit more by a co-ordination of materials, from the various divisions of learning, that is directed toward future probable needs.

THE GENERAL CURRICULUM. There has been a steadily increasing tendency in the last several decades for more and more schools to include a general curriculum among its various curricula. An increasing number of students in most schools have enrolled for the general curriculum. The general curriculum is not directed toward any specific vocation, nor does it include special provision for so-called college-preparatory subjects. Its chief weakness in the past has been its small number of required courses and large number of electives, which often have not been chosen wisely from the standpoint of a good, well-rounded education. The general curriculum has for this reason been severely criticized in recent years.

THE SINGLE, OR STEM-ELECTIVE, ORGANIZATION VERSUS THE MULTIPLE-TYPE ORGANIZATION. In junior high schools the number of electives is so small and the advisability of definite vocational training is so doubtful that the single, stem-elective type of curriculum is best adapted; practice has been almost uniform in this respect, though many schools employ, as a hangover from the old 8-4 plan of organization, the multiple type for ninth-grade students.

The single, stem-elective curriculum is recommended for junior high schools and four-year high schools of less than 200 or 250 students. As a matter of fact, in a great many high schools of greater enrollment, perhaps in a majority of them, multiple curricula are advisory and suggestive only, students changing curricula from year to year and the administration of the curriculum during registration time being anything but rigid.

Problems, Questions, and Exercises

1. Examine carefully the list of definitions of curriculum terms and pick one or two which you think may be improved. Add one term and its definition.
2. Be able to discuss in class the various limitations imposed upon curriculum offerings.
3. What do you consider to be the areas for a principal's greatest possible service in curriculum development in a school of 450 students?
4. Examine carefully the principles of curriculum organization given in this chapter; mention at least one or two that you question and see if you cannot add one or two.
5. What is the case for the multiple curriculum and the case for the single general curriculum? Which would you prefer for a school of 500 students?

Alberty, Harold, Adapting the Secondary-School Program to the Needs of Youth, Fifty-second Yearbook, Part I, National Society for the Study of Education, University of Chicago Press, 1953. [Current conceptions of programs designed to meet the common needs of adolescents are discussed in Chapter 7.]

Childs, Gayle B., "Supervised Correspondence Study," *Clearing House* (September, 1951), Vol. 26, pp. 3-6. [Offers a report on the effectiveness of supervised correspondence study, as compared with regular classroom instruction, in terms of subject-matter achievement only.]

Conant, James B., "Recommendations for the Junior High School," *Education Digest* (December, 1960), Vol. 26, No. 4, pp. 5-9.

Douglass, Harl R., *Education for Life Adjustment,* New York, Ronald, 1950.

Dulstead, William M., "How Can Summer Schools Improve the Total School Program?" *Bulletin of the N.A.S.S.P.* (April, 1958), No. 237, pp. 31-36.

Eckhardt, John W., "The High School Principalship in Its Relation to Curriculum Development," *Bulletin of the N.A.S.S.P.* (April, 1948), No. 154, pp. 101-109.

Education in the U.S.S.R., Washington, D.C., Office of Education, U. S. Department of Health, Education, and Welfare, 1957.

Education Policies Commission, *Education for All American Youth, a Further Look,* 1952, pp. 373-376; "Work Experience Programs," pp. 71-79, 248-252, 276-286, 298-307, 345-347; "Terminal Education," pp. 364-366; "Leisure and Recreation," pp. 119-176, 156-160; "Elective Subjects," pp. 232-237; "Citizenship Education," pp. 77-106, 216-253; "Common Learnings," pp. 223-260, 309-313.

English Language Arts in the Comprehensive Secondary School, National N.A.S.S.P., 1960, 16 pages, Grades 7-12.

"Foreign Language Instruction in Secondary Schools", California *Schools,* Vol. 33, (February, 1962), pp. 37-47.

Hand, Harold C., and others, "What Is The Role of the Principal in Curriculum Work?" *Bulletin of the N.A.S.S.P.* (April, 1956), No. 219, pp. 381-408.

Harnly, Paul W., and Lovelass, Harry D., "How Have Summer Schools Been Used to Enrich the Educational Program for the Academically Talented?" *Bulletin of the N.A.S.S.P.* (April, 1959) No. 246, pp. 182-186.

Hartshorn, Merrill R., "Current Critical Issues in Secondary-Education – Social Studies in the Comprehensive Secondary School," *Bulletin of the N.A.S.S.P.* (April, 1961), No. 264, pp. 312-326.

Hartshorn, Merrill F., and Gillespie, T. Marcus, *A Selected Annotated Bibliography to Assist Teachers in Teaching About Communism,* National Council for the Social Studies, 1201 Sixteenth Street, N. W., Washington, D. C.

Holt, Howard B., "Curriculum Problems in a Small High School? Imagination May Be the Answer," *Bulletin of the N.A.S.S.P.* (October, 1958), No. 240, pp. 70-75.

Ivins, Wilson H., *Adapting the Secondary-School Program to the Needs of Youth,* Fifty-Second Yearbook, Part I, National Society for the Study of Education, University of Chicago Press, 1953, Chapter 10. [The relation of work and outdoor experiences to youth needs, types of work experience, types of outdoor experience, initiating student programs of work experience or outdoor activities, and operating the programs for work and outdoor experiences.]

Ivins, Wilson H., and Runge, William B., *Work Experience in the Schools,* New York, Ronald, 1951.
Jackson, Arthur, "A Crash Program for the Education of Negro Youth," *Negro Educational Review* (July, 1958), Vol. 9, pp. 111-116.
Janet, Sister Mary (S.C.), "Highlights in Secondary Education," *Proceedings and Addresses,* 49th Annual Meeting, National Catholic Educational Association, August, 1952. [A well-phrased discussion of common secondary curricular problems and other high-school problems.]
Keller, Charles R., "The Twelfth Grade Problem," *Bulletin of the N.A.S.S.P.* (April, 1961), No. 264, pp. 342-349.
Krug, Edward A., Babcock, Chester D., and Fowlkes, John Guy, *Administering Curriculum Planning,* New York, Harper, 1956. [Chapter 5, "Teachers and Students in Curriculum Planning"; Chapter 6, "Public Participation"; Chapter 7, "Curriculum Experimentation"; Chapter 8, "The Use of Consultants"; Chapter 9, "Workshop, Work Conferences, and Institutes"; Chapter 10, "Curriculum Laboratories, Libraries and Study Centers in Local School System."]
Lally, Ann M., and others, "Art Education in the Secondary School," *Bulletin of the N.A.S.S.P.* (March, 1961), No. 263, pp. 1-102.
Latimer, Charles L., Jr., "What Kind of Education for Home and Family Living Is Needed Today?" *Bulletin of the N.A.S.S.P.* (April, 1956), No. 219, pp. 58-60.
Miller, Delmar F., and others, "The Principal's Role in Improving the Curriculum," *Bulletin of the N.A.S.S.P.* (February, 1959), No. 244, pp. 1-119.
Mitchum, P. M., *The High School Principal and Staff Plan for Program Improvement,* New York, Columbia University Press, 1958.
National Commission on Safety Education, *Driver Education and Driving Simulators,* Washington, D.C., National Education Association, 1960.
Olson, A. R., "Organizing a Faculty for Curriculum Improvement," *Bulletin of N.A.S.S.P.* (February, 1960), No. 253, pp. 94-98.
Parry, O. Meredith, "Use Summer School to Broaden Your Curriculum," *High School Journal* (January, 1959), Vol. 42, pp. 116-120.
"Patterns of Curriculum Practices," *Bulletin of the N.A.S.S.P.* (February, 1960), No. 253, pp. 73-166.
Punke, H. H., "Court Rulings on the Curriculum and Teaching Program," *Bulletin of the N.A.S.S.P.* (December, 1959), No. 251, pp. 137-151.
Rinker, Floyd, Auffenberg, Walter, Jones, Galen, and Dobbin, John E., "New Developments in Secondary School Programs and Services," *Bulletin of the N.A.S.S.P.* (April, 1961), No. 264, pp. 189-195.
Rosser, Neill A., "The Junior High School Program in Raleigh," *Bulletin of the N.A.S.S.P.* (September, 1959), No. 248, pp. 157-162.
Russell, Edward J., "Curriculum Design for Junior High School," *Nation's Schools* (August, 1952), Vol. 50, No. 3, pp. 60-62. [Curriculum revision a slow and deliberate process. A joint venture between Harvard Graduate School of Education and professional personnel in Pittsfield, Massachusetts.]
Scully, Mark, "Possibilities of a Summer Reading Improvement Program for Entering Sophomore," *High School Journal* (November, 1955), Vol. 39, No. 2, pp. 118-123.
Smith, Julia W., and others, "Outdoor Education for American Youth," *Bulletin of the N.A.S.S.P.* (May, 1957), No. 229. [Thorough discussion of school camp-

ing and other outdoor education (not including athletics); their relationship to high-school subjects, teacher preparation.]
Tracy, J. P., "Issues in Catholic Secondary Education," *Catholic School Journal* (September, 1960), Vol. 60, pp. 46-47.
Tucker, Hazel, "The Fresno High School Plan," *Bulletin of the N.A.S.S.P.* (March, 1960), No. 253, pp. 58-60. [Organization on the basis of different interests, abilities, and needs of groups of students.]
Tyler, Ralph W., "Next Steps in Improving Secondary Education," *School Review* (December, 1952), Vol. 60, pp. 523-531. [The advances which have been made in secondary education; in light of these, suggests eight important steps which now need to be taken to further improve the American school.]

8

Improving Curriculum Content

1. Leaders in Improving Curriculum Content

The great majority of teachers of the various subjects in secondary schools of the United States have had no appreciable amount of training in revising or constructing courses of study or selecting textbooks. It is therefore necessary that they have opportunity in service to acquire the fundamental principles and to develop skill in these fields of activity. While some of this training may be obtained in summer schools at institutions for teacher education, for the most part it must be obtained while in service and in connection with teaching responsibilities.

CO-OPERATION WITH OTHER LEADERS. While there must be co-operation in the process of improving the curriculum and a clear-cut understanding as to the respective fields of authority of the high-school principal and other leaders of the teachers, the process of curriculum improvement will differ from school to school, especially from small school to large school. In the small school the principal will work directly with the teachers and will operate very largely as an assistant to the superintendent of schools. In very large schools there will be individuals involved in the process who occupy one or more of the following positions: director of curriculum, director of instruction, assistant superintendent, assistant principal, and head of department.

In the larger school systems the principal will not have time to give the direction and assistance to teachers that they should have; thus, he will co-operate with and support other individuals whose chief responsibility will be that of improving the curriculum and instruction. In some schools, funds will be available for the employment of consultants from outside the school, specialists in various subject fields who have kept up with current thinking and practices and have sound professional backgrounds.

CO-OPERATIVE PROCEDURE. In the better schools today, the approach to course-of-study revision and construction is a co-operative procedure.

The teachers themselves work out changes in the course of study, curriculum guidance, and resource units. Since it will not be possible, except in small schools, for all teachers to participate in the developing of curriculum guides, resource units, etc., it will be necessary that leaders with creative ability and leadership be appointed as a producing committee and that other teachers serve as reviewing committees. The smaller number responsible for creative materials should have approriate reduction of their teaching loads so that the work of revision can be carefully and effectively done.

Revision of Basic Philosophy and Objectives. At the beginning of a project aimed at improving courses of study it is good procedure to have the teachers review, and probably revise, the basic philosophy of the school, including the objectives of secondary education in general and those of the particular school in each of the subject fields. If such review has not taken place in previous years, some time will be required to think through a practical, sound philosophy and a statement of objectives.

In this connection it is useful to review the problems that the American people as a nation face in international relations and in domestic affairs and to note particularly the recent changes and trends in these fields. Emphasis should be placed upon the fact that the school is a social institution which in a democracy is at least as much responsible for the education of an intelligent, effective citizenry as it is for the education of individuals for their own benefit.

The Objectives of Secondary Education. The school and each of the subjects taught in it should be analyzed in terms of growth objectives; such analysis should determine what information, what concepts, what social, physical, and intellectual skills, what physical, social, and intellectual habits, what ideals, what attitudes, and what interests should be developed.

If possible, a committee of carefully chosen teachers should be appointed and asked to present to the staff a statement of the more important characteristics of adolescents and adolescent growth, the more important current problems and ambitions of adolescents, and the types of activities most likely to interest them.

Furthermore, some individual or committee should present to the staff a carefully developed statement of the nature and characteristics of the student body for whom the course of study is being planned. This statement would include facts concerning the mental ability or I.Q. of the students, the college plans of a number of the students, and the general, social, and economic status of the homes from which the students come.

Still another individual or committee should prepare a statement of broad general principles, such as the following, which should be used in the selection of curriculum content:

1. The learning experience should provide the opportunity for attaining the objectives of the school.
2. The learning experience should be appropriate to the interests and needs of children.
3. The learning experience should provide for continuity and sequential development.
4. The learning experience should have much relationship to life and living.
5. The learning experience should permit a considerable variety of learning activities.

In connection with these various principles, there should be available for use by individuals charged with the responsibility of curriculum revision a wealth of curriculum materials gathered from other schools' curriculum units.

CURRICULUM UNITS. Curriculum materials need to be organized into divisions such as curriculum units; this organization may well be left to the individual teachers. For the benefit of those charged with the responsibility of curriculum organization, curriculum programs, mimeographed or printed, should be obtained from other schools. Where time is available, at least some resource units should be developed by the most imaginative and creative teachers for the guidance and help of others.

As progress is made, occasional reports should be made to the members of the staff who are teaching the subjects involved in the curriculum revision; these teachers will act as a reviewing committee and should be encouraged to make suggestions and criticisms for the consideration of the production committees which are revising the work and putting it in final form.

SHOULD CONTROVERSIAL ISSUES BE INCLUDED? Classroom discussion of controversial issues results frequently in criticism of teachers and teaching.[1] The administration has a difficult problem in keeping criticism at a minimum and preserving the rights of students to study controversial issues. Following is a statement of the position of the Elizabeth, New Jersey, schools, on this question:

A. *Definition*
   A controversial issue, as herein understood, is one in which there exist conflicting opinions among the citizens of the community, of the nation, or among the nations of the world.
B. *Criteria for Determining Appropriateness of Controversial Issues for the School Curriculum*
   1. The issue must not involve the indoctrination of religious beliefs, a practice prohibited by state law.
   2. The treatment of the issue in question should be within the range of the knowledge, maturity, and competence of the students.

[1]James B. Conant, in his *American High School Today,* definitely approved the discussion of controversial issues.

3. There should be study materials and other learning aids available from which a reasonable amount of data pertaining to all aspects of the issue may be obtained.
4. The inclusion of the issue should require only as much time as is needed for a satisfactory study by the class; but sufficient time should be provided to cover the issue adequately.
5. The issue should be current, significant, real, and important to student and teacher. Significant issues are those which, in general, concern considerable numbers of people; are related to basic principles; or, at the moment, are under consideration by the public, press, and radio.
6. The proper avenues by which arguments on controversial questions reach students in school are through qualified teachers, the students themselves, and the other curriculum channels approved by the Board of Education.

C. *Responsibility of the Teacher*

1. A teacher in a free society has the obligation to uphold, protect, and defend the fundamental freedoms as documented in the history of our American democracy.
2. The teacher is responsible for creating in the classroom an atmosphere of freedom for students to raise questions dealing with critical issues of the time and for maintaining an atmosphere conducive to the free, spirited, and friendly interplay of ideas.
3. If the teacher does not feel qualified for an exploration of a controversial issue, he should guide the pupils to the proper sources and qualified persons who can help them in arriving at their own opinions, based upon facts.
4. It shall be the duty of teachers to see that all facts, evidence, and aspects of an issue are presented honestly.
5. The teacher should acquaint pupils with books, newspapers, and other materials which present data on all aspects of a controversial issue under discussion.
6. Statements presented and opinions expressed during discussion on controversial issues are to be carefully scrutinized by the teacher to make sure they are based on substantiated facts or credible evidence. The teacher should exercise special care to avoid misunderstanding.
7. The importance of the authenticity of facts and the purpose for which they were gathered must be stressed. Propaganda, in any form, should be clearly identified as such by teachers and students, and its intent should be clearly understood.
8. Although it is the teacher's responsibility to bring out the facts concerning a controversial question, he has the right to express his opinion, providing his students understand that it is his own opinion and is not to be accepted by them as the authoritive answer.

D. *Responsibility of Administration*

1. The following assumptions are basic to the administration of a policy which provides for the inclusion of controversial issues in the schools' curriculum:
   a. That the teacher is competent to handle controversial issues in the classroom within the fields of his preparation and training only.
   b. That the principal, as the administrator of his building, bears a major responsibility for the administration and supervision of the curriculum, selection of materials, and methods of instruction, and therefore is alert to and continuously aware in general of what is being taught in his school.

c. That citizens have the right to suppose that controversial issues are being presented fairly, and to protest to the Board of Education if convinced that unfair, biased, or prejudiced presentations are being made.

2. A teacher who is in doubt concerning the advisability of discussing certain issues in the classroom should confer with his principal as to the appropriateness of the issue. If the principal and the teacher are unable to establish agreement, the issue shall be referred to the Division of Instruction. The Division shall refer the matter to the Superintendent of Schools if necessary.
3. No individual or group may claim the right to present arguments directly to students in schools. Such a "right" to present arguments directly would make the schools battlegrounds for all kinds of controversies. The teacher, with approval of principal and/or superintendent of schools, should feel free to invite representatives of various viewpoints to discuss issues with classes in order to inform students on all aspects of controversial questions.
4. The Board of Education shall provide a hearing in accordance with American principles of justice, whenever, in the judgment of the Board, materials of instruction or the work of an individual teacher are seriously attacked by individuals or organized groups in such manner as to interfere with the normal administration of this policy.

E. *Selection of Material*

1. At the direction of the Superintendent of Schools the Division of Instruction shall establish and maintain proper procedures for review and approval of educational materials, including textbooks, visual aids, library books, and other supplementary aids to teaching.
2. Whenever publications or materials which are suspected of not clearly, fully, and truly presenting the truth are received by teachers, administrators, principals, or librarians, such materials shall be submitted to the Curriculum Advisory Council for review and consideration. The Council will make recommendations to the Superintendent of Schools concerning what shall be done with these materials. In serious cases of this nature, the Superintendent of Schools shall present the materials in question and the recommendations of the Council to the Committee on Educational Management of the Board of Education for decision.

This policy is intended to clarify for all concerned the determination of the Elizabeth Board of Education to preserve, protect, and increase appreciation for the fundamental rights and responsibilities of good American citizenship through education.[2]

2. *Current and Recent Trends*

MATHEMATICS, SCIENCE, AND FOREIGN LANGUAGES. In recent years very important and well-subsidized studies have been conducted on the content of secondary-school courses in mathematics, science, and foreign languages. These studies have grown out of the increased importance being attached by leaders in the United States today to the preparation of people qualified to conduct national defense and international rela-

[2]Board of Education, Elizabeth, New Jersey, *A Policy for the Handling of Controversial Issues in the Elizabeth Schools*, Elizabeth, New Jersey, Laboratory Press, 1950, pp. 3-5.

tions. The results of these studies should be brought to the attention of teachers for their careful examination and evaluation.

The National Defense Act provides funds for the operation of institutes at various colleges and universities for improving the subject-matter background of teachers in the fields mentioned above. Furthermore, scholarships are available which will pay at least part of the expenses of teachers attending these institutes. The principal has an opportunity to serve his school by getting information about these institutes and by encouraging appropriate teachers to attend and to apply for the scholarships.

FEDERAL SUBSIDIES UNDER THE NATIONAL DEFENSE ACT. Passed by Congress first in 1958, the National Defense Act provides funds to enable local schools to improve their curriculum along lines that contribute to the national defense. As far as the curriculum is concerned, these funds go primarily to schools wishing to improve their program in science, mathematics, foreign languages, and vocational education. The funds are to be employed largely for the improvement of the housing and equipment for instruction in these fields, rather than for the payment of teachers' salaries. In the field of vocational education the grants are given largely to schools which are improving their offerings in such fields as electronics, tool-and-dye instruction, and industrial chemistry.

Applications for this aid must be made through the department of education of the state in which the school is located. Since the standards and provisions vary somewhat from state to state, the principal is advised to contact his state department and the U.S. Office of Education for information; no attempt will be made here to describe the details of processing the applications. There are each year two deadlines for applications, one of them usually in the early part of October and the other around the middle of April. The Federal grants must be matched by the state and the local school, the local school usually providing much more than the state.

CURRICULUM AND THE COMMUNITY. Among the most prominent curriculum trends in recent years have been those which tend to bring about a closer correlation between the curriculum and the community. This correlation takes several forms.

One of the forms is to attempt in every subject to relate the materials of the curriculum to the community by emphasizing community applications. A second approach is to use the community as curriculum, particularly in the field of social studies and also in subjects such as science and English.

In assisting teachers to improve their courses of study, the principal or the supervisor shall not fail to consider the use of lay individuals in the community. Since this use is such a new development, he should read much of the literature now available on the subject, especially the reports of procedures and experiences of various school groups in employing lay resources. Among the selected references for this chapter will be found some of the best publications on this subject.

Large Units and Resource Units. It has been a prominent course-of-study trend for several decades to organize each year's course of study into large units rather than daily units, units involving at least several days and usually several weeks. These units may be in terms of life problems or logical subdivisions of the course of study for the year. In many schools the units seem to be a mixture or compromise of the two approaches.

Instead of, or in addition to, the use of general outlines of subject matter with suggestions for teaching which are commonly called courses of study, there is a trend toward the use of what are called resource units. A resource unit, usually prepared by a group of teachers, contains broad general outlines for large units of learning activities, as well as reservoir of such things as suggested projects, discussion topics, supplementary readings, investigation problems for individual students or committees, possible audio and visual aids, and other suggestions for materials and procedures for possible use in the unit.

The teacher and students choose from all the resources mentioned those which appeal most to them. A few resource units are worked out for one year; additional units may be added in subsequent years.

Trends toward Integration. There has been for a long time a feeling on the part of many educators that organizing learning experiences solely on the basis of subject-matter divisions is not the most effective way of promoting student learning and student growth. There have been several types of reorganization to change this situation: the core curriculum, the unified-studies curriculum, the broad-fields movement, and the fusion of subjects. The form of organization which is most widely employed and which is most likely to grow and be followed in a larger number of schools is the core (including the unified-studies) curriculum. This form is employed now in nearly a thousand schools, the majority of which are junior high schools.

Usually the core curriculum involves four elements: (1) a combination of two or more subjects, usually English and the social studies; (2) integration of the subjects around life problems or other psychological units; (3) a greater participation of the students in planning and managing their own learning activities; and (4) the division of time into large blocks of two or more periods.

The unified-studies plan is generally regarded as a modification of the core curriculum. Its principal characteristic is the fusion of two or more subjects or subject fields—for example, English and social-studies courses. It usually does not go far in organizing learning activities around problems and projects, although it does employ that principle of organization to some extent.

Initiating a Core or Unified-Studies Program. Although the number of schools employing the core of unified-studies program is slowly increasing, it has not been successful in some of the schools in which it has been initiated. It seems fairly easy to discover the reasons for the failure of the progra; on the basis of these reasons, suggestions may be made for initiating the core program successfully.

In the first place, in all but a very few schools it is probable that not all the teachers of the subjects involved in the core – for example, English and the social studies – should be required or even urged to reorganize their subjects into a core. It seems to be true that better results are obtained where, especially in the beginning, only those teachers are encouraged to use the core plan of curriculum organization who are rather eager to do so and who seem to be prepared to make a success of the venture. Also associated with success in beginning the core or unified-studies program is a period of co-operative in-service preparation which lasts at least a year. This preparation usually involves participation of the teachers in a workshop, either a local one or one at some college, where together with other teachers with similar problems they may fully orient themselves and do much of the spadework in preparing their core outlines and courses.

It has also proved desirable in a number of instances to have an English teacher and a social-studies teacher co-operate, each taking a core block of pupils for two periods and each teaching both English and the social studies. The two teachers co-operate, each assisting the other as consultant and co-planner for the two groups of students involved.

Likewise, it is wise to enroll in the core-curriculum groups only those students who understand the plan and who wish to be included. It is probably a wise precaution also to attempt to explain the core curriculum to the parents of prospective core pupils and to put into the core groups only those students whose parents signify their willingness to have their children in such groups.

A core program usually involves guidance and counseling, as well as a closer relation between teacher and student and teacher and parent. It is therefore necessary to see that the teachers of core groups have some background, knowledge, and training in counseling and guidance and in the gathering and interpretation of pupil data; they also should have sufficient time for more than the usual number of individual conferences with students and with parents. It seems quite logical that teachers should not be required to do more teaching than is involved in two core blocks, or four periods a day.

Combining English and Social Studies. It seems natural to many people to combine social studies and English. Literature to be studied in English classes may be selected and taught largely from the point of view of developing understandings and attitudes in youngsters relative to problems in human relationship and social living. A certain kind of literature lends itself unusually well to such development and more of that type of literature might well be included in the English courses.

In the literature classes there should be discussion of the human and social problems and situations involved in the literature; such discussion should provide a considerable amount of training in speech and oral expression. Likewise, training in written composition might center around writing about the problems, the conditions, and the situations of human relations developed in the literature; also, there could be writing about the problems, conditions, and situations involved in the psychological, political, economic, and sociological aspects of the literature. In the core curriculum some time might well be given to special study of language (including some drill exercises) apart from the work connected with the social studies. Likewise, time might be given to some aspects of history or some social study which would involve only incidental training in English. While allowance should be made for particular needs, care should be exercised to discourage the normal tendency of a specialized teacher to teach one field apart from the other and to neglect the integration of the materials.

3. Textbook and Workbook Selection

LEADERSHIP IN THE SELECTION OF TEXTBOOKS. In the last analysis, for the great majority of teachers the textbook is a potent determinant of what and how they will teach. The high-school administrator should, therefore, do his part to see that the selection of textbooks is thoughtfully and painstakingly done. The following suggestions are a composite of suggestions made by those who have made a careful study of the selection of textbooks:

1. If there is much criticism of a textbook currently used, or a feeling that there should be a new text adopted, obtain from the teachers of the subject involved a statement of the criticism of the textbook to be replaced and a statement of what they would like to have as the fundamental characteristics of the textbook to be adopted. Have the teachers, probably under the direction of the head of the department or some other supervisor, do considerable reading with respect to the improvement of the course-of-study materials in their field; hold several meetings for the discussion of the trends and the soundness of the trends in the course of study in the particular subject.
2. There should then be several meetings of the teachers to hear the committees appointed to summarize and report on trends. These meetings should also include discussion of the proper aims and scope of the course in which the textbook is to be adopted.
3. If the high school is of considerable size, or if there is more than one high school in the city, there should be a committee of teachers appointed with the special responsibility of selecting several of what they think to be the best textbooks in the field, reporting to the teachers their recommendations, and getting from the teachers, either orally or in writing, their reactions to these

tentative recommendations. Copies of the newer textbooks in the subjects under consideration should be obtained from the publishers and made available to the teachers. A committee of teachers should be especially chosen to develop criteria for the evaluation of textbooks.

4. Finally the selection committee should recommend the textbook or textbooks to the principal, who will transmit the recommendation to the superintendent of schools.

Following is a list of criteria which may well be employed in the selection of textbooks:

1. The extent to which the topics or units of material can be justified on the basis of probable contribution to the objectives of secondary education in general and of the specific subject in particular.
2. The degree to which relative emphasis upon topics is proportional to:
   a. Probable contributions to the objectives of the course.
   b. The necessity of emphasis for adequate mastery in the light of relative difficulty.
   c. The value of the specific topics as a prerequisite to other topics or materials.
3. The validity of the materials—the extent to which the topic is treated truthfully and accurately in the light of the most complete and recent knowledge on the subject (in the case of a textbook, an indirect measure of validity is the reputation of the authors as authorities on the subject; the date of the copyright should also be a consideration).
4. The character of explanations, presentations, and illustrations and their conformity to the principles of learning and effective teaching.
5. The degree of adaptation of presentation, thought content, sentence structure, vocabulary, and style to the student for whom the textbook is intended.
6. The degree to which the text is free from material likely to be inflammatory in the local community.
7. The order and sequence of materials with reference to:
   a. The introduction of new ideas.
   b. The degree of difficulty.
   c. The logical organization facilitating grasp of interrelations.
   d. The best arrangement from the point of view of using some topics to pave the way for others.
8. The degree of adaptation or adaptability in the adjustment of instructional activities to the individual ability of the learner: e.g., the inclusion of supplementary topics, problems, exercises, questions, experiments, and references adapted to the more able students; provision for omission of more difficult and less important exercises and materials for the less able students.
9. The provision of opportunities for bringing into relief and remedying inaccurate and inadequate learning and for diagnostic and remedial instruction.
10. The degree to which the material in the book articulates with courses which have preceded and those which will follow it (in the selection of texts for any given grade, consideration must be given with respect to their adaptation to the students of other grades, so that gaps, duplication, and differences in terminology or general approach may be kept at a minimum).
11. The degree to which explanations, descriptions, problems, exercises, and other materials are likely to challenge and arouse interest and energetic study on the part of the students for whom they are intended.

12. The character and number of learning aids such as appendixes, indexes, glossaries, footnotes, section and paragraph headings, illustrations, and the like.
13. The degree to which the content and vocabulary are adapted to what practically all the learners for whom it is intended may have learned or may be reasonably certain to learn in other courses.
14. The degree to which the content and approach, the format and visual material, and, above all, the problems or learning activities are likely to engage the interest of youngsters of the age and grade of those with whom the textbook will be used. Although mentioned last in this list, this is perhaps one of the most important criteria of all.[3]

Score cards for evaluating textbooks may be general in nature (that is, they may be designed to judge texts in various fields) or they may be designed to judge textbooks in one subject only. The latter type is to be preferred, for these cards aid in directing attention to specific areas peculiar to textbooks in that subject. While teachers may develop their own rating scales, they should first examine carefully some of the published score cards or rating check lists.

PROCEDURE FOR THE SELECTION OF TEXTBOOKS. Following are recommendations of the Association of Secondary School Curriculum Coordinators of the California Education Association:

1. Textbooks and other educational materials should be adopted by democratic methods. Where all the teachers concerned can be used for such selection this is desirable, and where committees must be appointed, they should be made up of classroom teachers together with suitable representatives of the supervisory and administrative staff.
2. Emphasis should be placed on the importance of selection as a part of curriculum development. Procedures should be carefully organized and time should be allowed so that the best possible choices can be made.
3. A central and up-to-date file of materials used regularly and in quantity in the classroom should be maintained so that interested persons can determine what is available. Lists of approved textbooks should be provided upon request.
4. Where possible, central libraries containing copies of approved basic and supplementary textbooks and other materials should be established. It is recognized that in some schools the problem of maintenance makes this suggestion difficult to carry out.
5. Adoption procedures should be stated in writing so that persons who wish to determine how such selections are made will be able to obtain the information.
6. Because of its responsibility for the educational program in the schools, the board of education should approve all materials used regularly and in quantity in the classrooms. Audio-visual and pamphlet materials should have committee and board approval similar to that recommended for textbooks.
7. Books should be selected for a period of at least three years or longer so that full use can be made of them before they are discarded.

---

[3]Harl R. Douglass, Rudyard K. Bent, and Charles W. Boardman, *Democratic Supervision in Secondary Schools*, pp. 202-203.

8. All approved textbooks should be reviewed at regular intervals so that those that have been in use for a number of years can be compared with new materials that are available.
9. Criteria should be established for the selection of educational materials so that evaluations may be as objective as possible.
10. A scientific analysis of vocabulary difficulty seems desirable in the selection of textbooks.
11. Experimentation in the classroom with sets of texts under consideration for adoption is of benefit wherever possible. The reactions of students, and even of parents, are of importance in making a choice.
12. Samples should be in the hands of teachers for several months so that enough time is available for careful analysis of each book before a final choice is made.
13. Adequate time should be allowed in the regular schedule for teachers to devote to the problem of analysis, evaluation, and selection of textbooks.
14. Adoption procedures should be elastic enough to provide for differences in classes and in schools.
15. Publishing houses should be notified in writing of pending adoptions so that all who are interested can submit their samples.
16. Textbook salesmen should be accepted as competent professional persons who know their product and its place in education and who are able to make a definite contribution to the improvement of instruction.
17. Time and adequate space should be provided for committee members and others concerned to interview bookmen and discuss the merits of their publications.
18. Because a better understanding of each book will result in wiser selections, salesmen should be encouraged to present the merits of their publications to those making the recommendations for adoption.
19. Salesmen should not discuss a text or adoption of textbooks with individual teachers but should discuss them only with committees or other groups.

SELECTION OF WORKBOOKS AND OTHER MATERIALS. Workbooks and other printed materials to be employed as a part of the curriculum should be selected with care, using somewhat the same criteria as are used for the selection of textbooks. Illustrative of good procedure followed by many schools in the selection of printed workbooks, bulletins, and other similar materials are the criteria employed in the Denver Public Schools and described as follows:

Criteria for the Selection of Material Other than Textbooks

(A) Authorship
- (1) The writer is competent to write in this field.
- (2) So far as can be ascertained, the writer supports the principles of American constitutional government.

(B) Material
- (1) No material expressing partisan, sectarian, sectional, or factional bias shall be used unless such bias is openly expressed and supported by objective data.
- (2) Material shall treat with respect all differing views presented to the students.
- (3) The conclusions presented in the material shall be supportable by evidence.

(4) Material shall be in good taste and conform to generally accepted moral standards and spiritual values.

Procedure for the Selection of Material
Other Than Textbooks

(A) Material other than textbooks must be evaluated in terms of the above criteria by the person or committee in the school ordering the material. Such evaluation may be by means of reading the material or through careful consideration of reliable sources of information, including reviews, book lists, and other aids.

(B) On orders for materials other than textbooks the signature of the person making or approving the order signifies that, according to his judgment and best knowledge at the time, the material meets the above criteria unless the statement of exception (see paragraph C below) accompanies the order.

(C) If the material being ordered has special educational value and is to be used on a limited basis only, but does not meet the criteria in every respect, the following statement of exception must be completed and must accompany the order:

The material requested on the attached order does not meet the criteria for selection of material other than textbooks in the following respects:

\- -

The material has special educational value, however, and will be used only on the following basis:

\- -

The statement of exception must carry the signatures of the persons initiating and making the order and the signatures of the persons approving the order. This material shall be so marked as to indicate its limited area of usefulness.

(D) Orders for material that does not meet the criteria in every respect must have the approval of the Director of Library Services and the Director of Instruction.

(E) If for any reason questions are raised concerning such material, the Superintendent of Schools shall refer the questions raised to the reviewing committee herein provided for consideration and recommendation.

Review Procedures

(A) A reviewing committee shall be composed of representatives of school personnel, as follows:[4]

Seven senior high teachers Five junior high teachers Five elementary teachers	Elected by the appropriate committee on instruction for overlapping two-year terms
Director of Publications Director of Library Services Directors of Instruction for Elementary and Secondary Education	Ex officio

[4] The number and proportions adopted for the Denver schools might be different from those adopted for other school systems.

(B) The review made by the reviewing committee shall result in one of the following specific recommendations of which the reviewing committee shall immediately notify the Superintendent of Schools and the person or persons initiating the action:

(1) The material meets the criteria and should be used.

(2) The material does not meet the criteria in specifically stated respects and should be used only on the limited basis recommended by the committee.

(3) The material does not meet the criteria in specifically stated respects and its use in the Denver Public Schools is not recommended.

The Review Committee shall also prepare for general distribution periodic summaries of its actions.

(C) It is the intent of these procedures that such materials and text shall not be excluded from use in the Denver Public Schools without opportunity for consideration and recommendation by the Review Committee.[5]

4. Teaching Machines and Curriculum Material[6]

One of the more important and rapidly spreading developments in recent years has been the increase of various types of teaching machines. The administrator and supervisor, as well as teachers, will need to investigate carefully the various kinds of machines with a view to evaluating their usefulness. There is at present a need for much more data from carefully conducted research studies which will throw light on the degree to which teaching machines are effective, their limitations, and the ways in which they may be used to best advantage.

Among the various types of teaching machines are the following:

Simple Write-In Machine. This device, used mainly by Porter, is a write-in type of teaching machine. It merely controls the exposure of mimeographed sheets of paper so that only a line at a time can be shown. The student writes directly on the exposed line, then moves a lever which exposes the answer and the next line. He can still see his response under a sheet of glass; he indicates on the answer line whether he was correct or incorrect. The device is hand-fed but satisfactorily prevents cheating, which could be accomplished by looking ahead. It has been used by Porter to teach spelling to second-graders and sixth-graders, and by Schutz in Arizona for programming problems. Similar simple write-in machines are Rheem's DIDAK 501, the Foringer Machine, and the Bell device.

Computer. An IBM 650 digital computer was used with a typewriter input-output as a teaching machine. Knowledge of results was given by having the typewriter keyboard freeze if an error was made. Branching was also used: students who responded correctly could elect to skip items.

Punch Board. The Punch Board was developed by Pressey at Ohio State. It is a small board, about the size of a man's hand, which contains rows of holes.

---

[5]Quoted with permission from *Criteria and Procedures,* Department of Instruction, Denver, Colorado, Public Schools.

[6]See "Self Instructional Devices," *Audio-Visual Instruction* (April, 1961). This material includes articles on teaching-machine terms and the names and addresses of manufacturers with brief descriptions of their products.

Multiple-choice questions are presented on a separate mimeographed sheet, and the students respond to each question by pushing a hole in the appropriate row. If his choice is correct, the pencil goes deep into the punch board; if he is wrong, the pencil does not go so deep. Each punch, correct or incorrect, makes a hole in the paper, which can be preserved. Numerous studies have been done at Ohio State by Pressey and his graduate students, using this punch board. Navy Special Devices Center has developed a very similar punch board and has sent some to the fleet for utilization.

Scrambled Book. The Scrambled Book presents a problem situation on the first page with several multiple-choice answers at the bottom. The student responds to the question by selecting an answer at the bottom which gives a page number. He then turns to this page and is told whether or not his selection is correct and why. This device provides branching, which means that students making incorrect responses are given remedial help or are led to repeat a certain section of the main program.

Automatic Rater. The Automatic Rater is a multiple-choice type of teaching machine. It was used during World War II by the Navy for incidental training and currently is being used by Keislar at U.C.L.A. for experiments in teaching arithmetic to children. The subject looks at a question on a small screen, then responds by pushing one of five buttons. He is given knowledge of results before the machine will move to the next line. Items are stored on a film loop. There is no variation in sequencing or mode.

Programmed Text. This device, developed by Homme, Glaser and Evans, is a unique form of textbook. The top third, or panel, on a page presents a question. The student responds to the question subjectively and then turns the page to learn the next question on the top panel, continuing as before. After the student has worked through all of the top panels, he returns to the front of the book and works through the middle panel; then the lower panel.[7]

FILMS AND TELEVISION. In recent years there has been a really accelerated speeding-up of various types of audio-visual projection, especially in the field of television. Principals of larger schools for which buildings are being constructed should investigate the possibility of providing for closed-circuit television within the school. Principals also may contribute to the improvement of teaching by exploring carefully and having various members of their teaching and supervisory staffs explore carefully the various kinds of audio-visual projection, with a view to obtaining appropriate equipment for expanding their programs and to providing in-service or summer-school training of the teachers in the use of projection equipment within the school and of television programs that come from outside.

In recent years there has been a very great increase in the amount of audio-visual material used in secondary-school courses of study.

Among the films used, the following types have been identified by DeKieffer and Cochran:

[7] E. B. Fry, G. L. Bryan, and J. W. Rigney, *Teaching Machines: An Annotated Bibliography* (Supplement to the *Audio-Visual Communication Review*), Washington, D.C., National Education Association, 1960.

1. *Historical films.* To give a background knowledge of historical events; usually dramatized.
2. *Documentary films.* To document the living scene or story and, as defined by John Grierson (one of the originators of documentary films), to provide "creative treatment of actuality."
3. *How-to-do-it films.* To show how to operate a machine, how to work a problem, etc.; many types of technical films.
4. *Scientific films.* To depict scientific theory, such as the theory of flight, the theory of astronomy, or atomic theory, as well as similar scientific subjects.
5. *Appreciation films.* To teach an appreciation of art, music, literature, a way of life, etc.
6. *Personal- and social-adjustment films.* To present the problems of personal and social adjustment for the elementary, secondary, and college student; often of a discussional nature.
7. *Informational films.* To create a general understanding or give background in such areas as geography.[8]

General considerations in the selection of films include the following:

1. The availability of the film (possibility of obtaining the film when needed).
2. Mechanical and technical quality of the film.
3. Possibilities of correlating a film with the topic being studied.
4. Appropriateness of a film to the mental and social maturity of the students.
5. Distinctive contribution to be made by the use of the film, such as motivation, information, culminating activity.
6. Opportunities for follow-up procedures.[9]

The administrator should be active in the matter of seeing that teachers have available the appropriate projectors, which should include a 16-millimeter film projector, a projector for slides, and a projector for opaque projection, as well as adequate maps, models, mark-ups, and equipment for the construction of various kinds of materials, including graphs, cartoons, and diagrams.

In recent years there has been an increased use of television in secondary schools. Leaders and teachers should obtain, read carefully, and make available to appropriate members of the staff some of the material which has been coming out in large volume in recent years; examples of such material are *Design for ETV, Planning for Schools with Television,* published through a Ford grant by the Educational Facilities Laboratories, Inc., 477 Madison Avenue, New York 22, New York; *The National Program in the Use of Television in the Public Schools,* a report on a national workshop in 1959, published by the Fund for the Advancement of Education, 477 Madison Avenue, New York 22, New York.

In the Trump plan of teacher utilization, which involves lectures to large classes, television programs and tape recordings are found to be

[8]Robert DeKieffer and Lee W. Cochran, *Manual of Audio-Visual Techniques,* Englewood Cliffs, New Jersey, Prentice-Hall, 1962.

[9]*Ibid.,* pp. 128-129.

quite useful.[10] A great many teachers require training in the use of films, television programs, tape recordings, and other audio-visual equipment and materials.

There is a fast-growing use of audio-visual materials (particularly tape recordings) in the language laboratories which have been established in a great many schools.

Tape recordings are also used in:

1. Recording radio and television programs to be brought into the school and played back during class.
2. Recording music which is unusually appropriate for instruction but for which there is no record in the school.
3. Recording rehearsals of school plays for the purpose of diagnosis and improvement.
4. Recording community resources such as interviews, speeches, and music.

In order that curricula may be improved by the use of a wide variety of audio-visual materials, the administrator must see that there is ample provision for teachers to make and store various audio-visual materials of a variety of types.

Problems, Questions, and Exercises

1. Be able to give a 10-minute talk from notes on "The Community as a Curriculum Resource."
2. Be able to describe in class and give your opinion of resource units.
3. Mention five important advantages of work-experience programs and five important suggestions for their organization and supervision.
4. How do you account for the development and spread of core and unified-studies programs?
5. What is your idea of the best type of a core or unified-studies program?
6. Mention what you think are the six most important suggestions as to procedure in selecting textbooks for use in high school.
7. Be able to discuss in class several important trends relative to the relationship of the curriculum and the community.
8. Be able to describe fully your idea of dealing with controversial issues in the classroom.

Selected Supplementary Readings

Alberty, Harold, *How to Improve the High School Curriculum*, Columbus, Ohio, College of Education, Ohio State University, 1959. [A resource guide for curriculum workers.]

Ames, Maurice U., "Teaching Science by Television," *Education Digest* (December, 1959), Vol. 25, No. 4, pp. 38-40.

---

[10] See J. Lloyd Trump, *New Direction to Quality Education*, Washington, D.C., National Association of Secondary School Principals, 1960.

Anderson, Vernon, and Gruhn, W. T., *Secondary Education, Principles and Practices,* New York, Ronald, 1962. [See especially Chapters 10, 11, 13, and 14; written from a very modern point of view.]

Automatic Teaching: The State of the Art, Eugene Galanter, ed., New York, Wiley, 1959.

Becker, James M., "Education for Participation in World Affairs," *Bulletin of the N.A.S.S.P.* (September, 1960), No. 258, pp. 143-150.

Bossing, Nelson L., and Kaufman, John F., "Block-Time or Core Practices in Minnesota Secondary Schools," *Clearing House* (May, 1958), Vol. 32, pp. 532-537.

Brandes, Louis G., "The Core Curriculum in the Secondary Schools," *Progressive Education* (February, 1952), Vol. 29, pp. 141-143.

Bulletin of the N.A.S.S.P. (January, 1958, 1959, 1960, 1961). [Reports on experiments with team teaching (especially the Trump plan) and the use of tape recordings and other teaching machines for large-group instruction.]

"Business Education Program in the Expanding Secondary School," *Bulletin of the N.A.S.S.P.* (March, 1957), No. 225.

Chamberlain, Hope, "Continental Classroom—A Progress Report," *N.A.E.B. Journal* (September-October, 1960), Vol. 19, pp. 33-37; also *Education Digest* (January, 1961), Vol. 26, pp. 19-21.

Conant, James B., *American High School Today,* New York, McGraw-Hill, 1958.

Donaldson, Robert R., and others, *Science for the Academically Talented Student,* Washington, D.C., National Education Association and National Science Teacher Association, 1959.

Douglass, Harl R., and others, *Education for Life Adjustment,* New York, Ronald, 1950. [A symposium of how various subjects and other aspects of the high school may contribute to better education for life adjustment.]

Educators Guide to Free Tapes, Scripts and Transcriptions, Walter A. Wittich and Gertie Hanson, ed., Randolph, Wisconsin, Educators Progress Service, 1961.

"English Language Arts in American High Schools," *Office of Education Bulletin* (1958), No. 13, p. 122.

Erickson, Carlton W. H., *Administering Audio-Visual Services,* New York, Macmillan, 1959.

Faunce, Roland C., and Bossing, Nelson L., *Developing the Core Curriculum,* New York, Prentice-Hall, 1951. [Offers some valuable information drawn from practices in use throughout the country, including philosophy and purpose of the core, the role of the teacher, the core class in action, the role of the administrator, and steps in developing a core program.]

Frazier, Alexander, and Wigren, Harold, *Guidelines for Television,* National Education Association, 1960, 80 pages.

Grinnell, John E., "Our Most Dangerous Neglect," *Education Digest* (April, 1960), Vol. 25, No. 8. pp. 22-26. [A program for character building.]

Hale, Helen E., "Quality Science for the Junior High School," *Bulletin of the N.A.S.S.P.* (December, 1960), No. 260, pp. 36-40.

Halvety, Julius H., and others, *Mathematics for the Academically Talented Student,* Washington, D.C., National Education Association and National Council of Teachers of Mathematics, 1959.

Heaton, Margaret, "A Look at the Core Curriculum," *California Journal of Education* (March, 1959), Vol. 34, pp. 179-183. [A look at problems and difficulties which have beset the development and implementation of the core curriculum; considerations which should be studied in core-curriculum planning.]

Hogenmiller, Robert E., "A Science and Mathematics Curriculum for Terminal Students in High School," *Bulletin of the N.A.S.S.P.* (October, 1958), No. 240, pp. 109-117.

Kenworthy, Leonard S., and others, "International Understanding Through the Secondary School Curriculum," *Bulletin of the N.A.S.S.P.* (December, 1956), No. 224, pp. 9-247.

Kostbade, J. T., and Ball, J. M., "Geography and Education for Citizenship," *Bulletin of the N.A.S.S.P.* (February, 1960), No. 253, pp. 159-165.

McKibben, Margaret J., "New Developments in Secondary-School Science," *Education Digest* (March, 1961), Vol. 26, No. 7, pp. 34-38.

McLure, W. P., "The Future of Vocational and Technical Education," *Bulletin of the N.A.S.S.P.* (February, 1961), No. 262, pp. 7-12.

Morse, A. D., *Schools of Tomorrow,* New York, Doubleday, 1960. [A report on experiments with team teaching, television, tape recording, teachers' aids, and guidance.]

Mott, Kenneth, "Language Arts—Social Studies Fusion in the Junior High School Block Period," *Bulletin of the N.A.S.S.P.* (March, 1960), No. 254, pp. 124-131.

National Commission on Safety Education, *Driver Education and Driving Simulators,* Washington, D.C., National Education Association, 1960.

National Council for the Social Studies, *Social Studies for the Junior High School,* Washington, D.C., National Education Association, 1957.

Noall, M. F., and Winget, Lerue, "The Core Curriculum Project," *Bulletin of the N.A.S.S.P.* (January, 1959), No. 243, pp. 196-203.

Otto, Arleen C., *New Designs in Home Making Programs in Junior High Schools,* New York, Bureau of Publications, Teachers College, Columbia University, 1958.

Penna, F. J., "Vocational Education in Catholic Schools," *Catholic School Journal* (January, 1958), Vol. 53, pp. 3-6.

Public Vocational Education Programs (Pamphlet No. 117), Office of Education, U. S. Department of Health, Education and Welfare, 1960. [States plans and objectives of various fields.]

Remley, Frederick M., "T. V. Playback on Tape and Film", *Overview* (December, 1961), Vol. 2, No. 6, pp. 48-49.

Renner, John W., Brown, Kenneth E., Johnston, Marjorie C., Jewett, Arno, "Keeping Up to Date With Developments in Science, Mathematics, Modern Foreign Languages and English Language Arts," *Bulletin of the N.A.S.S.P.* (April, 1961), Vol. 45, pp. 248-254.

Rosskopf, Myron F., and others, "New Developments in Secondary School Mathematics," *Bulletin of the N.A.S.S.P.* (May, 1959), No. 247, pp. 1-189.

Shulz, Richard W., "Quality Science for the Senior High School," *Bulletin of the N.A.S.S.P.* (December, 1960), No. 260, pp. 77-82.

Schwartz, Bernard, "An Investigation of the Effects of a Seventh and Eighth Grade Core Program," *Journal of Educational Research* (December, 1959), Vol. 53, No. 4, pp. 16-25.

Snider, Robert C., and others, "Teaching Machines and Programmed Instruction Materials," *Nation's Schools* (February, 1961), Vol. 67, No. 2, pp. 70-79.

"Speech Program for the Secondary School," *Bulletin of the N.A.S.S.P.* (February, 1954), No. 199, pp. 1-169.

Stach, Edward M., *The Language Laboratory and Modern Language Teaching,* New York, Oxford University Press, 1960.
Strain, Frances Bruce, Eggert, Chester Lee, and others, "Framework for Family Life Education," *Bulletin of the N.A.S.S.P.* (December, 1955), No. 215, pp. 1-117.
Studies in Mathematics Education, Chicago, Scott, Foresman. [A brief survey of improvement programs for school mathematics.]
Subcommittee on Television of the Commission on Research and Service of North Central Association of Colleges and Secondary Schools, Chicago, *The Uses of Television in Education,* 1961, 32 pages.
Tarbet, Donald G., *Television in Our Schools,* New York, Ronald, 1961. [Equipment, facilities, administration, program planning, public relations, curriculum supplementation.]
Teaching Machines and Programmed Learning: A Source Book, Arthur A. Lumsdaine and Robert Glaser, ed., Washington, D.C., National Education Association, Department of Audio-Visual Instruction, 1960.
Thaddeus, Brother, "Teaching and Streaming Today," *National Catholic Educational Association Bulletin* (August, 1960), Vol. 58, pp. 321-327.
The Revolution in School Mathematics: A Challenge for Administrators and Teachers, National Council of Teachers of Mathematics, 1201 Sixteenth Street, N. W., Washington, D. C., 90 pages.
United Business Education Association, *Administering Business Education in the Sixties,* Washington, D.C., National Education Association, 1960.
Wittich, Walter A., "Teaching Machines – Practical and Probable," *Nation's Schools* (August, 1960), Vol. 66, No. 2, pp. 64-65, 84-90.
Wittich, Walter A., and others, *Nation's Schools* (February, 1961), Vol. 67, No. 2, pp. 63-96. ["Television in the Classroom," "Audio-Visual Tools of Learning," "Language Laboratories," "Programmed Instructional Materials."]
Wright, Grace S., *Block-of-Time Classes and the Core Program in the Junior High School,* Washington, D.C., U.S. Office of Education, 1958. [A survey of block-of-time and core programs in junior-senior and separately organized junior high schools.]

9

Improving Student Learning

RECENT INCREASE IN IMPORTANCE. From the beginning of schools one of the major problems has been that of stimulating prospective learners to the greatest possible effort, or at least to a reasonable amount of effort, in participating in the learning activities planned for them by instructors as a means of guiding and encouraging desired educational growth. This problem has, however, in recent years become somewhat greater by reason of two developments.

As years have gone by, there have been more youngsters attending high school who have less interest in study and academic attainment and who have less academic and intellectual ability. To provide learning activities appropriate for this type of pupil constitutes a great challenge to the teachers and principal, not only because of the desirability of serving these youngsters but also because of the fact that when the educational program is not appropriately adapted to them they constitute a hazard to the discipline of the school and to the opportunity of other students to study effectively.

Furthermore, as years have gone by, competition for the time and attention of young people has very greatly increased, first through the radio, more recently through television, and always through the social activities related to the automobile, the student hangouts, and the home. The reliance which teachers can place upon home study, ordinarily motivated, has definitely decreased.

1. Interests and Felt Needs

TYPES OF STUDENT INTEREST AND FELT NEEDS. The highest grade of student interest in learning activities is, of course, that which results from the fact that the learning activities are in themselves interesting, regardless of their value and their contribution to educational growth. The best teacher exhibits the highest ingenuity and understanding of young people, as well as of the subject matter, by planning learning activities and materials which are challenging to the interest of the learners. Nevertheless, this type of interest needs to be supplemented by what may be called motivation, or a felt need on the part of the learners to participate in learning activities because of the learning which may result from them. These felt needs are of a variety of types.

IMMEDIATE AND DEFERRED NEEDS. The needs for learning may be needs which are present at the time or they may be needs which the students will have later in life. An example of an immediate need is a student's need to acquire some type of learning as a means of increasing his ability to participate successfully in some type of leisure or work activity in or outside of the school. Another type of immediate need is that of satisfying the teacher with respect to efforts and achievements in learning assigned material for the immediate future.

Many of the more important needs are deferred needs. Among these are the needs to acquire information, skills, habits, understanding, interests, or attitudes which will be effective in increasing the student's satisfaction and effectiveness in participating as a citizen, as a worker, as a student in college, as a homemaker, or as a parent.

While it is quite obvious that immediate needs are more stimulating to learning efforts, a great deal of learning must be for future needs. Future needs and their importance must be made clear to the student.

GENERIC AND SPECIFIC NEEDS AND INTERESTS. Some types of learning are necessary for a particular purpose; for example, there is the need to prepare a chart in an art class or for some other subject, the need to earn a credit with a good grade in some subject that is required for entrance to college or graduation from high school, or the need to learn some specific thing in shop or science class in order better to operate, repair, or select a radio, television set, or some other mechanical device.

A generic need is a need for some type of learning which is not for a specific or special purpose. Of this type is the need felt for making a good average mark, for receiving the approval of teachers and parents, or for acquiring an education or knowledge in general. It should be clear that specific needs are more effective than generic needs in stimulating learning activities.

POSITIVE AND NEGATIVE NEEDS. Some felt needs focus on some desirable attainment or experience; others focus on the avoidance of something undesirable, such as the avoidance of criticism, bad marks, or embarrassment when called upon in class. While it cannot be said that positive needs are more effective in stimulating effort, it is definitely clear that positive needs are much superior and preferable by reason of the fact that they are much less likely to result in unfortunate attitudes towards teachers, subjects, and school in general.

2. *Artificial Incentives to Learning Effort*

While every effort should be made to plan learning materials and learning activities which are intrinsically interesting to learners, as well as valuable for their contributions to the goals of education, it should be recognized that this approach must be supplemented by the use of artificial incentives.

TYPES OF INCENTIVES TO SCHOLARSHIP. The various artificial devices for improving scholarship may be classified as negative or positive. Usually the negative and the positive are simply two aspects of the same device; yet one may be emphasized to the relative obscurity of the other. For example, posting a list of honor pupils emphasizes the positive aspect of the device, but the device also has the negative aspect of disappointing those not included in such a list. Posting a list of those in danger of failure emphasizes the negative aspect, though it also operates in a positive way to bring satisfaction to those whose names do not appear. Among the various devices employed by schools, at least partly for their supposed influence on scholarship, are the following:

1. Marks on report cards.
2. Medals, prizes, school letters, and other material awards to individuals on the basis of scholarship alone, or scholarship in combination with citizenship, participation in activities, or other items.
3. Honor rolls of names of pupils published periodically in a local paper or in the school paper, posted on a bulletin board, or announced in assembly or roll room.
4. Eligibility rules for interscholastic competitions and restriction of participation in other extracurricular activities on the basis of scholarship.
5. Exemptions from examinations.
6. Graduation honors: for example, valedictorian or salutatorian; graduation *cum laude* or *magna cum laude*.
7. Roll-room, class, or other group honors: for example, cups, banners, or other awards for the class making the highest average mark for the semester or the year.
8. Membership in honor societies similar to the National Honor Society.
9. Credit toward graduation determined by the quality of the work done.

It will be worth while to look into the merits and defects of certain of these and to examine the criteria by which we may judge the value of incentives.

CRITERIA FOR EVALUATING SUCH DEVICES. The relative value of any device intended as an incentive to action—study, good behavior, or other type of response—may be judged by observing the following criteria:

1. *Strength.* The degree of appeal the device possesses for those persons to whom it appeals; for example, fear of failure is a much more powerful stimu-

lus to young people than the desire to render service to mankind.

2. *Universality.* The extent to which the device will appeal to all pupils for whom it is intended; for example, marks appeal to many more pupils than the offering of a gold medal to the one best pupil.
3. *By-products.* The desirability of the concomitant educational effects upon pupils; for example, it is undesirable to arouse jealousies or dislike of teacher on the part of less able pupils and to place falsely high value upon the attainment of honors as compared with that accorded to interest in the subject matter and subject-matter values.
4. *Administrative Convenience.* The ease with which the device may be employed and the relatively small amount of time necessary to make use of it.

APPLICATION OF THE CRITERIA. Because of the fact that many types of school devices commonly employed do not scale high on the second and third criteria, they are of questionable value. Medals or other honors attainable by one pupil or by a definite and small number of pupils do not appeal to more than the upper 10 or 20 per cent of high-school pupils. Fear of failure does not influence many high-school pupils, since all but a few are reasonably certain of passing. The possibility of graduation honors does not appeal to many pupils, though a few may work diligently in an effort to win them. Almost any type of incentive which gives publicity to distinctions between individuals is likely to generate bad social attitudes and to give pupils an unfortunate perspective of the intrinsic value of a study as compared to its value as a means of winning distinction or avoiding humiliation.

There are few formal school devices or combinations of devices for stimulating scholarship which meet all four standards sufficiently to warrant much enthusiasm for them. In schools in which superior and interested teachers are to be found in the classrooms, these devices add little if anything to the net educational improvement of pupils. Perhaps the chief contribution of such devices is the satisfaction experienced by members of the faculty at seeing bright and industrious pupils officially rewarded and apparently lazy pupils punished.

Evidence that the relative lack of value possessed by such devices is becoming recognized may be seen in the facts that the custom of selecting valedictorians and salutatorians has been abandoned in a great many schools, that honor lists and medals are employed much less frequently than formerly, that less stress is being put upon marks, and that in general less attention is being paid to singling out individuals for artificial rewards or punishments on the basis of scholarship.

ADMINISTRATIVE CONSIDERATIONS. One of the criteria mentioned above concerns administrative inconveniences or difficulties involved in the use of artificial incentives. Prominent among these difficulties is the possibility of creating undesirable attitudes on the part of patrons, owing to the invidious distinctions which are frequently brought into relief by the use of artificial incentives. Such distinctions often give rise to the suspicion, if not the conviction, that the awards have been determined inaccurately or on a personal basis and to rationalization that occasionally leads disappointed parents to attempt to discredit the awards, if not the entire administration. The smaller the community, the greater is the possibility that such developments may be of significance. Of less importance, but not to be ignored, are the time and energy spent in administering these devices, in calculating records and averages, in discussing candidates in committee meetings, in preparing lists, and in similar activities.

Limitations of Artificial Stimuli. There seems to be a growing tendency to place less and less emphasis upon artificial incentives. It has been the experience of teachers and principals that artificial stimuli result in pushing those who do not need the incentive into undesirable effort, while those who do need the stimulation are more often harmed than helped. Devices for artificially stimulating enthusiasm, including honor societies, awards of merit, and honor rolls, have been somewhat overrated. The effects of such devices upon students of lesser abilities are either negative, objectionable, or both. There is need to do more thinking about arousing interest on the part of students. Interest will cause them to make achievement its own reward; they will participate in learning activities because they believe that the resulting growth is valuable or that the learning activities are in themselves pleasurable. Interest is brought about by improving the curriculum and the methods of teaching and learning.

However expedient artificial incentives to study may be or seem to be, the real effect of their use almost invariably includes a distortion of the learner's scale of relative values; more often than not, they serve to hinder rather than to accelerate the development of interest in the subject of study itself. The sharp distinctions resulting from their use often contribute to a dislike for the subject in the minds of some pupils and to an unbecoming attitude of superiority in others.

A century ago the keen insight of Horace Mann disclosed the following: "If a teacher desires that his pupil should be a great man rather than a good one, or that he acquire wealth rather than esteem; or that he should master Latin rather than ride his own spirit, or attain high official preferment rather than love the Lord his God with all his heart and his neighbor as himself—then he will goad him on by the deep driven spur of emulation or any other motive until he will outstrip his fellow, at whatever peril to his moral nature."

Fear of failure affects only those students in some danger of failure; that is, it affects only a few inferior students in each class. The bad effect upon these students with respect to their attitudes toward themselves, their teachers, the subject, and the school probably more than offsets the stimulating value of the fear.

TESTING AND SCHOLARSHIP CONTESTS. In recent years testing programs and contests have been more and more regarded as undesirable types of stimuli to scholarship. A very serious objection may be seen in the premium placed upon goals and methods of teaching which are of such a nature as will permit ready objective testing. Without doubt one effect of such contests is to obstruct the progress that secondary schools are making toward reducing the extreme and unfortunate overemphasis heretofore placed on information and other strictly intellectual outcomes of teaching, to the neglect of important outcomes which play a large part in determining qualities of citizenship, worthy home membership, leisure and culture, moral development, and health—namely, ideals, attitudes, interests, and habits. Teachers are prone to concentrate on temporary learning of names, dates, places, and other detached facts, subject-matter laws, rules, and principles—the easily taught and easily measurable outcomes. They need no further encouragement to neglect the more subtle yet more important types of outcomes.

THE HONOR SOCIETY. The National Honor Society is a project of the National Association of Secondary School Principals. Membership in it is limited to 15 per cent of the graduating class. The number of members elected should not exceed 10 per cent of the low twelfth and 5 per cent of the high eleventh grade. To be elected to membership, a pupil must rank in the upper third of his class in scholarship. A key is presented to be worn by members.

Various schemes are employed in different schools for the selection of prospective members of the society. The quotation below is from the report of a committee appointed by the National Council of the society. The quotation below is from the report of a committee appointed by the National Council of the society to report on methods of selecting members:

I. The principal submits, either to the entire faculty or to a faculty committee, an alphabetical list of seniors comprising the highest 33 per cent of the class in scholarship rank. In case a school uses a letter scheme of grading, it is well to use a weighted value as follows: 5 for Grade A; 4 for Grade B; 3 for Grade C; 2 for Grade D; etc.

II. Usually the executive committee of the local honor society defines for the faculty or faculty committee the meaning in their school of service, leadership, and character. The following definitions are suggested:

1. *Service* is interpreted to mean

a. A willingness to render cheerfully and enthusiastically any service to the school whenever called upon.

b. A willingness to do thoroughly any assigned service in school procedure or student government, such as acting as proctor or citizenship committeeman, or serving voluntarily on the staff of the school publication.

c. A readiness to show courtesy by acting as guide to visitors, selling tickets, looking after concessions, acting as big brother or sister to underclassmen, or assisting students behind in their work.

d. A willingness to offer oneself as a representative of his class or school in interclass or interscholastic competition.
e. A willingness to uphold scholarship and maintain a loyal school attitude.
f. A willingness to render any other worth-while service to the school, or through the school to the community.

2. *Leadership* is interpreted to mean
a. Demonstrating a degree of initiative in classroom activities which leads to higher scholarship for all.
b. Showing initiative in prompting any high-school activities.
c. Successfully holding school offices, committee chairmanships, and other positions of responsibility.
d. Contributing ideas which may be incorporated in the civic life of the school.
e. Exerting a type of leadership which actively and wholesomely influences others toward fine leadership.

3. A student may gain recognition in *character*
a. By meeting his individual obligations to the school promptly and completely.
b. By demonstrating an honest spirit in his class work and a spirit of cordiality and sincerity toward his teachers and student associates.
c. By actively helping to rid the school of bad influences or environment.
d. By upholding the ideals of the Christian organizations of the school whenever occasion affords opportunity.
e. By constantly demonstrating such qualities of personality—honesty, reliability, promptness, achievement, and morality—as are indispensable to the finest young manhood and womanhood.

In a large and increasing number of junior high schools there is now a chapter of the National Junior Honor Society, also sponsored by the National Association of Secondary School Principals.

MARKS AND CREDITS AS INCENTIVES. Since the earliest secondary schools in this country, marks have been used as incentives, as have credits toward graduation and college entrance, although incentive has not been their intrinsic purpose. Marks were originally designed to inform parents of the quality of a student's learning in a subject; credits were originally intended as units for recording educational achievement.

While no doubt the use of marks and credits has served to stimulate the efforts of students who otherwise would have applied themselves less diligently, marks and credits have tended to become substitutes for more educationally sound types of motivation. By reason of their appeal to deep-seated mainsprings of human action—the desire to excel, to appear well, and to satisfy the demands of parents—marks and credits have been effective in one sense as incentives. They have, however, tended to replace, with many teachers and in many schools, such appeals as recognition of the value of learning and interest in the learning activities themselves.

Reinforced by misinterpretation of the theory of formal discipline, marks, as rewards or punishments, have operated to relieve teachers of incentives to become good teachers. If the teacher fails and some pupils, therefore, fail to learn, the pupil receives a bad mark or loses his unit of credit. With better teachers and in better schools, pupils are motivated by the desire to grow, to learn, and to achieve and by interest in learning activities. An increasing number of supervisors, administrators, and teachers are placing less emphasis upon marks. Marks are discussed less and thought of less.

Furthermore, in many schools there is an effort made to assist parents in taking a sane and practical attitude toward the marks made by their youngsters and to assist them in making an appropriate interpretation of marks. In some instances conferences are carried on with parents who are insistent upon having their children make marks beyond the possibilities of their academic talents.

The tendency toward less emphasis on marks is being accelerated by the increased attention given to the concomitant effects, or by-products, of teaching and to mental hygiene. Fear of bad marks constitutes a source of worry which makes many pupils dislike schooling and teachers, quarrel with their parents, lose confidence in teachers and parents, develop nervous, digestive, and skin disorders, and develop lack of confidence in themselves. It has been observed by many teachers and principals that overemphasis on marks seems to stimulate student cheating on examinations and in other ways. Also it has been observed that young people convicted of vandalism with respect to school property are most often students and former students who have been unsuccessful in meeting the demands of the schools for academic achievement.

Methods of deflating marks and other artificial awards are various. In some schools, marks and report cards are not used at all—probably an unwise extreme. In others, marks include qualities of citizenship, industry, and personality, a practice limited by the small possibility that very accurate judgments of these qualities can be made by teachers who see the youngsters only one class period a day. In other schools, marks are reported to pupil and parents in the form of statements which, in addition to rating the pupil, offer suggestions for improvement. In still others, the conventional marks and reports are still employed, but pupils and parents are encouraged not to take them seriously.

A more detailed discussion of marking practices, report cards, and reporting to parents will be given in Chapter 17.

3. Supervising Students' Study and Teaching How to Study

RECENT TRENDS. Teaching methods in secondary schools in this country have been departing steadily from the traditional method of daily assignment and recitation that was characteristic of teaching a quarter or a half of a century ago.

There has also been a continued trend towards the substitution of a longer period, on the average about 55 minues, for the shorter class period of approximately 45 minutes. As a result, part of the time spent in classes is being used for what may be called supervised study. Indeed, in some junior high schools using the long period, much of the study is done in the class period, leaving little for study halls or homework.

In most schools in which the lengthened supervised study period is used, daily recitation as such has disappeared. The cycle of assignment, study, and recitation covers from three or four days to several weeks, depending on the unit. From one to three days may be spent in what would correspond to assignment in the old plan: in introducing the students to the new unit; in laying out, co-operatively or otherwise, the learning activities involved in the new contract, project, or unit; and in presenting or teaching materials which the pupil should know before beginning his study. The pupil's study of the unit, including the supervised study, may then be distributed over a number of days, possibly several weeks, with occasional group conferences, testings, or teaching periods of a few minutes to full periods in length. After this, some time, either one period or several daily periods, is given over to recitation or "checking up" in the form of oral or written reports, exhibition and explanation of projects, oral discussions, written tests, or co-operative evaluation.

As the result of a very general demand, there has been a tendency on the part of teachers to provide for more homework. In addition, there has been an improvement in homework assignments. The improvement has largely taken the form of providing homework assignments in which the assistance of parents or others may not be substituted for the independent efforts of the students.

TRAINING PUPILS IN STUDY METHODS AND SKILLS. Many principals have found it profitable to assist in training pupils in habits and methods of study by one or more of the following means:

1. Preparing lists of study helps.
2. Requiring students to prepare study schedules.
3. Requesting parents to examine and approve pupil's study schedules, particularly the study hours scheduled for home study.
4. Training students in classes in methods of studying particular subjects.

Lists of study helps and suggestions may be found in any one of a number of books on how to study. In many schools such a list is prepared by a committee of teachers, often with the help of students. Such study lists may be distributed to the pupils through assemblies or roll-room groups (with explanation and discussion), through the medium of student handbooks, or through both avenues. They may also be distributed through the teaching staff. Each instructor may modify the suggestions to fit his subject and may supplement them with additional suggestions peculiar to that subject.

As a leader in this area, the principal should become familiar with one or more of the books on how to study: *Teaching Study Habits and Skills* by Ralph C. Preston, published by Rinehart in 1959; *A Practical Guide to Effective Study* by Charles L. Gunthorp, published by the Exposition Press in 1957; *Learning to Learn* by Donald E. R. Smith and others, published by Harcourt, Brace and World, Inc. in 1961; and *Learning and the Teacher,* issued by the John Dewey Society in Washington, D.C. in 1959. Students may well be encouraged to read *Study Your Way Through School,* published by the Science Research Associates of Chicago.

Proven very useful to students are tests of study skills such as the Spitzer Study Skills Test and the Stanford Advanced Study Skills Test, the former being expressly adapted to grades 9 through 12 and the latter to junior high school grades. Both are published by the World Book Company of New York City.

STUDY SCHEDULES. The use of a form for study schedules, which has been prepared and distributed to each pupil soon after the opening of the semester, is thought by many principals to be well worth the effort required. After a copy of this form has been filled in and has received the approval and signature of the parent, it should be returned by the pupil to the principal or the group adviser for approval. The pupil schedules the preparation of some subject or subjects for each class period during which he has no class or laboratory; he also indicates on his schedule what hours he will spend in home study. The study schedules are ordinarily not collected from the pupils until two or three weeks after the beginning of the semester, allowing them that time to experiment and to orient themselves before finally formulating their study schedules.

STUDY HALLS AND SUPERVISED STUDY. The conventional study hall, while not emphasizing supervision of pupil study, is, nevertheless, related to the effectiveness of pupil study and may be modified so as to provide conditions for supervised study. In small schools the library and the study hall should be combined, thereby facilitating the use of the library by pupils and eliminating the necessity of employing simultaneously the services of two staff members for supervision which may satisfactorily be done by one.

Until very recently, as a consequence of the adoption of longer class periods and of permissions for students to take more subjects and to be in class more periods during the week, the use of study halls has greatly diminished. The student depends, therefore, much more on study in classes and out-of-school home study. This situation makes it necessary to take or send classes or groups of students to the library and to bring into the classroom and make available to students books which they need in connection with their study.

Experience has shown that even in small study halls it is not wise for teachers in charge to assist or attempt to direct the study of pupils not in their own classes. In large schools special-subject study halls may be provided.

In a few large high schools there are so-called departmental study halls, each equipped with departmental libraries—one for English, one for science, one for foreign languages, one for mathematics, and one for history, social studies, and commercial subjects. Teachers who are specialists in these fields are assigned to these study halls for two or more consecutive periods as a part of their regular teaching load. These teachers, being experienced in the study problems in their particular subject, are able to supervise study more effectively. The student can arrange his schedule in order to go to any one of these study halls that he wishes.

Under the leadership of the principal, uniform rules, conventions, and standards should be formulated for the management of study halls. Uniform procedure so arrived at is likely to be superior to that developed by each teacher on his own initiative; also, the very fact of uniformity assists the pupil to learn quickly what is expected of him, avoids the confusion likely to result when teachers employ different standards or conventional procedures, and eliminates undesirable comparisons of different study-hall teachers by pupils. Standard behavior in study halls today is good working behavior. Every member of each study-hall group is expected to study and to make it possible for others to study without distraction.

Study-hall teachers often attempt to agree on the details of what constitutes distraction (for example, noisy passage to and from seats, conversation other than very brief exchanges, and humming), but the general standard rather than the detailed interpretations of it should be kept in mind.

Many beginning teachers, and occasionally an older one, will profit from some supervision in connection with their management of the study hall. Often they tend to perpetuate practices which were born of a spirit quite dissimilar to that obtaining in the better schools today. Some are prone to take officious note of all petty and inconsequential infractions of conventions, some of which may have little relation to the work atmosphere of the study hall. Some employ public reprimands of a caustic nature, which are in the long run more likely to cause than to prevent distraction. Others seem helpless, lacking standards or confidence in their judgment or ability to cope with disorder. A few conferences and a visit or two to study rooms by more skillful teachers may be of great help to such teachers.

Insofar as possible, teachers assigned to study halls should be only those teachers who are interested and have above-average ability in study-hall management; they should preferably be those who have demonstrated their ability previously in study-hall supervision.

Principals will find it wise to develop, with the assistance of teachers, study-hall guides which include suggestions for organizing and directing student activities in the study hall and for setting up standards and rules for the supervision of study halls. The study hall should be located near the library and as far away as possible from noisy streets and playgrounds. Ordinarily, not more than 50 students should be assigned to study hall for any given class period.

Principals of a few senior high schools have reported that they have found it practical to offer study opportunities in the library in the evening, usually from 7:30 to 9:30. This practice proves very effective for students in whose homes are many distractions and no appropriate place to study. It also affords opportunity for students to get at materials not to be found in the home. It tends to offset the disadvantage of not having more time to study in the library during the regular school day. Provision must be made, however, to see that students do not abuse the privilege. In a small but increasing number of schools, provision has been made for study at school in the evening.

TRAINING STUDENTS FOR INDEPENDENT STUDY. Particularly in those schools in which plans of team teaching are being employed, with resulting demands for a considerable amount of independent study and for definite preparation, the training of students in independent study is necessary.

In any school, independent study will be carried on largely in the library, study hall, laboratory, shop, or typing room. The extent to which high-school students use the library depends largely upon the nature of the assignments made and the interest otherwise aroused by members of the instructional staff, but instruction and training in the use of the library are generally of practical service. In many schools lessons on its use are given either as a part of the instruction in English or as a part of the guidance program. The time given to such training varies from a few periods to as much as eighteen lessons or more.[1]

4. Adapting To The Individual

In the administration and supervision of high schools considerable attention has been given in recent years (and no doubt a greater amount will be given in the future) to developing plans and assisting teachers to adapt the instruction better to the needs, abilities, interests, and background of the individual student. This adapting ordinarily is done not by what is called individual tutoring but by other means which deserve attention here, including grouping, the adaptation of material and methods in the classroom, diagnosis and remedial teaching, variation in the student load, the use of electives, and special classes and instruction for the handicapped.

[1]See Chapter 20 for a more detailed discussion.

Acquiring Information about the Learner. For the purpose of adapting instruction to the individual learner, for the purpose of guiding him in respect to what subjects he should select and whether he should go to college, and for the purpose of easing other relationships between the principal or the teacher and the student (including matters of discipline), information should be gathered about each individual student. Among the more important types of data which are useful for these purposes are the following:

1. Data concerning abilities may be gathered from intelligence-tests scores, previous grades in school, and aptitude tests.
2. Information concerning interests may come from such sources as interest inventory, choice of electives, hobbies, and extracurricular activities, out-of-school experiences, statements made in class, and plans made for a vocation and further education.
3. Information should be gathered concerning character and personality traits, including such things as seriousness, frankness, extroversion, introversion, dominance and submission, sociability, resistance, neuroticism, and relative adjustment or malajustment to home and school companions. These data may be obtained by the use of special devices such as personality inventories and adjustment inventories, by means of recorded observations of pupil behavior, and by conferences and home visitation.
4. Educational status and achievement can be learned from placement tests, standard tests, and grades made in previous semesters of study.
5. Data should be recorded relative to cultural and economic status, including such matters as occupation of parents, education of parents, general tone of the home, neighborhood, and church experiences.
6. From records which are usually available in school there should be data available concerning the student's special abilities, talents, and physical, mental, and emotional health.

Home visitation by teachers, counselors, and others in the school may serve as one of the sources of data and one of the devices and procedures for better adaptation of the school to the individual. Home visitation is a rapidly growing practice, effective not only in the better adaptation of the school to the individual but also in better public relations. Through this practice data are exchanged between the school and the parents; a better understanding of the problems and needs of the youngsters on the part of both parents and teachers is most frequently its result. For home-visitation work to be done effectively, there is need for special in-service training of teachers. It is the responsibility of the principal to encourage teachers to become familiar with data about each of their students; he should give them some in-service training in the interpretation of various kinds of data about students.

If the principal and teachers are not familiar with the critical learning characteristics of the dull or slow learner and of the bright and rapid learner, they should read at least a few discussions similar to those given in Mills and Douglass, *Teaching in High School*.[2]

Is Grouping Desirable? After having lost some ground in past years the practice of grouping students has in recent years experienced a revival and increased use. This increased use has resulted in part from necessity and in part from the better adaptation of instructional materials and methods both to the more capable students and to the increasing number of those with less academic ability and intellectual interest.

Among the reasons for the former failure of grouping and its discontinuance in many cities were the following:

1. Naturally students placed in sections with those of less ability were somewhat stigmatized. In some schools this situation was handled not at all diplomatically: students were embarrassed and parents were disturbed.
2. The grouping was not well done: the students in each group were not much more homogeneous with respect to capacity and ability than those in so-called heterogeneous groups.
3. The teachers did not realize that within each group there was still a wide range of individual differences and that therefore other supplementary methods of adapting to individual interests, needs, and abilities must be employed.
4. The teachers most often in charge of the sections for the less able and for the more able lacked the adequate time, ingenuity, background, and imagination to adjust the learning activities to the student.
5. Students in most schools were not grouped separately for each subject, but were grouped for all subjects, ignoring the obvious fact that the student who might be somewhat inferior in ability, capacity, background, and interest in one subject might be average or even better in another subject.

In recent years there has been a growing feeling that when grouping was abandoned perhaps "the baby was poured out with the bath"; the problem of adapting learning activities to the capacities, abilities, and interests of students still confronts us, in an even more challenging form and degree. In the larger cities, at least, grouping has been slowly regaining lost ground. It is taking several forms, including (*a*) special remedial sections for those needing considerable training in reading, language arts, and, in the junior high school, arithmetic; (*b*) special sections in academic subjects for those of greater verbal abilities and capacity for dealing with abstractions and for those whose interests and abilities call for courses emphasizing applications and uses in daily life; and (*c*) groups at three levels—the least able 10 to 20 per cent, the ablest 10 to 20 per cent, and the middle group.

The percentage of students falling into the higher group and the percentage falling into the lower group will vary greatly from school to school. Schools located in communities in which people of upper eco-

[2]Hubert H. Mills and Harl R. Douglass, *Teaching in High School*, New York, Ronald, 1957, pp. 384-390.

nomic levels constitute the larger part of the population will enroll more students of the higher level and fewer of the lower level. Likewise, strictly agricultural communities and those populated largely by families in which the breadwinner is in the lower economic levels will enroll more students of the lower level and fewer of the higher level. In the very large high schools it is possible to set up sections of very gifted youngsters who are in the upper 2 to 5 per cent in academic ability. Such sections have already been formed in some schools.

CRITERIA FOR GROUPING. Grouping should be done separately for each subject. A considerable number of students may belong in one level in one subject and another level in another subject. Better grouping may be accomplished if special bases, especially valid for each subject, are used. Grouping should be done on the basis of these criteria: (1) a subject prognostic test, e.g. the Orleans Prognostic Test in Algebra, or grades made in the previous year or two in the subject: (2) mental age or I.Q.; (3) general average grade for the previous year; and (4) teachers' estimate of drive.

MANAGING GROUPING. Occasionally a student needs to be reassigned after once having been put into a group. Usually between 10 and 20 per cent of the students should be reassigned after the first month or six weeks. Except in case of obvious misclassification, reassignment should not be done at any other time except at the end of the semester.

To instruct sections other than the regular or conventional sections, teachers should be carefully selected on the basis of their special interest and given some definite inducement, such as a salary bonus, especially in the case of those teaching "slow" or remedial sections. They should be required to adapt markedly their courses of study and methods and they should be given special supervisory assistance. They should probably make special preparation by attending a workshop in which they give considerable time to planning and preparing a course of study of materials for their section.

Care should always be taken to avoid any remark or any action that serves to call attention to the fact that a "slow" group or a "superior" group is a special section or that it is inferior or superior. There will still be some stigmatization, but almost always the slow students will feel less discouragement than they would in a "regular" section, attempting to do work day after day that is both uninteresting and beyond them.

5. *The Academically Bright Student*

DIFFERENCES WITHIN CLASS SECTIONS. Whether or not students are grouped so as to be relatively homogeneous with respect to their academic ability, there will be the necessity for the teacher to discover the relative ability of each individual student and to make adaptations to the individual students in the class section. To determine the relative academic ability of the individual student, the same types of data may be employed as are employed in grouping: e.g., intelligence quotient or mental age, previous average over-all grade, and previous grade in the particular subject field.

In helping teachers adapt instruction to individual students, particularly to those of inferior and those of superior academic ability, the principal should bring to the attention of the teachers characteristics of the dull or slow child and characteristics of the bright child, such as those listed on pages 389 to 391 of *Teaching in High School* by Hubert H. Mills and Harl R. Douglass.

Furthermore, in assisting teachers to adapt to the academically talented student, the principal should make available and call to the attention of the teachers appropriate publications, including the publications on the academically talented student which are published by the National Education Association, 1201 Sixteenth Street, N.W. Washington 6, D.C. They include:

The Identification and Education of the Academically Talented Student in the American Secondary School (Conference Report), $1.50.
Administration—Procedures and School Practices for the Academically Talented Student, $1.25.
Mathematics for the Academically Talented Student, $.60.
Science for the Academically Talented Student, $.60.
English for the Academically Talented Student, $1.00.
Modern Foreign Languages and the Academically Talented Student, $1.00.
Social Studies for the Academically Talented Student, $1.00.
Summary of Research on the Academically Talented Student, $.50.

News of the National Education Association's project on the academically talented is issued several times a year, in publications costing $.25 each.

SECTIONS FOR THE BRIGHT STUDENT. In thousands of secondary schools throughout the United States today, sections of bright students are being formed and courses of study are being planned which make better provision for these students. Teachers assigned to teach such sections should be encouraged to prepare themselves to do so effectively, either through in-service activity or through attendance at summer school. In recent years summer schools have offered courses, quite commonly with subsidized scholarships, on methods of improving the instruction in certain subjects, particularly science, mathematics, and foreign languages.

The principal who wishes not to be left behind should become acquainted with the publications about courses of study and other provisions for the gifted that are published by the National Education Association, the U.S. Office of Education, and the National Association of Secondary School Principals, all with offices in Washington D.C.

For some time in many schools there have been offered two-track and three-track plans in various subjects, one track being for the more capable and college-going student and other tracks for the students who, though not so capable in a particular field, need to be conversant with the simpler things in that field. These plans are particularly suited to the fields of science and English. Some schools have a triple-track plan in mathematics in the ninth grade and a double track plan in grades 10, 11, and 12.

In many high schools there are two courses in physics: one course may be called applied or everyday physics and the other course may be called general physics. The college-going youngster and the youngster of fair capacities, abilities, and interests are naturally advised to take the general physics; the youngster with lesser abstract ability and the youngster not going to college are advised to take the applied or everyday physics.

The important feature with respect to these classes is that the student is not arbitrarily sectioned; he is advised by his counselors and the teachers of the subjects concerned as to which section he should take, on the basis of his previous school records, intelligence-test score, and other criteria. In other words, it is on a voluntary basis and compulsion is not employed. Students soon learn which section is best for them, in view of their interests and capacities and in general tend to get into the right section.

THE ACCELERATION OF BRIGHT STUDENTS. In the first quarter of the century there developed a practice of permitting bright students to complete high school and to graduate in three years, by (1) carrying extra subjects each year, (2) taking correspondence courses, (3) attending summer school, or (4) making extra credits by participating in extracurricular activities.

More recently there has been opposition by high-school principals to this practice on the grounds that (1) students of less than seventeen years of age are too young to go to college, (2) accumulating credits does not mean the equivalent of a full four-year education, and (3) it is not fair to the high school to lose its best students, who are often the school's leaders and best performers in many areas of school life.

However, careful investigations by Sidney L. Pressey of Ohio State University, and others,[3] seem to prove that young, bright college students (1) make better than average marks in college, (2) have an average social life, (3) adjust as well as others to college life in general, (4) stay in college and graduate school longer than bright students not so young, and (5) furnish their quota of student leaders.

Recently there has been a slight trend toward permitting bright students to complete high school in three years under certain stipulated

[3]Sidney L. Pressey, "Acceleration: Disgrace or Challenge?" *Science* (September 6, 1946), Vol. 104, pp. 215-219.

conditions, such as those set by the Manhattan, Kansas, schools and shown below:

1. The student is to present his plan in writing to the committee. He will make a statement of reasons for acceleration, and of vocational plans. An additional statement from the parents will be made, in which will be listed their reasons for making such request.
2. The request is to be reviewed by the committee. A joint conference of parents, student, and committee may be called for by either the committee or the student and his parents.
3. Work taken by correspondence, for any reason, must be recommended by the committee and approved by the Board of Education. No credit will be allowed for correspondence work if the grade is below a *C*.
4. The committee will recommend a plan to the Board of Education for each individual case.
5. Final approval shall be subject to the approval of the Board of Education.

One form of acceleration which is being used in a great many schools with considerable success is the starting of algebra in the eight grade for those students who are very superior in mathematics. Unless, however, a considerable number of students start this section, there will not be a sufficient number to maintain a section for them in the upper grades. In addition, there is the serious question as to whether eighth-grade general mathematics should be omitted from the learning experiences of these youngsters.

ADVANCED-PLACEMENT COURSES. In a rather large number of secondary schools in recent years there have been provided for seniors special sections of college level in one or more subjects, especially in the fields of English and chemistry. The course of study in these sections is usually quite similar to the conventional course of study taught in the freshman years in colleges and universities. Some colleges give college credit for these courses, but many others recognize them only through giving the student placement in advanced courses and relieving him from repeating material in the beginning course in college. The principal should definitely ascertain what adjustment will be made by each college which these students are likely to attend.

The New York State Education Department has prepared a series of syllabi in mathematics which is designed to encourage high schools to offer academically superior pupils instruction of postsecondary grade that may warrant advanced placement or credit upon college entrance. Like the advanced-placement series in English, American history, chemistry, and French, this series shows the relationship between the state standards for the high-school grades and the advanced-course material which must be offered to qualify pupils to take the advanced-placement examinations that are offered by the College Entrance Examination Board. The state publications include: *Mathematics 7-8-9* (Syllabus, 1955, $.15); *Mathematics 10-11-12* (Syllabus, 1954, $.25); *Math-*

ematics for All High-School Youth (Basic Skills Conference Clinics Report, 1953, $.50); *Measurement* (Resource Unit, 1958, $.50); *Solid Geometry* (Reprint, 1959, $.25); and *Advanced Algebra* (Reprint, 1959, $.25).

In ordering any of these publications, the check should be made payable to the New York State Education Department; the order should be sent to the Publications Distribution Unit, Finance Section, New York State Education Department, Albany 1, New York. Various mimeographed booklets supplementing the syllabi have been produced and distributed to teachers.

INDEPENDENT STUDY, RESEARCH, AND HONORS COURSES. In recent years in a great many schools there have been initiated special types of study for the more capable students. These types of study are called by various names, such as the independent-study course, the research course, the honors course, and the open-end seminar. Students are very carefully selected and admission is only by special permission. There ordinarily is no textbook in such a course; within the framework of an outline supplied by the instructor with suggestions for indivudal projects, students are pretty much on their own. As yet, it is a little early to assess the actual value of these provisions for abler students.

6. The Less Able Student

REDUCING NUMBER OF FAILURES. The rapid spread of the concept of universal secondary education to school people generally has, along with the results of elimination studies, served to focus attention upon means of preventing elimination and its close associate and chief cause, failure or retardation. In recent years the tendency has been to award fewer marks of failure in all subjects in the high school.

Attempts to discover causes of failure have not been very successful. Reasons assigned by pupils or by teachers are not sufficiently valid. Pupils do not know with exactness why they fail, nor do their teachers. Failure is most likely to come about through a combination of causes, not all of which are associated by the pupils with failure. They, even more than adults, are prone to rationalize, even deceiving themselves to a great extent. Teachers' opinions are probably of little greater validity than those of pupils. But from all the investigations of all sorts, it would seem that the principal cause of failure, somewhat in the order of their importance and the number of pupils they affect, are as follows:

1. The nature and difficulty of the subject matter and the learning activities.
2. Lack of provision for more active learning situations.
3. Lack of interest and lack of appreciation of the value of the subject.
4. Failure of teachers to interest the child.
5. Failure of teachers to understand the difficulties of the child.
6. Outside interests and activities, including work and social activities.

7. Marking standards of teachers.
8. Lack of good study conditions at home.
9. Lack of adequate previous preparation in the subject.
10. Lack of good study techniques and of vocabulary-building habits.
11. Lack of reading skills and habits.
12. Teacher-pupil difficulties—poor personal equation.
13. Distractions—worry, daydreaming, etc.

It should be apparent that the prevention of failure cuts across the whole field of teaching—teaching, management, guidance, supervision, measurement, etc. One thing is clear: if failures are to be reduced materially, class teaching must be both improved and individualized. Consequently, teachers must have an abundance of data concerning each pupil.

It is obvious that to attempt to discuss all the causes of failure would quickly carry us far beyond the scope of this volume, into methods of teaching, tests and measurements, supervision of health, and other fields. In other chapters of this volume, discussions and suggestions appear which are related to a number of approaches to the question of failure. We must confine the discussion here largely to topics not treated in other sections of the volume.

Improvement of Marking Practices.[4] In instances of more than ordinary proportions of failure, investigation should be directed to the marking practices of the teachers concerned. It has been shown in numerous studies that the percentage of failing marks assigned by different teachers in the same school and in the same subjects in different schools contain variations which could not possibly correspond to the variation in the abilities of the different groups of pupils.

Careful studies by committees of teachers of the marks assigned by teachers in school may serve to attract attention to discrepancy in marking standards and thereby reduce materially the number of failing pupils.

Adaptation of Instructional Materials and Learning Activities to the Lower Levels of Ability. There is probably much truth in the criticism that high-school courses of study and standards have not been readapted to take cognizance of the greatly increased percentage of students of inferior intellectual ability and interest now staying in secondary schools beyond the ninth grade.

Courses in mathematics and foreign languages are conspicuously involved in this criticism, as may be observed from the large percentage of failures in these subjects.

As a means of preventing failure as well as of providing for the most capable pupils, courses of study should, wherever possible, be differen-

[4]See Chapter 17. "Student Accounting and Reporting," for a more detailed discussion of marks, marking, and reporting to students and to parents.

tiated. Those for the less able pupils should consist largely of the simpler and more practically useful materials and tasks, which inferior pupils may be expected to assimilate with reasonable degrees of success. In junior high schools special classes should be formed for students who are definitely below the grade norm in arithmetic, reading, and language arts. Teachers should be placed in charge of these classes who will become, or already are, specialized in the matter of adapting learning activities to youngsters of lesser abilities. These groups, comprising from 10 to 20 per cent of seventh-grade and eighth-grade students, should not attempt to do the regular seventh-grade and eighth-grade work; they should be taken where they are and given courses of instruction adapted to their present abilities.

Indeed, there are coming into junior high schools and some times persisting in senior high schools a considerable number of youngsters with I.Q.'s of less than 75 or 80 who cannot profit much from even the classes organized for students of lower ability. In an increased number of schools some specific provision is made for children of so greatly limited ability.

The Mark Keppel High School, Alhambra City High School District, California, has established a special-education program for students with I.Q.'s of approximately 50 to 80. One class of two hours is for freshmen students and a second class of two hours is for sophomores and juniors. A special-education teacher is in charge. The teacher for this program possesses the Exceptional Children's Teaching Credential.

Beyond the two-hour core class, these students may be programmed into art, physical-education, industrial-arts classes of a special-education nature for boys, classes in clothing and cooking for girls, and a special-education mathematics course. The program attempts to present as natural a school day as possible for the special-education students.

Special classes are held only for ninth, tenth, and eleventh grades. Those students remaining to the twelfth grade are allowed to join their graduating peers in carefully selected slower groups. During the four years of the students' attendance in high school, the counselor and the special-education teacher work together to bring forth the educational and social potential of each individual.

In at least a few schools, dull students with antagonism towards academic subjects are permitted to devote a major part of their school time to shop and work experiences of various sorts for a semester. They are given intensive counseling and special training in reading and are then urged to shift back to a more conventional type of program. Those who will not shift back are given certificates instead of diplomas. In the public schools in St. Louis, less able students coming from areas of very low economic and cultural levels are grouped and given programs similar to that described above.

Diagnosis and Remedial Teaching. Teachers should be encouraged and trained to practice diagnosis and remedial teaching: to construct tests which will enable them to bring into relief the fundamental sources of pupils' errors and weaknesses and to formulate and administer learning exercises to eliminate such errors. Diagnostic-remedial methods are most fruitful in beginning classes in foreign languages, mathematics, and English. Teachers of shop and laboratory subjects may prevent much subsequent unsatisfactory work if they will observe their pupils closely in the first few weeks of their courses and note those who seem unusually inept at handling the equipment they are called upon to use.

GUIDANCE IN CHOICE OF ELECTIVES. One of the most prolific sources of failure is the tendency for large numbers of boys and girls of less than average ability to enroll for advanced mathematics and foreign languages. More care than has previously been exercised should be taken to prevent certain or probable failures from enrolling in college-preparatory mathematics and foreign languages. Such pupils may be located with a fairly high degree of accuracy if proper methods are employed. At enrollment time advisers should have at hand data which will enable them to render useful guidance in this connection. Most useful of such data are the following: mental age, I. Q., prognostic-test scores, and previous ranking in scholarship. Unless those lacking in ability, as indicated by these data, show special aptitudes in mathematics or foreign languages, as indicated by prognostic tests or previous marks, they should not be permitted to enroll for these subjects.

A principal should see that there are available and brought to the attention of his staff modern books on measurement evaluation and an up-to-date collection of catalogues of tests published by the commercial houses.

CASE STUDIES AND PERSONAL CONFERENCES. Case studies and conferences serve two important purposes: (1) to discover factors contributing to failure and (2) to establish personal contacts and attitudes making for the personal influence of the principal, counselor, or teacher with the pupil.

Case studies of individuals who are failing may bring into relief factors which may be remedied or which will make further efforts of the pupil seem useless. Case studies may include any combination of the following types of data:

1. Reasons for dislike of school.
2. Conditions at home: mental, emotional, and hygienic phases.
3. Outside employment: nature and hours.
4. Health records and medical-inspection data.
5. Temperament and moral character.
6. Vocational plans or interests.
7. General mental ability.
8. Reading ability and study habits.
9. Extracurricular participation.

In every school there should be someone to consult all the available data of these types, to gather other needed data by visitation or conference with pupil, parents, teachers, or associates, and to determine as far as possible why each pupil concerned is failing. In small schools the principal may carry on this work alone or assisted by the members of his staff who are interested in various individual cases; in larger schools counselors should be trained and encouraged for this work. With proper organization for guidance, the head of the guidance program should include this work as one of his major responsibilities. The visiting teacher, if there be one, should be utilized as an important agent for obtaining useful data.

Perhaps the most usable organization for such guidance is that of the home-room or group counselors—each for his or her group of pupils. Failing work or deficiencies likely to lead to failures should be reported directly to the counselors or to the office, from which the reports will be sent to the advisers concerned.

Careful analysis of data will locate the remediable causes for a considerable percentage of failures, many of which are otherwise not readily discernible.

The following cases are illustrative of the causes of poor work and the remedial treatment prescribed:

Pupil A. Inability to read effectively. Remedy: Training in reading.

Pupil B. General poor health and lacking of vitality. Remedy: Light program; tactful management.

Pupil C. Imaginary illness. Remedy: Enlightenment of parents and pupil on point; better attendance.

Pupil D. Stomach disorder, causing nervousness. Remedy: Medical treatment.

Pupil E. Worked in army store from 7 to 12 in evenings. Remedy: Lighter program; parents consulted about more sleep.

Pupil F. Engaged in milking and delivering milk from 5 to 8 A.M. Remedy: Lightening pupil's work program to from 6:30 to 8:30 A.M.

Pupil G. Dreamer in class—never paid attention. Remedy: Trained to check self; taking notes on trend of recitation; influenced largely by inspiration of adviser.

Pupil H. General lack of interest and of taste for school. Remedy: Personal interest of teachers.

Pupil I. Speech disability and emotional complications. Remedy: Special speech instruction; diplomatic handling by teachers.

Pupil J. Interested only in drawing—no interest in other subjects. Remedy: Change of program—dropping certain most distasteful subjects; talents employed in all school affairs.

Pupil K. Eyesight poor; headaches; disliked to study—made him nervous. Remedy: Glasses provided as loan from available fund.

Pupil L. General lack of interest. Parents, who were both employed, frequently quarreled, no check on boy, who spent time in pool halls and around depot. Remedy: Parents arranged to check more closely—to give more attention to boy and his interests; companionship and leisure in home.

Pupil M. Bright-looking girl with low I.Q.; fooled teacher as to intelligence.

Remedy: Changed program of study; teachers informed; given more help and attention in supervised-study period.

Pupil N. Disliked two teachers. Remedy: Transferred to other teachers.

In addition to uncovering useful data that may explain poor work, conferences of pupils with the principal, counselors, or instructors very often result (1) in causing pupils to see the importance of going on with school and doing satisfactory work, (2) in breaking down antagonisms toward the school, the teachers, or principal, (3) in causing the pupils to see and appreciate the importance of their own delinquencies, (4) in convincing them of the value of the subjects in which they are failing, and (5) in stimulating them to think through their plans rather than drifting as they have been doing.

CLOSE CO-OPERATION BETWEEN PARENTS AND SCHOOL. The administration of the school should proceed on the principle that the parents are even more concerned than the school with pupils' failure. The fact that not all parents appear to appreciate the interest of the school should not be taken to mean that they will not co-operate, or even that they are not actually appreciative. The disappointment and embarrassment of the parent often obscure the appreciation he feels and often serve to delay the feeling and expression of appreciation. In Chapter 17 forms for calling the attention of parents to failing or unsatisfactory work on the part of the pupil are shown and discussed. In order to obtain the co-operative effort which will be most helpful to the pupil, these forms should always invite conferences for exchange of data about the pupil. Statements of parents about the pupil's peculiar traits, favorable modes of approach, and failures of the school to reach the pupil in some way or another should not, as is often the case, be taken too lightly. Principals and teachers may often acquire from parents even more information about pupils which will be of practical use, if employed properly, than parents may learn from the school. Of course, allowances must be made for what may be known or thought to be the peculiarities of the particular parent.

Parents should not be interviewed with the sole purpose of discovering causes of failure; they should be advised frankly as to how out-of-school factors may be improved to advantage, if there is sufficient basis to validate such suggestions.

VARIATION IN STUDENT LOAD. Careful investigations have yielded two clear and very important conclusions: (1) abler students, the upper 25 to 35 per cent (in average mark and intelligence-test score) of the average high-school student body, may with diligence do superior work in five full-unit (solid) subjects, the upper 10 per cent being able to carry five and a half or six units; (2) students doing poor work with four subjects do very little, if any, better with the three subjects remaining after one is dropped.

For the student who is doing unsatisfactory work in his subjects, some approach ordinarily should be discovered that is more effective than having him drop a subject. Dropping a subject, to be successful, should be resorted to only in cases where the student is doing a great deal of outside work or possesses a violent dislike for a particular subject.

Where possible, when a subject is dropped, the student should be scheduled to enter some other class as a substitute.

Sometimes it will be found that the student's poor work in a subject grows out of a student's dislike of the teacher or his feeling that the teacher is unfair to him. Some of these cases should be investigated thoroughly with a view to scheduling the student with another teacher who teaches a similar section of the same subject.

ADAPTATION AND ADMINISTRATION OF COURSES OF STUDY. One of the best approaches to the problem of individual differences lies in provision for students to work in subjects or materials suited to their interests, abilities, needs, and backgrounds. It is unfortunate that teachers seem to be so inept in making such provision; they need much in-service training. Occasionally a specialist should be called in for a few days or a week, if not for a semester or a year, to lead the way. Many teachers seem to get little farther than prescribing more or less of the material of the regular course, usually pitched at the level of the high-middle group in class, or, at best, harder or easier materials, with little consideration of pupils' interests, tastes, needs, or backgrounds.

The chances of successful adaptation are much greater if the school is operating on a long-period supervised-study plan in which teachers spend not more than half of the class-period time in "recitation." This plan affords the teacher time for individual and small-group conferences in which special assignments are given and individual interests discovered. Also at this time, the teacher has opportunity to become better informed concerning the nature and causes of the weaknesses of the individual student and, perhaps, to give a little individual instruction. Better pupil-teacher relationships may be developed as the outcome of more personal contact and the opportunity afforded to demonstrate interest in the individual pupil.

APPROPRIATE TEACHING METHODS. Teachers also need to be encouraged and trained in methods of adaptation of learning materials and activities to the capacities, interests, and needs of the individual student. Fundamental to such methods is a wealth of knowledge about each individual, his tests and achievement record, his extracurricular and out-of-school interests and activities, and his opportunities at home and elsewhere for looking up topics, getting information from others, and carrying on projects.

The teacher should be encouraged to employ all sorts of adaptations in the distribution of individual assignments, in the distribution of questions in class discussions, in his methods of motivating the individual, of encouraging him, and of discouraging misconduct or undesirable tendencies, and in every other contact. He should be encouraged to employ supervised-study time in such a way as to have personal conferences and thus establish good relations, discover areas and causes of unsatisfactory achievement in terms of the individual's capacities, etc. He should be given every encouragement to do diagnostic testing and to provide remedial instruction, particularly in sequential subjects such as foreign languages and mathematics.

REMEDIAL-READING CLASSES. A type of special class which has been employed in a rapidly increasing number of schools in recent years is the class in remedial reading for defective readers. Because of the importance of reading ability in the study of nearly all subjects, one of the most common causes of unsatisfactory work has been found to be poor reading ability and reading habits. Remedial classes have been found to contribute materially to the scholastic success of most pupils enrolled in them. Reading tests should be given to pupils in the lowest half of the class and to all others whose achievement is well below what might be expected on the basis of their I.Q.'s. Those found to have reading ability definitely below that which is normal for their grade should be encouraged, if not required, to enter, at least for a few months, a remedial-reading class. Teachers of such classes, if not possessing special training for remedial-reading work, should be encouraged to read the recent literature in that field.

HOME VISITATION. In gathering information concerning the individual pupil, home visitation is one of the most fruitful procedures. Information of a type not otherwise available and special insights are obtained. This is particularly the case with problem youths. Information is obtained concerning not only the youngster but also the home and parents, which information may throw much light upon behavior at school and enable the teacher to think better in terms of what he can or cannot expect in the way of homework.

Frequently, too, a relationship of effective co-operation is thus established between home and school, enabling both to pool their resources in working with the individual boy or girl. Teachers need to be trained for home visitation. It can be harmful or wasteful, as well as very useful. Teachers must be most judicious in discussing children with parents. In fact, teachers must learn to be discreet listeners rather than talkers.

THE USE OF COUNSELORS AND COUNSELING. More and more in public schools counselors are being employed to assist teachers to solve problems relative to the progress of the youngsters and to assist the youngsters to solve their problems in this area. The counselors can render much valuable assistance to teachers by participating in the diagnosis of the causes of failure and by helping students to ameliorate or remove these impediments to achievement, be they environmental, emotional, or based on a lack of ability. The counselor's primary contribution should be as a consultant; care should be taken that he not be assigned responsibility for routine interviewing of failing pupils to the point where duty colors his relationships with pupils and prevents him from devoting the major portion of his energies to constructive and preventative activities.

The counselors may also carry on some home-visitation activities as a means of diagnosing pupil difficulty and problems and of assisting in educating the parents to the situation and obtaining their intelligent cooperation. They may assist parents in making more practical and intelligent interpretation of the marks which students of less ability may receive. They may also discuss with parents the advisability of putting students with limited ability into sections which are especially organized for them, sections in which the instructional material has been especially adapted to the needs of the youngsters who have limited abilities, limited background in a subject, or both.

THE UNDERACHIEVER. In every school there are some students who may be classified as underachievers. The underachiever is one whose intelligence quotient, mental age, and reading ability indicate that he is capable of doing definitely better work than he is doing. Underachievement represents a great loss of talent and underachievers should be investigated carefully by the counselor and principal; conferences should be held with parents to see if the cause or causes of the underachievement may be ascertained and if something may be done to result in the underachieving students' doing a quality of work which is in harmony with their potentialities.[5]

Problems, Questions, and Exercises

1. Tell what is meant by strength, universality, and administrative convenience as criteria for evaluating various procedures to stimulate learning activity. Apply these criteria to each of three different procedures used in school. Select your procedures so that they show up differently on the criteria.
2. Be able to discuss testing programs and scholarship contests as means of encouraging activities.
3. What is your opinion of the value and the limitations of the National Honor Society? Would you have a chapter in the school in which you are principal? If so, what would be its activities?
4. Be able to discuss marks as an incentive to study, emphasizing the dangers of marks and how to avoid them.
5. What do you think are the best ways to train high-school students in study habits and study skills—in class, out of class, or both?

[5]See *Factors Related to Scholastic Underachievement* by Paul H. Bowman, Quincy Youth Development Project, 25 North Seventh Street, Quincy, Illinois.

6. What do you think is the place of study halls in school today? What are the trends? What are the advantages and limitations?
7. What are the principal objections to ability grouping; how may they be minimized or avoided?
8. How would you proceed, as a principal of a school of 400 students, to make the best provision possible for adapting instructional materials and methods to the individual interests, capacities, educational background, temperament, home background, and present and future needs of high-school students? Consider each of these types of variation separately.
9. Prepare notes for a discussion of the desirability of offering honors courses and independent seminars; give suggestions for operating them.
10. Be able to discuss the acceleration of bright students, giving both sides of the question and your own conclusions.
11. What is the place of remedial instruction in high school and how is it provided for?
12. As a high-school principal of 480 students, how would you proceed to organize and carry on a program for reducing the number of failures in school?
13. In reducing the number of failures in a school, tell how you might employ home visitation and counseling by other than classroom teachers.
14. What is the relationship between courses of study and failure?
15. Make a list of what you think are five or six of the most important suggestions for planning learning activities for the bright students in a class of youngsters of varying ability. Do this for the teaching of dull students in a similar situation.
16. Be able to describe the Trump plan of team teaching and to point out its possible advantages, its limitations, and what you think are the important factors in its possible success.

Selected Supplementary Readings

"The Academically Talented," *School and Society* (April 11, 1959), Vol. 87. [Entire issue; several articles.]

"Administration Procedures and School Practices for the Academically Talented Student in the Secondary School," *Bulletin of the N.A.S.S.P.* (May, 1960), No. 256, pp. 1-224. [Identifying and providing programs for gifted and accelerated; enrichment and grouping programs; programs in use in the United States.]

"Advancement Placement Programs in Secondary Schools," *Bulletin of the N.A.S.S.P.* (December, 1958), No. 242, pp. 1-171. [Contains descriptions of programs in a number of high schools and syllabi for eleven different subjects.]

Anderson, Lester W., Fergason, J. E., and Atkinson, Stewart B., "How to Modify the Curriculum to Benefit the Academically Talented Student?" *Bulletin of the N.A.S.S.P.* (April, 1961), No. 264, pp. 243-247.

Applebaum, M. J., "A Survey of Special Provisions for the Education of Academically Superior Pupils," *Bulletin of the N.A.S.S.P.* (October, 1959), No. 249, pp. 26-43.

Arbolino, J. N., "What's Wrong with the Advanced Placement Program," *Bulletin of the N.A.S.S.P.* (February, 1961), No. 262, pp. 28-31.

Ball, R. A., Isacksen, R. O., Veit, Charles, and Woodbury, S. T., "How Can We Better Motivate the Under-Achiever and the Indifferent Student?" *Bulletin of the N.A.S.S.P.* (April, 1960), No. 255, pp. 174-180.

Bish, Charles E., "Teaching the Upper Fifteen Per Cent," *Clearing House* (May, 1959), Vol. 33, pp. 515-518; also *Education Digest* (October, 1959), Vol. 25, pp. 12-14.
Bish, Charles E., and Gilliland, Minnis, "A Program for the Academically Talented in Science," *Bulletin of the N.A.S.S.P.* (December, 1960), No. 260, pp. 138-144.
Bowman, Paul H., *Factors Related to Scholastic Underachievement,* Quincy, Illinois, Quincy Youth Development Project.
Brimm, R. P., Merz, Albert F., Jr., and Peebles, James M., "Thorny Problems—How to Weigh Student Marks in Honors Courses?" *Bulletin of the N.A.S.S.P.* (April, 1961), Vol. 45, pp. 43-48.
Broberg, Edith H., "The Study-Hall Supervisor," *Clearing House* (November, 1951), Vol. 26, pp. 154-156. [The possibilities of a specialist.]
Brock, C. A., Fitzpatrick, Dave, Mastin, A. W., and Northam, M. E., "How Can the Junior High School Provide Quality Education for the Academically Talented Student?" *Bulletin of the N.A.S.S.P.* (April, 1960), No. 255, pp. 139-145.
Carlsen, G. Robert, and Beck, Willard R., "How to Improve the Reading Skills and Habits of Junior High-School Students," *Bulletin of the N.A.S.S.P.* (April, 1961), No. 264, pp. 264-270.
Chaffee, Everett, "Programs for the Gifted in California Secondary Schools," *Bulletin of the N.A.S.S.P.* (February, 1960), No. 253, pp. 110-114.
Conant, James B., "Development of Talent in Europe and the United States," *North Central Association Quarterly* (April, 1960), Vol. 24, pp. 265-272; also *Education Digest* (September, 1960), Vol. 26, No. 1, pp. 16-18.
Cuony, E. R., "Integration for Educable Mentally Retarded Pupils in the Junior High School," *Bulletin of the N.A.S.S.P.* (November, 1960), No. 259, pp. 87-91.
Davis, L. R., and Davis, Jacqueline, "What Principals Should Know about Remedial Reading," *Clearing House* (January, 1955), Vol. 29, pp. 298-300.
Dodds, B. L., "What is a Good Program for the Slow Learner?" *Bulletin of the N.A.S.S.P.* (March, 1952), No. 185, pp. 329-336.
Dudley, D. A., and others, "Advanced Placement Programs in Secondary Schools," *Bulletin of the N.A.S.S.P.* (December, 1958), No. 242, pp. 1-183.
Dunn, Lloyd M., and others, "The Education of Handicapped and Gifted Pupils in the Secondary School," *Bulletin of the N.A.S.S.P.* (January, 1955), No. 207, pp. 3-154.
Educational Policies Commission, "Individual Differences," *Education for All American Youth,* 1952, pp. 23-28, 84-87, 45-46, 220-226, 288-314, 311-313, 376-378, and 256-259.
Feeman, Hyrtl C., "The Role of a Junior Honor Society in the Senior High School," *Bulletin of the N.A.S.S.P.* (March, 1951), No. 177, pp. 245-247.
Ferguson, W. J., "A Report on a Junior High School Program for the Gifted," *Bulletin of the N.A.S.S.P.* (November, 1960), No. 259, pp. 79-82.
Finding and Educating the Academically Talented Child in the Secondary School, Washington, D.C., National Education Association, 1958.
Flory, Vera, "A Working Program for the Gifted," *Bulletin of the N.A.S.S.P.* (September, 1956), No. 221, pp. 82-88.
Fry, Edward B., Bryan, Glenn L., and Rigney, Joseph W., *Teaching Machines: An Annotated Bibliography,* (Supplement to *AV Communication Review*), Washington, D.C., National Education Association, Department of Audio-Visual Instruction, 1960.

Gifted Child in California, Sacramento, State Advisory Council on Educational Research, December, 1955. [Brief description of programs in thirteen California cities.

Gluck, Harold, "The Study Hall; A Place to Study," *Catholic School Journal* (March, 1948), Vol. 48, No. 3, pp. 12-21. [Suggests ways and means of organizing the study hall.]

Gruhn, William T., and Douglass, Harl R., *The Modern Junior High School*, New York, Ronald, 1956. [Chapter 10, "Meeting Individual Differences."]

Havinghurst, Robert J., and others, *Education of the Gifted*, Fifty-seventh Yearbook, Part II, National Society for the Study of Education, University of Chicago Press, 1958.

Hook, J. N., "The Principal and the Superior English Student," *Bulletin of the N.A.S.S.P.* (February, 1961), No. 262, pp. 13-19.

Howell, Wallace J., "Grouping of Talented Students Leads to Better Achievement in the Secondary School," *Bulletin of the N.A.S.S.P.* (April, 1962), No. 272, pp. 67-71.

Jackson, Arthur, "A Crash Program for the Education of Negro Youth," *Negro Education Review* (July, 1958), Vol. 9, pp. 111-116.

Janes, H. Paul, "How About a Special Adjustment Coach in the High School?" *School Executive* (November, 1949), Vol. 69, p. 44. [Describes an experimental program organized to care for educationally frustrated children.]

Jenks, W. F., "The Mentally Retarded in High School," *Catholic School Journal* (January and February, 1960), Vol. 60, pp. 17-20, 34-35.

Jewett, Arno, Poe, J. Dan, and others, *Teaching Rapid and Slow Learners in High School*, Washington, D.C., U. S. Department of Health, Education, and Welfare, 1954.

Jones, Reginald, and Baxter, Joseph R., "Parents' Views on the Acceleration of Superior High School Students," *Bulletin of the N.A.S.S.P.* (March, 1962), No. 272, pp. 24-29.

Josina, Sister M. (F.S.P.A.), "An Honor Roll That Is an Honor Roll," *Catholic Educational Review* (November, 1950), No. 48, pp. 615-616. [A scholastic honor roll based on a deviation table; a plan for recognizing deserving pupils, which also affords an opportunity for objective guidance, since it takes into consideration the individual of low intelligence.

Long, Howard H., "The Relative Learning Capacity of Negroes and Whites," *Journal of Negro Education* (Spring, 1957), Vol. 26, pp. 121-134.

Long, Watt A., "Senior High School Study Halls—Their Educational Function," *California Journal of Educational Research* (March, 1952), Vol. 3, pp. 74-79. [Reports a study which surveyed 2820 students enrolled in 53 study halls to ascertain the external and internal conditions which affect the pursuit of satisfactory independent study.]

Maybee, G. Davis, and Myers, L. L., "How Can Junior High Schools Best Provide for Academically Talented Students," *Bulletin of the N.A.S.S.P.* (April, 1959), No. 246, pp. 19-23.

Meade, Mary E., Campbell, H. C., and Sorenson, R. K., "The Case For and Against Multiple High-School Diplomas," *Bulletin of the N.A.S.S.P.* (April, 1961), No. 264, pp. 29-33.

Mersand, Joseph, "Individualizing Instruction in Large and Small Classes," *Bulletin of the N.A.S.S.P.* (March, 1960), No. 254, pp. 111-123.

Miller, Leonard N., and others, *Guidance for the Underachiever with Superior Ability,* Office of Education, Bulletin 1961, No. 25, 85 pp.
Mills, Hubert H., and Douglass, Harl R., *Teaching in High School* (Second Edition), New York, Ronald, 1957. [Chapter 5, "Understanding the Student"; Chapter 23, "Adapting the Teaching to the Individual."]
Morton, M. S., "Teacher Load and the Gifted Pupil," *Bulletin of the N.A.S.S.P.* (March, 1960), No. 254, pp. 60-64.
Newton, D. E., "Curricular and Instructional Practices for Superior Students," *Bulletin of the N.A.S.S.P.* (February, 1961), No. 262, pp. 23-27.
Peake, Frank A., Janke, George, W., and Ortt, C. H., "Developing Tomorrow's Leaders Today Through the National Honor Society," *Bulletin of the N.A.S.S.P.* (April, 1961), No. 264, pp. 238-242.
Programs for the Gifted: A Casebook in Secondary Education, Samuel Everett, ed., New York, Harper, 1961. [A description of a number of programs in secondary schools.]
Silverman, Hirsch Lazaar, "Educational 'Unadaptives' and the Schools," *Bulletin of the N.A.S.S.P.* (October, 1958), No. 240, pp. 129-133.
"Teaching Rapid and Slow Learners," *High School Bulletin* (No. 5), Washington, D.C., U. S. Department of Health, Education and Welfare, 1954.
Thelan, Herbert A., "Classroom Grouping of Students," *School Review,* (Spring, 1959), Vol. 67, pp. 60-78.
Tolarro, Morris, "The Mentally Handicapped Child in High School," *Education Digest* (September, 1960), Vol. 26, No. 1, pp. 45-47.
Tucker, Hazel, "The Fresno High School Plan," *Bulletin of the N.A.S.S.P.* (March, 1960), No. 253, pp. 58-60. [A plan of curriculum organization for students of differing academic interests, abilities, and needs.]
Watts, Mrs. J. C., "A Study of High School Failure," *Bulletin of the N.A.S.S.P.* (October, 1959), No. 249, pp. 69-75.
Yorgan, D. G., "Lincoln Junior High School Administers an Accelerated Program for Superior Students," *Bulletin of the N.A.S.S.P.* (March, 1960), No. 254, pp. 65-70.
Zenner, E. A., "High School Honors Course," *Catholic School Journal* (March, 1959), Vol. 59, pp. 80-81.

10

Administering the Extra-Class Activity Program

1. The Place of Student Organizations In Secondary Education

A good percentage of the time spent by the typical secondary-school principal in his professional duties is related to problems of administration and supervision of the student activities or extra-class program. The amount of time spent in this area of activity has increased through the years, especially as the percentage of students of lesser academic interests and abilities attending schools has increased.

THE RELATION OF ACTIVITIES TO THE OBJECTIVES OF SECONDARY EDUCATION. One should bear in mind that stimuli to educational activity are not confined to textbooks, subjects, or organized bodies of knowledge. Any type of object, situation, or impression that stimulates in an individual mental or physical activity which results in modification or control of future behavior in the direction of the objectives of education is legitimate subject matter for education. Contributions to these objectives are made through the acquisition of information, skills and habits, ideals, tastes, and interests. To many it seems obvious that activities may be so managed as to make valuable contributions to these objectives. The lists on pages 199-200 illustrate the possible contributions of participation in extracurricular activities to the objectives of secondary education.[1] The lists are not intended to be exhaustive; they are merely illustrative of the possible educational values of activities.

OTHER DESIRABLE OUTCOMES OF PARTICIPATION IN EXTRA-CLASS ACTIVITIES. As important means of realizing the objectives of secondary education, well-managed programs of activities make contributions which should not be overlooked; they are important in: (1) exploring student interests and capacities for growth; (2) developing school loyalty and

[1]Athletics will be discussed separately in a later chapter in this book.

Contributions of Activity Participation to Objectives of Secondary Education

Objective	Type of Outcome	Contributing Activity
Health and safety	Information about sports, games, animals, flowers, plants, scientific basis of health and sanitation, first aid, fire and accident prevention. Habits and skills in games, sports, outdoor activities, dancing, first aid, avoiding accident; general bodily skill and strength. Ideals of sound, healthy bodies and proficiency in physical activities. Tastes and interests in outdoor sports and health.	Athletic teams of all sorts, hiking, outdoor clubs, biology clubs, nursing club, dancing, Junior Red Cross.
Vocation	Information concerning occupations (nature of work, rewards, chance for advancement, etc.) and concerning pupils' abilities in different pursuits—information underlying choice of vocation. Habits and skills: those general habits (honesty, industry, and ambition) that make for vocational success; skills in vocations or activities common to several vocations (salesmanship, accounting, writing). Ideals: of success, influence, independence, fair dealing, cooperation, and service. Tastes and interests: explorations of such as a basis for vocational choice.	Sports and games, musical and other fine-arts clubs, journalistic and forensic clubs, semiscientific clubs (radio, photography, automotive, aëronautic); semivocational clubs (printing, millinery, cartooning, agricultural, and commercial clubs).
Worthy use of leisure	Information about things of culture: art, music, drama, current and classical literature, and authors; about current social problems and events; about games and sports; about nature, scientific phenomena and laws. Habits and skills: in fine arts, games and sports, and reading. Ideals of culture, dignity, and self-respect; of approval of others in such matters. Tastes and interests in fine arts, sports, games, hobbies of various sorts.	Athletic and other sports; chess, checkers, and other games; musical and other fine-arts clubs; foreign-language clubs; mathematical clubs; dramatic clubs; reading clubs; history clubs; sewing and basketry clubs; short-story clubs; radio, motion-picture, and television clubs.

Objective	Type of Outcome	Contributing Activity
Command of fundamental processes	Information—how to read, to study, to write, to speak, to solve problems. Habits and skills in the application of computation, study methods, skills in written and oral communication. Ideals, tastes, and interests: continuation of desirable types begun in elementary school.	Practically every activity, particularly those involving reading books, writing reports, keeping accounts, giving oral reports, or participating in discussions (journalistic and forensic activity).
Worthy home membership	Information about things of culture, human nature and character, biology, sanitation, household decoration, purchasing, budgeting, diet and nursing, preparation of foods, construction and repair of clothing, household machines, children's reading. Habits and skills in fields mentioned above. Ideals: culture, monogamy, fair play, courtesy, co-operation, happy and beautiful homes. Tastes and interests in fields named above, in artistic things, and in games and sports.	All sorts of fine-arts clubs, household-arts clubs, and semi-scientific clubs. All clubs, insofar as they develop an understanding of human nature and psychology and of how to get on in close contact with others.
Citizenship and ethical character	Information about government (national, state, and local), public utilities, community organizations, results of unsocial acts or neglect. Habits and skills: in getting along in group activities as followers and as leaders, respecting feelings and rights of others, repressing unsocial impulses, thinking through consequences of behavior. Ideals and attitudes: "the group above the individual," fair play, service, patriotism, favorable social attitudes, and attitudes toward self resulting from "belonging" and participating. Tastes and interests: in local and other social institutions, in justice and fair play, in the welfare of others, in religious motivations and philosophies; antagonism toward unsocial ideas and acts.	All organizations involving group efforts: student government, teams, civic clubs, letter clubs, traditions clubs or committees, Girl Reserves, Girl Scouts and Boy Scouts, Hi-Y clubs, service clubs, religious clubs.

happiness in school life; (3) developing personality and contributing to its mental hygiene and health; (4) understanding the theory of democracy; (5) establishing habits of democratic action; (6) developing intelligent leadership and followership; (7) increasing the power of self-direction; (8) developing a sense of personal responsibility and favorable attitudes to and skills in social co-operation; and (9) developing respect for orderly procedures and duly constituted authority of a variety of types.

2. *Dangers and Limitations of Activities*

All plans for setting up and administering pupil clubs and organizations in schools should be thought through in full view of their dangers and alleged evils. Most prominent among these are the following:

1. Interference with scholarship.
2. Unwise increase in principal's and teachers' loads.
3. Failure of activities to achieve desirable outcomes.
4. Excessive costs to students.
5. Excessive emphasis upon competition.
6. Excessive emphasis upon developing perfection in activities which lead up to performance before the public, such as plays and operettas.

INTERFERENCE WITH SCHOLARSHIP. In view of the results of statistical studies reported, it is probable that the fear of the interference of participation in activities with the scholarship of participants has been largely without basis and that one must look to other factors for the explanation of inferior achievement of present-day high-school pupils, if indeed inferior achievement may be found actually to exist. Studies relating to the question seem to indicate rather clearly that participation to a moderate degree in activities has little or no undesirable effect upon scholarship. Participants in activities receive marks as high as those of nonparticipants, or even higher. Those instances in which the data show that leaders and participants in nonathletic activities seem to surpass the average of non-participants and that participants in athletic activities often do not do as well may be largely accounted for by the fact that on the average nonathletic participants score higher on intelligence tests than do athletes. It has been definitely shown in a number of high schools that students, with the exception of those participating in athletics, make as high marks while they are participating in extracurricular activities as when they are not participating.

OVERLOADING THE PRINCIPALS AND TEACHERS. When teachers give considerable time to assisting students in their activities, the school day becomes appreciably longer for them—for many teachers, an hour or more longer. Giving teachers extra pay for time spent in connection with extra-class activities in addition to their full teaching assignments is almost certain to lead to difficulties in determining the relative values of teachers' services in connection with different activities; the increased time spent on activities is likely to reduce the time that may be given to duties connected with the teaching assignment.

Apparently sponsors of extracurricular activities in many schools are given extra pay running from $200 to $600; the larger amounts seem to be paid to athletic coaches.[2]

The organization, the administration, and in smaller schools the actual advising of student organizations have added no small increment of responsibility and work to the burden of the already overloaded high-school principal. This condition is one more argument for freeing the principal in small schools from teaching and for providing the principal in large schools with executive, supervisory, and clerical assistance. There have already been established in an increasing number of secondary schools directors of activities, who relieve principals of the details of administrative problems connected with the activity program and who guide and train teachers in their advisory duties.

NONEDUCATIVE ACTIVITY. Just as in the selection of studies it is difficult to determine the ultimate relative value of various units or items, so it is difficult to say which phases of various activities have sufficient educative values and which do not. There is considerable probability that many activities involve an expenditure of time, without adequate educational return, in duplication of training and in relatively useless activity. It is very likely, for example, that the soliciting of advertisements or subscriptions in any given field and the selling of candy or other things to raise money soon exhaust their profitable educational possibilities for any one individual. It is also questionable whether the great amount of time spent in polishing many dramatic productions is economical from the standpoint of educational returns. On these points advisers will have to learn to do practical thinking in terms of educational values, and principals and other directors of activities will have to guide them in doing so.

STUDENT MISMANAGEMENT. Of the more prominent types of student mismanagement are the following: the mismanagement of funds and business contracts, excessive expenditures, the development of selfish cliques, and the participation in unconventional or undesirable activities which reflect discredit upon the school. Corrections of such mismanagement fall into these categories: a sound, businesslike system of fund administration and accounting; a careful, diplomatic but firm limi-

[2]*Extra Pay Provisions in 1959-60 Salary Schedules* (Educational Research Service Circular), Washington, D.C., National Education Association, May, 1960.

tation of expenditures by organizations and by individuals; countereducation and the development of a counterspirit against exploitation by cliques; a carefully administered system of chartering and approving organizations dependent upon good behavior; and a careful check upon organizations by advisers.

Much of the misdirection and overemphasis of activities on the part of both adviser and pupils is stimulated by state or district contests for championship typing, debating, and athletic teams; for prize annuals, journals, and newspapers; for championship glee clubs, orchestras, and bands; and for prize dramatic presentations. Though they are often sponsored by higher educational institutions in the interest of such activities, such contests usually lead to the overtraining of a few of the best participants to the neglect of others, as well as to the neglect of studies and other activities on the part of the contestants. Excessively expensive annuals may in many instances be attributed in part to such a stimulus of competition. The tendency to lower all activities to the plane to which athletics has fallen should be checked by principal and advisers.

COSTS TO PUPILS. It has been shown by Punke, Jacobson, Hand, and other investigators that the cost of participation in extracurricular activities in many instances is excessive and in a great majority of instances is sufficient to tend to bar from participation in extracurricular activities some students coming from homes of the lowest incomes.

At first including only admissions to athletic events and plays, class pins, and a modest school annual, the annual costs in many senior high schools have increased to more than $100 per pupil, including costumes, dues in clubs, school parties and dances, subscriptions to school papers and to periodicals for use in classes, rental fees for typewriters, laboratory fees, library fees, school jewelry, initiation into fraternities and sororities, use of automobiles for school functions, workbooks and materials for shop and instruction, and a school annual, which costs as much as college annuals used to and also involves costs for pictures.

As a result of these increased costs of participation in the normal activities of the high school, American secondary education is no longer free. It has been rapidly becoming a commercial commodity. When one also takes into consideration the increased costs of the clothing and extraschool social life of high-school pupils, one understands how it is that many splendid boys and girls, guilty of nothing more culpable than having been born to poor fathers and mothers, are made to feel most uncomfortable while attending high school. Such a situation has undesirable effects upon self-assurance and other aspects of personality development; it also develops unfavorable attitudes toward the school and public education, toward American democracy, and toward more fortunate classes of society.

In recent years measures have been taken in many schools to keep down the costs of participation in extra-class activities. Sponsors and student councils have exerted effective influence in this direction in many schools. In keeping down costs to pupils participating in pupils' organizations, the secondary-school administrator is rendering a valuable service to pupils, parents, public education, and American democracy.

In recent years there has been an increase in the number of schools in which some of the costs of various extracurricular activities are borne by public funds administered by the board of education. If the extracurricular program is definitely a part of the educational program, there is much logic in this practice.

3. Developing a Program of Student Organizations

WHAT ACTIVITIES SHOULD BE MAINTAINED. The following criteria should be considered in determining which activities should be represented in any given school:

1. No activity should be organized which requires stronger stimulus than casual suggestion and encouragement from the principal or another member of the staff.
2. No activity should be organized or maintained which, because of the lack of local support outside the school, the unwillingness of the board of education to assume financial responsibility, or the small number of pupils, requires excessive expenditure on the part of pupils.
3. No activity should be permitted to continue as a school activity which is not democratic in its membership, or which will not submit to school regulations for activities and respond reasonably well to advisory control.
4. No activity should be encouraged which does not promise a favorable excess of beneficial results over harmful educational results or difficulties of management, or which does not produce desirable educational returns in proportion to expenditures of time.
5. The number of activities should be kept down to such a point that a reasonable quality of work may be done in them without excessive activity loads upon the more talented pupils.
6. No activity should be maintained for which a capable and reliable adviser cannot be found.
7. Activities should be sufficient in number to provide opportunities for all pupils desiring to participate.
8. Within the bounds mentioned above, as wide a range as possible of types of activities should be organized and maintained.

Besides such conventional athletic teams as the school is large enough to support, ordinarily there should be maintained, in every school large enough to maintain them, one organization of each of the following types of activities:

Student associations.
Forensics.
Dramatics.

School-news departments or newspapers.
Glee clubs or other choral organizations.
Orchestra, band, or both.
One or more semiscientific activities: for example, camera, radio, automobile, and aëronautic clubs.
One or more character clubs for girls: for example, Girl Scout, Girl Reserve, and Camp Fire organizations.
One or more character clubs for boys: for example, Hi-Y, Boy Scout, and civic-improvement organizations.
Exercise and sport clubs: for example, golf, tennis, hiking.

A very useful means of surveying the need for various organizations is the interest-analysis questionnaire. This questionnaire and its use are described later in this chapter.

INITIATING OR CHARTERING ACTIVITIES. Activities should not be unduly urged upon pupils. If pointing out the possibilities of a new activity to a few pupils most likely to be interested does not result in their sincere desire to organize and maintain that activity, the matter should probably be dropped. It is more desirable that the idea of organizing an activity originate with a group of interested pupils. Activities in which the interest of pupils has ebbed should not be continued as prefunctory, lifeless formalities.

The approval of the principal for every new activity should be required. Consideration of a new activity should be contingent upon the presentation of a petition which states the objects of the organization and is signed by a number of interested pupils. It would not be a bad procedure to require annual petitions by each new group of students and officers as a means of bringing to their attention that activities exist by permission of the administration of the school.

In many schools there exists a practice, perhaps a good one, requiring the approval of the student council for the initiation of any new activities and the continuance of any activity the existence of which is under question.

4. Encouraging and Regulating Student Participation

The problem of reaching all pupils with at least one form of activity is as important and as baffling as that of maintaining a balance between the curricular and extracurricular activities of the more capable and versatile pupils. Unfortunately mistakes have been made in attempting to ensure that all students participate in some activity; for example, there has been the practice of requiring a certain specified number of activity points for graduation or of requiring a choice on the part of every pupil of at least one activity in which he will participate. Among the important sources of value of any activity as an educative agent are the interest, spontaneity, and initiative shown by the pupil participant. If pupils are required or pressed to participate in an activity, the activity is more than likely to give many of these students few of its unique advantages and all of its disadvantages.

Among methods of bringing about general participation are the following, which have been employed frequently with success:

1. Publicizing activities and the activity program through handbooks, bulletin boards, assemblies, and daily bulletins.
2. Employing interest-analysis questionnaires.
3. Allowing credit toward graduation.
4. Giving letters, awards, certificates, or prizes based on participation.
5. Developing student approval of participation in activities.

THE INTEREST-ANALYSIS QUESTIONNAIRE. In some schools, at the beginning of the year or the semester, a questionnaire similar to that reproduced below is handed to each pupil in the assembly room or roll room; he is asked to fill it out and return it within a few days. If a copy has been placed on the bulletin board a few days in advance, with notice of the purpose of the questionnaire, or if it has been explained in the assembly or roll room in advance, so that the pupil may have had opportunity to consider the matter, the questionnaire may be filled out when it is received and returned at once, thus avoiding difficulty in collecting the forms. The list of activities mentioned in the questionnaire should be made up from all activities or organizations which exist in the school, or which might be organized if there were sufficient demand. Excerpts from a widely used activity questionnaire are given on page 207.

On the basis of the tabulated returns of such a questionnaire, invitations should be extended, perhaps by means of the bulletin board and announcement in the roll room, to students interested in membership or tryouts for membership in the activities preferred.

THE STUDENT BULLETIN. In a number of schools there is issued to the students one or more times a week, through the public-address system or in mimeographed form, a bulletin containing news about the school, including news about various extracurricular activities. These announcements have been found to be effective in increasing interest in student activities.

CREDIT TOWARD GRADUATION. Despite the fact that as yet colleges and universities will not recognize for entrance any credits awarded for activities, many schools have arranged to grant credits toward graduation for participation in activities. Some administrators do not believe in giving credits for participation in activities, thinking that the student should participate through sheer interest or not at all. Some schools award fractional credits for specified major activities: for example, one quarter unit each semester for membership in the glee club. Others have

FORM 1. *Interest-Analysis Questionnaire*

Name________________ Sex__________ Age__________ Class__________

Directions. *Below is a list of possible activities. Draw a circle around the number preceding each thing you like to do.*

1. Draw cartoons. 2. Cook and serve luncheons. 3. Design and make costumes for plays and parties. 4. Make posters to advertise parties, games, plays, and so on. 5. Embroider, tat, and knit.

6. Learn about the city you live in. 7. Learn how to be a good officer. 8. Learn how to conduct an office successfully. 9. Study what is proper to wear at a dance, at a party, or when traveling. 10. Find out just what is best to eat, what exercises are best for health. 11. Belong to a boosters' club and help to boost our school.

12. Be an editor of the school paper. 13. Write items of different kinds for the school paper. 14. Write short stories. 15. Be a leader in our school activities. 16. Learn how to advertise a business. 17. Help students who have trouble with their lessons. 18. Be helpful to students having few friends.

19. Draw house plans. 20. Make cross-word puzzles. 21. Study the habits of fish, birds, animals. 22. Make such things as tables, candlesticks, cupboards, hatracks, and so on.

23. College postage stamps. 24. Learn how to take good pictures. 25. Make and use a radio set. 26. Learn how an automobile is made and works. 27. Learn military drilling.

28. Study the stars. 29. Find out what the people of other countries do and how they live. 30. Belong to a science club. 31. Learn how to give first aid. 32. Learn how to take care of the sick. 33. Learn more about space travel.

34. Dance. 35. Read good books. 36. Tell stories. 37. Hear good music. 38. Learn how motion pictures are made. 39. Attend good motion pictures. 40. Figure out queer mathematical problems. 41. Learn about people who lived in ancient times.

42. Play basketball. 43. Play baseball. 44. Play tennis. 45. Play volleyball. 46. Hiking. 47. Track. 48. Swimming. 49. Watch basketball games. 50. Watch baseball games.

51. Take part in a play. 52. Be on a debating team. 53. Take part in assembly programs. 54. Give readings. 55. Learn how to persuade people to do what you want them to do. 56. Learn how to sell things to people.

57. Sit in groups with other people. 58. Play an instrument in a band or orchestra. 59. Participate in student council, home-room committees, or other similar student groups. 60. Participate in a service club.

If there is something else you would like to do or like to learn to do, write it in here ______________________________

From those you mark select the one you would most like to do or like to learn to do and write it in here ______________________

Number of second choice ______________________

Number of third choice ______________________

developed point equivalents of credits similar to those employed for the restriction of participation. Each activity or office is assigned a specified number of points and specified numbers of points are regarded as the equivalent of a unit or fraction of a unit of credit; for example, eighty points for one unit, forty points for half a unit. The ratio of equivalents will, of course, depend upon the number of points assigned to various activities and must be determined after consideration of the time spent by earning activity points.

Point-credit accounting will be facilitated if the student organization or the principal's office furnishes "activity reports" on which the captain, the president, or the leader of each organization will report the participation of each student, an estimate of the time spent by him, and the quality of work done. Approved by the adviser and filed in the office, this report will entitle the pupil to the appropriate credit on his activity card, which is kept in the office file. A simpler method requires each student leader and faculty adviser to prepare and sign at the conclusion of the season's activities a report of the organization covering the participation of each pupil and recommending the points to be allowed to each. A suggested form to be used for that purpose is shown as Form 2.

The granting of credits for participation in activities is not without objections. Because of the varying amounts of time required by the same activity from year to year and required of different students in the same activity in the same year (for example, in different parts in a play), the

FORM 2. *Report of Activity Membership and Participation*

ACTIVITY REPORT

Name of activity or organization ______________________________

President or captain ____________ Secretary or manager ____________

Adviser ____________________ Semester ending ____________________

Approximate hours spent in meetings __ Period covered from ___ to ___

NAMES OF PARTICIPANTS	ESTIMATED HOURS OF ACTIVITY	NATURE OF ACTIVITY	QUALITY OF PARTICIPATION	POINTS RECOMMENDED

Etc.

number of points allowed will, of necessity, always be determined subjectively and be open to question. The system involves considerable bookkeeping, which is not likely to be well attended to. Activities will often not be reported and students will later ask to receive credit points for participation. The use of the system also tends to establish the atmosphere and feeling that the pupil is working for points, which is certainly not nearly so favorable a situation as that in which he engages in activities for sheer enjoyment. In schools giving credit for participation in extra-class activities, seventeen or eighteen year-units are usually required for graduation.

AWARDS OF LETTERS, INSIGNIA, AND CERTIFICATES. It is common for schools to award school letters, service stripes, and sweaters to first-string athletes. The practice in some schools has been extended to include not only managers of sports but also participants in other types of work, including debate and general leadership. This extension of the practice is of doubtful value. It is an obvious imitation of practice in athletics, and the letter has become so well associated with athletics that the wearer of a nonathletic letter is frequently subjected to such ridicule or more subtle contempt that his award does not seem to him of much value. Recognizing this fact, some schools have provided for interscholastic nonathletic team members other types of awards, with inscriptions designating the years and the type of activity.

Other schools encourage participation by awarding cups or medals to school or class champions in various activities, awarding activity certificates to participating pupils and arm bands to the school "knights" or ushers, and by considering activity records in selecting members for the honor society. Different degrees of certificates may be awarded, based on a point system. The certificate usually is an attractively printed form which bears the name of the pupil, the signature of the president of the student body, and that of the principal and designates the activities engaged in and the offices held. It constitutes a very attractive souvenir of high-school days. In general, letters and other awards are questionable devices, contributing as they do to the development of a false sense of importance in many of the recipients and to a dissatisfaction with school life and with themselves on the part of many of the nonrecipients.

In a large number of schools one or two assemblies at the beginning of the school year are given over to talks by student officers, faculty sponsors, or both, in which talks the nature of the activities is set forth and explained to the students. Serving, as it does, to orient the new pupil, to promote democracy in membership, and to provide an exercise in leadership, the plan is very commendable.

In many schools the leaders and chief participants in several different important activities are the same persons, often from a small group. For example, one lad is a member of the football team, the senior-class president, business manager of the annual, and a member of the student council. Another is editor of the newspaper, assistant editor of the annual, and a member of the dramatic club and of the glee club or orchestra. This condition is not an insuperable difficulty. Restriction of the participation in activities of any one individual to a defined maximum is not at all impossible to administer, as many schools have discovered, in spite of the pressure brought to bear when, for example, pupils desire to elect to a major office a candidate who already participates in two other major activities or, worse still, when it becomes necessary to require a pupil to resign from an office or membership in some activity in order to become eligible for an athletic or other team. In many schools clubs are scheduled so as to have two or more clubs meeting at the same time, thus forcing the students to make a choice.

THE MAJOR-MINOR PLAN. Two commonly employed plans for distributing participation are (1) the *major-minor plan* and (2) the *point system.*

The major-minor plan consists, briefly, of classifying all activities as major or minor, according to the responsibility and expenditure of time involved, and of restricting the participation of any one pupil to a specified number of majors and minors or their equivalents.

Below is an illustrative classification of types of participation as major or minor activities.

Major activities:

Major sports
Editor of annual
Business manager of annual
Debating team
President of student body
Secretary of student body
Editor of school paper
Manager of school paper
President of junior or senior class
Leader of orchestra, band, or glee club

Minor activities:

Minor sports
Membership in any club, orchestra, or band
Class officers
Participation in a play
Member of staff of annual
Member of staff of school paper
Cheerleader
Chairmen of student-body committees

Participation is usually limited to some such equivalent as two majors, one major and two minors, or four minors.

In a great many schools a point-scale system is used for the encouragement of participation in extracurricular activities and also for restriction of excessive participation and monopoly of the educational opportunities by overparticipators. In some schools a point system is set up, allowing points to various types of participating members or leaders in activities, and each student is restricted in participation on the basis of a maximum number of points. In other schools, and sometimes in the same schools, the point system is employed for the purpose of determining the basis for awards; in some schools it is used for determining the amount of credit that may be earned in extracurricular activities.

The point system requires a great deal of record-keeping and accounting. It also requires checking up to see if individuals are participating excessively. Sometimes, although a student exceeds the maximum number of points allowed, it is difficult to enforce the rule because of the fact that he is desired very greatly by coaches and sponsors of several activities; in this situation there is great pressure brought to bear to make an exception of the individual.

Following is an illustrative point system, one employed in the Beverly, Massachusetts, High School.[3]

1. In order to eliminate the possibility of overloading a student with official responsibilities, and in order to give more students the opportunity to benefit from holding positions of leadership, the following point system is established.
2. A student, under the system, may hold offices totaling not more than seven points during a school year.
3. Points will be scheduled as follows:

5-point positions
President of the Student Council
President of the Senior Class

4-point positions
Editor of the *Aegis*
Editor of the yearbook
Editor of the *B-Hive*

3-point positions
President of the Junior Class
President of the Sophomore Class
Secretary of the Student Council
Treasurer of the Student Council
Vice-President of the Student Council

2-point positions
Captains of major sports
Managers of major sports
Class officers, other than President
Chairmen of all general committees formed by the school or a class

[3]*The B-Hive,* Beverly, Massachusetts, High School, 1960-61, pp. 13-15.

Presidents of all clubs
Assistant editor, secretary, and managers of the yearbook staff
Members of the Student Council
Assistant editor, and secretary of the *Aegis* board
Head cheerleader
Lieutenants of the safety patrol
Student leader of the band

1-point positions

Captains of minor sports
Managers of minor sports
Homeroom officers
Members on all general committees formed by the school or a class
Officers, other than president, of any club
Cheerleaders
Head of the baton squad
Members of *Aegis* staff
Members of yearbook staff
Alternates

No person can be both president of his class and president of his homeroom. A person may not be captain of more than one athletic team during a school year.

4. It will be noted that only the highest-rated position held by a student in any organization will be credited to his point total. For example, the editor of the *B-Hive,* who must also be a member of the Student Council, would receive only four points for these two offices, not six points.
5. If any justified question arises regarding the interpretation of a person's total points according to this system, the principal will confer with a committee familiar with the system, to be appointed by the president of the Student Council. Then, he, as head of the judicial department, will interpret the case.
6. If a student finds that his offices exceed the point limit, he must, in order to come within the limit, resign from a position of his own choosing, provided that the duties of the office are not completed at the time of resignation. That is, a person may not resign a football captaincy after the playing season is over and expect to lose points for that position.
7. The homeroom officers are responsible for keeping an individual record of the offices and points of each member of the homeroom and of reporting them to the Student Council.

CONSTRUCTION OF CLASSIFICATIONS OR POINT SCALES. It is not probable that any one major-minor classification or point scale would serve all schools equally well. The relative demands made upon the time of participants by any given activity will vary from school to school and from year to year. Those responsible for the administration of activity problems in each school should work out a scheme for the classification or point-weighing of activities to fit local conditions. Perhaps this scheme should be based upon data gathered from a study of estimates of time spent by pupils on various offices and activities.

The weighting must take into consideration not only the total amount of time spent in the office or activity but also the amount that may be demanded daily by certain periods of intensified practice or by exigencies of the organization. It is probably wise to think first of the offices or activities requiring the least time and energy, assigning to these a value of one point and assigning proportionate point values to all the others. A classification or point system, once set up, should be revised from time to time on the basis of information obtained by continued study and collection of data on the relative demands of the activities. It should not be regarded as inflexible. The principal, the director of activities, or the committee on the administration of activities should hear and pass on petitions requesting that a different number of points be assigned for participation in specified activities for reasons stated. Ordinarily, however, the safe policy is to do as little tinkering during the school year as is consistent with justice.

5. *Administration and Supervision*

ADMINISTRATION OF MAJOR-MINOR AND POINT PLANS. For major-minor and point plans to be effective in controlling participation of students in extra-class activities, records of participation must be kept up to date, showing the extent of each student's participation at all times. A form for such records is shown as Form 3.

FORM 3. *Activities Record*[4]

EXTRACURRICULAR PARTICIPATION CARD

Manhattan, Kansas, Senior High School

Activities	1	2	3	4	5	6	Yr	Quality of Participation
Total activity points								
Permitted points								

[4]The figures 1, 2, 3, 4, 5, and 6 refer to the successive six-week periods in the year. Under "Yr" should be entered the number of points earned in each activity.

These forms should be checked over at the beginning of each year or semester; either they should be approved or students should be notified that their activity loads exceed the limit. It is not a bad practice to have a pupil specify at the time of registration the activities in which he intends to participate. Upon his applying for membership in any organization after the opening of the year or the semester, his application should be referred to the office for checking and approval before acceptance. Officers of activities organized after the beginning of the year should send to the office a list of proposed members so that each individual may be checked.

In some schools the pupil's activity load is measured by the number of points totaled from all activities engaged in during the semester; in others it is estimated from the activities being participated in at any given time. From the point of view of protecting the pupil from over-loading to the point of endangering his scholastic standing, the latter method is advantageous. It involves a more careful accounting, however; also, since the work incident to most activities is fairly well distributed throughout the semester or year, the disadvantages of the plan probably outweigh its peculiar values. From the standpoint of preventing monopoly of activities, whatever difference exists between the two methods is in favor of the semester or annual basis for accounting.

FUNDAMENTAL PRINCIPLES GOVERNING MEMBERSHIP. There should be established, understood, and observed certain principles governing administration to and continuance of membership in activities sponsored by the school. The following are suggested as being important among these:

1. *There should be complete democracy in the means of determining membership.* Membership should not be dependent upon the preference of members or leaders of cliques.
2. *Membership should be determined on the basis of the pupil's interest and ability in the work of the organization, in accordance with the objective rules of the organization.* If the organization does not stand ready to accept all candidates, there should be set up objective means of selecting candidates, such as tryouts conducted by faculty advisers, order of seniority of pupils, or formal application.
3. *Membership should be restricted to pupils in good standing.* No school organization should admit to membership or to participation in its activity any person not a bona-fide member of the student body. All members should be boys and girls subject to the discipline of the school. Outsiders almost invariably constitute unusual and unnecessary problems difficult to handle.
4. *Membership should be regulated by rules which prevent monopoly of activities by the more able or popular pupils.* Regulations should be provided and enforced that will make it impossible for a small number of pupils to enjoy a large share of the opportunities for training in the activities

of the school to the exclusion of those more in need of such training. Means of administration of such regulations have just been outlined and discussed.

5. *Membership should not depend upon any degree of scholarship beyond passing marks.* It has been shown that participation in activities (with the possible exception of certain types of athletics—notably football) has little or no effect upon the quality of work done by participants on their regular, conventional studies. In perhaps a majority of instances the pupil who is not capable of or interested in such studies will profit relatively more by participation in activities than the normal or superior pupil; in fact, many inferior pupils will profit very little from attendance in school except by means of activities.
6. *Membership should not be subject to severance in the interests of the highly specialized training of a selected few.* This principle is violated in almost every organization or activity which engages in interscholastic competition. Coaches or sponsors of such activities are prone to place a good showing of a picked team above the educational value of the activity. Pupils of lesser promise are frequently forced to discontinue. This practice is indicative of a perverted concept of values and should give way to a regime which makes provision for those who need the training most and are willing to acquire it, as well as for those who are most gifted or who have already reached a high degree of training.

In those schools in which the number of pupils desiring to become members of some organization exceeds materially the number that can well be accommodated in one group, favorable consideration should be given to the formation of two or more groups: for example, two bands, two debating clubs, or two dramatic organizations. This is an excellent policy. Divisions are sometimes made on the basis of maturity (for example, underclassmen and upperclassmen), sometimes on the basis of proficiency (the "first" and "second" teams or clubs), and sometimes on the basis of the choice of the applicant for admission.

If educational values are to be criteria, it is not possible to justify, on a practical basis, the provision of an inferior quality of opportunity, coach, sponsor, or equipment for the "second" or "third" squad or club. Only the feverish desire to win contests and the consequent failure to realize the true, practical values of activities can account for the impractical procedure of dismissing all but the abler pupils or of providing only inferior training for the less able.

Limiting Participation in Contests Originating outside the School. In recent decades hundreds of organizations, in order to promote their objectives or to indoctrinate young people, have organized contests and invited schools and students to participate. Many of these contests are of doubtful educational value and they have become so numerous as to constitute a serious disruptive force in American education.

The Indiana Activities Committee stated the objections to national contests as follows:

A. School time lost by teachers and pupils from classes for practice and contests.

B. Interference with the regular school program by keeping the staff and school in a state of unrest due to the contests or festivals.

C. Hazards involved in transporting pupils long distances on crowded highways.

D. Pupils being drafted from academic or regular classes for rehearsals and practices.

E. Conflicts in schedules necessitating oftentimes the chaperoning of individual pupils back and forth between events of two or three different contests.

F. Little uniformity of eligibility for events.

G. Frequently too much emphasis upon one department or division of a school.

H. The rise to popularity of certain good teachers in a school and community, while equally good teachers go unnoticed because their teaching field does not lend itself readily or easily to publicity or showmanship.

I. The use of a pupil or pupils for the personal aggrandizement of a teacher.

J. Exploitation and commercialization frequently in certain activities.

K. Constant pressure within and without the school for funds.

L. School policies oftentimes directed by out-of-school campaigns for funds.

M. Extra burdens placed upon teachers.

N. Outcomes frequently evaluated on false bases.

O. The desire to win sometimes developing unethical practices.

P. Motivation to educational accomplishment artificial.

Q. Contests sometimes influencing teachers to work specifically with those pupils known to have winning possibilities at the expense of other members of the class.

R. Many contests not professional and not contributing to the objectives and purposes of education.

S. Many groups sponsoring activities and contests far removed from the educational picture.[5]

In recent years state and national organizations of school officials have taken group action to protect the schools, if not the students. The National Association of Secondary School Principals has for some years had a continuing committee to study the problem, make recommendations, and prepare a list of approved contests of national scope.

The National Association publishes each year, usually in the September issue of the *Bulletin,* a list of approved national nonathletic contests.

A. RECOMMENDATIONS FOR PARTICIPATING IN NATIONAL CONTESTS AND ACTIVITIES IN SCHOOLS

It is recommended:

1. *Policy for All Secondary Schools.* That all secondary schools take a firm and consistent position against participating in unapproved national contests or activities.

[5]Paul E. Elicker, "Contests," *Bulletin of the N.A.S.S.P.* (February, 1952), No. 184, p. 189.

2. *School Participation*
   (a) On a national basis – That a school confine its participation to those national contests that are currently placed on the Approved List.
   (b) On a state basis – That schools limit their participation to contests and activities endorsed by their own state high-school organizations.
3. *Student Participation*
   (a) That, if a school participates in any approved contest or activity outside the state, no pupil should be absent from school more than five school days for a single contest or activity.
   (b) That no individual pupil should participate in more than one contest in each of the categories on the Approved List except where scholarships are involved.
4. *Essay Contests.* Unsupervised essay contests are of questionable educational value. If the essay contest is not given under secure conditions, we make the recommendation that:
   (a) A school announce or post notice *only,* but not promote an essay contest.
   (b) A staff member should not be required to serve as a judge for an essay contest.
   (c) A staff member should not be required to use class periods for conducting an essay contest.

B. GENERAL RECOMMENDATIONS

The Committee suggests that all secondary-school administrators give consideration to these recommendations:

1. Before a school agrees to participate in any national contest or activity, the principal should check this List to find out whether it is approved. If the contest or activity is not approved, *please do not participate in it.*
2. Approval by the Committee on National Contests and Activities does not give the sponsor the right to operate in any school. The school will determine the contests and activities in which it chooses to take part.
3. In regard to college scholarships, no sponsor should pay a cash award directly to the student. The award should be deposited with the treasurer of the institution selected by the student.

C. CRITERIA

Sponsors of contests and activities desiring official approval by the Committee on National Contests and Activities should read carefully the Criteria before filing an application.

1. *Primary Objective.* The primary aim of a national contest or activity is to benefit high-school youth in educational, civic, social, and ethical development.
2. *Types of Contests.* Contests that make it possible for individual students to work out contributions, solutions, and creations by their own efforts are preferred. Scholarship and achievement tests and contests involving original work by the contestant are highly recommended.
3. *Purpose.* The contest or activity should be educationally sound, worthy, and stimulating to the student.
4. *Values.*
   (a) The contest or activity should be well planned and have adequate evaluation.
   (b) The contest must emphasize either the development of intellectual competence, good citizenship, or high moral standards.

(c) The contest or activity must be of such a nature as not to be considered commercial, controversial and sectarian, or concerned with propaganda or advertising of any individual.

5. *Restrictions.*
   (a) No contestant may be excluded because of race, color, or creed.
   (b) The contest or activity must not place undue burdens on students, teachers, or school.
   (c) The student or school should not be required to pay an entry fee or to purchase materials to participate.
   (d) Teachers should not be required to judge or select contestants in any stage of a contest.
   (e) The contest or activity must not require frequent absences of participants from school. Special consideration will be given to an activity held during the summer vacation period.
   (f) Ordinarily, out-of-state travel during the school year should be limited to one student per state for any contest.
   (g) A new contest or activity should not duplicate one already sponsored by another organization.
   (h) An organization should not conduct more than one national contest or activity in the same school year.
6. *Awards and Prizes.*
   (a) Awards and prizes must be adequate in number and amount. The payment of cash awards directly to winners should be avoided.
   (b) Scholarships and educational trips are regarded as the most desirable types of awards.
7. *Sponsorship.* The organization sponsoring the contest or activity must be engaged in a creditable or acceptable enterprise regardless of the kind and amount of prizes offered, and must not use the contest or activity as a "front" for advertising a company name or product.

D. OTHER CONDITIONS AND REQUIREMENTS

1. If participation in a contest or activity is offered to schools in six or more states, it will be regarded as a national contest or activity and application for placement on the Approved List should be made to the Committee on National Contests and Activities.
2. If participation is offered to schools in only one state, or fewer than six states, separate applications should be directed to the appropriate organizations that approve contests and activities—the State Association of Secondary-School Principals, the State Activities Association, the State Department of Education, etc.
3. Organizations whose contests or activities are placed on the Approved List must include this statement on their publications or entry blanks: "The National Association of Secondary-School Principals has placed this Contest (or this Activity) on the Approved List of National Contests and Activities for 1960-61." Further, they should inform the Committee of the names of the national and state winners of contests as soon as they are determined.
4. Applications for placing national contests or activities on the Approved List must be filed with the Committee on National Contests and Activities on or before April 15 for consideration for the ensuing school year.
5. Approval of national contests or activities is for one year only. New applications must be submitted each year.[6]

STATE INTERSCHOLASTIC-ACTIVITIES COMMITTEE. In most states there exists a state interscholastic-activities committee, formed by the principals of secondary schools, which sets up guiding principles and regulations for interscholastic contests, acts as a commission for the approval of nonathletic interscholastic activities, and exercises some supervision over nonathletic interscholastic contests. The regulations of the Indiana State Activities Committee, as approved by the Indiana Association of Junior and Senior High School Principals, are given below:

1. Sanction must be secured for nonathletic meets, festivals, contests, tournaments, clinics, and assemblages involving participation of more than two schools.
2. Schools all of which are in the same county or the same school corporation or system need not apply for sanction of activities involving participation among their own schools.
3. When more than two schools in two or more states near a state boundary form a natural grouping for a meet, contest, festival, tournament, clinic, or assemblage, approval will be given provided distance traveled by participating schools from other states does not exceed 75 miles one way.
4. All school meets, contests, festivals, tournaments, clinics, and assemblages must be held at a time when there will be no interference with the regularly scheduled school day. Exceptions will be considered by the committee when requested in writing by all principals participating in a school-sponsored activity.
5. Schools wishing to hold a meeting involving schools of other states should first receive approval of their own Activity Committee and then that of the other states before sending word to schools themselves.
6. If a school wishes to attend a meet held in another state, it is necessary that the school holding the meet should first receive approval from its own state and then the participating Indiana school must submit evidence of this approval along with its application to the Indiana committee.
7. The cost of financing meets, contests, festivals, tournaments, clinics, and assemblages is to be kept to a minimum and should not be burdensome to the parents, pupils or community.
8. Applications for sanction should be made prior to August 1 for activities to be held between September 1 and December 31. Applications should be made before December 1 for activities to be held between January 1 and August 31.
9. Schools or organizations receiving sanctions for meets should make a statement of this in letters sent out in order that the school principals will know these events have been sanctioned.
10. An itemized report should be mailed to the Activities Chairman by the host principal following each event.
11. Approval for national and regional nonathletic activities must be secured from the National Association of Secondary School Principals. Nationally approved activities are automatically approved by the Indiana Committee.

[6]"Approved List of National Contests and Activities for 1960-61," *Bulletin of the N.A.S.S.P.* (September, 1960), No. 257, pp. 139-141.

This approved list is published in the September issue of the *Bulletin of the National Association of Secondary School Principals*. The committee chairman and his address are in the footnote of this *Bulletin*.

12. Approval for any athletic contests or play days should be secured from the Commissioner of the Indiana High School Athletic Association, 812 Circle Tower, Indianapolis, Indiana.[7]

Each principal should keep in touch with the interscholastic-activities committee of his state. Most state committees have a full-time paid secretary, who usually has his office in the quarters of the state education department or teachers' association.

6. *Activity Meetings*

PLACE OF MEETINGS. As far as possible, all meetings of school organizations should be held in the school building or on the school grounds and be attended by the faculty adviser. Meetings should be held in other places only with the consent of the principal. By their very nature some organizations will have need to meet or carry on activities in other places: for example, rehearsals of plays or entertainments in downtown theaters or in churches. Even in such instances exceptions to the general rule should be held to a minimum. When meetings are held in the school building, students naturally feel that the authority of the school, even though it is not being ostentatiously displayed or exercised, is, nevertheless, extended to such meetings. The conduct of students is much less likely to be questionable and advisers may more easily be on hand to supervise the work.

TIME AND FREQUENCY OF MEETINGS. As is desirable, many organizations may reduce their meetings to a set schedule of once or twice a week, or once or twice a month, for periods of uniform length. Among organizations which should be able to do so are the debating club, the band, the nursing club, the cartoon club, Boy Scouts and Girl Scouts, Girl Reserves, the Hi-Y, the civic club, the commercial club, the honor society, the camera club, all semicurricular clubs (such as the French, German, Latin, history, mathematics, and art clubs), the orchestra, the glee club, the chorus, the printing, agriculture, household-arts, and other semivocational clubs, and the roll-room organizations.

Other organizations, such as the staff of the school annual, class organizations, dramatic clubs, and athletic teams, cannot do this so easily. As far as is practical, clubs should be required to meet on set schedules, those schedules to be arranged by a committee of the student organization and the principal or director of activities. Such schedules

[7]Application for Sanction of Non-Athletic Interscholastic Activity, Indiana Association of Junior and Senior High School Principals, John M. Hougland, Principal, Marion High School, Chairman of Activities Committee.

will reduce the amount of conflict between meetings of clubs with overlapping membership, as well as the confusion resulting from meetings held on call.

In a very large number of schools there is a definite activity period on the daily schedule. While practice varies greatly among the schools, the general practice is to have two activity periods a week and to have some activities meeting both periods, others meeting only one period, and some meeting only once every two weeks. Nevertheless, many schools designate only one period a week as an activity period and in some schools there is an activity period three, four, or five times a week. Provision for an activity period is difficult in schools in which there are only six periods in the day; provision for an activity period is found much more often in schools which have seven or eight periods a day.

Administrators in those schools which do not have activities meeting during the regular school day claim the following advantages for scheduling activities outside the daily schedule:

1. It extends the school day for the work on the curriculum subjects.
2. It extends the school day only for those participating.
3. It permits the individual pupil to engage in a larger number of activities.
4. It does not complicate the daily schedule.
5. It permits the time given to activity meetings to be as long or as short as desired.

However, the disadvantages of having activity meetings after school have been pointed out by school administrators as follows:

1. It tends to reduce the number of students participating, making it impossible for some to participate.
2. It often forces pupils to choose between extra-class and personal nonschool activities.
3. It often results in an unco-ordinated activity program.
4. It is likely to result in lack of co-ordination of home-room activities with other activities.

THE SCHOOL CALENDAR. With the multiplication of organizations and their activities, the necessity develops for careful management with respect to the dates for performances, contests, and social and other events. In order that these may not conflict and that they may be distributed properly throughout the year, there should be kept in the principal's office a calendar for scheduling in advance all sorts of events, thereby preventing conflicts. Each organization must make application for a place on the calendar.

Certain types of events are fixed by their nature and should be the constants on the calendar, leaving as variables the events for which suitable dates are not predetermined. Athletic schedules, commencement events, final examinations, school holidays, and certain local nonschool activities are examples of constants.

Activities or organizations that have had certain days regularly for a period of years should have priority in application for those dates; otherwise, a rule for awarding dates on the schedule on the basis of priority of application should be followed, thus forestalling disputes likely to occur over desired dates.

There should also be worked out agreements as to when the intensive work of some organizations should take place: for example, an operetta in January, the senior-class play in April, a series of glee-club concerts in March, and an intramural debating tournament in December. The exercise of foresight will operate to reduce the number of possible conflicts, as well as to distribute the calls upon versatile students and the demands upon local out-of-school support at public exhibitions.

The following is an excerpt from a school calendar followed for the month of February at Central High School, Evansville, Indiana:

Date	*Activity*
Mon., Feb. 3	Meeting of Councils
Tues., Feb. 4	Club Schedule B
Wed., Feb. 5	Guidance
Thurs., Feb. 6	College Week Assembly
	Lunch Hour Movies
Fri., Feb. 7	College Week Assembly
	Basketball-Bloomington (There)
Sat., Feb. 8	Basketball-Jasper (Here)
Mon., Feb. 10	Meeting of Girl Reserves and Hi-Y
	Big Broadcast Practice – 7:00-9:30 P.M.
Tues., Feb. 11	Club Schedule A
	Big Broadcast Practice – 7:00-9:30 P.M.
	P.T.A. Meeting – 3:15 P.M.
Wed., Feb. 12	Guidance
	Big Broadcast Practice – 7:00-9:30 P.M.
Thurs., Feb. 13	Scholarship E Assembly
	Lunch Hour Movies
Fri., Feb. 14	Pep Assembly for Bosse Game
	Basketball-Bosse (Here)
Sat., Feb. 15	Senior Open Dance (Away)
Mon., Feb. 17	Meeting of Councils
	Big Broadcast Practice – 7:00-9:30 P.M.
	Stage Crew Practice – 3:00-5:00 P.M.
Tues., Feb. 18	Club Schedule B
	Big Broadcast Practice – 7:00-9:30 P.M.
	Stage Crew Practice – 3:00-5:00 P.M.
Wed., Feb. 19	Guidance
	Student Council Assembly
	Faculty Meeting
	Big Broadcast – 8:00 P.M.
Thurs., Feb. 20	Student Council Assembly (In Front of Curtain)
	Lunch Hour Movies
	Big Broadcast – 8:00 P.M.

SPONSORS OR ADVISERS. Each organization should have a faculty adviser or sponsor as a part of its organization. Occasionally, in a smaller school where no one of the staff is competent to act as adviser to a desirable organization, the principal may appoint some responsible, competent individual in the community who is willing to give the time and attention necessary. This practice should be regarded as a makeshift to be employed only in rare cases: advisers should be in more direct contact with the administration, in closer touch with the life and operation of the school, and not so likely to be involved in local factional differences.

Although advisers should be chosen on the basis of their capacity for leadership and management, their special experience and subject-matter qualifications should also be considered. Teachers of English usually make the best advisers for journalistic and public-speaking enterprises; teachers of the sciences and industrial arts, for semiscientific and semivocational activities; and teachers of history, for debate. However, wide differences exist between English teachers in their training and qualifications for acting as advisers to school-publication staffs, dramatic clubs, and other activities. Teachers trained only in literature are very often not as valuable as history teachers with some training in journalism or foreign-language teachers with some training in dramatics.

Though the principal may well consult pupils' preferences and requests, the selection of faculty advisers should, for several reasons, rest largely with him. In the first place, he must see to it that advisers are well qualified to assist in the activity, which is often of a semitechnical nature, and are well adapted by personality and character to assume and exercise the desired leadership in the activity. Then, too, it is he who must attend to the matter of keeping the teachers' loads equalized. Again, since he is most likely to have assisted in the selection of his teachers, taking care that advisers be provided for different types of activities, he knows what teachers are best fitted for relations with each activity. Finally, selection by the principal is not conducive to disagreement among pupils or to the development of delicate situations among teachers incident to the choice of advisers by pupils. For example, no teacher will be "second choice" as adviser.

THE DIRECTION OF FACULTY SPONSORS. In the small school the principal is in all likelihood the logical individual to head the activity program and to direct it through his staff of advisers. He is best oriented in the various contacts, events, and related problems of management of the school. In larger schools he may delegate a considerable portion of the details of administration to vice-principals or other assistants. In a very small but steadily growing number of schools a qualified individual is selected to serve, with or without teaching duties, as director of activities. To him the principal may commit the whole program of activities, making officers and advisers responsible to him and charging him with the complete responsibility for the success of the program.

Faculty advisers should be brought to understand that supervision which borders on domination operates to destroy pupils' spontaneity and interest. Many advisers are prone to look upon the material product rather than the educational growth of the participants as the most important result of the activity. They are, like athletic coaches, inclined to assume almost complete responsibility for leadership and initiative, reducing pupils to low levels of participation. Such guidance fails to arouse purposeful interest and responsibility and serves to reduce activities to the status of traditional classroom teaching, characterized by perfunctory, uninterested pupil performance and a lack of opportunity for the development of initiative, leadership, and skills in democratic, co-operative undertakings.

Not a little time should be spent in training advisers in the correct point of view and procedures for their work. Meetings of advisers at which problems relating to activities are discussed should be held from time to time, especially during the first month or two of the school year. Advisers who have not had formal training in the management of activities should be encouraged to do considerable reading in comprehensive treatments of the subject, such as those listed at the end of this chapter.

The necessity of developing a balanced point of view on the part of advisers, as well as of leading them to study the details of management, should not be overlooked. Many teachers were not in their own student days leaders in activities, being more inclined to "book study." Many have little sympathy with and no adequate understanding of the educational value and purpose of activities. They need to be brought to understand a modern and practical philosophy of the values and principles of organization and administration of extra-curricular activities. They need to be caused to think through clearly and somewhat specifically the possible contributions to the aims of education and the possible harmful or wasteful effects which result from participation in each activity. In some larger schools it has been found helpful to assign a teacher without experience in sponsoring extra-class activities as an assistant to a more experienced teacher in charge of an activity.

GENERAL PRINCIPLES OF SUPERVISION. It is difficult to define in detail what should be the degree and nature of the supervision of organization activities by the faculty adviser. It is, perhaps, equally useful and certainly simpler to set up certain general principles which the adviser should translate into specific practice in the light of the particular activity, the local situation, and the personnel of the organization.

Among such principles are the following:

1. The supervision of activities should not amount to domination. Opportunity must be provided for the development and exercise of pupil initiative, leadership, imagination, and thinking through of consequences. Pupils must be permitted to make some mistakes as a part of their training. The educational value derived from an activity depends largely upon its incidental training value and by no means entirely upon success in the ostensible purpose of the organization.
2. Supervision must circumvent the influence of immoral and unsocial practices: for example, the mismanagement of funds, the domination of social cliques, undemocratic selection of members and officials, and unethical business and competitive practices.
3. Supervision should be, as far as possible, by suggestion rather than by authoritative direction.
4. Supervision must include co-operation with the central administration and the general activity program, especially in matters of accounting (records and reports) and in the management of activities in such a way as to ensure loyalty to the administrative policies.
5. Supervision must include recognition of the exploratory value of activities as a factor in guidance. Advisers should be constantly on the lookout for evidence of special talent and should advise pupils concerning the possibilities of training and employing such talent.
6. Supervision should have as one of its primary objectives the integration of curricular studies and extracurricular activities.

PUPIL SELF-MANAGEMENT. In addition, the pupil officers of the various organizations may well have a large part in the organization and management of the whole program of activities. In many schools all the organizations, or a great many of them, are subdivisions of the general student association; they receive their charters from it and are subject to its constitution and the legislation passed by its suffrage or by its designated representative councils. As far as possible, organizing and managing should be left to pupils acting through their central organization and their different organization officers and committees. The school committee on activities should be composed of both pupil and faculty representatives. In large schools with very many activities subcommittees of the council for the administration of groups of activities are advisable.

MANAGEMENT BY COMMITTEES. It has been found effective in many schools to make use of a committee of students and faculty, or a committee made up of students alone, which has the following responsibilities:

1. To study the activities program in operation, to recommend changes, and to inform the principal and staff of any developments which should be given consideration.

2. To formulate principles and policies for directing the activities program in such areas as regulation of student participation in activities, accounting for activity funds, setting of time and place for meetings, and making of policies relative to matters such as requiring sponsors to attend meetings of organizations, etc.
3. To help in obtaining sponsors for the activities.
4. To help plan and schedule activities, to formulate policies, to govern scheduling of assemblies, etc.

SUPERVISION OF FINANCES. A discussion of financial accounting in student organization and its supervision will be found in Chapter 17, "Student Accounting and Reporting."

Problems, Questions, and Exercises

1. What additions could you make to the table of the objectives and types of outcomes of curricular activity?
2. What is your opinion as to the degree to which and the conditions under which participation in extracurricular activities may interfere with students' learning in the school subjects?
3. Examine the list of criteria for determining what and how many activities should be represented in any given school; offer suggestions for the revision of the list.
4. For a school of a size selected by you, what activities do you think ought to be offered?
5. After reading the material in this book and some of the references on the subject, propose a program for encouraging and regulating student participation in extracurricular activities.
6. Make up a point system for use in controlling participation in extracurricular activities.
7. Examine the fundamental principles given in this text for governing membership; note to what extent you agree or disagree with each of these. Could you add another principle?
8. Think through carefully the problem of contests in the schools that are suggested by outside agencies; tell what you think the high-school principal ought to do about invitations to participate in such contests.
9. To what extent and under what conditions should the meeting periods of extracurricular activities be in the regular school day, on some sort of schedule?
10. What help in supervision do you think the principal should give the sponsors of various extracurricular activities?

Selected Supplementary Readings

Campbell, Walter H., "The Daily Bulletin in Action," *Bulletin of the N.A.S.S.P.* (February, 1957), No. 226, pp. 219-228. [Description of a device helpful in the smooth operation of the Queen Anne Junior-Senior High School of Seattle, Washington.]

Flury, A. H., "Essay Contests are Educationally Undesirable," *Bulletin of the N.A.S.S.P.* (February, 1960), No. 253, p. 35.

Frederick, Robert W., *The Third Curriculum,* New York, Appleton-Century-Crofts, 1959. [See Part II, "Managing the Activity Program."]

Gastineau, Jerry, and Martin, George B., "The Assignment of Extra-Curricular Advisors," *Educational Administration and Supervision* (January, 1952), Vol. 38, pp. 42-47. [A set of positive steps for the selection and assignment of the staff.]

Graber, Ralph E., "How Extensive an Activity Program in the Junior High School?" *Bulletin of the N.A.S.S.P.* (March, 1952), No. 185, pp. 250-261.

Gruber, Frederick C., and Beatty, Thomas B., *Secondary School Activities,* New York, McGraw-Hill, 1954. [Chapters 1, 3, and 4, on the importance and the administration and supervision of activities.]

Hand, Harold C., "Hidden Tuition Charges in Extra-Class Activities," *Educational Forum* (November, 1949), Vol. 14, pp. 95-103.

Johnston, Edgar G., "Critical Problems in the Administration of Student Activities," *Bulletin of the N.A.S.S.P.* (February, 1952), Vol. 36, pp. 1-12.

Johnston, Edgar, and Faunce, Roland, *Student Activities in Secondary Schools,* New York, Ronald, 1952. [A concise, modern, comprehensive treatment of activities both general and specific.]

Joseph, Sister Mary, "Guidance Through Extra Curriculum Activities," *Catholic School Journal* (March, 1960), Vol. 60, pp. 38-39.

Keller, Ruth Maynard, "How to Keep Elections from Becoming Popularity Contests," *School Activities* (April, 1952), Vol. 23, pp. 243-245. [Specific suggestions for more efficient choices of able and competent student officers, as well as for the inclusion of more people in school organization.]

Kilzer, Louis R., Stephenson, Harold H., and Norberg H. Orville, *Allied Activities in the Secondary School,* New York, Harper, 1956. [Chapters 1, 2, 8, and 11, on the philosophy of and participation in the athletic program; the program's financing.]

McKown, H. C., *Extra-Curricular Activities,* Macmillan, 1952. [An excellent comprehensive treatment by a long-time outstanding authority in the field.]

Manning, George A., "What Are Sound Policies for Controlling Non-Athletic National Contests and Activities Offered to Schools by Outside Organizations?" *Bulletin of the N.A.S.S.P.* (March, 1952), Vol. 36, pp. 29-33. [Reports on the work and recommendations of the National Contest Committee of the N.A.S.S.P. by the chairman of the committee.]

Miller, Norma R., "What Is A Good School Contest?" *Bulletin of the N.A.S.S.P.* September, 1959), No. 248, pp. 28-31.

Punke, Harold H., "Cost to High School Seniors," *Bulletin of the N.A.S.S.P.* (February, 1957), No. 226, pp. 202-212. [Survey of costs in twenty-six medium-sized high schools in southern states.]

Pupil Activities in Junior High Schools—A Bibliography, Washington, D.C., Department of Health, Education and Welfare, Office of Education, February, 1955.

Susanne, Sister M. (I.H.M.), "Extra-Curricular Activities and Intellectual Virtues," *Catholic Educational Review* (December, 1952), Vol. 50, No. 10. ["Extracurricular" does not mean "noncurricular."]

Tompkins, Ellsworth, "The Relation of Activities to the Curriculum," *Bulletin of the N.A.S.S.P.* (February, 1952), Vol. 36, pp. 13-24. [The advantages and disadvantages of three ways of organizing pupil activities: (1) activity period, (2) core program, and (3) before school and after school.]

Tompkins, Ellsworth, "How Can We Administer an Activities Program for All Pupils?" *Bulletin of the N.A.S.S.P.* (April, 1950), Vol. 34, No. 170, pp. 17-23.

Trump, J. Lloyd, *Extra-Class Activities and the Needs of Youth,* Fifty-second Yearbook, Part I, National Society for the Study of Education, University of Chicago Press, 1953. [Chapter IX, "Adapting the Secondary-school Program to the Needs of Youth."]

11

Administering the Extra-Class Activity Program (Continued)

8. School Clubs

In some schools students are asked at the beginning of the school year to indicate various types of extra-class activities in which they would be interested. This procedure tends to arouse interest in various clubs and to assist students to get into club activities in which they would like to participate. Scheduling a number of clubs at the same time tends to distribute participation among the students. If a student is unable to get into a club of his choice one semester, he may get into it another semester.

TYPES OF CLUBS. Johnston and Faunce have identified the following types of clubs; under each of the types they mention are given some activities found in high schools in the United States.

A. *Clubs closely related to school courses or departments.* The largest number of clubs fall in this category. They serve both to motivate class activity and to provide opportunity to develop more fully interests originating in the classroom. Frequently they reflect particular interests within a subject field. The examples are illustrative rather than comprehensive.

Agriculture: Dairy, Forestry, 4-H Club, Future Farmers of America, Garden, Poultry.

Art: Art Appreciation, Cartoonists, Handicraft, Illustrators, Photographers, Sketchers.

English and Speech: Booklovers, Debate, Dramatics (under many names), Forum, Library, Parliamentary Law, Poetry, Short Story, Writers.

Foreign Language: French, German, Latin, Spanish—frequently with special names, such as Le Cercle Francais, Der Deutsche Verein, Club Español.

Homemaking: Art Needlework, Costume Design, Camp Cookery, Fashion, Future Homemakers, 4-H Club, Home Nursing, Knitting, Little Mothers (a club for baby-sitters), Luncheon, Millinery, Weaving.

Industrial Arts and Vocational Education: Automobile, Blueprinting, Book Repair, Electricity, Household Mechanics (for girls), Machinists, Model Airplane, Printers, Radio, Woodworkers.

Mathematics: Applied Mathematics, Junior Financiers, Mathematical Games, Surveyors.

Music: *A Cappella* Choir, Band, Chorus, Dance Band, Glee Club, Music Appreciation, Orchestra, Record Players.

Physical Education: Archery, First Aid, Folk Dancing, Golf, Hiking, Life Saving, Modern Dance, Skating, Skiing.

Science: Airplane, Bird Study, Biology, Camera, Chemistry, Conservation, General Science, Inventors, Physics, Radio, Wild Life.

Social Studies: Biography, Current Events, Community Improvement, History, Know Your City, Know Your State, Museum, National Geographic, Stamp Collectors, Travel.

B. *Clubs promoted by national character-building organizations and sponsored by the school.* In this group will be found Boy Scouts, Camp Fire Girls, Future Teachers, Girl Reserves, Girl Scouts, Hi-Y, Junior Red Cross, and the clubs for boys and girls developed to correlate with vocational agriculture—the 4-H Clubs, Future Farmers of America, and Future Homemakers. (This last group is appropriately listed also under the departments indicated.)

C. *Hobby and recreation clubs.* A few examples may suggest the almost inexhaustible range of possibilities: Checker and Chess Clubs, Collectors, Fencing, Fun, Hooked Rug, Marionette, Model Coach, Outdoor Life, Puzzle, Santa Claus (a toy-making club), Scrapbook, Tap Dancing, Woodcraft.

D. *School and community-service clubs.* In this classification may be included organizations having the aim of social service to the school or to the community. They provide an opportunity to capitalize on and develop the natural altruism and social consciousness of youth; they may range from the "pep club," concerned with developing support for school teams, to constructive community projects. Among the organizations in this group are Big Brother and Big Sister Clubs (to help the orientation of new pupils), Boosters, Hospital Visitors, Safety, Social Service, and Welfare.

E. *Honor societies.* The most widely known of these is the National Honor Society, sponsored by the National Association of Secondary School Principals and based on the four aims of scholarship, leadership, citizenship, and service.[1]

In addition to the organizations mentioned above, there has spread widely in recent years the Junior Achievement Club. This club usually operates a small business, quite frequently manufacturing some product which is sold by members of the club. Participation in the club tends to develop in young people an understanding of some of the problems related to business and to give some training in very common business activities. This club is usually sponsored by the local Chamber of Commerce or some other group of businessmen.[2]

CLUB SPONSORS. One of the important factors in the success of a club and the attainment of the potentialities of this educational enterprise is the sponsor. In many high schools it is difficult to find a sufficiently large number of sponsors, particularly with variety of experience, to provide adequate leadership and guidance for a wide variety of clubs, particu-

---

[1]Edgar G. Johnston and Roland C. Faunce, *Student Activities in Secondary Schools*, New York, Ronald, 1952, pp. 121-123.

[2]For information, write to Junior Achievement, Inc., 500 Fifth Avenue, New York 36, New York.

larly the newer types of clubs. It is probable that in many schools much care will have to be exercised in the selection of teachers in order to ensure that there will be qualified sponsors for a desired variety of clubs. In addition, it is likely that in many high schools it will be found necessary to encourage teachers already on the staff to attend summer sessions or in other ways to obtain in-service education which will enable them to act more efficiently as sponsors of clubs. The principal qualifications for a successful sponsor may be set forth as follows:

1. Does he really like to associate with boys and girls of high-school age?
2. Does he enlist the confidence of boys and girls?
3. Is he keenly interested in the world around him?
4. Has he contagious enthusiasm?
5. Does he seek to become expert in some of the fields of activity in which the club is engaged?
6. Is he able to give constructive suggestions for activities of the club?
7. Is he able to guide without dictation?
8. Has he the ability to plan systematically?
9. Is he willing to give time and thought to making the club work a success?
10. Is he democratic in spirit?
11. Has he a sense of humor?
12. Is he able to find his chief satisfaction in pupil growth, rather than in appreciation of his efforts?

In some school club sponsors are given extra pay for their activities and responsibilities as sponsors of clubs.

9. Speech and Music Activities

SPEECH ACTIVITIES. Speech activities are of two types: (1) forensic activities, including oratory, debating, extemporaneous speaking, and discussion; and (2) interpretative activities, such as dramatics and oral reading. The oration as a type of speech activity, either in the assembly or in clubs, has almost passed out of the picture. There are few opportunities in everyday life for people to deliver orations, and young people have indeed rare opportunities. Orations have been replaced by discussions, reading of papers, debates, informal talks, and other types of forensic activities.

Debating is still very commonly found in the high school, particularly scholastic debating. The limitations of scholastic debating, particularly of interscholastic debating, have received much attention in recent years; however, certain modern trends in debating enhance its educational value. These trends are as follows:

1. The use of debating in a way which will diminish the overemphasis placed upon winning: e.g., having debates without decisions.
2. Employing intramural debating in place of or in addition to scholastic debating and thereby increasing the number of students participating in debating.

3. Having students speak from notes rather than from written or memorized speeches, thus training youngsters for extemporaneous speaking and speaking of the type that is more often done in everyday life.
4. Having youngsters select the subject for debate and the side on which they wish to debate so that they have a specific interest in making a case for the position they take.
5. Reducing the amount of help given by coaches to debaters and increasing the responsibility of the youngsters for the preparation of their own speeches.

In recent years there has been a tendency to increase extemporary speaking to include a variety of speech activities, thus training the youngster to express himself without much previous preparation. There will be many times in life when extemporary speaking will be employed. The student should be given some training in discussing a topic about which he has not been informed in advance; also he should have experience in situations in which he is expected to read widely in a particular field but is not permitted to use any notes or to know in advance the exact wording of the topic.

Discussions of various kinds are being employed much more in student activities, as well as in the classroom round table: the small group discussion, the buzz session, the open-forum discussion, and especially the panel discussion, in which atopic is opened up and discussed by a selected small group of people and which is sometimes followed by an open-forum discussion.

The principal types of interpretative activity found in schools today are the school play and the school operetta. These types of activity appeal to a very large number of youngsters and possess great potentialities as educational opportunities. The plays are put on not only by dramatic clubs and classes but sometimes by the combined junior and senior classes, by instructional sections in English, and even by history classes (particularly one-act plays and short sketches). Plays are being employed more in assemblies and less as entertainments to which admission is charged. A splendid development in many schools is that of having several casts put on the same play, thus increasing very materially the number of students who benefit by participation. Participating in school plays and school operettas is thought by many to be of considerable value in the mental hygiene of youngsters who may be frustrated otherwise in self expression.

The educational opportunities of dramatics are not confined to the parts in the play. There are splendid opportunities to participate and to get training in connection with the preparation of costumes, stage setting and lighting, construction of scenery, make-up, care of properties, business management (including advertising and the sale of tickets), and social participation (such as ushering). Sometimes students are even permitted to direct or assist in directing plays.

One thing seems quite clear: the educational objectives of speech activities, as of other kinds of activities, seem to be best served when the emphasis is shifted from competition and winning and from concentration on perfect performances toward the participation of a larger number of youngsters and toward attention to what happens to the youngster in terms of his educational growth.

MUSIC ACTIVITIES. Like speech activities, musical activities were among the first types of student activities in the secondary schools. They include concert and marching bands, orchestras, instrumental ensembles, the *a cappella* choir, the assembly sing, and particularly the operetta. It has been observed by many that the quality of the music of young people, both choral and instrumental, has increased greatly in recent decades and that the improvement is largely attributable to the development of bands, orchestras, and singing organizations. Opportunities for participation have increased greatly, since the youngsters are not dependent upon the ability of their parents to pay for music lessons. The administration of music groups is beset with the same problems that are attendant upon most organizations.

One of these problems is the increased cost of participation. This cost may be reduced by subsidies by the board of education for uniforms and even for the more costly instruments. The school may buy the instruments, which become the property of the school, and rent them on a nonprofit basis to the youngsters. This practice may be justified by the fact that the school band, school orchestra, and choral groups are called upon frequently to give programs without charge to the school and to the community. In some schools instruction in small groups is provided for beginners.

Many supervisors of music activities are far more interested in impressing the public than they are in educating the youngsters. Such supervisors need careful and firm guidance. The young people participating in musical as well as other activities need to be protected from excessive demands upon their time.

In recent years the practice of having musical organizations travel long distances to give performances and participate in contests has become so excessive as to be almost incredible. Principals need carefully to consider this practice and to restrict very materially the amount of time and expense involved in travel. The practice has gone a long way toward raising serious questions in the minds of taxpayers and others as to the value of the school education missed while the youngsters are away. The expenses involved have taxed excessively a considerable number of parents, who feel that they must not let their youngsters down; they have made sacrifices unwillingly that they should not have been called upon to make.

As is true in a great many activities, provision should be made for as many students as would care to participate. There should be in large schools several bands, several orchestras, several choral groups, and several casts in operettas. In this connection, principals have a great responsibility for seeing to it that the teachers of music and the sponsors of musical organizations do not sacrifice the educational growth of larger numbers in an attempt to perfect the performance of a small number and thereby impress the community with the outstanding competence of the music teacher or director.

10. School Publications

The principal types of school publications are the newspaper and the annual. In small communities schools cannot afford to print their own newspapers and may make arrangements for space in the local newspaper, space which may carry a title and include material produced by students under the guidance of a teacher. School papers may also be mimeographed papers. Some school papers are not published at all but read orally. This is particularly true of the home-room or class paper.

There is always the problem of guidance and censorship in connection with the school newspaper. Some youngsters' sense of humor is not quite developed or is developed along freakish lines; a young daredevil may confuse originality and humor with violation of the canons of good taste, particularly along the lines of sex, and overemphasize news materials which pertain to sex or drinking. Also, in many schools there is a principal, sponsor, or teacher who is easily shocked by youngsters, who exercises such censorship as to destroy a great deal of the natural interest of the youngsters in their newspaper, and who creates unfortunate conflicts and disturbances.

THE SCHOOL ANNUAL. As stated by Johnston and Faunce, the principal limitations of the school annual are as follows:

1. *The annual is frequently too costly.* The school staff is often under pressure, on one side by printers and engravers and on the other by the seniors who want their annual to be more ambitious and impressive than any previous issue. The results of such pressures are expensive paper, leather bindings, and costly engravings.
2. *Too often the annual is a stereotyped imitation of the older college yearbooks.* Literary features which belong in the magazine rather than in the yearbook are included as space fillers. Humor is often clipped from joke books and newspapers, and modified by using names of teachers and pupils. Meaningless quotations following the pictures of seniors, lists of pet peeves, and designations of "most (or least) popular," "most handsome," "sophisticated," "good-natured" add little to the historic value of the annual, and detract from its dignity. This might be said also of the special senior items, such as the class prophecy, class will, class poem, and graduation addresses. The chief objection to the imitative annual is that it provides little opportunity for originality or educational experience for those who produce it. If this type of annual is to be published, it may be well to engage a commercial company to prepare it, and free the time of students for something more important and educational.

3. *The annual is often almost exclusively for and about the senior class.* While it is appropriate for the yearbook to give increased attention to the class which is spending its last year in the school, it need not confine its emphasis to the seniors and neglect the rest of the school.
4. *Pictures are often stiff, posed, and unnatural.* Often the pictures in the annual are as awkward and unnatural as those of Great-aunt Ella and Uncle John in the family album.
5. *The annual is often a miscellaneous collection of items rather than a planned production.* The weight of tradition induces the inclusion of much inappropriate material, and no relationship or central theme appears to give the book unity.[3]

Johnston and Faunce have given suggestions for management of the school annual which tend to reduce the effect of these limitations:

1. Costs can be reduced by careful planning. As a last resort, a June issue of the school paper or magazine can be devoted to the senior class record and serve as a low-cost annual. This device is not entirely satisfactory, however, for achieving the purposes of the annual. Offset printing can produce a highly satisfactory yearbook at low cost. Competitive bidding can cut the engraving and printing costs if a printed annual is desired. A reasonable budget, carefully planned and rigidly adhered to, will help.
2. The yearbook can be planned by the whole school through representation on the advisory board, and built up in original fashion around some appropriate local theme. Pictures and other *décor* can be developed on this central theme.
3. The annual can devote space to all students and all activities, thus enhancing the general appeal of the book. The test of the success of an annual lies in its appeal to the average reader, who makes its publication possible by his support.
4. The faculty adviser's schedule should be so arranged as to allow sufficient time for supervision of this task. If a yearbook is important to have, it is important to schedule time for guidance of the project.
5. The yearbook should be a student product, with every piece of copy, photography, and layout the work of students. The same should be true of the business and circulation work. Engravers, printers, and photographers can help with advice, but the actual decision and the real planning must be in the hands of students under the guidance of a competent, interested sponsor.
6. Plans should be made to get the kind of photographs which tell an action story. Informal pictures in a natural action setting are much more interesting than portraits. Individuals and groups should be presented in their characteristic settings: the principal at his desk, the biology class on a field trip, the football team lined up for the big game.
7. There is an excellent opportunity for educational planning in presenting the various activities in such a way as to interpret the spirit and life of the school. The Grosse Pointe (Michigan) *View Pointe,* for example, carries on its cover an artistic photograph of some feature of the school – the clock tower framed by trees, the flagpole seen through the columns of the school entrance, a

---

[3]Johnston and Faunce, *op. cit.,* pp. 185-186. Quoted with permission of the publishers, The Ronald Press Company.

winter view of the school, three graduates in uniform with the school as background. The book then has eighteen pages of vivid photographs of students and faculty at work and play, arranged under suitable captions, and with accompanying interpretation and comment.

8. In illustrating and describing the educational activities of the year, the annual incidentally can help the parents to understand better the total program of the school. It can be a potent public relations instrument, without diverting it from its major function of providing a souvenir record for students.[4]

FINANCIAL PROBLEMS. Publications are financed in various ways, including: (1) subscriptions by the youngsters; (2) subsidy by the activity budget for the entire school; (3) sale of advertising space; and (4) subsidy by the board of education.

Sale of subscriptions and single copies adds to the so-called hidden costs of schooling and is not to be desired for this reason, as well as for the reason that much time is wasted on subscription campaigns. Definitely the best financial support for school publications is subsidy by the activity budget or the total student-body funds of the school, as well as material subsidy by the board of education which believes in the educational value of school publications.

11. The Home Room

FUNCTIONS AND PURPOSES. Perhaps, from the educational point of view, the most valuable extracurricular activity is the home room, when it is organized and operated in accordance with a high-grade modern plan. The home room serves the following four types of functions:

1. *Administrative.* It serves as an agency for distributing notices, report cards, textbooks, and materials; for making announcements and checking on tardiness and absence; for collections of scrap paper and other materials; for sales campaigns; for discussion of school policies, new rules, and the like.
2. *Curriculum supplementation.* It furnishes an opportunity for teaching important topics which are not adequately treated in the regular curriculum subjects, or which may be better learned by home-room procedures—for example, safety education, personality development, occupations, social conventions, current events, study habits and techniques, home relationships; it is an excellent place for emphasis upon social and character education.
3. *Guidance.* (1) It is an organization for group guidance in such fields as health, selection of courses, selection of an occupation, personal appearance, making friends, use of leisure time, securing, holding, and getting ahead in a job, boy-girl relationships, school citizenship, matters of ethics and of sportsmanship, and problems of going to college; and (2) it is an arrangement for guidance of the individual pupil by a home-room teacher, who comes to know the individual pupil better than the typical teacher of his classroom subjects can and to whom a few pupils are assigned as protégés for guidance.

[4]Johnston and Faunce, *op. cit.,* pp. 186-188. Quoted with permission of the publishers.

4. *Promotion of extracurricular activities.* The home room may contribute to this function in two ways: (1) by contributions to the all-school program of activities and (2) by its own program of activities. In the home-room clubs, the programs of school organizations and other activities may be brought to the attention of home-room members, their value discussed, and the students' participation encouraged. Certain types of administrative routine may be carried on—for example, announcements, election of home-room representatives, rally programs. The home room may also have athletic, debate, or other teams to participate in interhome-room competition. The home room may carry on its own activities by putting on programs at the school assembly; it may have programs, either for its own members or with another home room as its guest, including musical numbers, talks, debates, vaudeville stunts, or reading of the home-room "paper."

The home room is particularly useful in larger schools, where each class is too large a group to work together with the most effective group dynamics. It is particularly valuable, too, in schools that have no core program in which the students are broken up into groups sufficiently small for good group activities and group dynamics.

The home room should not be confused with the roll room (often miscalled home room), where youngsters meet in relatively small groups at some period in the day for from 5 to 10 minutes, usually at the beginning of school, and where attendance is checked, absence excuses are administered, announcements made, textbooks distributed, and other routine management and administrative needs taken care of. Home-room groups should be sufficiently small, their meeting periods sufficiently long, and their operating philosophy sufficiently appropriate to make them, to a considerable extent, community units and living groups. In these home-room groups there will be discussion of school policies and various other matters of more than ordinary and immediate interest to the students involved.

The home room also provides an excellent opportunity, which has been exploited in a small but increasing number of schools, for developing effective parent-school relationships. It is quite possible for the home-room teacher to come to know the parents of every youngster in the room. Indeed, in some schools it is made a point for the teacher to pay a brief visit to the home of every youngster in his home-room group. This visitation is particularly useful in cases in which it is difficult to get the parents to attend meetings in school.

In many schools the home-room sponsor organizes the home-room parents and has them meet several times during the year, in the afternoon or evening (the latter is probably better, because of the fact that fathers may attend then). At these meetings the work of the youngsters may be explained to the parents. Parents may have an opportunity to raise questions and to make criticisms which may be passed on to the appropriate teachers, supervisors, or administrators. It has been observed that in schools where home-room parents and other groups have been formed and where they meet with home-room sponsors or representatives of the school, there is definitely a better school-parent relationship and much less serious criticism of the work of the school.

HOME-ROOM SPONSOR. In some larger schools the very reasonable practice is employed of assigning to the same home rooms, at least for one semester, students who are seriously considering going to college; in these home rooms they can be provided with specialized sponsors.

In most schools where home rooms exist, all or practically all teachers are assigned home-room groups. Unless a sponsor is assigned to two groups, or the groups are very large, almost every teacher is needed. If it were not for schedule difficulties, it is very likely that many principals would much prefer to employ for this important work only those teachers who by training, personality, and interest are best qualified. In fact, such a practice is actually employed in some schools, two home-room groups usually being counted as the equivalent of one class taught.

Sponsors need to be interested in boys and girls as individual human beings, rather than merely as "students," and they should be the kind of persons with whom pupils will co-operate and develop a confidential guidance relation; also they need to have developed a modern practical philosophy of pupil-teacher relations and of home-room practice. They should also have had some training in such fields as guidance, extra-curricular activities, modern secondary education, mental hygiene, psychology of personality, and intelligence-testing.

Where home rooms have not succeeded, the failure has been attributed in most instances to the lack of preparation of the home-room sponsors. They have not been trained in college for home-room leadership and planning, nor have they had sufficient in-service training and time to understand how to develop a program of activities for pupils and themselves that is in harmony with the fundamental philosophy of home-room organization. In addition, many others have not the time during the school year to make the investigations and do the planning necessary for a successful home-room program; in cases in which they have not made considerable preparation during the period of the school year, in summer workshops, or otherwise, the extra time required by home-room activities has been a burden and they have been unable to plan and care for the home-room program during the year.

In some schools it has been planned to have two groups of home rooms that meet at different times, so that one teacher may handle two home rooms; home-room sponsorships are thus assigned only to those who are most suited by reason of educational philosophy, personality, interest, training, and experience. Where two home rooms, each meeting twice a week, are given to one sponsor, they might well be counted the equivalent of a class taught, particularly in the first few years, giving the sponsors some time for planning, for conferences with the youngsters, for studying the data about each individual youngster, and for conferences at school or at home with parents.

In some schools sponsors are assigned to the same groups for several years. Sponsors under this arrangement come to know their pupils much better. Where this is done, pupils should be permitted to change groups at the end of any semester.

Time Allotment and Schedule. In a majority of schools home rooms meet two or more class periods a week. Home rooms which meet for periods of 15 minutes or less are not really home rooms; they are roll rooms, serving only an administrative function. It is a common practice to fit the home-room meetings into a daily activity program—for example, home rooms twice a week, clubs twice a week, and school assembly once a week.

It is becoming generally recognized that home-room or activity periods should not be scheduled for the beginning or the end of either the morning or the afternoon session. To schedule them so, it has been discovered, is to invite nonattendance at these periods.

Officers and Committees. A good home-room organization is very likely to include a president, a vice-president, a secretary, a treasurer, a representative on the student council and his alternate, the executive committee, and other committees to carry responsibilities as they develop. The vice-president should have definite responsibilities, in addition to assisting the president and presiding in his absence. Among such duties frequently are the following: director of safety, director of campaigns, chairman of the reception committee, receiving visitors, and looking after new students.

Among the committees most likely to be useful are the following: citizenship, scholarship, programs, finance and auditing, welfare and visiting, entertainment, and the committee on relationships with the all-school program.

In some home-room organizations there is an auxiliary parents' organization, in which all parents of pupils in the home room are eligible for membership. Parents are encouraged to attend home-room assemblies, to sponsor home-room parties, and to get acquainted with the sponsor, who will introduce them to other teachers upon request or upon need.

Fundamental Principles. The most important elements in the success of a home-room program include the following:

1. The staff should study home-room plans and philosophy and should plan materials for a year before launching the home rooms.
2. A collection of not less than one book per pupil in the school should be made available, including books on vocations, vocational guidance, educational guidance, social conventions and etiquette, and the various topics likely to be discussed in the home room. Hundreds of books very suitable for this use have been published in recent years. In recent years, too, there have been published many valuable pamphlets and bulletins, particularly by the Science Research Associates in Chicago.

3. New teachers should be selected partly on the basis of their ability to be good home-room sponsors.
4. When new teachers are employed, there should be an understanding that home-room sponsorship is an important part of the regular teaching load. Of course, this same understanding should prevail with all teachers engaged in home-room sponsoring.
5. There should be available to all home-room sponsors collections of outlines, manuals, and units for home rooms, already worked out in other schools; these should be kept up to date.
6. Sponsors should recognize that home-room discussions should be characterized by freedom to express opinion, spontaneity, and naturalness.
7. Lectures should be avoided, particularly lectures by school personnel. When opinions are expressed by the sponsors and others, they should be identified as such. Presentation should be short, to the point, and delivered in a conversational manner; opportunity should be afforded for questions and discussion.
8. The sponsor should from time to time suggest appropriate things to read—for example, short, interesting bulletins and articles that are very likely to be of interest to home-room groups. This suggesting should not be done in the spirit of assignment, and checking up should not be done by quizzes.
9. Use should be made of the learning device of having individual students or small committees volunteer to make special investigations and reports on various problems and topics.
10. If it seems necessary to add dignity to home-room work, credit toward graduation may well be given, usually one fourth of a year unit or one half of a semester unit for each year in programs in which there are two to three periods a week of not less than 30 minutes each. Giving credit is hardly practical when home-room meetings do not involve as much time as 60 minutes a week.

HOME-ROOM GUIDES. In places where home rooms have functioned more effectively, there has been a guiding outline. In places where home rooms have been abandoned, there usually has been no guide. Teachers became confused, turned home rooms into study periods, and fell far short of conducting functioning home rooms.

The outlines need not be too detailed and can be used as a resource rather than as a "course of study." A guide assists in reducing the duplication between grades or years.

Following is a typical outline of topics suitable for home-room discussion in the ninth or tenth grade:

LIVING AND PLANNING YOUR LIFE

UNIT 1. Meeting School Situations

Section 1. What Is Your School Trying to Do for You?
2. What Values May You Expect from Continued Schooling?
3. How Does Your Success in High School Affect Your Future?
4. How Does Your School Evaluate Your Success?
5. What Is the Best Method of Study?
6. How Can You Use the Library to the Best Advantage?
7. Who Pays for Your Education?

53. How Does Your Personal Economics Affect Your Life?
54. How Can You Most Profitably Use Your Leisure Time?
55. What Hobbies Will You Cultivate?

UNIT 5. Looking to the Future

Section 56. What Agencies Are Available to Help You to Secure Employment?
57. What Opportunities for Employment Does Your Local Community Offer?
58. How Will You Conduct Yourself When Applying for a Job?
59. How Will You Conduct Yourself on the Job?
60. How Will Social-Security Laws and Union Organizations Affect You on the Job?
61. Will You Go Into Business for Yourself?
62. What Will You Do if You Are Unable to Secure Employment?
63. Which College Will You Attend?
64. What Procedure Will You Follow to Get Admitted to College?
65. How Will You Finance Your Post-High-School Education?
66. What Will Be Your Initial Adjustment to College?
67. How Will You Conduct Yourself While Living Away from Home?
68. When Will You Marry?
69. What Community Organizations Will You Join?[5]

12. The School Assembly

PROGRAMS. Successful assembly programs can hardly be expected to materialize except as the result of a well-organized schedule planned several weeks in advance. Types of material suitable for assemblies are:

1. Announcements and explanations of interest to the entire school relative to the various administrative procedures.
2. Announcements and reports relative to the achievements and honors of pupils, teams, classes, and organizations and the awarding of letters, honors, and prizes.
3. Programs growing out of curricular activities: dramatizations, pageants, demonstrations, presentations by means of projecting machines, style shows, exhibits of products of classes in household arts, fine arts, and industrial arts, and readings of original or other poems or prose.
4. Programs growing out of extracurricular activities: concerts, exhibitions, demonstrations, pageants, and dramatizations presented by glee clubs, orchestras, bands, and by radio, first-aid, history, foreign-language, debating, dramatic, and other clubs; reports, exhibitions, and final interclass contests of various types of teams, such as typing and debating; rallies for athletic and other contests.
5. Business meeting of the general student organization: elections, nominations, and discussion of school problems and enterprises.
6. Programs from outside sources: informational, entertaining, and inspirational talks and lectures by qualified local speakers, speakers from state edu-

[5]N. William Newsom, Harl R. Douglass, and Harry L. Dotson, *Living and Planning Your Life,* New York, McGraw-Hill, 1952, pp. v-vii.

cational institutions, and occasional distinguished visitors in the city; club programs given by local service clubs, parent-teacher associations, and musical, literary, and civic organizations.

7. Programs of music, or drama, or exhibits, produced by the organizations and clubs of other schools.
8. Programs for special days or movements: patriotic and biographical occasions, thrift days, Thanksgiving, Armistice Day, Christmas, and Memorial Day.
9. Mass singing by the students.
10. Miscellaneous programs: appropriate movies and sets of slides (e.g., those taken in other countries), especially desirable radio and television programs, faculty programs, miscellaneous debates, and reports by students of trips and interesting experiences.

Though the first consideration in the selection of assembly-program material is its possible administrative and educational value, it must without question be of interest to high-school students. Too much speaking must be avoided, as well as speakers whose talks are not adapted to the vocabulary, maturity, and interests of high-school boys and girls.

Learning experiences in both class and extra-class activities may result in student-centered assembly programs. For example, a homemaking, agriculture, or science class may put on a demonstration of work done in the class; or students in the music, art, and speech departments may combine to present a Thanksgiving program. Students in the Rochester, Minnesota, Senior High School have used the "town meeting" idea in assembly programs in which student problems and responsibilities are discussed. At Drury High School, North Adams, Massachusetts, the students presented a panel discussion, with audience participation, on student interests in movies, radio programs, and comic books. Prior to the assembly program the 800 students in the school were polled to secure views on those topics. At Lincoln High School, Wisconsin Rapids, Wisconsin, an assembly on etiquette was presented the week preceding the junior-senior prom. In the East High School, Aurora, Illinois, an assembly program including use of ballet and pantomine depicted "A Day at East High," in which actual school situations and scenes were presented. Such programs as the foregoing may have considerable significance in the efforts or schools to meet youth needs more adequately.[6]

Assemblies should provide a socializing influence and educational profit, not merely an opportunity to make announcements. Among the types of activities found most frequently in secondary-school assemblies are the following:

1. Installation of student officers
2. Group singing

[6]J. Lloyd Trump, *Extraclass Activities and the Needs of Youth,* Fifty-second Yearbook, National Society for the Study of Education, University of Chicago Press, 1953, Chapter 9.

3. Orchestra programs
4. School plays and pageant features
5. Occasional outside speakers
6. Promotion of worthy school projects.

Types of programs which are appearing less in school assemblies are those sponsored by various commercial groups and "pep" assemblies preceding athletic contests. The "pep" assembly has been found in many schools to develop excessive emotionalism and to have a harmful effect upon classwork in periods immediately preceding and following the assembly.

MANAGEMENT. The assembly may be regarded not only as a student activity but also as an important administrative device of the principal—an educational agency especially useful for certain types of education not employing student activity and for the establishment of favorable contacts between the central administrative staff and the students as a whole. For this reason it has been a common practice to make the assembly a dual-purpose activity, presided over jointly by the high-school principal and the president of the student body or his assembly-program chairman. In some schools the responsibility for the assemblies is entrusted to an assembly committee composed of both faculty and pupil members, who co-operate with the principal and the president of the student body in arranging the programs for assemblies.

Although any day of the week is used for assemblies in some schools, Friday and Wednesday are the more popular days. An assembly usually lasts a full class period, although in a considerable number of schools the period is shortened.

Practically all secondary schools today have a calendar planned in advance, the majority of them planning it for a semester ahead and a considerable number making a tentative plan for a full year.

In about half of the schools some provision is made for assembly expenses. The funds come both from the student-activity budget and from appropriations by the board of education. A practice of providing fees for out-of-school speakers and entertainers, which developed in a considerable number of schools particularly in the 1940's and 1950's, seems to be on its way out. The use of funds for professional entertainers is certainly open to very serious question and criticism.

Planning and rehearsing for assembly programs is done at a variety of times, both during school hours and after school: for example, during home-room activity period, during the other activity periods, and in a few instances during class periods.

The principal problems that must be faced with respect to planning and administering assemblies include finding a time for rehearsal of programs, avoiding the overburdening of teachers in connection with planning and preparing for assembly programs, completing assemblies with the time limit, providing sufficiently interesting programs, and dealing with individuals or groups who wish to use the assembly for a special religious, political, or commercial purpose.

An important problem in some schools, though not the major one in most schools, is the insuring of appropriate behavior on the part of all students. In most schools the principal, teachers, and student leaders share this responsibility.

STUDENT PARTICIPATION IN CONTROL. As far as possible, the assembly should be managed by student representatives under faculty direction. Teachers should not dominate assembly programs. These periods should constitute opportunities for developing responsibility and skill in management. In addition, student leaders, if not the bulk of the students, should share in feelings of responsibility for making the assemblies successful. The appearance of students in positions of leadership serves as an inspiration to other students in the areas of responsibility and leadership. Principals may always arrange to be introduced for whatever announcements or talks they may wish to make without interfering with student management. Student leaders may be advised and assisted behind the scenes as much as is necessary to make the assemblies interesting and otherwise worth while. The success of student management, however, depends upon reducing to a minimum close or arbitrary supervision by faculty or principal. The ideas of student leaders should be considered on their merits and at times actually given consideration beyond their real value.

PRESIDING OFFICER. In the majority of senior high schools today the presiding officer of the assembly is a student officer, although the principal may open the assembly and turn it over to the student officer. Frequently, however, the student officer presides over the entire program, calling upon the principal and others to make announcements or statements that have been arranged for in advance. The president of the student body or of the student council is usually the presiding officer.

In a majority of the junior high schools the principal presides at least for part of the time, although there is an increasing tendency to rely more upon student presiding officers.

ASSEMBLY PERIODS. If an activity period is provided for, the assembly should probably be scheduled for this period. If assembly periods are provided by dismissing classes for a period, they should be alternated among the various class periods in order that certain classes will not be dismissed a disproportionate number of times. The last period in the day is useful for assemblies which are wholly or in large part rallies. For other assemblies the last period is the least desirable, offering, as it does, a temptation to pupils and parents which results in more absences than would occur if classes were held at that period.

Evaluation of Assembly Programs. The assembly program should be constantly evaluated by the principal and by committees especially appointed for the purpose. They should consult students, and possibly parents, to get their opinions. A very valuable evaluation of the school assembly can be made by teachers with good background, who will have regard to the educational development of the youngsters: the development of desirable and valuable information and understandings, of social, emotional, and intellectual habits and skills, and physical habits, skills, ideals, attitudes, and interests. Such an evaluation cannot be made objectively; it must depend upon the background and expert insight of those who are to make it. It must involve also careful study throughout the year as the programs are developed. It is also possible to use interest and attitude questionnaires which are given to students at the end of each year. The scores for different years give a rough indication of the development of assemblies.

13. Class Organizations and Commencement

Class Organization. Particularly in the small schools, but also in many of the larger ones, grade-year classes are often organized and function for some extracurricular activities, both to facilitate administration and management and to promote educational purposes and functions. Such class organizations carry on various sorts of desirable and necessary activities, participation in which is educational. In larger schools the class organization must employ committees for handling various types of activities and for exploring matters, discussing them, and making reports to the class, since the membership of a class is too large to permit adequate discussion in class meetings of all the matters that may concern a class. Committees may also be used to carry on the management and administration of various types of activities which relate, for example, to the class social life, including picnics, dances, and parties. In the smaller schools in which there are no home-room organizations, the class organization may serve reasonably well some of the functions of the home room.

One of the dangers of class organization is the temptation to purchase expensive class rings or pins. Rarely does the purchaser wear the ring or pin more than a year. In recent years principals have discouraged the purchase of class jewelry as being an unwise investment and constituting one of the contributing features of excessive and undemocratic costs of attending school.

Selection of Sponsors. In many schools sponsors have been identified who are particularly good at working with a particular class —for example, the ninth grade, or the seniors—and these are kept on as sponsors year after year. In some schools a class will have two sponsors, one male teacher and one female teacher; in a few schools each class will have several sponsors. In other schools the sponsor moves along each year with his class, thus coming to know them quite well, to know their parents personally, and to have knowledge about and attachments for a particular class and the individuals which compose it. There is much to be said for this last plan.

Because the principal knows the relative effectiveness of sponsors in various types of activities and is in a good position to distribute the load of teachers, it is best for him to choose the sponsors for the various activities; before doing so, however, he should probably confer with some of the student leaders in each activity and with members of the staff. In some schools the choice of sponsors is made jointly by the student council and the principal; this is not a bad plan.

TYPES OF CLASS ACTIVITIES. It is impossible to catalogue all the activities which classes carry on. They are too numerous and too diverse for detailed treatment. A list of sample activities actually engaged in by high-school classes may suggest some of the trends. The purely routine, administrative functions, such as roll-taking, have not been listed.

Social Activities

Class parties
Hay rides
Sleigh rides
Dances
Proms
Theater parties
Banquets
Picnics
Senior skip day
Class trips

Fund-Raising Activities
Sales of candy, soft drinks, pie, popcorn
Christmas-tree sales
Sale of publications
Motion pictures
Rummage sales – clothing

School Service

Class gift to school
Editing paper, annual school handbook
Orientation program for incoming classes
Senior or sophomore "guides," "buddies"
Landscaping school grounds
Repairing school property
Developing school camp

Putting on school assemblies
Presenting commencement pageants
Writing school history
Intramural programs in athletics, forensics
Presenting music or drama festivals
Building up school library
Presenting class plays
Organizing grade-level parent clubs
Conducting follow-up studies of school graduates and dropouts
Teaching in nursery school, or in elementary or junior high school
Community Service
Landscaping public grounds
Conducting public-opinion polls
Making surveys of housing, recreation, or traffic
Planting trees
Conserving soil and game resources
Advertising and promoting for the community
Surveying job opportunities in the community
Presenting festivals
Organizing speakers' bureau
Putting out town newspaper
Conducting town theater
Distributing Christmas baskets
Organizing community clubs
Obtaining traffic lights
Conducting campaigns on health, malaria control, chest X rays, and safety
Campaigning for change in form of city government

EDUCATIONAL TRAVEL. There has been in recent years an increased amount of school travel, particularly by senior classes. This travel in some instances has been made possible by school busses. In some instances the amount of time taken for the trip and the amount of expense involved have been thought to be excessive and the project of the long trip has been abandoned.

Different policies are used for financing such travel. Sometimes a class or club uses funds accumulated through social events, sales of commododities, or receipts from an entertainment to offset the charges in part or completely. Although the possible contributions of planned tours to individual students and to the school they represent are obvious, care must be exercised that tours do not require too large expenditures of student and faculty time, energy, and money. Undoubtedly some trips constitute undertakings which are too ambitious in view of their contribution to educational objectives, including especially the objectives of public relations, education of those participating, and the good will and pleasure of the students and their parents.[7]

---

[7] *Ibid.*

SENIOR CLASS ACTIVITIES. In practically all four-year and senior high schools the senior class participates not only in commencement and in baccalaureate services but also in such activities as class plays and class dances. Other activities of the senior class may be farewell assemblies, senior-class trips, senior banquets, and senior picnics. Few schools have all of these activities. In some schools the costs of such activities have become very excessive and call for corrective measures on the part of the administration of the schools. In many schools the costs are somewhat difficult for students who come from homes of lowest income.

THE COMMENCEMENT. There has been in recent years a tendency to draw away from the old, formal, traditional commencement exercise and to foster the new, vitalized, student-participation type of exercise. The characteristics of the old and the new commencements may be set forth as follows:

The Old Commencement:

1. Was planned by school officials.
2. Consisted chiefly of an "address" by an imported speaker.
3. Centered about no special or helpful topic.
4. Was indentical from year to year.
5. Was used chiefly as an opportunity for "preaching" to the graduates.
6. Secured the passive interest of the graduates and community.
7. Made no effort to interpret the school to its patrons.
8. Received no advance preparation.
9. Did not utilize the available resources.
10. Merely ended another year.

The New Commencement:

1. Is planned by the graduates.
2. Consists of a program by the graduates.
3. Centers about a topic of interest to pupils, parents, and community.
4. Is original and attractive.
5. Is used as an opportunity for graduates to train themselves for self-activity.
6. Secures the active interest of the graduates and the community.
7. Interprets vital school activities to citizens.
8. Receives preparation by large numbers of people throughout the year.
9. Utilizes the resources of the school, home, and community.
10. Makes a large contribution to graduates, school, and community.

Quite frequently the commencement centers around a particular theme which furnishes the motif of the program. Themes that are used fairly widely are the following: Our Town and Our People, The Story of Democracy, Our School of Today and the School of Yesteryear, Peace and Goodwill to Men, Challenges to Negro Youth, The Space World Today, Our Great American Heritage, Our School, One World, Let Youth Speak, Beyond the Horizon, and Our Constitution Lives.

The National Association of Secondary School Principals[8] issues

[8]Address: 1201 Sixteenth Street, N.W., Washington, D.C.

from time to time excellent bulletins concerning commencement exercises, particularly of the new type. These bulletins describe in detail a great many commencement programs and related senior-class activities, including formals, orations, demonstrations, pageants, tableaus, motion-picture presentations, musical numbers, choric speaking, and community participation.

It is coming to be believed by school administrators that commencements for junior high schools serve no good function and that they should be discontinued since they are likely to encourage the idea of dropping out of school either at commencement time or soon thereafter. In their place in many schools there are now operated year-end assemblies which honor the graduates. Frequently these are held at night and special invitations are sent to parents and friends.

The following principles seem to be sound and contributory to achieving the functions of the commencement program and exercises:

1. Opportunities should be utilized to emphasize the achievements, honors, and high quality of the student body in general, the graduates in particular, and incidentally the faculty.
2. Acknowledgment of the co-operation of the community should be sincere, clear, and definite.
3. Praise for, or exhibition of, individual students should not be such that by comparison some pupils will be humiliated or parents disappointed.
4. Some mention should be made in some way of the special features, philosophy, and objectives of the local school program, especially of those emphasized currently—in the year just past and the year to come.
5. The program should not be too long, should be carefully planned, and should be devoid of dry or uninteresting features. Commencement speakers should be carefully chosen and instructed.
6. A considerable amount of formality and ceremony is very appropriate, if not too time-consuming and if carefully rehearsed.
7. The commencement exercises should be in an attractice hall, which is adequately decorated and has superior acoustical properties.
8. The costs of commencement to the individual student or family should be held to a minimum which should not embarrass any student or his parents.
9. Care should be taken not to arrange a program which will offend any individuals or groups, any church, or any prominent local musician.
10. The board of education should be given adequate recognition and opportunity for participation. The superintendent or principal should not be too conspicuous.
11. Consultation should be held throughout the year with members of the senior class, representative parents, members of the teaching staff, and the student council. These council sessions should be for the purpose of getting suggestions which will improve the commencement exercises in the light of their objectives.
12. All commencement activities should be built on the basis of their contribution to educational objectives, including especially public relations, education of those participating, and the good will and pleasure of the students and their parents.

14. Social-Life Activities

TYPES OF SOCIAL ACTIVITIES. Of the kinds of social activity which are carried on in addition to the activity of ordinary clubs and organizations, the following may be mentioned as examples: gatherings with refreshments at homes of students, informal dances in the school gymnasium, social activities in the lunch-hour period, picnics, sleigh rides, and square dancing.

There are several important suggestions which should not be lost sight of and which are the result of careful study and experience with social activities. Among them the following may be mentioned:

1. Social activities must not prove to be too expensive, particularly for the students participating in them.
2. Parents should be brought in to participate in the planning, management, and chaperoning of such social life.
3. Care must be taken not to offend too seriously even small minorities in the community who are opposed to certain types of social life—for example, dancing and card playing. This does not mean that there must be no dancing or card playing where any parents object; on the other hand, it does mean the situation must be handled diplomatically and that perhaps some contact with parents should be made in a friendly way to attempt to reconcile them to the program.
4. Care should be taken by both parents and members of the school staff that the social activities do not excite deserved criticism by permitting such things as too late hours, drinking of beer or other intoxicants, petting and necking on the part of students, destruction of property, or the dangerous use of automobiles or other conveyances.

All school social functions should be channeled through regular organizations of the school; such things as the following should be attended to:

1. Getting a place on the school calendar and avoiding conflicts.
2. Applying for a permit for a party, with definite evidence of appropriate arrangements, such as the names and signatures of parent-faculty sponsors.
3. Checking up and reporting by the students in charge and by the sponsor.

A typical form for application to hold a party or a social event is shown on the next page.

CHAPERONS FOR SOCIAL FUNCTIONS. Administrators of most secondary schools wisely insist upon chaperons for school social functions. The chaperons should be selected or at least approved by the principal or someone designated by him (for example, by the dean of girls).

Members of the staff and their wives may serve as chaperons and parents of some of the students involved may well be selected and share the responsibility for chaperoning. The number of chaperons needed will depend upon the nature of the social event and the number of students involved; for events involving both boys and girls, at least one male and one female chaperon should be assigned (preferably, two of each sex should be assigned).

FORM 4. *Application for Holding School Social Affairs*

REGISTRATION OF EVENTS

Date ______________

Date reserved ______________ Organization ______________

Type of event ______________

Place ______________

Time: From ______________

To ______________

Purpose of event ______________

Guests ______________

____

Committee chairmen: Head chairman ______________

Decoration ______________

Reception ______________

Program ______________

Refreshments ______________

Clean-up ______________

Others ______________

Faculty sponsors ______________

Plan of event ______________

____

____

Invitation or publicity arrangements ______________

____

Refreshment arrangements ______________

____

Transportation arrangements ______________

____

Estimated expense. Total ______________ Method of financing ______________

Estimated expense. Per person ______________

____

Final report:

Total receipts ______________

Expenses ______________

Net profit ______________

Disposal of proceeds ______________

____

____

Suggestions for next time ______________

____

____

Approved ______________

____

The administrator or the dean of girls should prepare instructions for chaperons which will indicate their duties and responsibilities and contain suggestions for them. These instructions should cover such items as smoking and non-smoking areas, minimum lighting allowed, hours during which the building may be used, use of automobiles during the time of the event (involving students leaving the building without a chaperon), and the acquaintance of the chaperon with such matters as exits, fire doors, fire extinguishers, and the fire-alarm boxes. It should be made clear to the chaperons that they should remain at the social event until it is over and the students have dispersed and that they should prepare a report on the event. Chaperoning should be distributed among suitable members of the faculty and parents.

Undemocratic Social Organizations. For half a century or more the high schools of the United States have had to contend with the problem of undemocratic social clubs. These clubs and organizations seem to possess all the bad features and few of the reasons for existence of college fraternities and sororities, which in recent years have themselves been very seriously criticized. A safe criticism of these organizations is that they are undemocratic. In many instances the organizations tend to interfere with the normal democratic processes within the school—for example, by attempting to influence and control elections and the selection of team representatives. They tend to dissatisfy and discourage those boys and girls who are not given an opportunity to belong to them and thus often bring criticism upon the school from parents. Various approaches have been employed in an effort to meet this problem, including the following:

1. Prohibition of the organizations by state law and by rules and regulations of the local boards of education. This prohibition has been very hard to enforce; in many instances the parents and even the administrators and board of education have winked at the law rather than enforce it and bring penalties upon the youngsters and their parents.
2. The attempt to bring the organizations in as regular social clubs of the school and to give them supervision. This does not work too well, since the youngsters do not want supervision and usually want secret societies. In addition, undemocratic features of the organizations cause them to be in violation of several of the more important fundamental principles and ideals of student organizations in the modern high school.
3. Discouraging the formation of such clubs and membership in them by communicating with the parents, pointing out the position of the school, and giving the reasons for it; the refusal to permit students belonging to such unrecognized organizations to participate as representatives of the school in any way, whether by holding an elective office or by being a member of a team or any other group representing the school before the public.

In many schools, after having conferences with parents, the board of education has passed legislation to establish and to enforce the administration of student activities, including the requirement of a pledge by each student who is a candidate for any school office or who wishes to represent the school on any team that he is not a member of any such organization and will not join one.

Whether or not this device is used, it is very desirable to give considerable attention to the matter of discussing with parents the limitations, dangers, and bad features of high-school fraternities and sororities; perhaps some representative of a college or university might be present at the discussion in order to bolster the case against the organizations. In addition, there has been developed in many schools a constructive program which includes such things as: (1) developing a rich student-activity life, including much provision for parties, dances, and other social life; (2) refusing to provide a meeting place or in any other way to recognize any activities except those definitely sponsored by the school; (3) having students in the school themselves discuss clubs and programs for social life, including secret societies, with a view to developing student opinion against these societies; (4) providing good sponsorship and other favorable conditions for the success of clubs and extracurricular activities; and (5) guarding carefully against the participation of cliques that include the secret organizations in elections, athletics, or other organizations of the school.

Because these clubs usually narrow the interest and social contacts of the youngsters, give them an artificial status of personal worth and thus develop snobbishness, create bitterness and dissatisfaction on the part of those who are not invited to become members, and result in an unfair distribution of honors and positions of importance in the student body, administrators and educators, as well as educational sociologists, have been very much opposed to them and have been working on ways to eliminate them from secondary schools.

A PRACTICAL PLAN. In many schools a practical compromise plan is employed which is aimed at converting fraternities and sororities into legitimate student organizations. The following letter employed in the Ponca City, Oklahoma, schools indicates the nature of the plan and constitutes an approach to the problem of obtaining parent co-operation.

Dear Patron:

One of the questions that is asked most frequently of the high-school principal and of other members of the senior high school faculty is "Should my son or daughter join what is generally known as a 'high-school fraternity' or 'high-school sorority'?" The purpose of this letter is to present a frank discussion of this subject. We believe the best way of presenting the various phases of the problem is by answering a number of questions pertinent to the situation.

I. What is the origin of these high-school groups?

[*Ans.*] The present groups were organized from fifteen to thirty years ago. Some of them were first connected with national high school fraternity organizations having secret rituals, initiations, and insignia, which were similar to those of college fraternities and sororities.

II. What is their present legal status?

[*Ans.*] The State legislature has a regulation outlawing high-school fraternities and sororities and "other secret societies." Exception is made for the Order of De Molay, the Rainbow Girls, and the junior organizations of other fraternal orders that have responsible adult leaders. In a test case, brought before the Board of Control of the Oklahoma High School Athletic Association in order to determine what was "a fraternity, sorority, or secret society," it was decided that students could band themselves together in "co-operative groups" if they met the following provisions:

A. This organization does not use the "black ball" method of exclusion wherein twenty per cent or less of the membership may deny admission to any individual, the active body of which [the organization] is essentially made up of pupils attending the public schools. *B.* This organization has no affiliation with a national, regional, or district organization which has a secret order or ritual. *C.* This organization has a responsible adult adviser who assists in the forming of its policies and in the supervision of its activities. *D.* This organization shall not engage in any activities, the nature of which might tend to disrupt the morale, routine, or best interests of the school.

III. To what extent have these provisions been met by the Ponca City "Co-operative groups"?

[*Ans.*] *A.* Those groups that existed as chapters of national fraternities surrendered their charters and reorganized as local organizations. *B.* Membership lists, copies of constitutions and by-laws, and initiation ceremonies are on file in the principal's office. New membership lists are provided at the first of each semester. *C.* Each group files a statement that it will conform to the regulations set up by the state legislature and the Ponca City Board of Education. This statement is signed by the president of the group and by the "responsible adult adviser."

IV. In what respects have the groups failed to live up to their agreements?

[*Ans.*] *A.* In some instances the "responsible adult adviser" has not assumed, or has not been allowed to assume by the membership of the organization, the necessary guidance and leadership. *B.* On a number of occasions the groups have indulged in practices and activities which "tend to disrupt the morale, routine, and best interests of the school."

V. What has been done to improve the situation?

[*Ans.*] *A.* The Board of Education authorized the sending of a letter similar to the present one to the parents of the incoming sophomores as well as to the parents of those students who were then members of the "high-school fraternities and sororities" in order that there should be a general understanding of the problems which existed.

B. The superintendent of schools and the high-school principal have held meetings with the membership of the organizations at which the following points were discussed:

1. It was recommended that the groups disband *(a)* because it was believed that the school and other agencies in the community provided ample opportunities for wholesale social activities; and *(b)* because of the failure of the groups to meet all of their obligations in the past.

2. If the organizations were to continue as "co-operative groups" it would be necessary for them to meet in full all of the provisions listed under section II. It was stressed that the most important of these obligations would

be the securing of a responsible adult adviser who would be willing to take an *active interest* in the affairs of the group.

3. In the event that an adult adviser could not be found who would be willing to assume the full duties of his sponsorship, or if the group would not be willing to conform to the regulations of the Board of Education, the members of such group "would not be eligible to participate in any extra-curricular activity, nor to hold any school office, nor to receive any school honor."

C. As a result of the group meetings and subsequent meetings with the sponsors, some improvement has been made. The most noted improvement was in the scholarship of the sophomore members and pledges. The organizations conformed almost without exception to the suggestions that had been made regarding the chaperonage at club parties and dances, etc. Most of the sponsors took an active interest in seeing that suggestions and recommendations made by the Board of Education were carried out. However one group was asked to disband because of its failure to abide by the rules and regulations governing co-operative groups.

VI. Is the "need" for such organizations as great at the present time as in former years?

[*Ans.*] We do not believe that the need is as great, for the following reasons: *A*. The Ponca City Senior High School sponsors a very comprehensive program of extracurricular activities, which includes the following: (1) interscholastic and intramural athletics; (2) band, orchestra, boys' and girls' glee clubs, mixed chorus, and vocal and instrumental ensembles; (3) school plays, assembly programs, and all-school stunt night; (4) school publications, the *Poncan* and the *Cat Tale; (5)* Student Council meetings and dinners, home-room parties, picnics, and other activities; and *(6)* membership in clubs, such as Home Economics Club, Penguin Club, Latin Club, Art Club, Biology Club, the F. F. A., and the T & I Club.

B. In recent years the Ponca City Board of Education has given permission for the school to sponsor dances and other social activities in the field house. *C*. The organization of the Loft has provided another outlet for social and recreational activities. *D*. The Boy Scouts of America through its new program of Senior Scouting also provides for a number of social activities during the year. *E*. To a greater extent than ever before, the Ponca City churches are recognizing the need for wholesome recreation and are making provisions for it in their youth programs.

VII. What is the attitude of the college fraternity and sorority toward the high-school groups?

[*Ans.*] A recent issue of the *School Board Journal* states, "the National Interfraternity Conference is unalterably opposed to the existence of high-school fraternities and sororities. Officials of this conference regard these societies as inimical to the purpose of fraternities and sororities at the college level." The same article further states, "they affect the life of the school where they exist, whether they are under the supervision of the school or whether they exist without such supervision; their effects are bad in terms of personality growth of the individual students who are members and of many students who are not elected to membership."

This has been a lengthy explanation of a problem that has existed for many years. It is only through the co-operation of parents and school officials that the situation can be improved. If the organizations are to continue under the rules and regulations established by the Ponca City Board of Education, the "responsible adult advisers" will need to assume more responsiblity than many of them have in the past, and they will need greater support and assistance from the parents of members.

Yours sincerely,
J. WIN PAYNE, Superintendent of Schools
HOMER S. ANDERSON, High-School Principal

Problems, Questions, and Exercises

1. Write out what you think is a good definition of a club, as distinguished from some other kind of extracurricular activity.
2. Examine the list of clubs mentioned in the text and make a list of clubs which you think might well be encouraged to exist in a school of 150 students.
3. Select one club and write a description of how you would apply the suggestions for operating a club.
4. What suggestions can you offer in addition to those given in the book for supervising and managing various kinds of school clubs?
5. Do you believe that there should be any scholastic or other requirement for membership in a particular club or extracurricular activity?
6. Select either speech, journalistic, or music activities as a field and prepare a paper on how to organize and manage them, going into more detail than is done in the chapter in this book.
7. For a school of any size to be selected by you—for example, about 125 students, or 500 students—describe the program of school publications and how they might be managed, including the question of whether or not there should be any form of a school paper, a school annual, or a student handbook. Discuss how participation in producing these might be distributed among the members of the faculty and students and how costs might be kept at a minimum.
8. Develop a list of criteria for evaluating some club or activity—for example, debate team, plays, orchestra, or a hobby club.
9. Write out the five most important principles for the management of assemblies.
10. Describe four types of assembly programs which you think are excellent and discuss how they might be prepared.
11. To what extent do you believe there should be class organizations—for example, freshman or senior class organizations—and what do you believe are their values and limitations?
12. Draw up a list of activities for the last semester in school of the senior class and under each of the activities list a few suggestions for making them more successful.
13. Discuss the values, dangers, and procedures of educational trips.
14. To what extent do you believe that the school should undertake responsibility for providing social life for youngsters, *(a)* during school hours and *(b)* outside of school hours. What are the best methods you can think of for doing this?
15. How serious do you believe are the dangers and objections to school sororities and fraternities? How would you go about eliminating or managing them? Evaluate the Ponca City plan.

16. How could a principal see that home-room sponsors are prepared to discharge their responsibilities; what help could he give them in this connection?
17. Draw up a list of half a dozen of the most important suggestions for management of home rooms, considering the following: *(a)* student composition of membership, *(b)* frequency of meeting periods, *(c)* types of programs, and *(d)* fundamental principles of management by the sponsors.
18. Draw up and be prepared to discuss a list of reasons why home rooms might not be a success and why in some places they have been abandoned.

Selected Supplementary Readings

Agnesine, Sister M. (S.S.N.D.), "A Hobby May Lead Anywhere," *Catholic School Journal* (June, 1950), Vol. 50, No. 6. [Shows by illustration that hobby development is education in a broad sense.]

Daly, C. A., "Social Clubs at Southeastern," *Bulletin of the N.A.S.S.P.* (September, 1956), No. 221, p. 142.

Drake, C. E., "How Should Administrators Deal With School Fraternities and Sororities?" *Bulletin of the N.A.S.S.P.* (May, 1949), No. 163, pp. 21-26.

Dugan, Lucille, "How to Plan the Social Program in a Large High School," *Bulletin of the N.A.S.S.P.* (November, 1955), No. 214, pp. 104-107.

Eugene, Sister (S.C.), "The School Paper Is Important," *Catholic School Journal* (October, 1950), Vol. 50, No. 8. [The sponsor for the school paper presents her case to the other members of the faculty.]

Fleischer, Robert D., "Secret Societies: An Administrative Problem," *Bulletin of the N.A.S.S.P.* .(October, 1952), Vol. 36, No. 188, pp. 131-133. [In this article the author brings together more of the literature on this subject.]

Frederick, Robert W., *The Third Curriculum—Student Activities in American Education,* New York, Appleton-Century-Crofts, 1959. [See Part III, "Types of Student Activities."]

Gray, Martha, "Student Clubs," *Bulletin of the N.A.S.S.P.* (February, 1952), Vol. 36, pp. 80-93. [Good treatment of secret societies and of club officers.]

Gruhn, William T., "The Administration of Club Activities in the Junior High School," *Elementary School Journal* (October, 1934), Vol. 35, pp. 107-114.

Gruhn, William T., and Douglass, Harl R., *The Modern Junior High School,* New York, Ronald, 1956. [Chapter 12, "The Homeroom"; Chapter 13, "Extra Class Activities."]

Heiss, Elwood D., Oburn, Ellsworth S., and Hoffman, Charles W., *Modern Science Teaching,* New York, Macmillan, 1950. [Chapter 10, "Extracurricular Activities in Science," pp. 233-244, shows how many clubs and other extra-class activities can be developed by the science teacher.]

Hess, Walter E., "The Commencement Program," *Bulletin of the N.A.S.S.P.* (February, 1952), No. 184, pp. 195-203. [Reviews recent trends in regard to such commencement factors as type of program, responsibility for planning, use of valedictorian, and others.]

"How to Use Punch Cards to Solve Your Ticketing Problems" *School Management* (December, 1959), Vol. 3, No. 12, p. 60.

Koss, H. A., "How Free Is It, for the Kids?" *School Activities* (October, 1955), Vol. 27, pp. 45-47.

Olsen, George S., and Moore, J. D., "How Can the School Administrator Deal with Fraternities and Sororities?" *Bulletin of the N.A.S.S.P.* (March, 1951), No. 177, pp. 320-332. [Presents a list of reasons showing the unwholesome effects of such organizations, suggests various plans to combat such organizations, and describes how one particular school handled the problem.]

Reid, Noma, "Educational Trips," *Bulletin of the N.A.S.S.P.* (February, 1952), No. 184, p. 127. [Treats fully all aspects of educational trips, including organization, objectives, evaluation, problems, and types.]

Ross, Vivian, *Handbook for Homeroom Guidance,* New York, Macmillan, 1955. [A small book, very practical for the classroom teacher who has not had a course in guidance.]

Thompson, Nellie Zetta, "School Assemblies," *Bulletin of the N.A.S.S.P.* (February, 1952), No. 184, pp. 157-176. [Presents studies showing the typical practices in regard to organization, responsibility, direction, preparation, length, place, equipment, financing, problems, types of program, evaluation trend, and improvement. Examples to illustrate various phases are cited from numerous schools throughout the country.]

Thompson, Nora B., "A Latin-American Club in High School," *English Journal* (May, 1947), Vol. 36, pp. 260-261.

Van Pool, Gerald M., "The Case Against High School Secret Societies," *Bulletin of the N.A.S.S.P.* (May, 1961), No. 265. [An excellent statement of the points for and against.]

Van Pool, Gerald M., "The Home Room," *Bulletin of the N.A.S.S.P.* (February, 1952), Vol. 36, pp. 150-156. [Objectives, administration, assignment of pupils, and internal organization of home rooms.]

Vredevoe, L. E., "How Should Administrators Deal with School Fraternities and Sororities?" *Bulletin of the N.A.S.S.P.* (May, 1949), No. 163, pp. 15-21.

12

Organizing and Improving Guidance

1. The Place of Guidance in the High School

INCREASED NEED FOR GUIDANCE. There is a very much greater need for guidance of young people today than there was a decade or so ago. In the first place, because of the fact that young people are with their parents much less and spend a much larger part of their life with young people of their own age, there is less opportunity for them to receive the counseling that they very much need. Secondly, the world today has become a very uncertain one for the development of young people; sex and violence pervade newspapers, television, and other mass media of communication, as well as much of the observable behavior of adults. Furthermore, the greatly increased number of young people thinking about going to college has expanded the need and the opportunity for service in the area of guidance for college.

There is a definitely increased need for guidance for Negroes and other nonwhite boys and girls, particularly in the schools where integration has taken place or is taking place. Maintenance of wholesome attitudes towards themselves and towards the people of the white race has become a much greater problem in recent years. Young people are now definitely less inclined to accept discrimination; however valuable in the long run this new attitude is, it creates very serious problems for a large number of young people in the period of transition.

The greatly increased heterogeneity of ability and of future occupation of high-school students, large numbers of whom will soon pass from their school days into the vocational world, challenges high-school officials and teachers to new types of responsibilities and activities. The professional study of education has brought these responsibilities into relief, and the development of the technique of guidance has made it possible for the high school to function effectively with respect to them.

AREAS FOR GUIDANCE SERVICE. The school should provide young people with experiences and counsel which will enable them to make intelligent choices in decisions about their educational problems and their vocational futures; in addition, as a result of the greatly increased percentage of boys and girls of high-school age who now go to school and the greatly increased need for moral and social guidance owing to the changed conditions of present-day society and the lack of effective guidance by home and church, the high school may perform a most valuable service in providing guidance.

The modern secondary school, with specially trained workers and with facilities for health and physical examinations, is in an excellent position to render valuable guidance toward the improvement and preservation of health and physical excellence. In a great many instances, it is in a much better position than the home to render such service. In many instances there appears to be a genuine need for the protection of young people from the ignorance and indifference of their parents as well as from their own immaturity.

Similarly, it is apparent that there is a splendid opportunity for the school to assist pupils in developing interests and the ability to satisfy them, which will tend to ensure pleasurable and profitable expenditure of leisure hours in ways not inimical to the interests of others.

MENTAL HYGIENE IN GUIDANCE. In recent years much more has become known about mental hygiene – the development of a sound, healthy personality – and the experiences which tend to contribute to an unhealthy personality and unfortunate mental, emotional, and social adjustment. In addition, much more attention has been given to the relationship of mental hygiene to school problems, particularly to the matters of guidance and discipline. Many of the problems of young people, which seem at first to teachers and principals to be merely discipline problems, apparently have their roots in, or are closely related to, matters of emotional and social maladjustment and call for guidance to promote human relations between teachers and students and among students which are in harmony with modern principles and practices of mental hygiene and personality development. Thus, not only have guidance services in the schools expanded but the nature of guidance services has been definitely changed.

TYPES OF PROBLEMS CALLING FOR GUIDANCE. For the purpose of classification, we may group guidance activities with reference to their objectives. However, in rendering the service of guidance it is neither desirable nor possible to separate guidance activities completely as to type of outcome desired or as to the nature of the activities themselves. It is, for example, almost impossible to think of any guidance activity or service which is not "educational" guidance. For the purpose of discussion, however, the following classification, with illustrative activities, may be serviceable.

1. Vocational guidance

a. Furnishing the pupil with knowledge of occupations, particularly relating to rewards, conditions of employment, opportunities for advancement, and requirements for entrance to, and success in, occupations.

b. Furnishing the pupil with opportunities to discover and reveal to himself his general and special capacities and aptitudes, his interests, and his traits of personality and character as related to vocational life.

c. Furnishing the pupil with a point of view and a method of study of occupations which will assist him in making his vocational decisions.

2. Educational guidance

a. Furnishing the pupil counsel and the opportunity to discover his interests, abilities, and capacities in various studies.

b. Furnishing counsel as to what studies will contribute best to the realization of his probable vocational and educational plans and where such studies may be best pursued.

c. Providing courses of study adapted to the abilities of atypical children, as well as guidance in electing such courses.

d. Furnishing pertinent information concerning the possibility and desirability of further schooling and stimulating the pupil to consider these carefully.

e. Acquainting the pupil with the curricular and extracurricular opportunities of the school and with conventions relative to the life and management of the school.

f. Acquainting the pupil with the opportunities and methods of using the school library most effectively.

3. Leisure or avocational guidance

a. Providing opportunities, curricular and extracurricular, for the pupil to discover or develop tastes and interests which will provide avenues or fields of reflection, enjoyment, and recreation and thus make life more worth while to the individual and the individual more worth while to society.

4. Moral and social guidance

a. Furnishing counsel, example, and learning situations in private conference, in the classroom, or by means of extracurricular activity which will contribute to the development of right ideals and habits of conduct and living.

b. Furnishing opportunities for training in extracurricular group situations, which will result in information, attitudes, habits, and abilities which will contribute to the tendency and ability to work and play effectively with other people with satisfaction—as leader, follower, or colleague—in the home, in school, at work, or at play.

c. Furnishing training in correct social conventions.

d. Developing adjustments to other people, particularly young people of both sexes of the pupil's own age.

5. Health guidance

a. Providing situations which will call attention to any infirmities, defects, or tendencies that should be corrected or removed.

b. Developing an interest in health and in a strong, healthy body.

c. Developing interest, habits, and skills in games and other activities which will operate to promote health.

d. Assisting the pupil to develop sound mental and emotional health and hygiene, partly through expert counseling in this field.

6. Personal guidance

a. Providing, under favorable conditions, hints or suggestions that are likely to make for improvement of personal appearance and traits of personality.

b. Providing advice and counsel on personal problems of all sorts which the boy or girl may desire to receive: sex problems, problems of family relationships, etc.

c. Providing the inspiration and encouragement which come from personal interest of an older individual who "understands" and is "interested."

7. Military-Service Guidance

a. Assisting the boy in senior high school to become informed about his responsibility for military service.

b. Assisting the boy in senior high school to understand the nature of and the opportunities in the various armed forces.

c. Assisting the boy to approach the problem of deciding what time in his life to give the required military service.

PROVIDING FOR THE TYPES OF GUIDANCE. The foregoing classification of the functions of guidance by types should not be taken to mean that each type is to be carried on separately or that different machinery must be set up to carry on each type. As a matter of fact, the same person, subject matter, data, and activities may contribute simultaneously to different types of guidance. The high-school principal, for example, in a small school may serve in all the types of guidance. Subjects of instruction may be taught in such a manner or made the basis of such discussions that contributions may be made to all types of guidance. Test scores and personal history may be useful in connection with each type. In fact, it is practically impossible to think of each of these types of guidance as being carried on independently, without reference or material contribution to one or more of the others.

GUIDANCE RELATED TO JUVENILE COURT CASES. More and more counselors and administrative officials of the schools are beginning to take an active part in assisting in the counseling of young people who have gotten into trouble with the law. The following would seem to be good modern practice in respect to relationships between the schools and the courts and police in connection with such cases:

The school system through its chief administrator or other representative may be expected to:

1. Be informed of all legal actions involving school children.
2. Co-operate with arresting officers and the court in establishing the facts of the case.
3. Interview promptly the child involved in the legal action.
4. In the event of detention following arrest, visit the place of detention to make certain that the child is receiving satisfactory treatment.
5. Co-operate with parents and others in making certain that the child will be given a hearing and consideration in keeping with his age and the facts in the case.

6. Observe at court hearings, standing ready to offer the advice of the school system and other services in the interest of the child.
7. Arrange for the acceptance by interested teachers of parole custody of the child.
8. In cases of institutional commitment of the school child, investigate conditions under which the child is being held through visits made periodically during the confinement.
9. Through the advisement services of the system, assist in the rehabilitation of the offender.
10. Undertake, through the school program, preventive and remedial measures against juvenile delinquency.
11. Educate the community through news releases, parent-teacher organizations, conferences, and home bulletins in the reduction of community influences toward juvenile delinquency and the better treatment of offenders.[1]

BASIC PRINCIPLES AND PHILOSOPHY OF A MODERN GUIDANCE PROGRAM. As thought of by a majority of principals and teachers twenty years ago, guidance consisted of little more than assisting youngsters to make tentative vocational decisions and to solve some of the problems of educational guidance, (such as selecting courses, deciding whether or not to go to college, and learning how to adjust to a new school) and those of health guidance. As commonly conceived, the place of the counselor or other agent of guidance was that of one who furnished young people the solutions to their problems, or at least guided them rather energetically in making their own decisions.

Today there is a definite trend in the following directions:

1. To broaden the scope and the field of guidance.
2. To realize that many of the problems of young people, if carefully studied, do not fall into one area of guidance but are complicated problems having ramifications in several areas.
3. To place less emphasis on making decisions for young people and much more emphasis upon assisting the youngsters in making their own decisions.

Certain other basic assumptions or fundamental principles of modern guidance are as follows:

In many cases the problem is one which cannot be solved directly. For example, a girl may worry excessively about being too tall. There is no way available for her to lessen that height. The problem is therefore an indirect one: namely, to assist her (1) to develop a philosophy of concentrating upon her advantages rather than upon her handicaps and (2) to make compensations which will enable her to be happy, even though she is taller than she would like to be. Another example is that of the youngster who does not possess the general abstract or verbal intelligence necessary to succeed in a curriculum in a medical school or a law school. There is little that can be done in the way of increasing the student's

[1]Harlan L. Hagman, *The Administration of American Public Schools,* McGraw-Hill, 1951, p. 237. Quoted with permission of the publishers.

natural intelligence. The problem is one of assisting the student to substitute other goals and to realize that happiness and satisfactions in life are not materially lessened by reason of one's exclusion from a vocational life which calls for more abstract and verbal intelligence than he has.

In many such cases as these, it is very important for the student to find someone to whom he may talk about his problem, some sympathetic individual to whom he may get it off his chest. Even though no constructive plan is laid down, there is a cathartic effect in discussions of this sort, which effect has been noted by many counselors as being tremendously worth while.

A problem is frequently met which is recurrent or chronic and which cannot be solved once for all time. For example, the matter of the vocational decision is ordinarily one that is not settled once for all. There are tentative decisions, sometimes made as early as the latter years of the elementary school or in the junior high school—decisions which are revised if not completely abandoned in later years. Likewise the student whose personal appearance is not what he would like it to be will probably find that his problem is one that cannot be solved within a few days or even a few months. The problem may last throughout a lifetime and may become a critical one at various times, calling for counseling and sympathetic discussion.

In many instances, particularly in the case of vocational choices, a definite decision is not the most important thing. For example, in the selection of vocations it probably is far more important for most youngsters to learn how to approach the problem, how to think about it, how to gather the data for solution, and how to interpret the data. Counselors realize that young people continue to have problems long after they have left school; the solution of the immediate problems, even if possible, does not constitute all or perhaps even the major part of guidance services. The student will be faced throughout life with a variety of problems; the important thing is training in how to approach them and how to take a sound philosophical attitude, in order to avoid the unfortunate effects of experiences which grow out of problems occurring when there is no counselor at hand.

In most counseling situations it is also necessary to acquire much more data about the problem and about the counselee than is readily available. Although valuable data for counseling may be found in the school records already available, in many instances it is desirable and a prerequisite to good counseling to find out more about individual counselees. The modern, effective counselor strives to assist young people in getting and interpreting data about themselves and about vocations, colleges, social situations, health, and other areas of life with which a problem seems closely associated.

If counseling is to be of a high order and if students are to continue to bring their problems to counselors, a confidential relationship must be established between counselor and counselee. The student must know that information he gives the counselor will be strictly confidential, will not impair the confidence and respect which the counselor has for him, and will not be held against him in any way. Otherwise, by giving inaccurate, partial, or false information, or by withholding information, he misleads his counselor.

Group Counseling. In certain groups (particularly home-room and core groups), it is possible to hold discussions about problems that are more or less common to the group and to assist the members of the group in thinking through solutions to these problems. It is possible in home rooms, core classes, assemblies, and elsewhere to give very useful group guidance by having a teacher or counselor assist the youngsters in thinking through and considering possible solutions to various problems which are more or less common to young people.

Preparation of Counselors. In recent years there has been a definite increase in the preparation which is required for a counseling career. Ordinarily, only those counselors are employed who have had a year of graduate training in the appropriate aspects of guidance and counseling and the nature of young people and their problems. In general, a counselor is not employed who has not had at least two or three years' experience as a classroom teacher.

Guidance of Nonschool Youth. Slowly but certainly, schools in the United States are assuming more responsibility for the guidance of boys and girls who have dropped out of school. Such guidance needs to be carefully planned since the problems of these youngsters are definitely different from the problems of those who are still in school. Among the more serious problems of out-of-school youth are those of vocational relocation and additional vocational training and problems incident to married life and homemaking.

Unless there is a very successful government placement bureau operating locally, the secondary-school administrator should think seriously and, in most cases, favorably of extending the service of the school placement bureau to out-of-school youth.

2. Guidance About Schooling

Registration. Registration offers one of the most effective opportunities for rendering guidance service to high-school students, as well as one of the easiest to administer. Recently principals have realized more fully than before the importance of preregistration as an opportunity for guidance; the trend of practice is clearly in the direction of providing adequate counsel at this important time, though inertia and tradition still conserve the laissez-faire procedure.

Provision should be made for preregistration during the previous semester. Sufficient time should be allowed for careful study and reflection on the part of pupils and parents. It is not too much to allow two or even three weeks. Perhaps the best plan is to provide for preregistration during the spring for the entire following school year, allowing a day or so at the beginning of the first semester for changes in registration and for the registering of new students. This supplementary registration may well be taken care of during the week just preceding the opening of school. When it is thus taken care of, it is possible to begin regular classwork on the second day of school.

Registration for the second semester may be confined to a few days toward the latter part of the first semester, during which pupils desiring or compelled to make changes may petition to do so and confer with their advisers about such proposed changes.

Both the students and the registration advisers should have at hand either a handbook or mimeographed material prepared for students which includes all the offerings of the school, requirements for graduation, various curricula (if more than one curriculum is offered), and other information of a similar sort.

It is becoming increasingly common in secondary schools today to have students in the first semester of their stay in the high school make a tentative educational program, including subjects to be elected in each year of their stay in the school. Many schools are now providing blanks for this purpose: for each year there are appropriate blanks in which to indicate the required courses as well as the elective courses.

PROVIDING USEFUL INFORMATION. During the preregistration period, all possible means should be used to provide advisers and students with information which may be useful in the choice of studies. Many principals prepare, or have a committee of advisers prepare, a chart of the entrance requirements of all colleges and universities to which students of the community usually go. This chart is reproduced so that a copy may be placed in the hands of each adviser and one or more copies may be posted on bulletin boards in the halls. Talks may be delivered before school assemblies or roll-room groups on the advisability of studying the relative values of the subjects offered by the school. These talks should not be sales talks which center vaguely around values of doubtful reality. There should be talks in assembly or in roll room on the various curricula offered, their constants, and the futures for which they prepare.

Information regarding the value of continuing in school should be given in roll-room meetings or assemblies. Care should be taken that this information is interpreted properly; it should be indicated that not all of the difference in the income of various groups may be attributed to differences in amount of schooling but that part of the difference may be the result of the greater academic intelligence of those who stayed in school longer. Such results of education as the ability to command the respect of one's fellows, an understanding of public affairs and current topics of conversation, enjoyment of life on a high level, and the ability to mingle with ease and pleasure with other educated people should be emphasized. Discussions are most useful in this connection if the pupils are permitted to participate freely.

Pupil Data Needed by Registration Advisers. Data which should be organized and placed in the hands of advisers at registration time should include intelligence-test scores, M. A. (mental age), I. Q. (intelligence quotient), previous school marks, data from health and physical examinations, data resulting from questionnaires or analyses of vocational interest, character ratings of previous teachers in junior and senior high schools, family data (for example, occupation and nationality of father), tentative occupational choice, tentative decision relative to going to college, tentative four-year enrollment plan, and data available relative to citizenship and other personality traits.

The usefulness of such data in the hands of those who understand their significance is great. Pupils whose ability to do school work is distinctly above the average should be urged to carry heavier than normal programs and to select college-preparatory subjects. Those who will in all probability never finish high school may be located with some precision by means of their age, their I. Q., occupation of father, school marks, and intention to graduate and should be encouraged to elect non-college-preparatory subjects. Students with low I. Q.'s should not be encouraged to enter a vocational curriculum, particularly one preparing for secretarial work. Those whose chances of any real success in mathematics or languages are not promising, according to intelligence and prognostic tests and previous school marks, may be identified and so advised, in order that months of discouraging toil rewarded only with failure and humiliation may be avoided. Those not in good health should be given programs which will not overtax them. Students with definite vocational goals may be given valuable assistance in selecting subjects of most value to them. These examples are illustrative of the many purposes for which pupil data may be used. In schools that enjoy the services of a vocational counselor, the records of pupils kept by the counselor should be made available.

It is not enough that data be available for reference in the office or some other central place; they should be put into the hands of the registration advisers, who should be called into conference in advance to consider the most effective use of the information, as well as other questions and problems of educational guidance connected with preregistration.

In addition to the data mentioned above, there are tests available for use in assisting pupils to decide whether they should take a foreign language, algebra, or geometry, the subjects most responsible for the percentages of failure; it is possible for highly pertinent data to be gathered through the medium of prognostic tests for special subjects: for example, Luria-Orleans Modern Language Prognosis Test, Symonds's Foreign Language Prognosis Test, Orleans-Solomon Latin Prognosis Test, Orleans Geometry Prognosis Test, California Algebra Aptitude Test, Rich Algebra Prognosis Test, Lee Test of Geometry Aptitude. Also, there are the Turse Clerical Aptitude Tests, Turse Shorthand Aptitude Tests, Whistler and Thorpe's Musical Aptitude Test, Differential Aptitude Test Battery by Bennett, Seashore, and Westman, and Flanigan's Aptitude Classification Tests and Multiple Aptitude Tests.

It is useful for the principal to have at hand catalogues listing various kinds of tests for adjustment, aptitude, intelligence, interests and attitudes, personality, and mental health. These catalogues are obtainable from such companies as the California Testing Bureau (with offices at Del Monte Research Park, Monterey, California; 206 Bridge Street, New Cumberland, Pennsylvania; 110 South Dickinson Street, Madison, Wisconsin; and 2114 Irving Boulevard, Dallas 7, Texas), the Cooperative Testing Division of the Educational Testing Service (with offices at 20 Nassau Street, Princeton, New Jersey and at 4640 Hollywood Boulevard, Los Angeles 27, California), the Psychological Corporation (304 East Forty-fifth Street, New York 17, New York), and the World Book Company (with offices at Tarrytown-on-Hudson, New York; 6 Beacon Street, Boston 8, Massachusetts; 441 West Peachtree Street, N.E., Atlanta 8, Georgia; 2126 Perry Avenue, Chicago 16, Illinois; 703 Browder Street, Dallas 21, Texas; and 2054 University Avenue, Berkeley 4, California). These companies distribute tests, check lists, and inventories in other fields which are of use to counselors: for example, in the fields of behavior rating, personality adjustment, delinquency proneness, personality diagnosis, social adjustment, social relations, temperament, mental health, and health.

Approval of Registration by Parents and Counselors. At the beginning of the registration period, parents should be urged to counsel with their children. Information about curricula and courses should be sent to them, and publicity should be given to the preregistration period in the local newspapers. Parents should be invited to visit the school for conference and should be informed of office hours at which they may find the principal, counselor, dean, or advisers available. When the pupil's registration is complete, the signature of the parent indicating approval should be obtained on the registration card.

Immediately upon the completion of registration, the counselor, or in small schools the principal, should check over all registration cards with a view to suggesting improvement in the selection of studies for individual pupils and to making sure that each pupil has registered for the constants in his chosen curriculum and has not registered for courses for which he is not eligible.

WHO SHOULD BE REGISTRATION ADVISERS. Advisers should be chosen, as far as possible, from those who have had special training and who understand the significance of data and how to use it. It is better to employ a smaller number of advisers and to take more time for registration than to assign as advisers teachers who are not properly prepared to render effective service. In many schools where the latter condition obtains, the advisership is a perfunctory, mechanical position, which often, though held in the best of conscience, is of very doubtful value if not actually harmful. The practice of employing heads of departments or the regular class advisers for preregistration guidance is not always wise, nor are all home-room teachers competent registration advisers. Before preregistration the principal, if properly trained himself, may give valuable training to some members of his staff for advisory responsibilities.

GUIDANCE IN THE NEXT LOWER SCHOOL. Many schools are beginning to realize the possibilities of guidance in the last year of the next lower school: for example, guidance in the eighth grade for a four-year high school, in the ninth grade of the junior high school for the senior high school, and in the sixth grade for the junior high school. This guidance may take the form of co-operative guidance, in which officials and teachers of both schools pool their efforts.

There have developed in a great many schools throughout the country practices of guidance in the elementary school for the junior high school or the high school, and in the junior high school for the senior high school. These practices have proved to be very valuable and to serve in helping to bridge the gap between the lower and the upper school. Among the various types of service that can be rendered are the following:

1. Study by counselors in the lower schools of the cumulative records and the case history of every pupil about to leave. These include reports of the pupil's scholarship in previous years, his scores on subject-matter tests, his attendance, attitudes toward school work, and general mental capacity; scores on any aptitude test he may have had, his citizenship record, any records that may be of interest, vocational plans, and data that may be available concerning his parents and home situation.
2. Conferences between the counselor of the lower school and the counselors of the upper school for exchanging information and particularly for acquainting the counselor of the lower school with problems and opportunities in the upper school.
3. Visitation of the upper school by the students of the lower school, where they are entertained by assemblies or athletic contests, addressed perhaps by a principal, advisers, or student officers of the upper school on curricular and extracurricular opportunities of the school, and taken by student guides to visit the various portions of the building, particularly the shops, laboratories, libraries, gymnasiums, and other special rooms.
4. The sending of speakers from the upper school to the lower school to explain the opportunities in the upper school and to give advice on such points as selection of courses, participation in activities, and social life.

5. The assisting of the student to make a selection of subjects to be studied in the first semester in the higher school, which selection is to be submitted to a counselor in the higher school. This selection involves acquainting the students in the lower school and their parents with what the higher school has to offer and with its requirements and standards. Quite frequently handbooks about the higher school are available.

In many secondary schools something similar to the following procedure is observed, with excellent results:

1. A counselor from each school studies the cumulative card or data sheet and the case history of every pupil.
2. A conference is held between the counselors of the junior and senior high schools for a careful study of the problems and opportunities in the senior high school.
3. The pupil's program for the first term in the senior high school is made out. This involves:
   a. A careful study by every prospective student and his parents of the bulletin "What the Senior High School Has to Offer."
   b. A conference between the pupil and his parents with reference to high school courses as explained in the bulletin. This conference may be supplemented by a general meeting of the parents of prospective senior high school pupils with a senior high school counselor. Here opportunity is given for parents to ask questions concerning the new school in which they expect to enroll their children and about which they have every right to know.
   c. The pupil's selection of the program in which he is most interested and which he thinks will best fit his needs and capacity.
   d. A conference between the senior high school counselor and the pupil with reference to the subjects chosen. Here the counselor checks carefully to see that the student has the proper prerequisites for the subjects he has selected, that the subjects meet the matriculation requirements of the college in which the student expects later to enroll or that they offer training for the specific vocation which he may have selected, and, finally, that enough interests are being developed.
   e. A revision of the program by the pupil and his parents in the light of any suggestions brought out in conference with the counselor.
   f. A second conference between the counselor and the pupil for final decision with regard to the program. The final choice of subjects is recorded on the "introduction card," which becomes the child's admission card to the senior high school.
   g. The signature of the parent on the back of the introduction card. This indicates the parent's approval of the course chosen.
   h. The signature of the junior high school counselor on the introduction card.
4. Each incoming student's case record is carefully studied by the senior high school counselor. Students are placed in differentiated sections in certain subjects, depending on whether they are of limited, average, or superior ability. In the classification of students seven points are taken into consideration: (1) previous scholastic accomplishment, (2) teacher's estimate of ability, (3) industry, (4) health, (5) home co-operation, (6) chronological age, and (7) mental capacity, as measured by a standardized test of general intelligence.

A similar program may be developed for students about to transfer from an eight-year elementary school to a four-year high school and for students about to transfer from a six-year elementary school to a junior high school.

Principals of lower and upper schools do not always agree as to who should have charge of the guidance with respect to the upper school. Without noting here the arguments advanced on either side, it would seem correct to state that the guidance leadership would depend largely upon which school was better prepared to render the desired service. As between schools in which one maintains a competent counselor and the other does not, the responsibility should be borne by the school better equipped to render effective service. If neither maintains an especially trained worker in the field of guidance, it is very likely that better results and less friction will be obtained by utilizing representatives of the upper school as sources of information about their school and by leaving in the hands of the lower-school principal and advisers the actual guidance. The lower-school principal and advisers have a personal knowledge of the individual pupil which it would be difficult to commit to records or otherwise transfer to any representative of the upper school. It is awkward for representatives of the upper school to make use of the records of the pupils still attending the lower school and to schedule individual conferences with them.

3. Guidance in Adjusting to a New School Unit

ORIENTATION IN THE LOCAL SCHOOL. Very closely related to the type of service which has just been described is what, for want of a better term, may be called school orientation. In many high schools a series of discussions has been devised to be given during the first month or first semester to all incoming new pupils. Illustrative units covering one or more days are given below.

I. *The school day, building orientation, and more important rules.* Information about the opening time of school, the length of periods, the schedule of bells, assemblies, and lunch period; explanation of the roster card; plan of building; the numbering and the location of rooms; lunch rules; excuses for absence and tardiness; books and material for classes.

II. *Traffic regulations.* Need for; standards and ideals; rules.

III. *Student material, equipment.* Lesson book: specifications and how kept; other equipment for all classes; care and arrangement of books and material.

IV. *Personal appearance.* Cleanliness; neatness; clothes; conventions; posture.

V. *Lunchroom ethics.* Standards and ideals; regulations; after lunch.

VI. *Group meeting: parliamentary procedure.* Order of business and parliamentary form.

VII. *Aims, purposes, and functions of the junior high school.* The curriculum: special aims and functions.

VIII. *Home study.* Proper environment; rules for effective study.

IX. *Attendance.* Meaning and importance; proper excuses; details of routine.

X. *Punctuality.* Importance in business world; school punctuality.

XI. *Student organizations.* School government; student agencies for government, their activities and duties.

XII. *Ethics of the auditorium.* Advantages of auditorium privileges; means of entrance, seats, and exit; behavior.

Much of the time spent on these topics is given over to discussion by pupils. Attempts are made to lead them to form the desired attitudes as well as to develop and to acquire useful information. A collection of supplementary reading material is made available for voluntary reading and special reports. Such a series of discussions might well be substituted in the junior high school for instruction in some seventh-grade subjects for two or three weeks.

THE STUDENT HANDBOOK. In many schools student handbooks are prepared, often with the aid of student representatives. They include such things as the following:

A. Introduction

1. Students' creed
2. Location, how to reach school
3. Names and assignments of faculty members
4. School emblems, colors, mottoes
5. Aims of the school and accreditation
6. Flag salute
7. Picture of school
8. Greetings: principal and president of Student Council

B. School Organization

1. Attendance laws
2. Excuses
   - Absences
   - Tardiness
   - Leaving class
3. Building plan
4. Grounds plan
5. Calendar of school year
6. Examinations
7. Fire and traffic rules
8. Library information
9. Transfers, procedure for
10. Reports to parents
11. Study-hall regulations
12. Advisers
13. Assemblies
14. Lockers
15. Daily bell schedule
16. Marks
17. Registration
18. Admission
19. Books; bookstore
20. Air-raid shelters
21. Placement bureau
22. School bank
23. Cafeteria
24. Activity tickets
25. School parties
26. Lost and found
27. Parking
28. Nurse, doctor, hospital
29. Offices

C. Program of Studies

1. Classification, promotion
2. College admission requirements
3. Graduation requirements
4. Curricula
5. Required and elective courses
6. Guidance program

D. Student Organizations and Activities
1. Clubs and organizations
2. Alumni association
3. Athletic records and schedules
4. Names of club, class, and school officers
5. Letters and numerals
6. Scholarships
7. Band, orchestra, glee clubs
8. Student council
    Description of plan
    Names of officers
    Roster of past presidents
9. Debating
10. Dramatics
11. Constitution of school
12. Regulations for clubs
13. Rules—office holders
14. Awards
15. Home-room plan
16. Elections
17. School publications
18. Noon-hour program
19. Ushers
20. Court
21. Commissions and committees

E. General Customs and Traditions
1. Care of personal property
2. Care of school
3. Dress, appearance
4. Manners and courtesy
5. Use of telephone
6. Obtaining working permits
7. Yells
8. School songs
9. Book exchange
10. Bulletin boards
11. Homework
12. Study suggestions
13. Trophies
14. Visitors
15. Citizenship marks
16. "Did you know"
17. Good sportsmanship
18. History of school
19. Parent-teacher-student association
20. Fees and other costs
21. Index[2]

In recent years there has been a tendency for these handbooks to be written in a more informal and otherwise attractive style. In the Dayton, Ohio, schools the handbook bears the title *Take It from Me, Joe!* Published especially for the incoming or prospective first-year student, it includes information and advice on the following questions: Why should I go to high school? What shall I do in high school? How important is my high-school record? When and how shall I get my lessons? Shall I work after school? Who will help me with my problems? How can I get along with other people? How shall I use the library? How can I help build a better world? What course shall I take? Should I go to the co-operative high school? What will my subjects teach me? What subjects shall I take? Also including a description of a day at school, some final details, and some information for parents, the handbook is written in a style attractive to young people.

[2]Edgar G. Johnston and Roland C. Faunce, *Student Activities in Secondary Schools,* New York, Ronald, pp. 190-192. Quoted with permission of the publishers.

Improving Educational Adjustment of New Students. In at least a few good schools a procedure similar to the following is employed as a means of improving the educational adjustment of new students in the school:

1. At the close of the first six or seven weeks, when the first report cards are issued, each individual student's scholarship grades are studied. An individual conference is held with each new student who has not done as well as he did in the lower school. The student's own statement as to the reason for his failure is always asked for and is recorded on his record. The counselor always notes any circumstances that in his judgment are explanatory.
2. After each report period, during the student's first year in the high school, the senior high school counselor holds a conference with the principal, the counselor, and the ninth-grade teachers of each junior high school, and the case record of each problem case is carefully considered.

Guidance service should include the counseling of students, particularly at registration time, with reference to the selection of the extraclass activities in which they will engage. Some students, who otherwise would not do so, should be urged to take part in at least one kind of activity; some students should be urged to take part in fewer activities; and some students should make a better choice of the activity in which they will engage.

4. Guidance for College

Since the college-preparatory group is the largest group of high-school students who are homogeneous as to plans for immediate postschool occupation, it is necessary to adopt administrative procedures and to provide counseling that will satisfy their needs.

Giving Scholarship and Loan Information. In an increasing number of secondary schools, pamphlets or booklets are being prepared for students and advisers which contain information concerning scholarships, grants, loans, and awards for those planning to go on to college. Such a booklet, published by the Hibbing, Minnesota, High School, contains information concerning scholarships offered by the following, among others: Elks National Foundation, Fannie and John Hertz Engineering Foundation, Gaige Merit Scholarship, General Motors Corporation, General Motors Institute, National Foundation, National Honor Society (NEA), National Merit Program, Westinghouse Science Talent Search, Junior Achievement of Hibbing and National Junior Achievement, Minnesota State Elks Association, General Motors Corporation, Great Northern Railway Company, Minnesota AFL-CIO Federation of Labor, Minnesota Bankers Association, State of Minnesota (for nursing), Minnesota Academy of Science, Minnesota Congress of Parents and

Teachers, Inc., United Steelworkers of America-Oliver Local, United Steelworkers of America, and Women of the Moose.

In the Hibbing booklet, information is given relative to the name of the sponsor, the number of scholarships, loans, or awards available, eligibility qualifications, mode of selection, stipend, final application dates, and application blanks. For some of these scholarships, particularly the approximately six hundred National Merit Scholarships[3] which are awarded each year, tests are given which applicants are required to take. Counselors and principals should see that these matters are brought to the attention of all students, particularly those likely to make application.

GIVING HELP IN THE CHOICE OF COLLEGE. The most likely future college students should be located and, from the beginning of their high-school course, furnished with special advice and data calculated to assist them in making adequate preparation for college entrance.

When the students have become seniors, another very valuable type of service may be rendered (and is being rendered by many secondary schools): namely, guidance in the selection of the institution which they will attend upon graduation from the high school. Important as the decision is, young people are influenced in making it by factors which are either trifling or unreliable. Teachers and alumni of colleges and universities exploit the students in the interest of building up the enrollment of their institutions. The students are influenced by older friends, now students in college, who likewise are operating more in the interest of their institutions or Greek-letter organizations than in the interest of the prospective college freshmen. Athletic, debating, dramatic, musical, and many other types of tournaments held at institutions of higher education are organized, as are special "high-school days" or "high-school week ends," largely for the purpose of recruiting students. Many colleges and universities which would prefer not to engage in such activities are forced to do so by the competition furnished by other institutions which draw students from the same communities.

The methods of helping a student to choose a college are not at all uniform among the schools. In some it is handled entirely by the group advisers of senior students. In many small schools the principal undertakes the service. In some schools one or more special groups of prospective college entrants are scheduled for conferences with an adviser and for weekly or occasional meetings throughout the spring, at which group discussions are conducted or opportunities provided for study of catalogues and other material. In still others the counselor, the head adviser, or the principal leads a few discussions, usually including consideration of "How to Choose My College," and invites students to make appointments for personal conferences. No matter what procedures are em-

[3]National Merit Scholarship Corporation, 1580 Sherman Avenue, Evanston, Illinois.

ployed, the catalogues and other pertinent material of all the schools in which the students are likely to be interested should be collected early in the year, made available, and called to the attention of the senior class. Discussion of such topics as the possibilities and opportunities of earning all or part of college expenses, the importance of a good start in college life and studies, the choice of roommates, scholarships, and the costs of a college education should prove useful to prospective college students.

WHO SHOULD GO TO COLLEGE. While principals and counselors should exert every effort to see that students of distinctly superior academic and creative ability become interested in and enter appropriate colleges and universities, it should be remembered that there is no such thing as determining who should go to college. This is true for two reasons: (1) there is a very great variation among colleges with respect to the amount of intellectual ability required for success; and (2) there is material variation in the degree, the nature, and the pattern of abilities required in different curricula in the same college. In other words, if a high-school graduate has anything like normal intelligence and is interested in further study, the question is not so much whether he should go to college but to which college he should go.[4] The student of average intelligence among high-school seniors might be a quick failure in any one of the institutions in the upper 5 or 10 per cent of colleges and universities, rated on the basis of the intelligence of the student bodies.

Because of the raising of the standards for entrance in a considerable number of the stronger colleges and universities, there has been in recent years an increase in the variation of the standards for entrance to colleges and universities.

As is clearly indicated by studies made by the author of this book and by many other investigators, not only is there a difference in the *degree* of ability required for success in the various curricula offered by institutions of higher education[5] but the *pattern* of background and abilities required also differs significantly. For example, it was discovered that for success in the School of Law at the University of Minnesota reasoning ability and certain kinds of vocabulary abilities were very important, much more so than they were in the College of Dentistry or the School of Medicine; in the College of Dentistry, certain types of ability in finger manipulations and spatial judgments were important for success.

---

[4]"Getting Into College," *Coronet* (January, 1961), Vol. 51, pp. 141, 144-147, gives names of colleges with moderate entrance requirements.

Two college placement centers for students not accepted by colleges of their first choice are: College Admissions Center, Glenbrook High School, 2300 Shermer Road, Northbrook, Illinois; and College Admissions Assistance Center, 535 East Eightieth Street, New York 21, New York. Another helpful agency is the Catholic Admissions Information Center, Assumption College, 500 Salisbury Street, Worcester, Massachusetts. These centers charge each student a small registration fee.

[5]Greater intellectual ability is required for success in schools of medicine and law; somewhat more than average ability is required in schools of dentistry and engineering.

For success in the curricula in medicine, dentistry, pharmacy, nursing, and engineering, background interests and abilities in science were much more important than they were in other curricula.

THE PROPER APPROACH FOR THE COUNSELOR. It should be clear to the high-school counselor that, for all but the least capable and the least interested, it is not a question of "Can I succeed in college?" but one of "In what college or branch of a university or college can I succeed?" In almost every region there is at least one college in which the mediocre student can be reasonably sure of success. It is to be hoped that high-school counselors will not guide their inferior graduates into teachers' colleges merely because their chances of survival there are good. Junior-college terminal curricula, the nonuniversity music schools, the independent business colleges, the trade schools, and curricula in agriculture should not be overlooked as appropriate schools for the student of limited intellectual abilities.

The able student should be steered toward schools preparing him for college teaching, medicine, or law, a higher-grade college of engineering, or a graduate school of business, depending upon his interests, pattern of abilities, and personality.

The principal and the counselor should gather all available data about the requirements for entrance and the standards and types of ability apparently necessary for academic success in colleges, universities, and junior colleges and be able therefrom to advise the students effectively. Special attention should be given to the requirements which apparently are preferred for entrance and required for success in the terminal curricula in the junior colleges.

In an increasing number of states there is held at least once a year a state-wide conference between representatives of the secondary schools and representatives of each or several of the institutions of higher education in the state. At these meetings there are discussions of entrance requirements, articulation, and other problems of common interest relative to attendance of secondary-school graduates at the institutions of higher education.

Stimulated and supervised by the Educational Testing Service of Princeton, New Jersey, there are developing state-wide co-operative plans for testing the aptitudes of students looking for admission to college. The first of these plans was developed for the state of Georgia in 1959-1960, and plans for similar co-operative organizations in other states were under way by 1962.[6]

The Montclair, New Jersey, High School has a printed folder of information about the school which is sent to admission officials at colleges to which Montclair graduates apply for admission. It contains in-

---

[6]Educational Testing Service, *The Cooperative Plan for Guidance and Administration.* This pamphlet contains description of these plans.

formation about: the community, the high school, the faculty, the curriculum, grouping for instruction, classes for the academically gifted, advanced placement, the summer-school enrichment program, and how Montclair students rate on the National Merit Scholarship Test.

THE NATIONAL SCHOLASTIC APTITUDE TESTS. Fees for the Scholastic Aptitude Test, the Achievement Test, and the Preliminary Scholastic Aptitude Test were substantially reduced beginning in 1960-1961. Beginning with the test administered in December of 1960, the Scholastic Aptitude Test fee was changed from $6 to $4 and the Achievement Test fee fell from $9 to $6; the fee for the Preliminary Scholastic Aptitude Test given in October was reduced from $1 to $.50. These reductions were made possible by the College Entrance Examination Board in co-operation with the Educational Testing Service. The Scholastic Aptitude Test is given six times a year in more than 1700 cities in the United States and provision may be made for students who happen to live a long way from any center.

National Merit Scholarship Corporation officials and many other college and testing services have discovered that decisions about awarding scholarships and loans and about admission to college are not favorable to a great many young people who possess creative abilities and qualities of personality and character, factors which contribute heavily to superior service and vocational success after graduation from college.

FACTORS RELATED TO SUCCESS IN COLLEGE. It has been shown time and again by careful investigations that the pattern of subjects taken in the high school has little relationship to success in college, although, of course, for a few technical curricula, such as those of the engineering college, certain subjects like mathematics are indispensable.

In the more than fifty investigations (including the eight-year study of the Progressive Education Association) that have been published relative to the college-entrance requirements of units in various high-school subject fields, there has been revealed a lack of substantial correlation between the amount of work taken in any particular high-school subject field and the grades made by students in college and university.

Counselors and principals should remember, however, that because of the lack of credits in certain fields (for example, foreign language, science, or mathematics) some doors may be closed in colleges and universities. Students may not be able to take the courses or to follow the curricula which they want if they lack preparation in certain required subjects.

Teachers and principals who wish to enhance the possibilities of success of their students when they go to college may use the following means:

a. Development of a large vocabulary, with specific and precise meanings of words.

b. Development of the ability to express oneself orally and in writing.
c. Development of the ability to find materials and to organize them from a considerable number of sources.
d. Development of study habits and skills.
e. Development of skill in arithmetical and simple algebraic computation and problem solving.
f. Development and maintenance of intellectual and other cultural interests—in science, in public affairs, in good reading, in music, in art, in writing, and in history.

Hundreds of studies have been made to determine the degree of correlation that exists between various factors and the marks made in college. In the order of magnitude of the coefficients of correlation, the correlation of various factors is given in Table 5.

Table 5. Coefficients of Correlation Obtained in Investigations of the Correlation between Certain Variables and Average College Mark of the First Year or Two Years

Variable	Approximate Central Tendency of Coefficients
Average high-school mark	.55
Average College Entrance Examination Board examination	.50
Average mark in high-school science courses	.48
Average mark in English or social-studies courses	.45
Intelligence or college aptitude test	.42
Average mark in mathematics	.40
Number of units in foreign language	.15
Number of units in mathematics	.10

Factors correlating less than .40 with college marks are worthless when used alone to predict college success. Those correlating between .40 and .60 are of some value, but they must be interpreted only as very rough approximations of the student's ability to do well in college. Even those between .60 and .70, while very useful, are not highly accurate and will involve some remarkable exceptions. Coefficients of correlation greater than .60 are obtained only by combining two or more of the more valid predictive variables—for example:

High-school average and intelligence-test score	.60 to .75
High-school average and average College Entrance Examination Board score	.60 to .70
Average College Entrance Examination Board score and intelligence-test score	.55 to .65

It should always be recalled that these coefficients of correlation are based on marks made in the first year or two of college. Coefficients of correlation between various factors and the marks made in the later years of college are not so great. More predictive of success in medical school, law school, or college of dentistry, for example, are specialized aptitude tests given just before entrance, combined with the average college mark made in the first two years.

RECENT TRENDS. In the light of experience and scientific studies of the relationship between scholastic success in college and patterns of subjects pursued in high school, there has been in recent years a tendency to place less and less emphasis upon the pattern of high-school subjects and more upon the ability of the student, as judged from intelligence-test scores, high-school record, and qualities of character and personality.

In a considerable number of colleges and universities, including some of the stronger Midwestern and Pacific Coast universities, there has been in recent years a tendency to develop flexibility in regard to the subject matter of units taken in high school. The newer trend has been toward requiring a minimum of some ten or eleven units in academic subjects, including either two majors of three units each (one of which must be English) and two minors of two units each in other academic fields or three majors of three units in each of three academic fields.

In recent years in the larger and stronger universities and in some of the colleges, there has been a tendency to require greater evidence of scholastic ability, as expressed in terms of the rank in the graduating class, on the basis of average marks made in subjects taken in high school, and in scores made in scholastic aptitude tests. Information about college requirements should be kept up to date and the counseling of prospective college students should be made in the light of changes in requirements.

In assessing the potentiality of the high-school student for academic success in college, it should be borne in mind that college aptitude tests, high-school averages, and college-entrance board scores taken separately afford a very meager and unreliable basis for prediction; even taken all together, they do not constitute a basis for accurate predictions. Among the things which should also be taken into consideration are evidence of drive and evidence of leadership.

RECRUITING AND GUIDANCE. Although the expansion of college and university facilities has not been comparable in recent years to the growth of the number of students wishing to enter college, many colleges and some universities still compete openly for students. Institutions for higher education send representatives into high schools in large numbers with a view to encouraging students to attend the institutions with which the representatives are connected. The institutions are particularly interested in students with unusual talent of an intellectual type or with apparent unusual potentiality in athletics, music, or other fields.

Among the protective devices employed by secondary schools are the following:

1. Requiring college field agents to interview students upon a voluntary basis after school hours.
2. Setting aside a day or two, or in some cases a week, to which visits and the interviewing of seniors during school hours must be confined, colleges being informed that their representatives are not welcome at other times.
3. Limiting, through regulations adopted by associations of secondary schools, the number and extent of trips to college campuses. (For guidance purposes, these trips are on the average worse than useless, giving false impressions to most high-school students.)

PROVIDING GUIDANCE RELATIVE TO COLLEGE ATTENDANCE. In recent years secondary schools have built up a number of excellent provisions calculated to assist prospective college students. Among them may be mentioned the following:

1. The library collection of (a) college catalogues and (b) reliable books on college life and how to get the most out of college.
2. The discussion unit, usually lasting a semester, frequently employed in home rooms composed of seniors likely to go to college to consider various problems of getting into college, social life, finances, and college curricula.
3. The appointment of an adviser who may become a specialist in matters of college selection, entrance requirements, college life, and the relationship of various factors to success in college.
4. The acquisition and making available for students and counselors (particularly for the college counselor) of catalogues and reference books about colleges and the selection of colleges.
5. The development of the best types of cumulative record to be used in guidance in the high school and sent on to college to be used in guidance there.
6. Special attention in the senior year to students who have declared their intention of entering college, the attention taking the form of training in note-taking, preparation for examinations, writing of long papers, English composition and grammar, laboratory procedure in science, review of arithmetic and algebra, and use of the library.

Following are listed a few publications of practical value in guiding college-bound seniors:

Bowles, Frank H., *How to Get Into College* (Revised Edition), College Entrance Examination Board, New York, Dutton.

College Entrance Counsellor. Barnes and Noble, Inc., New York 3, New York.

College Entrance Examination Board, *The College Handbook,* William C. Fels, ed., New York, College Board Publications, 1951.

College Entrance Examinations. Barnes and Noble, Inc., New York 3, New York.

Facing Facts About College Admissions. A guide for pre-college students and their parents. The Prudential Life Insurance Company, Education Department, Box 36, Newark, New Jersey. 27 pp.

"Getting Into College," *Coronet* (January, 1961), Vol. 51, No. 3, pp. 137-159. [Concise, reliable information on various aspects of subject: sources of information, small-college requirements, scholastic aptitude tests, scholarship talent search, costs of attending various colleges, how to pay for college, loans. Reprints are available in quantity at very low cost.]
How About College Financing? Washington, D. C., American School Counselor Association.
Making Plans for College? Washington, D. C., Kiplinger's *Changing Times* Reprint Service.

5. *Vocational Guidance*

Among the various methods employed in rendering vocational-guidance service in the high school, the following may be mentioned:

1. The occupational survey of the community, carried on usually by high-school students under the supervision of someone interested in vocational guidance.
2. The vocational-information shelf or alcove in the high-school library, in which are placed pamphlets, bulletins, reports, books, etc., readable by high-school pupils and dealing with vocations and the choice of a vocation.
3. Vocational information taught through the high-school studies: theme work in English; side trips and incidental information in general science, geography, history, manual and household arts, vocational subjects, and special try-out courses.
4. Talks and lectures on vocations before assemblies, roll rooms, or classes by members of various professions and callings.
5. Formation of junior chambers of commerce.
6. Life-career, or occupation, classes meeting regularly, with preparation as in any other class, usually four or five times a week for a semester.
7. Advisory activities of the counselor and teachers.
8. Films and other audio-visual methods of presentation.

The activities of counselors should not be thought of as intended to determine the decisions of the pupil. The very large part of vocational guidance should be, in fact, the assisting of pupils in making vocational choices. It does not involve the direct influencing of decisions; rather, it is indirect, attempting to stimulate, inform, and guide the pupil in the study of himself and his vocational future. When giving information about vocations, a counselor should bear in mind that the occupational structure of workers in the United States has undergone a very great change in recent years and is still undergoing rapid changes. For counseling there are two important implications of these changes: in the first place, there are many types of new occupations resulting from developments in science, technology, business, and the field of personal service; secondly, requirements in the way of preparation for the types of work to be done in many occupations have undergone a change.

THE COURSE IN OCCUPATIONS. The course in occupations, or the life-career class, may play an important part in the program of vocational guidance. It serves a threefold purpose: (1) to arouse in the pupil an interest in the matter of vocational choice, so that information from any source in the next few years of his life will be utilized for the light it may throw upon his problem of choosing a life occupation; (2) to furnish the pupil with standards, criteria, and a method of approach to the study of a vocation as a possible occupation for him; and (3) to furnish the pupil with information about the more important occupations, especially those in which he is interested.

The course in vocations is usually offered in the eighth or ninth grade as the equivalent of a one-semester solid subject. There is much to be said in favor of offering in the first semester of the twelfth grade a second course in which vocations are studied in more detail and more emphasis is placed upon actually making a vocational decision. At this advanced stage of maturity, the pupil should be able to arrive at some definite, if tentative, conclusion as to what his vocation will be and should set about preparing himself for it. In this grade, the course should include a study of college and university facilities available for training for the prospective life work.

CAREER NIGHTS. Of a certain limited value as means of vocational guidance are the career nights being arranged for in a considerable number of high schools. Programs differ somewhat from school to school, but a typical program is to have several speakers talk on choosing a career in general and a number of other speakers discuss particular vocations with groups that split up after the general program. It has been discovered pretty generally that the people who speak on the opportunities, requirements, and means of training for particular vocations or groups of vocations need to be very carefully briefed and coached; in many instances they should have materials put into their hands. Otherwise they speak in quite a general way and confine their discussion to their own experiences, opinions, and biases. Time is too short and the speakers are too limited in experience and background to make this approach very valuable. It does seem, however, to serve very well to arouse interest which may be followed up in the next few weeks in guidance counseling and group discussions.

While the number of vocational groups must be limited and will vary from school to school and from time to time, there will probably be a relatively large number of groups in all but the smaller high schools. Some schools issue to the students a mimeographed list of the possible groups and the students check the two groups in which they are most interested. On the basis of returns from this check list, a plan for grouping student interest groups with appropriate speakers or consultants may be set up for career days or career nights. It might be wise to furnish each speaker with an outline which is similar to the following:

Career Conference
Ponca City Senior High School
Suggestions for Consultants[7]

The following general outline has been found helpful to speakers discussing the various vocations with high school students. The outline will not be followed in detail since some of the subjects are of no consequence to some of the vocations. Knowing your subject as you do, it is suggested that the one important thing for you to do is to outline the points you want to cover and budget your allotted time to the various points. We realize that in the time allotted you will not be able to touch upon every point listed. We have tried to indicate which topics seem to be of the most interest to our students. The items marked with an asterisk should probably be stressed.

*I. Description of the vocation.
   A. Nature of the work.
   B. Attractive features—associations, social status, pensions.
   C. Advantages and disadvantages.
      1. Working conditions.
      2. Are there opportunities in smaller communities as well as in metropolitan areas?
      3. Is the work solitary or does one meet and work with many types of people?
      4. Supply and demand.

II. Requirements of the vocation.
   *A. Education and training—amount, nature, time and expense.
      1. School and subjects most essential.
      2. Skills and abilities most needed.
      3. Recommendations of where to obtain training, credentials, licenses.
   B. Additional training necessary.
      1. Graduate work.
         a. How long?
         b. Where available?
         c. Approximate expense.
      2. Other professional training.
         a. Suggested schools.
      3. Apprenticeships or internships necessary.
         a. How to secure them.
   C. Desirable aptitudes or skills.
      1. Examples—manual dexterity, stenographic training, etc.
   *D. Personal qualifications.
      Mental ability, personality types, special interests, appearance, age, sex, ability to get along with people, ability to follow directions, ability to lead other people, common sense or good judgment, orderliness, system and neatness, initiative, resourcefulness, punctuality, perseverance, industry.
   E. Physical qualifications.
      Any special demands upon health, nerves, lungs, feet, endurance, vision.

[7]Quoted with permission of Homer S. Anderson, Principal, Ponca City, Oklahoma, High School.

*III. Starting.
  A. How does an inexperienced person get a start in this field?
  B. What kinds of jobs may a beginner expect?
  C. Would you advise volunteer experience? If so, how may one obtain it?
  D. What is the salary range for the beginner?
IV. New developments in this field.
  A. What are some of the problems now unsolved which challenge workers?
*V. Rewards of the vocation.
  A. Financial – pay scale or reasonable income.
    1. How paid – salary, commission, wage, bonuses.
  B. Security – pensions, retirement allowance, tenure.
  C. Possibility of transfer to related vocations.
  D. Opportunity for advancement – promotions.
  E. Personal – service to others, associations, prestige, self-expression.

It is desirable also to collect and put into the hands of invited speakers bulletins and other publications furnishing data along the lines indicated in the foregoing outline. Opportunity should be furnished for questions from the students. It is useful to place in the library a list of references relating to each field at the time each talk is made and to make some announcement of such provision when the talk is given, or a few days before it is given.

EXTRACURRICULAR ACTIVITIES. Coaches and advisers of extracurricular activities should be brought to think of the guidance possibilities of such activities. Talents and interests of many a boy and girl have been disclosed to the young people themselves, as well as to advisers, as the result of their participation in debating, in art, and in dramatic, journalistic, musical, athletic, and other types of extracurricular activities. Cases without number could be furnished of boys and girls who, through participation in extracurricular activities, have found themselves to be talented and interested in a particular field or activity and have thus been led into profitable and satisfying vocational lives; there are, in addition, tens of thousands of young people who have discovered themselves to be lacking in talent or interest in activities representative of vocations which they had thought of entering. Usually qualified to recognize unusual talent, the coach or advisor should be urged to be on the lookout for it and to encourage those who appear to possess it to think of obtaining further training and of engaging in life activities which will capitalize on it. Demonstration by any pupil of unusual talent in any line should be made a part of his permanent record for future use by principal and advisers.

TESTS AND INVENTORIES IN VOCATIONAL GUIDANCE. The usefulness of aptitude and prognostic tests and interest inventories in vocational guidance has been consistently exaggerated in books on guidance and high-school administration. A number of the tests and inventories, however, are of some value and should always be used in any careful program of vocational guidance. Among them should be mentioned the following:

Aptitude Tests for Occupations, by Roeder, California Testing Bureau (Del Monte Research Park, Monterey, California; 206 Bridge Street, New Cumberland, Pennsylvania; 110 South Dickinson Street, Madison, Wisconsin; and 2114 Irving Boulevard, Dallas 7, Texas).

Differential Aptitude Tests, by the Psychological Corporation (304 East Forty-fifth Street, New York 17, New York).

Kuder Preference Record—Vocational, Science Research Associates (57 West Grand Avenue, Chicago 10, Illinois).

Lee-Thorpe Occupational Interest Inventory, California Testing Bureau.

Prognostic Test of Mechanical Ability, California Testing Bureau.

Strong Vocational Interest Blank for Men and Strong Vocational Interest Blank for Women, Stanford University Press (Stanford, California).

SOURCES OF INFORMATION CONCERNING OCCUPATIONS. Any successful program of vocational guidance must be based upon three fundamental approaches: (1) an analysis, including self-analysis, of the student's aptitudes, interests, personality potentialities, and character traits; (2) information concerning occupations and methods of analysis of occupations for purposes of guidance; and (3) training of the pupil in combining his information and insights in (1) and (2) so that he may formulate one or more tentative programs for himself.

One who is to render service with respect to pupil analysis must have had considerable technical training in that area, both in college and on the job. One who is to render any real vocational-guidance service must know a good deal about vocations, their financial and other rewards, conditions of work, and demands upon workers with respect to abilities, personality and other character traits, general education, and special training. In addition there must be available, for student reading and study, books or pamphlets of reliable information concerning all the vocations engaged in by any considerable number of people in the United States.

Bibliographies that cite the many sources of information available from private publishers, government agencies, schools, and industrial concerns are the following:

Career Index. An annotated bibliography of current materials published monthly, September through May, by Chronicle Press, Moravia, New York. $8 a year.

Counsellors Information Service. Published twice a month by B'nai B'rith Vocational Service Bureau, 1640 Rhode Island Avenue, N. W., Washington, D. C. $3 a year.

Occupational Index. An annotated bibliography of current materials published quarterly by Personnel Services, Inc., Jaffrey, New Hampshire. $7.50 a year.

Personnel and Guidance Journal. Book reviews and regular columns listing new publications and journal articles, some of which bear on occupational information, published monthly, October through May, by the American Personnel and Guidance Association, 1605 New Hampshire Avenue, N. W., Washington, D. C. $9 a year.

Vocational Guidance Quarterly. Articles and reviews on occupational information, published quarterly by the National Vocational Guidance Association, University of Michigan, Ann Arbor, Michigan. $3 a year.

At intervals the U. S. Office of Education, of the Department of Health, Education and Welfare in Washington, D. C., publishes the *Occupational Outlook Handbook,* in which information is given concerning more than six hundred occupations. Also the Science Research Associates of Chicago have published a series of booklets with very useful information for both counselors and students.

Problems, Questions, and Exercises

1. Under each of the areas of guidance try to add one more activity.
2. Think of at least two or three problems requiring guidance which involve two or more of the areas of guidance.
3. Think of an actual or hypothetical problem of the type that cannot be solved directly: a chronic problem, one which a student needs to talk over with someone.
4. Be able to discuss in class "Guidance and Juvenile Delinquency."
5. Outline a procedure for adequate guidance in connection with registration.
6. Mention one type of service that can be rendered in the next lower school, in addition to those given in the book.
7. Think of any type of guidance service, in addition to those in the chapter, that can guide youngsters in their adjustment to a new school unit.
8. Discuss the matter of how to assist a youngster in deciding whether or not he should go to college.
9. Make one suggestion, in addition to those given in the book, for deciding what college the student should attend.
10. Describe a complete plan for advising college-going students about college.
11. Make one additional suggestion for assisting a student in connection with vocational guidance.
12. Make notes of the points that you would use in preparing a talk on the following topic: "Modern Practices in Guidance for College."

Selected Supplementary Readings

"Administering Guidance in the Secondary School," *Bulletin of the N.A.S.S.P.* (November, 1954), No. 205, pp. 1-136.

Brewster, Royce, *Guidance Worker's Certification Requirements,* (Bulletin No. 14), Washington, D. C., Office of Education, U. S. Department of Health, Education and Welfare, 1960, [Requirements for certification of counselors, psychologists, psychometricians, and other guidance workers, by states in 1959.]

Brown, J. E., and Dolen, R. A., "What Constitutes an Adequate Guidance and Counseling Program for the Junior High School?" *Bulletin of the N.A.S.S.P.* (April, 1960), No. 255, pp. 40-44.
Camden, Blanche, "For a Better Understanding of Entering Students," *School Review* (January, 1953), Vol., 61, pp. 39-42.
Christensen, Thomas E., "Responsibilities of the High-School Principal in the Guidance Program," *School Review* (March, 1949), Vol. 57, pp. 149-154.
Clark, Kenneth B., "Some Principles Related to the Problem of Desegregation," *Journal of Negro Education* (Summer, 1960), Vol. 23, pp. 339-347.
Donovan, Bernard C., "Military Guidance in New York City High Schools," *Bulletin of the N.A.S.S.P.* (February, 1957), No. 226, pp. 138-145.
Educational Policies Commission, "Guidance," *Education for All American Youth,* 1952, pp. 289-301, 46-47, 49-59, 250-253, 356-359.
Elicker, Paul, and others, *Guidance and Counseling in the Secondary School,* Washington, D.C., National Education Association, 1959. [Several good articles.]
English, Walter H., "Minority Group Attitudes and Implications for Guidance," *Journal of Negro Education* (Spring, 1957), Vol. 26, pp. 99-107.
Evans, James C., and Parker, Albert J., "ROTC Programs and Negro Youth," *Journal of Negro Education* (Spring, 1956), Vol. 25, pp. 130-139.
Gardner, John W., "From High School to Job," *Education Digest* (April, 1961), Vol. 26, No. 8, pp. 1-4. [Summary of a very timely point of view, originally printed in the 1960 annual report of the Carnegie Corporation.]
Gerritz, E. M., Stahl, Edgar, Halladay, R. E., and Fields, G. H., "How Resolve the Hot Issue: Early Decision Plans for College Admission?" *Bulletin of the N.A.S.S.P.* (April, 1960), No. 255, pp. 101-109.
Gordon, Ira J., *The Teacher As A Guidance Worker,* New York, Harper, 1956. [Chapter VIII, "The Teacher as a Counselor," describes the opportunities and responsibilities of the classroom teacher in guidance.]
Harvey, C. C., "Most Serious Problems of Seniors," *Bulletin of the N.A.S.S.P.* (September, 1956), No. 221, pp. 52-57. [Survey of 1674 Utah Students.]
Hendrickson, Harry C., "The Secondary School Principal – Key to a Good Guidance Program," *Bulletin of the N.A.S.S.P.* (February, 1957), No. 226, pp. 188-201.
Hill George E., "What Kind of Guidance and Counseling Services in the Small High School?" *Bulletin of the N.A.S.S.P.* (March, 1952), Vol. 36, pp. 47-56. [Impressions gathered from a year's intensive study and from the subsequent two years of work with a group of small high schools on a consultative basis.]
Hines, William E., "A Vocational Guidance Score Card for High Schools," *California Journal of Secondary Education* (February, 1949), Vol. 24, pp. 114-119.
"How to Raise a Teenager," *Coronet* (March, 1961), Vol. 49, No. 3, pp. 149-172. [Authentic and concise. Useful for counselors, administrators, and teachers. Good to recommend to parents.]
Johnson, G. B., "Comparison of Two Evaluation Instruments for the Analysis of Academic Potential of Negro Children," *Phylon* (Spring, 1957), Vol. 20, pp. 44-47.
Johnson, Mauritz, Jr., Busacker, William E., and Bowman, Fred, Jr., *Junior High School Guidance,* New York, Harper, 1957.
Jones, Arlynne L., and Parrey, Charles A., "The Predictive Values of the Tests

of the National Freshman Testing Program," *Negro Educational Review* (January, 1958), Vol. 9, pp. 23-33; "A Further Note on the Predictive Value of the National Freshman Testing Program," *Negro Educational Review* (July, 1960), Vol. 11, pp. 120-125.

Kitzhaber, Albert R., Garrell, Robert M., and Robert, Paul, *Education for College,* New York, Ronald, 1960.

Marshall, Fred R., "A Guidance Handbook," *Bulletin of the N.A.S.S.P.* (October, 1959), No. 249, pp. 17-18. [Describes a handbook used in West Junior High School, Downey, California.]

Nancarrow, J. W., and others, "Guidance Procedures in the Secondary School," *Bulletin of the N.A.S.S.P.* (May, 1961), No. 265, pp. 1-168. [A series of short, practical articles by secondary-school administrators and counselors.]

"Orientation of New Students to High School," *School Review* (February, 1956), Vol. 64, pp. 64-66. [Techniques and evaluative program at Sheboygan, Wisconsin, High School.]

Peters, H. J., "Guidance Reading for Teachers, Counselors, and Administrators," *Bulletin of the N.A.S.S.P.* (December, 1959), No. 251, pp. 168-170.

Phillips, Waldo B., "Counseling Negro Pupils: An Educational Dilemma," *Journal of Negro Education* (Fall, 1960), Vol. 39, pp. 504-507.

Riccio, Anthony C., and Wehmeyer, Donald J., "Guidance Services Recommended by Public- and Parochial-School Teachers," *National Education Research Bulletin* (January, 11, 1961), Vol. 40, No. 1, pp. 12-16.

Roeber, Edward C., Smith, Glenn, and Erickson, Clifford E., *Organization and Administration of Guidance Services,* New York, McGraw-Hill, 1955.

Rushing, F. E., "What Kind of Guidance and Counseling Service for the Small School?" *Bulletin of the N.A.S.S.P.* (March, 1952), No. 185, pp. 38-47.

Saalfeld, Lawrence J., *Guidance and Counseling for Catholic Schools,* Chicago, Loyola University Press, 1958.

Saunders, Juliet, "Organizing and Supervising a Junior High School Guidance Program," *Bulletin of the N.A.S.S.P.* (March, 1960), No. 254, pp. 132-134.

Segel, David, *Guidance and Pupil Personnel Services in the Junior High School —A Bibliography* (No. 426), Washington, D.C., U.S. Department of Health, Education and Welfare, Office of Education, February, 1955.

Stoops, Emery, and others, *Guidance Services, Organization and Administration,* New York, McGraw-Hill, 1959.

Strang, Ruth, "Guidance to Meet the Needs of Youth," *Adapting the Secondary-School Program to the Needs of Youth,* Fifty-second Yearbook, Part I, National Society for the Study of Education, University of Chicago Press, 1953, Chapter 11. [Today's views of guidance, contribution of the classroom teacher, teacher-counselor, club sponsor, administrator, and specialist.]

Tanneyhill, Ann, *From School to Job: Guidance for Minority Youth,* New York, New York City Public Affairs Pamphlet, 1960.

Traxler, Arthur E., *Techniques of Guidance* (Revised Edition), New York, Harper, 1957. [See Chapter 2, "Essentials in Launching a Guidance Program"; Chapters 4 through 7, on the information needed for appraisal of data.]

Walsh, Mary Belle, "An Organized Guidance Program in the Catholic High Schools of the Diocese of Kansas City," *Proceedings and Addresses,* 49th Annual Meeting, National Catholic Educational Association, August, 1952. Outlines the plan used in these secondary schools.]

Wechsler, Louis K., Martin, Blim, and Friedman, Sidney, *College Entrance Counselor,* New York, Barnes and Noble, 1960. [A paperback of counsel for the college-bound with directories of two-year and four-year colleges and a guide to scholarships.]

Wilson, Eugene S., and Bucher, Charles A., *College Ahead!* New York, Harcourt, Brace, 1961.

Wilson, Eugene S., Keim, Edwin B., and Martin, Robert A., "What's Ahead in the College Admissions Scramble?" *Bulletin of the N.A.S.S.P.* (April, 1961), Vol. 45, pp. 48-52.

Zeran, Franklin B. and Riccio, Anthony C., *Organization and Administration of Guidance Services,* Rand McNally, 1962.

13

Organizing and Improving Guidance (Continued)

6. Organization of Personnel

TYPES OF GUIDANCE PERSONNEL. A variety of staff officers has been developed to carry on guidance in high schools. Among such officers are the director of guidance, the vocational counselor, the placement director, the dean of girls, the dean of boys, the school counselor, registration advisers, and home-room or group advisers. In addition to these, there exist in a number of schools directors of health and directors of activites, who perform guidance service in these specialized fields. The nature and organization of the personnel employed in a given school vary, not only with the extent to which the school has gone into the development of a guidance program but also with the size of the school and with the individuals whose services are readily available.

Conant, in his highly publicized report to citizens on the American high school, recommended that there be one full-time qualified counselor or guidance officer for every 250 to 300 pupils in high school.[1] This is not too high a standard.

An excellent organization for larger schools includes a director of guidance and one or more counselors. In the largest schools the organization might include a special counselor for girls, a vocational counselor, a college-problems counselor, a staff of registration advisers, and a staff of home-room advisers. The director of guidance heads and directs the entire guidance program. The vocational counselor is one of the director's chief lieutenants. Under the director's general direction he assumes responsibility for developing a program: bringing the pupils of the school into contact with information on vocations, with special reference to the local community; assisting them to bring together all available vocational information and data concerning themselves, their abilities and

[1]James B. Conant, *The American High School Today,* New York, McGraw-Hill, 1959, p. 44.

interests, so that they may deal with the problem of choosing a vocation; and assisting them to initiate and perfect their early adjustments in vocational life. The dean of girls is in many schools the major counselor for girls. She not only assumes the leadership in directing the social life of the school but also plays a large part in personal contacts with the girls of the school. The director of guidance, or head counselor, personally directs the activities of two groups of staff assistants: registration advisers and home-room, or group, advisers. The former are teachers who are chosen for special guidance duties at registration periods; the latter are advisers who are assigned each to a group of pupils and who function throughout the year.

The duties and responsibilities of each of these officers in any given school depend upon the number and character of other members of the guidance staff. This point will be amplified and illustrated in the discussion of the duties of the different guidance agents.

THE DIRECTOR OF GUIDANCE. In all but the smaller schools an effort should be made to obtain on the staff, even if only on a part-time basis, one individual who is especially trained in guidance theory, organization, and techniques and in underlying psychology and psychological testing; on this individual responsibility may be placed for organizing and supervising a modern, functioning guidance program. The director of guidance should be charged with setting up the plan of organization and the machinery for guidance, with training registration and home-room advisers, and with supervising their activities.

In many school systems the director of guidance also has the responsibility for planning, administering, and interpreting the various types of tests, inventories, and check lists for gathering data about counselees.

PSYCHOLOGICAL SERVICE. In recent years many more schools, particularly in large cities, are providing on a limited basis psychological and psychiatric services for young people who are emotionally disturbed or have other unusual needs for psychological or psychiatric help.

FEDERAL AND STATE SUBSIDIES FOR GUIDANCE. Through the George-Barden Act for Vocational Education and the National Defense Act, there have been made available substantial funds for the improvement of the guidance services in local school systems. Very little of this money is available for the payment of salaries of counselors in service, but substantial funds are available for improving the guidance training of counselors and for providing similar aid in testing programs. The aid for the test programs, which are on a state basis, may be obtained in the form of tests which may be given in the local schools and scored by machine in the offices of the state department. The superintendent, the principal, or both should, if possible, have a personal conference with the appropriate representative in the state department of education and get information and guidance in making application for the aid in testing programs, the scoring of tests, and the training of counselors.

COMMUNITY RESOURCES. There are in every community some resources which may be employed or co-operated with in the development and operation of the guidance and counseling programs. For example, there are agencies which are carrying on counseling programs which may be to some extent co-ordinated with the school programs. Among the community agencies of this type are the local employment agency, the service clubs (particularly Kiwanis Club), 4-H Clubs, Girl Scouts, Boy Scouts, YMCA, YWCA, YMHA, pastors, priests, and rabbis.

CERTIFICATION OF GUIDANCE WORKERS. In recent years state after state has made definite provision for the special certification of counselors, school psychologists, and psychometricians. In 1961 thirty states required that those engaged especially in counseling work have a state counselor's certificate. In eight other states certificates were issued but were not required for counselors. The number of states requiring certificates is certain to increase.

The certification requirements vary greatly from state to state, but in every state at least a year of experience and some course-work training in the field of counseling are required. The requirements range all the way from the requirement of a single course in counseling to the requirement of a master's degree in the field of counseling and guidance.

There are several types of certificates, but in most states they fall into two classifications: (1) the provisional or temporary certificate, which is good for a limited period – that is, two, three, or five years; and (2) the permanent or professional certificate, which is good for life. In general, a master's degree in counseling and guidance is required for the latter type of certificate. Each principal should ascertain what the requirements are in the state in which he is working or planning to work.

The movement toward setting up and requiring special certificates for school psychologists and psychometricians is more recent; in 1961 only thirteen states required certificates for these workers.

HOUSING AND FACILITIES FOR GUIDANCE WORKERS. The principal must, either by requesting some remodeling of older buildings or by demanding appropriate planning of new buildings, see to it that guidance workers have adequate office space, equipment space, and conference rooms. Buildings built in recent years provide much more adequate space for guidance than those built prior to 1950.

Excellent suggestions for housing and equipment are given in the bulletin issued by the U.S. Office of Education and prepared by Don P. Twiford. Since space is not available here to present his many suggestions and diagrams for housing, the reader is referred to the publication by Dr. Twiford (see readings listed at the end of this chapter).

7. *The Vocational Counselor*

THE COUNSELOR'S DUTIES. The duties of vocational counselors vary from school to school, but in general the better-trained and better-supported counselors attempt to:

1. Provide information about vocations:
   a. By placing books, magazines, bulletins, monographs, and other related material in the school library or in the hands of interested students.
   b. By organizing and giving courses in occupations.
   c. By organizing and supervising local occupational surveys.
   d. By arranging for speakers to talk about occupations before assemblies or groups of pupils.
   e. By giving talks before such groups.
   f. By arranging for students to visit places where occupations are carried on and by conducting follow-up discussions.
   g. By having personal conferences with students.
   h. By stimulating pupils to make intensive studies of one or more vocations in which they are interested individually.
2. Study the capacities and interests of students as individuals:
   a. From the scores of tests of intelligence and achievement and from the scores of prognostic (or aptitude) tests.
   b. From extracurricular-activity records.
   c. From interest or occupation questionnaires and analyses on interests or occupations.
   d. From the rating of teachers as to character and personality.
   e. From the personal data of students and family data.
   f. From data gathered from conferences with students.
   g. From part-time or summer vocational experience of students.
3. Assist students in tentative choice of occupations:
   a. By a study of students' records with a view to vocational advice.
   b. By conferences with students about their vocational futures.
4. Supervise and direct related types of research:
   a. By determining the prognostic value of various types of data for educational and vocational prediction.
   b. By analyzing data for recommendations regarding curricula.
5. Co-operate with the following groups in mutual problems:
   a. The attendance department in connection with work permits and certificates on leaving school.
   b. Placement agencies within or without the school.
   c. Social agencies or workers interested in the vocational problems of young people.
   d. Parents and friends interested in assisting children in making good vocational adjustments.
6. Gather data and conduct follow-up guidance with graduates and former pupils to determine:
   a. "Dropouts": where they go, why they dropped out, etc.
   b. Occupational success of those leaving school.
   c. Degree of occupational adjustment.
   d. Efforts at self-improvement.

Selecting and Installing a Vocational Counselor. That these responsibilities may be discharged properly, the right type of counselor must be selected and provided with favorable working conditions. For high-grade work a man of considerable technical training should be obtained. This training should include a good background in psychological and aptitude testing and statistical methods, in educational and vocational guidance, and in vocational education. It is important to obtain a man who by his personality and appearance, as well as by his training, will command the respect and good will of all high-school boys and girls (particularly problem cases) and of the professional, business, and industrial men of the community. Such a man will naturally command a salary in excess of the classroom teacher or department head, a salary equivalent to that of a vice-principal or an assistant principal.

The counselor should be given proper office quarters and equipment, as well as funds for tests and for scoring tests. He should be given an adequate fund for vocational-guidance materials in the way of books and other printed matter. He should receive the complete co-operation of all other agencies, officials, and instructors in the school. Those in charge of the administration of the school should in every way assist him in making contact with outside forces of value to him, such as commercial and service clubs, social-service organizations, parents' organizations, and parents as individuals. He should not be given teaching or other duties to such an extent that he will not be able to spend much time in conference with students, parents, and employment executives and in the study of his records and data.

Placement and Follow-up Service. School administrators interested in secondary education have come to realize that the school may make to society and to young people as individuals a contribution which is broader than instruction. They have been impressed with the fact that, for a great many pupils, the school may render a service, in getting them safely started in their vocational careers, that their parents are unable to render for them effectively; the school may give valuable assistance to parents in this important function. The idea has become generally accepted that the school should seriously consider assuming responsibility for any type of service necessary or highly desirable in the preparation of young people for life when no other institution or agency is functioning in that particular type of service, provided, of course, that the school can reasonably render the service. It is obvious that industries, trades, professions, businesses, and other branches of productive life are rarely impartially interested in guiding boys and girls into those occupations in which they as individuals will be most happy and useful. Nor are they in a position to render service equal to that of the school. The idea that the school should maintain guidance influence and contacts even after a boy or girl has withdrawn from school is gaining adherents rapidly. An outgrowth of such thinking in educational philosophy is the placement service now furnished by many schools, particularly for withdrawals from junior and senior high schools.

Briefly, the placement service should involve five types of activities:

1. The gathering of all information possible about the boys and girls to be served which will throw light on their abilities, capacities, interests, temperaments, and health and which will therefore be of use in most effectively locating them.
2. The establishment of contacts with employing concerns or individuals which will result in opportunities to place at work and in training the boys and girls to be guided.
3. The accumulation of such local information about vocations as will be useful in advising young people.
4. The continuation of contacts with young people after they are placed, for the purpose of guidance, counsel, and advice on matters vocational, moral, educational, and personal; also hints may be obtained through these contacts for the improvement of placement service.
5. The administration of details relating to employment certificates and other phases of the compulsory-attendance laws as these relate to employment.

Since placement service—its technique, records, and forms—constitutes a somewhat specialized field, the principal should place it in the hands of someone who has been able to give it careful study or is willing to do so. The personal qualifications desirable are similar to those mentioned in connection with the counselor and will not be repeated here. Principals installing placement service for the first time should visit and study the organization of the service in schools maintaining it successfully.

As a result of very careful study of placement services in large-city school systems, Margaret E. Andrews[2] concluded that the director of placement should:

1. Be provided with a budget adequate to meet the needs for personnel, time, physical facilities and supplies, both in the schools and in the central office, to carry on this program.
2. Understand and actively support activities necessary to carry out this program.
3. Foster the understanding and cooperation of the school principals through allowing the central office placement worker to meet with them from time to time to discuss placement problems.
4. Establish, with the aid of the school staff, an advisory committee on student employment made up of representatives of labor, management and education. This committee should assist in formulating policies and procedures, on a city-wide basis, which affect student workers and which are acceptable to the groups affected.
5. Plan, with the school staff, for the preparation, distribution and use of materials and forms necessary for carrying out the placement function.
6. Develop a plan for the systematic follow-up of all students at work whether or not they were placed by the school.

[2]Consultant in Business Education and Placement in the Minneapolis, Minnesota, schools; Ed. D., University of Colorado, 1954.

7. Develop, on request and with advisory committee approval, plans to meet special local employment needs.
8. Establish, with the advice of the advisory committee, effective, cooperative relationships with the State Employment Service.
9. Develop plans for year-round employment service for students and employers.
10. Promote plans for making full-time student help available at varying times throughout the year.
11. Develop working relationships with all agencies in the community which can be of value in placement, such as other junior placement agencies, social and welfare agencies, civic organizations, employer groups, and unions.
12. Plan, with school placement workers, in-service training for them and for teachers working on pre-placement units and in trade classes.
13. Plan city-wide program of group guidance activities for students to avoid exploiting employers and civic leaders receiving conflicting requests from many schools.
14. Keep informed of, and inform other central office staff members of, developments with significance for placement, particularly in relation to needed curriculum changes.
15. Coordinate activities related to the issuance of work permits and age certificates so that schools may recommend their issuance where feasible, may make the work experience a part of the cumulative record, and may follow-up students on the job.
16. Develop a professional committee from among school placement workers to work continually on the evaluation of the placement program and to develop plans to meet future needs.
17. Serve as a clearing house on wages, hours, and working conditions of job orders which are received.
18. Refer all acceptable job orders for students to the placement counselors in the schools to be filled.
19. Promote understanding of the placement program in the school so students will use its services, and faculty and administration will understand and accept its worth.
20. Provide students with the opportunity to register for work, both full-time and part-time, regardless of their apparent need or their academic status.
21. Accept employer calls for student workers which have been cleared through the central office and refer students listed in the file of active applicants, or seek out qualified students.
22. Maintain adequate records of job orders and job applications, and make proper entries on cumulative records when students are working.
23. Refer calls received from employers who are not known to the central office for clearance.
24. Promote good employer relationships with small, neighborhood employers who cannot be known by the central office.
25. Carry on systematic follow-up as part of the city-wide plan.
26. Promote in-service training in the school which will be of help to teachers in understanding and cooperating in the placement program.
27. Assist teachers by suggesting methods and in providing materials for group guidance in pre-placement and vocational classes.

28. Provide for the counseling which is necessary before, during, and after placement is made.
29. Establish a personal pattern of work which allows for regular field contacts of employers and for observation of students at work.
30. Set up a policy of encouraging employers to come to the school to discuss employment problems, interview students, and observe the school training programs.
31. Work with vocational teachers in utilizing their training and experience in the preparation of skilled workers and in giving them up-to-date information on job market trends in their trade.
32. Provide each teacher with the opportunity to have a part in the placement program through allowing them to recommend students for employment, conduct preplacement training activities, and through utilizing the vocational implications of their own work.
33. Understand student interests and needs and interpret them to the school curriculum committee and to individual staff members as the basis for a school offering which will hold students in school and at the same time prepare them for work when they leave.

FOLLOW-UP. Many schools keep contact with their former students in order to (*a*) continue guidance service to them and (*b*) obtain information upon the effectiveness of the school's program of vocational education and vocational guidance. The National Association of Secondary School Principals has prepared and published a form for this purpose, "Post School Inventory."

8. The Girls' Counselor and the Boys' Counselor

DUTIES OF THE GIRLS' COUNSELOR. A realization of the importance of guidance, the difficulty of finding among the regular teaching staff sufficiently trained counselors with favorable personality and temperament, and the need felt for the special guidance of girls by one of their own sex have been largely responsible for the establishment, in a majority of schools of over 200 pupils, of a dean of girls (or girls' counselor) or a vice-principal who performs the duties of a counselor of girls. Properly supported with needed data, equipment, and working relations, an adequately trained girls' counselor may become the most useful member of the principal's administrative staff.

The duties and opportunities of the girls' counselor include all those mentioned in connection with the discussion of counselors; in addition, there are other duties and responsibilities which pertain particularly to the position of counselor of all girls' affairs in the school and which are peculiarly suitable for a woman who counsels girls. Among the most important of these the following may be mentioned as typical:

1. Personal and group advice in the matter of health and hygiene.
2. Responsibility for organization and assistance in the social and recreational program of the school: dances, parties, and hikes in which girls participate, with or without boys.

3. Sympathetic and wholesome advice to girls in their social life outside the school: romantic and personal, as well as formal.
4. Special responsibility in bringing social and personal development to the backward, ignorant, shy, and uncultured girls of the school.
5. Responsibility for assisting the girl to arrive at a true understanding of the place and activities of the modern girl and woman of today, touching upon such things as:
   a. Friendships of various kinds.
   b. Leisure and recreation.
   c. Formal social life.
   d. Attitudes toward older people: parents, teachers, and others.
   e. Conventions that mark "good breeding."
   f. Dress and appearance.
6. Analysis and remedial measures for personality and mental "twists" and nervous handicaps: for example, hypersensitiveness and sulkiness, pugnaciousness, abnormal fears, phobias, and suspicions, extreme extraversion or introversion, and morbidity.
7. Advice and counsel on financial problems, such as self-support, loan funds, employment, and working one's way through college.
8. Advice and counsel on matters of boarding or rooming houses, hygiene of home quarters (food, diet, and sleep), and unfortunate personal relationships in the home.
9. Vocational counseling in those schools in which there is no vocational counselor.

Even to a less extent than in the case of the group counselor should the girls' counselor be charged with duties which operate to spoil the fundamental relationship of confidant and friend. The administration of disciplinary cases referred to her should be such as permit her to refer them to some other official if formal punishment is necessary. The girls' counselor must be admired, esteemed, and respected—not feared, disliked, or avoided.

INSTALLING A GIRLS' COUNSELOR. The responsibility of counseling girls should be assigned only to one who is fully familiar, by means of formal training or study in service, with the purposes and possibilities of the position and with techniques and procedures which have proved successful; she should be one who is familiar with the points of view of high-school girls and who possesses the appearance, personality, and manner to attract girls. Superannuated teachers with no qualifications other than a "motherly" appearance or attitude should not be designated for the position. The problems involved not only require intellect and professional training but also make tremendous demands on the ability to win the confidence and admiration of girls. All too often the woman selected proves to be too stern or too prone to criticism of low standards, prizing the prestige of lost battles in a worthy cause even more highly than compromises which lead to progress; she may put her own reputation among the women of the community above the character of her girls; she may be a social censor or policewoman, beneath whose external pleasantness there lies, after all, the traditional "schoolmarm."

The girls' counselor should be given adequate office room, strategically located and affording desirable privacy. She should be given clerical and stenographic assistance proportionate to the size of the school; she should have record forms and filing cabinets. She should be given every possible favorable working relationship with the school physician, the nurses, the directors and instructors in physical education, the attendance department, the building custodian, and the faculty in general. All counselors in the school should clear their social activities and program through her. She should be placed in close working relations with the vocational counselor, if there is one. She should be given every opportunity to make social and personal contacts with parents. As the representative of the school, she should be put in touch with others in the community who work with and for girls—juvenile-court authorities, social workers, and religious and similar organizations.

She should not be so heavily loaded with teaching or with other duties not pertinent to her work as counselor as to prevent her from having ample time for many personal conferences with pupils and parents, for visits to pupils' homes and to the nonschool officials and agencies mentioned above, and for planning the details of her work.

If she is relatively untrained or inexperienced, she should be stimulated to give much study to her position, its possibilities and techniques, and to fit herself for graduation from the apprentice class as soon as possible. Appointments or increases in salary should be contingent upon such self-improvement, as well as upon apparent success in the work.

THE BOYS' COUNSELOR. Very few schools have separate deans of boys, or boys' counselors. Since most principals are men, there is much less need for a separate administrative office for boys corresponding to that of the dean of girls. The duties of the boys' counselor are similar to those of the dean of girls. He stands ready to talk over with the boys as individuals or as groups problems of almost any sort which they bring to him; he is also constantly on the lookout for opportunities to offer counsel to individuals or groups in any of the numerous problems which are likely to arise in the lives of boys at this age and with which few are ready to cope unaided—problems of conduct in school and out, problems of home, financial problems, and problems of social life. In the large majority of schools there is no dean of boys; many of the home-room, or group, counselors are women; and not all the men counselors are qualified to meet the requirements. In such schools the director of guidance, or in smaller schools the principal, is the logical individual to perform counseling service.

9. Home-Room Guidance

THE HOME-ROOM OR GROUP COUNSELOR. The home-room or group counseling system spread rapidly in the thirties. Its spread has been very materially slowed down in recent years. Under the home-room or group counseling system the teacher is assigned one or two groups of youngsters, usually of approximately 30 pupils each. The home-room counselor furnishes two types of guidance: (*a*) group guidance (discussed in this chapter) and (*b*) individual guidance. The functions performed by these counselors vary with the guidance program of the principal or director of guidance and with the number and duties of other guidance agents. If there are on the staff a competent girls' counselor, a vocational counselor, and a director of guidance, or head counselor, the duties of the home-room counselor will naturally be less varied and will involve fewer of the more complex and technical tasks, which will be performed by the more highly trained members of the staff.

INADEQUACY OF MANY HOME ROOMS AS ADVISORY ORGANIZATIONS. Except in those schools in which there are competent and forceful head counselors or chief counselors with the authority and the time to direct the activities of the counselors, the home-room, or group, counseling organization has rarely been very successful as an instrument for guidance. The home-room period is in many schools no more than a place and time for taking the roll, for making announcements, for electing home-room representatives and preparing home-room programs, for checking on absences, and for unsupervised study. In many high schools the reasons for this condition lie largely in the lack of training, competence, and interest on the part of those assigned as home-room counselors, in the lack of constructive supervision of counselors and their activities by someone who can outline a working program of principles and techniques of home-room guidance and who can interest counselors in the program, and in the failure to supply home-room counselors with necessary data. In many instances the home-room counselor knows no more about the pupil than does any teacher with whom the pupil has a class; and he has little opportunity to learn any more about him, meeting him, as he does, in a group of from 25 to 40 pupils daily from 5 to 15 minutes or for 15 to 30 minutes two or three times a week. Often the counselor regards the responsibility as just another chore, to be completed with as little effort as possible. He is furnished with meager documentary data in regard to his charges, or with none at all, and feels that there is not much that he can do. To call this sort of thing "advisory group-guidance service" approaches travesty. However useful home-room activities of the prevailing type may be in supplementing a really professional type of guidance carried on by a trained counselor, they do not in themselves constitute other than a very primitive type of guidance.

FUNDAMENTALS OF A SUCCESSFUL GROUP-COUNSELING ORGANIZATION. In the following paragraphs are presented briefly certain suggestions for setting up a group-guidance program either on the basis of home-room organization or in some other setup.

1. *The counselors must be by training, personality, and interest*

fitted to render guidance services. In those schools in which the home-room counselor is expected to render professional service, the position should be made more than an "extra." Either a bonus should be given for counseling services which will make appointment to such work desirable or, better still, a sufficient reduction should be made in the teaching load. The counselor should then be required to make a formal study of his problems and of the principles and techniques of guidance. Summer-session or extension courses in guidance are most valuable, but unsupervised professional reading will go far to give the counselor training in the possibilities and procedures of that work. The principal may be of assistance by providing bibliography and books. Especially useful should be books which discuss actual techniques of guidance and the case method of guidance and which illustrate with many types of individual cases and guidance follow-up.

2. *Time and opportunities should be provided for conferences between the counselor and each pupil allotted to him.* Where a daily activity period of from 30 to 45 minutes is provided, one or two such periods a week should frequently be given over to the meeting of counseling groups, at which times the counselor not only may carry on group-guidance discussions of various sorts but may also find opportunity for conferences and counsel with individuals about problems of school progress, school attendance, citizenship, health, student activities, or dress. In schools where no activity period is scheduled, one or two regular periods a week or several shorter periods should be given to counseling or home-room meetings.
3. *The counselors must be furnished with adequate data and with equipment for the care and use of it.* The professional home-room counselor should be provided with all possible types of data regarding the pupil: previous school record, scores on tests of intelligence and achievement, prognostic tests of aptitude, personal and family history, citizenship, character ratings, health and medical or physical-examination records, present program, interest and vocational questionnaires, and any other data available. An idea of the possible detailed items of data and forms for recording data may be had from forms illustrated in Chapter 17. From time to time reports of unexcused absences, delinquency in scholarship or in citizenship, participation in extracurricular activities and special achievements, and all other similar current data should be regularly and promptly forwarded to the appropriate counselors. It is important for counselors to be prepared to congratulate the student on his achievements as well as to confer with him about his delinquencies or difficulties. To fail to do so weakens very materially the influence of the counselor with the student. The student should feel his counselor is interested in him as an individual, truly rejoicing at his successes and truly grieved at his failures.

4. *Counselors must be trained not to neglect the counseling activities in favor of routine or other noncounseling activities.* Meetings of counselors should be held from time to time by the head counselor or the principal. These meetings serve to impress counselors with the importance of their work, to afford opportunity for exchange of ideas on making counseling activities effective, and to provide special training. If possible, speakers from teacher-training institutions or other high schools who are well versed in the details of counseling-group activities should be brought in to discuss techniques successfully employed elsewhere. Counseling or home-room periods should be visited even more frequently than regular classes in an effort to perfect techniques in this new type of educational service. Counselors should be requested to make case reports on all important special cases, and these reports should be made a part of the pupils' permanent records to be passed on to all future counselors. Counselors should also, at the conclusion of the semester or year or at any time when pupils are transferred to other counselors, file a brief report on each counselee and longer ones on special cases which will assist other counselors in being of most service. Such reports should include pertinent character traits, individual interests, and avenues of approach which have proved successful with the student.

ACTIVITIES OF GROUP COUNSELORS. Only in a volume entirely devoted to guidance is it practical to discuss in detail the activities and techniques of home-room or group counselors. Much may be inferred from the foregoing discussion. Space will permit here merely a brief summary. Among the responsibilities borne by the counselor in at least a few schools are those listed below:

1. A careful study of all the available records of each individual assigned to the counselor.
2. Advice and assistance in counseling-group organizations, activities, and programs.
3. Discovery of reasons for absences; assistance to pupils in bringing about more regular attendance.
4. Guidance in registration for subjects to be studied for the coming year or semester.
5. Comparison of student's scholastic marks in relation to capacity as judged by intelligence-test scores and previous scholastic record.
6. Discovery of reasons for a student's failure to progress in his studies in proportion to his apparent capacity.
7. Conferences with students relative to citizenship in school.
8. Instruction in "school guidance" appropriate to the maturity of counselees.
9. Conferences with and advice to students upon any matter brought to him by the students: health, social problems, employment, and preparation for college, for example.
10. Conferences with parents of students about excessive absences, matters of health, or citizenship in such instances as suggest the need of co-operation or information of parent.

11. Supervision of home-room activities: election of officers and the preparation and presentation of programs.
12. Visiting the homes of the students in the counseling group and having the parents visit the school individually and in groups, for the purpose of better acquaintanceship and better working relationship between the parents and the group counselors and for the exchange of information between the parent and the home-room counselor, enabling all of them to discharge more successfully their responsibilities in advising and guiding boys and girls.

Counselors should not be charged with responsibilities which involve the punishment of pupils or with other contacts or relations that are not consistent with establishing and maintaining friendly and confidential relations. The ideal to be kept in view is the establishment of counselors as guides, friends, and confidants. The influence of such individuals in the lives of many boys and girls at high school age may often exceed that of the pupils' own parents, who, because of the apparent necessity of much nagging and checking, have come to be regarded as persons who "do not understand." Ideals and ambitions may be engendered and fostered by counselors. Facts explaining various types of delinquencies may be discovered, difficult diagnoses made, children saved to good citizenship, educational careers prolonged, and intelligent choices of subjects or vocations contributed to; counselors may increase the happiness and dispel undesirable worries of troubled boys and girls. Yet the functioning of the counseling system demands the utmost care in organization and supervision by the high-school principal.

10. The Principal and the Guidance Program

According to Dean Franklin R. Zeran of Oregon State College, the administrator who wishes to have a superior guidance program must:

1. Administrative.
   A. Make adequate provision in the budget for carrying on the guidance program.
   B. Establish and maintain a cumulative record system. See to it that it is kept cumulative and that it is used in the counseling process.
2. Organizational.
   A. Recognize the need and importance of a comprehensive guidance program and give it his unqualified personal support.
   B. Make his staff cognizant of the value, functions, and problems of guidance services. The work of the guidance program cannot be carried on in any school, no matter how well provided with specialists on the staff, unless the entire faculty understands and sympathizes with the objectives of the program and, in fact, participates in many of the activities required. There must be an acceptance of the administrator and the staff of guidance principles and active participation in the program by all.
   C. Work out and coordinate the guidance program co-operatively with members of the staff.
   D. Provide for a guidance committee.
   E. Coordinate all available co-curricular resources to aid in the program.

F. Coordinate and use all available community resources to aid in the program.

G. Give desirable publicity to improve school, home, and community relationships.

3. Personnel needs.

A. Select best qualified workers as counselors.

B. Offer special inducements and recognition to counselors in the guidance program where special services and training are required.

4. Scheduling.

A. Arrange the school schedule so that *every* pupil may have an opportunity for counseling services.

B. See that ample time is allowed the counselor.

5. Equipment, supplies, and quarters.

Provide suitable quarters and facilities for the counseling service. Counseling is on an individual basis and quarters should be provided to meet this individual need.

6. Evaluation of the program.

Provide for continuous evaluation of the guidance program.[3]

THE PRINCIPAL AS COUNSELOR. In the small school an elaborate organization for guidance is often not possible and to a certain extent not necessary. In schools in which it is possible for every student to have immediate personal conferences with the principal and in which the principal may find time to give careful study to all the pertinent data and to call into his office students apparently most in need of guidance, much valuable guidance service may be rendered. In some ways he is in the best position to render it, being most likely to come naturally into contact with all the various types of data desirable for guidance—through records of various sorts, knowledge of attendance, and misdemeanors, and contacts with parents. On the other hand, it is difficult for him to assume the double role of "terror" to evildoers and "friend" of the sinners. If the principal will, as far as is possible, handle disciplinary cases more as guidance opportunities and endeavor to solve problems on the basis of good mental hygiene, he may go a long way toward dissolving the duality of the role of one who must punish in some cases but also act as a counselor. In a situation where the student must be punished by the principal, the principal should transfer the student to some other counselor and not attempt to carry on the dual role. The principal of the small school, however, will miss golden opportunities and will labor under a distorted perspective if he becomes so busy maintaining discipline and carrying on routine and subject-matter supervision that he does not find the time and the occasion to come into the lives of many boys and girls at critical moments with sympathy and advice, encouragement and caution, and assistance in arriving at right decisions.

[3]Franklin B. Zeran, "The Roles for the School Board Member, Superintendent, Principal, and Classroom Teacher in an Effective, Well-Integrated Guidance Program," *Bulletin of the N.A.S.S.P.* (December, 1959), No. 251, pp. 96-98.

Even in larger schools, when certain conditions obtain, the principal may well act as chief guidance officer. Such conditions are the following:

1. The assistance of a capable dean of girls who can relieve the principal of at least a great share of actual conference with girls.
2. An assistant principal who will relieve him of much of the office routine or of the major burden of supervision of instruction.
3. The lack of funds or qualified candidates for the position of counselor.
4. Adequate training on the part of the principal.

These conditions should be regarded as relative. For example, in a school not too large the failure to have either a dean of girls or an assistant principal need not discourage the principal from building up a good guidance program centered about himself, especially if department heads may be relied upon to assist with supervision of instruction.

Unless funds are available for a real counselor, it is likely that the principal may find it advisable to delegate to teachers or department heads duties which require less in the way of personality and special training, rather than to delegate counseling to a less able individual. Where the counseling is performed by the principal, it is fortunate if an assistant principal may be given responsibilities for the details of "discipline," punishment, and other activities where appeal to fear must be made. If these are handled personally by the principal, it may weaken his position materially as an adviser and a counselor.

If the untrained principal finds it impossible to obtain the services of a properly trained and fitted counselor and must himself assume the functions of guidance, he should apply to the department of education of a college or a university for a bibliography of the soundest, most readable, and most practical references on guidance and for a bibliography of materials to place in the library or in the hands of students. Practically all the larger institutions, through their bureaus of research or reference or their departments of vocational guidance or secondary education, are prepared to render this service gratis or at very little cost. The principal may be able to pursue a correspondence course which, if he has sufficient time to complete it, will be of assistance in organizing his reading and reactions. He should, at any rate, realize that there is much to learn. For the principal possessing little special training in guidance, it will be helpful to make a careful study of several treatises.[4]

In smaller schools, where for one reason or another home-room or group counselors or other guidance agents cannot be relied upon to look after such matters, the principal should arrange to hold personal conferences with pupils falling far short of their possibilities in their subjects, with those most likely to fail in two or more subjects, and with those most in need of personal or civic guidance. At such conferences efforts should be made to encourage the pupils not only to exert efforts in their own behalf but also to seek to discover the underlying causes for the

[4]See "Selected Supplementary Readings" at the end of this chapter.

difficulties or delinquencies (of which the pupils themselves are often not conscious) and, upon ascertaining these, to initiate a constructive effort at rehabilitation. Such conferences should not be looked upon merely as opportunities for rebuking apparently lazy or indifferent pupils and for appealing to fear, an approach which, though effective in many cases, is too crude and superficial to get at the heart of most difficulties and yields only temporary improvement, if any at all.

11. The Teacher as Counselor

The General Counselor and the Specialist. There has been much debate as to whether guidance should be made by general counselors or by specialists. Experience seems to indicate that both are necessary. As the school becomes larger, there should be several specialist counselors. The important thing is for the home-room counselor, the classroom teacher, and the general counselor to realize the limitations of their competence, to be able to spot quickly the cases where the services of a specialized counselor are indicated, and to see to it that the student and the counselor get together for the solution of the student's problem. In some schools a report by the teacher, giving the names of students who seem to be in most need of counseling service, is sent weekly to the principal or director of guidance.

In an increasing number of schools there is prepared and put into the hands of each teacher data concerning each youngster in his classes. These data commonly include, among other things, information concerning the youngster's general academic intelligence, his previous scholarship, and his scores on such special aptitude tests as might be useful for the teacher of the subject concerned.

In the Ponca City High School there are furnished every teacher the following types of data for every youngster in school: average marks so far; attendance record; I. Q.; geometry aptitude test; scores on each part and the total of the Stanford Achievement Test, Science Research Associates Verbal Test, Science Research Associates Primary Mental Ability Test, Social and Science Development Test, and Kuder Preference Test.

In recent years the teacher has come to participate more in guidance. Not only has he come to participate more effectively as home-room counselor and sponsor but also he has come to employ more of the philosophy of guidance in his teaching and has come to see more and more opportunities in his normal classroom contacts with pupils to render guidance services not closely associated with the teaching of his subject.

The more modern classroom teacher gathers and uses more data than his predecessor. He wants to have reliable data concerning the individual pupil – his general intelligence, his special abilities, something of his home environment, his vocational, social, and hobby interests, his vocational, extracurricular, and work experiences, and his social and emotional adjustment. He takes more pains to locate the areas of the pupil's limitations, so that he may adapt instruction to his needs and interests.

It must be admitted, however, that in most schools there are one or more teachers who have not learned to perform these services; and quite

Functions of Teachers and Specialists in Guidance Services[5]

Principal (or designated representative) co-ordinates administration of services

Functions of Classroom (and Home-Room) Teachers	Special Services to Individual Youth	Functions of the Guidance Specialists
Provides learning situations Collects data about interests Confers with youth on interests Plans studies related to choice	1. Choosing a vocation	Maintains occupational materials, files, records Observes youth at work Gives aptitude tests Helps teachers prepare resource units on vocations
Maintains records for specialists Helps youth with applications and interview preparation Helps youth with work habits and techniques	2. Finding a job	Maintains records for prospective employers Makes opportunity analyses Places youth in jobs Helps in adjustment on job Maintains records of follow-up studies
Collects data about interests Maintains records for specialists Confers with youth about needs Studies school's total curriculum	3. Planning an educational program	Maintains records of college requirements Gives intelligence and other tests Studies success in school and college Advises faculty on curriculum changes
Studies youth's total activities Maintains personal histories Confers with youth regarding problems and refers to specialists	4. Solving personal problems	Maintains contact with non-school sources of help Confers with individuals Arranges for special help
Observes difficulties in skills Administers diagnostic tests Confers with youth and recommends sources of help Gives remedial instruction Advises other teachers of needs	5. Overcoming academic difficulties	Recommends or gives tests Refers to clinical agencies Confers with youth and teacher Advises teachers on remedial instruction

often, unfortunately, there are some who have learned to perform them—but not very aptly or wisely. Quite commonly, teachers attempt to give

[5]William M. Alexander and J. Galen Saylor, *Modern Secondary Education*, New York, Rinehart, 1959.

answers in situations where it is not necessary to give an answer at all; equally commonly, they attempt to give answers in areas in which they are not competent. It is a very common occurrence for teachers to give youngsters misinformation relative to the factors related to success in college and college-entrance requirements. It is also quite common for teachers to give misinformation about job opportunities and about the factors related to success in specific vocational lines. In fact, there is hardly an area in guidance in which it is not a frequent occurrence for teachers to give too many answers, to mislead and misinform youngsters on important matters. In-service training of teachers in guidance constitutes an important responsibility of the principal who is competent to lead. Principals must inspire teachers to self-improvement along the lines of guidance services and to attendance at summer schools, where adequate training is now becoming available. The following are fields in which the teacher who is to be effective in personalizing his instruction and in other guidance services should have had courses or have read carefully: mental hygiene, guidance, adolescent psychology, elementary statistical methods, intelligence and aptitude testing, and sociometry.

12. Counselee Data: Sources and Interpretations

Scores on intelligence and achievement tests and on prognostic and aptitude tests constitute one of the most valuable types of data for educational and vocational guidance. Taken in connection with one another and with previous school records, they are, in the hands of a thoroughly trained worker, perhaps of more value than all other sources of data taken collectively. However, because of the great amount of technical training required for the most effective use of tests and because of the comparative recency and inadequacy of the training afforded even in the best teacher-training institutions, the use of tests in schools, especially for purposes of guidance, has usually been marked by bungling and poor craftsmanship. What training in this field is demanded for skillful work is not generally understood. A first course in tests and measurements should be regarded as only an introduction to the possibilities of tests, just as a first course in statistical methods is nothing more than an introduction to the techniques of treating test scores. Adequate training for research and guidance offices should include advanced courses in the details of giving and interpreting intelligence tests, achievement tests, and prognostic tests on aptitude and, in addition, advanced courses in statistical methods. What now usually passes for research and guidance with these instruments, so simple in appearance but so complicated in interpretation, will, no doubt, in the course of the next twenty-five or thirty years seem most stupid and ineffective.

Such tests are very useful in guidance programs, when properly selected and interpreted and taken into consideration with other data, and help in the following situations:

1. Identifying students who in all probability will not enter college.
2. Identifying students who will probably not graduate from high school.
3. Sectioning students into groups for instruction on the basis of ability.
4. Determining in a general way the intelligence level of occupation which a student should think most of following: for example, discouraging some students from entering occupations beneath their possibilities and others from aspiring to callings in which their chances of success are remote.
5. Determining whether a student is capable, under favorable conditions and with reasonable effort, of doing better work in class than he is doing.
6. Guiding students into courses for which they show special aptitude and away from those in which they show little promise.

Check List for Identifying Pupil Interests. As important in guidance as tests of general intelligence and of school achievement are the means of discovering economically the present interests of the individual student and the types of problems and areas of greatest maladjustment which are causing him excessive worry or personality difficulties. There are available a number of check lists for gathering data on these matters.

Among the best of the many interest blanks developed for this purpose is one by Professor W. G. Brink of Northwestern University, part of which is reproduced on the next page.

Adjustment Inventories. Guidance workers in many schools have prepared check lists or questionnaires, some of which are very useful. A few very superior ones have been published and are readily available commercially. Among them are Bell's Adjustment Inventory and School Inventory, Personal Adjustment Inventory, Science Research Associates' Youth Inventory, Bonney's Socio-Graph, and Mooney's Problem Check List.

By means of these check lists pupils are asked questions concerning their opinions, attitudes, and relationships which are very likely to reveal maladjustments at home, with teachers or a certain teacher, or with other young people of the same sex or opposite sex; conflicts involving religion; sex worries; health worries; and other types of maladjustment. When given under favorable conditions, professionally interpreted, and skillfully employed, these instruments are most valuable in gathering critical data for guidance workers.

These inventories are not scored as are standardized tests; they merely furnish factual information which needs to be interpreted very carefully and intelligently by the counselor. Of course, this information must be treated absolutely confidentially and not discussed with the student until a very opportune occasion arises. The inventories should be filed and the results of each inventory should be compared with those of others given previously.

Form 5

INTERESTS OF HIGH-SCHOOL STUDENTS

Boy ________ Girl ________ Age: years ______ months ______

Grade ________________ High School ________________

Teacher ________________ Date ________________

To the Student: Your teachers would like to obtain some information about your interests. They believe that such information would be of great value to them in making your high-school life most enjoyable and profitable to you. Will you, therefore, answer *frankly* and *truthfully* the questions listed below? Answer *only* those questions that will give a clear picture of your interests. You may do this with the assurance that your answers will be kept strictly confidential and will have no bearing on your grades in any subject. You need not sign this report.

1. *(a)* What sports do you like to watch? ____ *(c)* What team games (of 5 or more persons) do you play? ________________

2. *(a)* Have you made any collections within the past few years? ____ *(b)* If you have, what kinds of collections have you made? (Example: stamps.) Place a *1* before the one you liked best; a *2* before the one you liked next best; etc. ____

3. *(b)* What parts of the newspaper do you most enjoy? (Place a *1* after the part you enjoy most; a *2* after the part you enjoy second best, etc.) World news ____; local news ____; news about war ____; editorials ____; the comics ____; sports ____

4. *(d)* What types of articles and stories in magazines do you like best? (Rank them as you did above.) Love stories ____; adventure ____; travel ____; sports ____; detective ____; science ____; technical ____; politics ____; current news ____; religion ____; arts ____

5. *(b)* What types of books do you like best? (Rank the following types according to your interest.) Travel ____; science ____; sports ____; religion ____; poetry ____; humor ____; biography ____; adventure ____; drama ____; romance ____; mystery ____; art ____; music ____; history ____; homemaking ____; aviation ____; personal appearance ____; politics ____; etiquette ____

7. *(a)* Name the occupation or occupations which you are interested in entering upon after you will leave school. (List them in the order of your preference.) ____ *(f)* Are there things you like to construct, make, or build? (For example: knitting a sweater, constructing an engine, etc.) ____ *(g)* Check no more than 3 of the following activities in which you have great interest: playing a musical instrument ____; acting ____; dancing ____; drawing ____; speaking ____; modeling clothes ____; home-making ____

8. *(g)* What institutions, museums, buildings, or industries would you like to visit if you had only two weeks more to stay in Chicago? ________________

9. *(e)* Where do you have the best times? (Check not more than five.)

on a hike ____	riding ____
at games ____	roller-skating ____
at parties ____	dinner dances ____
at the movies ____	tea dansant ____
at school socials ____	meeting celebrities ____
on a date ____	giving a party of your own ____
at clubs ____	or what else? ____

Record Forms. The success of guidance depends not a little upon the data gathered and made available for counselors and advisers. Forms for gathering and keeping records of the various types should be prepared with care and kept systematically for use by guidance agents.

Many of the records needed for purposes of guidance are available in the form of records gathered for other purposes: for example, marks, credits, attendance, test scores, age, family history, activity records, health, and disciplinary records. If a thorough, careful program of guidance is to be carried out, it is convenient to duplicate the entries on each of these records on a single card called the counselor's card. What should be included on such cards would depend upon the nature of the program of guidance contemplated. Ordinarily the cards should include at least the items mentioned above. In addition, if teachers' estimates of personality traits are available, these should be entered. In a number of schools all these records for each pupil are kept together in a folder or packet file.

Special Forms and Records. Types of forms and records not always found among school records, but useful in schools attempting a more efficient guidance program, include:

1. Employers' requests for help.
2. Introduction card to employers.
3. Individual employment or follow-up records.
4. Records of permits for working and for leaving school.
5. Employers' reports on advisees—occasional and terminal.
6. Forms for requisition of information about individual pupils from principal's office.
7. Interest-analysis questionnaire.
8. Memoranda of counseling conferences.
9. Conference notices (invitation to pupils to call for conference).
10. Forms for advisees to report contracts for employment.
11. Records of interviews with pupils.
12. Report by teachers of names of students in special need of counseling.
13. Records of participation in co-curricular activities.
14. Records of work experience during school year and in summer vacations.
15. Records of data gathered in follow-up studies of former students.
16. Records of personality and character tests and ratings.
17. Records of social adjustment and sociometric devices.
18. Records of home background, including social-welfare data.
19. School disciplinary history, including nature of offenses, treatment, and follow-up.
20. Records of out-of-school citizenship, including juvenile and other court experiences.

Which of these should be employed will depend upon the types of guidance procedures employed. Examples of types of pupil records now being kept which are most valuable are shown in Chapter 17.

Office equipment should include filing cabinets for the safekeeping of all types of records, as well as index cards containing references to material on vocations, classified by vocation. Provision should be made for placing under lock and key, or in vaults, confidential information concerning high-school students. This is far more important than many principals and some counselors seem to realize.

Records should be rarely kept unless there is assurance that they will be used. Continuously over a period of years, teachers and counselors should grow in their ability to interpret expertly a greater body and variety of information concerning pupils.

THE TESTING PROGRAM. There should be developed in every school system a program of giving, scoring, and interpreting tests, check lists, and inventories covering all phases of the growth and the problems of young people. A program should include provision for giving, scoring, and interpreting several instruments for gathering counselee data in each grade through the twelfth. This program needs to be worked out on a co-operative basis so that it is integrated and co-ordinated with adequate space. The program should not involve excessive testing of young people, but it should be the means of gathering important counselee data and school-achievement data which are needed for various types of counseling and pupil personnel problems. In this program there should be developed, and stated clearly, provisions for making appropriate data available to the director of guidance, to trained counselors, to home-room sponsors, to the teachers in general, and to parents. Also there should be developed rules and provisions under which data may be made available to interested persons in the community. These provisions must protect the interests of the pupil according to the degree to which the data concerning the pupil may be regarded as confidential.

In recent years, particularly in connection with the selection of students for admission to college, there have been developed more than a dozen national testing programs. Any one school must make careful choice among these testing programs, since it is not wise to have a considerable number of students participating in more than a very few of them. The emphasis upon the aptitude tests has been greater than it should be; indeed, in some schools teachers have become coaches instead of teachers, believing that their chances for recognition are closely related to having their students do well on testing programs. There are many reasons why this thinking is not sound. Those who construct the national aptitude tests say that coaching helps the student very little. The national organizations dispensing scholarships will place less emphasis upon test results. Dr. John L. Holland, Research Director of the National Merit Scholarship Corporation (the largest single dispenser of scholarship funds, dispensing $20,000,000 in 1960-1965), says that "generally scores on aptitude and achievement tests and on high-school grades are only moderately accurate for predicting college grades and they have very little relationship to post-college achievement since they do not measure creative talent."

EVALUATION OF GUIDANCE PROGRAMS AND SERVICES. Many state departments of education and state boards of vocational education, through their divisions of guidance and counseling, have developed criteria for the evaluative study of guidance programs. These criteria include such matters as the provision for facilities, the training of the guidance staff, guidance services including individual inventory, educational and occupational information, counseling services, placement services, follow-up services, and, lastly, guidance services as an influence on the total school development. Furthermore, in *Evaluative Criteria, 1960,* published by the National Study of Secondary School Evaluation (1785 Massachusetts Avenue, Washington, D.C.) for the co-operative evaluation of secondary schools, there are set forth excellent criteria and procedures for evaluation of the guidance program.

Problems, Questions, and Exercises

1. Write out a plan for organization of personnel for guidance in a high school of 250 (or 150, or 1000) students, indicating what people would be involved in it and what might be their major duties and responsibilities.
2. Be able to give in class a 10-minute talk on the duties and qualifications of, and the principal's responsibilities in connection with, a vocational counselor.
3. Make a list of suggestions for the organization and operation of a vocational placement service for a high school of 250 to 750 students.
4. What is the place of the girls' counselor in a high school; in what way would her activities and responsibilities be different from those of a typical counselor? Answer the same questions with regard to the boys' counselor.
5. What are the types of problems or areas of guidance in which substantial contributions can be made by group guidance? Make a list of six to ten of these.
6. Be able to discuss in class the activities of home-room or other group counselors.
7. What are some of the chief differences between the guidance activities of a principal in a school of 100 to 200 students and those of a principal in a school of 500 or more students?
8. Make a list of all the different types of data that you think a teacher should have about his students in order to render the guidance service which should be rendered by a classroom teacher.
9. What uses might be made as a result of an interest inventory? Adjustment inventory?
10. Make a list of several types of records about pupils that would be kept or used for guidance purposes only.

Selected Supplementary Readings

Arbuckle, Dugald S., *Guidance and Counselling in the Classroom,* Boston, Allyn and Bacon, 1957.
Beals, L. M., and Sorenson, T., "Guidance Practices Used by Junior High School

Homeroom Teachers," *Bulletin of the N.A.S.S.P.* (October, 1956), No. 210, pp. 120-123.

Brewer, A. L., "Experiment with Multiple Counseling," *Bulletin of the N.A.S.S.P.* (November, 1958), No. 241, pp. 152-157.

Christensen, Thomas E., "Responsibilities of the High School Principal in the Guidance Program," *School Review* (March, 1949), Vol. 56, pp. 149-154. [Procurement of facilities, selection of counselors, public relations, avoidance of overlapping functions, and distribution of duties.]

Educational Policies Commission, "Counselors," *Education for All American Youth,* 1952, pp. 109-113, 162-163, 289-304.

French, Will, Hull, J. Dan, and Dodds, B. L., *American High School Administration* (Revised Edition), New York, Rinehart, 1957. [Chapter 19, "The School's Responsibility for Post-High School Placement."]

Gordon, Ira J., *The Teacher As a Guidance Worker,* New York, Harper, 1956. [Chapter VIII, "The Teacher as a Counselor," describes the opportunities and responsibilities of the classroom teacher in guidance.]

Janet, Sister Mary, *Catholic Secondary Education,* Washington, D.C., National Catholic Welfare Conference, 1949. [Chapter 8.]

Lloyd, R. Grann, "The Interview as a Research Technique for the Classroom Teacher," *Negro Educational Review* (April, 1953), Vol. 14, pp. 57-63. [How to interview for gathering knowledge about a pupil.]

Long, V. E., "Guidance and the Classroom Teacher," *Clearing House* (March, 1958), Vol. 32, pp. 419-421.

O'Neill, John J., "The Cumulative Record as a Guidance Service," *Catholic School Journal* (December, 1954), Vol. 54, pp. 317-319.

Ramstad, W. K., and Reiss, William, "The Teacher—Counselor Program," *Bulletin of the N.A.S.S.P.* (October, 1959), No. 249, pp. 10-14.

Roeber, Edward C., Smith, Glenn S., and Erickson, Clifford E., *Organization and Administration of Guidance Services,* New York, McGraw-Hill, 1955.

Ryce, Ruth B., "A Program of Guidance at the Macon, Georgia, High School," *Negro Educational Review* (April, 1957), Vol. 8, pp. 52-69. [Principles and practices of a supervised guidance program for Negro youth.]

Saalfeld, Lawrence J., *Group Guidance Units for Catholic High Schools,* Chicago, Loyola University Press, 1957.

Segel, David, Wellman, Frank E., and Hamilton, Allen T., *An Approach to Individual Analysis in Educational and Vocational Guidance,* Washington, D.C., U.S. Department of Health, Education and Welfare, Office of Education, 1958. [Contains many useful and practical suggestions.]

Stack, Philip L., *Guidance Services in the Catholic Secondary Schools,* Washington, D.C., Catholic University of America Press, 1958. [Counseling and testing programs.]

Strang, Ruth, *The Role of the Teacher in Personnel Work,* New York, Teachers College, Columbia University, Bureau of Publications, 1953.

Thompson, Orrin G., "Parents: Unused Allies in Guidance," *Educational Leadership* (May, 1949), Vol. 6, No. 8, pp. 536-538. [Practices in the Elgin, Illinois, school. A preschool workshop before school opens; teachers and parents participate in planning; psychologists, guidance specialists, and authorities on child development appear on the program with parents, interrogating.]

Turrell, A. M., "The Classroom Teacher and Guidance," *California Journal of Secondary Education* (October, 1948), Vol. 23, pp. 330-338.

Twiford, Don D., "Physical Facilities for School Guidance Services," Washington, D.C., U.S. Department of Health, Education and Welfare, Office of Education. [Suggestions for offices, equipment, and conference rooms; illustrative diagrams.]

Wright, E. N., "Multiple Counseling. Why? When? How?" *Personnel and Guidance Journal* (April, 1959), Vol. 31, pp. 551-557.

Zeran, Franklin, "The Role of the School Board Member, Superintendent, Principal, and Classroom Teacher in an Effective, Integrated Guidance Program," *Bulletin of the N.A.S.S.P.* (December, 1959), No. 251, pp. 88-101.

14

Improving School Citizenship

1. Current and Recent Trends

Increased Importance of Discipline Problems. If for no other reason, school principals and teachers must give careful consideration to the problems of discipline because of the increased criticism of the schools, teachers, and administrators with respect to what many parents seem to think is inferior discipline and student behavior today. There are many who draw a connection between what they consider to be a recent tendency of teachers and administrators toward softness and the use of progressive education and what they consider to be a deterioration of student behavior in the schools. Although many parents insist that teachers and principals should be stricter and more severe with youngsters, many of these same critics are quick to protest vigorously when their own children are punished. Nevertheless, the individual principal is faced with the problem of seeing that there is less basis for criticism of his school on this point.

In addition to the increasingly vigorous volume of criticism, there are other important reasons why problems in student behavior have become more critical than formerly. Among the students in junior and senior high schools today there are many more students with less maturity and less intellectual ability and interest, who rebel in one form or another against the imposition by adults of intellectual, and what are to them disagreeable, tasks. Furthermore, young people in general today have attitudes toward standards and practices of social behavior which are unlike those formerly accepted. Young people are now much more highly respectful of the opinions of their peers than those of their elders. Indeed, largely because of the peer stratification in social activities today and the lack of close parent-child association, there has developed on the part of young people a hostility towards their elders and lack of respect for their standards and opinions.

Moreover, there is a tendency today for many parents to be indulgent, and perhaps overindulgent, with their children; these parents thereby create problems for teachers and administrators who are attempting to set up and enforce standards of good social and ethical conduct. Many boys and girls attending secondary schools today live with parents who, in the rivalry for the good will of their youngsters, are inclined to be lax in matters of conduct and the development of good ideals. The greatly increased number of students in senior high school who drive automobiles has further contributed to delinquency and further aggravated the problem.

In practically all communities there is an alarming amount of juvenile delinquency in some form or other. The youngsters who are more definitely lacking in morals and standards of social conduct are likely to cause problems in school, not only with respect to the relationships between themselves and teachers and administrators but also for the great majority of boys and girls attending school. Indeed, there are in almost every school youngsters whose behavior is such as to constitute a definite distraction and an impediment to the learning of students.

2. *Objectives of Discipline*

EARLIER CONCEPTIONS OF DISCIPLINE. Until the last decade or so, the objectives of discipline were thought to be the maintenance of order in the school and the development of fear on the part of pupils in regard to violating the rules set up by the faculty for student behavior. Even today, the merit of teachers is judged by many principals, as is the effectiveness of principals in many communities, largely by the order maintained in the classrooms, in the building, and at all school activities conducted outside the school. The criterion apparently considered by many to be the most important for rating teachers and principals is the degree of fear that they are able to develop in pupils in regard to doing other than those things which are acceptable to the staff of the school.

Another objective that is still important, though in much lesser degree, among those influencing the choice of standards and the measures of discipline, is the winning of parents' approval. Measures that are in themselves quite ineffective as means of influencing pupil conduct are often employed because they meet with the approval of the people in the community. Harangues in assembly against smoking, joy-riding, the use of cosmetics, and various other practices against which older people are warmly prejudiced usually have little effect upon the pupils, other than to cause them to lose confidence in the principal's understanding of young people and the times; yet such harangues serve to let the community know where the principal stands on these matters. Concern with what people will say controls procedures in many schools to such an extent that the influence of any procedure on pupils' character and behavior is dimly considered only secondarily.

In days gone by, the authority of the principal was not conventionally accepted as a matter of course. In fact, in small schools it was often put to the test for each new principal. The methods of discipline and, indeed, the whole spirit of discipline were such as to invite the antagonism of the pupils, solidifying them in the common cause of resisting oppression. With the development of saner methods of school government, we are rapidly emerging from that state, so that principals may be less conscious of the necessity of immediate girding for the battle for supremacy. The passing concept of the educative value of discipline was associated very closely with the training of young people to obey authority, do distasteful things without protest, and develop patience, endurance, and self-restraint.

Though theory and practice as to government of the school are still in the stage of transition, new values, changes in relative emphasis, and methods adapted accordingly characterize the disciplinary program and procedure of the modern secondary school.

MODERN OBJECTIVES OF DISCIPLINE. The changes which have taken place in the objectives and principles of discipline center very largely around the increased emphasis on permanent educational values, rather than on maintaining order in the school; on training boys and girls to desire to do acceptable and useful things, rather than destructive and harmful things; on training individuals to govern each his own conduct, rather than to be dependent upon government by others.

Modern philosophy of school discipline does not contemplate disorder in the school; it does not lose sight of the value of having pupils respect authority; and it does not entirely deny the necessity of keeping in mind the prejudices of the local community and the tendency of parents and citizens to criticize the administration of the school for the failure to do with 25 to 30 pupils per teacher what they as parents are failing to do with an average of 3 children per family. It does, however, insist that these considerations move over and make room for a new type of objective, an educational objective to which the others should be secondary: order is largely incidental to the primary educational objective, to be maintained in and of itself only so far as is necessary to maintain satisfactory work conditions. Respect for authority should be at least partly the deserved result of leadership, not merely a forced tribute from a less mature group; the approval of the school community should be the natural outcome of the more modern and effective program of character development, not a primary objective.

MODERN STANDARDS OF DISCIPLINE. Consistent with the modern conceptions of the goals of discipline, there has been a marked change in what are considered to be desired standards of conduct in school. There has been a relaxation of the strain experienced by teachers and principals in trying to prevent all whispering, writing of notes, and gum chewing and in trying to insure all the minor externals of conformance and respect. A more constructive program has now been adopted, looking forward to development by positive rather than negative means: to growth, rather than repression; to initiative and freedom governed by acceptable ideals and interests, rather than self-restraint and inhibition actuated by fear and accompanied by resentment and other emotions and attitudes unfavorable to the development of qualities of good citizenship.

The modern principal or teacher well oriented in the philosophy and objectives of discipline does not ask: "Is this conventional? Should pupils be permitted to 'get away with that'? Was I permitted as a pupil to do that?" In the order of their importance, he raises the following questions:

1. What relative net educational results, direct and indirect, for this pupil and for all others, will the various reactions I may cause have upon the development of ideals and habits that are consistent with good citizenship and self-government?
2. Of what condition or development is misconduct a symptom?
3. What will be the effect upon the conditions for carrying on profitable educative activity?
4. What will people say?
5. What will be the effect upon the "authority" of the teacher or principal (beyond the indirect results mentioned in 1)?

In schools and classrooms where such standards prevail, mechanical and deadly quiet, which was the goal of many teachers of the passing generation, will rarely be found; in its place will be found groups of busy, happy pupils, ready to join with authority to disapprove really objectionable behavior. Perfection in conduct will not be found, but the perfecting of conduct will be in evidence. Practice and growth in citizenship and self-direction will be guided, but not deprived of opportunity for development.

3. Encouraging Acceptable Student Behavior

COUNTERATTRACTION THROUGH TEACHING AND MANAGEMENT. After a long and unsuccessful trial of the treating of symptoms—the repression of undesirable behavior through various negative means—we have been turning to the use of constructive agencies. Wise and patient parents have learned, as teachers are now learning, to guide young people away from undesirable activities and habits by guiding them into activities which are desirable and which will lead to the formation of desirable habits. By such a program of developing interests, of keeping boys and girls busy doing things which they like to do and which are at least harmless, disciplinary crises are avoided. As is often said of successful teachers, "You couldn't tell how good a disciplinarian she was, for she never had any disciplinary situations."

Careful study of misbehavior and the development of unfortunate practices and attitudes on the part of the students has revealed that among the more important causes are such matters as boredom and lack of confidence in the subject matter taught, failure of learning activities to provide for pupil initiative and self-management, uninteresting methods on the part of the teacher, and antagonistic reactions to what is thought to be injustice on the part of the teacher, particularly with reference to marks received by the student. It seems rather obvious that, in schools or classes where subject matter seems more useful and practical, the students behave in ways more conducive to learning and with less interference to the learning of others. This is true not only in such places as industrial-arts shops, typewriting and shorthand classes, agriculture classes, and home-economics classes but also in more academic classes in which a great deal of attention is given to practical applications in everyday life.

The studies that have been made of why students like some teachers much better than others and of the characteristics which they attribute to their best-liked teachers have shown that the students respond better to teachers who are clearly fair, who have a good sense of humor, who do not assign impossible tasks, who give some help to students in difficulty, who seem to have no favorites among the students, who are interested in each student as an individual, and who are fair in the marks and grading. It is also apparent that, in schools in which less interest and importance is placed on and attached to grades and marks, student attitudes are better and student behavior is more acceptable.

Douglass, Bent, and Boardman[1] listed the following effective means of avoiding situations which call for special disciplinary measures:

1. Carefully planned classroom procedure, in which continuous challenging activity is provided.
2. Classroom procedure which evokes interest and includes exposition and, supplementary to material already studied, facts, illustrations, and other materials new to the students.
3. Poise and self-control on the part of the teacher in the face of inattention, incipient disorder, minor infractions of standards of order, or disappointing lack of adequate preparation on the part of the class.
4. Active and interested participation on the part of the instructor.
5. Successful demonstration of fairness, and a respect for the personality of each student.
6. Careful preparation of classwork and good scholarship on the part of the teacher.
7. Uniformity of disposition and of reaction to minor misbehavior.
8. Avoidance of sarcasm and unnecessary humiliation of students.
9. Refraining from pedantic or preaching lectures on behavior or attention.
10. Provision for activities which cast students in the role of doers and contributors, as well as "study-ers" or "reciters."
11. A friendly and reasonable attitude toward students' questions and tendency to divert discussion into worthwhile related areas not precisely included in the lesson.
12. A good sense of humor.
13. Development of group and individual standards, rather than imposition of arbitrary rules and regulations.

[1]Harl R. Douglass, Rudyard K. Bent, and Charles W. Boardman, *Democratic Supervision in Secondary Schools,* Boston, Houghton Mifflin, 1961, page 261-262.

Among the types of inadequate procedure which are likely to contribute to unsatisfactory behavior of young people are the following:

1. Subject matter and assignments are too easy or below the mental maturity of the student.
2. Subject matter and assignments are too difficult, resulting in frustration to the less able student. This and the above weakness in teaching result chiefly where the same assignment is made for all youngsters regardless of their ability.
3. The explanations and the vocabulary and language used by the teacher are too advanced for the student's intellectual level.
4. Assignments are not well planned, not made clear to the students, and their efforts are criticised, thus frustrating and antagonizing them. The types of learning activities and materials are on a level beyond which the students have passed with the result that they are uninterested, even contemptuous of the materials and activities.

It has been observed that student behavior is better in classrooms in which the teacher has made better adaptation to the individual, to his abilities, to his interests, and to his particular characteristics of temperament and disposition. It has also been observed that students usually are better behaved in situations in which they are at work in small groups under the direction of teachers.

DEVELOPMENT OF SCHOOL IDEALS AND SPIRIT. Assemblies, home-room discussions, and other group meetings of pupils should be employed for developing ideals that make not only for character and good citizenship of a general nature but also for a good school spirit. Programs should be provided which will include stimuli to the growth of an interest in the achievements of the school and the pupils, to group and individual loyalty, and to pleasant and friendly relations between faculty and pupils.

In many schools home-room discussions include the topics of what constitutes good school citizenship and good behavior. In some schools criteria for evaluating school behavior are developed and employed. Shown in Form 6 are excerpts from a check list of this type developed by students in the Folwell Junior High School of Minneapolis.

DEVELOPING FAVORABLE RELATIONS. Upon all occasions the principal and his staff must remember that their influence is conditioned largely by the attitudes taken toward them by their pupils. While it is in no way suggested that either the principal or the teacher should approach the unethical by condoning offenses or low scholarship, or by playing cheap politics for personal preferment by the students, or lose dignity by becoming too intimate, the success of discipline will depend in a large measure upon the relative willingness of students to accept in a favorable spirit advice, counsel, and even rebuke and punishment. Pupils will not accept ideals from those whom they dislike. They are ready to resent attempts by such persons to restrict or even to counsel

Form 6

MINNEAPOLIS PUBLIC SCHOOLS

Folwell Junior High School

Minneapolis, Minnesota

Date ____________________

______________________ ______________________

Pupil's Last Name First Teacher's Signature

SELF-EVALUATION of Student Growth and Adjustment

The Student Rates Himself

TO THE PUPIL: This rating of yourself is intended to help you be successful in your school work. Your teacher has spent class time explaining what these questions mean. In case you do not understand the meaning of a word or question, please ask for help. Check each of the numbered items according to this KEY: 1 Almost always; 2 Occasionally; 3 Never. Use the column of blanks nearest to the number of the questions.

II. Appearance and Manners (1, 2, or 3)

______________ 8. Are you careful about your appearance (hair, clothes, fingernails)?
______________ 9. Do you wear a smile instead of a frown?
______________ 10. Are you able to remain calm instead of hurried and unsettled?
______________ 11. Do you keep your voice down?
______________ 12. Do you sit and walk with erect posture?
______________ 13. Do you avoid chewing gum while in the presence of others?
______________ 14. Are you courteous, cheerful, and pleasant?
______________ 15. Do you say "please," "thank you," and "excuse me"?
______________ 16. Do you avoid being rude?

IV. Co-operation and Good Will (1, 2, or 3)

______________ 26. Do you like most of the people with whom you live and work?
______________ 27. Are you fair and reasonable with people?
______________ 28. Do you like to help others?
______________ 29. Do you consider the rights and wishes of others?
______________ 30. Are you willing to help the group instead of doing just as you please?
______________ 31. Do you refrain from being impudent and disrespectful?
______________ 32. Do you refrain from acting smart and showing off?
______________ 33. Do you refrain from talking when you are expected to be quiet?
______________ 34. Do you refrain from seeking attention?
______________ 35. Do you refrain from being negative, antagonistic, and bitter?
______________ 36. Do you refrain from being belligerent?
______________ 37. Do you refrain from acting too important or too sophisticated?

Form 6 *(continued)*

V. Consideration and Respect for Others (1, 2, or 3)

_______________38. Do you treat others the way you like to be treated?

_______________39. Are you sympathetic and kind?

_______________40. Are you agreeable and friendly?

_______________41. Are you clean and considerate in the things you say?

_______________42. Are you generous with people instead of always being critical and petty?

_______________43. Do you treat the opposite sex with respect?

_______________44. Do you refrain from throwing snowballs at people, windows, streetcars, and cars?

_______________45. Do you refrain from making repeated telephone calls that disturb homes?

_______________46. Do you try to help pupils new to the school?

_______________47. Are you decent and respectful toward substitute teachers?

_______________48. Do you refrain from walking in the streets and making it difficult for cars?

_______________49. When in the auditorium do you grant respect to the person on the stage?

_______________50. Do you refrain from using the pressure game, "The other kids do it"?

_______________51. Are you thoughtful of and loyal to your family, your school, and country?

VII. Taking Responsibility (1, 2, or 3)

_______________62. Do you refrain from giving alibis and excuses for not doing what you should do?

_______________63. Do you like to take responsibility instead of having others take care of you?

_______________64. Do you do what is right, even though someone is not watching?

_______________65. Can you adjust to changes without someone telling you what to do (substitute teacher—changing rooms)?

_______________66. Do you like to take initiative and leadership (serve as committee chairman)?

_______________67. Are you able to do things without relying too much on others?

_______________68. Do you pick up your own things without being told?

_______________69. Can you take the streetcar or bus and be decent to people aboard?

_______________70. Can you go down the hall, enter the lunchroom, enter the auditorium, or leave the building without running or pushing?

_______________71. Do you refrain from blaming others for your difficulties?

_______________72. Do you use time effectively instead of wasting it?

_______________73. Do you refrain from throwing paper or waste material on the floor?

XIV. Comments or Suggestions from Parents

____

Parent's Signature

them, to the point of completely misinterpreting their actions and words. The desire to have the good will and respect of teachers and principals who are well liked and respected actuates most pupils to behave in a way that will merit approval.

Consequently, the principal should exhibit, wherever possible, at least a casual interest in every pupil and in all pupil activities, congratulating pupils upon their successes and sympathizing with them in their misfortunes. He should avoid all unnecessary sarcasm and reproof. He should be extremely cautious in attempting to punish large groups of pupils, even for group offenses. He must insist also that teachers and others do not make him responsible for all disciplinary cases and thereby weaken his influence in his school. In his conferences with erring pupils he should be careful to avoid a show of temper and personal antagonism, leaving each pupil with the knowledge that, in spite of the necessity for rebuke or even for drastic action, he bears no personal ill will.

REMOVAL OF TEMPTATION AND THE POSSIBILITY OF MISBEHAVIOR. A great many disciplinary situations may be avoided by careful planning on the part of the principal and his staff. Opportunities for pilfering should be as few as possible. Challenges in the way of threats should very rarely be employed. Careful checking of absences should forestall the feeling on the part of the youngsters that they may be able to beat the game. Periods of enforcement of rules should not be interspersed with periods of indifference. Opportunities for cheating on written examinations or in papers, notebooks, and experiments should be reduced to a minimum. In crowded buildings the use of exits and halls should be so planned as to prevent congestion likely to lead to disorder. Careful checking should eliminate the possibility of pupils' absenting themselves with impunity from classes or portions of class periods. Friendly relations with pupils should develop in such a manner as not to lead them to believe that they can take advantage of such relations to transgress. Routine should be so planned as to prevent confusion leading to what will be regarded as misbehavior.

Careful students of adolescence and adolescent behavior conclude that "good" behavior is much more common if the individual feels secure, accepted, and liked and if he is achieving and succeeding a good part of the time. "Bad" behavior, they conclude, seems to be common when these conditions are not present.

REWARDS FOR GOOD CITIZENSHIP. In many schools good citizenship is rewarded with more than the satisfaction of doing right. Citizenship is taken into consideration in conferring many types of awards and honors: for example, in choosing members for honor societies and in selecting the best all-round student for individual honors at commencement.

Frequently, however, mistakes are made by teachers and principals desirous of expressing their appreciation of good behavior. School marks, for example, should not depend directly upon behavior. Anything that might appear to be conspicuous favoritism toward good school citizens serves to embarrass the "good citizen" by making him appear to be a favorite of the principal or the faculty.

In many high schools the records of student behavior are kept and made a part of the data supplied to employers when the school is asked to furnish data regarding its pupils or to make recommendations for positions. Particularly in schools which operate employment bureaus for their students, there is material incentive for the student to avoid behavior which may be recorded and which may militate against his getting a superior position.

Home and School Co-operation. Parents usually do not like to be bothered by teachers or school authorities concerning the misbehavior of their children. They are almost certain to be depressed, if not irritated or even antagonized, by such news. Nevertheless, it has been found to be definitely of advantage in many cases, particularly in cases in which the student is becoming an unusual problem, for someone who is skilled in such matters (the principal, the assistant principal, the home visitor, or, especially, the counselor) to confer with one or both parents and to see if together they can discover what is at the bottom of the misbehavior of the student and what can be done to improve his attitudes and his conduct.

This discussion must be skillfully managed. It should not begin with a complaint about the student; nor should the representative of the school at any time appear to be hostile to the student, antagonized by him, or motivated by any consideration other than the welfare of the individual child. Of course, it is often necessary to assist the parent to see that the child's behavior interferes with the morale of others, interferes with the rights of others, or is contrary to acceptable standards of property rights of the school or other pupils. Counter complaints or defenses set up by parents should be received diplomatically and in good faith, investigated thoroughly, and reported back to the parents.

Not always should the principal support the teacher, right or wrong. To do so is not only unjust but unwise. It results in arousing hostility toward the administration and in encouraging teachers of warm temper, domineering personality, or poor judgment to continue to make serious mistakes. Under no circumstances, however, should incidents appear to be handled in such a way as to make the principal "solid" with parents at the expense of the instructor or the standards of the school; as far as is consistent with fair treatment of the pupil and parent, the confidence of the parent in the teacher should be maintained.

Personal and Group Conferences. Conducted properly, the conference may be so employed with individuals and occasionally with groups as to bring to those whose behavior has left much to be desired a perspective on their actions and to make clear and logical to them the reasons for asking that such undesirable and unfair behavior be eliminated. If the conference be personal and managed with such an end in view, it may frequently terminate in the development of a more favorable personal relationship, which generates in the pupil a desire to obtain or maintain the respect and good will of the principal.

In personal conference with the student offender the principal should attempt to lead the student's thinking along the lines of the explanation of his conduct; in doing this, he should appear to be interested in and not too critical of the student's statements or reasons for his behavior. The principal should bear in mind the truth of the old statement, "A man convinced against his will will be a sinner still." A student should not be pushed aggressively in his self-analysis but lead in a friendly manner to attempt sincerely to find the reasons for and to evaluate his conduct, rather than to establish a defense for his behavior.

Group conferences should rarely, if ever, be of the scolding type; group scolding serves usually only to solidify the group. The group conference should aim to help the individuals of the group to understand the true meaning of their acts and to develop their attitudes toward more acceptable behavior. At group conferences care should be taken to avoid sarcasm, display of emotion, and, particularly, display of anger. Otherwise it is very probable that group antagonism will be engendered and will make the situation worse rather than better.

Individual conferences particularly may be employed to discover the real reasons for misbehavior, which will prove very illuminating in guiding the prescription of remedial treatment. It should be remembered that only in a relatively small minority of instances does the pupil fail to feel that his conduct is justifiable and that in many instances his behavior is the outgrowth of complex causes which are not all on the surface. In order that he may take adequate time to study each case, the principal should discourage the sending of large numbers of pupils to him for correction.

4. Disciplinary Training: Negative

NEED OF NEGATIVE MEANS. There will always exist the necessity for artificial discouragement of unsocial behavior. There will always be institutions of correction and punishment. The mistake that is often made in employing negative means is in making punishment the fundamental program of moral and disciplinary guidance. The correct procedure, of course, is that of cultivating constructively good behavior as the natural activity of pupils, thereby reducing, as far as possible, the necessity for punishment. It is impossible, however, to reach all pupils by the preferred means, and growth in the desired directions will be gradual and slow. It is necessary, therefore, to supplement the regular program with punishments as the second line of defense for order and morals.

The number of types of possible punishments is so great that it would be impractical to attempt to catalogue them here. The following are the more important types: detention after school, demerit systems, threats and warnings, ineligibility for participation in activities, forced apologies and promises to do better, suspension and expulsion, and corporal punishment.

DETENTION AFTER SCHOOL. Detention after school has been abandoned as a form of punishment in many secondary schools. The pupil detained does not feel that this punishment is much to be feared. It affords him time and occasion to rationalize his conduct and a stimulus to nurse his resentment and dissatisfaction. Yet in many schools it is employed apparently with some success as punishment for minor offenses and is so managed that the pupil has the feeling of being a good sport in "taking his medicine" as a matter of course. In such schools the "sentencing" member of the staff refrains from displaying any evidences of feeling.

THREATS AND WARNINGS. A distinction may be made between threats and warnings. The threat is essentially a dare to do wrong and is ordinarily a dangerous and foolish weapon, serving to challenge the offender and to widen the gap between the student and the one who makes the threat. It should be employed only when the penalty threatened will be certain, proportional to the offense, and of a serious nature. Warnings should occasionally be given, not as a display of irritation or impatience, or as a challenge, but as a friendly or matter-of-fact picturing of what the continuance of the offense will lead to and of the penalty to which the pupil renders himself liable. Pupils who apparently fail to see that serious penalties lie ahead of them are entitled to warnings, but these would rarely take the nature of threats. Warnings should be used sparingly.

FORCED APOLOGIES. As an alternative to a more severe punishment, it seems clearly an unwise procedure to require pupils to make apologies, even in private (and certainly in public), to a teacher or pupil against whom the offender has transgressed. Being forced to make an apology is more than likely to lead to hypocrisy, to the feeding of fires of resentfulness, antagonism, and vengeance, and to further complications growing out of the manner of the apology. It should be remembered that few offenders consider themselves entirely to blame and that frequently they are not. Some pupils will regard the apology as an easy way to escape any significant punishment and the procedure becomes education in hypocrisy.

Of course, if the pupil has come to see that he has been wrong, has done an injustice, or has been discourteous, a subtle suggestion that he can regain the good will or respect of the instructor by a statement that he is sorry, or that he now sees that he was in the wrong, possesses none of these limitations. If safeguarded from exploitation by deceitful pupils, the apology can do no harm and often leads to a marked improvement in the relations between pupil and instructor.

SUSPENSION, EXPULSION, AND TRANSFERS. These punishments should be reserved for the most serious offenses or the most chronic and incurable cases. So long as the pupil is not seriously corrupting his companions, dismissal from school should rarely occur. Throwing the erring pupil into a nonschool environment, except in such cases as those in which the misbehavior grows directly out of a lack of interest in school, does not contribute to the solution of the problem from the standpoint of the development of the pupil or of the welfare of society as a whole; it merely transfers the problem from the school to a less favorable environment. Almost invariably, expulsion from school should occur only after a very careful consideration of the case, after repeated attempts to appeal to the pupil, and after warnings to parents and consultations with them upon the occasion of at least one previous offense.

Suspension or probation may often be employed as a warning of impending expulsion, a means of calling attention to the seriousness of the offender's situation. Suspension may be employed to remove an apparently seriously objectionable boy or girl from school during investigation of his or her case. Since it often seems to give the offender desired freedom from attending classes and to cause him to fall behind in his work, it is not always effective, being much less so for pupils who are not interested in school and who have little intention of graduating than for pupils who expect to receive diplomas.

Because of the seriousness of these penalties they should be invoked only after careful investigation and after the establishment of clear-cut proof of guilt. Complete records of all suspensions and expulsions should always be kept, giving details of each offense and of the evidence; such objective records may prove very useful for guidance in the consideration of future offenses, or in case action is brought by parents.

In some cases it will seem desirable to have the student transferred to a different situation with different companions, to a class where he may start with a clean slate. In cities where more than one high school is operated, it has proved in a considerable number of cases to be advantageous to transfer the student to another school. This transfer should be carried out with a minimum of publicity; and the student should know that he is welcome in the new school, that he will be given every opportunity to establish himself as a good citizen, and that there will be no prejudice against him. On the other hand, he should also know that if in the new school his behavior becomes markedly unacceptable it will be clear-cut evidence that any disciplinary difficulties in which he finds himself can be attributed with all logic and fairness to him rather than to the school or to the teachers. In a way, the student transferred is on probation.

Because of the fact that he has to give up his old friends at the other school and is likely to be quite resentful of it, transferring should not be done in many instances and perhaps almost as a last resort. It should be discussed with the parents first and, if possible, their approval should be obtained. It should also be discussed with the student; it is questionable whether it should be carried out in case he is very vigorously opposed. Of course his opposition cannot be taken too seriously if his situation is a very critical one in the school, one which would be likely to result in his suspension or expulsion from the school unless material improvement occurred in the very immediate future. The counselor and principal in the new school should have a full history of the case of the transferred youngster, including all aspects of his record, so that he may be dealt with intelligently. The success of the transfer of a student will depend, however, upon the skill and caution of the principal and counselor in their dealings with the incoming transferring student.

Parody, who has made a very careful study of the philosophy and practices of discipline in high schools, recommends a plan of dealing with serious offenders which consists of the following steps:

Procedural Plan.

1. If a student behaves in such a way that the teacher cannot carry on instruction, the pupil is to be sent to the office where he must fill out a "misbehavior slip." The pupil is required to write his answers—on the slip—to these questions: "Why were you sent from the room?" "What do you intend doing about it?"
2. It is the pupil's responsibility to arrange for a conference with the teacher involved before he can return to class. These conferences are to be held at the convenience of the teacher and in the privacy of the classroom.
3. The teacher indicates the outcome of the conference on the misbehavior slip. If the conference is satisfactory, the pupil may return to class; if not, the pupil is referred to the vice principal.
4. The vice principal follows up with the students who have been unable to straighten out their problems in the pupil-teacher discipline conference.
5. If the vice principal is unable to clear up the difficulty, then the student must report to the Discipline Committee. This committee meets weekly during school time.

The Committee at Work. The Discipline Committee consists of the school principal who serves as chairman, the vice principal, and the faculty chairman of the Discipline Study Group. The director of guidance and the visiting teacher attend all discipline meetings as observers but do not participate directly. The procedure is as follows:

1. When a student appears before the Discipline Committee, he is encouraged to state his problem as he sees it. An effort is made to point out behavior "limits" and to explain the reasons for such limits. The point is then made that pupils who exceed these limits will be dealt with firmly. The pupil is

encouraged to think through his problems and to make an effort to understand the *why* of his behavior. He is urged to seek help from the guidance director or the assistance of the visiting teacher.

2. When a pupil first appears before the Discipline Committee, he is given a white card which is labeled "Report." The pupil carries this card with him every day and leaves it on the teacher's desk at the beginning of each period. The teacher marks the card "S" if the pupil's behavior has been satisfactory and "U" if unsatisfactory. The pupil reports weekly to the Discipline Committee and his card is used as a basis for measuring his progress. The Committee decides whether to (a) release the pupil from card-carrying; (b) have him continue with the white card; or (c) place him under "warning."
3. When a student is placed under "warning" a letter is sent to his parents inviting them to the school for a conference, at which time the contents of the pupil's discipline folder are discussed. The pupils carry a yellow "warning" card to class. They understand that if their behavior fails to improve, they will be placed on school "probation" and lose their school-citizenship privileges.
4. When a pupil is placed on school "probation" the parents are again invited to school for a conference at which time the pupil's discipline history is once more reviewed. The parent is urged to offer suggestions and the problem is looked at coöperatively. While on school probation, the pupil is not permitted to vote in homeroom meetings; attend school assemblies; engage in club activities; represent the school in any program; participate in intramural activities; nor play or sing with any out-of-class music group.
5. If the student fails to make a more satisfactory adjustment while on school "probation" then additional agencies and services are called upon: attendance department, psychology department, Children's Court and others.
6. The entire faculty is kept informed of the activities of the Discipline Committee through the weekly publication of a "Discipline Bulletin" which lists the current status of all pupils reporting to the Committee.[2]

CORPORAL PUNISHMENT. In senior high schools corporal punishment had disappeared. The prejudice of people generally against corporal punishment has grown so steadily that, whatever may be said in its favor, it is not wise to use it in most communities. In addition, with few exceptions it is not effective for older children, since it serves to antagonize not only the pupil punished but other pupils as well, to arouse the "martyr" attitude, and usually to arouse parents to fever heat. It is likely to be more effective in junior high schools, but it is equally undesirable there from other points of view. It is becoming more and more out of harmony with the modern spirit of instruction and pupil management. Its chief value at any time is as a warning to other pupils.

When corporal punishment is employed, there are certain precautions which should be carefully observed. The pupil should be proved guilty beyond any reasonable doubt. The charges against him must be serious and proportionate to the punishment. Corporal punishment should be

[2]Ovid F. Parody, *The High School Principal and Staff Deal with Discipline,* New York, Teachers College, Columbia University, 1958, pp. 67-71.

invoked only after repeated failures of more acceptable methods. There should always be at least one adult witness. It is wise procedure for the principal to obtain in advance the permission of a parent for corporal punishment to be administered. Where parents refuse consent, they should be asked to assume considerable responsibility for improvement in the conduct of the offender. Care should be taken to confine the punishment to such a form as may not be considered brutal or vengeful, or in any way likely to result in permanent injury. The principal should familiarize himself with the state laws and with the regulations of the board of education relating to corporal punishment, many of which forbid it or prescribe conditions under which it may be administered. Perhaps the situation in which the use of corporal punishment is more excusable is that in which the parent suggests or agrees to this type of punishment, probably in lieu of expulsion, long-time suspension, or withdrawal of privileges.

WITHDRAWAL OF PRIVILEGES. One fairly effective negative approach to improving the behavior of some students in the school is that of withdrawing certain types of privileges. In many schools it has been found to be an effective approach particularly if the student knows that the withdrawal of privileges is a temporary matter which will come to an end upon a period of good behavior on his part.

The kinds or types of privileges which may be withdrawn include that of representing the school in any teams, contests, or exhibitions. The penalty may involve revoking the student's permit to drive his car to school or park it on the school grounds, if his type of misbehavior is associated with his driving or his parking of the car. In a few instances students who have become very great nuisances at the cafeteria have been denied the privilege of eating in the main dining room.

In all instances of withdrawal of privileges there should first be a conference with the parents so that they understand why it is being done; an effort should be made to convince them that the major objective is to improve the conduct of the student and to save him from a more severe type of punishment.

Each individual case should be considered on its merits. In some instances the withdrawing of a certain type of privilege, such as that of participating in an extracurricular activity, may aggravate the situation rather than improve it. The student may find life in school without participation in any extracurricular activities relatively intolerable for him and may thus be goaded into more flagrant misconduct. The student should, except in the most aggravated cases, be given a warning and put on a period of probation before his privileges are actually withdrawn.

While it is not wise to speak much to the students as a whole or in large groups of this policy, it should, nevertheless, be known to them that withdrawal of privileges is a logical outcome of long-continued or very serious misbehavior. The knowledge that such things can happen operates as a check, at least to some extent, to a considerable proportion of high-school students.

TREATMENT OF GROUP OFFENSES. One of the most perplexing and complicated situations confronting high-school principals is the group offense: for example, the concerted cutting of school by a considerable number of pupils, the student strike, or the "hard times" or "kid" days, on which all the pupils by arrangement come to school in unusual costumes. The problems of class-room supervision, of accounting for supplies, and other phases of the day's work seem to sink into insignificance in the presence of these situations, which are often poorly managed, resulting in serious consequences to the school and to the principal.

The usual mistake made is to regard such occurrences as a critical challenge to the authority of the principal. In two high schools in the same week boys and girls came to school in unconventional costumes. In one of the schools they were sent home to change their clothes, were given unexcused absences, and were required to make up the time. Those refusing to make up the time, about 40 students in all, were suspended. Public opinion was almost unanimously with the "martyrs." At a public meeting attended by most of the parents and other influential citizens, the students appealed to the board of education, which reinstated them. The principal's influence was materially weakened.

In the other school no attention was paid to the costumes, except in the case of a few students whose conduct constituted a distraction. These few students were handled as individual offenders. They were sent home and an explanation was given over the telephone to the parents of each offender. The whole group, upon being relatively unnoticed by the faculty, felt much like a group pulling hard on a rope which has suddenly become unfastened at the other end. Very little school time was lost and no antagonisms resulted. Contrary to the prediction of two or three excited teachers. who were all for accepting the challenge, the authority of the principal suffered no undesirable effect.

Ordinarily it is not wise to attempt to punish large groups of students, especially for such offenses as concerted absence. If they miss school, it is their misfortune as individuals, especially if they have a number of previous unexcused absences. As long as the management of the school has not contributed to such wholesale absences, the responsibility is more that of the parent than that of the school. To attempt to assume the responsibility in the hope of receiving firm support at home is often the mark of courage and optimism rather than of discretion and wisdom.

In the instances in which groups of students attempt to dictate, under threat of strikes or other group action, policies or details of administration, they should politely but firmly be told that requests coming under such conditions cannot be considered. Threats of groups of students to strike or to take other group action should be first referred to the student council and possibly to home rooms for discussion. Requests not coming as threats or demands should be given adequate consideration, with the benefit of the doubt going to the students. It is definitely unwise as well as unjust to punish groups for the offenses of a few.

SUMMARY OF PRINCIPLES UNDERLYING PUNISHMENTS.[3] Among the more important principles upon which punitive policies and measures should be based are the following:

1. Employ punishments only as a supplementary part of the program, distinctly secondary to the fundamental program of counterattraction and civic education.
2. Attempt to prevent the necessity of any but the nominal punishment attaching to conferences, by bringing the offending student or students to see the reasons for the standards which have been violated.
3. Attempt to analyze the causes for offenses, particularly by chronic offenders.
4. Appeal always, even in punishment, to the self-respect of the offender and his desire for the respect of his fellows and teachers.
5. Avoid threats and challenges.
6. Employ warnings merely as counsel or advice.
7. Do not employ punishment except after definite and conclusive proof of guilt.
8. Avoid sarcasm and the public humiliation of students.
9. Reserve long-time suspension and expulsion for very serious and chronic cases.
10. Avoid the use of corporal punishment; if it is employed, observe certain precautions carefully.
11. Avoid the frequent use of any except a nominal type of punishment—for example, slight expressions of disapproval or disappointment, given in any ordinary tone of voice.
12. Consult parents in cases of major or chronic offenders as a means of aiding diagnosis and obtaining the co-operation of parents.
13. Carefully avoid conflicts with large groups—group punishments and scoldings.
14. At no time in any punishment, verbal or otherwise, reflect directly upon the parents or home training of individual students.
15. Avoid making punishments of any kind in anger or with the appearance of anger and thus avoid the animosity often resulting from a teacher's anger.

5. Discipline and Counseling

Since most chronic cases of misbehavior, misconduct, and unnecessary and excessive absence are the results of maladjustments of some sort, it is important that the administrator enlist the services of the counselor in probing the causes of these deviations from the norm, understand the motivations of the individual, and apply measures designed to remove the causes, manipulate the environment, improve pupil attitudes,

[3]See Chapter 9 for a discussion of criteria by which to judge the value of devices intended to operate as incentives.

and ameliorate or cure the difficulty. Careful thought and planning must be applied to the question of how these ends may best be attained, so that discipline may be effectively maintained, teachers strengthened and supported in their disciplinary efforts, pupil morale and attitudes effectively enlisted, and the counselor's position in the schools, as viewed by pupils, parents, and teachers, enhanced.

THE COUNSELOR AS DISCIPLINARIAN. Seeking simple solutions which avoid elaborate procedures, some administrators resort to what appears to be a promising procedure by assigning to the counselor the administrative responsibility for the enforcement of discipline. That is to say, disciplinary cases are referred directly to the counselor by the teacher and, on occasions, by the principal; the counselor is charged with the responsibility of effecting a cure, by guidance techniques if possible or by whatever coercive steps are necessary to maintain order in the school and proper conduct by the pupil. While such an administrative assignment may be indicative of confidence in the counselor and counseling, it may also be conscious or unconscious "buck-passing" of an unpleasant duty which definitely handicaps the counselor in his relations with the students. Extremely serious harm may be done to the guidance services in that the status and prestige of the counselor may be weakened and his office viewed by both pupils and teachers as the "doghouse." His success as a counselor is based on confidence, respect, and good will. The most essential element in his relation with pupils is voluntary and permissive, and his office should be one into which all pupils may come without fear or ill feeling.

Serious disciplinary cases constitute a definite responsibility of the principal, or, in larger schools, of his assistant. Final solution of a case and the meting out of punishment, when necessary, are his responsibility and should always be discharged by him. Pupils in serious difficulty may well be referred to the counselor by the principal, and a tradition can be developed in a school whereby a pupil involved in a serious infraction will voluntarily go to his counselor for assistance in resolving his problem. Although the counselor will always uphold the school's rules and policies, he will act as an interpreter, but not an enforcer, of them and will also serve as an interpreter of the pupil to teachers and the administrator. His approach must always be advisory, never punitive or administrative.

In schools where there is available the service of a school psychologist, a chronic or serious offender should be referred to him for conference and study. The psychologist should be supplied with all the data available about the youngster. The service of the psychologist may be of two varieties: (1) to counsel with the offender, after careful study and analysis, and (2) to advise the principal and teachers concerned relative to methods of dealing with him.

In some schools there is available the service of a psychiatrist. Any student should first be referred to a psychologist and then to a psychiatrist only after the consent of the parents is obtained. In some instances parents should be advised to have their child consult a psychiatrist.

DISCIPLINE AND MENTAL HYGIENE. One of the most unfortunate aspects of the school discipline problem is the insufficient thought given to the effect of disciplinary measures upon the personality of pupils. Out of primitive practices, particularly when they are misunderstood or thought not to be deserved by the pupil, the most unfortunate attitudes, somewhat permanent, are known to arise. Teachers and principals are prone to seek order at the expense of pupil growth.

The teacher, as well as the principal, needs to be trained to observe such principles as the following:

1. Study the individual child: his type of temperament, his previous disciplinary history, his interests, his adjustment to school, friends, and home, and his home background, including opportunities available there for study and sleep.
2. Adapt the treatment to the child, not merely to the offense. Keep in mind a growing personality and administer to its special needs and status; do not attempt to develop standard treatment for types of pupil behavior.
3. Above all, try to keep the confidence and good will of every pupil. The pupil must believe in you as one who understands, is fair, and is interested in him and who firmly refuses to be run over.
4. Always remember that not a day, and rarely an hour, passes in which one or more pupils do not behave in ways that are displeasing to you. Do not be quick to take offense, to be self-conscious, or to be too "observing"; learn to react with some sense of humor to minor irritations.
5. Try always, when confronted with a bad or chronic case of misbehavior, to understand why the pupil behaves as he does. Look beneath the surface for causes. Very few pupils are by nature incurable or noneducable.

The goal of intelligent discipline is neither perfect order and respect at all costs nor the freedom of the pupils to do as they please; it is, rather, the guiding of pupils to do what they should, without too much compulsion, and the keeping of a keen eye on the probable long-time effects upon the individual pupil. The goal is rarely attained when pupils are caused to fear or dislike anyone intensely. The school treatment must be planned in the light of factors outside the school which are also influencing the pupils' behavior. Most important of all is to keep pupils busy doing worthwhile things that they like to do. This is both the calories and the vitamins for the nourishment of a healthy personality.

DEAN OF BOYS AND DEAN OF GIRLS. In a considerable number of secondary schools the dean of boys and the dean of girls are the principal individuals, other than the classroom teachers, to deal with infractions of discipline. This situation is to be recommended only when the deans are concerned primarily with discipline and management of social affairs and in those schools in which there is ample additional counseling service.

GIVING STANDARDS TO TEACHERS. One of the important functions of a high-school principal in connection with discipline is to aid members of the staff in obtaining orientation in the philosophy of discipline which will enable them to appreciate the relative importance of the objectives or purposes of discipline. In addition, he should assist them to arrive at practical standards of order consistent with those objectives. He should assist them to think through for themselves the relation and significance of any act or behavior on the part of a pupil to the morale of the school and the growth of the pupil. He should bring them to see the necessity of assisting pupils to become independent and self-directing as well as conforming. He should enable them to free themselves from outworn prejudices and conventions about "order for order's sake" only and to react to disciplinary situations without emotional excitation or the feeling of combat or of being challenged. He must assist them in looking at discipline from an impersonal point of view. He should not be apologetic in presenting the modern philosophy. Instead, with smiling confidence he should display a mildly indulgent attitude toward "immature" points of view.

The means of accomplishing these aims are the usual supervisory agencies: teachers' meetings at which discussions of these points and reports of individuals and committees are made, personal conferences, suggested readings, addresses by speakers, and routine contacts incidental to specific cases of discipline.

DISCIPLINE POLICY COMMITTEES. Many principals have found it useful to appoint a carefully selected committee usually including a counselor, assistant principal (if there is one), psychologist (if there is one), two or three teachers, and student representatives. This committee is responsible for the careful study of policies, rules, and procedures for student behavior and discipline and makes recommendations to the faculty for consideration and possible adoption. It is quite clear that there should be a well-known basic philosophy, a set of clearly defined policies, and a set of standards and rules for behavior of students in school.

STUDENT PARTICIPATION IN SETTING STANDARDS OR POLICIES. Principals of high schools and their staffs have discovered that good educational experience which adds materially to the development of good behavior by students in high school is offered by the provision for student participation in setting standards and determining policies of acceptable behavior at school. This participation is ordinarily carried on through the student council and through related activities of home-room groups, where there is opportunity for the students to consider the problems involved from all angles, to have free and full discussion of what constitutes acceptable student behavior, and to decide on the policies that should be adopted in order to insure that unacceptable behavior is kept at a minimum.

Supporting Teachers. Every student and every instructor should feel that all the staff stand together on all matters of discipline and that the principal stands squarely behind the staff in all cases in which the student is wrong. The staff and the principal should have uniform standards of discipline. Except in cases of gross injustice, the principal should not give definite evidence of his unwillingness to support the teacher in the presence of the students, even though the teacher may not have used the best judgment. Not only should the student's confidence and respect for the teacher be maintained but also a student's belief in the fairness of the teacher should be maintained or developed.

Teachers who frequently send or bring students to the principal for conference and who have not acted wisely and fairly with the student should be given in private conference some very good advice, with a hint that in the future it is to be hoped that cases will be handled differently. Teachers who frequently send students to the office and, therefore, seem unable to handle their own disciplinary situations as well as an average teacher should be given warning that the continued failure to be adequate in the matter of student management will call for transfer or dismissal of the teacher.

In cases where there is serious doubt or gross injustice, or where there is at stake something of importance (for example, serious punishment), the principal should attempt to help the teacher to see his mistake and to correct it; failing in this, however, he must see that the student is protected from serious injustice. In doing so, he should observe every precaution to maintain the prestige of the teacher, even though the teacher's attitude in the matter may not be at all pleasing. Justice to the student and not reproof of the erring instructor should be the aim.

A few principals of large schools have found it useful to appoint a committee to pass on cases which the principal may refer to it for report and on appeals by students from penalties imposed by instructors. This plan ensures the instructor of consideration by his peers and at the same time avoids the possibility of having him feel or assert that he does not enjoy the deserved support of the principal in matters of discipline. Perhaps in some schools the plan would reduce the temptation for weak principals to give way under pressure from students and parents.

Teachers should be well informed as to where they stand with respect to discipline and, with the guidance of the principal, they should develop a philosophy and common standards of discipline in the classroom. In the San Bernardino, California, High School a handbook on discipline has been developed by and for the teachers for their guidance. Such a handbook has probably been developed in other schools as well and is to be highly commended.

Dealing with Students Sent to the Principal's Office. The principal is usually at a loss to know what approach to use to the student who has been sent to his office. Without any question, the first time or the first few times that the student comes to the office a very sincere and careful attempt should be made to discover what is at the bottom of the student's misbehavior. An attempt should be made to enlist the student in analyzing the situation, giving him the definite impression that he should be truthful and help the principal to get as accurate a picture of the situation as possible. Ordinarily there should not be scolding by the principal in an obvious display of temper or irritation.

The principal should not rely much upon threats; but, when the student has been in the office several times for misbehavior or has a record of continued misbehavior, the principal must assist the student to see that a continuation of this kind of misbehavior will lead to suspension or expulsion, if withdrawal of privileges and complaint to parent are not effective. The principal must avoid the strictly do-nothing policy, on the one hand, and a hasty use of threats and punishment, on the other. Where there are good counselors, he may bring a counselor into the situation to assist him and the student in making an analysis of the student's misbehavior.

The teacher should assume rather full responsibility for discipline in his classroom; failure to do so should be regarded as an indication of professional weakness. Perhaps the majority of pupils sent to the office are sent there as a result of poor and uninteresting teaching, poor personality and judgment on the part of the teacher, or both. There is little in the way of punishment or of counseling that the principal can do that cannot be done by the teacher.

All cases of clear and unjustifiable insubordination should be referred to the principal of the school as possibilities for suspension or expulsion. After all other methods have failed, chronic, major offenders should be required to come to some understanding with the principal as to what their future conduct will be. Sending pupils to the office, if practiced to any appreciable extent by a number of teachers, results in putting up to the principal more cases than he can investigate closely enough to justify the use of harsh measures, even in those cases which merit it. As a consequence, he dismisses manh of them with a perfunctory admonition, and the prospect of being sent to the office is no longer a deterrent to potential mischief makers. Teachers then complain of the failure of the principal to "do something." Often the pupil sent from the room does not find the principal in his office, and the matter goes no farther. Better practice than sending the pupil from the classroom is that of requiring him to report to the principal at an hour designated for that purpose. For every pupil referred to the office, the teacher should file with the principal, preferably in writing, a statement of the circumstances of the case.

Pupils are many times sent from the room in the heat of the moment of misbehavior for lack of a better solution, in order to remove the disturbing pupil so that the classwork may proceed. A procedure that has worked in some schools is one in which the teacher, when dismissal from class is unavoidable, give the offender a pass to the study hall with the understanding that he will report back to the teacher after school. In most instances, difficulties can then be ironed out in private and after tempers have cooled. Only if such a conference fails of results should the teacher send the pupil or refer the case to the principal.

Problems, Questions, and Exercises

1. Be prepared to give from notes a talk of 5 or 10 minutes on the transition from the old to the new idea of discipline.
2. What do you think are the ways in which students can participate in setting standards for their own behavior?
3. Be able to explain what is meant by each of the questions determining the objectives of discipline which are given early in the chapter.
4. What is your reaction to the plans for evaluating behavior used in the Folwell Junior High School.
5. Be able to discuss for at least 5 minutes home and school co-operation in connection with student behavior.
6. Be able to discuss the treatment of group offenses, indicating if possible one kind of situation where group punishment might be practical.
7. Be able to give a talk of 5 or 10 minutes on the relationship between counseling and guidance.
8. Be able to state your position clearly in class in respect to the principal's position in backing up teachers in disciplinary cases.
9. Under what conditions do you believe students should be sent to the principal's office? What should be done by the principal when they are sent there?
10. Mention a number of ways in which a principal might help members of his staff individually or collectively to meet better the situation of discipline.
11. To what extent do you think misbehavior is the normal outgrowth of an inadequate curriculum and inadequate methods of instruction?
12. With the help of two other members of your class acting with you as a committee, draw up a statement of the philosophy and fundamental policies relative to discipline that you think would be sound enough to recommend to the faculty of a typical secondary school.

Selected Supplementary Readings

Bowman, Herman J., "A Review of Discipline," *Bulletin of the N.A.S.S.P.* (September, 1959), No. 248, pp. 147-156. [Types and causes of unacceptable behavior.]

Brandes, Louis G., "Meeting the Discipline Problems of Our High School," *Bulletin of the N.A.S.S.P.* (September, 1956), No. 221, pp. 104-109.

Broberg, Edith H., "Discipline in the Study Hall," *Clearing House* (March, 1953), Vol. 27, pp. 397-400.

Brown, Edwin J., "Punishment: 14 Rules for Handing It Out," *Clearing House* (February, 1949), Vol. 23, pp. 345-347.

Butterworth, Ivan, "Discipline," *Bulletin of the N.A.S.S.P.* (November, 1954), No. 205, pp. 70-78. [Contains check list for teachers of factors affecting teacher-pupil relationships.]

Chamberlain, Robert J., "The Role of the Principal in Discipline," Bulletin of the N.A.S.S.P. (September, 1959), No. 248, pp. 139-143.

Finkler, M. R., and Battrick, D. H., "What Are Good Practices in Handling Student Discipline?" *Bulletin of the N.A.S.S.P.* (April, 1959), No. 246, pp. 190-194.

Goldman, Martha, "School Vandalism," *Education Digest* (December, 1960), Vol. 26, No. 4, pp. 1-4.

Havinghurst, Robert J., "Dealing With Problem Youth," *Nation's Schools* (May, 1958), Vol. 61, No. 5, pp. 43-45. [Some inviting approaches to the problem.]

Hill, A. S., Miller, L. M., and Gabbard, H. F., "Schools Face the Delinquency Problem," *Bulletin of the N.A.S.S.P.* (December, 1953), No. 198, p. 181-221.

Kvaraceus, William C., "School and Home Co-operate to Meet Juvenile Delinquency," *Educational Leadership* (January, 1953), Vol. 10, pp. 223-228.

Mayer, Theodore H., "What Are the Characteristics of a Good Citizenship Program?" *Bulletin of the N.A.S.S.P.* (March, 1952), Vol. 36, No. 185, pp. 10-17. [Gives definitions, characteristics, and descriptions of a project in Columbus, Ohio.]

Mills, Hubert H., and Douglass, Harl R., *Teaching in High School,* New York, Ronald, 1957. [Chapter 8, "Discipline and Good Human Relations in the Classroom," is a good discussion to recommend to teachers, who should note especially the suggestions for teachers found on pp. 135-136.]

Oliva, Peter F., "Corrective Measures and Punishment," *Bulletin of the N.A.S.S.P.* (January, 1956), No. 216, pp. 73-84.

Oliva, Peter F., "High School Discipline in American Society," *Bulletin of the N.A.S.S.P.* (January, 1956), No. 216, pp. 1-96.

Parody, Ovid F., *The High School Principal and Staff Deal with Discipline,* New York, Teachers College, Columbia University, 1958.

Patterson, W. G., "Smoking in High School: Report of Ten Years' Work with the Smoking Problem," *Bulletin of the N.A.S.S.P.* (September, 1956), No. 221, pp. 125-128.

Phi Delta Kappan (December, 1959), Vol. 41, No. 3. [Includes "Discipline and Delinquency," "Training for Responsibility," "Discipline in the Good Old Days, Ten Imperative Obligations of Youth," "Work Education – The Missing Link? N.E.A. Delinquency Project Reviewed," "School's Responsibility for Discipline," and "Discipline in the Classroom Today."]

Punke, Harold H., "Exclusion of Pupils from Public Schools," *Bulletin of the N.A.S.S.P.* (September, 1958), No. 239, pp. 41-59. [Legal aspects of the problem.]

Symonds, Percival M., "Classroom Discipline," *Educational Digest* (March, 1950), Vol. 15, No. 7, pp. 5-8.

15

Using Students in Government and Management

1. Values and Limitations of Different Forms of Student Participation in Government

VALUES OF STUDENT GOVERNMENT. It is often stated that the "citizenship" aim of education can be truly achieved only by "living it." It is claimed that, more often than not, whatever loss in orderliness may result (if, indeed, there is loss rather than gain) is more than compensated for by the social training afforded by student government. It is difficult to make any reliable or objective comparisons on this score. Benefits which are often mentioned as resulting from student government include the impression upon students of the similarity of school and life experiences, better co-operation between the home and the school, and provision for more intelligent majority rule.

Among the values of student government, which its proponents commonly claim may be realized under careful management by competent and skillful principals and under favorable conditions, are the following:

1. Essentially temporary:
   a. Provision of a channel through which the principal and the faculty may educate the leaders and the students to civic responsibility and to the ideals and attitudes of good citizenship.
   b. Development of feelings of good will, friendliness, and fellowship between students and faculty.
   c. Reduction of the necessity of supervision and pressure by the faculty, relieving them for more professional duties.
   d. Increased happiness of school life for students.
   e. Improvement in the discipline and moral tone of the school.
   f. Removal of the tie that often binds students together in unsocial attitudes and conduct in school: namely, the feeling of common opposition to oppression by outside force.
   g. Opportunity and machinery for students to solve their own problems.
2. Essentially permanent:
   a. Development of ideals of right conduct, self-control, co-operative efficiency, and fairness.

b. Provision for practice contributing heavily to the development of habits of co-operation, self-control, right thinking, and responding favorably to questions involving civic righteousness.

c. Provision for training in leadership—for learning the means of bringing others to see the right side of civic issues and for acquiring skill in doing so.

d. Preparation of the student better to understand and appreciate the necessity for, and the virtues of, fair and ethical co-operation, as demanded in adult activities in business life.

e. Development of a sense and appreciation of individual responsibility for the welfare of all group interests.

f. Development of habits of, and skill in, substituting behavior that is socially ethical for individualistic behavior in situations in which the demands of social and civic life conflict with instinctive reactions.

g. Provision of valuable training in situations which are similar to those to be met in later life, which training is much more likely to be effective in influencing conduct in later life than mere information or even ideals, acquired in classroom or elsewhere, which are divorced from concrete practical situations in the life and immediate conduct of the pupil.

PROBLEMS OF STUDENT PARTICIPATION. It has been the general opinion of administrators and most teachers that student participation in management and, in a limited way, in government has been successful in high school. It is claimed especially that there is less disciplinary trouble when there is student participation, that the attitude of the student toward the school and toward the teachers is better, and that student participation correlates school and life, facilitates crystallization of school opinion, tends to maintain a democratic situation, and assists the students in developing mature attitudes toward self-management and self-government.

The administrator has commonly reported that there are dangers and problems in managing student participation and that these must not be taken too lightly. Most common among the dangers and problems mentioned by administrators are the following:

1. There may be a lack of intelligent faculty co-operation, resulting primarily from what seems to be the inevitable tendency for a great many teachers to want to dominate student opinion and student activities rather than assist them to be self-directing.
2. Many students are much more interested in other things, such as special problems, their social life, and out-of-school activities, and take a relatively minor interest in student management and responsibilities. This may be attributed in part in many schools to the domination of the teachers and the lack of opportunity for the students to have complete expression of opinion and have the challenge of important activities.
3. In many schools it seems, at least occasionally, that the students elected to positions of leadership have failed to fulfill their responsibilities, by reason of either incompetency or lack of appreciation of the importance of responsible leadership and co-operation.

It has been the experience of many schools that, with more intelligent co-operation of teachers and administrators, careful preparation of students for student government, and gradual introduction of student participation and expansion of student powers and areas of activities, the difficulties mentioned above are not insuperable and do not mean that student government is necessarily certain to be of doubtful success in any school.

DANGERS AND LIMITATIONS OF STUDENT RESPONSIBILITY FOR DISCIPLINE. The greatest dangers of student participation lie in situations in which students are given responsibility for enforcing rules and regulations and have, therefore, responsibility for what we ordinarily think of as the discipline of the school.

Student government which is given responsibility for the direct discipline of the school has proved so unsatisfactory in many places that great care should be exercised in making use of it. Students often resent discipline by their peers much more than that dispensed by the staff of the school; parents frequently have even less confidence in its justice and efficacy and may complicate the situation greatly. Infrequently, the faculty or administration of a high school, after having delegated certain of its powers or responsibilities to organized students, come to believe it necessary to reassume them. These instances of "Indian giving" quite regularly result in much more undesirable situations and relations than would exist if no responsibility had been delegated in the first place.

Students tend somewhat to settle cases on a personal or clique basis, departing obviously from the uniform treatment of all individuals. Officers are often elected or appointed who for one reason or another function spasmodically or not at all. In some instances groups defeated in elections have refused to submit to their fellow students who were victorious.

Even where penalties are administered by the principal or the faculty, the onus of detecting and reporting offenses is not a welcome one and is likely to result in unpleasant feelings between individual students, or groups of students, divided on the question of whether it is ethical to "tell." As a consequence, the responsibility for detecting and reporting or recommending for punishment is like the responsibility that exists in connection with certain laws toward which the opinions of the people of this country are divided—a responsibility which is not felt by all but which rests heavily upon a few individuals, thus ensuring a doubtful degree of enforcement and provision for justice.

If student government is employed at all for disciplinary responsibilities, it should be built upon a foundation of student guaranty of co-operation to ensure success. Its charter, verbal or written, should center around the principle that student authority must be in proportion to the ability and willingness of the organization to exercise it effectively. Admission of student government to the control of various phases of school life should come gradually and as the result of a careful consideration of the best means and time for ensuring continued success in the broader field.

Student Participation in Matters of Discipline: Legislative Rather than Administrative Functions. Though self-government or self-control is to a considerable extent a function of one's own conscience and sense of what is right and fair and socially efficient, it is influenced in large measure by the opinions of one's fellows. It is important, therefore, that such effort and attention be given to the developing of student opinion and sentiment as will place a premium upon right conduct. In this function, which is legislative rather than administrative in nature, student co-operation will usually be found very useful.

By means of student councils, committees of the pupils on cafeterias, halls, assemblies, fire drills, extracurricular activities, social affairs, athletics, and clubs, and other representative bodies, there may be provision for an exchange of points of view between faculty and students. This may often be enlightening to the faculty, as well as to the pupils, and should be so regarded. In the meetings of these bodies, at which faculty representatives are present either as members of the committees or as sponsors, questions of what are reasonable and desirable standards of conduct in specific school situations, conventions, regulations, privileges, and similar matters may be considered and discussed, bringing into relief all the pertinent considerations and reasons. Decisions of such bodies do not have the appearance of being arbitrary rulings of the faculty, who "naturally" may not be expected to be in sympathy with or to understand the pupil's point of view. Indeed, they should never be rulings of the faculty approved by puppet pupil committees. As long as such bodies seem to be reasonably unbiased and open in their consideration of matters brought before them, their sincere decisions should in general prevail, subject to little pressure other than the appeal to reason, fairmindedness, and the ideal of efficiency, even though their decisions may fall short of the ideal standard.

When convinced of the fairness and reasonableness of rules, restrictions, and standards, such committees constitute a powerful nucleus in converting their fellows; even if they are not entirely successful, the lines of division are drawn not between faculty and students but between the leaders and a portion of their constituency. If these leaders are not mere puppets, students are much less likely to react unfavorably to their decisions than they are to decisions which come as edicts from the "ruling class"—the faculty.

Student Codes. In many schools it has been found practical and useful to have student groups draw up suggestions for rules and pupil behavior in the following places connected with the school: classrooms, corridors, toilets, playground, assembly hall, gymnasium, cafeteria, library, study hall, and bus or streetcar. In many schools the student body has adopted codes of behavior developed by their representatives—in some instances the student council, in others a special committee appointed for drawing up tentative codes for discussion and approval by the student body as a whole. Quite frequently the tentative drafts of the codes are discussed in home rooms or in other small groups for a considerable length of time before a final vote is taken by the student body as a whole. It is not difficult to see the educational advantages of this sort of procedure. They do not lie entirely in the student code itself. They lie to a great extent in the influence upon opinion and the development of understandings that result from the activities of the students in constructing the code and amending it, in the discussion activities that go on in the home room and in other groups, and in the discussions of the student body relative to its final adoption. These codes should be thoroughly reviewed, reconsidered, revised, and perhaps completely rewritten every two or three years, not only because of the educational values involved in the construction of the code and the discussion of it but also because conditions and opinions change with the times.

2. *Fields of Activity and Student Participation in Management*

One of the phases of the movement toward the more democratic participation of all concerned in the management of the activities and relationships in which they are engaged is the greater participation of high-school students in formulating policy for the government and management of the school actually managing some aspects of the activities of the school.

STUDENT PARTICIPATION. There are areas in which student participation has been more of a success than it has in others. Responsibilities which students have been made to assume in at least a few schools are as follows:

A. *Governmental*

1. *Assemblies:* developing the spirit of order; handling cases of discipline.
2. *Study halls:* developing the spirit of order; handling cases of discipline and tardiness.
3. *Libraries:* developing the spirit of order; handling cases of discipline.
4. *Social functions:* developing the spirit of good citizenship; handling cases of disorder.
5. *Classrooms:* handling cases of breach of discipline.
6. *Cafeterias or lunch rooms:* making policies for order; handling cases of breakage, etc.
7. *Lockers and locker rooms:* handling cases of untidiness, damage, etc.
8. *Tardiness:* bringing pressure to bear upon offenders.

9. *Vice defense:* detecting, reporting, and recommending punishment for offenses of gambling, drinking, etc.
10. *Trial courts:* trying offenders and recommending punishment for them.
11. *Grounds and games:* administering rules and regulations.

B. *Managerial*

1. *Assemblies:* providing programs; presiding; making seating arrangement.
2. *Study halls:* attending to bookkeeping incident to pupils' leaving and entering, attendance, etc.
3. *Libraries:* maintaining bulletin boards; charging books; working out policies and plans for managing.
4. *Social functions:* arranging and managing plans and details.
5. *Lockers:* assigning keys, etc.
6. *Lost-and-found service:* managing bureau, bulletins, etc.
7. *Book exchange:* managing plant and details of operating; managing funds, etc.
8. *Tardiness:* recording tardiness and administering excuses and admissions.
9. *Fire and safety:* developing plans; managing drills, etc.
10. *Employment service:* planning and operating bureau.
11. *Supervision of elections:* determining procedures and means of supervision.
12. *Grounds and games:* planning policies and regulations.
13. *Student clubs and organizations:* chartering; governing; managing.

The experience has quite generally been that participation in managerial functions has been far more successful than participation in governmental functions. The range of potential student activities and the possibilities for service are nearly limitless. Listed below are a few of the many student activities that have been carried out successfully in the public secondary schools of Levittown, New York:

1. Underwriting of expenses for operation of Citizenship Day, plus participation in programs as discussion leaders, panel members, guides, and members of hospitality committee.
2. Sponsorship of the formulation of student-parent-teacher council.
3. Sponsorship of a Christmas family through an "Adopt a Family" program in the local newspaper, *Newsday*.
4. Sponsorship of attendance by Future Teachers of America at "Life" Conference in Great Neck, New York.
5. Purchase of armbands for Future Teachers of America to designate them as official hosts and hostesses.
6. Sponsorship of a variety show and international hop.
7. Donation of money to the biology club to purchase scientific equipment.
8. Purchase and distribution of school newspapers.
9. Award of an annual scholarship to a high-school senior.
10. Sponsorship of school representation at New York State School of Music Association.
11. Sponsorship of a delegation of students and an adviser to Future Teachers of America conference.
12. Participation in regional conference for general organizations.

13. Approval of recommendations of a student committee for landscaping grounds for a high-school Arbor Day.
14. Loan of a sum of money to the school's store for anticipation of purchases.
15. Purchase of varsity pins for distribution to members.
16. Sponsorship of a mathematics team in county competition.
17. Purchase of a variety of scripts for the dramatic club.
18. Purchase of an award for the Citizenship Education Department.
19. Presentation to each teacher of a yearbook as a gift for Teacher Recognition Day.[1]

TABLE 6. *Areas of Student Participation in Management*[2]

AUTHORITY IN STUDENT ACTIVITIES	PER CENT OF EXPERTS AGREED ($N = 35$)	PER CENT OF STUDENTS AGREED ($N = 47$)
a. There should be some definite areas in which the council has *complete* control, i.e., chartering clubs, administering the intramural program, assemblies, traffic in the halls, and traffic and conduct in the lunchroom	72	85
b. There should be some areas in which the council *shares responsibility* with the faculty, i.e., classroom behavior, public relations, offerings of elective courses, and parking on or near the school grounds	72	87
c. There should be some areas in which the council has *no voice whatever,* i.e., required school attendance, holidays, program of studies, studies, and faculty selection	69	80

THE ROLE OF THE STUDENT COUNCIL. In some schools student participation is largely through the student council; in others it is through committees appointed for special purposes; and in still others it is through both the student council and special committees. The student council

[1]Irving Ratchick, "The Student—The School Is Evaluated Through His Actions," *Bulletin of the N.A.S.S.P.* (September, 1960), No. 257, p. 47.

[2]George F. Walters, *An Analysis of Selected Principles and Practices Related to the Organization and Activities of High School Student Councils,* Doctoral dissertation, University of Colorado, 1951, p. 83.

has been active in the largest number of schools in matters relating to social affairs and to the chartering and management of clubs. Experience has also revealed the fact that governmental functions are rarely employed in junior high schools and that the degree of responsibility in managerial functions is greater in senior high schools and in four-year high schools than in junior high schools, although in practically all junior high schools privision is made for very material participation by the students as assistants in managerial and routine matters in which the individual student or student groups can be successful.

In general, there is common agreement that the most important purposes of the student council and student participation in government and management are (1) to furnish citizenship training, (2) to allow pupils to participate in or manage extracurricular affairs, and (3) to promote good student-faculty relationships.

TABLE 7. *Extent of Council Responsibility in Certain Areas*[3]

Activities	Schools in Which the Student Council		
	Has Complete Control (Per Cent)	Shares Responsibility (Per Cent)	Has No Voice Whatever (Per Cent)
Chartering clubs	26.0	35.6	38.4
Administering the intramural program	4.4	39.3	56.3
Assemblies	16.5	76.0	7.5
Classroom behavior	0.8	41.3	57.9
Traffic in the halls	17.9	60.7	21.4
Traffic in the lunchroom	9.0	51.5	39.5
Conduct in the lunchroom	7.9	55.1	37.0
Parking on or near school grounds	3.6	30.5	65.9
Selection of "pep" song and cheer leaders	27.5	40.2	32.3

[3]Walters, *op. cit.*

The data assembled by George F. Walters, in his careful national study of student councils in four-year and senior high schools, throw light upon (1) the opinions of experts in the field of student participation in government and the opinions of student officers themselves as to what should be the fields of authority and participation of student councils, as well as upon (2) related practices as they exist in secondary schools. Data on these points are furnished in Tables 6 and 7.

THE COUNCIL ACTIVITIES IN RELATION TO DISCIPLINE. The earliest student councils were given responsibilities for discipline; many of them set up student committees for discipline and student policemen. With experience, this practice was seen to be questionable, if not definitely objectionable, and the tendency has been to confine the activities of councils to policy forming and to co-operation in setting up rules, customs, and standards; co-operation in enforcing these rules occurs only through the formulation of public opinion and student attitudes. Data relative to opinion and practice in the area of council participation in discipline matters are shown in Table 8.

TABLE 8. *Council Participation in Matters of Discipline*[4]

PARTICIPATION IN DISCIPLINE	PER CENT OF EXPERTS AGREED (N= 35)	PER CENT OF STUDENTS AGREED (N = 47)	PER CENT PRACTICING
The student council should be concerned with student discipline *a.* Only in a guidance capacity through activities to develop school morale	86	62	90.4
b. In an administrative capacity: (1) Through a code of offenses and resultant punishments	0	25	12.0
(2) Through a student court which investigates, tries, and punishes the offender......................................	0	45	14.0
c. In a referral capacity, in that it refers the offenders to the principal or the official responsible for behavior after an investigation of the case	11	38	13.5
d. In a co-operative capacity with the faculty in all aspects of the problem of discipline...	43	76	49.5

[4]Walters, *op. cit.*

COUNCIL RESPONSIBILITY IN THE ADMINISTRATION OF THE STUDENT-ACTIVITY PROGRAM. From the beginning, one of the principal functions and areas of activities of student councils has been with respect to the management and administration of student activity. Data relative to opinion and practice indicate that the council participation in activities should and does consist largely of the selection or approval of activities for the year and the scheduling of time and place for activities. Such data are shown in Table 9.

TABLE 9. *Council Participation in Administration of Student Activities*[5]

ACTIVITY IN ADMINISTRATION OF ACTIVITY PROGRAM	PER CENT OF EXPERTS AGREED ($N = 35$)	PER CENT OF STUDENTS AGREED ($N = 47$)	PER CENT PARTICIPATING
The council should organize and operate the pupil-activity program, including the following areas:			
a. Selection of activities for the year	57	53	53
b. Schedule of time and place for activities	40	45	51
c. Selection of sponsors	9	32	23
d. Administration of credits toward graduation for participation in activities.	9	19	9

COUNCIL ACTIVITY IN ORIENTATION AND OTHER GUIDANCE SERVICE FOR NEW STUDENTS. Recently student councils have concerned themselves more with the orientation of new students in the school. Three fourths of the experts and of the student jurors believed that the council should make provision for the orientation of new students in the schools. However, in only 38 per cent of the schools do they practice giving personal attention to the new students during a time set for orientation; in only 44 per cent of the schools do they distribute a handbook or similar material containing the necessary information; and in only 40 per cent of the schools do they bring students from lower grades to the high school for special assemblies and events intended to give a picture of high-school life.

COUNCILS, CHARITY DRIVES, AND COMMUNITY GROUPS. The majority of Walters' jurors believed that the council should promote and conduct charity drives by the school as a part of community drives; this practice is carried on in about one half of the schools. Walters' jurors also believed

[5]Walters, *op. cit.*

that the council should participate in various community group activities; this participation is evident in a small percentage of the schools. In about 36 per cent of the schools they participate in community "Clean Up" and "Paint Up" campaigns. In from 9 to 15 per cent of the communities the school council participates in (1) community safety councils, (2) community recreation committees, (3) service or luncheon clubs (Kiwanis, Lions, Rotary), (4) "Get-out-the-vote" campaigns, (5) promoting school bond issues, and (6) UNESCO activities.

STUDENT-MANAGED HONOR STUDY HALLS. In a considerable number of secondary schools the student organizations have taken over the responsibilities of promoting good study conditions in the study halls. In schools where honor study halls exist successfully there has been cultivated a feeling among the students that being a member of the honor study hall is an honor and an achievement and that, therefore, the students should want to be permitted to become members of such a group. The honor study halls may be of any size, but naturally those which are of not more than 20 or 30 students have a better chance of success.

In some schools which have honor study halls, students wishing to be in the honor study hall are asked to sign an application which states:

1. Membership in an honor study hall is entirely voluntary on my part; I may ask to be returned to a regularly supervised study hall at any time. This request must be made to the student council.
2. Membership in an honor study hall requires from me respect for and observance of the following rules and regulations: (a) individual work, (b) no conversation, (c) movement about the room only as is necessary and then quietly, and (d) co-operation with any student-council member in taking attendance, giving pass slips, etc.

When a pupil has been a member in good standing for one semester in an honor study hall, that fact is placed on his permanent record card. Failure to comply with the foregoing requirements makes him liable to dismissal from an honor study hall. Such dismissal is regarded as a disciplinary offense, and a record of the dismissal becomes a part of his permanent record.

By agreement, the honor study hall may be discontinued at any time by the principal.

OTHER FORMS OF STUDENT PARTICIPATION. In addition to the central organization of student government and its various branches, there exist in many schools certain special forms of organization for the control of student behavior in certain limited aspects of school life, usually those aspects somewhat related to the question of discipline. These special forms frequently exist as separate units, although sometimes they are part of the general student organization.

Most prominent among the responsibilities assigned to such student groups are these:

1. School traffic officers to regulate traffic at street intersections near the school at periods in the day when pupils cross streets at these places in large numbers.
2. School guides to conduct visitors through the building.
3. Assistant librarians to serve in the libraries, sometimes with and sometimes without the presence of a faculty librarian.
4. Study-hall presidents to preside over study halls, taking attendance, attending to traffic permits, and maintaining a morale appropriate to study conditions.
5. Fire patrols and chief to supervise fire drills and to man fire hose.
6. Assistants in the cafeteria to guide traffic, to discuss infractions of good manners with offenders, etc.
7. Traffic directors to assist in loading school busses and in conducting school excursions.

Usually in those schools in which students are given the above responsibilities, the students carry on all of their duties under the direction of some member of the staff, student leader, or both.

3. Organization of Student Participation

MEMBERSHIP ON COUNCILS. From the beginning, student councils have been representatives of groups of students in the schools and have been elected by the students. Walters, in his investigation of 750 student councils in various parts of the United States, found that the groups electing members to councils were home-room and class groups, separately, in combination with each other, or in combination with club groups.

Walters found that in almost two thirds of the schools the student body elects the officers of the council; in slightly more than one third the council elects its officers.

QUALIFICATIONS FOR MEMBERSHIP. In the Walters study the experts indicated quite clearly that there should be no qualification for eligibility for membership to the student council other than that of being a bona-fide member of the school. The student jurors somewhat disagreed, as indicated in Table 10.

The actual practice is more in line with student opinion than with the opinion of the experts. In about one third of the schools there is a minimum scholarship requirement; in one eighth of the schools there is questionable practice of requiring the approval of some member of the faculty. In a majority of the secondary schools in the United States as a whole, eligibility for membership in the student council is contingent upon an announced minimum quality of scholarship. Practices relative to re-election to the student council are indicated by the data of Table 11 from Walters' study. In the majority of schools students may be re-elected to

TABLE 10. *Requirements for Eligibility for Membership in the Student Council, as Reported by the Jury*[6]

Requirements for Eligibility	Per Cent of Experts Agreed (N = 35)	Per Cent of Students Agreed (N = 47)	Per Cent Practicing
Requirements for eligibility should be based *a*. Only upon being a bona-fide member of the school	74	55	33.6
b. Only upon being in good standing in the school	20	57	33.7
c. Upon the attainment of certain marks in the subjects	3	40	32.6

the council; in the substantial majority of schools a student may hold office on the council and also be an officer of some other student-body organization. The opinions reported by Walters seem to approve of the practice as existing in the schools.

TABLE 11. *Practices of Automatic Election, Holding More than One Office, Re-election of Members, and Faculty Representation in the Responding Schools*[7]

Practices	Per Cent
Students are elected automatically to the council if they are officers of groups represented in the council	47.7
No student is barred from holding more than one office at the same time (one in the council, others in the school)	64.9
Re-election to any council office is allowed	80.0
The faculty is represented on the council as a bona-fide group of the school population (not counting the sponsor who represents the administration)	12.1

There is a very general opinion that there should be some means for removal of inefficient or inept members of the student council. A summary of the opinions of the experts and student jurors on this matter, as reported by Walters, is given in Table 12. Practice in the schools is in conformity with the belief that there should be a method of removing in-

[6]Walters, *op. cit.*
[7]Walters, *op. cit.*

efficient and inept members of a student council. This is indicated by the data shown in Table 12.

TABLE 12. *Provision and Requirements for Removal of Inefficient or Inept Members of the Student Council, as Reported by the Jury*[8]

PROVISION AND REQUIREMENTS FOR REMOVAL OF COUNCIL MEMBERS	PER CENT OF EXPERTS AGREED ($N = 35$)	PER CENT OF STUDENTS AGREED ($N = 47$)	PER CENT PRACTICING
Provision should be made for the removal of grossly inefficient or inept members of the council	77	93	76.4
a. A requirement for the removal of the member should be a majority vote of the council	17	64	51.8
b. A requirement should be a directive to the group who elected the member requesting his recall	14	30	27.7
c. A requirement should be the action of a student-faculty committee which has such authority from the council	37	43	13.7
d. A requirement should be a petition, signed by a certain number of students, upon which the council must act	14	32	11.1
e. The principal or a faculty member alone can remove him	0	0	18.1

A typically good high-school student council includes in its membership a representative of each of the important school-wide committees. These representatives may be elected by the committee or appointed by the council president and their eligibility checked by the sponsor of the council or the principal of the school.

Among the committees which should have representatives on the student council are the following: assembly committee, grounds committee, hall and building committee, noon-hour committee, athletic board or committee, publications board or committee, and forensic board or committee.

ADMINISTRATIVE VETO POWER. There is some disagreement in respect to whether or not the principal should have veto power over the actions of the council, as indicated in Table 13. In practice the principal has in

[8]Walters, *op. cit.*

the majority of schools the power to veto any proposal of the council. This constitutional right of the principal has over past years been restricted and is coming to be used very sparingly.

TABLE 13. *Principles Concerning the Administrative Veto Power, as Reported by the Jury*[9]

PRINCIPLE	PER CENT OF EXPERTS AGREED ($N = 35$)	PER CENT OF STUDENTS AGREED ($N = 47$)	PER CENT PRACTICING
a. The principal should have the right to veto *all* proposals of the student council	63	38	64.5
b. The principal should have the right to veto any proposal which is in conflict with administrative policies	49	98	35.7
c. The council should be able to make some proposals which relate to its activities, which are not in conflict with other administrative policies, and which are free of administrative veto	46	80	32.5

SELECTION OF COUNCIL SPONSOR. In the large majority of schools the sponsor for the student council is appointed by the principal. In a few schools the students select the sponsor, their decision being subject to the approval of the principal; in a few schools the sponsor is selected by the superintendent of schools or by the superintendent and the principal; and in a few schools the sponsor is selected by the faculty.

LENGTH OF TERM OF SPONSOR. Practice with respect to the term of the sponsor is about equally divided between a tenure of one year and indefinite tenure. In a few schools the sponsor is selected for a period of two, three, or four years.

NUMBER OF COUNCIL MEMBERS. The number of members on the student council ranges from half a dozen to more than a hundred. The most common (and the best) size, however, is somewhere between 21 and 25 student representatives in the larger schools and less than that in the very small schools.

LENGTH OF TERM OF THE COUNCIL. In most schools the councils are elected annually, though a few are elected once a semester. When elected for the year, about half of them are chosen at the beginning of

[9]Walters, *op. cit.*

the school year and about half at the end of the school year. When elected for the year, a student council has a term of two semesters.

SUMMARY OF PRINCIPLES UNDERLYING STUDENT-COUNCIL ORGANIZATION. In summary, the following principles might be applied in appraising the organization and operation of student councils or in developing new ones:

1. The need for a student council must be felt by the students before one is started.
2. The demand for a council should come from the pupils.
3. Council authorities and responsibilities should be introduced and developed gradually.
4. The organization should be such that the entire school is directly represented in the council.
5. The council should not be so large as to be cumbersome in operation, nor so small that the duties and responsibilities are centered in a few people.
6. Definite powers and duties should be specified in the constitution.
7. Each member of the council should assume some definite responsibility.
8. The plan of organization of the council should be simple and functional.
9. The plan of organization should be geared to the purposes of school government, not municipal, state, or federal government. Guidance and supervision by faculty sponsors of the council's activities are necessary. The council should have definite, singificant work to do.
10. The plan of organization should be developed to meet the local school's needs, not copied from some other school's plan.
11. The principal should retain a limited veto power.
12. The council should not be a disciplinary device.
13. The financial activities and policies should be well organized and supervised.
14. All clubs and other student organizations should be chartered by the council or other central body.
15. The council should give continuous and adequate publicity to its problems and actions.

SCHOOL COMMUNITY COUNCILS. It is the opinion of the author that experimentation is needed to test out the practicability of a school community council, composed of students, teachers, and parents, with students constituting a definite majority of members and with alternate parent members to serve when it is inconvenient for the regular parent members to attend meetings. With real democracy prevailing, there are apparent advantages in a council made up of representatives from all groups having a stake in the school community. The school community council should probably not supersede the student council. Instead, it should take over, especially at first, only a few functions, such as those dealing with auto driving, social affairs, community relations, costs of student activities, and other problems in which parents have a special interest. Such a council would be definitely in line with the trend toward increased lay participation in school matters.

4. Essential Principles for Successful Operation of Student Participation in Government and Management

The following is a list of principles which have grown out of the experience of school administrators of student councils as those most likely to result in the successful operation of pupil participation in government and management:

1. The principal and the majority of the high-school teachers must be thoroughly in sympathy with the fundamental philosophy of the idea.
2. The principal and those to be associated with the council as sponsors or advisers must be well read in the theory and practice of student participation in management and administration, as organized in secondary school.
3. There must be a desire for student participation on the part of the great majority of students.
4. Both students and faculty must have a clear idea of the plan, its scope and its limitations. This is especially true with respect to the degree to which the control of the students and their representatives is complete and co-operative.
5. The development and extension of student participation, particularly in organized form, must be practiced; the students participating must be prepared in advance by discussions and, perhaps, by reading materials before each successive step in the development and expansion of participation, or before the initial organization for participation.
6. The faculty advisers must be carefully selected on the basis of their sympathy, understanding, and training and upon the reading they have done in the field of student government and management; as far as possible, they should have personalities which are attractive to young people and will cause them to be readily liked, accepted, and respected.
7. A carefully worked out constitution should be adopted. This constitution should be the result of a great deal of deliberation by various groups especially appointed for the purpose. Its various drafts should be discussed by small groups of the students and later by the entire student body at the time of its adoption.
8. It is necessary that the students have confidence in the council, its operations and its officers, and in the attitudes of the faculty in the matter of noninterference.
9. From the outset there should be cordial co-operation and constructive criticism on the part of members of the faculty.
10. As far as is practical, considerable numbers of students must be given responsibilities of some importance, though not onerous ones, in connection with the activities of the council.

THE INTRODUCTION OF STUDENT PARTICIPATION. Whereas certain phases of student government may be introduced rather directly, in general student government should grow out of a sincere desire for responsibility on the part of the pupils; the responsibility should be transferred gradually and only after careful advance preparation. The organization of classes, clubs, or the entire student body, which would (within limitations of the general policies of the school) transact pertinent business and be largely self-governing, is safely undertaken without much prefatory training, though guidance may be necessary in the earlier stages; if responsibility for conduct, for enforcing rules, and for awarding punishments is involved, however, a more cautious policy is wise.

Responsibility for maintaining the standards of conduct in a school, or even for fulfilling such duties as are typical of student councils, may be wisely assumed by pupils only after considerable preparatory ground has been covered. Students should be made ready for being induced to give such consideration to the matter as will enable them to see clearly what is involved and what their responsibilities really will be. The most successful pupil organizations have been allotted responsibility gradually and in proportion to their demonstrated ability to discharge it satisfactorily. Added responsibilities have come at the desire of the pupils to widen their scope of self-direction and have been granted only as tentative arrangements, subject to readjustment in case results do not justify a continuance of the arrangement.

To thrust powers of self-government upon any pupil organization by some means more abrupt than evolutionary progress is to violate the lessons learned from the history of sudden changes from autocratic to democratic government and is to invite failure, anarchy, and the necessity for a dictatorship of the faculty. The unfortunate experiences of many schools bear out the wisdom of the conservative procedure. In many other schools the time and effort taken to stimulate pupils to grow normally to the concepts, orientation, and attitudes which form a secure foundation for democratic government have been justified.

Sound policy requires the gradual transfer of responsibility. It also requires a careful study of the implications and possible consequences of a shift in responsibility. The latter is often the natural result of the careful study by pupils and their committees, together with faculty representatives, of the desirability of enlarging the scope of student government and the possible schemes for putting it into functioning and effective practice.

Problems, Questions, and Exercises

1. Give your opinion of the various different values claimed for student government or participation in school government or management.
2. Why do you think that student government does not succeed well in some high schools?
3. Discuss the place of student government in matters of discipline. What, if any, is the place of the student council in discipline and punishment?
4. What do you regard as the appropriate general field of student councils? Make a list of seven or eight of the principal areas in which you think student councils would be most successful.
5. Make a list of seven areas in which, according to Walters' study, it seems that student councils take responsibility in the greatest number of schools.

6. Discuss the relationship between the student council and extra-curricular activities. Take from such areas as activity funds, chartering of activities, and general supervision.
7. What are the advantages and dangers of the honor study halls? How do you think they ought to be organized and managed?
8. What are your ideas about membership on student councils; how do your ideas compare with opinion and practice as reported by Walters?
9. Discuss the use of veto power by sponsors and principals, its advantages, its dangers, and how you think it is actually administered in a typical school.
10. Examine carefully the list of principles underlying student-council organization and see which you think are the most sound and which the least sound
11. Be able to describe how you would set about introducing student government in a school of 300 students.

Selected Supplementary Readings

Allingham, Bruce, "Students, Faculty and Principal Manage a High School," *School Review,* (November, 1950), Vol. 58, pp. 450-457. [Traces the development of student government from a feeble start to a strong organization capable of doing much useful work.]

Anderson, Stuart A., "Where Students Maintain Much of Their Own Discipline," *Nation's Schools* (May, 1961), Vol. 67, No. 5, pp. 70-79, 168-170.

Bick, Kenneth F., Hurley, Nelson F., and Wright, C. P., "The Student Council—Partner or Plaything?" *Bulletin of the N.A.S.S.P.* (April, 1961), No. 264, pp. 259-263.

Dugan, Lucille, "The Popular Projects of a Student Council," *Clearing House (September, 1953), Vol. 28, No. 1, pp. 15-17.*

Dungan, Ralph A., Jr., "Student Government—A Question of Attitudes," Report of the Proceedings and Addresses, 46th Annual Meeting, National Catholic Educational Association, 1949. [Emphasizes that student government in any form is only as effective as the student body thinks it is.]

Frederick, Robert W., *The Third Curriculum,* New York, Appleton-Century-Crofts, 1959. [Chapter 31, "The Student Council," contains a good example of the constitution and bylaws of the council of a large high-school.]

Johnson, James H., "What is the Function of the Student Council in the Secondary Schools?" *Bulletin of the N.A.S.S.P.* (May, 1952), No. 187, pp. 243-247.

Lucas, Frank L., Vardon, Helen L., and Perry, J. Wallace, "The Groundwork for Student Government," *California Journal of Secondary Education* (May, 1951), pp. 268-275. [After working for three years to initiate a student-government program, the authors listed the events and work involved in obtaining a workable organization.]

McKown, H. C., *The Student Council,* New York, McGraw-Hill, 1944. [One of the best treatments of the subject.]

Marden, Freda W., "Current Practices Relating to Student Council Sponsors," *Bulletin of the N.A.S.S.P.* (May, 1955), No. 214, pp. 164-170.

Mathes, George E., and Johnson, James H., "What Are the Functions of the Student Council in the Secondary School?" *Bulletin of the N.A.S.S.P.* (March, 1951), No. 177, pp. 221-249. [The relationship between student government, citizenship education, co-curricular activities, school administration, the curriculum, and community relations.]

Meyer, Frank, "A Junior High Student Council, Some Practices and Principles," *Bulletin of the N.A.S.S.P.* (March, 1944), No. 121, pp. 79-86.

National Association of Student Councils, *The Student Council in the Secondary School,* Washington, D.C., Handbook of the National Association of Secondary School Principals, 1950.

Ringkamp, Brother Henry C. (S.M.), "Student Government in the High School," *Catholic School Journal* (December, 1948), Vol. 48, No. 10. [Sets up a framework of three divisions similar to that under which the Federal government operates. Asks and answers questions pertinent to the problem.]

Shipp, Frederic T., and Faunce, Roland C., "How Can the Student Council Function More Effectively in the Secondary School?" *Bulletin of the N.A.S.S.P.* (March, 1950), No. 169, pp. 28-39. [Factors involved in increasing effectiveness of the student council.]

Smith, Joe, *Student Councils for Our Times; Principles and Practices,* New York, Teachers College, Columbia University, New York, 1951. [A summary of 112 articles on student councils appearing 1939-1949, supplemented by visits to ten selected high schools where councils were in operation.]

Story, M. L., "Pupil Participation in Administration," *High School Journal* (March, 1951), Vol. 34, pp. 87-90. [Providing for effective and continuing pupil participation in the administration of schools. A survey of opinions of 1817 educators, including 920 teachers and 897 central administrators.]

Student Council Yearbook: Proceedings of the Twenty-fourth N.A.S.C. Conference, Washington, D.C., National Education Association, 1960.

Van Pool, Gerald M., "The Student Council," *Bulletin of the N.A.S.S.P.* (February, 1952), Vol. 36, pp. 43-52. [Definition of student council, delimitation of authority, standards, facilities, supervisors, relationship to the school, types of projects, faculty responsibilities, and sources of information.]

Van Pool, Gerald M., "What are the Functions of the Student Council in the Secondary School?" *Bulletin of the N.A.S.S.P.* (March, 1951), No. 177, pp. 213-220.

Walters, George F., "Evaluating Student Council Procedures," *School Activities* (October, 1952), Vol. 24, pp. 59-63. [Results of a 1951-1952 study of selected principles of high-school student organizations and activities. A comprehensive report of the more important problems in this area.]

16

Constructing the Schedule

Many important adjustments must be properly worked out in connection with schedule construction. Teachers must be assigned to appropriate duties—types of instruction for which they are best fitted. Their loads should be approximately equalized. Building space in many schools must be economized without disadvantage to instructional efficiency. Assemblies and other activities must be adequately provided for. Above all, students must be able to enroll without conflict for instruction in the subjects they need. To make a schedule that fully meets these conditions, that stands the test of operation from the first day of the school term, and that is free from delays and confusion resulting from necessary amendments and revisions requires some skill and great care. Success in constructing a good schedule is an indication to many teachers, pupils, and patrons that the new principal "knows what he is about." Success in this project may lead to respect and confidence and to an auspicious launching of a professional administration of a school. Failure to make a good schedule may lead to suspicion and a lack of confidence which will disappear only after continued and unquestionable demonstration of skill in other phases of the principal's work. The ability to arrange a satisfactory schedule is the first major test of administrative competence.

A schedule is ordinarily made for a semester, but the schedule for the second semester of a year ordinarily is only a modification of the schedule for the first semester. Nevertheless, preregistration of the students for the second semester must have been made in advance before the schedule can be modified to meet the conditions of the second semester.

1. Gathering the Preliminary Information

The principal or his schedule committee either must already have acquired the following information, which is fundamental to schedule-making, or must now acquire it.

1. The structure and plan of administration of various curricula: which subjects are constants and which are variables.
2. The probable number of enrollments in each subject.

3. The standard, minimum, and maximum size of class sections in various subjects.
4. The number of class sections necessary in each subject. (Derived from 2 and 3 above.)
5. The plan for forming class sections.
6. The number, types and seating capacity of rooms available.
7. The organization of the school day: the length and number of periods, the beginning and dismissing hours, and the length and hour of the lunch period or periods.
8. Special problems: for example, overlapping sessions made necessary by building congestion; time available of part-time instructors or supervisors.
9. Data concerning teachers: preparation, experience, preferences as to duties, and special fitness for different types of duties.
10. What shall be regarded as the standard teaching load.

OFFERINGS AND CURRICULA. It is obvious that, before the construction of a high-school schedule is begun, it must be known what subjects are offered in the semester or year involved. In smaller schools the practice of offering certain subjects only in alternate years is often followed. What subjects are to be omitted from the schedule must be known. Frequently, enrollments for subjects are smaller than the minimum number for which class sections are maintained. Omissions because of such conditions may be determined only after registration or preregistration, though in the smaller schools they may be estimated fairly accurately in most cases.

The schedule-maker must be familiar with the placement of the offered subjects in the curricula and with the list of subjects required for each curriculum. He must also know from what year-classes or grades enrollments for each subject may be expected: for example, whether first-year typing is open to sophomores, juniors, and seniors, to juniors and seniors, or to juniors only.

ESTIMATING REGISTRATIONS IN THE VARIOUS SUBJECTS. Estimating the probable number of students who will enroll for instruction in each of the various subjects is best accomplished by a preregistration held at least four to six weeks before the close of the semester. The selection of the subjects likely to be of most value is a very important decision for pupils. Because of a fuller realization of this in recent years, much more time and attention have been spent in many schools in assisting the students in making their choices. The preregistration process should include probable students in the highest grade of the next lowest unit: that is, the sixth grade of the elementary schools contributing students to a given junior high school or the ninth grade of junior high schools contributing to a given senior high school.

Though changes in the selection of subjects will occur between preregistration and the beginning of the next semester, with failures, withdrawals, additions of new students, and changes of plans of students, these will ordinarily affect only slightly the estimates based upon preregistration. The possibility of changes should be considered in advance and revised estimates made. When this is done, the changes will represent only a small percentage of the total registrations and will to a considerable degree be self-compensatory. By good counseling at preregistration and estimates of probable failures, such changes may be kept to a minimum. The principal or a committee in charge of schedule-making should review carefully the possibilities of a considerable number of changes; if there are reasons to believe that registration will be materially affected, revised estimates should then be made.

Some schools do not employ preregistration, but principals in these schools may arrive at close estimates by taking the enrollments of the previous year as a base and making modifications in the light of pertinent known trends. Although fairly reliable results are usually obtained by means of this type of procedure, they are subject to errors of judgment which may occasionally prove serious; for that reason, as well as for other reasons, a preregistration is to be preferred.

ESTIMATING THE NUMBER OF CLASS SECTIONS REQUIRED—CLASS SIZE.[1] From the preregistration the probable enrollment in each subject is readily tallied. The next step is to calculate the number of class sections which will be required. In doing this it is first necessary to determine the minimum, the standard, and the maximum class-section size. Ordinarily, the minimum number of pupils required for a section should be in the neighborhood of 10 or 12. Only in certain subjects required for college entrance should a smaller minimum be justified. In second-year or third-year classes in a foreign language a smaller minimum should possibly be observed, on the theory that the pupils desiring the section have taken the one or two years of the language in good faith, under the impression that the second or third year would be offered.

The decision as to the number of sections will depend definitely upon the size of each class; this will vary with the nature of the instruction, being slightly smaller, for example, in shop work, in home economics, and in instruction that requires much individual help and supervision, such as in remedial work. The number of pupils that can be well taught in a class will also depend upon the experience of the teacher and the ability of the teacher to handle large classes. These things vary from teacher to teacher and are hard to determine, except on the basis of a statement of the teacher and on the knowledge of the principal about the teacher.

Studies of classes of various sizes have not shown that large classes reduce materially the achievement of students as measured by objective tests. Nevertheless, most teachers and administrators believe that overall results in large classes are inferior. They believe that large classes

[1]In schools employing a plan of team teaching similar to the Trump plan, different standards for class size are observed.

do not offer opportunities for working with individuals for guidance and for various types of educational growth which depend more or less upon personal contacts between individual students and individual teachers or small groups of teachers. The load imposed upon teachers by large classes is considerable. If large classes are to be scheduled, the teaching load in terms of number of class periods should be appropriately reduced and arrangements should be made for the teacher to have conferences with individual students.

If teaching students in very large classes is to be successful, there must be certain provisions made which are somewhat different from those made for smaller groups. Among the most important of these are the following:

1. Teachers instructing very large classes must be given special training, or they must individually give much thought and attention to the principles and practices which have proved successful in teaching large classes.
2. Provision must be made for personal access by students to the teacher at other than class time.
3. The instructors in large classes must be chosen carefully on the basis of their qualifications as interesting and effective lecturers.
4. In teaching large classes it is necessary to employ audio-visual and mechanical aids.

The respective enrollments having been estimated for each subject in the program of studies to be offered and the standards as to class size having been set up, it is a matter of arithmetic to calculate the number of sections.

NUMBER OF CLASS PERIODS.[2] The introduction of supervised study, with the consequently lengthened class period, and of manual types of activity and physical education to break and shorten the "mental" or verbal day has tended to increase the practicability and the use of a longer school day. There is a great discrepancy in practice with respect to the length of the school day. A number of factors have operated to shorten the school day in some districts. Among these factors are (1) a desire of many teachers to get away from the school as early as possible, (2) the necessity of taking students home from consolidated high schools in busses, and (3) the desire of the youngsters to get out of school as quickly as possible to get at such activities as automobile riding, "coking," social hours at the drugstores and other places, and radio and television.

On the other hand, there are many strong arguments for lengthening the school day. Among them are the following: (1) the desirability of keeping youngsters in school rather than having them dismissed for the hours that parents cannot have adequate supervision of them and having them engage in questionable leisure pursuits; (2) the lessening reliance

[2]For statistical data on practices in Midwestern high schools relative to number and length of periods, opening and closing time, etc., see the article by A. W. Sturges listed at the end of this chapter.

that can be placed upon home study, as the result of the very greatly increased number of hours youngsters spend with radio, television, and social activities; (3) the desirability of incorporating within the school program adequate time and opportunity for all extracurricular activities; (4) the tendency toward the longer class period of between 52 and 57 minutes net, which has grown principally out of the tendency to incorporate less recitation and more study and laboratory type of work in the classroom, and (5) the need for more time in the library.

In recent years there has been a trend towards a longer school day, especially in senior and four-year high schools. The prevailing practice today is to have a seven-hour school day, from 8:30 in the morning to 3:30 in the afternoon, including a lunch period of approximately 30 minutes.

In a considerable number of schools operating on the six-period schedule, it has been found necessary, or at least desirable, to have what has been called in some schools the "zero" period and in others the "early bird" period—a period which comes before the first regular period in the school day. In this period are scheduled usually one section of classes in which there are several sections, certain student activities (particularly student council), and classes for students who are carrying more than the usual load. The principals of John Marshall Senior High School in Rochester, Minnesota, and Manhattan, Kansas, Senior High School are among those who report favorably about this practice.

In some schools classes are scheduled after the last regular period. This practice accommodates classes that are similar to those that come in other schools before the regular schedule. This practice is followed in a number of schools on the very western edge of the time belts, where in the winter daylight comes late in the morning and sunset late in the afternoon.

In general, there seems to be a growing feeling of necessity for a longer school day and it is quite probable that more and more schools will adopt a school day of more than six hours, exclusive of the lunch period.

LENGTH OF CLASS PERIODS. In recent years there has been a very pronounced trend toward a longer class period as well as a longer school day. Most schools operate with a class period of approximately 55 minutes net in the four-year and senior high schools; in junior high schools practice has been shifting toward a day of seven periods of approximately 48 to 50 minutes each and away from a day of six periods of approximately 55 minutes. In a few schools class periods are of different lengths: for example, 60, 65, 75, and 90 minutes. At the San Angelo, Texas, Central High School different kinds of classes are scheduled for periods of different lengths; for instance, typing, household arts, and shop classes are scheduled for longer periods.

In schools in which the long period is in operation, the question arises as to whether those subjects which have previously been allotted double periods should still be scheduled with double periods. It seems clear that to do so would favor such subjects disproportionately and would result in serious difficulties in scheduling and registration. Instructors in those subjects often oppose the substitution of the single longer period for the double short period. However, after trial of the plan, the vigor of opposition diminishes markedly, though, of course, the reduction in class-time allotment will always constitute a tempting way to explain any unsatisfactory results. In science classes it has been found satisfactory to dispense with the double period entirely, though certain experiments requiring more than an hour have to be eliminated, modified, or carried on by a special committee rather than by each member of the class. In schools arranged on a period basis of from 55 to 60 minutes, subjects to which daily double periods of 90 minutes had been given previously are frequently scheduled for single periods, with one or two additional laboratory or practice periods a week. In the schools employing the long period, the teaching load should be slightly reduced, either in the number of periods taught per week or in the amount of time spent on extra-class co-operative duties. Some schools operate on a schedule of five 70-minute or 75-minute periods, with classes meeting two to four times each week.

Most principals of senior or four-year high schools employing a plan which permits many or all students to carry five subjects plus physical education report that the achievement of students is as good or approximately as good as when they carried only four.[3]

Under skillful leadership, lengthening the class period may be a means of realizing in greater degree the following aims:

1. Making each class a laboratory or a workshop, rather than a recitation room.
2. Encouraging more thought in the "doing" subjects and more doing in the "thought" subjects.
3. Directing pupil growth and improving pupil behavior through increasing the time teachers spend with pupils and increasing the opportunities for observing pupils systematically.
4. Developing greater class interest and providing for individual differences through more differentiation of assignments.
5. Securing greater dividends on required homework by using more time in class to show pupils how to study.
6. Providing more favorable opportunity for class visitation to educational resources in the community.

In a few schools the experiment has been tried of scheduling some classes for a double period for a semester instead of for one period for a year. While there seem to be good arguments in favor of this plan, students seem to be divided sharply in their attitudes toward it. The author of this volume believes that the plan should be especially effective in the teaching of mathematics and foreign languages.

[3]M. E. Gardner, "Study of Subject Loads and Marks," *Clearing House* (November, 1960), Vol. 35, pp. 145-146. [Report by Director of Guidance and Pupil Services, Homewood-Flossmoor, Illinois, High School.]

The passing time between classes almost always ranges somewhere from 3 to 6 minutes, the latter time being necessary in large school buildings or in campus-type housing.

NUMBER OF PERIODS PER WEEK. Unlike secular schools in practically all other countries, with the notable exception of Canada, subject classes in high schools in the United States usually meet five times a week; so-called nonsolid classes—physical education, art, and music, for example—usually meet two or three times a week. It seems that the question of the number of class meetings a week should be thoroughly reviewed and studied. In a considerable number of schools in New England, in some on the Pacific Coast, and in a few elsewhere, so-called solid subjects meet longer periods, but only four times a week. The advantages of this system are easy to see, as indeed is one important disadvantage. There is advantage in this type of scheduling in that it reduces both the teacher and the student load and thereby is likely to decrease the expense of the school and the cost of teaching each class and permit the students to carry eighteen to twenty-two units of work a year.

The obvious danger of the plan is the difficulty of getting as much work done during the semester or year in the class which meets only four times a week as the teacher would like to do and as was customarily done when the class met more often.

FLOATING-PERIOD SCHEDULES. In a relatively small but increasing number of schools floating-period schedules are being constructed. In these schedules a class does not meet in the same period each day. It is argued that the floating-period schedule tends to equalize among classes the advantages of different times of day. However, a great many careful students of the problem of the effectiveness of learning activities during various times of the day believe that any difference in effectiveness is inconsequential. In some secondary schools, like the Edward M. Cope Junior High School of Redlands, California, a floating schedule is employed in which many of the classes do not meet on the same days each week. By use of the floating schedule it is possible to schedule more classes through the day that do not conflict, particularly classes that do not meet daily.

LIMITATIONS OF CONVENTIONAL SCHEDULES. The conventional schedule of from six to eight periods a day, with each period lasting from 45 to 57 minutes, possesses some serious limitations, among the most important of which are the following:

1. The schedule does not permit the students to go on field trips or other educational excursions for sufficiently long periods of time without being absent from classes other than those with which the field trips or excursions are associated.
2. The conventional daily schedule does not permit adequate time for conferences and co-operative planning by instructors.

3. The conventional schedule does not provide adequate opportunity for students to have access to teachers for conferences.

It is difficult even in flexible schedules to overcome these limitations. They are overcome in part by provision in the schedule for larger blocks of time to accommodate core classes or classes that meet two periods a day or two or three times a week.

OPENING AND CLOSING TIME. What constitutes the best time for beginning and closing the official school day is hard to specify for any given community. The first period might easily begin before 9 o'clock in most communities, probably as early as 8:30 in schools in which there are no transported pupils. Beginning earlier than 8 o'clock is likely to meet opposition on the part of parents and to result in hastily eaten breakfasts and considerable tardiness. Beginning at 8:30 makes possible in the morning session four periods of 42 minutes net or three periods of 55 minutes net, as well as a period of 30 minutes for home rooms and activities.

THE LUNCH PERIOD. The lunch period, which is discussed in Chapter 20, may be one long period of approximately 60 minutes for the entire school in those schools in which a considerable number of the students go home for lunch; it may be a shorter period, usually 30 minutes; in many schools there have to be two consecutive periods for lunch; and in some three consecutive periods are required. In some schools there is what is known as the "sliding lunch period," in which a group of students is sent to the cafeteria every 15 minutes, thus reducing the length of lines and the length of time spent waiting in lines.

THE ACTIVITY AND ASSEMBLY PERIOD. Studies show that, in approximately two thirds of the secondary schools of the United States, provision is made for extracurricular activities during the scheduled school day. Sometimes a period shorter than the regular period length—usually between 30 and 40 minutes—has been set aside for clubs, home-room meetings, assemblies, and other extracurricular activities. A fairly common plan is to have a period two days a week for clubs and extracurricular activities, two days for home room, and one day for assembly. When this period is used for assembly, it is usually lengthened and some time is taken from other periods. There is considerable variation in practice, as well as in opinion, as to what is the best spot in the schedule for the activity and home-room period. There are many principals who have eventually come to the conclusion that it should be in the middle of the afternoon schedule, in order to prevent students' parents from underestimating the value of the period, as they are inclined to do if it comes at the beginning of the morning or afternoon session or at the close of the session. Since in the afternoon the student is likely to be less alert and maybe a little drowsy, the period serves to stimulate students by means of activities which are somewhat more exciting than the usual class learning activities.

Scheduling the Core Block. The core block requires at least twice as long a time as the conventional class period. Since in most schools using the conventional class period there are conventional classes as well as core classes in the schedule, there is a tendency to schedule the core for two consecutive class periods, although a few schools, particularly junior high schools with a seven period day schedule it for three class periods.

Data Concerning Rooms. Before making or completing a schedule, it is necessary to know what rooms are available, as well as their size, location, and nature of equipment. For this purpose blueprints of each floor, showing major equipment, size, and number of seats, are very serviceable. In lieu of these, rough floor plans on which brief notations with respect to each room have been made will be found useful. Perhaps sufficient (especially in the smaller schools) is a diagram with columns for periods in the day and for rooms. In such a diagram some notation concerning the capacities of each room and its general nature should be entered in the column at the left, along with the room number.

Data Concerning the Staff. As may be inferred from the discussion relating to the assignment of the teaching staff in Chapter 5, the schedule must provide for the assignment of class sections that will bring about (1) the best possible assignment of subjects and extracurricular activities with regard to the preparation and interests of teachers and (2) an equalized teaching load.

In order to make such a schedule, the schedule-maker must obtain data as to the preparation and previous experience of teachers. The material collected concerning the teacher at the time of appointment, including transcripts of his college credits, should be available for reference, as should data concerning his training in service or in summer school since appointment and reports of supervisors or heads of departments regarding the suitability of members of their departments for various types of classes. Department heads should be consulted or asked to make recommendations concerning the assignment of classes in their departments.

Consulting Parents, Teachers, and Students. It is desirable at least every other year, and probably every year, before beginning to work on the schedule, to obtain comments, criticisms, and suggestions from parents, teachers, and students with respect to the schedule. A questionnaire or structured blank form could be employed, by which they might indicate any objections they have to the type of schedule being used during the current year, including such matters as the time of opening and closing the school day, the time and length of lunch periods, the schedules of bus routes, and the scheduling of clubs, teams, and other extracurricular activities. There should also be a place for writing constructive criticism. Points of dissatisfaction should be investigated by means of personal or group conferences.

2. *Constructing the Schedule: the Mosaic Plan*

MATERIALS NEEDED. The schedule-maker should obtain a drawing board or a large sheet of heavy cardboard about 20 inches wide; its length in inches should be one and one-half times the number of teachers in the school. The schedule-maker should also have thumbtacks, a sheet of heavy paper or light cardboard of the size mentioned above, a ruler or T-square, and a paper of small pins.[4] On the paper or cardboard should be ruled as many columns about 2 inches in width as there are teachers and as many rows as there are periods in the school day. The name of each class section should be typewritten on a small rectangular piece of

English IV (Robinson) 24 D

cardboard about 1 inch by ½ inch. On this card, as shown above, should also appear the probable number of students who will be assigned to the section and an abbreviation designating the days of the week on which the section will meet. On those cards representing classes which must be assigned to certain teachers, of which there are very likely to be instances in a small school, the name of the teacher should also appear on the card. Cards for all class sections meeting for double periods on one or more days a week should be twice as deep as ordinary cards, so as to extend over the spaces assigned to two consecutive periods. The cards should be arranged in rows or columns on desk or table, by class grade and by subjects: for example, seniors, juniors, sophomores, and freshmen in four different rows; English in one column, mathematics in another, and so on. The cardboard or heavy paper should be fastened to the drawing board with thumbtacks. Everything is now ready for filling in the "mosaic."

BLOCKING IN THE MOSAIC. It is well to start first with the sections which will be composed largely of seniors, sections which have no duplicates, and those which require double periods. Sections which fit into all three of these categories should be located on the chart first, followed by those belonging to two such classifications. Sections are located by passing a pin or thumbtack through the small card representing the section and fastening it to the chart in a square which is in the column headed by the name of the teacher who will teach the section. Care must be taken not to place in one row (that is, at one period) two

[4]For large schools the use of a composition blackboard is recommended. Instead of cardboard and pins, a pocket chart, such as is often used as a seating chart and sold by several school-supply houses, may be used to excellent advantage.

or more sections in which any given pupil will be enrolled. Likewise, no two sections assigned to the same teacher should be placed in the same row.

After all the senior sections, the nonduplicated single sections, and the double-period sections have been located, the schedule-maker should locate the sections of which there is only one duplicate, taking these in the order of seniority: for example, junior sections, then sophomore, then freshman or high ninth, low ninth, high eighth, and so on. The sections of which there are two or more duplicates will rarely cause any difficulty in scheduling and may be blocked in later. Where overlapping sessions obtain, as many sections as possible should be scheduled in the early-morning and late-afternoon periods. In small schools an effort should be made to avoid bunching recitations for any one group of students.

It will frequently seem impossible to locate all sections without conflicts. For example, one may be confronted with scheduling in six periods sections in the following twelve senior subjects: Latin, French, English, social problems, mathematics, second-year shorthand, bookkeeping, chemistry, household arts, agriculture, industrial arts, and second-year typewriting. It should be obvious that a number of nonconflicting combinations may be selected for scheduling in one period row: for example, shorthand and either agriculture, industrial arts, French, Latin, or mathematics. As many as three or even four such sections may sometimes be scheduled in a period—for example, agriculture, Latin, and shorthand, it being very unlikely that any pupil will be enrolled for two of these subjects at the same time. Fourth-year or even third-year foreign language should rarely conflict with senior-year commercial subjects.

Checking for Conflicts. After the mosaic has been completed—that is, after all section cards have been placed on the chart—it is ready to be checked for conflicts. This may be done by going through the preregistrations, selecting those that are somewhat irregular, and taking note of all conflicts. In small schools the proposed schedule may be exhibited at assembly and pupils asked to note their conflicts. There will be several types of conflicts and they should be classified. Most conflicts will be occasioned by irregular students or those desiring to take subjects not planned in the program of studies for the year in which the student belongs. If in either case students may hope to program one of the conflicting subjects the following year, less consideration should be given to them than to more deserving cases.

Often, after several possible schedules have been formulated, it will become obvious that there is little chance of eliminating all conflicts and that a schedule will have to be adopted which involves the least number of serious conflicts. The best schedule may not be the last one arranged; hence, it is desirable to have a record of all reasonably satisfactory solutions. Frequently, conflicts may be removed by consulting with the student or students concerned and discovering that there is no considerable margin of preference between one of the subjects causing the conflict and another which will not result in conflict.

MAKING A CONFLICT CHART. The schedule-maker should go through the entire proposed schedule and, ignoring subjects in which there are two or more sections, make a list, period by period, of all the subjects in which there is only one section. A conflict chart then should be made (see Form 7) for each period in the schedule. In the conflict chart there are rows and columns, with one row for each subject in which there is only one section and one column for each subject in which there is only one section; the abbreviations of the names of the sections should be put in the appropriate rows and appropriate columns. Then two people should take the students' subject-selection cards, one of them going through the cards and the other doing the tallying; wherever a student has selected any two of the subjects in each of which there is only one section, a tally should be recorded in the appropriate cell (see Form 7). Taking in turn each period of the day, as many charts should be made as there are periods in the day.

FORM 7. *Example of a Conflict Chart for Third-Period Sections*

	PHYSICS	FRENCH III	LATIN II	SHORTHAND	SHOP		HOME ECONOMICS
Physics							1
French III							
Latin II							
Shorthand I							
Shop II							
Home Economics II	1						

There will, of course, always be the possibility of conflicts in the case of a few students, even when the classes which seem to conflict with other classes have two or more sections. Conflicts on pupils' schedules can, however, be eliminated in all but rare cases in the process of assigning pupils to sections.

When conflict sheets are made separately for classes of each grade level, there are always possibilities of conflict in the case of students who carry some subjects in one grade-level group and one or more in others (for example, seniors carrying second-year or third-year subjects) and in the case of classes intended for students of two year levels (for example, home economics for both juniors and seniors). That is why, in all but the very large schools, it is better to make one conflict sheet for all classes in the school.

After all sections have been assigned to class periods and teachers and the schedule in this stage has been checked for conflicts, it is then ready for the filling-in of room assignments.

As far as possible, sections of the same type of work should be scheduled for the same classrooms: for example, all sections in American history, in order to avoid the necessity of moving maps from room to room. For convenience a teacher should have as much of his classes as possible in one room. By scheduling one or two sections taught by each of two teachers to other rooms, perhaps small sections to small rooms, it is usually possible to assign all other sections of those two teachers to the same room. It should be obvious that to tie up one room for each teacher, with the result that rooms are not scheduled for classes in periods in which the teachers assigned to them are not teaching, is wasteful and calls for a plant much larger than is actually needed. As noted in Chapter 22, a high-school principal may feel that the buildings are crowded before the utilization of the possible number of seatings or pupil stations has reached 60 or 70 per cent. This condition is brought about partly by poor schedule-making.

With a little care it is possible to reduce materially the amount of vertical traffic—that is, traffic from one floor level to another. If there are classrooms of different sizes in the building, very small sections should be assigned to smaller classrooms and very large sections assigned to larger classrooms. Although such assignments may improve class morale, they often conflict with the principle of assigning classes to rooms appropriately equipped to teach particular subjects.

Where buildings are crowded, it is necessary, in assigning sections to periods, to keep in mind the maximum number of classrooms available at each period and to distribute the sections among the periods in such a way that the finished schedule will not call for more rooms than are available. Likewise, it is necessary to avoid assigning to any given period more sections calling for the same type of special room (for example, physics laboratory) than there are rooms of that type available.

THE BLOCK METHOD. The block method, a variety of the mosaic plan, is so called because it consists in arranging all sections of students in nonconflicting units which are frequently referred to as blocks. The blocks may correspond to the periods in the school day, exclusive of the activity period, or a block may be made up of a different period each day, thus equalizing among the different blocks whatever differences there may be in the desirability of the different hours of the day. The distinguishing feature of the block system is that the pupils of each year or semester class are distributed to class divisions which are assigned as units to class sections.

Each year group or semester group—for example, the tenth-grade group—is divided into subgroups of equal numbers, each of from 25 to

35 pupils, according to the limit set as the "full" class size.[5] The division may be made merely by assigning the first 30 pupils, let us say, to group *A*, the next 30 to group *B*, and so on. Conflicts may be better avoided, however, if the class is first divided into curriculum groups and then subdivided in a manner similar to the following:

Class Groups: Grade 12—238 Pupils

Group *A*.	College preparatory	A through Marsters
Group *B*.	College preparatory	Masters through Z
Group *C*.	General	A through Rowell
Group *D*.	General	Sapley through Z
Group *E*.	Commercial	A through Milligan
Group *F*.	Commercial	Moore through Z
Group *G*.	Home Economics	
Group *H*.	Industrial	

In very large schools, such as senior high schools of 1200 or more students and junior high schools of 700 or more, the block plan (1) goes far to equalize sections and to eliminate the labor involved in equalizing sections, (2) reduces materially the labor involved in reducing conflicts, and (3) reduces materially the time spent in blocking out a schedule, by substituting a systematic approach for a more or less "trial and error" method. Principals of very large high schools or junior high schools should not be prevented, by the apparent complexity of the procedure, from giving the plan a trial. Its complexity is more apparent than real and disappears quickly when the schedule-maker attacks it in a concrete, practical situation.

3. The Individual Pupil, or Yardstick, Method

For very small schools a third plan is more useful. In these, because of the practice of offering some subjects only in alternate years and because of the high percentage of one-section subjects, the scheduling has to be carried on with each pupil in mind. A very convenient device for such schools is often referred to as the yardstick, or individual-pupil, method.

MATERIALS NEEDED. The materials needed are the registration cards of the pupils, as many yardsticks and thumbtacks as there are to be class sections offered (counting twice all sections requiring double periods on one or more days a week), and crayons of different colors. If yardsticks are not available, long strips of very heavy cardboard of about the same length will serve as well. To each yardstick attach with a thumbtack a

[5]In the senior class of a high school in which no subject is required of or likely to be elected by all pupils, the number may be increased to 40 or 45 pupils, so that resulting groups will be likely to furnish, on the average, full sections in the subject of greatest enrollment—usually English. Further description of the block plan may be found in Harl R. Douglass, *Organization and Administration of Secondary Schools*, 1932 and 1945 editions. It is practical only in very large schools.

small piece of cardboard bearing the name of the section and the instructor most likely to be assigned the section. (If cardboard strips are used, crayon marks should be used instead to indicate the sections.) Each yardstick should be consecutively numbered at each half-inch interval, and these numbers should be assigned to individual pupils. If the method is used in schools with more than 72 pupils, smaller intervals and more numbers must be used.

It is economical of time to arrange the names of the students alphabetically within each class. Taking each stick in turn, mark with the crayon a heavy line at the space corresponding to each of the pupils enrolled in that section, using different-colored chalk for each grade. Then lay off, with chalk lines on a table or with pieces of string on the floor, intervals wide enough to contain as many yardsticks laid side by side as there are likely to be assigned sections at any one period. These intervals should be numbered, one interval for each period in the school day.

PROCEDURE. The procedure of schedule construction itself is quite simple. The problem is to distribute the sticks approximately evenly among the intervals so as not to have in any one interval two sticks bearing marks at the same places—that is, so that no pupil will have a conflict. Yardsticks representing the two divisions of double periods should, of course, be laid in adjacent intervals. Care must also be taken that the sticks are so distributed as not to schedule at the same hour two classes requiring the same room or the same teacher.

The general principles of procedure are similar to certain of those of the other two methods. The sticks representing sections in which seniors are enrolled should be placed first; those for sections containing freshmen should be placed last. The sections having a duplicate (if there are any) should be left to the last.

As the size of the school increases, this method becomes cumbersome; the existence of duplicate sections helps to prevent conflicts and to render the individual-pupil check unnecessary. If the school is large enough to have two sections in many subjects or three sections in any one subject, the method becomes complicated. If the marks on the sticks are closer together than two to the inch, it is difficult, in watching for conflicts while constructing the schedule, to follow the lines over from stick to stick and to distinguish from one another the lines representing different pupils.

4. Putting the Schedule into Operation

PUNCH-CARD PROCEDURE. In an increasing number of large secondary schools there are punch-card machines available for use in schedule construction. By use of machines a great deal of time may be saved in large schools, not only in connection with making pupil schedules but also in connection with various types of guides and research services.

Machines may also save much teacher time in connection with the preparation of report cards and the recording of grades. To discuss the operation of these machines would require more space than is available in this volume. Full directions may be obtained from any office of the International Business Machines Corporation, the Todd Company, or the Royal McBee Company. The directions may be obtained prior to any purchase of machines, so the administrator may understand their operation and their time-saving qualities before he makes up his mind about whether to purchase them. The machines may also be rented by the month or the year. Several references at the end of this chapter contain useful information concerning the use of machines.

STUDENT SCHEDULES. In all but the smallest schools it is good practice for the principal, the home-room advisers, roll-room advisers, or school clerk or secretary to fill out a student schedule card for each student on a form similar to that shown as Form 8. If students are per-

FORM 8. *Student Schedule Card*

PUPIL-SCHEDULE CARD

NAME OF PUPIL Cawsky, Mary Jane — SEMESTER 1st

CLASS Junior — LOCKER NO. ____

STUDY	PERIOD	DAYS	ROOM	INSTRUCTOR
Algebra 3	1	D	16	Miss Blake
Study hall	2	D	B	Miss Andrews
Physics	3	M W F	28	Mr. Smith
Physics lab.	3 & 4	T Th	29	Mr. Smith
Physical ed.	4	M W F	Gym	Mr. Hansen
Music	5	M W	Art	Miss Fawkes
Study hall	5	T Th F	B	Miss Wilkins
English 5	6	D	21	Miss Jones
Amer. Hist. 5	7	D	14	Mr. Auld

mitted to make their own schedules, many will choose sections for trivial reasons, the sections of more popular teachers will be overcrowded, cliques of students will arrange to go into the same sections, and some sections will be too small. In very small schools, where there are few duplicate sections, these dangers are not of importance.

If the block method has been employed, the assignment of students to sections is in the main a mechanical procedure. With the exception of students who have been transferred for one or more classes to blocks other than the one in which they naturally would classify according to the scheme for forming divisions, the section, the classroom, and the hour are shown by the class-group letters. When either of the other methods is used, each student's schedule is a problem in itself, though it ordinarily presents no great difficulty. When the mosaic plan has been employed in assigning students to sections, a tally sheet should be provided so that the enrollment in each section may be tallied as students are assigned to it and the enrollment equalized among sections. It is very desirable that two persons work together in this task, one to make the entries on the tally sheet. In making the student schedules, care should be exercised to avoid erasures. It is better to prepare the card in duplicate, one copy being retained as a part of the school records.

CHANGES OF SCHEDULE FORMS. In the larger schools it is desirable that students desiring to drop or add courses or to rearrange their schedules be required to write out for record an application for such change. As a matter of convenience for correcting students' registration forms or schedule cards as filed in the office, as well as for furnishing records and registration changes, a proper application form is very serviceable and may be very inexpensive, as illustrated by Form 9. Where a written application is not required, students who are not pleased with their schedules are tempted to lose their cards.

FORM 9. *Applying for Change in Registration or Schedule*

CHANGE OF SCHEDULE APPLICATION

NAME OF PUPIL ____________________ Date ____________

1. I desire to add ______________________________
2. I desire to withdraw from ______________________
3. I desire to change the hours of my schedule as follows:

____

____

____

Approved ____________________
Signature of parent

Approved ____________________
Adviser

Approved
Rejected ____________________
Principal

The preparation of schedule cards is the last stage at which any changes in schedule should be made. All conflicts should be eliminated before the cards are completed; in fact, it is serious if any are necessary at this late time.

At the beginning of the first day of school the home-room advisers or teachers designated for that purpose should distribute these cards to the students and make such explanation as seem desirable with reference to rooms, periods, and other matters. Students desiring changes in their schedules should be permitted to petition for them, but with the understanding that only petitions based upon serious problems will be granted.

In the smaller schools a staff meeting should then be called to explain or discuss apparent and unforeseen difficulties in the operation of the new schedule. Since all students' programs are based upon the schedule as now formulated, revisions should be avoided as far as possible; before making changes, the effects of doing so upon students' programs should be thoroughly investigated. In this connection the method of tallying students' names by sections at the time of making student schedules is often seen in a very favorable light, since such tally sheets facilitate the study of the effect of shifting sections.

Testing and Revising the Schedule. After the designated period for distributing and explaining the students' schedules has elapsed, the schedule should be run through with abbreviated periods of approximately 15 minutes each. At this time assignments should be made and instructions given as to textbooks and materials needed in the various courses. Students having difficulties in following their schedules should report to the office, where someone should be stationed to assist them. Students may be dismissed at noon for the day.

Teachers' Rolls. Two common practices for preparing class-section rolls may be noted. At the time the student schedules are made, the student's names may be entered on the tally sheets; the rolls may be made up from these sheets and sent to the teacher. An alternative practice is to have a list made from the cards of students who attend the first meeting of the class. Since it is likely that some students will not be present at the first meeting of the class, the first method is preferable. The only advantage of the second plan lies in the fact that it lessens the clerical work at the time of making the student schedules. Teachers' rolls may be made with a great saving of time by the use of punch-card machines.

Scheduling Examinations. In a great many secondary schools several days each year are set aside for scheduled written examinations. Practice with respect to this varies a great deal. In some schools two or three days are set aside at the end of the year for examination; in a considerable number of schools several days are also set aside at the end of the first semester. In some schools a double schedule is run through—in other words, the morning schedule is on one day and the afternoon schedule on the next day and the examination periods are twice as long as regular class periods. In other schools the regular schedule is run through for both days, or for three days where they use three days for examinations, and final examinations are divided into two, or three, parts. There are no data available relative to the numbers of percentages of schools following any one of these practices; indeed, there is apparently not any decided preference in theory for one practice as against another.

In a considerable number of schools, though perhaps not quite so many as formerly, final examinations have been done away with as such and teachers are permitted to use some of their periods during the last week of school for examinations if they wish. There have been a considerable number of teachers and administrators who have believed that the bad effects or disadvantages of final written examinations outweigh the advantages. Among the bad effects are the following: (1) they put a considerable number of youngsters under a great strain at the end of a semester; (2) because of the amount of variation among youngsters with respect to effects upon them resulting from the strain imposed by final examinations, some youngsters are more greatly handicapped than others in being able to show what they have gained from their course; (3) there is always a large chance-factor in examinations and, if considerable weight is given to examinations, youngsters' grades may be a matter of luck as much as of growth in achievement; (4) final examinations, being largely paper-and-pencil affairs, measure only a part of the types of growth of individuals in the class and therefore should not be given too much importance.

On the other hand, there are several important advantages and reasons for conducting final examinations: (1) such examinations tend to stimulate careful reviews at the close of the semester, reviews which may be so conducted as to give the pupil a picture of the semester's work, to bring out the intercorrelation of various parts of the work, and to stimulate strengthening of the weak points in the pupil's growth during the semester; (2) final examinations constitute an incentive to students to master work as they go and to make up work missed because of absence, rather than to pass over points not well understood, since they will be held responsible for them at the end of the semester; (3) preparation for these final examinations at the end of the semester involves reviews and types of study which are not ordinarily followed throughout the year and which would be valuable to the students, particularly to those students going on to college; (4) with the final examinations at the end of the semester, it is possible for the teacher to spend less time quizzing and checking in the daily recitations and to devote much more of the class recitation time to teaching and supervising growth of youngsters.

There is fairly universal agreement that not too much importance should be attached to final examinations and that greatly increased attention should be given by most teachers and in most schools to evaluation of types throughout the semester or year. As a part of the training of teachers in service and in preservice education, there should be definite training which would cause teachers to be constantly alert to behavior on the part of youngsters which gives evidence of their growth toward the well-rounded objectives of education: emotional and social adjustment; ability to use what is learned in the class; development of attitudes, ideals, and interests; development in habits of use of intellectual skills, particularly in the matter of English; and clear thinking. Teachers also should be stimulated and trained in types of examination items which measure something other than information and subject-matter skills. They should also be trained in developing new types of evaluation procedures to be used in connection with various units throughout the year, evaluation procedures which would involve such things as self-evaluation on the part of the students and group evaluation of the work of groups of students, as well as evaluation of individual students.

Equalizing Teaching Loads. It is desirable after the schedule has been put into operation for the principal or one of his assitants to measure the probable teaching load of the members of his staff. This probably may be best done by use of the teaching-load formula described in Chapter 5. In those cases where it is obvious that teachers are materially overloaded, some adjustment is indicated. With experienced use of the formula and study of the factors and principles involved, principals can estimate roughly the probable teaching load at the time the assignments are made in the spring and schedule construction is begun. However, actual class size cannot be determined with great precision at that time and the principal's judgment should be checked by use of the formula after the classes are under way. Adjustments in teaching loads may be made by giving the teachers additional help of some sort or another, by decreasing their assignment for co-operative or extracurricular work and work on committees, and perhaps by adjusting the study-hall load. Those underloaded may be asked to assist with more co-operative work of various types.

Length of School Year. In recent years there has been much agitation for and discussion of a longer school year. There have been many uninformed individuals who have advocated a four-quarter plan, with students ordinarily attending only three quarters of a year. This plan, it is thought, would enable a district to meet its educational needs with reduced expenditure for buildings and possibly for teachers. Some advocates have thought of the plan as a means of getting youngsters through school in fewer years. The plan has not proved successful, however, it having been exceedingly difficult to get youngsters to attend the summer quarter. During the summer quarter, parents take vacations and wish their children to be with them; also, during this period it is too hot in practically all cities of the United States for teachers and students to be comfortable in the school.

In many districts in the last few years the school term has been lengthened from nine months to nine and one-half or ten months.

5. Scheduling for Team Teaching

THE TRUMP PLAN. Team teaching involves special difficulties and arrangements in scheduling. Under the Trump plan, for example, approximately 40 per cent of the student's time is to be spent in large classes taught preferably by the lecture method. This will mean that, instead of several sections of the class meeting at different times, two or more sections of the class must meet at the same time for at least one and probably two periods a week. Furthermore, there is the necessity for scheduling many small sections of various classes with groups of from 12 to 15 students each. This scheduling involves a housing problem which may be solved in many schools only through a new building or through the subdivision of some classrooms. In the case of the large groups in some schools whose buildings have not been constructed for this plan of teaching, the cafeteria, the gymnasium, and the auditorium are used – a not too satisfactory situation. Below is a schedule for a biology teacher in the Golden, Colorado, High School, which employs team teaching:

Period	Monday	Tuesday	Wednesday	Thursday	Friday
1.	Section A-F (150 pupils)	Section A	Section D	Section A	Section A-C
2.	*Planning*	Section A	Section D	Section B	Section D-F
3.	*Planning*	Section B	Section E	Section C	*Planning*
4.	*Planning*	Section B	Section E	Section D	*Planning*
5.	*Planning*	Section C	Section F	Section E	*Planning*
6.	*Planning*	Section C	Section F	Section F	*Planning*

The program of a typical tenth-grade student might look like this:

Period	Monday	Tuesday	Wednesday	Thursday	Friday
1	Medium group Math	Physical education	Resource center, or library	Medium group Math	Physical education
2	Large group Chemistry	Large group Math	Medium group Chemistry	Medium group Chemistry	Small group Math
3	Resource center, or library	Small group Chemistry	Small group Chemistry	Resource center, or library	Small group Chemistry
4	Small group Social Studies	Small group Conversational French	Small group Social Studies	Medium group Social Studies	Large group Social Studies
5	Small group English	Individual project work: music, art, shop; *or,* Large group Driver Education	Large group English	Medium group English	Medium group English
6	Language laboratory French; *or,* Sports, recreation, music, drama		Language laboratory French; *or,* Sports, recreation, music, drama	Large group French; *or,* Individual, tutorial, and planning with teachers	Resource center, or library; *or,* Sports, recreation, music, drama

A teacher's program might look like this:

Period	Monday	Tuesday	Wednesday	Thursday	Friday
1	Preparation of material	Preparation of material, professional study, student evaluation, etc.	Medium group	Small group	Small group
2	Large group		Large group	Individual tutorial	Small group
3	Medium group	Medium group	Planning	Small group	Small group
4	Teacher team conference	Small group	Medium group	Medium group	Medium group
5	Medium group	Small group	Small group	Small group	
6	Individual tutorial, in-service training, or faculty meeting	Medium group	Team conference	Small group; Tutorial or student conference	Preparation of material and planning

Problems, Questions, and Exercises

1. Be able to discuss clearly how you would estimate registrations for various subjects offered in the schools.
2. What are the relative advantages and disadvantages of preregistration; how would you go about carrying it on?
3. Discuss the optimum length of the class period and the school day and the optimum opening and closing time. Explain how one or more of these might be different at different schools.
4. What do you think should be the length of the lunch period in a school of 75 students? Of 200 students? Of 700 students?
5. Be able to explain and evaluate a plan of having classes meet only four times a week instead of five times.
6. Discuss scheduling of the activity period.
7. Be able to describe in class the mosaic plan of schedule construction.
8. What do you think is the best way of locating and eliminating conflicts?
9. Be able to describe the block plan; mention its advantages and where it is most suitable.
10. Be able to describe the use of the individual-pupil, or yardstick, method of schedule construction.
11. Be able to give in class without notes a discussion of how you would put a schedule into operation.
12. After a schedule is once made, what are some of the ways in which it might have to be modified?
13. Make a list of subjects for schedule construction in a school operating on a Trump or similar plan of team teaching.

Selected Supplementary Readings

Abel, F. P., and Gill, D. R., "What is the Most Effective Way of Organizing the Number and Length of Class Periods and the Length of the School Day?" *Bulletin of the N.A.S.S.P.* (April, 1960), No. 255, pp. 8-11.

Baker, William, "Streamlined Individualized Programming by Hand Punch Card," *Bulletin of the N.A.S.S.P.* (December, 1959), No. 251, p. 160-166.

Brandes, Louis Grant, and Forsheit, Samuel, "The Extended Session Schedule," *Bulletin of the N.A.S.S.P.* (September, 1959), No. 248, pp. 166-176.

Brandes, J. S., "Report on the Closed Campus," *Bulletin of the N.A.S.S.P.* (October, 1959), No. 249, pp. 44-51.

Bridges, E. W., "We Did Away With Study Halls," *Nation's Schools* (September, 1960), Vol. 66, No. 3, pp. 67-68, 110.

Bush, Robert N., and others, "Using Machines to Make the High School Schedule," *School Review* (Spring, 1960), Vol. 69, No. 1, pp. 48-49.

Byrne, David F., and Steel, Wade A., "Leyden High School 'Early Bird Period'," *Bulletin of the N.A.S.S.P.* (March, 1962), No. 272, pp. 79-82.

Clemmer, Elwin F., "A Fresh Approach to a Longer School Day," *School Management* (June, 1960), Vol. 14, No. 6, pp. 61-63.

Davis, C. D., "IBM Methods in Registration and Grade Reporting," *Bulletin of the N.A.S.S.P.* (December, 1953), No. 198, p. 123.

Diederich, Paul B., "Simplifying a Crowded Schedule," *School Review* (March, 1945), Vol. 53, pp. 162-169.

Ellis, V. Berkley and Dick, Stanley B., "Scheduling the Practical and the Fine Arts in the High School," *Bulletin of the N.A.S.S.P.* (April, 1962), No. 273, pp. 36-41.

Eveslage, Donald J., "Scheduling Balanced Classes," *Bulletin of the N.A.S.S.P.* (October, 1950), Vol. 34, pp. 47-60. [Deals with (1) registration, (2) sorting cards and tabulating choices, (3) making the schedule, (4) balancing the class, (5) writing out registration slips, and (6) opening-day procedure.]

Feldman, Louis G., "Programming Classes by Means of a Punch Card System," *Bulletin of the N.A.S.S.P.* (October, 1950), Vol. 34, No. 172, pp. 23-32. [Description of plan used at New Utrecht High School.]

Forshert, Samuel, "The Extended Session Schedule," *Bulletin of the N.A.S.S.P.* (September, 1959), No. 298, pp. 166-168.

Gwiden, Noble, and Austin, David B., *The High School Principal and the Staff Develop the Master Schedule,* New York, Teachers College, Columbia University, 1960, p. 104.

Haggerson, Nelson L., and Smith, Haskel B., "The Seventy-Minute Period Schedule Contributes to More Effective Staff Utilization," *Bulletin of the N.A.S.S.P.* (April, 1962), pp. 51-58.

Hemeyer, Will, and McGrew, Jean B., "Big Ideas for Big Classes," *School Review* (Autumn, 1960), Vol. 68, pp. 308-317. [Plans used at Rich Township, Illinois, High School.]

Janet, Sister Mary, *Catholic Secondary Education,* Washington, D.C., National Catholic Welfare Conference, 1949. [Chapter 9.]

Johnson, R. H., Lobb, M. D., and Patterson, Gordon, "Continued Study of Class Size, Team Teaching, and Scheduling in Eight High Schools in Jefferson County, Colorado," *Bulletin of the N.A.S.S.P.* (January, 1959), No. 243, pp. 99-103.

Karslake, James S., and Kirby, Thomas J., "Schedule-Making Made Easy," *School Review* (December, 1938), Vol. 46, pp. 754-759. [Includes description of a practical, mechanical device for saving time in location of conflicts.]

Kindred, L. W., and Standard, C. C., "How Have Schools Met the Problem of Eliminating Study Halls?" *Bulletin of the N.A.S.S.P.* (April, 1960), No. 255, pp. 190-194.

Klemmer, D. F., "The Rotating Schedule at Claremont Junior High School," *Bulletin of the N.A.S.S.P.* (March, 1960), No. 254, pp. 56-59.

Loats, Norman R., "Breaks Between Classes," *School Management* (September, 1959), Vol. 3, No. 9, pp. 74-75.

Nord, Gerald E., "Our School Tested 6 and 8 Period Days," *Clearing House* (October, 1941), Vol. 16, pp. 108-110. [Comparison of the good and bad features of each type of organization.]

O'Brien, James F., "A New Look in Schedule Building," *Bulletin of the N.A.S.S.P.* (September, 1958), No. 240, pp. 102-106.

Oliver, Eugene, "What Price Double Sessions," *School Management* (November, 1959), Vol. 3, No. 11, pp. 5-16.

Palm, Reuben R., and Ylvisaker, H. L., "How Effective is the All-Year Secondary School?" *Bulletin of the N.A.S.S.P.* (April, 1950), No. 170, pp. 63-73.

Patterson, Gordon E., Swenson, Lloyd G., and Johnson, Robert H., "Classes of 10, 20, 35, and 70 Under Varied Conditions are Taught in Jefferson County, Colorado, to Discover Effects on Students and Teachers," *Bulletin of the N.A.S.S.P.* (January, 1958), No. 235, pp. 165-167.

Price, J.W., "More Experience with Utilizing a New School Plant at Syosset, New York, in Contributing to Staff Use and Curriculum Development," *Bulletin of the N.A.S.S.P.* (January, 1959), No. 243, pp. 167-180.

Purnell, Dale, Harper, Paige S., Oliver, E. Eugene, Gott, Clyde M., Simmons, John W., and Noall, Matthew F., "The Daily Schedule—Shorter Periods, Longer Periods, Variable Periods, or What?" *Bulletin of the N.A.S.S.P.* (April, 1961), No. 264, pp. 12-17, 110-115.

Shipp, Frederic T., "A Flexible Daily Schedule for a Modern High School," *American School Board Journal* (October, 1945), p. 58. [Gives illustrations of the use of "floating period" without subject-period interruption or elimination.]

Simney, Lucille, "A Teacher Looks at the Double-Period Program," *California Journal of Secondary Education* (March, 1952), Vol. 27, pp. 146-147. [Relates reactions and cites advantages and disadvantages of the double-period program at the junior high school level.]

Sturges, A. W., "The Midwestern High-School Schedule," *Bulletin of the N.A.S.S.P.* (February, 1961), No. 262, pp. 91-95. [A survey of practices in 938 secondary schools..

Templeton, Frank L., "The Use of IBM Techniques in Program Making and Class Scheduling," *Bulletin of the N.A.S.S.P.* (October, 1950), Vol. 34, pp. 15-22. [An explanation of the use of the IBM system in class scheduling at Bloomington, Illinois, and its advantages.]

Tompkins, Ellsworth, "The Daily Schedule in Junior High Schools," *Bulletin of the N.A.S.S.P.* (May, 1956), No. 220. [A study of the committee on junior high school education.]

17

Student Accounting and Reporting

1. Purposes and Organization

PRINCIPAL PURPOSES OF STUDENT ACCOUNTING AND RECORDS. The need of records has increased greatly in the last few decades as the purposes for which they are used have multiplied and become more important. Among the most important purposes of student records the following may be listed:

1. Keeping the records of attendance for purposes of collecting state financial aid.
2. Keeping records for the purpose of certifying the credits earned, the marks received, attendance, participation in extracurricular activities, scores on aptitude tests, and qualities of citizenship and character for colleges and universities in connection with the selection and admission of college students.
3. Keeping records such as those mentioned in the paragraph above and others for prospective employers who are considering the applications of students for employment.
4. Keeping records for the purpose of assisting students in their applications for scholarships, loans, and awards when attending college.
5. Keeping records for assisting representatives of juvenile courts, police, and welfare organizations in connection with enforcement.
6. Keeping records to provide guidance and counselee data to counselors, teachers, and administrators.
7. Keeping records to assist teachers in determining final marks and in sending reports to parents.
8. Keeping records for the purpose of guiding those interested in problem youngsters who have become disciplinary cases.
9. Keeping records to improve attendance and promptness.
10. Keeping records for health guidance and the administration of immunization and other health programs.
11. Keeping records to supply data for a wide variety of research investigations.

FUNDAMENTAL PRINCIPLES UNDERLYING RECORDS AND ACCOUNTING. In deciding upon serviceable procedures in the various types of accounting, it is necessary to keep in mind the school for which they are intended and the conditions under which the procedure, forms, and records will be employed. The principal should bear in mind that the conditions existing in his school, any unusual projects or procedures, and any peculiar demands by outside authorities will necessitate modification and adaptation of the suggestions to fit his particular needs and conditions. Whatever procedures or forms are employed, there are several simple fundamental principles which should be observed. Among them are the following:

1. Every form or procedure should be thought through in the light of the administrative, supervisory, guidance, or instructional activities it is intended to facilitate.
2. Forms and accounting procedures should be as few, conservative, and simple as will adequately take care of the needs. There should be no forms, items on forms, or record-keeping for which there is not sufficient need to warrant the expense and time involved in their use.
3. Corollary to 2, forms should be employed in all situations in which their use will result in a net saving of time and money in the management and administration of the school.
4. The use of records and accounting should be sufficiently ample to ensure effective and honest stewardship of all property and funds.
5. The records, forms, and associated procedures should involve the least possible expenditure of time and afford the least opportunity for neglect and carelessness on the part of teachers and all others involved.
6. As far as possible, the use of forms, records, and accounting procedures, should make a minimum demand upon the members of the staff for work of a clerical nature. As far as possible, the clerical phases of all accounting should be performed by clerical help.

General-Information Record. All students should be required immediately upon entering school for the first time to furnish certain miscellaneous information for various types of uses from time to time. What information should be furnished for the records may be inferred from the form (Form 10) suggested for that purpose.

Form 10. *Form for General Information concerning Pupil.*

GENERAL-INFORMATION CARD

Richmond High School

Pupil ______________________ Address ______________________
Last name First name
Date of birth ________________ Place of birth ________________
Name and address of parent ______________________________
Home telephone no. or telephone no. of neighbor ______________
Which parent, if either, is not living ______________________
Occupation of parent or parents ____________________________
Last school attended ____________ Last grade passed ____________
Date of last vaccination for smallpox ________________________
Occupation you think you are most likely to follow ______________
Do you intend to graduate? ________ go to college? ____________

The cards in this form should be collected from students or advisers at the beginning of the term and filed alphabetically by classes. In a great many schools pupils are asked to fill out such cards at the time of each semiannual or annual registration. This practice serves to keep the cards up to date and to put into the hands of advisers information useful in advising in the selection of courses.

THE FILING OF RECORDS. Practically all records employed in educational accounting are kept on cards of standard size, ranging from 3 by 5 inches to 8½ by 11 inches. These are commonly filed in filing cabinets, each type of record by itself.

Many schools employ what is called the packet, or folder, system. In this plan most of the records of one child are kept in one packet or folder. The packet system has one outstanding advantage and several limitations. More often than not, when it is desired to investigate the records of a pupil, more than one type of record is needed. Where the packet system is employed, it is necessary to look in only one file – the packet file – to locate all the records. However, the packet system makes the recording of records cumbersome and requires more time. Moreover, when one investigator wishes to examine one complete set of records (for example, the records from achievement tests), he ties up the entire file, preventing other workers from employing any of the records of the same pupils unless he takes the trouble to remove all the achievement-test cards, with the intention of returning them when he has finished with them. In some schools, two sets of records, one of each type, are used.

MECHANIZED AIDS. During the 1950's and early 1960's, there has been a great increase in the number of schools which have employed mechanized aids for recording data about students and for pulling out the data desired for various types of investigations and reporting. Although the punch-card systems are somewhat expensive, in schools of more than a few hundred students the systems pay for themselves within a few years because they save teachers a great amount of time. Furthermore, these systems make possible certain types of investigations and services which are quite difficult to carry on without them.[1]

2. *Tests, Scores, Records, and Marks*

THE TESTING PROGRAM. It has become the custom in practically all schools today to develop a program of giving, scoring, and interpreting various kinds of tests. These testing programs should be unified and coordinated and should include the giving, scoring, and interpreting of tests throughout the school system, from the first grade through secondary school. In order to be of assistance in guidance, teaching, and research,

[1]See Chapter 16.

a testing program should include tests of school achievement, tests of general mental ability, tests of scholastic aptitude, tests of specialized aptitudes of various sorts, interest inventories, social-adjustment devices such as sociograms, and tests of vocational interest and preference such as the Kuder Preference Record.

Testing programs vary a great deal from school to school, not only in their completeness but also in the variety and grade level of tests given. Following is a typical program of testing for grades 7 through 12; it is quite similar to those found in a great many systems today:

Grade 7. If not given in grade 6, a complete battery of achievement tests should be given in the seventh grade—such tests as the California, Iowa Every-Pupil, Metropolitan, and Stanford achievement tests. If one of these batteries of tests has been given in grade 6, then there should be given a reading comprehension test and an arithmetic-skills test; also, sometime during the seventh grade there should certainly be given a mental-abilities test or some other type of intelligence test.

Grade 8. If achievement tests were not given in the seventh grade, they should be given at the end of the eighth grade.

Grade 9. During this year the student should take the Greene Reading Comprehension Test or the Co-operative Reading Comprehension Test, the Kuder Vocational Preference Record, the Otis Quick Scoring Mental Ability Test, the Gamma, and the Essential High School Content Battery, or comparable tests.

Grade 10. There should be given some form of intelligence test (if not given in the ninth grade), a differential aptitude test, and a test of fundamental skills in arithmetic.

Grade 11. The Co-operative English Test should be given, testing mechanics for effectiveness of expression and reading comprehension.

Grade 12. The Essential High School Content or similar battery should be given, as well as the Kuder Vocational Preference Record and a scholastic-aptitude test.

In addition to these tests, there should be some means of gathering data concerning the problems of the students in school; the Mooney Problem Check List and the SRA Youth Inventory List should be given at least once, preferably in grade 10 or in grade 12, or in both grade 9 and grade 12.

Some individual in the school system should be, and usually is, made responsible for formulating the testing program, seeing to its administration, supervising the scoring, and assisting teachers and others in its interpretation. Such a person might well be the director of guidance, the director of evaluation, or a psychometrician. If there is no such individual in the local school, then the principal or assistant principal, with the help of a committee of teachers and counselors, should take over these duties until the time that the services of a specialized individual are available. Necessarily the testing program under these conditions will be somewhat limited.

SUPERVISING THE SUBJECT-MATTER TESTING OF CLASSROOM TEACHERS. The principal should make a point of becoming informed about the means of evaluation employed by each of his teachers and of becoming familiar with the types of tests that the teachers use. This does not mean that the teachers should submit their tests to him for approval; but it does mean that in some instances he will discuss with the teachers the possibility of improving their test construction, scoring, and interpretation, as well as their program of evaluation of student educational status and progress.

Modern Concept of Place and Use of Marks. Since teachers' marks play so important a part in the administration and management of high schools, it is incumbent upon the principal to see that marking is so done that the marks will be as valid and reliable as possible for the purpose to which they are put. A review of the purposes which school marks serve seems to support the following principles underlying an adequate system of marks and marking:

1. The marks assigned in school subjects should measure achievement in the subject concerned. Subject marks should not be directly based upon attendance, behavior, effort, or any characteristic of achievement other than progress or status in the course. Any other procedure is certain to result in or contribute to:

a. The misleading of investigators in educational research.
b. Lack of objectivity and validity of marks:
(1) As measures of achievement and progress.
(2) As bases for promotion and classification.
(3) As data for educational and vocational guidance.
(4) As bases for college recommendations.
c. The misleading of pupils and parents as to pupils' achievements.

When it is desired to reward industry, citizenship, or achievement in proportion to ability, supplementary marks and oral praise to parents and students should be employed for this purpose. In an increasing number of schools two sets of marks are employed both for reports to students and parents and for the records. This dual marking system involves (1) an objective evaluation of the student's progress and status and (2) a second evaluation which is an attempt to rate the student's educational growth in terms of his apparent ability, as judged by intelligence-test and aptitude-test scores and previous marks. Certainly, the use of the latter type of marks only is not to be recommended; it would be most difficult to interpret such marks for the purposes of guidance and for most problems of college admission and research investigations.

2. Marks assigned by different teachers should represent as nearly as possible the same relative degree of achievement. Since there is no reliable method of directly equating degrees of achievement in different subjects, efforts in that direction must employ some indirect method. The method employed with greatest success is that of basing the distribution of marks on the assumption of approximately normal distribution of ability in typical classes.

3. The distribution of marks should be based upon the assumption that the courses of study for different year levels are equally well adapted to

the ability of students for whom they are intended. Ninth-grade pupils should receive about the same proportion of low and of high marks as seventh-grade pupils in junior high schools and about the same proportion as eleventh-grade or twelfth-grade pupils in the traditional four-year high school. Any other condition implies one of two things: either (1) that marking is improperly done or (2) that the courses of study need revision and a rebalancing of their relative difficulty.

4. Final marks for a semester, quarter, month, or six-week period should represent the best possible estimate of achievement and status in the subject. This objective is not best attained by recording as the final mark the mechanical mathematical average of weighted or unweighted selected factors, such as daily class grade, final examination, written quizzes, and notebook work. The practice of assigning arbitrary weights to different factors of a group and employing them mechanically in the determination of a final mark is not valid. Such weightings should be employed only to give pupils a general idea of the relative importance of different factors; they should be used in only a general way in averaging the factors for final marks. Weights should vary with the size of the class, the nature of classroom procedure, and, indeed, from individual to individual, depending upon what data may happen to be available for each individual. Frequently a pupil, after getting off to a poor start, will improve markedly, not only doing the later work better but mastering that which he failed to master earlier in the course. The safe criterion to employ is that which uses whatever evidence is available in whatever way will result in the most accurate estimate of the progress and status of each given pupil at the time when the mark is assigned.

In the marks given at the end of monthly or six-week periods or at the end of the semester or year, secondary schools have rather generally replaced the use of numbers with the use of letters, usually A, B, C, D, E, and F. F signifies failure; E, where used, refers to a conditional or exceedingly low pass; D represents below-average performance; C stands for average performance; B means somewhat superior performance; and A signifies outstanding performance. C's are the most commonly given marks; A's, D's, and F's are uncommonly given.

MEANING OF MARKS. It is highly desirable that, under the direction of the principal, assistant principal, or director of instruction, the faculty of every secondary school give considerable consideration to the matter of what marks are to mean. They should draw up a written statement upon which there is fairly general agreement about the marks that are to be used in the school. The statement of the meaning of marks should outline what the marks measure: whether they will be based solely upon subject-matter information (or subject-matter information and skills) or upon apparent interest, attitudes, and habits as well. A brief summary of this statement of the meaning of marks should be placed upon forms for reports to parents in order to assist parents in the interpretation of the marks brought home on the report cards of their children.

It is useful, at least in reports to parents, to indicate in some way whether a student has the ability to do much better work. Such an indication may take any brief and arbitrary form agreed upon, such as a circle around the mark, underscoring, or the use of colored ink. If the pupil is achieving as well as may reasonably be expected for his mental age, intelligence, or previous school record, the lack of a notation will indicate that fact. It is not necessary to distinguish between those who are doing as well as is to be expected and those who are doing better than that, nor is it practical to attempt finer distinctions with data no more reliable than those ordinarily available. In fact, even to make a general indication, teachers should have at hand such data as the mental ages, intelligence quotients, and previous grades of the students.

THE STANDARDIZATION OF TEACHERS' MARKS. Most principals are aware of the fact that teachers' marks, even final marks, are unreliable, different teachers assigning different marks for the same quality of achievement and even the same teacher sometimes assigning different marks for the same achievement at different times. It has also been shown that supposedly equivalent examinations covering the same subject matter vary so much in difficulty that the mark of the pupil is determined largely by the relative difficulty of the examination.

Because of the fact that in schools where departmentalization exists each pupil is marked by several teachers, there is unusual need for a coordination of the marking of members of the faculty so that marks of different teachers will indicate about the same degree of effort and achievement. Studies of marks in various schools have shown that in a given school one teacher may assign so many more high marks and so many fewer poor marks than another teacher assigns to the same pupils that the B of one teacher is equivalent to a C or an A of another. Various means have been employed to remedy this undesirable condition. Among the best is the practice of basing the distribution of marks on what is frequently called the normal distribution, or normal curve, though there still exists much misunderstanding with respect to the merits of this practice and the technique of its use.

There should be agreement on whether marks are to represent educational status and total attainment at the time of the marks or whether they are to represent progress during the period for which the marks are being given. Information about the significance of marks should go to students and their parents on the report form.

FUNDAMENTALS OF NORMAL-DISTRIBUTION MARKING. Space will not permit here an extended discussion of the theory and the application to marking systems of the normal distribution principle. It is based upon very sound fundamental principles, although the applications of these principles by teachers in many instances are not sound or desirable. Investigations have shown that intellectual abilities, aptitudes, and educational attainments, as well as many other qualities or characteristics of human beings, have a tendency to be distributed among people with a large number of individuals in the middle of the distribution; as deviation from the middle increases, the number of individuals represented decreases, so that there are very few at the extremely low levels and the extremely high levels of abilities and attainments. Because this distribution is found normally in scores and measures of a very large number of human traits, especially abilities, it has been called the normal distribution.

When one represents in a graph the distribution of various mental abilities among people that are more or less representative of the population, the result is a bell-shaped curve—the curve of normal distribution. As the people tend to be nonrepresentative, the measures of their ability and attainments tend to deviate from the normal-distribution curve. For example, in a group that is composed largely of youngsters with I.Q.'s below 95 and youngsters with I.Q.'s above 105, test scores of their ability, achievement, and aptitude will tend to be grouped toward the ends of the graph, resulting in two peaks with a dip in the middle.

Measures of ability, aptitude, and achievement in groups of 25 to 30 individuals (groups which are similar to typical secondary-school sections) tend to be distributed more in the fashion of the normal-distribution curve than in any other characteristic type of distribution curve; the presumption is therefore that achievement will be distributed somewhat after the fashion of normal distribution. Measures of achievement in small groups of 10, 12, or 15 youngsters are very likely to deviate materially from the normal distribution. However, it is very unlikely that the abilities or achievements of these youngsters are very superior or very inferior, unless they have been selected to constitute a group that is very superior or very inferior in native ability.

The misunderstandings concerning the application of the normal curve to marking ordinarily center around the following points:

1. The erroneous belief that the use of the concept and fact of normal distribution in marking implies that the marks assigned to each class must be proportioned exactly according to true normal distribution.
2. The erroneous belief that the use of the normal curve should be confined to the distribution of marks to pupils of many classes and not applied to any one class.
3. The erroneous belief that achievement in some subjects is distinctly not normal in distribution: that is, that all typewriting students are either good or bad, that there are no excellent pupils in Latin, or that all pupils in shop work are of equal ability—no failures and no outstanding pupils.
4. The erroneous belief that the use of the normal curve forces pupils' marks to conform to a theoretical curve and thereby prevents the assigning of marks according to the pupils' deserts.
5. The erroneous belief that the application of the normal-distribution idea to marking implies a certain relative proportion of marks to each level: for example, 7 per cent A's, 23 per cent B's, 40 per cent C's, 23 per cent D's, and 7 per cent F's rather than 5 per cent A's, 20 per cent B's, 50 per cent C's, 20 per cent D's, and 5 per cent F's.

IMPROVING AND ADMINISTERING THE MARKING SYSTEM. Every department head and principal should study the marks assigned in his department or school. Very often this duty may well be assigned to a committee for study and report in group conferences. Unless the distribution of the marks of the various members of the staff has in the natural course of events come to approximate normality, as it often does, the peculiarities of the situation should be studied closely with a view to changes in the marking practices. If it is decided that the reforms needed in the marking of the school call for a change to another plan, the principal should not only familiarize himself thoroughly with the theory and practice of the new plan but should also spend some time in orienting his teachers thoroughly to it, since practice has shown that a change in marking is easily misunderstood.

From time to time, probably about once a year, the distribution of marks by various teachers and departments should be made the subject of study. Teachers whose marks vary consistently from the plan may be asked to account for the deviations, and effort may be made to convince them of the fairness and the desirability of uniform standards throughout the school.

Other types of peculiarities should also be studied: for example, the tendency to base marks upon factors not a part of the marking system as agreed upon or prescribed for the school (such factors as attendance, effort, or others not essentially a part of school achievement) and the tendency to favor pupils in more advanced classes over younger pupils.

It should be impressed upon teachers that the final marks in courses should bear a close relationship to those assigned at the conclusion of six-week or monthly periods. It is difficult for parents to understand why a pupil who has been receiving passing marks for the greater part of his work in a semester or year should be given a final mark of failure.

THE PERCENTAGE OF FAILURES. Neither the normal-distribution nor any other plan of marking enables one to decide definitely what constitutes a reasonable percentage of pupils who should fail. Nor are there available any scientific data that will justify placing the failing mark at any given point or the percentage of failures at any given number. In recent years there has been a strong trend to the practice of failing few pupils, especially in required subjects, and the general average in most high schools does not exceed 5 per cent. It would seem that much could be said for failing no pupils who stay in a course to the end of the semester if some form of weighting credits according to quality were employed, so that those of poorest achievement would be given less than full credit for their work (perhaps one-half normal credit) and others of better performance would be given full credit.

If unusually large percentages of pupils or no pupils fail, the reasons should be studied and ascertained in so far as is possible; efforts should be made at readjusting courses of study, finding better methods of instruction, or adjusting marking practice. It has been found to be much better if committees of teachers are employed to study the distribution of marks by each individual teacher and by each department, rather than if the study is made in the principal's office by the principal or assistant principal.

Reporting and Recording of Marks. The variety of effective methods and forms used for reporting marks by the instructors to the central office and recording them on report cards and in the office is so great as to defy classification. A most effective procedure calls for a form which may be referred to as a section-mark sheet. A portion of this form, sufficient for illustration, is shown on page 398.

If desired, provision for reporting personality and social adjustment, attendance data, class standing, or final-examination marks may be made by substituting appropriate column headings for "Citizenship" and "Industry," or by providing additional columns.

These class-section sheets should be kept on file in the office until a few days before the close of each marking period, when they should be delivered to the appropriate instructors with instructions to make the appropriate entries and return to the office on or before a given date. As soon as enough of these sheets arrive in the office, clerical help may be employed in entering the marks upon the report cards of the pupils.

The data on this form:

1. Provides a record of the work covered by various sections, with the names of the pupils in each section, so that a record of the curricular materials to which any pupil has been exposed is always available.
2. Provides an office record of pupils' marks other than the final mark, from which record duplicate report cards may be prepared when necessary.
3. Provides a convenient source of data for checking up on the marks assigned by teachers.

At the end of the semester the section-mark sheets should be filed as a permanent record of curricular materials.

Marks in Grouped Sections. A perplexing problem is that of deciding upon what basis the marks will be distributed to students in sections of bright students, in sections of slow students, and, indeed, in sections of other students, when ability grouping is being employed. If something like normal distribution is employed in each of the sections, it is obvious that students of less ability are given an advantage and that students of greater ability are penalized. For this reason it seems logical that most students in the sections for more capable individuals should receive grades of A and B, the proportion of A's depending largely upon the basis of selectivity employed when the students were selected; many students in the sections of less capable students should receive D's, E's, and F's,

Form 11

SECTION-MARK SHEET

Class Subject ______ Section ______ Instructor ______

Schedule Period ______ Year ______ Semester ______

Name of Pupil	1st Period			2d Period			3d Period			Final Examination	Final Mark		
	Subject	Citizenship	Industry	Subject	Citizenship	Industry	Subject	Citizenship	Industry		Subject	Citizenship	Industry
1. ______													
2. ______													
3. ______													

[Etc., to 35 or 40]

Summary:	A	B	C	D	E	Inc.	Total
Number of marks							
Percentage of pupils . .							100%

Work covered and text used during semester:

______

______

______

the number receiving the lowest grades again to be determined by how carefully the students were selected. Of course, in both the sections for bright students and the sections for less capable students there will be a considerable number receiving C's; also, occasionally a student in a slow section may receive a B and a student in a bright section receive a grade lower than a C.[2]

THE USE OF STANDARD ACHIEVEMENT TESTS. When teachers wish to use standard achievement tests in determining marks, the principal, the assistant principal, a head of department, or preferably a director of testing or a psychometrician (if there is one available) should render assistance to teachers in selection and interpretation of tests. This responsibility in connection with subject-matter tests is not a great one. However, the administration and interpretation of any test other than those used for determining students' subject-matter achievement should be approved and closely supervised by the principal or someone designated by him. This is particularly important in the use of aptitude tests, general-intelligence and academic-ability tests, sociometric tests or devices, personality-rating devices, and interest inventories.

TEACHERS' RECORDS. It has been found desirable in most schools for teachers to be furnished with bound classbooks in which they record for each student in each class all the more important grades, such as test scores, marks on papers, tests, and examinations, and final course grades for the semester or the year. These classbooks should be collected at the end of the school year and stored for the future reference of the central offices. There will be occasions in every school when it will be desirable to go back into these records, particularly in the cases of individual students who claim that errors have been made or who have been given grades of "Condition" or "Incomplete" and in cases where investigations of marks of various teachers are being undertaken. In these classbooks there should also be kept records of absence and of the receipt of admission slips showing excused absences.

3. Records and Reports of Students' Achievement

PERMANENT CUMULATIVE RECORDS. In every school there should be provided and kept a file of permanent records bearing a complete statement of the credits and final marks of every pupil for every subject. These records should be card files or files of the loose-leaf ledger type. There should be a card or page for each individual pupil. The card should provide spaces for recording: the title of every subject taken by the pupil, the final-semester mark, the amount of credit earned, and the year in

[2]In some schools, e.g., Clover Park High School of Tacoma, Washington, H is used to designate very outstanding achievement of students in sections of very bright students.

which the subject was taken; subject-achievement, intelligence, aptitude, and other test scores; health records; records of participation in extracurricular activities; records of employment; interest and vocational preference records; citizenship and personality ratings; and the method by which the pupil has finally withdrawn—for example, graduation, expulsion, suspension, transfer to another school, or withdrawal without transfer. In recent years there has been a tendency to begin the records in the elementary school and to pass them along with the student to junior high school and then senior high school.[3]

Credits earned in any other school should be entered in ink of a different color and the name of the school entered in an appropriate place. Permanent-credit cards should be filed in separate active and inactive files. It is convenient to maintain two types of inactive files, one for graduates and one for students who have not graduated. The active file should be subdivided into year or semester classes. The inactive files of nongraduates may be grouped in periods of five or some other number of years. Files of graduates should be arranged by years or classes of graduation. All files should be kept in alphabetical order. If desired, the standard-test record, the activity record, or both may be printed on the reverse of the permanent-credit card.

GRADES AND DIPLOMAS. It has been repeatedly suggested that since the percentage of students who fail has become so small (in many schools the percentage is approaching zero) there should be at least two kinds of diplomas: (1) the so-called earned diploma for those who really reached a fair degree of mastery of the subjects, perhaps those who acquired the required number of units for graduation with an average grade of C+; and (2) for those whose average was no better than straight C, a diploma which in reality would be a certificate attesting to attendance for four years and a reasonable degree of citizenship. This plan of separating the sheep from the goats by awarding different kinds of diplomas has been tried in some schools and has usually been soon abandoned because of the development of very serious complications. Parents whose youngsters got the inferior type of diploma were quick and aggressive in their protests at what seemed to them unfair discrimination.

In some schools each diploma carries on the back of it a transcript of the credits and the grades made in the school. There is very much to recommend this procedure, and it seems surprising to the author of this volume that not more schools have awarded diplomas with such transcripts. Some schools employ the commendable practice of including also a brief statement of the student's participation and leadership in extracurricular activities.

[3]Excellent permanent cumulative-record forms may be purchased from the National Association of Secondary School Principals at very reasonable prices.

Reports to Parents. In recent years there has been a greatly increased and very keen interest on the part of a great many parents in the reports that they receive of the educational progress of their children. Many parents object to a report of any type which does not emphasize a supposedly objective measure of the student's achievement in the subject taken.

Where the system has been used of reporting only "Satisfactory" and "Unsatisfactory" or "Satisfactory," "Unsatisfactory," and "Honor," there has been most generally a vigorous protest by many parents and the system has been abandoned in most places where it has been employed. There has also been a demand on the part of a minority of parents to return to the numerical system of marking, but this protest has not been thought to be significant or meritorious and has in most instances gone unheeded.

The most prevalent practice today in secondary schools operating with a nine-month term is to send home reports at the end of each six weeks throughout the school year; reports are sent at slightly greater intervals in schools operating with a longer school year. In addition to information about the courses and, in some instances, supplementary comments on such matters as citizenship and social behavior, the reports usually include a statement of the number of half-days the student has been absent and the number of times he has been late to school, although there has been a slight tendency in recent years to omit this type of statement. There has been a tendency in recent years for report cards to provide space for brief communications to parents which set forth the probable reasons for the pupil's failure to receive higher marks. There has been an increased tendency to do at least some reporting to parents by means of conference—at the school, by telephone, at the home of the parents, or a combination of these forms. There is excellent reason to recommend this procedure. Not only is it a higher type of reporting to parents and much more useful in establishing co-operative guidance by parents and the school but also it is distinctly better public relations. It is very desirable to have some in-service training of teachers in the best techniques, as well as the dangers, of personal or telephone reporting to parents.

If there is insufficient clerical help available to record marks on the report cards of the pupils, the principal has the problem of seeing to it that the report cards get circulated to various teachers. For this reason and also for the purpose of more complete reporting, a great many schools have developed a reporting system in which every student has a separate report card for each class in which he is enrolled. This means either that the teachers hand out to the students the report cards for their classes or that the teachers turn the cards in at the central office, where they are collected and placed in an envelope to be given to the students to take home. An example of this type of report is shown as Form 12.

Form 12

COLLEGE HIGH SCHOOL
COLORADO STATE COLLEGE

Suggestions For Improvement

NAME	GRADE I	GRADE II	DATE
CLASS			TEACHER

SPECIFIC REASONS FOR BELOW AVERAGE OR UNSATISFACTORY GRADES ARE CHECKED BELOW.

SCHOLASTIC ACHIEVEMENT

_______Needs to prepare written assignments more carefully.
_______Needs to hand in assignments on time.
_______Needs to prepare oral assignments more carefully.
_______Needs to improve test scores.
_______Needs to contribute constructively to class activities.
_______Needs to show more improvement in specific class knowledge and skills.
_______Needs to attend class more regularly.

ATTITUDE AND EFFORT

_______Needs to make better use of leadership ability.
_______Needs to pay attention.
_______Needs to do work consistent with his ability.
_______Needs to cooperate better with students and faculty.
_______Needs to respect the rights and feelings of others.
_______Needs to take better care of materials and equipment.
_______Needs to stop wasting time.
_______Needs to follow directions.
_______Needs to stop interfering with learning of other students during class.

BASIC SKILLS

_______Needs to speak more clearly and effectively.
_______Needs to improve in reading.
_______Needs to improve written expression.
_______Needs to improve spelling.
_______Needs to apply previous learning to new problems.
_______Needs to use mathematics correctly.

WORK HABITS

_______Needs to organize work more effectively.
_______Needs to have materials ready for work.
_______Needs to use class notes more effectively
_______Needs to use outlines more effectively.
_______Needs to use reference sources more effectively.
_______Needs to do work more neatly.

INDIRECT INCENTIVES.[4] School can seldom be made so attractive that, through the pupils' sheer preference of school activity to all alternatives at all times, all cases of excessive absence may be avoided. Artificial incentives seem to be a necessary supplement.

One positive device which may be mentioned is that of having conferences with pupils, in which the relationship of attendance to progress is discussed and the co-operation of the pupil in contributing to the record of the school is requested. Pointing out in individual conference that courtesy demands punctuality puts tardiness in a new light for some pupils. Some high schools award special recognition to punctual and regular pupils.

Irregular attendance may be symptomatic of the pupil's problems of personal adjustment. Names of habitually absent or tardy pupils should be brought to the attention of the school counselors. Procedures for close liaison between the counselors and the official in charge of attendance should be established. Although a counselor should not be administratively responsible for attendance, he should concern himself with cases of continued absence and tardiness, try to learn by conference with the student and the parents what are the real causes, and see if he can make recommendations to the appropriate teachers or school authorities. Above all, he should attempt to assist the student with the pertinent aspect of his personal and social adjustment, conferring with the parents and others if necessary, so that he may really get at the bottom of a student's lack of attendance.

Frequently, a lack of attendance is associated with such things as the following: (1) maladjustment of the student with some particular teacher; (2) fears related to grades or failure in one or more classes; (3) a feeling of not belonging and insecurity in the school; (4) a student's lack of acceptance by his peers; (5) some severe disappointment in school life, perhaps involving a love affair or a failure in athletics or some other extracurricular activity or competitive situation; (6) the development of associations with companions not attending school, who keep a student in more thrilling, if not illegitimate, activities outside the school; (7) worries or problems related to home conditions, or himself, which may make it difficult for a student to concentrate on school activities and thus lead to embarrassment in class; (8) a lack of personal attractiveness or clothing comparable to that of the other youngsters in school; (9) inability to meet the financial cost of participating fully and freely in the activities of other students; (10) a lack of opportunity both in school and out to give vent to an unusual amount of energy of a physical and social sort; and (11) the impractical nature of the content of the curriculum.

[4]See Chapter 15 for a discussion of activities of student councils in connection with attendance and tardiness.

As a means of orienting and indoctrinating students relative to absence and tardiness, the following sheet of instructions is circulated at the beginning of each school year to all students in the Classen High School of Oklahoma City:

CLASSEN HIGH SCHOOL

Attendance Bulletin

DO YOU KNOW ALL THE ANSWERS?

What should you do,
1. IF YOU ARE ABSENT FROM SCHOOL?
2. IF YOU ARRIVE TARDY?
3. IF YOU BRING AN EXCUSE FROM HOME, ASKING THAT YOU BE EXCUSED FROM SOME OF YOUR CLASSES?
4. IF YOU ARE TAKEN SICK DURING THE SCHOOL DAY, AND HAVE TO GO HOME?
5. IF YOU LEAVE THE BUILDING FOR LUNCH, AND ARE TAKEN ILL?

Here are the answers:
1. Bring an excuse from home, explaining the cause of your absence. Show this excuse to your first hour teacher, then give it to your adviser, who will give you an admit to your following classes. When each of your teachers has signed this admit, return it to your adviser.
2. If you arrive at school *tardy,* report to attendance office and sign the "tardy sheet." This is important in order to prevent your being placed on the "cut" list, and to prevent your home being called.
3. Present your excuse at the office, and you will be given "Form 11" which must be signed by all teachers whose classes you will miss. Be sure that this form is completely filled out, then return it to the office.
4. If you are taken ill during the school day, report to the clinic or, if necessary, the office, *BEFORE LEAVING THE BUILDING. Failure to do this causes you to forfeit your connection with the school;* you must in this event be reinstated by the principal before you will be allowed to attend classes.
5. If you go home for lunch and are taken ill, be sure that your parents call the attendance office, before the close of the school day. Phone 58-4453, -54, -55.

REMEMBER THESE FIVE RULES AND KEEP IN GOOD STANDING.

Co-operation with the Parents. Quite frequently, the counselor or other person responsible for solving the problem of poor attendance may discover that by pooling the knowledge and resources of both parent and counselor more effective analysis and procedure may be accomplished. Parents may very frequently furnish information and data the counselor does not have, and frequently the counselor may assist the parent with information and understanding of the situation.

In many schools the attendance is checked promptly at the beginning of each morning and afternoon session; if a student is absent, an attempt is made to reach the parent on the telephone, notify him of the absence, and ask if the student is ill or has been injured or if something serious has happened to prevent him from attending school. This exhibition of concern for the welfare of the youngster promotes good school-parent relationships and frequently brings promptly to the attention of the parent the fact that may be unknown to the parent at the time—that the student is not in school—permitting the parent to deal with the situation promptly before the student has compounded his error.

The most common means of bringing the absence or tardiness of a pupil to the attention of his parents is by requiring the pupil to present, shortly after returning to school after absence or tardiness, an application for the excuse of the delinquency. This application should be made on a form especially prepared for the purpose. Such a form should furnish the parent with information about the absence or tardiness, carry a statement of the importance of punctual attendance, and provide for a statement by the parent of the cause of absence or tardiness.

Reasons for absence or tardiness which constitute valid excuses in most schools are confined to the following:

For absence

1. Illness of pupil.
2. Serious illness or death of a member of the family.
3. Grave emergencies calling for the services or the presence of pupils at home.
4. Unusual opportunities for educational experience, such as trips and excursions not available at other times.

For tardiness

1. Occasional (not frequent) unavoidable and unforeseen delays in transportation—failure of automobile or unusual congestion or delay of traffic owing to accidents, storms, bad roads, detours, etc.
2. Occasional emergency calling especially for services of pupils before school—fires, accidents, escaped livestock, etc.

The co-operation of parents may also be stimulated by material in bulletins sent to the home which is concerned with the attendance records of the school or of groups and the relation of punctuality and attendance to achievement in school. Similar information may be furnished at meetings of parent-teacher associations. Parents may also be impressed when report cards are sent by having their attention called to poor progress owing partly to absence.

In many schools the telephone is employed as a means of reaching parents. As soon as the report of absence reaches the office, the office clerk is instructed to call the home and to announce that she is calling in behalf of the principal. She informs the parent that the absence has been noted and expresses the hope that nothing serious has caused it. The reasons given for the absence should be recorded on blanks provided for that purpose and be made a part of the pupil's attendance record. This service may be rendered as well by the roll-room or group adviser. It is more effective than the use of the written application for excuse, owing to the greater embarrassment of the parent in reporting trivial causes for absence over the telephone. It also precludes the possibility or forged or delayed applications. Another advantage lies in the fact that the parent is aware of the absence at the time that it occurs and, in cases of truancy, may make prompt and more intelligent investigation. Short letters may be sent to those parents who have no telephone. Telephoning is somewhat more expensive, but it is more personal and prevents the use of forged notes purporting to be from the parent. As a means of checking up for forgeries, some principals keep a file of parents' signatures on cards obtained at enrollment time and occasionally compare these with signatures on excuses, especially in cases that arouse suspicion.

PENALTIES FOR UNEXCUSED ABSENCES AND TARDINESS. Unfortunately, it must be admitted that positive means will not reach all absentees and tardy pupils, and recourse must be had to negative devices. Such devices include the requirement that time be made up for unexcused absences and tardiness, detention after school for a half-hour or some such period for each offense of tardiness, the withholding of the privilege of making up work missed while absent, the requiring of excuses from parents, and the setting up of "red tape" for admission to classes. In many schools a set number of unexcused absences during a given period automatically places the offender upon probation for a given period. Additional offenses of a similar nature call for suspension from school. The wisdom of such measures is questionable, since they are no deterrent to the worst offenders, who usually welcome the opportunity to terminate their school careers. Similarly dubious is the practice of artifically deducting from the pupils' marks as a punishment for absence; there are some schools in which each half-day of absence carries with it automatically a reduction of 1 per cent in term standing, unexcused absences being penalized by greater reductions. Preferable to such penalties is the revocation of exemption from examinations and similar privileges.

THE ATTENDANCE OFFICER OR HOME VISITOR. The services of the attendance officer should be employed only as a last resort. Many parents are greatly offended at the use of such an officer; also it is expensive. The majority of schools no longer have the services of such an officer; at any rate, he is effective only in connection with absences of children of compulsory-attendance age.

Nothing in the foregoing paragraph should be thought of as applying to the new type of attendance officer, the visiting teacher. This type of official, trained for his work and going into the home to discover causes of absence in a helpful way, is likely to be of considerable assistance to the principal in diagnosing not only attendance problems but many other (including disciplinary) problems, as well as the failure of pupils to achieve in school subjects according to ability.

The older type of official, now passing out of the picture, was more often than not a political appointee or pensioner—a man, untrained for his work, who often performed perfunctory and ineffective service or employed crude and threatening methods and language. Resort to such an officer puts the matter on a low plane and invites antagonism rather than co-operation. At most he should be employed only in the most extreme cases, where all other means have failed.

Records and Forms. The two most commonly employed forms for keeping records of pupils' attendance in high school are (1) individual cards and (2) group registers. The individual card, ordinarily 4 by 6 inches, is ruled so as to provide a square for each school day of the semester or year. In these squares notations of absences and tardinesses are made, usually by the following marks: – (dash), absent in A.M.: / (slanted line), absent in P.M.; + (plus), absent all day; and T, tardy. Space is provided at the top of the card for the pupil's name and the semester number. Compared with the register, the card record requires more time for making entries and furnishes a less convenient form for computing attendance data for reports to the superintendent's office. Among the preferable types of attendance registers is one with pages measuring about 12 by 18 inches, each double page of which resembles that shown in part as Form 13.

Form 13. *Attendance Record*

ATTENDANCE REGISTER

Salem High School

Semester ______________________ Year ______________________

Name of Pupil	Grade	Sex	First Month from															To				
			M	T	W	T	F	M	T	W	T	F	M	T	W	T	F	M	T	W	T	F
1. Abel, W. A.	10	M																				
2. Ash, Joan	10	F																				
3. Etc.																						

Space similar to that above is provided from left to right for five months or, if desired, for nine or ten months, thus making it necessary to write the pupils' names only once for each semester or year and facilitating computations for those periods. At the extreme right are provided columns for totals of school days and days attended by each student; at the bottom of each page are lines providing for totals of absences and tardinesses. To facilitate entry on report cards or reports to the superintendent's office, columns may be provided after each month or six weeks for subtotals of absence and attendance and there should be space at the bottom of the page for page totals. The register may also be made up into longer pages, each containing many names, thus reducing the amount of page-turning involved in locating students' names.

It is also very desirable to employ with either the card or the register notations for designating, with dates, the students who enter after school begins, those who have dropped out or withdrawn, and those who re-enter; for example, E, D, W, and R are often used as notations. Such data are useful for many obvious purposes, including the determining of the number of students belonging at any given time to the school. It is customary to drop names of students from the roll after a number of successive days of absence, the number varying with different schools from three to five days. Students returning after such periods have elapsed are recorded as "re-entered" students. The practice results in reducing the number and percentage of absences.

In some of the larger schools a number of such registers or files of cards are kept, each home-room adviser keeping a register or file of cards for his group. Except where attendance is checked only at roll-room periods, this method is not very desirable.

THE TEACHER'S ATTENDANCE REPORT. Entries on such registers or cards are normally made from attendance reports made by teachers. Common practice is divided between (1) having such reports made daily or for half-days by roll-room or home-room advisers, to whom pupils report at the beginning of each daily or half-day session, and (2) having reports come from each teacher each period. Many principals prefer to keep in close touch with absences and therefore provide for the collection of reports during each period from hooks (placed near the doors of the class-rooms) on which the teachers file their reports shortly after the beginning of the class. Others prefer to have the reports collected only at the close of each daily or half-day session and checked on that basis. In order to discourage the practice on the part of students of "cutting" study halls, study-hall supervisors should make reports similar to those made by the classroom teachers.

For these reports, forms similar to Forms 14 and 15 are serviceable. By employing the symbol T for tardiness, an economy is made possible: the instructor at the time of class may record the names of those not present, later entering a T after the names of those who come in late. Attendance reports should be printed on medium-weight paper and furnished the teacher in packs of fifty or one hundred.

FORM 14. *Daily-Attendance Report*

CLASS-ATTENDANCE REPORT

DATE ________________________ A.M. / P.M.

INSTRUCTOR ________________________

NAME	PERIOD	LATE
1.		
2.		
3.		
4.		
5.		

(Up to 35 or 40)

To the instructor. Designate the period in the appropriate column.
Designate tardiness with a T in the last column.

FORM 15. *Period-Attendance Report*

CLASS-ATTENDANCE REPORT

DATE ________________________ CLASS ________________________

INSTRUCTOR ________________________

PERIOD ________________________

To the instructor. Mark absence in the column at the right with an A.
Mark tardiness with a T.

Absence reports should be posted daily in the register by the office clerk. From these reports a list of pupils absent should be prepared. After this list has been used for posting absences and tardinesses, it should be preserved and each absence on it checked off as it is excused.

Application for Excuse for Absence. Many principals prefer to provide blanks to be used by parents in "writing excuses" or applying for excuse of absence. Though the use of such forms complicates the procedure, since it compels the student to obtain a blank form upon his return and to take it to his parents so that they may apply for excuse, it insures the statement of reasons for absence and prevents any misunderstanding with respect to the dates covered by the excuse. Parents usually prefer filling in a form to writing a note. The student should be required to obtain a copy of this form when he applies for a slip for admission to class upon his return after absence; when the form is received with the proper entries and the signature of the parents, it should be filed in the office.

Application for Excuse for Tardiness. If so desired, the form for application for excuse for absence may also be used in connection with tardiness by printing the words "tardy for" or "tardiness" beneath the words "absent from" and "absence" in such a way that one of the two expressions, "absent from" or "tardy for," may be canceled by the principal or office clerk at the time when the slip is issued. Many principals, particularly those of senior high schools, deal directly with the pupils, by passing parents except in a case of repeated tardiness. Many principals employ a form similar to Form 16.

Form 16. *Application for Excuse for Tardiness*

APPLICATION FOR EXCUSE FOR TARDINESS

Centralia High School

Name of Pupil ________________ Date of Tardiness ________________

Times tardy this semester ________________________________

Will you be kind enough to excuse my being late at class? My tardiness was caused by ________________________________

____

Realizing that tardiness causes inconvenience to others and is not courteous to instructors, I will endeavor to be on time in the future.

____

Signature of pupil

Excused } in office ________________
Filed }

Date

ADMISSION TO CLASS AFTER ABSENCE. In many schools teachers are instructed not to admit pupils on the second day after absence without an admission slip from the office. A form useful for this purpose is given as Form 17.

Teachers should be trained to consult the attendance records in their classbooks at the beginning of each class period and to require appropriate admission slips. When the admission slip indicates that no application for excuse has been received from the parent, the slip serves to admit for the day only; the instructor should insist upon a temporary admission slip on each of the following days until the admission slip indicates the

FORM 17. *Admission Slip after Absence*

ADMISSION SLIP–ABSENCE

[*This slip is to be presented in each class from which the pupil was absent; the signature of each teacher is to be obtained, and the slip filed by the pupil in the office.*]

Name of pupil ______________________ Date ______________________

Date of absence ______________________ Periods ______________________

Reason given for absence ____

Application for excuse {has / has not} been received from parent.

Acceptable ____________

Not acceptable ____________

PERIOD SIGNATURES OF INSTRUCTORS

1. ____
2. ____
3. ____
4. ____
5. ____
6. ____
7. ____

____

Principal or clerk

receipt in the office of the application from the parent. Slips of different colors, one to indicate temporary admission and another to indicate receipt of application for excuse, will be a convenience to classroom teachers.

The absence is not regarded as excused in the office until the pupil returns his admission slip signed by all the instructors concerned. This procedure places the burden upon the pupil and enables the office to check on the co-operation of instructors.

Many principals who do not desire to force teachers to take the time to sign such slips employ similar forms in which no place for signature is provided except for that of the principal or the attendance clerk. It is convenient to have this slip in two colors—one for "satisfactory" authorization of admission and the other for "unsatisfactory" authorization.

In some secondary schools students are encouraged to anticipate absence from school for more than one day and to make arrangements for keeping up in their studies during absence when possible (see Form 18). This is particularly useful in schools in which absence for several days is likely to happen during harvest or other peak work periods.

FORM 18. *Request for Leave of Absence*

Renton Junior-Senior High School

I would like permission for a leave of absence from school on (date) ______
____________________ for (reason) ______________________________

____

I promise to turn in my assignments in advance, or to make suitable arrangements with the teacher for make-up work. I understand that if the schoolwork missed by this absence is not satisfactorily completed prior to the end of the quarter, I may receive failing grades and loss of credit. I further understand that it is extremely difficult to make up the work in some classes.

Signed ____

Grade ____________________ Date ____________________

In many schools special and definite provision is made for make-up work in cases of excused absence; the forms which are given to students upon their return to school have a space for a report on the make-up work for each subject, including the dates the work is completed in each subject and the signature of the teacher in each subject. These forms are usually sheets 8½ by 11 inches. On the form used by the Downers Grove, Illinois, Community High School this statement appears at the bottom of the report:

> Make-up work that is to be written out for the teachers should be listed on this report. Pupils who have been absent one day are required to have their work made up within three days; those who have been absent for two or three days must have their assignments completed within six days. If pupils are out of school for more than three days, the time in which the work must be made up will be left to the discretion of the counsellor. All pupils who fail to return these reports to the counsellor will have their six weeks grades lowered.

5. *Other Records and Forms*

BUILDING PASS. Carrying on the work of the day in a modern high school involves the passage of pupils to and from classrooms at times other than the time for the regular passing of classes and, in addition, the occasional permission of students to spend a period in some room to which they are not regularly assigned for that period, such as the library, the laboratory, the gymnasium, or a rehearsal room. In order that this privilege may not be abused and that the pupil may not be reported as "cutting," it is necessary to provide some method of checking on irregular traffic. A most serviceable plan in common use is that of providing a form of pass such as Form 19.

FORM 19. *Building Pass*

BUILDING PASS

______________________ CHECK: *Day* *M T W T F*

Name of pupil

Period *1 2 3 4 5 6 7*

Excused from ______________________ to ______________________

Purpose ______________________

Time of leaving ______________ Time of arrival ______________

Signature of person authorizing pass ______________________

[To be collected by the receiving teacher and filed in the office at the close of the day.]

By the use of such permits teachers may be protected from exploitation by adventurous pupils; pupils may be protected from oversuspicious teachers; and the principal or any instructor, by asking pupils to show their passes, may check on any pupils found about the halls or grounds when they may reasonably be expected to be in class or study hall. By this means, principals may also check on the extent of interruption of regular classes or study hall for various purposes: rehearsal of plays, athletics, or errands for teachers.

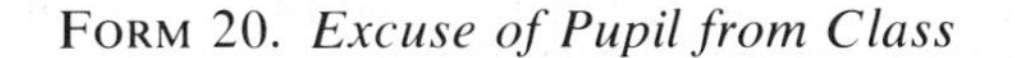

FORM 20. *Excuse of Pupil from Class*

EXCUSE FOR ABSENCE FROM CLASS

To ______________________:

Name of instructor

Please excuse ______________________ from

Name of pupil

______________ from ______________ to ______________

Class or study hall

On account of ______________________

____

Principal (or clerk)

The consideration of this item brings to mind the necessity of notifying instructors and study-hall supervisors in regard to pupils who for various purposes have been excused from class or study hall by the principal's office. When pupils are excused from class, study hall, or a part of either, the instructor concerned deserves the courtesy of a notice. This notice may well be in a form similar to the one shown as Form 20.

TELEPHONE-CALL SLIPS. Another type of form found useful in most schools is the telephone-call slip (Form 21). Since in most schools pupils or teachers are not called from classes to answer the telephone except for very important calls, the need for this form is obvious. The notice is sent to the instructor of the appropriate classroom at the close of the period. Usually pupils are not permitted to use the telephones during school hours, except in emergencies, though in many schools they are permitted during study-hall periods to respond to calls from their parents.

FORM 21. *Telephone-Call Message*

TELEPHONE CALL

For ______________________ Date ______________________
Room ______________________ Period ______________________
Called by ______________________
Message:

____
Name of person answering telephone

DRIVER PERMITS. In a large and increasing number of secondary schools students who drive their cars to school are required to obtain from the principal's office a permit to drive the car to and from school.

FORM 22. *Student Driver Permit*

ARTHUR HILL HIGH SCHOOL
Student Driver Permit

School year ______________ Permit Number ______________
Name ______________________________________
Address ______________________________________
Age ____________ Height ____________ Weight ____________
This student has permission to drive a motor vehicle to and from Arthur Hill High School

______________________ Principal

This permit is usually a revokable permit and contains information such as that shown on the form used by the Arthur Hill High School of Saginaw, Michigan (Form 22).

Usually a student is required to make a written application for a student driver permit (Form 23). Over the signature of the parent is the statement of permission by the parent for the student to drive a car to school.

FORM 23. *Application for Student Driver Permit*

ARTHUR HILL HIGH SCHOOL

Application for Student Driver Permit

Student ______________ Advisor ______________

Address ______________ Telephone ______________

License No. ______________ Driver's License No. ______________

Make of car ______________

(son)
I hereby grant permission for my (daughter) to drive a motor vehicle to Arthur Hill. It is understood that this privilege shall be withdrawn if it is abused.

(Signed) ______________
Parent

Date ______________

____
Student

1. Car is to be driven to and from school only by the owner or a member of of his family.
2. Students are not to sit in parked cars.
3. No horn blowing, loud exhausts, or noisy starting near the school.
4. No cruising around on streets adjacent to the school.

HEALTH, ATHLETICS, AND BUSINESS ACCOUNTING. A discussion of accounting related to health programs and to athletic contests will be given in Chapter 19; business administration and accounting will be discussed in Chapter 18.

Problems, Questions, and Exercises

1. Mention one or two other items that should be included in the uses and purposes of personnel records.
2. Which do you think is superior, the packet system or the card system of personnel records?
3. What are the purposes of student schedule cards and files and where should they be kept?
4. Are you in favor of the use of the normal-distribution concept in high-school marking? Explain your position and give your reasons for it.

5. In what ways do you think marks are not well used in dealing with high-school students?
6. Discuss the use of marks with classes grouped on the basis of ability.
7. Discuss the use of marks in terms of ability and effort.
8. What uses do you think should be made of standard test scores in the modern high school?
9. Discuss the problem and make suggestions for better reporting to parents about students.
10. What items of personality do you believe should be recorded; what use should be made of the records?
11. What uses should be made of intelligence-test scores, including derived scores such as mental age and intelligence quotient? By whom should the scores be used?
12. Discuss "A Dual System of Marks and Their Administration."
13. What do you think are some improvements that can be made in the most commonly used procedures for reporting to parents? Include personal conference and use of the telephone and letter.
14. Examine the list of factors with which the lack of attendance is commonly associated; be able to explain them and give your opinion on their relative importance.
15. Discuss co-operation between school and home in improving attendance, particularly in reference to problem absentee cases.
16. What punishments, if any, do you think there should be for absence and for tardiness?
17. What is the sound modern philosophy of the work of the attendance officer? Give some suggestions as to how he may proceed.
18. Outline for a school of a given size, let us say 230 students, a good procedure for checking and recording absences and for admitting students after absence. Make rough sketches of forms to be used.
19. For a school of similar size, outline a plan for handling the excusing of students from class for various causes.

Selected Supplementary Readings

Anderson, Harold A., "Early School Leavers," *School Review* (October, 1953), Vol. 61, pp. 388-389.

Barrows, E. F., "Grades vs. Scores: Students Prefer Best-Effort Scoring," *Clearing House* (January, 1952), Vol. 26, pp. 271-274. [Describes a system of marking which utilizes scores similar to the point systems in most popular sports and defends its utility in factual subjects.]

Bates, G. S., "A Two-Way Reporting System," *Bulletin of the N.A.S.S.P.* (September, 1956), No. 221, 68-71. [School-to-home-to-school reporting.]

Bent, Rudyard K., and McCann, Lloyd E., *Administration of Secondary Schools*, New York, McGraw-Hill, 1960. [Chapters 14 and 15 include discussion of married couples, transfers, and requirements for graduation.]

Bolmeier, E. C., "Administrative Aspects of the Standardized Testing Program," *Bulletin of the N.A.S.S.P.* (January, 1952), No. 183, pp. 62-69.

Bolmeier, E. C., "Principles Pertaining to Marking and Reporting Pupil Progress," *School Review* (January, 1951), Vol. 59, pp. 15-24. [Ten good underlying principles and two good report forms.]

Braun, Catherine H., "Attendance Officer: There's the Human Side," *Clearing House* (November, 1952), Vol. 27, pp. 141-43.
Burrup, Percy, "How to Free Teachers from Student Absence Accounting," *School Management* (August, 1960), Vol. 4, No. 8, pp. 47-49.
"Call for Halt on Misuse and Overuse of Tests," *Nation's Schools* (May, 1961), Vol. 67, No. 5, p. 136.
Coleta, Sister M. (O.P.), "Cumulative Records for a High School of 250 Students," *Catholic School Journal* (May, 1949), Vol. 49, No. 6, pp. 49-60. [States the general features requisite to a good general record and enlarges upon the procedure for setting such a plan up.]
Davis, C. D., "IBM Methods in Registration and Grade Reporting," *Bulletin of the N.A.S.S.P.* (December, 1953), Vol. 37, No. 198, p. 123.
Educational Policies Commission, "Drop-outs," *Education for All American Youth,* 1952, pp. 361-373.
Educational Policies Commission, "Evaluation of Students' Work," *Education for All American Youth,* 1952, pp. 59-80, 300-312, 345-349.
Flood, Mary Louise, "How Can the Results of a Testing Program Be Used Most Effectively?" *Bulletin of the N.A.S.S.P.* (April, 1956), No. 219, pp. 325-327. [Practical suggestions.]
Foster, E. C., "The Use of Evaluative Instruments," *Bulletin of the N.A.S.S.P.* (March, 1960), No. 253, pp. 15-18. [Interpretation of scores.]
Gerberich, Raymond J., *Specimen Objective Test Items,* New York, Longmans, Green, 1956. [Items for different kinds of growth, such as attitudes, skills, appreciations, and concepts.]
Green, Harry R., Jorgensen, A. N., and Gerberich, J. R., *Measurement and Evaluation in the Secondary School,* New York, Longmans, Green, 1954. [Chapters on each of the subject-matter fields.]
Gruhn, William T., and Douglass, Harl R., *The Modern Junior High School,* (Second Edition), New York, Ronald, 1956. [Chapter 14, "Evaluating, Reporting, and Recording Pupil Progress."]
"High School Record Forms," *Bulletin of the N.A.S.S.P.* (December, 1958), No. 242, pp. 236-250.
Holt, Charles C., "External Testing Programs," *Bulletin of the N.A.S.S.P.* (April, 1961), Vol. 45, No. 264, pp. 402-407.
Hudson, C. H., "Absences Cut 43 Per Cent, Plan Also Reduces Number of Failures," *Clearing House* (February, 1950), Vol. 24, pp. 328-330.
Kamena, Viola I., "The Role of the High School Registrar in Administration," *Bulletin of the N.A.S.S.P.* (April, 1962), No. 273, pp. 63-66.
Keller, I. A., "More Comprehensive and Significant Marking System," *Bulletin of the N.A.S.S.P.* (January, 1952), No. 183, pp. 70-78. [Argues for a dual system of marks: (1) individual and (2) comparative.]
Kern, Willis P., "Teachers Need Not Be Clerks," *School Management* (May, 1960), Vol. 4, No. 5, pp. 76-84. [Use of data-processing machines.]
LaFranchi, Edward H., "High School Marks: Comparative or Individual," *School Executive* (July, 1952), Vol. 71, pp. 51-54. [Suggests that high-school courses in any one school could be divided into two groups: those that will be evaluated and marked on an absolute scale and those in which varying individual capacities will be considered.]
Lindecamp, Charles P., "How Should the Secondary School Evaluate and Record Student Progress?" *Bulletin of the N.A.S.S.P.* (May, 1952), No. 187,

pp. 135-142. [A workshop program on marking at Garfield Heights High School and the results of the group's work.]

Manley, C. Benton, "How Should the Secondary School Evaluate and Record Student Progress?" *Bulletin of the N.A.S.S.P.* (March, 1952), Vol. 36, pp. 130-135. [Enumerates seven steps in developing a program of evaluation.]

Morrell, Radcliffe, "Are Your Parent-Teacher Conferences Worthwhile?" *School Management* (December, 1959), Vol. 3, No. 12, pp. 52-62. [Scheduled conferences as reports to parents.]

Murray, Thomas R., *Judging Student Progress,* New York, Longmans, Green, 1954. [Chapter XI, "Rating and Checking Student Progress."]

Odell, C. W., "The Earmarks of Good Marking Systems," *High School Journal* (April, 1953), Vol. 36, pp. 197-202.

Ramseyer, John A., "Effective Ways of Measuring, Recording, and Reporting Pupil Progress," *Bulletin of the N.A.S.S.P.* (March, 1951), No. 177, pp. 125-130. [A good summary of the major items of the three most prevalent types of grading used in the United States today.]

Raub, S. L., "A Testing Program for a Small School System," *Bulletin of the N.A.S.S.P.* (December, 1959), No. 251, p. 171.

Reporting Pupil Progress to Parents, Education Briefs, No. 34, Washington, D.C., U. S. Office of Education, December, 1956. [Report on practices and changes in seventy school systems throughout the country.]

Roeber, Edward C., "Cumulative Records: Plan Lifts Burden from Teachers," *Clearing House* (May, 1950), Vol. 24, pp. 543-545. [A plan for saving time.]

Schwartz, Alfred, and Tiedeman, Stuart C., *Evaluating Student Progress in the Secondary School,* New York, Longmans, Green, 1957. [Especially Chapters 1 through 5.]

Smith, E. R., and Tyler, R. W., *Appraising and Recording Student Progress,* Adventures in American Education Series, Vol. III, New York, Harper, 1942. [The evaluation procedures employed in the Eight-Year Study of the Progressive Education Association.]

Snepp, Daniel W., "Why They Drop Out," *Clearing House* (April, 1953), Vol. 27, pp. 492-494. [Eight clues to greater holding power.]

Traxler, Arthur E., "15 Criteria of a Testing Program," *Clearing House* (September, 1950), Vol. 25, pp. 3-7.

Warner, Frank B., "Pros and Cons of External Testing Programs," *The North Central Association Quarterly* (Fall, 1961), pp. 201-210. [Suggestions for improvement of the situation.]

White, M. Judson, "New Procedures in Marking and Reporting," *High School Journal* (April, 1953), Vol. 36, pp. 202-207.

Wooley, John, "Ironing Out the Problems of St. Paul's New Report Card," *Clearing House* (February, 1952), Vol. 26, No. 6, pp. 368-370.

Yeager, William A., *Administration of the Non-instructional Personnel and Services,* New York, Harper, 1959. [Chapter 13, "The Attendance Service As an Aspect of the Pupil Personnel Function."]

18

Business Accounting and Administration

1. Purposes and Principles of Business Accounting

The principal purposes of business accounting in the high school are:

1. Preventing theft and waste of material, equipment, and funds.
2. Furnishing a record for the purpose of freeing teachers, administrators, and students from suspicion of mismanagement or bad stewardship.
3. Effectively allocating equipment and supplies to departments and teachers.
4. Furnishing a basis for a budget entry.

As treated in this chapter, business accounting will be discussed in terms of the following problems:

1. Relating to supplies and equipment:
   a. Budgets and requisitions.
   b. Inventories.
   c. Records of receipt.
   d. Requisitions and distributions.
   e. Library records.
2. Relating to funds entrusted to principal, teachers, and students:
   a. Petty-cash funds.
   b. Student-activity and other student-body funds.
   c. Payments made by pupils for materials, supplies, deposits, and fines.

THE HIGH SCHOOL AS A UNIT IN CENTRALIZED BUSINESS ADMINISTRATION. In every school district there should be sufficient centralization of control and uniformity of procedure to prevent duplication, waste, and confusion, to ensure articulation, and to develop lines of responsibility. On the other hand, there should be sufficient freedom of initiative to allow for the capitalization of the personality and ingenuity of individuals.

The application of these two important principles will have to be determined in the light of the particular field in which they are to be applied and in light of the size and organization of the particular school system. It should be obvious, for example, that complete uniformity in method of instruction is not to be desired, whereas complete lack of centralization in the purchase of chalk and erasers would result in loss and waste with no compensating benefits. It is clear also that the value of centralization in purchases and of uniformity of records and related procedures increases with the size of the school system and the consequent increase in the number of schools and quantity of supplies.

The principal should co-operate fully with the central administration. If it is inadequate in some respects, two courses are open for him to follow in conserving the interests of his school and his own administration. He should feel free to make suggestions for the improvement of the central or uniform system and, at rare times, when the occasion seems clearly to demand it, to request that his school be permitted to deviate from the district system. This request should be made only if careful deliberation has resulted in the constructing of an irrefutable case for an exception.

There are two fundamental principles to be kept in mind: (1) centralization in matters of business administration is desirable and, where it exists, it should take precedence over local initiative of the individual school; (2) in the large number of schools in which a uniform organization or system of accounting forms and procedures is but partly developed, the principal and his staff should set up such supplementary forms and procedures as will enable them properly to discharge their responsibilities for the conservation and accounting of supplies, equipment, and funds.

2. The School Budget and Its Administration

THE SCHOOL BUDGET REQUEST. The principal (or in small schools the superintendent) should ascertain when the budget for the schools of the district will be presented to the board of education. Sufficiently far in advance, he should begin the study of the needs of his school for the coming year. He should survey general needs, such as additional housing, repairs, office equipment, and general reference works and other library needs. He should attempt to estimate the specific needs of the various members of his staff, including the librarian. If authorized by the superintendent of schools, he should ask each department head or, in the smaller schools, each teacher to prepare and submit a list of needs for the coming year. At the time this request is made, it should be made clear that each teacher or head should be prepared to justify every item on his list and that only in very exceptional instances will it be possible to obtain supplies and equipment beyond what is allowed in the budget, even though the budget necessarily includes provision for unforeseen needs.

The principal should study these lists, questioning teachers about items for which the need does not seem obvious. In coming to conclusions as to what recommendations he will make concerning the proposed items, he should be mindful of the following considerations:

1. The total cost of the items on the lists, as compared with expenditures for similar purposes the previous year.
2. The financial ability of the particular district, as compared with other districts: the school tax rate, the assessed valuation behind each pupil, and similar data.
3. The relative proportion between amounts requested by different departments, making allowances for differences to be expected in the light of the nature of the subject taught. Larger expenditures are necessary for instruction in science and shop work than are necessary for mathematics, English, and history; in the schools where the most modern instruction is found, however, the library facilities for the last two subjects are decidedly superior to those of the average school.
4. The probability that the teacher or teachers will make effective use of the materials or equipment involved.
5. The number of pupils served and the number of times a year the materials of equipment will be of service. For example, the expenditure of several hundred dollars for various expensive units of laboratory equipment for certain experiments in physics, which units will be employed once or twice a year by a few pupils, is illustrative of the lack of good business sense in some teachers and principals.
6. Most important of all, the probably increased effectiveness of instruction resulting from the proposed addition of equipment.

In many schools there is a desirable, though time-consuming, practice of having each instructor (in small schools) or each head of a department (in large schools) present his request to the principal not only in writing but also orally. Sometimes discussion is postponed until the principal has had time to examine the written request.

THE COMPLETED BUDGET. After having been informed by the superintendent of schools or the board of education of the maximum appropriation he can hope to receive, the principal should prepare two lists from the items turned in by his teachers, one made up of the items selected for approval for the coming year and the other made up of those items which apparently will have to wait for at least a year. On the basis of the former list, he can submit his estimated minimum needs in the form requested. This form may involve estimates by departments or by nature of items to conform to the central accounting system, or it may call for an unsummarized list of items. He should also present a list or summary of the requested items which were omitted from the budget even though they were desirable and which probably have to go over to another year. In some districts it may seem desirable, because of a practice of having all original budgets returned for reduction, to submit at first a complete list of needs. When the budget has been approved in final form, the principal should discover what proportion of his original budget he should be able to count on. With this figure in mind he is able to pare his original estimates, if it should prove necessary. He is then in a position to allot to his various departments the amounts for which he will approve requisitions during the year.

REQUISITIONING. At all times the requisitioning of equipment, supplies, and materials should be approved by the principal's office or, in the smaller schools, by the office of the superintendent of schools. Having supervised the preparation of the budget estimates for various departments in his school, the principal is familiar with the allotments to departments and other units in the construction of the budget as finally approved. He should install a method of accounting by means of which he may know at any time what portion of the funds intended for each department still remains unexpended. He should also be in a position to act as technical adviser in requisitioning, in discouraging the purchase of relatively unnecessary or expensive equipment (at least until it is certain that more practical needs will be taken care of), and in preventing unnecessay duplication in equipment.

Times without number, suspicion has attached to teachers, principals, and superintendents, usually without basis, in connection with purchases charged to the board of education. As a protection to teachers and school administrators, as well as to the district funds, a definite system of requisition accounting should be employed.

The installation and administration of a businesslike system of requisition accounting will tend to:

1. Eliminate the possibility of, and the temptation to, dishonesty on the part of teachers and principals.
2. Restrict expenditures to the amounts intended for each department when the budget was constructed.
3. Make possible careful supervision by the principal of expenditures and thus make for the correct apportioning of the available funds to the needs of the entire year.
4. Bring about closer contact of principal with teacher and department heads, and with their plans, through discussions of the needs of the various teachers or departments.
5. Strengthen the position of the principal as the head of the school.
6. Eliminate politics or favoritism as frequently practiced by school clerks when teachers make all requisitions directly through the clerks.

REQUISITION FORMS AND BUDGET RECORDS. Requisition forms should be prepared and employed, showing the date, nature, and amount of the purchase, the name of the dealer, and the department or teacher recommending the purchase. The principal should have these forms made out in sufficient duplicates so that he may retain one for his records. If there is no form in use in his school, the principal should devise such a form or, in lieu of that, a record book in which requests for supplies and equipment are set down as they pass through his office. He should collect and keep in his office, for his own use and the use of his teachers, catalogues of all dealers in, and manufacturers of, all types of school equipment, books, and supplies.

Form 24 is illustrative of the better type of requisition blank employed in many schools.

In school systems in which all purchases are made by the school clerk or business manager, the requisition may be addressed to that individual, with a blank provided for the signature of the superintendent of schools just below that of the principal.

FORM 24. *Requisition for Supplies or Equipment*

REQUISITION

Glassboro High School

No. ______________________ DATE ______________________

To the superintendent of schools:

There will be needed by the ____________ Department of the Glassboro High School the items described below before the dates indicated. To be purchased from

______________________ ______________________

(Name of dealer) (Teacher or head of department)

______________________ ______________________

(Address of dealer) (Principal)

QUANTITY	DESCRIPTION OF ITEM (CATALOGUE NUMBER)	DATE NEEDED	ESTIMATED COST	ACTUAL COST

THE FILING AND RECORDING OF REQUISITIONS. The requisitions should be made in triplicate, one copy being filed in the office of the principal and the other two going to the superintendent or clerk. One of these will be returned later with accurate information as to the cost of the items ordered, thus enabling the principal to keep accurate records of the expenditures of the various departments in the school. In those districts in which the principal is authorized to make small purchases without resort to the superintendent or clerk, one of the forms given above should be used with a statement written on its face that the goods have been ordered directly by the principal.

The copies of the requisitions retained by the principal should be filed in one of two files—that for goods received and that for goods not received. By consulting the file of requisitions from time to time for goods not received, the principal may render valuable service to teachers by checking up with the clerk or dealer on goods ordered but not delivered, when the time for needing them is close at hand.

THE PRINCIPAL'S BUDGET BOOK. The amounts of requisitions should be recorded in what may be called the principal's budget book. In larger schools this book should include separate accounts for each department. The accounts should be in two columns, one for "balance of budget remaining" and the other for entries of requisitions with their numbers. Statements from these accounts are, in most larger schools, sent to department heads. In smaller schools such a record should probably be a single account for the school as a whole, serving the purpose of informing the principal as to where he stands with reference to the amount of his budget allowance remaining unexpended. Form 25 illustrates such a record. In schools in which competent clerks or secretaries are employed, the keeping of such a record may be delegated to them.

The amounts of requisitions may be entered in pencil at the time of issuance, permanent entries to be made in ink when the actual costs are known.

FORM 25. *Budget Record*

DEPARTMENT OF PHYSICAL EDUCATION			
DATE	ITEMS	CREDIT	DEBIT
August 1 September 2 September 9	Budget allowance Parallel bars, Requisition No. 412 Playground supplies, Requisition No. 418	$400.00	 $ 46.90 112.00
			$158.90
October 1	Balance, $241.10		

3. *Storage and Accounting of Supplies and Equipment*

THE RECEIPT OF SUPPLIES. Upon the delivery of supplies to the building, the principal, or some appropriate person designated by him (for example, the school secretary or the head custodian), should examine them as well as possible before the package is opened; if they are in bad order, note should be made of this in the receipt given to the delivering agent. The principal or his agent (preferably the person at whose instance the supplies were ordered) should check the contents of the package when it is opened to note: (1) what contents are delivered (that is, to check on shortages), (2) whether contents are exactly as specified in the requisition, and (3) whether contents are complete and in good condition.

A ledger for the purpose of recording the receipt of all supplies and equipment should be provided, and each delivery should be entered. Such enteries should include the date, the name of the person or concern furnishing the supplies or equipment, a description of the supplies or equipment, and any notes that may seem desirable with respect to the three points suggested above.

These records should be kept with respect to supplies received from the central office. Likewise, records should be made of the transfer to or from the school of any supplies, equipment, or furniture which is coming from or going to other school districts.

THE STORAGE AND DISTRIBUTION OF SUPPLIES. In the larger city districts storage places and plans for the requisitioning and distribution of supplies will probably be worked out for the entire school system. In districts where no such plans are in operation, the principal should install some simple, practical system which will safeguard the supplies from theft and waste and enable him to make accounting for them.

Storage space should be provided that will give adequate protection to supplies and equipment not in use. Supplies stored in the principal's office, in a storage room, in laboratories or shops or in their stockrooms, or in the janitor's quarters should be kept in rooms, cases, or cabinets that can be locked. Keys to places of storage should be in the possession of those responsible for the safekeeping, distribution, or use of supplies—janitors or heads of departments of science, household arts, manual arts, fine arts, commercial and physical education, etc. Supplies left over from the previous year should be used before those for the current year, to prevent deterioration, annual inventories should be prepared.

FREE AND RENTED TEXTBOOKS. In schools furnishing free or rental textbooks at least three types of records are necessary: (1) a record and an annual inventory of all textbooks belonging to the school; (2) a record of all books lent to each pupil, which should include a notation of the book, when loaned, and when returned; and (3) an account of all funds received for lost or defaced books and the disposition of such funds. The first record may consist of a card catalogue, the card for each title showing the number of copies purchased for the school and entries made at the time of the annual inventory. A record book is clearer and simpler. Comparisons from year to year are facilitated if columns for successive and yearly inventories are provided.

The second type of record may be a card or loose-leaf system, one card or leaf for each pupil, showing the books received and those returned or paid for; the card is delivered to the pupil as a receipt on the annual closing of his account. However, if a permanent ledger is employed for these records, it will facilitate auditing the accounts of funds received from pupils. These records should include the dates, numbers, and names of books delivered to pupils, credits with dates of books returned, and sums paid by pupils.

In some schools, books are distributed through the home-room teachers. If so, the teachers must be instructed carefully about charging and crediting the individual pupil's account. It is better to have books issued through the store or the office.

EQUIPMENT ACCOUNTING. An accurate description of all major pieces of portable equipment should be recorded in the principal's office for future reference. In this category fall typewriters, computing and duplicating machines, dictaphones, phonographs, radios, pianos and other musical instruments, television receivers, filing cabinets, machines for use in shops, sewing and washing machines, household furniture and other equipment for instruction in household arts, batteries, transformers, microscopes and other equipment for instruction in science, projection machines of all kinds, cameras, expensive drawing sets, office furniture, athletic and gymnasium equipment, etc.

The record kept should include the trade name of the article, model name or number, serial number if it has one, and the name of the manufacturer, as illustrated by the hypothetical entries reproduced in Form 26.

FORM 26. *Form for Recording Inventories*

INVENTORY OF EQUIPMENT	Inventory Date			
1. Efficiency Duplicator – Model 4, No. 1634				
2. Superba Radio – Model 91A – Superba Mfg. Co.				
3. 6 microscopes – Model 13A, 2341, 2369, 2370, 2963, 2994, and 3465. Jones Lens Co.				

When any piece of equipment is removed from the building or returned to the building after having been removed, appropriate notation should be made and attached to the record. At the close of each school year the principal should conduct an inventory to ensure that all equipment remains in the building or is otherwise satisfactorily accounted for.

SUPPLY AND EQUIPMENT ACCOUNTING BY DEPARTMENT HEADS. The careful principal will also require the heads of various departments to keep equipment records for their various departments (as shown in Form

27) and to file at the close of each school year inventories of the more valuable supplies and portable pieces of equipment (see Form 26). This is no more than good business procedure and is based on principles almost invariably observed in business institutions, the inventory in the schools in June corresponding to the annual inventory in business concerns in early January.

Such records discourage waste and theft; protect teachers, department heads, and principals from rumors or accusations of waste or misappropriation by careless or mischievous pupils, patrons, or others; furnish a means of locating lost or stolen supplies and equipment; and provide an excellent basis for estimating the need of replacements and supplies in connection with budget-making.

FORM 27. *Pupil Athletic-Equipment Record*

ATHLETIC-EQUIPMENT RECORD

NAME OF PUPIL ______________ LOCKER NO. ____________
SPORT: Football ____ Basketball ____ Track ____ Baseball ____

ARTICLE	NO.	DATE ISSUED	CONDITION	DATE RETURNED	CONDITION	CHARGE	PAID
Pants							
Jersey							
Shoes							
Socks							
Helmet							
Shoulder pads . .							
Sweat shirt							
Blanket							

No teacher or principal should object to such a procedure on the grounds that it implies lack of confidence in his honesty, care, or efficiency in the management of supplies. To do so would only make him appear ridiculous, in view of the extent to which such practices are uniformly observed in all phases of the business world, even when most successful, responsible, and reliable bankers or business heads are concerned. These matters are part of the business side of school administration and should be administered in a businesslike manner.

Those phases of supply-accounting which involve payments by pupils will be discussed in the next section as one of the types of situations calling for the accounting of intraschool funds.

Accounting for School Equipment Furnished to Pupils. For shop, household-arts, commercial, athletic, physical-education, and other departments in which equipment and supplies are lent or sold to pupils, there should be carefully kept adequate records of the nature and amounts of supplies and equipment issued and similar data relative to supplies or equipment returned. Form 27 is a practical form for a card-catalogue record of athletic equipment issued.

Inventory at the Time of Taking Over a New School. Upon taking over the responsibility for a new school, a principal should never fail to take an inventory of all equipment and funds turned over to him. If his predecessor has kept an inventory book, it should be verified and any discrepancies noted and reported to the superintendent of schools, in order that disappearance of any equipment may be charged to the proper administration. If no such record is available, an inventory should be taken at once. In the case of funds, receipts should be given to the preceding principal or treasurer in duplicate, and he should be asked to return one with his signature as a memorandum.

4. Financial Accounting

The problems of financial accounting involved in secondary-school administration are various and may be classified as belonging to one of two types: (1) those which are problems of the whole school system or those which are so completely removed from the immediate administration of the high school that they are not problems of the principal or his staff; and (2) those which are essentially problems of the immediate administration of the school. In the latter category are the following problems:

1. Those associated with accounting for petty school funds which are not deposited with the treasurer of the board of education—for example, collections, funds resulting from entertainments, and library fines and fees.
2. Those associated with accounting for funds collected for supplies and materials of instruction in various departments, particularly in household-arts, manual-arts, and art departments.
3. Those associated with accounting for funds of the student-body or student-organization activities.

It is the principal's responsibility to see that funds of these three types are systematically accounted for by a system which will permit easy, objective auditing. In no instance should the management of any fund falling in any of the types given above be carried on without adequate accounting, consisting of a complete, detailed record of all receipts and expenditures. No principal, teacher, or pupil should be placed in the position of not being able to account adequately for every penny of any fund or of not being subject to an objective auditing of any funds in his care.

Funds Entrusted to the Principal. The principal should maintain an account of all receipts and expenditures in connection with any funds in his care. These records should show separately each amount received, with the date of receipt, the person or organization from whom received, and the occasion for the receipt of the amount. They should also show the amount of each expenditure, to whom paid, the purpose or object of payment, and the date. The principal should insist upon being able to render a statement of such funds once a year and, if they total any significant amount, upon having his account audited and approved, such audit and approval to be recorded in his account book.

Moneys Collected by Teachers. The principal should insist upon similar accounts from all teachers or department heads to whom any moneys are paid or entrusted in connection with the sale of books, materials, or supplies. These also should be audited annually and the audits properly recorded. The principal should either specify or examine and approve the accounting systems employed. A good type of record system provides a card for each individual pupil in each class where supplies and equipment are charged to pupils. On such a card should be entered all charges for supplies, the dates, the nature of the supplies, and all credits for supplies returned and payments made by pupils for any purpose, showing from whom received, for what, and to whom paid.

It is much more satisfactory in larger schools that all moneys paid on such accounts be paid to the chief high-school clerk, who issues receipts to be presented to the instructor in charge. When this is done, it is perhaps better for instructors to use as records of payments made by pupils slips which may be made in duplicate, rather than cards. The duplicate, upon which the amount due to the school will appear, is then presented by the student to the clerk along with a payment to cover the amount. The use of such a plan relieves the instructor of the responsibility of carrying and accounting for money paid in by pupils. The clerk is required to keep such an adequate ledger of receipts and disbursements as will facilitate ready summaries by departments of amounts paid in, as well as a ready reference to payments made by any pupil or pupils.

Problems Related to Tuition. In many high schools there are students attending who do not live in the district and who are required to pay tuition. While the amount of tuition to be paid for attendance in high school is always determined by the board of education, usually upon the recommendation of the superintendent of schools, the high-school principal should be prepared to furnish information concerning the costs per student for his instruction. Basic per-student instructional costs may be fairly easily determined by dividing by the number of students enrolled the total budget for teaching, counselling, and other personnel and expenditures for supplies, plus a prorated amount for supervisory costs of service from the general city administrative and supervisory offices and costs for permanent instructional equipment. A fairly accurate estimate of total cost may be made by including also costs of repairs, replacements, custodial and secretarial help, fuel, insurance, and depreciation on the building.

A second type of responsibility is that of seeing to it that the nonresident students attending the schools have paid their tuition. Procedures commonly followed are: (1) to have the payments made at stated intervals, usually at the beginning of the semester, at the general administrative offices and (2) to have the payments made at the office of the principal of the high school. Care should be taken that appropriate receipts are given and that ample records and accounting are definitely provided for. The principal should insist that rules be made by the board of education, leaving little discretion to him as to amount of time that a student may continue to attend school after the date his tuition is due and payable if it is not paid on that date. In all instances great care should be taken that the student may not be embarrassed. It is much better to discuss the matter over the telephone or by letter with the parent than to send messages to the parent about it through the student; embarrassment to the parent in the presence of his son or daughter should be avoided.

Textbooks and Instructional Supplies. If pupils are furnished materials at cost—for example, materials in home economics, laboratories, or industrial-arts shops—careful accounts must be kept for each pupil of all supplies disbursed and of all amounts paid. Ordinarily, payments should not be made to teachers. It is much better if payments are always made to the principal's secretary or to someone else who is trained and accustomed to keeping accounts and handling funds. The administration should organize a system of accounting. In addition, the administration should see that accounts are audited at least once a year and the funds deposited. Practically all schools furnish some supplies free. The majority of schools furnish no free textbooks and others supply materials at cost and textbooks on a rental basis. All these accommodations involve accounting responsibilities on the part of the administration.

If supplies are furnished free, there should be developed some per-pupil amount as a reasonable allowance. Otherwise per-pupil costs may be excessive or unwisely distributed among teachers or departments. Among free supplies are such things as paper, chemical supplies, and art supplies.

The School Store and Miscellaneous Sales. In many schools, stores are conducted for the convenience and benefit of students, supplying books, paper, pencils, composition books, art supplies, etc. Usually the store is operated on a co-operative basis, selling at cost or converting profits into dividends to purchasers or contributions to a fund. The store should be put on a strictly business basis so far as accounting is concerned. There is no such thing as the "honor plan" in business. To pretend that there is in school is bad business training and an inducement to immature students to forget where the lines are that separate their own property from that of others.

Even if stores are temporary and operated by some pupil organization or club, the administration of the school should insist upon strictly businesslike methods, including rigid accounting and the auditing of the records of everyone who handles either cash or goods. Such requirements apply to the selling of tickets for any type of event, candy, refreshments, sandwiches, and all such things. Any pupil who undertakes selling must be made to realize that he is financially responsible for careful accounting and for any shortage of funds he collects. With the development of cafeterias and low-cost lunches, there has been a trend toward banning the sale of candy and soft drinks in the school building.

REGULAR AUDITS IMPERATIVE. There should be an annual audit by a competent and disinterested person or committee of all funds collected and disbursed. The new principal should always insist upon getting from his predecessor an audit and report on all funds not deposited with the treasurer of the board of education.

STUDENT-ACTIVITY FUNDS—THE CENTRAL-TREASURER PLAN. It is most important that the principal see that every fund of any sort entrusted to any student officer or faculty adviser of any student activity is the subject of an adequate accounting system. Experience has definitely shown that the failure to do this constitutes an invitation to dishonesty or carelessness, which not only is distinctly harmful training for young people but reflects discredit on the administration of the school.

A plan suggested by specialists in extracurricular activities and employed in a large number of secondary schools involves the depositing of all funds with a school or student-body treasurer and the keeping of separate accounts of receipts and expenditures by the treasurer of each organization. The school treasurer, preferably a member of the high-school teaching staff, should be bonded. In this plan, as it is frequently administered, each organization treasurer deposits all receipts immediately with the school or student-body treasurer, taking a receipt therefor. All receipts are recorded as separate items in the account kept by each organization treasurer; numbered and signed receipts showing amount, date, and person for each payment are given by him to all persons making payments, often in the form of entries in books which are similar to bank books and kept by the treasurer of each organization.

Pupils or officers are authorized to incur indebtedness only by means of requisitions signed by the president or the secretary (whichever has been designated by the charter or constitution) and the adviser for a particular organization. The requisition form should on its face advise the person or firms to whom it is issued to file it as the basis for statements rendered to the organization or student body. It should be issued in triplicate, one copy for the central treasurer and one for the organization treasurer. Payments for goods or services are provided by means of requisitions upon the central treasurer for warrants or checks. These are to be issued only for items for which, as shown by his records, authorizations or requisitions have been issued by the officials authorized by the particular organization and its faculty adviser. At stated intervals (probably monthly) the central treasurer should send to each organization treasurer a statement of the account of his organization showing receipts, expenditures, and balance. Such a system calls for the following records or forms:

1. A ledger kept by each organization treasurer, showing all receipts of funds with dates, amounts, and the names of the contributors; deposits with the central treasurer; and requisitions for warrants addressed to the central treasurer.
2. Forms for requisitions or authorization to incur indebtedness made in triplicate, showing the date, the person or company whose goods or services are to be purchased, and the signatures of the authorized official of the organization and of the principal or adviser.
3. Forms for authorizing warrants to be drawn upon the central treasurer, showing the name of the person or the company to whom the warrant is to be made payable, the date, the amount, the purpose or object of expense, the number of the requisition, and the signatures of the organization treasurer and the adviser. These requisitions are to be made out in triplicate, one copy being retained by the organization treasurer as part of his records and another copy going to the central treasurer.
4. The ledger of the central treasurer, in which are entered in separate accounts for each organization all receipts, showing the amount, the date, the person and organization from whom payments are received, and all warrants or checks issued, showing the payee, the amount, the day, upon whom drawn, and the object of payment.
5. Forms for receipts to be made out to the organization treasurer for all money deposited with the central treasurer. These should show the amount, the date, and the organization from which received and should be made in duplicate, one copy being retained by the central treasurer as a part of his records.
6. Forms for receipts to be issued by the organization treasurer to all individuals paying money into the funds of his organization.

The accounts of the central and organization treasurers not only should be audited by a competent person frequently (perhaps quarterly) but should also be supervised by some competent member of the faculty. Frequently a member of the staff of the bookkeeping department is asked to assume the responsibility for general overseeing of the accounts and the audits and for prescribing the types of account books and instructing treasurers how to keep their books.

Such a system of accounting ensures all the safeguards of adequate accounting already mentioned and, in addition, introduces student officials to the responsibilities and procedures of business with a minimum of opportunity for carelessness or dishonesty, the funds themselves not being carried on the person or otherwise constituting a danger of loss and a temptation to divert for private purposes. In some schools provision is made for the payment of all funds directly to the central treasurer instead of to the treasurer of the organization, the former

BOULDER HIGH SCHOOL STUDENT BODY
Report of the Treasurer
Month of October, 1960

Account Title	Balance Sept. 30, 1960	Receipts	Disbursements	Balance Oct. 31, 1960
Activity Tickets	43.50	45.50	2.50	86.50
Assembly Fund	1256.23	3.00	50.00	1209.23
Athletic Association	3296.81	1039.75	1447.87	2888.69
Band and Orchestra	139.89			139.89
Band Fees	140.00	3.00	1.00	142.00
Book Deposits	51.69			51.69
B. R. B. C.	137.65		16.85	120.80
Choir	207.13	51.15	21.03	237.25
Choir Fees	144.00			144.00
Class of 1960	101.00			101.00
Class of 1961	223.13		143.83	79.30
Concessions	278.81	496.35	209.50	565.66
Cubs	227.97	47.00	25.16	249.81
Dramatics	707.98		4.60	703.38
Faculty Fund	22.11	45.00	15.45	51.66
F. H. A.	56.30			56.30
F. T. A.	28.82	6.00	7.25	27.57
G. A. A.	100.36	64.10		164.46
General Fund	1376.31	344.11	235.77	1484.65
German Club	12.20			12.20
Insurance	900.00	11.00	879.00	32.00
Jr. Unesco	237.29	40.60	24.21	253.68
Latin Club	95.40			95.40
Library Fines	61.23	35.00	43.40	52.83
Locker Fees	528.60	2.50		531.10
Men's Club	131.84		131.84	none
N. F. L.	30.90		5.10	25.80
Odaroloc	5237.90	28.00	4011.66	1254.24
Office Petty Cash	200.00			200.00
Owl	2483.77	60.75	470.50	2074.02
Rifle Club	67.24			67.24
Russian Club	3.05			3.05
Science Club	9.00			9.00
Ski Club	124.00			124.00
Spanish Club	49.66			49.66
Student Council	1001.78	365.00	530.63	836.15
Student Welfare	46.50	25.00		71.50
Trampoline Club	6.45			6.45
Vocational Dept.	1404.47		748.42	656.04
Y-Teens	317.82		14.95	302.87
TOTALS	21488.79	2712.81	9040.53	15161.07

Respectfully submitted,

Christian F. Recht,
Treasurer

issuing numbered receipts therefor in triplicate. One copy is forwarded to the organization treasurer, who enters it on his ledger as a credit against which, when duly authorized, he may issue requisitions drawn upon the central treasurer.

Types of Accounts in a Large High School. In a large high school the central treasurer keeps books for each fund and checks up to see that students follow good accounting procedures in their own organizations. All checks for any student-body fund have to be signed by the school treasurer as well as by the treasurer of the particular fund. Following is a report of the treasurer of the Boulder, Colorado, High School for the month of October, 1960. From this report it may be seen what clubs and other organizations are included in the scope of the work of the high-school faculty treasurer. In some schools there is also a student co-treasurer who works with the faculty treasurer. This co-operative system is to be highly recommended.

The various organizations should make annual statements which are similar to those indicated in the Boulder High School report. Supplementary statements should be attached to these statements, showing miscellaneous expenses under such items as "Football, miscellaneous," "Basketball, miscellaneous," etc.

Procedure Where There Is No Central Organization. When any or all organizations manage their funds separately, the same general principles of accounting should apply. It will be found wise to authorize expenditures only by means of requisitions signed by the student officer designated by the organization to be in charge of requisitions and by the faculty sponsor. All checks should also require the signature of the organization treasurer and perhaps that of the faculty sponsor and should be issued only for properly requisitioned items. Copies of all requisitions should be filed with the treasurer at the time of issuance as memoranda to support the authorization for issuing checks when statements are rendered the organization.

Event or Ticket-Sale Accounting. It may be found desirable to authorize managers of entertainments or athletic events to receive funds and to make expenditures in connection with a particular event without formal authorization for each item. Every such person receiving funds for any student activity should be required to submit a report of receipts and expenditures. He should submit a receipt for all bills paid other than by check.

The student council or other central organization (or, in the absence of any such central organization, the principal) should require from the manager or treasurer a report for each event or sale. In instances of athletic contests, debates, plays, entertainments, sales, or trips made by representatives of the school, a form similar to that shown as Form 28 should be employed.

Under the disbursements should be listed expenditures for fees of officials of athletic contests, traveling and other expenses of such officers, supplies, transportation of contestants or participants, meals and rooms of contestants or participants, miscellaneous labor, printing of programs and tickets, rental fees for costumes, halls, or fields, royalties, and other items. Disbursements should be segregated as suggested by the foregoing list of headings.

FORM 28. *Financial Report on School Affairs*

FINANCIAL REPORT ON SCHOOL AFFAIRS

Bedford High School

NATURE OF CONTEST OR EVENT ______________________

DATE HELD ______________________ PLACE ______________

Receipts

From sale of tickets ______________

From other schools ______________

From other sources ______________

TOTAL ______________

Disbursements ______________

Advertising ______________

Transportation ______________

__________ ______________

__________ ______________

__________ ______________

__________ ______________

TOTAL ______________

TICKET REPORT

Number of tickets issued	Adult ________	Student ________
Number of tickets sold	Adult ________	Student ________
Price of tickets	Adult ________	Student ________
Tickets returned	Adult ________	Student ________
Tickets unaccounted for	Adult ________	Student ________

______________________ ______________________

Signature of approving officer Signature of reporting officer

Such a form may be used both for contests or events held at home and for those held in other cities to which the local school has sent representatives. To make exceptions to the regular system of requisitioning all purchases, however, operates to create confusion on the part of local merchants and others selling to school organizations; it is very likely that employment of blanket authorization should be restricted to expenses incurred upon trips away from home. Reports on receipts of money for ticket sales may be employed separately and the form correspondingly adapted.

THE ACTIVITY BUDGET. Many schools have adopted a budget plan for extracurricular activities. As it is usually operated, there is only one student fee for all activities of the semester or year. This feature reduces the amount of time spent in selling tickets and operates to insure better attendance at less popular activities. On the basis of expenditures and receipts from various sources in previous years, with due allowance given for new activities or factors which may be expected to increase or decrease receipts or expenditures, the estimated receipts for the school year are distributed to the various activities or organizations according to their needs and the programs planned by each for the year. A portion of the total receipts is reserved for emergency or unforeseen expenditures. The officers of an organization should be warned that help from this fund is very difficult to obtain. All unexpended allotments revert to the central fund at the close of the season of activities of the organization.

The budget should be approved in final form by the student council and the faculty sponsors only after representatives of every organization have had the opportunity to submit budget requests for their respective organizations and to protest against what seems to them to be inadequate budget allowance. This often necessitates budget "hearings." When the budget is finally approved, organizations should not be allowed to exceed their budget allowances, though from time to time requests for budget increases to take care of unexpectedly small receipts or large necessary expenditures should be heard by the council or whatever central organization is provided for that purpose.

AN OUTLINE OF A PRACTICAL PLAN. Following is a synopsis of the bookkeeping and accounting system of the student-activity funds for Manhattan Senior High School, Manhattan, Kansas:

I. Accounts under the Student Activity Funds. Controlling Account, General Account, Athletic Account, Mentor, Blue M, Hi-Y, Y-Teens, Senior Class, Junior Class, Sophomore Class, Student Council, Activity Ticket Account, State Tax Account, Federal Tax Account, F. F. A., F. H. A., Music Club, Art Club, Pep Club, Science Club, M-Etts, M-Club, Spanish Club, Printing Club, Senior Memorial, Photography Account, other special accounts.

The accounts under the direct control of the principal shall be: General, Athletic, Activity Ticket, State Tax, Federal Tax, Senior Memorial, Photography, other special accounts.

II. Officers. The principal shall be treasurer of the student-activity funds. A teacher approved by the principal shall be sponsor for each pupil organization. The sponsor shall approve all purchases and all payments made by the organization, and supervise the work of the organization treasurer.

Each organization treasurer shall keep a record book and make regular checks with the account book maintained by the principal.

III. Receipts. All receipts shall be issued in duplicate, with both original and carbon copies serially machine numbered. One copy shall be given to the person depositing funds and the other copy placed on file.

All receipts shall include, in addition to the serial number, the date, the name of the person to whom issued, the amount, the description or source, and the account designation, and shall be signed by the principal or his secretary.

Organization treasurers shall issue receipts for all money received. These receipts are to be issued in duplicate and serially numbered, one copy to be retained by the organization treasurer and the other copy going to the person turning in the money.

IV. Authorization of Purchases. 1. Pupil Organizations. All authorizations for the expenditures of funds of pupil organizations shall be on forms signed by the teacher-sponsor, the president, and the treasurer of the organization. Purchase orders shall be in triplicate. One copy shall be transmitted to the vendor, one shall be retained by the organization treasurer, and one transmitted to the principal.

2. Funds Controlled by the Principal. All authorizations for the expenditure of monies from funds under the control of the principal shall be made on purchase forms signed by the principal. Purchase orders shall be in duplicate. One copy shall be submitted to the vendor, and one shall be retained by the principal.

V. Disbursements. All disbursements shall be by bank check with supporting voucher or check order.

1. Pupil Organizations. The principal shall issue checks in payment for services or commodities only upon receipt of properly prepared payment orders signed by the sponsor, president, and treasurer of the organization.

2. Funds Controlled by the Principal. The principal shall issue checks in payment for services or commodities based on invoices properly signed by the vendor or properly signed vouchers.

VI. Budgets. A budget shall be adopted for each account at the beginning of the school year which shall be approved by the group sponsors and the principal and a copy filed with the superintendent of schools.

Organization officers and the faculty sponsor of each organization shall prepare the budget for said organization.

A committee of two teachers and two members of the student council shall assist the principal in preparing the budgets for accounts that do not have officers who control them.

VII. Recording. The principal shall record or cause to be recorded under his direction all payments made in the accounting book, and make or cause to be made all necessary entries involved in each payment. The principal will file all payment orders numerically under the title of the organization or fund upon which the order has been made.

The principal shall record or cause to be recorded under his direction all receipts in the accounting book, and make or cause to be made all necessary entries involved for each receipt. All receipt blanks shall be filed numerically under the title of the organization or fund receiving the money.

The accounting book employed is to be a columnar book providing for the recording of receipts, expenditures, and bank balances.

VIII. Transfers. The principal shall cause monies to be transferred from one account to another within the activity fund on the basis of a properly executed transfer order.

IX. Bank Deposits. Bank-deposit slips shall be made in duplicate and a copy placed on file. An itemized record shall be made of each deposit, showing serial number of the receipts, organization or fund in receipt of the money, amount, and source of money deposited.

Bank reconciliations shall be made on the back side of each monthly bank statement. All outstanding checks shall be listed by number and amount.

All cancelled checks shall be filed in numerical order.

X. Expense Money Advanced to Sponsors in Charge of Trips. When it is desirable, expense money shall be advanced to teachers in charge of out-of-town trips. Checks are to be issued with supporting vouchers. The teachers, in making their reports, shall present an expense memorandum including receipts for all money paid out. Any unused balance of the expense money is to be redeposited, together with any guarantee receipts.

XI. Activity Tickets. A separate activity-ticket account shall be kept. A budget for the distribution of the receipts from the sale of activity tickets shall be determined at the opening of the school year by a committee composed of the principal, director of athletics, sponsor of the school paper and the school yearbook, sponsor of the student council, and two students from the student council. The principal shall distribute the funds in the activity-ticket account in accordance with the budget adopted by the committee.

XII. Tax Accounting. A state and a federal tax account shall be maintained. At the time of the receipt of any monies subjected to either of these taxes the principal shall prepare a detailed financial statement of the event, showing ticket count, number of admissions, base price, state tax, and federal tax. Tax money shall be deposited in the respective tax accounts. Commercial forms will be used in preparing tax statements.

XIII. Safeguarding of Funds. 1. Bonds. The Board of Education shall designate the depository for all such funds. The principal as treasurer shall procure a surety bond for the protection of the funds in his charge in the amount of the largest anticipated amount of money on hand at any time during the school year. The cost of such bond shall be paid by the Board of Education, and the bond shall be made in favor of the Board of Education.

2. Auditing. The student-activity fund shall be audited annually by an auditor designated by the Board of Education. One copy of the auditor's report shall be placed on file, with the account book, in the high-school principal's office, and one filed with the clerk of the Board of Education.

XIV. Reporting. The principal shall prepare, or cause to be prepared under his direction, (1) A monthly report of the status of each account, to be transmitted to the superintendent of schools, who shall present a copy to each member of the Board of Education with his monthly report to the Board. Monthly reports will also go to the organization treasurers and sponsors. (2) A monthly report of all funds and accounts controlled by the principal. This report shall show:

a. A detailed statement of all bills due and unpaid.
b. A detailed statement of all bills paid.
c. A detailed statement of all money received.

This monthly report shall be transmitted to the superintendent of schools, who shall present a copy to each member of the Board of Education with his monthly report to the Board.

Payment of bills due and unpaid is to authorized by the Board of Education.

XV. Annual Reports. The principal shall prepare an annual report of the status of each account or organization in the student-activity fund. This annual financial report shall be part of the principal's annual report to the Board of Education. Organization treasurers and sponsors will also receive a copy of the annual report.

Each organization shall file an annual financial account with the principal. A copy of each of these annual financial reports shall be filed with the superintendent of schools.

Problems, Questions, and Exercises

1. Make a list of all the different types of business accounting about which you think the local school and its principal should be concerned.
2. Outline what parts you think the principal should play in developing a budget for a particular school.
3. Discuss the requisitioning of supplies and the principal's responsibility in connection with it.
4. Be able to discuss how to store and account for supplies and equipment.
5. Outline how you would proceed as a principal to see that all funds collected by high-school students and members of the teaching staff were properly handled and properly accounted for.
6. Discuss the relative advantages and disadvantages of having someone in the school, such as an assistant principal or someone in the business department of the school, be responsible for funds, bookkeeping, and accounting.
7. What part and responsibility should students have in connection with collecting and accounting for receipts of extracurricular activities?
8. For a school of 500 to 1000 students, discuss (1) the purposes of operating a school store, (2) how a school store might be well managed, and (3) the lines of goods it should handle.
9. Draw up a plan, to be presented in class, entitled "Financial Management and Accounting in Extracurricular Activities."
10. What should be the place of the school secretary or head clerk in business accounting and handling funds?

Selected Supplementary Readings

Bent, Rudyard K., and McCann, Lloyd E., *Administration of Secondary Schools*, New York, McGraw-Hill, 1960. [Chapter 16, "Business-management Functions."]

Burrup, P. E., "Handling Finances of Student Activities," *Nation's Schools* (November, 1955), Vol. 56, pp. 87-88. [Identifies twelve basic principles for handling such funds.]

Flood, Elizabeth, and Laslett, H. R., "A Study of High-School Stores in a City School System," *School Review* (November, 1949), Vol. 57, No. 9, pp. 490-496.

"How Schools Are Using Mechanized Accounting," *Nation's Schools* (May, 1958), Vol. 61, No. 5, pp. 65-68.

Ivins, W. H., and Anderson, H. I., "Extra-curricular Funds Accounting in the Various States: A Preliminary Report," *Bulletin of the N.A.S.S.P.* (March, 1954), No. 201, pp. 122-126.

Julie, Sister Marie, "Financial Practices in Catholic Private Schools," *National Catholic Educational Association Bulletin* (August, 1959), Vol. 56, pp. 246-249.

LaFranchi, Edward H., "The Administration of Student Body Funds," *California Journal of Secondary Education* (October, 1950), Vol. 25, pp. 352-356.
McCann, L. E., "Practices of High Schools in the Management of Concessions," *Bulletin of the N.A.S.S.P.* (May, 1956), No. 220, pp. 46-49.
Olsen, Ola A., and Rieke, Lola E., "Manual for Treasurer of Class or Club," *School Activities* (January, 1956), Vol. 27, pp. 154-156.
Powers, L. J., "Financing With Student Funds," *Bulletin of the N.A.S.S.P.* (February, 1961), Vol. 45, No. 262, pp. 124-126. [Chapter 19.]
Ryan, L. V., "Accounting, Budgeting and Purchasing in Catholic High Schools," *Catholic Educational Review* (May, 1958), Vol. 56, pp. 306-318.
Ryan, L. V., "Appraisal of Business Management in Central Catholic High Schools," *Catholic Educational Review* (April, 1958), Vol. 56, pp. 251-258.
Samuelson, Everett, and others, "Financial Accounting from School Activities," *Office of Education Bulletin* (1959), No. 21. [A very thorough treatment.]
Stevens, H. John, "An Easy Way to Keep Textbook Records," *School Management* (September, 1960), Vol. 4, No. 1, pp. 76-78.

19

Physical and Health Education and Athletics

1. Physical Education

PROVIDING APPROPRIATE LEADERSHIP. The first obligation of the administration should be to select well-qualified persons to direct and teach in the physical-education program. Because of the peculiar interests of the adolescent, his tendency toward hero worship, and his impressionable irresponsibility, the coach or physical-education teacher can have a very strong influence, not only on the pupils in his immediate classes but also upon the youth of the entire community.

It is important that the physical-education teacher be adequately trained in his subject-matter field at a recognized and approved teacher-training institution. Coaches or other persons not adequately prepared in physical education should not be given responsibilities for physical-education and health-education duties and activities or coaching assignments.

PHYSICAL-ACTIVITY CLASSES. Physical-education activity classes should be learning, not merely exercise, periods. A wide range of activities should be offered to meet the needs and interests of each of the students. There should not be an annual repetition of activities; progression should be offered in activities as well as in a variety of sports. Instruction and participation should be provided in sports in which students may develop interest and skills that will continue to meet leisure and exercise needs after the students have completed their schooling; also there should be provision for activities that meet more immediate physical, emotional, and social needs.

Factors which should determine class size are the type of activity, the facilities, the characteristics of pupils, and the competency of the instructor. The same principles that govern the size of academic classes should obtain in physical education. If many more than 35 pupils are permitted in class, activity will need to be restricted to formal exercise or free play, little individual attention can be given, and the teacher can only act as an organizer or supervisor. As class size increases, more restrictive organization is required, with less opportunity for individual development and expression. If the class is to serve properly as an instruction period and attention is to be focused on the individual, class enrollment must obviously be limited. Classes in remedial or corrective activities probably should be restricted to not more than 20 pupils.

Periods of less than 45 minutes, during which students must undress, bathe, and dress, are too short to permit anything more than intensive exercise. Periods of at least 50 minutes are recommended. In senior high school, physical-education classes should meet at least two periods a week; in junior high school, such classes should meet at least three times a week; and when the junior high school operates on a day of seven periods, physical-education classes might well meet daily.

Classification of Pupils and Individual Needs. Pupils are not sufficiently homogeneous with respect to needs and interests to be assigned at random for the purposes of physical education. The following types of classification are frequently used:

1. *Sex.* Interests, as well as capacities and abilities, of boys and girls are so different that few schools have boys and girls in the same classes.
2. *Height and Weight.* In some schools larger boys are classified together and smaller ones together. This plan is subject to the limitation that pupils of the same size may not necessarily be of the same physiological maturity.
3. *Tests of Skills.* Perhaps the best criterion is a test or rating of motor skills and athletic ability, with age and size as subsidiary criteria. Several batteries of performance tests are available for this rating.
4. *Grade in School.* In order to avoid conflicts in scheduling, it is desirable that students in each physical education class be of the same grade.

One of the most important contributions to modern practice in physical education is the tendency to study the individual pupil for physical defects and limitations, recommending to him remedial exercises or prescribing certain types of activity likely to be profitable to him. For this, medical-examination results are useful.

Physical Fitness as a Goal. In recent years much attention has been given to data which seem to indicate strongly that young men in the United States do not possess physical fitness comparable to that of previous generations. These data are stressed in the unfavorable comparisons made between physical fitness in the United States and that in certain other countries, particularly Russia.

There is fairly general agreement that the physical fitness of young people in the United States has declined in recent years. The American Association of Health, Physical Education, and Recreation, a department of the National Education, and Recreation, a department of the National Education Association, issued in 1958 the AAHPER Youth Fitness

Test, which includes a manual and a record card with the following items: age, height, weight, grade, pull-ups (boys), modified pull-ups (girls), sit-ups, shuttle run, standing broad jump, 50-yard dash, softball throw, 600-yard run-walk, and three types of swimming tests. There is room on the card to record the appropriate scores and percentile range, as well as a graph upon which a profile record may be drawn.

Athletic Competition as Physical Education. Under sound leadership athletic competition may provide opportunity for rich educational experiences in leadership, followership, co-operation for a common goal, reaction to victory and defeat, and physical, mental, and emotional adaptation and adjustment in the face of adverse conditions.

Athletic competition should be made available to all boys. This can be accomplished by providing competition in more sports, as well as by encouraging participation in "B" squads, junior varsities, class teams, lightweight contests, and intramural competition. If more competition in more sports is provided, more individuals will have the opportunity to learn through doing and there will be less probability of the exploitation of a given team, player, or coach by a sometimes uninformed, inconsiderate, and demanding public. It is obvious that qualified leadership and adequate facilities and equipment should be provided for these activities.

Excusing Students from Physical Education. If well-trained instructors are available, no pupil should be excused from all physical-activity classes. Adapted or restricted activities should be included in the activity program; those unable to participate in normal activities should, after consultation with nurse or physician, be assigned to activities adapted to their needs. It may well be that the handicapped child will benefit most from physical education, provided that the activities offered are those that can help the exceptional child to overcome his difficulties. This may be particularly true as we learn through more effective health programs to recognize conditions due to rheumatic fever, poliomyelitis, general debility, and convalescence. To excuse athletes, bandsmen, or members of ROTC units from physical-education classes may deprive them of a well-rounded education. Members of varsity teams may well be excused from physical-activity courses, with the exception of those who need special, remedial physical education and those who need to reduce their weight.

It has been the common experience of high-school principals that a considerable number of youngsters wish to avoid physical education and are able to reason, beg, or intimidate their parents into co-operating with them in a plan to avoid required physical-education courses. There have been several common trends in practice that can be recommended for dealing with this situation. One is that schools have students report to the school physician, if one is available, rather than to the family doctor.

The second and growing practice is to send the student to his physician with a blank form similar to that shown as Form 29, which does not require a choice between nonparticipation and full participation.

FORM 29

EMPORIA CITY SCHOOLS

The physical-education program is planned to promote recreational and social interests as well as physical development.

NOTE. A screening examination by the physician will be accepted by the school, but a complete physical is recommended.

Discuss this with your physician. Type of examination: Screening ____ Complete physical ____

NAME ________ ADDRESS ________ BIRTH DATE ________ GRADE ________

Have you had a successful smallpox vaccination? ____ (year); typhoid inoculation? ____ (year)

Nutrition: Good ____ Fair ____ Poor ____ Skin and scalp ________

Nose and throat ________ Glands ________

Heart ________ Lungs ________

Spine or other orthopedic defect ________ Nervous disorders ________

Hernia ________ Other defects ________

Recommendations for medical care ________

____

Please check he group or groups of activities which this pupil's physical condition would permit him to participate in.

____ REGULAR PROGRAM: Gymnastics apparatus, touch football, tackle football, soccer, basketball, track and field, volleyball, tumbling, swimming, diving, tennis, social dancing, boxing, wrestling, water polo, relays, rope climbing, softball, and teniquoits.

____ MODERATELY ACTIVE: Horseshoes, table tennis, badminton, paddle tennis, casting, golf putting, archery, foul shooting, bowling, hiking.

____ MODIFIED ACTIVITIES: Dartball, shufflboard, individual calisthenics.

Remarks ________

____

Date ________ ________

Examining physician

Rather, it requests that the physician recommend the type of program which the pupil's physical condition would permit him to participate in. Surely there are very few students who could not participate at least in dartball, shuffleboard, or some form of individual calisthenics especially adapted to cripples or those needing special treatment. Such a form, indicating the physician's recommendation, might well be employed for each student enrolled in physical-education classes of any kind.

The difficulty with this approach is that in recent years there has been a great shortage of doctors and physicians and, therefore, they are extremely busy. Also, because of the trebling and quadrupling of doctors' fees, many youngsters find that their parents do not wish them to consult a doctor. In these instances if the local board of education has approved compulsory physical education, the person on the school staff best qualified to judge whether the student can participate in strenuous activities. limited activities, or very modified activities should make a recommendation; the student should be held responsible for attendance until such a time as the student has gotten a report from his physician.

The principal, the adviser, the coach, and the instructor in physical education should always take great care to see that students with certain types of limitations, particularly heart weakness, hernia, and spinal or other orthopedic defects, are definitely excluded from those types of physical activities which would be a hazard for them. For example, to permit a boy with any one of certain kinds of heart difficulties to play basketball on a gym floor, whether on a regular team or not, is distinctly dangerous to the student. It is an unethical practice on the part of the school and officials, one which is likely to bring down a great deal of criticism upon the principal and other officials if the youngster suffers a serious heart attack, particularly if it should prove to be fatal.

There are certain religious sects which have conscientious objections to physical education on what they believe to be religious grounds. Exceptions to the rule of compulsory physical education may well be made in the cases of children who belong to such religious groups, but in each instance a parent should be required to fill out a form or to write a letter requesting an excuse for the student in question.

First Aid. Several individuals should be located on the staff of every high school who have had training in various types of first aid, including resuscitation; they should be designated as individuals who would render first aid or take charge of emergency situations occuring to students on the campus and on trips away from the campus for which the school has responsibility and authority.

There must be some plan in schools in some sections of the country for finding very quickly the safest place accessible to each student at any time of the day for shelter against raids from the air, including the dropping of atomic bombs; there must also be information given and leaders designated not only for the quick transfer of students to places of shelter but also for the rescue work which is to be carried on after the raid has passed.

It is particularly important that the students have instructions for action in emergencies and that the staff members know their responsibilities for handling situations in case of a fire[1] or panic in a room containing a large number of youngsters, such as the auditorium or gymnasium. All students should be taught, preferably before reaching the eighth grade, the fundamentals of first aid.

It is also desirable in most communities today that the high-school students be organized and instructed in taking care of community disasters, including, of course, military disasters as well as such things as floods, storms, or a large community fire. Wherever community organization is present, the school should be part of the organization rather than completely independent of it. At least there should be liaison with the rest of the community; co-ordination and co-operation should be planned for in advance.

[1]See Chapter 22 for a discussion of fire drills and alarms.

2. *Health Services*

PLACE OF HEALTH SERVICE IN SECONDARY EDUCATION. In addition to education for health in special classes for that purpose, as well as in classes in science, home economics, and other subjects, there have been developing in the last several decades a greater variety and number of special health services. These services include medical and physical examinations, immunization services, school-nurse service, and medical and dental service.

The variety, amount, and quality of health service naturally vary with the size of the school and with the financial ability of the district to support the school. They also vary with the relative modernness or conservatism, and somewhat with the political affiliations, of the people of the individual community. It seems quite clear that whether or not the trend be regarded as socialistic, society, through its schools as well as through other agencies, is tending to render more health service to young people. This seems particularly desirable and necessary in view of the shortage of physicians and surgeons in the country, the great increase in their charges, and the increase in costs of hospital service.

It has become increasingly clear that society has its choice of either providing for better health education and health services or paying greater costs for not doing so in the form of illness, loss of work, decreased physical capacity for production, delinquency, and crime. In addition, it is also increasingly clear that the defense needs of the country cannot be served by health services during the brief period of compulsory military training or draft service. Since future wars will be fought by entire populations, it is not only sensible but imperative that the health and physical well-being of the young people of the schools be protected and developed as far as possible from an early age through adolescence.

CO-OPERATION WITH COMMUNITY HEALTH AGENICES. While the schools are somewhat independently rendering more and more specific health services, there should be developed co-ordination and liaison between the school services and other health services of the community, particularly those of the city and county health units and the various social-welfare agencies that may be operating in the area. Likewise, as far as possible, it is very desirable to co-operate fully with and to obtain the full co-operation of physicians and surgeons with the community, individually and collectively. There should be active co-operation with local health agencies whenever there develops what might become an epidemic of communicable disease.

Students in school discover, in their courses in science, social studies, and physical education and elsewhere, that opportunities exist in the community for the improvement of sanitation and health, the protection of the food and water supply, and the control of communicable diseases.

As they so learn, they should be helped in making diplomatic approaches to various health agencies and to others responsible for health, such as city councils.

School Health Staff. In all but the smallest high schools there should be someone on the staff who is designated for a position of leadership in the school health program. If there is not someone especially trained in health education, it may be that a committee may perform valuable services and leadership in this area. Among the individuals who might serve as leaders or on committees are those teaching the courses in science, home economics, and physical education. The extent of leadership and authority of these individuals naturally must be in proportion to their training. For example, principals of high schools should not charge or entrust teachers of physical education, home economics, or science with responsibilities which involve specific and fairly extensive training in health education which the individuals do not have. It is desirable that all members of the school staff, including administrators, teachers, and custodians, become aware of the implications their own areas of responsibilities can have on the health of each school child.

In larger school systems school physicians, serving at least on a part-time and in many instances on a full-time basis, are becoming leaders in school health service. The success of the participation of the physician depends largely upon his sympathy for this type of service and his understanding of school situations. It is doubtful whether school authorities should ever abdicate completely in favor of a physician, even though he be a school physician.

There should be, and generally is, available to all but the smallest high schools, on at least a part-time basis, the service of one or more school nurses. These nurses may assume many of the duties for which a fully trained physician is not necessary and they may assist a physician in various ways. School nurses or other individuals with special interest or training may be assigned the responsibilities of counseling young people relative to their health problems, discussing with them the results of medical and physical examinations, and in a mild and diplomatic way discussing with parents health problems of their own children, particularly those shown by physical and health examinations to have health and physical defects, with a view to encouraging them to remedy them.

Among the principal duties of the school health nurse are that of examining children who show symptoms of illness, with a view to protecting other individuals in the school from communicable diseases, and that of protecting the health of the individual student by sending or taking him home, if that seems to be indicated, or by calling for the services of a physician. A school nurse also renders valuable first-aid service in case of injuries. If there is no school nurse, one or more teachers should be identified who can render first aid quickly in emergencies.

In an increasing number of schools there are not only free dental examinations but also free or relatively inexpensive dental services for unusual cases, particularly those in which for reasons of health the youngster needs dental service and the parents are able to pay only part of the cost for service and materials. Care should be taken that neither dental nor medical services are rendered which duplicate medical or dental services available for little or no cost through other health agencies in the community.

Physical and Health Examination. Except in the very smallest schools, it has become customary for students to have periodical physical and health examinations. This practice is followed in schools in more than 90 per cent of the districts which contain more than 2500 people. These examinations are not given by teachers, but by well-trained physicians, with the assistance of school nurses and other qualified teachers and school personnel. A thorough, meaningful medical examination is to be preferred to more frequent routine, superficial check-ups. It is recommended that medical examinations be given to pupils upon their returning to school after a prolonged absence, upon referral, or upon entering school, as well as to those who graduate or leave school for employment. Special examinations should be given to determine fitness to participate in strenuous forms of athletics.

The value of the examination will depend on the extent to which health attitudes and habits are improved and on the effectiveness of the follow-up program in treating or removing remediable defects.

Time for Giving Examinations. It is probable that medical and physical examinations should be given at the beginning of the year, in order that the follow-up may be more effective; on the other hand, local physicians and dentists have often noticed that the response from parents and pupils in attending to defects is greater when the examination is given at the close of the year, owing, no doubt, to the tendency to have medical and dental matters looked after at a time when school work will not be interfered with by absence. The difference in response, however, is not so marked in high-school boys and girls who are employed in large numbers in the summer months. Examinations given at the beginning of the school year may better be followed up with appropriate contacts by school nurses and communications from the school to parents; also the results of the examinations can be more regularly recorded. This choice of time also operates to furnish examinations to new pupils from other schools who might otherwise go through the year without adequate attention. Owing to lack of service and equipment, it may be necessary to give examinations throughout the year. However, in schools not having complete equipment, it is better to schedule examinations in such a manner that borrowed equipment will be employed for a short period only.

WHO SHOULD GIVE EXAMINATIONS? If the school enjoys the services of a school physician and a school dentist on full time or part time, as well as the services of one or more school nurses, the responsibility for planning and directing the examinations should be assigned to the physician and the dentist, assisted by the nurses. If the school employs a physician (but no nurse) and a trained director or instructor of physical education, the latter may examine or interrogate pupils with respect to matters less technically medical, such as weight, height, posture, hearing and vision defects, and health history, leaving to the physician the examination of tonsils, heart, lungs, skin, and nose, the inspection for symptoms of goiter and nervous disorders, and the laboratory tests of urine and blood if such are made. If there is no school physician or school dentist, one of two plans may be followed: (1) an arrangement may be made with the local physicians and dentists (preferably through their local professional society, if one exists) for co-operative free services; or (2) additional responsibility may be placed upon the instructors, appropriate to the degree of their training. If the first plan can be arranged, it is, of course, to be preferred. If there are no properly trained instructors, an appeal to the local physicians and dentists may result in obtaining examination services at a minimum cost.

Medical examinations may well be performed in the following order of priority:

a. Pupils who have returned to school without a medical certificate after prolonged or frequent absence.
b. Pupils referred by the school staff.
c. Pupils entering school for the first time.
d. Pupils leaving school before the next scheduled health examination. (N.B. This should include examinations for employment certificates where required.)
e. Pupils entering junior high school.
f. Pupils ready to graduate from senior high school.[2]

GIVING THE EXAMINATION. Examinations must be conducted with great care. A physical and medical examination is a very delicate matter to which many people are extremely sensitive. No person must be assigned any detail of examination which he may not by training be expected to perform carefully, with observation of all sanitary precautions. Children should be examined in the nude, if at all, only by

[2]"Suggested Standards for Health Services in Secondary Schools," *American Journal of Public Health Year Book* (May, 1952), Vol. 42, No. 5. Reprints are available; copyright is held by the American Public Health Association, Inc., 1790 Broadway, New York, New York. This report was prepared by the Committee on Health Service Programs for Secondary Schools.

physicians and under such conditions as are likely to be least objectionable to them and to their parents. If parents so desire, examinations by private physicians should be accepted in lieu of school examinations if the data are recorded in the same manner as in the school examinations and are furnished to the school as a part of its records. Although the enforcement of the rule calls for unusual diplomacy, all pupils should be required to undergo an examination, either by the school examiner or by a private physician or dentist.

Proper rooms and equipment must be planned and provided for the examinations. The examining officer should be asked to designate the equipment needed, its arrangement, and the necessary supplies.

HEALTH RECORDS. Every school should keep records of all physical and health examinations; these should be referred to on all subsequent examinations.

FOLLOW-UP OF EXAMINATIONS. The purpose of examinations is not merely to acquire data or fill out forms. It is for the purpose of improving the health of those examined. This means that there must be a follow-up which will result in the improvement of health in some way or another. This follow-up may take various forms, including the following:

1. The school may provide health counseling by a competent person to the individual student with remediable health or physical defects. Competence will depend upon the nature of the area of the counseling: for example, a teacher might discuss with the youngster such things as posture; indeed, if trained in the testing of vision and hearing, a teacher might discuss with the youngster the necessity of consulting someone who is by training and law qualified to remedy defects in those areas. Also, teachers may discuss matters relative to eating, care of the skin, rest habits, and things of the type that do not necessitate a physician, surgeon, or dentist. On the other hand, the individual who does health counseling should have sufficient background to know his limitations and refrain from attempting to counsel and render advice which should be given only by a person with professional training which the counselor does not have.
2. The school may make provision for some sort of correctional training. For example, corrective exercises may be included in the physical-education program for certain types of physical defects. Here again, caution must be exercised in seeing that the individual who prescribes the activities has adequate preparation and that he avoids exaggerating the defect in his attempt to cure or ameliorate it.
3. The school should report to parents the results of the examinations, including, of course, mention of physical and health defects and needs for treatment. After a diplomatic request by the school, the parent should be allowed to take initiative in obtaining treatment or making adjustments in the home living of the student. Reports to parents should as far as possible be made in conferences; there should also be memoranda to the parents in a form developed especially for that purpose.

4. There should be an adaptation of the school life of the youngster in cases where it is clearly indicated—for example, less pressure for scholarship in some instances, special seating of youngsters with visual or auditory defects, and restricted or modified physical-education and athletic programs. School records should be kept of interviews with parents and conferences with youngsters, of things recommended, of referrals to physicians, surgeons, optometrists, opticians, etc., and of measures taken in the school to correct physical weaknesses or defects and to make appropriate adjustment to them.

IMMUNIZATION MEASURES. To prevent the spread of contagious diseases, it is necessary when cases of certain diseases occur in the district to require that every child attending school be immunized. In some large city districts, in smaller districts in which a fairly large number of the inhabitants live in crowded sections, and in districts located in parts of the country in which smallpox is usually very severe, it may be wise to insist that all pupils be vaccinated against the disease. Immunization facilities should also be provided for and strongly urged, if not required of youngsters in the schools, at times when there are more than a normal number of cases of contagious diseases such as typhoid fever. Immunization may be provided for the modern children's diseases, but it should not be required and perhaps need not even be provided. Immunization against rabies may well be provided in neighborhoods in which animals with the disease have been discovered, but at other times it probably should not be offered. Immunization services relative to lockjaw should be provided only in the case of the youngster who has had some sort of wound which might be dangerous.

Requirements of immunization should in every instance be authorized by the local board of education *after* it has been ascertained that the state laws and court decisions support such a requirement. The parents should first be notified and then given ample time to obtain the immunization treatment privately before the child is excluded from school. Many schools arrange through the school physician or the city or county health officer to provide immunization at cost to pupils. The consent of the parents in writing, on a form similar to that shown as Form 30, should always be obtained before immunization is given.

FORM 30. *Parent's Consent to Immunization*

To parents of pupils of the ________________________________ *School:*

The school is prepared to offer immunization against ________________ at the nominal cost of ____ cents per pupil. If you desire to take advantage of this service, please sign below and return this slip to us.

JAMES F. AHORN
Principal

____

Signature of Parent

Reports to Parents. The results of the health examination should be reported at the earliest convenience after it has been held. Such reports should not be extensive, detailed, or technical but should be confined to the more important and remediable defects: for example, defective vision or hearing, undernourishment or underweight, heart defects, infected or enlarged tonsils, acne, teeth needing straightening, adenoids, goiters, etc. A simple form, such as Form 31, will suffice.

Form 31. *Report of Health Defects to Parents.*

HEALTH-EXAMINATION REPORT

Dear ____________________:

Name of parent

Within the last few days ____ was examined and found to ____

____

Name of defect, disease, or weakness

We feel sure in the interests of the health of your son / daughter you will want to investigate the matter further. Will you be kind enough to report to us that you

have consulted a physician.

are giving the child attention at home.

(Please check one or both.)

____

Principal

Mental Health Service. As a corollary to the greatly increased attention being given to the mental health of young people as well as older people, schools not only have been giving consideration to developing good mental health but also have been avoiding situations which may contribute to emotional disturbances or other types of mental disorder. In many schools there now is a psychologist available to see youngsters who seem to be emotionally disturbed or otherwise definitely in need of psychological help.

In some schools there is a psychiatrist available to whom students may be sent if there is an obvious need for psychiatric help. However, students should never be sent to a psychiatrist until a psychologist or a physician has recommended it and the parents have agreed to it. Psychiatric service is very expensive and schools are not in a position to finance psychiatric service for young people, but a considerable number of schools take financial responsibility for the first interview with the psychiatrist.

3. Problems of Competitive Athletics

THE DEVELOPMENT OF COMPETITIVE COMMERCIALIZED SPORTS. In recent decades many developments in the field of interscholastic and intercollegiate athletics have been very alarming to thoughtful educators. In the earlier days of interscholastic and intercollegiate athletics it seemed necessary, as a means of providing financial support for the athletic programs, to charge admission from the relatively small number of spectators who would come to the games. In order to increase the financial support, considerable efforts were made to interest a larger proportion of the general population in attending contests. With an increased number of people becoming interested, newspapers first developed sports columns, later a sports page, and then several pages in a sports section. This served to increase and intensify the interest of the public in competitive athletics. With increased interest there was greatly increased public demand that athletics be managed in such a way as to produce winning teams; this development has proved to be a painful thorn in the side of school administrators.

Not only have coaches of athletic teams been employed and discharged on the basis of the success of their teams but also some superintendents, in order to hold their positions or at least to avoid active opposition on the part of sports fans in their communities, have yielded to pressures in ways that were unthinkable a few decades back. In some instances the salary of a coach has been increased far beyond that of a typical teacher; in some schools it has been increased beyond that of the head of a department or even the principal. Indeed, in some places coaches are paid more than the superintendent of schools. In many schools teachers are under enormous pressures from students, out-of-school sport fans, and in some instances from administrators to give athletes grades on a level that will let them remain eligible for participation in athletics.

In an increasing number of instances football coaches backed by students and sports fans have openly defied the administration; in altogether too many instances, in pitched battle between the sports crowd and the school administration, they have been able to win their struggle. In a typical high school today there is at least one game in the season, if not several, in which the student body becomes keyed up, particularly after a rousing assembly, to a pitch which is alarming to the casual observer and which distracts the students from their educational activities. Demands are made upon team members to spend time in practice and in trips, making it impossible for many of them to carry on a high quality of work in their educational program. In addition, the betting at games has increased to the point where not only college athletes but even high-school athletes and coaches are approached in some instances to play so as to influence results. In communities where a win-at-any-cost philosophy prevails, competitive athletics indeed present a sordid picture;

school administrators have a bear by the tail and do not seem to know how to let go. State athletic associations have been a most valuable force in keeping these excesses and dangers at a minimum, but they have only been able to counteract in small part unrestrained and uncontrolled forces in local communities.

While claims have been made for the great values of competitive athletics, it seems to the careful analyst of the above-mentioned situation to be quite clear that most of these claims have little basis in fact and that they constitute a rationalization of a situation which is pleasant to the primitive urges in human beings. In some schools everything, including sportsmanship and the physical welfare of the participants themselves, is subordinated to the desire to win. Attention and financial support are often diverted from the health and physical-education program of the school. Indeed, in many schools the direction of the physical-education program is placed in the hands of coaches who have little training and background and less interest in a general health-education program. Youngsters whose normal development would call for active participation in physical sports are trained to content themselves with emotional sprees at games and pep assemblies. Claims that the interscholastic athletic program develops friends for the school are questionable. These are usually fair-weather friends who become severe critics in a losing season and who at best are interested only in the athletic aspect of the school program; they are often not any more likely than others of the community to attend P.T.A. meetings or to work for the passage of increased tax rates or bond issues as these apply to the total school program.

In addition, the efforts to obtain good material for a team have caused administrators, as well as coaches and some teachers, to resort to aggressive and active recruiting tactics and, in many instances, to ape the colleges in unethical practices.

FUNDAMENTAL POLICIES. There should be drawn up for every school system a statement of fundamental policies with respect to interscholastic competition, particularly athletic competition. Participating in developing this policy, or reviewing it from time to time, should be the superintendent of schools, the principals of the schools, the athletic directors or coaches, one or more parents, and one or more students. If the policy is drawn up for a particular junior or senior high school rather than for the city as a whole, then the committee should include the principal, the coach, one or more parents, and one or more students. The policy should be submitted to the board of education, adopted, and published; mimeographed or printed copies of the policy should be made available for distribution to everyone concerned in the year it is adopted and in subsequent years. This policy should include statements about the eligibility of students, interference with other school work, trips away from home, management in the accounting of funds, the responsibilities of coaches and athletic managers, the responsibilities of principals, assistant principals, or both, responsibility for and insurance against injuries, recruiting, and awards.

REDUCING ATHLETIC OVEREMPHASIS. In general, educators are agreed that, when properly managed, athletic competition has values that justify its existence. Educators have also in recent years become quite generally agreed that in many schools, perhaps a majority of schools, athletic competition has been overemphasized and bad practices have developed. The following is a list of suggested practices or positions with respect to practices which have been set forth by a number of educators as contributing to the reduction of overemphasis and other evils in interscholastic athletic competition:

1. Secondary schools should not participate in tournaments or in championship postseason games.
2. There should be no dismissal of school for travel to games away from home.
3. There should be no game rally.
4. There should be no dismissal of school to celebrate a victory.
5. There should be appointed committees of parents, students, and staff to evaluate and to make recommendations for each of the major sports.
6. Awards by nonschool groups should be discouraged.
7. There should be constructive effort made to build up other activities such as plays, operettas, band, choral groups, forensics, etc.; in these the mistakes which have been made in athletics should be avoided.
8. Awards should be made on the same basis as in other activities and should not consist of more expensive items.
9. There should be constructive public-relations policies and practices educating the public to the better type of athletic competition, exposing the evils and the unfortunate practices that have developed. Definite attention should be given to developing ideals and practices of good behavior and good sportsmanship, both at home and at games away from home, not only by members of the team but by members of the student body who may attend games away from home.

In recent years the overemphasis on athletic competition has crept down into many junior high schools; in many of these there is need to cut back the interscholastic athletic programs. Indeed, there are many educators, including some coaches and others trained in physical education, who definitely believe that there should not be interscholastic athletic competition between junior high schools.

PROBLEMS RELATED TO FUNDS. The problems of principals relative to the funds of athletic organizations fall into two main categories: (1) the obtaining of funds and (2) the supervising and accounting of expenditures. In recent years there has been a tendency for the board of education to assume more and more financial responsibility for all extracurricular activities, including athletics; as a result, there is less reliance upon getting out large crowds to support the teams financially as well as otherwise. In some schools, although in altogether too few, athletic funds are placed in a general fund for extracurricular activities and are distributed in proportion to the needs of the various activities. In a great majority of schools, however, funds for athletics are kept separate from the other funds. There has been a strong tendency for coaches and members of athletic teams to oppose the expenditure of funds received from athletics for any purpose other than athletics. Indeed, in a great many schools there has been a strong pressure, to which administrators have in some instances yielded, to place the expenditure of athletic funds almost completely in the hands of the student managers and the coaches, with little more than a perfunctory audit for the purpose of seeing that funds are not stolen or used for the personel benefit of any individual. The funds have been employed, in many instances, to purchase awards and gifts of one kind or another for the competing athletes. Under any circumstances, a high-school principal must insist that there be followed a definite and business like accounting system for all receipts and expenditures and that these accounts be audited at least twice a year. He should also insist that businesslike methods of purchasing be followed through the use of requisition forms and payment vouchers duly signed by the accredited officials of the organization.

Responsibility of the Principal. The supervision of athletics has been a serious responsibility for secondary-school principals. Indeed, it is regarded by many as their biggest "headache." People in the community, as well as students in the school, become much more emotional about interscholastic competition than they do about almost any other phase of the work of the school. The principal can ill afford to neglect his responsibilities in this area. Among the more important responsibilities are the following:

1. The principal should give leadership in determining eligibility requirements and see that they are lived up to. The principal must get from the coach prior to each game a list of players, which he may use in the game and see that each is eligible.
2. The principal should see that there is no recruiting of students from other districts in which there are similar secondary schools.
3. The principal should inform himself and supervise directly or through an assistant principal all trips made away from home for athletic events.
4. The principal should participate in the construction of the schedules of games for each athletic team and should arrange the schedules for practice sessions.
5. The principal should see that there is installed and employed correctly an appropriate system for caring for and accounting for funds and equipment.
6. The principal should exercise leadership in working out a plan for the insurance of participants in athletic events against injuries.

These responsibilities will be discussed in the following pages of this chapter.

COMPETITIVE EVENTS. Among the problems in which the principal is particularly interested are those relating to the competitive events themselves. The principal must play a prominent part in determining when the season shall begin and when it shall end for any particular athletic sport. Beginning practice for football a considerable time before the beginning of classes should be avoided; the prolonging of competition past the normal football or basketball season should be opposed. Over the last few decades various kinds of tournaments have been encouraged and sponsored, in fact urged and promoted, by institutions of higher education and by newspapers. These tournaments serve to extend the season, at least for the better teams, and thereby also to prolong and increase a distracting influence upon the students of the schools. Because of the increased recognition of these evils, there has been a growing feeling on the part of thoughtful educators that all postseason contests and tournaments of any kind should be avoided and that each school should refuse to participate in them.

The principals also have a very great responsibility for the student spectators in connection with trips of the teams. There should be someone besides the coaches to go with the teams on all out-of-city trips and to have the responsibility for seeing that the students behave in a definitely moral way so as not to bring discredit and criticism upon the school they represent. There is a growing feeling that the attendance of student spectators at the games away from home should be discouraged. With the development of high-speed automobile travel, the number of deaths and serious injuries which occur each year on trips accompanying athletic teams has become alarming and challenging. In addition, of course, on the day of the trip and at least one day before, there is a great amount of excitement on the part of the students who are planning to go on the trip and a corresponding amount of discouragement and depression on the part of many who are not able to go. This interferes seriously with the purpose for which the school was originally established.

RECRUITING AND ELIGIBILITY. The principal has a very definite responsibility for seeing that each student who participates in any interscholastic contest meets the eligibility requirements of the school and of the league or conference in which the team is playing. While this duty may be delegated to some member of the staff other than the coaching staff, the principal is definitely responsible for seeing that no ineligible player represents the school.

It is the responsibility of the principal to see to it that the recruiting of athletic material stays within normal bounds and that efforts to persuade young people to attend particular high schools are mild, involving no financial inducements of any type. In general, the participation of athletes at schools other than those located in the high-school district in which the students reside is definitely frowned upon and should be prohibited by state athletic associations.

College Recruiting. The school administration also has a responsibility to provide advice and information to prospective college athletes who may be bombarded by alumni and representatives of certain college athletic departments that are more interested in the contributions which the athlete can make to the athletic program of the college than in his educational development. Most colleges offer scholarships of various types to outstanding students in many areas of achievement. Many authorities believe that those students interested in the athletic activities of the college program are as entitled to aid as those active in other phases, as long as they are making normal progress toward a degree suited to their vocational interests and abilities.

However, the athlete is often lured, by false promises, excessive scholarship offers, and other flattering inducements, to enter certain colleges where little heed is paid to his educational development except to encourage his enrollment in such courses as will assure his athletic eligibility. After graduation his athletic achievement is soon forgotten, and he may find his training has not fitted him for the business and vocational opportunities that present themselves.

The moral integrity and honesty of an athlete and a college are challenged when, through some subterfuge, an athlete is given a "feather-bed" assignment or paid excessively for work he does not perform.

Perhaps the most damaging feature associated with the bidding for athletic talent is the false sense of values and the dissatisfaction developed in student bodies and the rank and file of varsity-team members by exaggerated rumors regarding aid to various athletes.

Public Relations. The high-school principal of today finds himself frequently between two groups. One group is made up of the rabid, win-thirsty sports fans; the other consists of the conservative individuals who are irritated, if not actually disgusted, at the excesses of modern interscholastic competition. The principal, therefore, has a difficult problem maintaining good public relations. He should definitely indicate his interest in sports for young people—in particular, sports for all the young people of his high school, as well as for the selected representatives on teams; he must also do what he can to appease the righteous indignation of those who still feel that schools were established for educational purposes and that the schools have become far too deeply involved in the public-amusement business. The principal should co-operate with the local newspapers in providing information about sports and games, but he should minimize the amount of other publicity, ballyhoo, and emotion-stimulating events in the school. Such minimizing may be said to have occurred in many schools where they no longer hold pep rallies or pep assemblies during the season.

The behavior of many team members and student spectators at games, especially at games away from home, leaves much to be desired. The students' dress and behavior at hotels, in eating places, and on busses often reflect badly upon the school, as well as upon the homes from which the young people come. Reckless driving of cars also constitutes an unacceptable form of behavior. Efforts must be made by coaches and principals to develop the ideals and practices of acceptable behavior. Students attending games at home and away from home should be regarded as still "being in school" and subject to regulation of authorities of the school.

Suggestions by the National Committee on Interscholastic Athletics. In recent years there has been an increased recognition of the serious problems of athletics on the part of various national and regional educational organizations, such as the National Association of Secondary School Principals, the American Association for Health, Physical Education, and Recreation, and the National Federation of State and High School Athletic Associations. These agencies, acting cooperatively through a joint committee, have studied very carefully the problems of interscholastic activity and have submitted the following recommendations:[3]

1. The program of athletics should be developed with due regard for the following standards of health and safety standards:
   a. A health examination should be required previous to participation, preferably on a seasonal basis, with annual examination a minimum.
   b. A physician should be present at all contests involving activities where the injury hazard is pronounced.
   c. A contestant who has been ill or injured should be readmitted to participation only on the written recommendation of a physician.
   d. A contestant upon returning to participation after illness or injury should be carefully observed and, if there is any doubt as to his condition, he should immediately be referred to a physician.
   e. The coach (faculty member in charge) should be competent in first aid and thoroughly versed in sports conditioning and training. It is also strongly recommended that all players be given basic instruction in first aid.
   f. In case of head, neck, or spine injury or suspicion thereof, the player should be removed from play, placed at rest, and be given the immediate attention of a physician.
   g. Every school should have a written policy regarding the responsibility for injury incurred in athletics, and this policy should be known to all participants, their parents, and other responsible adults. Arrangements should be made for obtaining and paying for medical and hospital care of injured participants, in accord with local policy.
   h. The best obtainable protective equipment should be provided for all participants, and special attention should be given to proper fitting of such equipment.

---

[3]See *1960-1961 Handbook of the New York State Public High School Athletic Association* (John K. Archer, Secretary, Malvern, New York, High School); and the *1960-1961 Handbook of the National Federation of State and High School Athletic Associations* (Clifford B. Fagan, Executive Secretary, 7 South Dearborn Street, Chicago 3, Illinois).

i. Competition should take place only between teams of comparable ability, and playing seasons should be limited to reasonable duration.

j. No preseason games should be played until players are well drilled in fundamentals and have had a minimum of two weeks of physical conditioning.

k. Playfields should meet standard requirements for size of area, playing surfaces, and facilities for safety, and all reasonable precautions should be taken to prevent accidents.

l. Contests should be selected, and rules and lengths of playing periods should be such that they will not overtax the physical abilities of high-school students.

2. Good citizenship must result from all coaching and from all interschool competition. The education of the youth of the nation fails unless it creates the proper ideals and attitudes, both in the game and off the field.

a. The contribution of athletics to citizenship—indeed to life itself—will be judged according to the contribution they make to fine living.

b. Athletics should contribute a feeling, on the part of the athlete, of personal worth, excellence in performance, self-respect, and desirable personal and social growth and development.

c. Educationally, winning is not the important item. While the will to win within the rules of good sportsmanship is an important attribute to good citizenship, there is always a tendency to overdo the importance of winning in athletics. Other important contributions are those desirable changes made in skills, habits, and attitudes of the participants.

d. Athletics are responsible jointly with education for establishing among boys and girls those standards of behavior that represent the best in good citizenship. Athletics must contribute to those virtues which are socially sound for a democracy, such as truthfulness, fair play, honesty, modesty, give-and-take, courtesy, self-discipline, courage, generosity, self-restraint, and loyalty to team, state, and nation.

3. The "ten cardinal athletic principles" are accepted as expressing the policies of our organizations, and it is urged that these be displayed in the literature of our organizations. To be of maximum effectiveness, the athletic program will:

a. Be closely co-ordinated with the general instructional program, and properly articulated with the other departments of the school.

b. Be such that the number of students accommodated and the educational aims achieved justify the use of tax funds for its support, and also warrant the use of other sources of income.

c. Justify the time and attention which is given to the collection of "other sources of income" which will not interfere with the efficiency of the athletic program or of any other departments of the school.

d. Confine the school athletic activity to events which are sponsored and supervised by the proper school authorities so that any exploitation or improper use of prestige built up by school teams or members of such teams may be avoided.

e. Be planned in such a way as to result in opportunity for many individuals to explore a wide variety of sports and to set reasonable season limits for each listed sport.

f. Be controlled in such a way as to avoid the elements of professionalism and commercialism which tend to grow up in connection with widely publicized "bowl" contests, barnstorming trips, and interstate or intersectional contests which require excessive travel expense or loss of school time, or which are claimed to be justified by educational travel values.
g. Be kept free from the type of contest which involves a gathering of so-called "all-stars" from different schools to participate in contests which may be used as a gathering place for representatives of certain colleges or professional organizations who are interested in soliciting athletic talent for their teams.
h. Include educative exercises to reach all nonparticipating students and community followers of the school teams in order to insure a proper understanding and appreciation of the sports skills and of the need for adherence to principles of game ethics.
i. Encourage a balanced program of intramural activity in grades below the ninth to make it unnecessary to sponsor contests of a championship nature in these grades.
j. Engender respect for the rules and policies under which the school conducts its program.

4. All schools shall use reasonable care in avoiding any participation in a contact sport between participants of normal high-school age and participants who are appreciably above or below normal high-school age.

Senior-high-school competition should be limited to participation in games, meets, and tournaments between participants enrolled in grades 9 through 12. Junior-high-school competition should be limited to participation in games, meets, and tournaments between participants enrolled in grades 7 through 9. These games, meets, and tournaments should be approved and conducted by appropriate secondary-school authorities.

a. All school personnel should utilize *every precaution and procedure* to assure competition in secondary-school athletics on the basis of comparable parity.
b. A significant phase in the growth of a living organism is maturity. Wide difference in maturity places in jeopardy the well-being of athletic competitors. School personnel should permit competition between teams of comparable maturity.
c. Certain stages of maturity can be distinguished and should be utilized as one of the bases for determining parity in athletic competition.
d. Outstanding features of adolescence are insecurity, awkwardness, and excessive competitiveness. One can adjust himself to these factors of environment only by becoming more mature, wiser, and more self-reliant. These are additional evidences that parents and school personnel should use protective procedures in setting up competition between individuals and groups of preadolescent and adolescent age.
e. A high-school pupil or team should not compete with members of a college or university, a preparatory school, or other schools which include postgraduates on their teams, or against any independent team sponsored by an "outside" organization.
f. A junior-high-school pupil or team should not compete with members of a team representing a senior high school, elementary school, or an

"outside" organization. This would not, however, exclude the participation of ninth-grade pupils as members of a senior-high-school team if the ninth grade was under the administrative direction of the high-school principal and if the other conditions stated above are met.

g. Appropriate secondary-school authorities consist of all legally certificated teaching, supervisory, and administrative personnel directly under the superintendent of schools. These personnel should see that the items noted above are observed.

5. All schools shall fully observe and abide by the spirit and letter of established eligibility requirements which have been democratically developed by each of the state athletic associations.
6. Each state athletic association should attempt to secure the co-operation which would provide a plan of continuous eligibility from high schools to college.
7. For competition in which only one state is involved, no school shall participate in a meet or tournament involving more than two schools, unless such contest has been approved by its state high-school association or its delegated constituent or allied divisions.
8. The use of school facilities or members of the school staff shall not be permitted in connection with any postseason or all-star contest unless such contest has been sanctioned by the state athletic association.
9. A school shall not permit any employee or official to encourage or collaborate in any negotiations which may lead a high-school athlete to lose his eligibility through the signing of a professional contract.
10. The solicitation of athletes through tryouts and competitive bidding by colleges and universities is unethical, unprofessional, and psychologically harmful. It destroys the amateur nature of athletics, tends to commercialize the individual and the program, promotes the use of athletic skill for gain, and takes an unfair and unjust advantage of competitors.
11. In all interstate athletic contests, each athlete shall compete under eligibility rules which are at least as restrictive as those adopted by the state high-school athletic association of his state, except in the case of nonmember schools which are not eligible for membership in their state associations.
12. No school shall compete in any of the following contests unless such contest has been sanctioned by each of the interested state high-school athletic associations through the National Federation: *(a)* any interstate tournament or meet in which three or more schools participate; *(b)* any interstate two-school contest which involves a round trip exceeding 600 miles; *(c)* any interstate two-school contest (regardless of the distance to be traveled) which is sponsored by an individual or an organization other than a member high school.
13. No basketball tournament which is purported to be for interstate high-school championship shall be sanctioned, and no basketball tournament involving schools of more than one state shall be sanctioned unless the tournament is purely community in character.
14. No contest which is purported to be for a national high-school championship in any sport shall be sanctioned.

These recommendations were developed for junior high schools, as well as for senior high schools and four-year high schools. Nevertheless, they seem a little more appropriate for senior and four-year high schools and some modification probably should be made for junior high schools. At any rate, the recommendations seem to presuppose a type of interscholastic competition in junior high schools which is very seriously questioned by many educators, including junior high school principals and, indeed, many junior high school coaches. Nationally accepted authorities in the field of junior high school education have made the following recommendations for junior high school athletics:

A. From the health aspect, there is invaluable merit in emphasizing the practice of *touch* (or flag) football in grade 7 and in grades 7 and 8. Some states advocate *touch* football, but do not prohibit contact football.

B. The American Medical Society has held that body joints are too tender and under-developed to warrant any degree of contact, especially in the contact sports.

C. Most junior high-school contests should be played between 2 o'clock and 6 o'clock in the afternoon, and on Saturday.

D. For contests played during school time, spectator groups, pep groups, bands, and so forth should be prohibited from following the team to another school.

E. Visiting teams should not arrive at the host school more than one hour before game time. In Iowa, the I. H. S. A. A. has definite regulations relative to dismissal time and travel time for teams playing away from home.

F. In some states where the junior high-school maximum age is 17, there is a movement underway to lower it to 16, or from 16 to 15. Iowa's maximum junior high-school age is 16.

G. Adequate physical examinations are strongly recommended prior to each sport season. In other words, athletes, therefore, are to be required to have physical examinations more than once during the year, and for each sport.

H. Eligibility requirements may be higher than the minimum required by the respective athletic association.

I. Transportation of teams and spectator groups should be strictly supervised. The players should be transported in one bus and all others in another bus, or other means of transportation.

J. The junior high-school program also gives an opportunity to place emphasis on proper dress, grooming, poise, etc.

K. Health practices and good housekeeping in the classroom, dressing room, as well as at home, can be strongly emphasized in a junior high-school program.[4]

A good discussion of the various aspects of the interscholastic athletic program in junior high schools will be found in the November, 1958, issue of the *Bulletin of the National Association of Secondary School Principals* (No. 241, pp. 1-47). This survey of interscholastic athletic programs in separately organized junior high schools, reported by Ellsworth Tompkins and Virginia Roe, was based upon the practices of 2278 junior high schools. Some of the principle findings of this survey are as follows:

---

[4]Harold Schmickley, *National Trends and Good Practices in the Junior High-School Athletic Program,* Des Moines, Iowa High Schools Athletic Association, November 8, 1957.

1. While the majority of junior high schools have interscholastic athletic contests the healthy minority of their principals are opposed to them.
2. Tackle football is played in 60 per cent of the schools and baseball in about 35 per cent, softball in about 15 per cent, basketball in about 80 per cent, track in about 60 per cent, and swimming, wrestling, soccer, tennis and volleyball only in less than 5 per cent each.
3. In more than half the schools the Board of Education contributed to the support of interscholastic athletics and in about 30 per cent of the schools they are supported entirely by the Board of Education.
4. In about half of the schools the participant pays the entire insurance premium and in about 15 per cent the school pays the entire premium, while in about 10 per cent the school and the participant contribute to pay the premium.
5. In 95 per cent of the schools the uniforms and equipment are provided by the school.
6. In a large majority of the schools 9th-grade pupils in junior high schools do not play on senior high school teams, although in about one-third of the schools they participate in one or more sports.
7. In about half of the schools the players are transported to out-of-town games in school buses, while about 25 per cent use commercial transportation and another 25 per cent provide cars.
8. In about half of the schools the teams participate in interscholastic athletic tournaments, the principal type being basketball although rather a large number participate in tournaments in track and tackle football.
9. In approximately 75 per cent of the schools there are few interscholastic teams for girls. Interscholastic competition for girls is principally in softball, basketball and volleyball.
10. About 70 per cent of junior high schools report having both interscholastic and intramural programs.
11. Slightly more than half of the schools have their interscholastic events in the afternoon only, about one-third in both the afternoon and night, about 10 per cent night only, and about 7 per cent on Saturday morning only.
12. With respect to eligibility standards about 40 per cent abide by the standards of the state athletic association, 29 per cent develop standards for their own junior high school, and 23 per cent abide by standards set by the local school system.

Athletic Permits. The principal or assistant principal must make sure that students participating in athletics or strenuous sports or exercise of any kind, including intramural sports, are in such physical condition that they are not risking serious injury or illness by participating.

In most secondary schools principals have required students wishing to participate in athletics to obtain a permit signed by the family physician and the parent (Form 32).

Such a permit should be obtained not only for participation in interscholastic athletics but also for participation in intramural athletics. A considerable but decreasing number of schools do not require the signature of a physician, but they do require a statement of permission from a parent.

NONSCHOOL COMPETITION. In many communities, when the schools have failed to provide for the competitive needs and interests of school pupils, other groups have organized competition for school-age children. Sometimes, well-meaning but misinformed industrial and commercial groups have sponsored teams and leagues. The leaders in many cases have not been trained to direct school-age players, and many educators believe that much harm can come from nonschool-controlled competition. It would seem that, if an adequate athletic program were provided by the schools, pupils would not be obliged to go elsewhere for training and playing experience.

FORM 32

COLORADO HIGH SCHOOL ACTIVITIES ASSOCIATION
Statement for Physician and Parent for
Athletic Participation

I hereby certify that I have examined ______________________ and that he was found physically fit to engage in high school baseball, basketball, cross country, football, golf, gymnastics, skiing, swimming, tennis, track, wrestling. (Please cross out any sport in which the boy should not participate.)

Date______________ Signed______________________
(Physician)

****

Parent or Guardian Permit

I hereby give my consent for ______________________ to compete in athletics for ______________________ High School, in Colorado High School Activities Association Approved Sports, except those crossed out below. (Baseball, basketball, cross country, football, golf, gymnastics, skiing, swimming, tennis, track, wrestling.)

Date______________ Signed______________________
(Parent or Guardian)

This statement should be on file in the principal's office for every student participating in inter-school athletic competition.

Surrounded by modern living conveniences and prevented from employment in the current industrial pattern, young people naturally turn to sports and recreation programs for leisure-time and developmental activities. If the schools do not furnish a comprehensive enough sports program for school-age pupils, it is only natural that youth will turn to other agencies. If sports that are organized and managed by out-of-school agencies flourish in a given community, there is a strong suggestion that the physical-education program of the school is failing to meet the needs and interests of youth in that community.

INTERSCHOOL COMPETITION FOR GIRLS. Most authorities believe that interscholastic competition does not lend itself well to the development of desirable social, emotional, and physical characteristics for the adolescent girl. Instead, play days are recommended as a means whereby girls from two or more communities may meet and compete with others of their own sports interests. Nevertheless, many schools sponsor extramural athletic activities for girls; in the handbooks of a considerable number of the state athletic associations will be found facts dealing with participation, supervision, and control in connection with girls' activities. The following example, is taken from the handbook of the New York State Athletic Association, Albany, New York.

1. *Supervision and conduct.* All extra-mural athletic activities for girls shall be conducted under girls' rules sanctioned by the Division for Girls' and Women's Sports and under standards established by that organization. (See appropriate D.G.W.S. Guide.) Women shall act as referees, umpires, and officials.
2. *Types of participation.*
   a. *Sports day:* A day when pupils from two or more schools meet and engage in a *variety* of competitive sports events.
      Type 1. Two schools competing in more than one sport, but with each girl participating in only one sport.
      Type 2. More than two schools competing in one sport.
      In all of these, both team and school identity are retained.
      Type 3. Two or more schools competing in more than one sport, but with each girl participating in more than one sport.
      In all of these, both team and school identity are retained.
   b. *Invitation activities:* Those games or other events dealing with one sport, arranged by invitation of one school to one or more other schools, without leading to any formal schedule or championship.
      Type 1. Two schools competing in one sport.
      Type 2. More than two schools competing in one sport.
      In all of these, both team and school identity are retained.
3. *Acceptability of types of participation.*
   a. Sports days and approved invitation activities are acceptable for girls.
   b. While the following types of participation are not mentioned in the Regulations of the Commissioner, it is our belief that it is the intent of the Regulations to permit such extra-mural activities, since they are of generally recognized value:
      1. clinics
      2. workshops
      3. play days (2 or more schools competing in activity [ies] in which neither team nor school identity is retained)
4. *Amount of participation.*
   a. *Per day.* Maximum participation of any one girl in any of these activities shall not exceed one full-length game or its equivalent for one day.
   b. *Per time division.* The maximum total of sports days and invitation activities shall be *6 per girl* in a given time division and may not exceed 6 per girl in a given sport in adjacent time divisions; in either case, only 4 of these may be type 1 sports days and/or type 1 invitation activities.

Note: 4b. applies to girls in grades 9-12. The needs of girls in grades 7 and 8 are more appropriately met by the basic intramural program, although an occasional informal extra-mural event may be desirable.

INTRAMURAL ATHLETICS. The intramural program offers an opportunity for many who may not have the time or ability to compete in interschool contests to gain educational experiences through games and sports. Because these participants may lack the skill, natural ability, experience, or training of the varsity athlete, superior teaching or coaching ability is required to direct these activities.

In many junior high schools either there is no interscholastic athletic competition or it is limited to a very few games with other junior high schools in the same district. In these schools an intramural program has an excellent opportunity to develop the values that derive from participation in athletics.

The intramural program provides an opportunity for academic teachers in the school system to direct activities in their sports interest. The academic teacher who is qualified may find a refreshing outlet for his athletic interests through the direction of intramural activities which do not involve the pressures of interschool competition. Instructors in physical education who are not involved in coaching teams in interschool competition usually make excellent leaders for intramural groups.

An intramural program needs to be very carefully organized, supervised, and supported. There need to be adequate playing fields and adequate gymnasium space. There needs to be adequate equipment, particularly first-class protective equipment in football. Adequate provision must be made for first aid and for immediate examination of any injuries that seem at all serious.

The type of classification used in composing intramural teams varies greatly from school to school, but ordinarily teams are composed on the basis of one or two of the following criteria: by weight, by age, by grade. The intramural program presents an excellent opportunity to teach the student rules and sports appreciation.

Intramural activities which may be considered for boys include the following: archery, badminton, baseball, basketball, golf, gymnastics, handball, ice hockey, ping-pong, horseshoe pitching, shuffleboard, skating, skiing, soccer, softball, speedball, swimming, tennis, touch or flag football, track, volleyball, water polo, wrestling, and square dancing.

Intramural activities for girls may well include any of the following: archery, badminton, basketball, modern dancing, ping-pong, horseshoe pitching, shuffleboard, skiing, softball, skating, speedaway, swimming and lifesaving, tennis, and volleyball.

INSURANCE PROGRAMS. Very generally, secondary schools have adopted some sort of insurance program which provides reimbursement to parents who have to meet expenses for injuries received by students in athletic competition. This program has come in many schools to include insurance not only for interscholastic competition but also for intramural competition. In an increasing number of schools the insurance covers injuries of any kind occurring to young people while they are in school or on the way to and from school. In many instances the board of education contributes to the cost of these insurance plans, which plans in many cases prevent suits against the board by parents. A large majority of state activities associations and state athletic associations have developed plans for athletic insurance. For example, Colorado developed a plan for insurance against injuries in athletic participation which was later underwritten by a company handling life insurance and accident insurance. The athletic-insurance program should be one in which the premium is low enough that any school can afford to carry it; also the insurance should cover the major share of the cost of any injury.

Problems, Questions, and Exercises

1. Be able to present in class what you think is a good fundamental philosophy of physical education in the schools.
2. Be able to discuss classification of students for physical education and the excusing of students from physical education.
3. What is the responsibility of the school in connection with first aid; how should that responsibility be discharged?
4. For a school of a size selected by you, discuss the school health program, including basic theory, staff, types of staff members and their responsibility, and physical-health examinations.
5. Be able to present to the class in some detail a plan for organizing and managing the physical-health examination, including such matters as personnel, records, and follow-up.
6. What do you believe are the principal effects upon the school and its program of the present interscholastic participation now found in a typical high school? Mention both good and bad effects.
7. Make a list, somewhat in the order of their importance, of the principal's responsibilities in connection with interscholastic competition.
8. Examine carefully the recommendations by the National Committee on Interscholastic Athletics; divide their recommendations into four groups: (1) those that are outstandingly sound and important; (2) those that are fairly sound and important; (3) those that are questionable or of little importance; and (4) those that are either unsound or of no importance.
9. What do you think about the place of interscholastic competition in junior high schools? What should be its scope or its limits?
10. What do you believe about interscholastic competition for girls?
11. Make a list of the advantages and the dangers of intramural athletic competition. Discuss fundamental principles for setting up and supervising a program of intramural athletics.
12. Outline and be prepared to discuss a program of athletic competition for junior high schools.
13. Obtain from some secondary-school principal or state athletic or activity association information concerning the insurance plan in operation in your state and evaluate it in a report to the class.

Archer, John K., "Athletics for Girls," *Bulletin of the N.A.S.S.P.* (April, 1956), Vol. 40, No. 219, pp. 125-126.

Archer, John K., "Standards in Athletics for Boys and Girls," *Bulletin of the N.A.S.S.P.* (March, 1952), Vol. 36, No. 185, pp. 322-325. [A brief but to-the-point discussion of how the athletic end of the school might be put back on an education basis.]

Brownell, Clifford Lee, and others, "Administration of the Health, Physical Education and Recreation Program in Secondary Schools," *Bulletin of the N.A.S.S.P.* (May, 1953), Vol. 37, No. 195, pp. 1-136.

Bucher, Charles A., *Administration of School Health and Physical Education Programs,* St. Louis, C. V. Mosby, 1958.

Bundesen, Herman N., and Bergmann, John C., "A Dental Health Program in a Large Mid-West School System," *American Journal of Public Health* (March, 1955), Vol. 31, pp. 67-71.

Educational Policies Commission, "Health and Health Services," *Education for All American Youth,* 1952, pp. 108-110, 113-114, 157-160, 179-181, 255-264, 362-363; "Physical Education," pp. 228-238, 255-264.

Forbes, Ted, "Physical Fitness and Our Youth," *Bulletin of the N.A.S.S.P.* (March, 1962), No. 272, pp. 156-162.

Forsythe, Charles E., *The Administration of High School Athletics* (Third Edition), New York, Prentice-Hall, 1954. [Chapters 1, 5, and 7.]

Hughes, William L., "The Place of Athletics in the School Physical-Education Program," *Education Digest* (February, 1951), Vol. 16, No. 6, pp. 34-37.

Janet, Sister Mary, *Catholic Secondary Education,* Washington, D.C., National Catholic Welfare Conference, 1949. [Chapter 10.]

Maybee, G. D., and McCracker, Oliver, Jr., "Do Interscholastic Athletics in the Junior High School Aid or Retard a Desirable Educational Program?" Bulletin of the N.A.S.S.P. (April, 1960), No. 255, pp. 96-100.

Research Committee of the Pennsylvania State Association for Health, Physical Education, and Recreation, "A State-wide Survey of the Insurance Protection of Pennsylvania Public Secondary School Students," Bulletin of the N.A.S.S.P. (September, 1958), No. 239, pp. 60-70.

Sellery, C. Morley, "Where Are We Going in School Health Education?" *Journal of School Health* (June, 1950), Vol. 20, pp. 151-159. [Gives the objectives of health education.]

Usilaner, Hiram, "Suggestions in Administering Health Programs in Secondary Schools," *Bulletin of the N.A.S.S.P.* (May, 1958), No. 230, pp. 88-91. [Helpful to principals who must set up a program without the aid of an expert's advice. Lists sixteen suggestions for organization and administration.]

Vernier, Elmon L., and others, "Health, Physical Education and Recreation in the Secondary School," *Bulletin of the N.A.S.S.P.* (May, 1960), No. 256, pp. 1-196.

Wagner, Marsden G., "The Medical Basis for School Health Programs," *The School Review* (Autumn, 1961), Vol. 69, pp. 322-337.

Yeager, William, *Administration of the Non-instructional Personnel and Services,* New York, Harper, 1959. [Chapter 14, "The School Health Services: Objectives and Organization," and Chapter 15, "The School Health Services, Specialized Personnel."]

20

Administering Library, Lunch, and Transportation Services

1. The Library

IMPORTANCE OF THE SCHOOL LIBRARY. Half a century ago the instruction in secondary schools was largely a textbook type of instruction; beyond a few general reference books such as dictionaries, encyclopedias, and atlases and perhaps a few books in history and in English, there was not much need for a school library. While it is true that many teachers today employ methods of instruction centering upon one book in a subject, the trend has been toward the use of many books, as well as the use of pamphlets, booklets, periodicals, bulletins, and other reference materials, in classes other than those in mathematics and foreign languages. As the trend in this direction has developed, the importance of libraries has increased and the functions of the school library have changed.

REQUIREMENTS OF A GOOD LIBRARY. While it follows naturally that what can be provided in the way of library service and facilities will vary greatly with the size of the school and the wealth per capita of the community in which the school is located, there are certain standards or ideals toward which all schools should work. It is the responsibility of the administrator to take leadership in the developing of a school library which meets good standards. Outstanding among the requisites for a good library are the following:

1. The library is under the direction of an individual with adequate training in school-library work. In small schools this person may of necessity be one of less than complete library training, perhaps a teacher with library training of six or eight semester hours who devotes only part of the day to library work.
2. The library has a sufficient number of good reference books (including encyclopedias, atlases, and dictionaries, the contents of which are not too old), an adequate number of books on all subjects taught in the high school (suitable for use as reference and supplementary reading by students in high-school classes), and general reading materials of various kinds which have been selected by people who know the interests and needs of adolescents.

3. There is employed an adequate system for classification, preferably the Dewey Decimal System; and all books are classified, labeled, and shelved on the basis of that system.
4. There is adequate provision in the form of space, equipment, and materials for the repair of books and for their accessioning as they come into the library.
5. There is provided and operated adequately a record system which maintains a record of orders and acquisitions to the library, a record of all loans and returns of the library, a record of all fines paid and the disposal of the money, and a record of books lost, destroyed, or discarded.
6. There are provided a number of facilities for purchasing books, including publications of the Library Association and other information about new books which have been published.
7. There are adequate provisions for students to use the library, including:
   a. A schedule which provides free study periods.
   b. Facilities for bringing whole classes into the library at times.
   c. Provision for easy access to the library by students in study halls, this taking the form in small schools of having combined study halls and library and in larger schools of having study halls adjoining or close to the library.
   d. Provision for keeping the library open for short periods before school in the morning, after school in the afternoon, and during the lunch period.
8. There are provided as part of the library suite one or more listening rooms and one or more conference rooms.

There should also be the following equipment and furnishings:

1. Shelving for books which will be put out on the open shelf for the students to examine.
2. Stacks for books which it is not advisable to put on the open shelf.
3. Shelves near the library attendant for books or materials which are placed on reserve—for example, books which may not be withdrawn from the library or kept out more than one class period.
4. Suitable desk space and chairs for the librarian and assistants.
5. One or more large bulletin boards, in places where they may be seen by the students, to call attention to new and interesting additions to the library and to display bulletins of information about the library.
6. Card catalogues, including adequate cabinets.
7. Magazine racks for periodicals.
8. An atlas stand and one or more dictionary stands or small tables.
9. Display and exhibit case.
10. One or more charging trays.
11. Portable blackboard.
12. Typewriter and typewriter desk.
13. Box files for clippings and small pamphlets.
14. Picture-mounting materials.
15. Complete set of reporting materials.
16. Library and dating stamps.
17. Sufficient number of book pockets.
18. A floor covering of coarse carpet or linoleum to ensure quiet in the room.
19. A small workroom or repair room, or, in smaller schools, a desk and materials which may be used by those working on accessioning and repair.

Library Personnel. The success of the library as an educational aid to the school depends greatly upon the quality of its personnel. In every library of any size there should be at least a half-time librarian with some library training. Libraries and schools of more than 250 or 300 students should have a full-time librarian who has the equivalent of a master's degree in library science with emphasis upon school libraries. In larger schools the librarian should have assistants, including in very large schools one or more well-trained assistant librarians. Other assistants will include aides from the community, usually college graduates who will spend at least part of each school day in the library, and student assistants, who will spend one period a day in the library. The aides and student assistants will, of course, need to be given training by the librarian so that their work will be helpful.

In small schools of less than approximately 150 students, it conserves staff time and encourages student use of the library to have the library used as a study hall. There should be a trained librarian in the library at least several periods a day; at other periods there should be the most nearly qualified member of the staff (probably an English teacher), aides from the community, or the best student assistants.

The librarian should have had adequate training in library science and practice; a full-time head librarian should have had not less than sixteen semester hours of training and assistant librarians should have had not less than eight to ten hours. While this training may be taken as an undergraduate, it is usually postgraduate training. The librarian should have had special training for service in school libraries. The graduates of most general library-science curricula are lacking in understanding of the functioning and the management of school libraries. The librarian should also have had at least two or three years of experience as a high-school teacher.

If the library is included in an instructional-materials center with audio-visual equipment and materials, there should be, in all but the very smallest schools, either a head of the instructional-materials center who is familiar with both library management and audio-visual aids or an assistant to the librarian who is familiar with audio-visual equipment and materials.

The head librarian should have at least one or more part-time assistants who are competent to relieve her, at least one period in the day, so that she may attend to duties other than those of charging books, advising students, etc. In large libraries the head librarian should do very little work directly with individual students.

The multitude of services performed by a librarian may be classified under such headings as the following:

Classifying and cataloguing
Assisting pupils in using library
Selecting and ordering books
Maintaining loan routine
Maintaining routine of closing library
Assisting teachers in using library
Instructing pupils in library science
Filing clippings and materials

Selecting and processing periodicals
Processing and accessioning books and pamphlets
Supervising library staff
Weeding out unused library materials
Carrying out inventories
Maintaining routine of opening library
Mending and binding old books
Publicizing new books
Storing and issuing audio-visual materials
Sponsoring library club

TRAINING NEW STUDENTS IN USE OF LIBRARY. In a considerable number of schools a series of lessons is given to all students at some time, usually in their first year. In a number of schools this series is given through the home room. Following is an illustrative outline of lessons.

LESSON I. OVERVIEW

1. Introductory talk on libraries in general.
   a. Reasons for using books. *b.* The kind of books necessary to make a library useful.
2. The general arrangement of the library.
   a. Charging desk. *b.* Card catalogue. *c.* Books on one subject placed together. (No explanation of classification here.) *d.* Reserves. *e.* Magazines. *f.* Picture collections and pamphlets. *g.* General reference books.
3. Comparison of school and public libraries.
4. Method of handling books.
   a. Borrowing and returning of general and reserve books. *b.* Overdues. *c.* Fines.
5. General hints on using the library.
   a. Reasons for rules. *b.* Why one should know how to find material himself.

LESSON II. BOOKS AND HOW TO USE THEM

1. History of the book.
2. The physical make-up of the book. (An old book dissected is necessary to make this lesson clear.)
3. Care of the book.
   a. Opening. *b.* Marking place. *c.* Rough handling. *d.* Effects of moisture and heat. *e.* Cleanliness. *f.* Replacement (loss of time, expense).
4. Parts. (All pupils have the same textbook for this study.)
   a. Frontispiece. *b.* Title page. *c.* Preface. *d.* Table of contents. *e.* List of illustrations. *f.* Introduction. *g.* Body. *h.* Appendix. *i.* Index. *j.* Bibliography. (Examine other texts for these parts.)
5. How to judge a book without reading it. (Each student gives a report on some book he has examined, but not read.)

LESSON III. ARRANGEMENT OF BOOKS ON THE SHELVES

1. Explanation of the Dewey Decimal System of Classification. (Each student should have a mimeographed copy of a brief outline of the ten classes. These outlines may be purchased in quantity at very small expense.)
2. Explanation of class and author number (known as the call number).
3. Explanation of call number on book and on book card corresponding. (When the book is out of the library, it is represented by its book card in the charging tray.)

Lesson IV. Cataloguing

1. Explanation of various methods.
2. The card catalogue.
   a. As an index to the library. *b.* Kinds of cards made for each book (depending on number used in the library). *c.* Arrangement of cards in the trays, with guides. *d.* Questions that one can answer by using the card catalogue. *e.* Connection with lesson on classification.

Lesson V. General Reference Books, Dictionary

1. Unabridged dictionaries.
   a. What one may find out about a word: spelling, pronunciation, definition, part of speech, capitalization, etc.
   b. Other things to be found: phrases, biographical information, noted names in fiction, foreign words and phrases, etc. Arrangement, completeness, date of publication, thumb index, guide words, divided page, addenda.

Lesson VI. Other General Reference Books

1. Encyclopedia.
   a. Examination of those in the library for scope, date of publication, arrangement, length of articles, reliability, signed articles, cross references, methods of keeping up to date.
   b. Look up one topic in all the encyclopedias and compare in interest and comprehensiveness.
2. Atlases, Directories, Gazetteers.
   a. Scope. *b.* Key for using. *c.* Most reliable ones.
3. Yearbooks.
   a. *World Almanac:* general idea of contents and arrangement; index.
   b. Other yearbooks: *Daily News Almanac; American Yearbook; New International Yearbook; Statesman's Year-Book.*
4. *Who's Who in America.* *a.* Scope. *b.* Arrangement. *c.* Abbreviations. *d.* Comparison with *Who's Who.*
5. Special indexes.
   a. *Index to Poetry,* Edith Granger: key, arrangement, author, title, first lines, how to use.
6. *Reader's Guide to Periodical Literature.* *a.* Key. *b.* Arrangement. *c.* Value *d.* How published.

Lesson VII. Magazines, Newspapers

Kinds: literary, current news, general. Classify those taken by library. Relative objectivity and reliability.

Use of the Public Libraries. There are public libraries which in many ways may be thought of as adjuncts to school libraries, at least insofar as the reading of students is concerned. There should be developed much more liaison and co-ordination between the public library and the school library. To be sure, it is not to be expected that the public library can be relied upon as a place where a student can go regularly to study. Nevertheless, there are facilities in the public library that ought to be discovered and made available to teachers and students. Students should be encouraged to use the public library, even to the extent of being definitely assigned activities which will carry them into the library. Among the important purposes of such assignments is to acquaint the student with the location of the public library, its facilities, and the means and procedure for utilizing it, thus adding to the probability that after the students have been graduated from high school they will use the library services. Co-operation between the school library and the public library may also be useful in the exchange of information; indeed, in some instances there may be an exchange of books for a limited period of time.

Broadened Concept of School Libraries. In a small but rapidly increasing number of schools the library itself is only a part of an instructional-materials center which involves (in addition to library books, pamphlets, and clippings) various kinds of educational materials, including audio-visual aids of various kinds, collections of textbooks, collections of courses of study of states, cities, and counties, resource units, professional books and journals for teachers, and projection machines. The instructional-materials center should have a small room with a screen for the prevision projection of films and slides. This room, of course, should be relatively soundproof so that workers in other areas in the instructional-materials center will not be disturbed.

The librarian has a definite responsibility in connection with the use of library books in various classrooms. In schools operating with a long class period there has developed a tendency to bring appropriate materials into the classroom so that the students may have them available for study. This development has certain limitations and imposes responsibilities upon the librarian. Any books withdrawn from the library are used only a very limited time during the day; thus there is a reduction in the resources available for students who come to the library. The librarian must use tact and judgment in dealing with this problem; the principal must work with the librarian and teachers in deciding which materials should be withdrawn from the library for use in the classrooms.

The Administrator and the Library. With respect to the school library, the principal has a variety of important responsibilities and opportunities. He should:

1. Realize that the school library's efficiency, scope, and service depends on his knowledge of its functions and services.
2. Choose a librarian who is more than a dispenser of books—an organizer, administrator, personnel worker, and teacher.
3. Arrange the schedule to permit effective service for classrooms; instruct and guide individuals; provide necessary clerical assistance.
4. Provide adequate financing on an annual basis, so that wise purchase plans can be worked out. Set order dates, with sums allowed to meet emergency needs and take advantage of good buying opportunities.
5. Expect his teaching staff to know what the library should have, how to use the materials.
6. Establish a professional collection within the school library, specially budgeted.
7. House and equip the library adequately and attractively.
8. Become acquainted with the community, county, state, and national library agencies.

9. Realize that it is his attitude, his planning and interpretation of the library to teachers, pupils, and librarian, that establishes the library in the school.
10. Recognize and develop the role of the library in the development of the instructional program.
11. Work through the supervision of instruction to develop the use of the library.
12. Schedule for the most advantageous use of the library.
13. Establish a working relationship between the classroom and the teachers, seeing the librarian as having a senior-teacher status, thus automatically putting the librarian on instructional and curriculum committees.
14. Spend time in the library observing the students' ability to use materials and their scope of usage.
15. Recognize the reading guidance in progress, and check with the librarian before interrupting a student's reading.
16. Appoint a faculty library committee with rotating membership. Committee serves to develop rules and schedules, and in book selection.
17. Develop a student library representation in the student government, and the election of a student library committee.
18. Assist the librarian in developing policies of routines, staffing, and discipline in the library.[1]

SELECTION OF LIBRARY BOOKS AND MATERIALS. The administrator of the secondary school has the responsibility for stimulating and guiding appropriate members of his staff to co-operate with the librarian in the selection and ordering of new books for the library. Members of the staff in the various departments should meet and make a list of books recommended for library purchase. If the list is long, it should be divided into at least two or three categories on the basis of the desirability of the respective books; thus, if not all the books may be purchased immediately, the librarian and the principal may make a good decision with respect to the postponement of the purchase of some.

The librarian should, of course, make recommendations for various kinds of reference materials and general reading materials to be ordered; perhaps these too should be similarly divided into two or more categories.

While respecting the judgments of the librarian and the members of the various departments, the principal must exercise some responsibility and be able to make effective decisions. Both for his use and for the use of the librarian and other staff members, two or more books similar to the following should be available:

Amdeff, Ruby Ethel, *Recommended Reference Books for the High School Library,* Nashville, Tennessee Book Company, 1955.

American Association for the Advancement of Science and the National Science Foundation, *An Inexpensive Science Library,* Washington, D.C., American Association for the Advancement of Science, 1958.

American Association for the Advancement of Science and the National Science

[1]Prepared by Mary Louise Lyda and Martha Mae Marsh, Department of Library Service of the University of Colorado.

Foundation, *The Traveling High School Science Library,* Washington, D.C., American Association for the Advancement of Science, 1958.

Bermen, Elsa P., and Sacro, Mabel, *A Basic Book Collection for Junior High Schools* (Second Edition), Chicago, American Library Association, 1956. [More than 600 books classified and annotated.]

Cook, Dorothy E., Eaton, Anne T., and West, Dorothy H., *Standard Catalog for High School Libraries* (Seventh Edition), New York, Wilson, 1956. [A carefully selected list suitable for junior and senior high school libraries; excellent buying guide; indispensable to the high school library; kept up to date by supplements.]

Hall, Elvajean, and others, *Books to Build On,* New York, Bowker, 1957. [A book list for high schools; books for the gifted child; paperbound books.]

McAllister, Mariana K., and others, *A Basic Book Collection for High Schools,* Chicago, American Library Association, 1957. [More than 1500 books classified and annotated.]

Library Accounting. The trained librarian should recommend a system of library accounting for books and for funds, as well as for the forms employed in library accounting. These forms should include the following: order slips or cards, book cards, book pockets, borrower's cards, charging guides, check-list guides, date-due cards, catalogue cards, preferably a borrower's register, and daily-record slips. In addition, the library should have an accession book (preferably of the loose-leaf type), a circulation record book, and a book for recording inventories.

Recommended Policies and Practices. The following are policies and practices which may well be used in the school library:

1. Students enrolled in a regular study hall should be able to use the library a full period or part of a period if they so desire.
2. Admittance to the library should be by regular printed forms properly executed, with only one name per slip. Special groups may be admitted without slips, provided a teacher accompanies a group.
3. The library should be a place for constructive reading and work. Only conduct conducive to good library practices should be acceptable.
4. Students should be permitted to browse.
5. Students should be allowed to use the library during a supervised study period at the discretion of the classroom teacher.
6. A maximum of 3 minutes should be allowed for passing to and from the library. The librarian should handle those who are tardy in arriving at the library and the classroom teacher should handle those who are tardy in returning to the classroom.
7. Students should be allowed to check books in and out before and after school hours.
8. An advisory library committee should be appointed.
9. The library should be open at least 15 minutes before the opening of school, continuously throughout the day (including the lunch hour), and as long after the close of school as demand justifies.
10. Clerical workers and library assistants should be provided for the librarian in the number necessary.

11. Library books and materials should be loaned to classrooms or to the study hall as need arises.
12. All monies handled by the library should be properly accounted for.
13. Library funds should be properly apportioned to new books, periodicals, repairing, binding, etc.
14. Books should be properly shelved and frequently checked to prevent or correct misplacement.
15. Books should be repaired and rebound as need requires and a record should be kept thereof.
16. In case the library also serves the general public, special arrangements should be made for hours the library is open, needed additional staff, and other necessary adaptations.
17. In case the community also supports a public library, arrangements should be made for mutually advantageous use of both library facilities, the conditions of use being clearly specified.

2. *Lunch-Period Problems*

SCHEDULING LUNCH PERIODS. Before the establishment of cafeterias in high schools, the most common lunch period was an hour in length—time enough to walk a mile and a half and eat lunch. In recent years there has been a pronounced tendency for a great majority of students to have their lunch at school. Indeed, in a large and increasing number of schools all of the students eat lunch at school; some schools, whether legally or illegally, require that everyone eat at school. The fact that the Federal government subsidizes school lunches and thus reduces their cost very materially has encouraged parents to have their children eat lunch at school; also, more children eat at school because most fathers are no longer home at lunch and approximately half of the mothers are at work or at social engagements during the lunch period.

In recent years the typical lunch period has been 30 minutes. In many larger schools there are two consecutive lunch periods of approximately half an hour, thus enabling the cafeteria to serve virtually twice its seating capacity. In a few schools three lunch periods are necessary. While in most schools students are not required to eat lunch in school, those who go home find it difficult, if not impossible, to make the trip to and from home and eat lunch in the single lunch period of 30 or 35 minutes; in schools with two lunch periods students going home almost always miss out in some extra-curricular activities held during the lunch period.

In schools in which three lunch periods are provided, one of three common practices is employed: (1) a staggered schedule, with some classes meeting only 30 to 40 minutes before the second lunch period and other classes similarly shortened which meet just after the first lunch period: (2) no classes scheduled for either lunch period, but various kinds of clubs or other social activities meeting at least some days at each lunch period; and (3) sliding lunch arrangements in which groups of youngsters going to the cafeteria are staggered in a manner to reduce the number lined up for food at one time and to reduce the length of the total lunch-period time. Under this last arrangement groups of students are sent into the cafeteria at intervals of 10, 12, or 15 minutes. The sliding period is certainly to be recommended in schools where otherwise three or more consecutive lunch periods would have to be employed.

In a considerable and growing number of schools there has been established what has come to be called the closed lunch period. In schools operating with the closed lunch period the youngsters are not permitted to leave the school building during the lunch period. In those schools in which some students go home for lunch, special permission, granted only upon the application of the parent, must be obtained and the student may not re-enter the school until after a specified time.

In schools in which the closed lunch period is not used, there is always the danger that youngsters will patronize questionable concerns in the neighborhood, where pornographic material will be offered for sale to them, where gambling is permitted, where dope peddlers are looking for victim customers, and where the students are not likely to get a balanced or healthful diet. There is some question as to the legality of the closed lunch period, but apparently the question is rarely raised.

Rules developed for the closed noon hour at the Manhattan, Kansas, Senior High School are as follows:[2]

1. The cafeteria will serve lunch to students and teachers each day that we have an all day session.
2. All students and teachers are expected to eat in the cafeteria. However, anyone is most welcome to bring his lunch from home and eat in the cafeteria.
3. A basic plate lunch is served which can be supplemented by ice cream, fresh fruit, and extra milk. Menus for the week are published in the Sunday paper. Watch the menu board for the items included in the plate lunch and the extras each day.
4. There are two serving lines with the same menu; please use either line to facilitate serving.
5. Meal tickets are on sale for your convenience.
6. YOUR COOPERATION IS URGED IN FOLLOWING A FEW REGULATIONS:
   a. Students are to report to fourth hour for roll check before going to lunch. Your group will report and return to class as directed by your fourth hour teacher.
   b. In going to and from lunch, please use the cross walks or the inside corridors. Students are not to go to and from lunch through the courts.
   c. Get into line promptly without running or pushing. Take your turn. Entrance to the serving line from the main hall ONLY.
   d. Choose your food quickly; the person behind you is hungry, too!
   e. Carry your meal ticket with you. NO CHARGING AT THE CASHIER'S STATION. If you forget your meal ticket or lunch money, please go to the office and secure a loan.
   f. There is to be no eating of lunch in any areas other than the cafeteria. This applies to sandwiches, fruit, ice cream, etc. NO EATING IN

[2]Furnished by Herbert H. Bishop, Principal.

THE LOBBY OR OUTDOOR AREAS. Exception: Food purchased at school organization bake sales may be eaten in the lobby.

g. Please clean your table, take your tray, dishes, and refuse to the disposal window – place all waste paper in the waste containers.

h. Students may leave the cafeteria upon finishing lunch and may have access to the main lobby and the main entrance walks and steps.

i. Please use the rest rooms adjacent to the cafeteria.

j. Students are not to go back to their respective rooms until they meet as a group with their teacher in the main lobby. Students eating lunch during the last serving period are to report to their fifth hour class at 1:15.

k. During the lunch period students are directly responsible to their fourth hour teacher, the cafeteria hostess, and the hall supervisors.

l. It is your responsibility to return to class on time as directed by your fourth hour teacher.

NOON-HOUR ACTIVITIES. The development of the cafeteria has created both a serious educational problem and a very important educational opportunity. In many schools with long lunch periods (in which no adequate provision was made for youngsters to expend their time and energies during that portion of the lunch period when they were not in the cafeteria) the lunch period proved to be a headache to administrators and those assigned to supervision of the lunch hour. Property was destroyed or damaged; the activities indulged in were reported to the home and the community; and there was much damage done to the reputation of the school, its administrators, and its teachers.

In very small schools with no cafeteria and in schools in which a considerable number of the youngsters go home for lunch, there is a real problem in providing harmless things for the students in the building to do until the lunch period is over. Through a co-operative approach, employing the suggestions and the managerial activities of the students, a great many schools have developed social programs for the noon hour which eliminate most of the difficulties and which have definite educational advantages. The programs developed include various sorts of sports in the gymnasium (such as volleyball, basketball, and wrestling), other less strenuous games (such as table tennis, softball, shuffleboard, chess and checkers, canasta, gin rummy, bridge, horsehoe pitching, and square dancing), regular dancing in the gymnasium, the showing of films of interesting, attractive types in the auditorium, and group singing in a music room. Good study conditions are maintained in the library, certain rooms are available for meetings of committees of various types, and one or more conversation rooms are open to couples or small groups. There are opportunities provided for youngsters to practice on the typewriter and to work in the shops and home-economics laboratories.

Not all of these activities exist in any one school. Committees of students and faculty should develop over a period of years a functional and satisfactory program for all concerned. Care should be taken that noon-hour supervision does not constitute an extra load without extra pay for some members of the staff. Those working in their lunch hour at supervision should be given extra pay or appropriate credit on their teaching load, their teaching load being reduced in other areas.

Some schools have provided special rooms as recreation centers for students during the noon hour. The Winfield, Kansas, High School, for example, has set up the equivalent of three classrooms as a recreation center, which consists of a fully equipped snack bar, poolroom, ping-pong area, and dance floor. Principal William Medley reports that in the 63-minute lunch period there is a minimum of trouble with students and that the recreational facility is used for other purposes during the day and for school parties and adult groups during the evening.

The success of such a program depends mainly on the way it is organized. In the first place, there must be some key faculty members who believe in the program and will accept certain responsibilities to make it go. Secondly, there must be a staff of dependable student assistants to do much of the routine management of the program, which management provides, incidentally, some good opportunities for training in leadership. The program, to be successful, must grow out of the needs and the interests of the pupils themselves.

CAFETERIA MANAGEMENT. In the large or medium-sized cities, where there are several cafeterias, it is the usual practice to have them under the management of a city-wide cafeteria specialist, one who is experienced and trained in the management of cafeterias and in the diet of young people. The technical aspects of management, particularly matters of financial accounting, are therefore not the direct responsibilities of the principals of the buildings in which the cafeterias are located. This arrangement relieves the principals of responsibilities which, in most instances, are not to be desired. The principal should, however, be consulted frequently on many matters relative to the cafeteria: for example, the employment of people to be assigned to his building, their re-employment from year to year, and the formulation of rules governing their activity in the building.

In districts in small towns and villages, where the only cafeteria is in the local school, much greater responsibility rests upon the high-school principal, or, in the very small districts, upon the principal and the superintendent jointly. Under any circumstances, there are responsibilities and opportunities for the principal in connection with the services that may be rendered. The cafeteria is coming to be regarded not only as a place for the serving of food but also as an educational auxiliary of the school. The educational opportunities relate not only to diet and health but also to social training, social adjustment, and etiquette.

There should be, at least once a year, a meeting of students and faculty or a meeting in each home room devoted to discussing cafeteria practices, services, and opportunities. In a meeting of students and faculty the principal should participate, as well as someone directly representing the cafeteria, maybe someone representing the faculty committee on the cafeteria and lunch hour, and, of course, someone representing the students. No doubt there should be a student committee, perhaps a subcommittee of the student council, constantly studying the problems and opportunities of the cafeteria and the lunch period in general. It has been found in a great many schools that co-operation in policy making and the developing of rules and customs pays off well, as indeed it seems to do in many phases of group life.

In the very small schools the cafeteria manager may be the home-economics teacher, using the part-time help of one or more adults employed for cooking. In many schools the collection of trays, dishwashing, and other types of routine duties for which little training is necessary are done for pay by students who need the opportunity to earn money.

EDUCATIONAL VALUES OF THE CAFETERIA. Many administrators have pointed out that students' experience in the cafeteria may have distinct educational values. The students may, with wise and not too brusque advice and counsel from selected faculty members, learn to improve their etiquette at the table. A film might also be of use in this connection. Secondly, the school lunch may improve the eating habits of many youngsters. In a large and increasing number of schools the cafeteria is operated on a school-lunch basis: that is, the student does not select merely what he wants; his choice is restricted in such a manner as to make certain that he gets a balanced lunch. Extra dishes, in addition to the basic lunch, cost extra.

Thirdly, under favorable circumstances and with a little guidance, the social experiences in the cafeteria are valuable educationally.

In a great many schools there is appointed, with or without a faculty adviser, a student committee to study problems of the cafeteria and student behavior and to make recommendations to the administration, including recommended standards of behavior for students.

In most cafeterias there is a separate room for members of the faculty which offers them some privacy; in some cafeterias there are little conference rooms which may be occupied by student committees who may wish to combine lunch with work. It has been found that it is advisable to have such rooms signed up for and scheduled in advance, giving definite preference to groups of students who are known to constitute committees and withdrawing the privilege of such rooms from groups of students who do not use them for the purpose intended.

3. Problems Related to Transportation

The development of transportation has increased the scope, complexity, and number of the problems of administrators of secondary schools. In many schools transportation not only constitutes a major problem in itself but affects many other aspects of the administration of the school, particularly the extracurricular activities and the organization of the school day and school schedule.

Co-operation of Principal and Superintendent. The city superintendent of schools will naturally take the leadership in stimulating and guiding the board of education with reference to providing transportation; the principal will naturally serve only as a lieutenant in that area. The superintendent will naturally be in charge of such matters as the employment of drivers and the purchase of busses and fuel, a field which is primarily that of business and personnel. The principal will naturally assist the superintendent in connection with the supervision of the drivers who bring the students to the school. The principal and superintendent will work jointly on many matters. Since the principal is in the building and is giving particular attention to the effect of the transportation upon his students, his teachers, and his program, he will feel free to discuss with the superintendent many aspects of the supervision of the drivers and the transportation program. When so delegated by the superintendent, he will supervise the drivers and the transportation in certain respects agreed upon by the superintendent and the principal.

Getting Information and Establishing Standards. The secondary-school administrator will find it very desirable to obtain from various sources materials which will assist him in thinking about the problems of transportation. There is available now such valuable information which should be studied by the administrator. A number of circulars have been prepared by Dr. E. Glenn Featherston (of the Office of Education of the U.S. Department of Health, Education, and Welfare) which provide information very useful to administrators and boards of education. Among these circulars might be mentioned the following: *Characteristics of State Plans for Financing Pupil Transportation, Pupil Transportation—State Laws, Plans for and Procedures in Purchasing School Busses, State School Bus Standards* and *State Provisions for Transporting Pupils.* Most state departments of education or public instruction also issue publications on transportation problems.

Every state has passed some laws relative to the organization, financing, and operation of transportation systems and an increasing number of states are providing special state subsidies for transportation. Consequently, the administrator should become quite familiar with the laws of his state that apply to transportation. The bulletin referred to above on state laws concerning the transportation of pupils provides excellent information on some legal aspects of transportation, including the use of busses for educational and student-activity trips. This information is given for each state separately. In addition, many state departments of education are providing information about school-transportation laws and stand ready to answer various legal questions related to transportation of students.

State laws relative to pupil transportation usually cover the following subjects: pupils who may or must be transported, curricular and extracurricular use of school busses, allocating or computing of state funds for transportation, special tax levy for transportation, standards for busses, school-bus inspections, school-bus maintenance, standards for school-bus drivers, licensing of drivers, training program for school-bus drivers, school-bus routes and route standards, school-bus operating regulations, speed limit specifically for school busses, stopping at railroad crossings, passing school busses on the highway, school-bus purchase procedures, contracts for transportation, insurance or liability, records and reports for transportation, and registration of school busses.[3]

Administrators should contact the office of the state commissioner or the state department of education for the laws in particular states, including laws relative to state plans for financing pupil transportation and state laws on stopping for and passing school busses.

SUPERVISION OF THE BUSSES AND BUS DRIVERS. The principal will want to keep well informed as to the general behavior of the students on the busses, particularly with respect to anything that borders on immorality, anything likely to be criticized by a considerable number of parents, anything likely to endanger the health and safety of other pupils, or any of the more serious violations of property rights of the other bus riders.

The principal will also want to keep informed relative to such matters as whether or not there are long waits at corners where the bus picks up the youngsters, whether the bus is overheated or underheated, and the amount of time spent on the bus by the students who are on the longest routes. The principal will want occasionally to inspect the bus and its equipment together with the driver to make certain that it is in such condition as will ensure safety and that the students are not defacing or harming school property. It is good practice for the principal to ride each bus route with the driver and transported pupils at least once a year.

The principal should work out with the superintendent the problem of his relationship to the bus driver. Perhaps the three of them should work out rules in advance and write them into a document so that there can be no misunderstanding. Naturally, the principal must insist on some system which will prevent transportation from operating disadvantageously to the education of the youngsters.

In some schools older and more responsible high-school students have been employed as bus drivers. In North Carolina, for example, there were fewer accidents per mile involving student drivers than there were involving adult bus drivers. The success of this plan is likely to vary somewhat from high school to high school. In some school districts

[3]E. Glenn Featherston, *Pupil Transportation—State Laws,* Washington, D.C., Office of Education, U.S. Department of Health, Education, and Welfare, October, 1955.

teachers have taken on the additional responsibility of driving the bus; this arrangement has also been reported successful: it gives the high-school teacher an opportunity for making extra pay and the high-school teacher understands high-school students well enough to simplify the problems of maintaining morale and order.

In a circular by Dr. Featherston and John B. Murray of the U.S. Office of Education, *Requirements in Training and Programs for School Bus Drivers,* there are listed the various state requirements. In general, states require a minimum age of seventeen or eighteen years, experience in driving, one year or more of experience in driving automobiles, good character and morality, good physical condition (including use of hands, arms, feet, and legs), good eyesight and hearing, and a knowledge of first aid. In many states a physical examination is required and the driver must have a special school-bus driver's license.

Following are recommendations which may be applied, subject to the laws of separate states and the conditions under which a given school system must provide transportation:

1. Busses should be painted standard school-bus chrome with black trim and lettering.
2. Busses should have all-steel bodies or the equivalent and have safety glass in all windows, doors, and windshields.
3. All seats should face forward; all seats should be securely bolted to the floor.
4. The bus should be clearly identified as a school bus by large lettering on the front, rear, and sides, and by flashing warning lights.
5. Doorways should be kept clear; the emergency door should be easily opened from inside and out but be guarded against accidental opening; the service door should be controlled manually from the driver's seat and by a release button outside at the front of the bus but away from the door.
6. The aisle should have a minimum width of twelve inches.
7. Windows should have guards preventing children from extending their arms out of the bus.
8. Rear-view mirrors should be placed on each side of the bus outside and at the center front inside.
9. Special equipment should include a safe heater large enough to heat the bus comfortably during the average winter weather of the region, fire extinguisher, first-aid kit, and tool kit.
10. Busses should carry thirty passengers or more to effect economy in operation but should never carry more than the rated capacity; standing should not be permitted.
11. Busses should have such chassis and power plants that a good margin of safety is provided; the underpowering of school busses has been a common fault.
12. Maximum speeds should be controlled by a governor attached and sealed at the factory where the bus is built.[4]

---

[4]Harlan L. Hagman, *The Administration of American Public Schools,* New York, McGraw-Hill, 1951.

Instructions for Drivers. In many schools regulations and instructions have been developed similar to the following:

1. The driver shall keep his person neat and clean. He shall not use tobacco in the bus, and shall abstain from the use of intoxicating liquor.
2. The driver shall see that the inside of the vehicle is kept clean and comfortable at all times. Surface bearing lettering on the front and rear of the bus shall be kept clean, so that all markings are clearly visible.
3. The driver shall keep the service door closed at all times when the bus is in motion.
4. The driver should not leave the bus while the motor is running.
5. The driver should never turn or swerve suddenly. He should avoid jerky starts and sudden stops, and travel slowly over rough places. When stopping to load and unload pupils along the roadway, the driver shall pull as far to the right as is safe, and at a place on the roadway where the visible clear distance to the front and the rear is sufficient to allow the approaching motorist to stop his vehicle.
6. The driver should not back up the bus on school grounds, unless the rear is guarded by a school patrol or an adult and the driver is advised that the way is clear.
7. No animals shall be permitted on school busses.
8. No loaded weapon of any sort shall be permitted on the school busses.
9. In case of accident or breakdown while the bus is loaded with children, the driver should not leave the bus to go to a telephone or to summon help. He should send two patrol boys or older responsible children for these purposes. Flares or red flags should be used to warn of a disabled bus on the roadway.
10. The driver shall assume control of all children while they are being transported and shall require from them respectable and orderly behavior. Any continued disorderly conduct should be reported to the proper school authorities.
11. The driver shall be instructed in administering first aid.

Rules and Safety Regulations for Pupils. The following are typical of useful rules and regulations to enforce on bus routes:

1. The driver is in charge of the pupils and the bus. Pupils must obey the driver promptly and cheerfully.
2. Pupils should obey and respect the orders of monitors or patrols on duty.
3. Pupils must be on time; the bus cannot wait beyond its regular schedule for those who are tardy.
4. Pupils should never stand in the roadway while waiting for the bus.
5. Unnecessary conversation with the driver is prohibited while the bus is in motion.
6. Classroom conduct is to be observed by pupils while riding in the bus, except for ordinary conversation.
7. The use of tobacco is not permitted in the bus.
8. Pupils must not throw waste paper or other rubbish on the floor of the bus.
9. Pupils must not at any time extend arms or head out of the bus windows.
10. Pupils must not try to get on or off the bus, or move about within the bus, while it is in motion.

11. Pupils must observe the directions of the driver and the patrol when leaving the bus.
12. Any damage to the bus should be reported at once to the driver.

School-Bus Patrols. In a great many elementary-school systems and in a fairly large number of secondary-school systems there are student bus patrols; in other words, some students are designated on each bus trip to assist the driver in maintaining order and in case of emergencies which may develop.

Tranportation and the Bus Schedules. The principal must seek to avoid some of the unfortunate effects of transportation upon the educational opportunities of youngsters. He must be careful to keep at a minimum the effect of the transportation plan upon the participation of students in various types of extracurricular activities. If possible, he should incorporate in the daily schedule an extracurricular period and have as many meetings of student organizations as possible within the regular school day. It is usually poor management for extracurricular activities to be carried on after some portion of the youngsters have left the school to go home on the busses. Sometimes this means providing extra bus or transportation service for some youngsters who are on athletic teams which perforce must have long practice periods after school.

It is also unwise to split the youngsters into two groups: those who come on the busses and those who do not. It is a distinct challenge to the high-school administrator and his staff to cause the transported youngsters to become assimilated with the nontransported youngsters, so that the tendency to fall into two groups is avoided. Every effort should be made to see that they do not get into classes composed respectively of transported and nontransported pupils. This same principle should be applied to guidance services and conferences. The transported youngsters should have the same opportunities for conferences with counselors and advisers that are available to the nontransported youngsters.

The principal should participate in planning the routes for the busses, so that he may be familiar with the routes and where the homes of the pupils are with respect to the routes. He should study the problem and attempt in whatever co-operative way he can to see that the transportation of the youngsters does not require more than 45 minutes. It should certainly not require more than an hour, even in areas of sparsely settled population or in bad weather. In order to shorten the transportation routes in some communities, two trips in the morning and two trips in the afternoon have been planned. To work out this sort of double-trip plan requires very careful attention by the driver and the principal and considerable contact and discussion with the parents.

When two trips are made, there must be some sort of program at the school to take care of the youngsters who arrive early at the end of the

FORM 33. *School-Bus Schedule*[5]

Bus No. ________________

1. Driver ________________ 2. Administrative Unit ________________
3. Bus seating capacity[a] ____ 4. Total miles to cover this schedule in A.M. ____
   a. Distance from initial starting point of bus to point where pupils are first picked up: ________ miles (unloaded mileage).
   b. Distance from point where pupils are first picked up to point where pupils are last discharged: ________ miles (loaded mileage).

5. Schools – listed in order first served in morning:

	Time Bus Unloads at Each School	Time School Opens, A.M.	Time School Closes, P.M.
School A			
School B			
School C			
School D			

6. Pupils to be transported:

Bus Stop No.	Time Scheduled for Stop, A.M.	Name of Each Pupil Loaded in the Morning	Miles from Home to Bus Stop	Miles Pupil Rides Bus to School	Grade	School Attended[b] (check)				Time Scheduled for Pupil Unloading, P.M.	Dates Pupil Transported	
						A	B	C	D		First Date	Last Date
1	2	3	4	5	6	7	8	9	10	11	12	13

[Continue this part of the form on the back of the sheet]

[a] According to state standards.

[b] Or busses served by this bus; for example, if pupils are transferred to another bus instead of being taken to a given school, this schedule should be modified by writing in the number of the bus to which pupils are transferred.

[5]E. Glenn Featherston and Andrew H. Gibbs, *Records and Reports for Pupil Transportation,* Washington, D.C., U.S. Office of Education, 1949, pp. 5-8.

FORM 34. *School-Bus Driver's Report*[6]

(To be filed, when necessary, with principal)

School____
Driver____
Bus No.__________________________ Date______________

1. Names of non-co-operative pupils

a.		*d.*	
b.		*e.*	
c.		*f.*	

2. Pupils riding bus for first time[a]

	Name of Pupil	*Date of First Trip*
a.		
b.		
c.		
d.		

3. Pupils no longer riding bus

	Name of Pupil	*Date of Last Trip*
a.		
b.		
c.		
d.		

4. Remarks:[b] ______________________________

[a] Additional data required for modification of the school-bus schedule should be obtained by the principal from either the driver or the pupil, and should be transmitted to the supervisor of transportation.

[b] The names of pupils consistently failing to ride the bus during the past week should be reported here.

first trip. This program may be in the form of making available to them libraries, study halls, the gymnasium, and the playgrounds. Perhaps the youngsters who made the first trip in the morning should be the first to leave in the afternoon, although in some schools they have developed the double-trip idea so as to use the second trips for the students who are participating in athletics, operettas, or plays and who need to practice

[6]*Records and Reports for Pupil Transportation,* p. 6. On page 7 of this publication there is a form on which a driver may report any need of repairs or inspection of specific types. On page 8 is a form for authorizing a special trip and for the driver's report on it.

after school. It is not at all an easy and simple matter to plan the transportation schedule; care must be taken to see that the parents understand the reasons for making a certain plan and that their objections are met in part, so that they will not oppose vigorously any plan of transportation proposed.

The school-bus driver's report should include a space for remarks and he should be instructed as to what sort of data should be put in that part of the report. The report probably should include space for his observations or suspicions about the condition of the motor and other parts of the bus.

SUPERIOR PRACTICES. In a careful investigation of what administrative practices seem to characterize the most effective pupil-transportation programs, Dr. Walter G. Hack,[7] Assistant Professor of Education at Ohio State University, reported the following practices to be associated with effectiveness:

1. Driver qualifications exceed State minimum requirements.
2. The driver's contract or agreement in a continuing contract includes a definition of responsibility and authority and sets limitations in regard to conduct with pupils.
3. Women are employed as regular bus drivers.
4. Written and codified transportation policies, incorporating legal requirements, have been developed and approved by the Board of Education.
5. The transportation policy statement establishes the maximum walking distance to the bus.
6. The transportation policy statement establishes the earliest time a pupil is to board the bus.
7. Requests for instructional use of busses are made in writing.
8. Each driver completes a special report on special trips.
9. Each driver immediately completes an accident report following each accident.
10. A continuous student-involved safety program is conducted within the school.
11. Adequate loading and unloading facilities are used at the schools.
12. Rules governing pupil behavior while waiting at the pick-up points, at school, and while riding the bus are distributed to parents.
13. A program of planned instruction in the rules is provided in the classroom and involves teachers, administrators, and drivers.
14. Incidents of misconduct on the bus are reported by the driver to the principal.
15. Repeated misbehavior results in a loss of riding privilege as determined by the principal after consultation with the driver.
16. Insurance protection is provided for all pupils transported.
17. A report is maintained for supplies used in each bus, i.e., gasoline, oil, grease, antifreeze, etc.

---

[7]Ed. D., Dissertation, Ohio State University.

The School of Education, University of Mississippi, published a check list for good administrators under the title "The Do's of School Transportation." Among the "Do's" not mentioned previously in this chapter were the following:

1. Prepare and use spot maps and charts to locate pupils who are entitled to transportation and to assist in establishing and changing bus routes.
2. Check distances in establishing bus routes and the eligibility of children to ride the busses.
3. Establish and relocate bus stops, setting up a definite time and place for pupils to be picked up.
4. Involve parents in working out transportation problems.
5. Arrange bus routes so that they cover the lowest possible mileage.
6. Have a staff member ride over bus routes to check on the routing and scheduling.
7. Consider the rearrangement of bus routes in order to shorten the school day of transported pupils.
8. Inform parents of the necessity for changing bus routes.
9. Periodically review bus routes and make changes when necessary.
10. Secure the help of personnel from the State Department of Education in surveying the transportation system.
11. Discuss with bus drivers their duties, responsibilities, special problems, and role in the educational program.
12. Provide lists of pupils and have bus drivers check attendance each day.
13. Obtain suggestions from bus drivers concerning the improvement of safety conditions.
14. Have bus drivers check the mechanical condition of the busses daily and turn in check list forms.
15. Have all busses inspected periodically by experienced mechanics or state police to check safety devices.
16. Publish information in the local paper concerning bus routes and schedules.
17. Have police officials come to the school and discuss safety with pupils.
18. Discuss with pupils the rules and regulations for school bus safety.
19. Give parents and pupils a set of safety rules and regulations for the transportation system.
20. Warn pupils and parents that transportation will be denied those pupils guilty of unsafe conduct at bus stops.
21. Organize a pupil safety patrol to assist bus drivers in improving transportation safety by helping with loading and unloading, etc.
22. Provide a special area on the school grounds, out of traffic, for loading and unloading busses.
23. Instruct bus drivers to report the license number of motorists who violate the law by passing busses which are stopped to load or unload pupils.
24. Meet with parents, pupils, and bus drivers to instruct them concerning conduct on the school busses.
25. Involve the staff, parents, and bus drivers in establishing codes of conduct for pupils on school busses.
26. Post bus rules and regulations on each school bus.
27. Issue passes or identification cards to transported pupils, and permit no unauthorized persons to ride school busses.

28. Allow pupils to board and leave the school bus only at their regular bus stops unless they have written permission to do otherwise.
29. Have bus drivers and pupil monitors report acts of disobedience by pupils to the proper authorities.
30. Assign seats on the bus if such action is needed to improve pupil conduct.
31. Hold individual and group conferences with pupils guilty of misconduct on school busses.
32. Involve parents in conferences with pupils who are guilty of repeated misbehavior on busses.
33. Arrange, when necessary, for privately owned vehicles to transport isolated pupils to the main school bus route.
34. Arrange for public transit busses to transport pupils living in the city but far enough from school to be entitled to transportation at school expense.
35. Work to secure a special rate for school pupils who ride public transit busses.
36. Provide assistance in improving the conduct of pupils riding on contract school busses.

Problems, Questions, and Exercises

1. With respect to each of the eight requisites given for a good library, consider its relative importance and the degree to which you think that requisite is met in the typical high school in the United States.
2. Be able to discuss the library personnel—staff and student—their duties and their supervision, in a school of a size selected by you.
3. Revise the list of lessons for training youngsters in the use of the library, or at least make a number of suggestions for its improvement.
4. Expand on the use of the libraries beyond the discussion in the textbook.
5. Discuss the library as a storage and distributing center for audio-visual aids.
6. Classify the suggestions of important responsibilities and opportunities for the administrator in the library into three categories: (1) most important, (2) of considerable importance, and (3) of relatively less importance.
7. For a school of a size selected by you, outline in some detail the plans for the lunch hour.
8. In what ways does the high-school principal have opportunities and responsibilities in connection with the high-school cafeteria?
9. Draw up a list of suggestions for the principal's supervision of transportation, busses and bus drivers. Divide your list of suggestions or designate them in some way so as to differentiate between those that are absolutely fundamental and most important, those that are of some importance, and those which may not apply in all situations.
10. What use can the principal make of the material on the form for the school-bus driver's report and on the form for special-trip authorization and driver report?
11. What are some of the problems created for the high school and its principal by transportation? Tell how you might approach the solution of each of these problems.
12. What do you think of using high-school students or high-school teachers as bus drivers for transporting students to junior or senior high school?

Selected Supplementary Readings

Ahlers, E. E., Dieckmann, W. C., Greiner, B. E., and Wagner, R. A., "What is the Role and Function of the Library in Quality Education?" *Bulletin of the N.A.S.S.P.* (April, 1960), No. 255, pp. 248-256.

Batchelor, L.L., and Amsden, R.L., "What Library Services for the High School in the New Era?" *Bulletin of the N.A.S.S.P.* (April, 1959), No. 246, pp. 62-68.

Bent, Rudyard K., and McCann, Lloyd E., *Administration of Secondary Schools,* New York, McGraw-Hill, 1960 [Chapter 17, "The Administration of Whole-school Services.]

Bookhout, Hamilton, "Teacher Aids for Lunch-Hour Activities," *School Executive* (February, 1959), Vol. 78, No. 7, pp. 136-140; or *Education Digest* (May, 1959), Vol. 24, No. 9, pp. 26-29. [Discusses an hour of freedom for teachers.]

"Buses for Catholic Students," *United States News* (March 15, 1957), Vol. 42, pp. 16-20.

"Catholic School Lunch Managers Organize Food Service Group," *Catholic School Journal* (November, 1959), Vol. 59, pp. 80.

Eckel, Howard, "School Lunch Management Practices, Part III," *School Executive* (February, 1952), Vol. 71, pp. 129-130. [Ideas are presented on what is thought to be the outstanding feature of good school lunch programs. Major problems connected with the plan are also presented.]

Educational Policies Commission, "School Lunch," *Education for All American Youth,* 1952, pp. 340-341.

Education Policies Commission, "Vocational Education," *Education for All American Youth,* 1952, pp. 148-151, 232-236, 264-299.

"The Effective Secondary School Library," *Bulletin of the N.A.S.S.P.* (November, 1959), No. 250, pp. 3-172.

Featherston, E. G., "Transportation of Pupils – A Growing Problem," *School Life* (January, 1949), Vol. 31, No. 1, pp. 4-6.

"Five Steps to a Prosperous Cafeteria," *School Management* (March, 1960), Vol. 4, No. 3, pp. 102-104.

"Health Service Program for Secondary Schools," *Bulletin of the N.A.S.S.P.* (September, 1957), No. 230, 224 pp.

Jordan, T., "Use of the Library by the Faculty and Students," *National Catholic Educational Association Bulletin* (August, 1960), Vol. 57, pp. 128.

Josey, E. J., "The Library of Three Comprehensive High Schools," *Negro Educational Review* (July, 1960), Vol. 11, pp. 105-114. [A study of three high schools for Negroes.]

Kaye, Bernard W., "Parents Like Library Work," *School Executive* (February, 1955), Vol. 74, No. 7, pp. 52-53.

McKeough, Reverend Michael, *The Administration of the Catholic Secondary School,* Washington, D.C., Catholic University of America Press, 1948. [Chapter 7.]

Marita, Sister Charles, "A Librarian's Message to Teachers," *The Catholic School Journal* (February, 1960), Vol. 60, pp. 23-24.

National Commission on Safety Education, *Minimum Standards for School Busses,* Washington, D.C., National Education Association, 1959.

Punke, H. H., "Recent Court Rulings on Pupil Transportation," *Bulletin of the N.A.S.S.P.* (February, 1961), No. 262, pp. 49-61.

Rosita, Sister M. (S.S.N.D.), "Organization and Management of the School Lunchroom," *Catholic School Journal* (September, 1951), Vol. 51, No. 7. [Among other details summarized clearly, the basic features of the National School Lunch Act.]

Schachter, Norman, "Maintaining a Clean Lunch Area," *Bulletin of the N.A.-S.S.P.* (September, 1958), No. 212, pp. 104-112. [Practices used by the author's junior high school in Van Nuys, California—practices revolving around the use of a Cadet Corps which works with the school safety program.]

Xavier, Sister Mary, "Some Educational Trends in School Activities," *Catholic Journal of Education* (January, 1957), Vol. 55, pp. 18-26.

Yeager, William A., *Administration of the Non-instructional Personnel and Services,* New York, Harper, 1959. [Chapter 16, "The Food Service," and Chapter 17, "The Pupil Transportation Service."]

21

The Administrative Offices and Their Management

1. The Principal's Office

As the program of secondary education has become more comprehensive, including such things as guidance, extracurricular activities, health education, and school nurses, it has become necessary to have more central offices. The number and character of these will of course vary with the size of the school and the program.

THE SMALL SCHOOL. In the very small schools there is need for no more than one administrative office. In schools of less than 150 the superintendent usually serves as principal, perhaps with the assistance of one of the teachers. Such a teacher may even carry the title of principal, although this seems to be in many instances an unwise practice, since it tends to waken in the heart of the teacher the desire to be a principal in practice, even though in such small schools there is no place for two administrative officers. In the small school the administrative office may be of one or two types. In very small schools in which the superintendent is not in the office all of the time and the principal is there only part of the day, a single office with a single desk, occupied alternately by the superintendent and principal, may serve. The second type of office is one in which the superintendent and the principal have desks in the same room, with a partition or screen between.

In a combination office the principal and the superintendent may make common economical use of the space, secretaries, records, telephone, reception space, and materials. Note that in these office plans there is ample space for keeping permanent records and, in fact, all records of consequence, at times when they are not in use and especially when no one is in the office. There is also a typewriter desk for a stenographer, even though a stenographer may not occupy the desk for more than part of the day. There are seats for visitors and a wardrobe for hanging their coats and wraps; there may well be storage space under the counter tops to supplement the filing cabinets.

In the secondary school of from 200 to 300 students, there should be a separate principal's office. There should be special storage and work space, including space for the use of duplicating machines. There should be ample space for filing cabinets, books, and supplies.

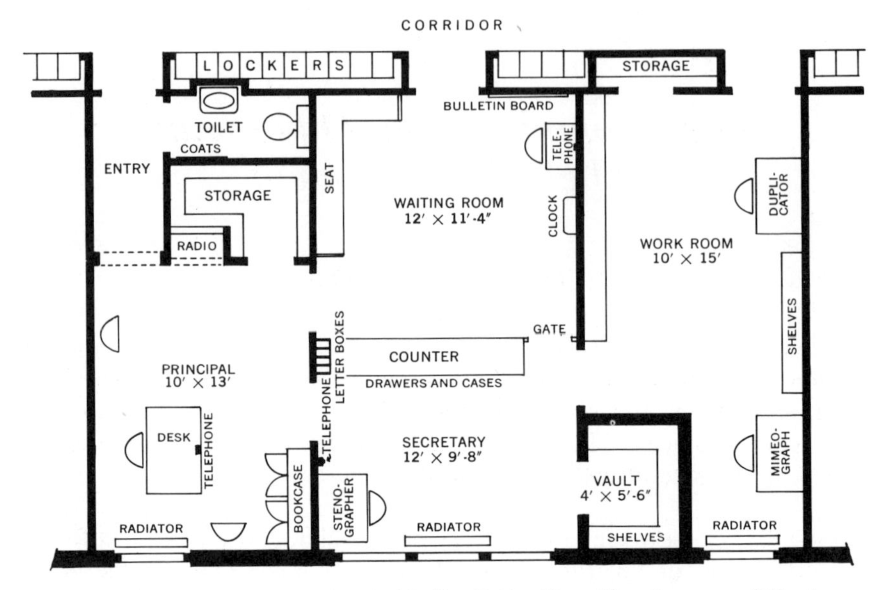

Reproduced through the courtesy of the School Building Division, Missouri State Department of Education

FIG. 1. *Office Layout Recommended for High School Enrolling from 300 to 700 Pupils*

THE LARGER SECONDARY SCHOOL. In schools of more than 300 students the principal's office should be somewhat larger, provided with a more or less private area for the principal and special work space. For the principal of a school of from 300 to 700 pupils, for example, the office layout shown in Figure 1 is a useful type. Suggestive of good office space and arrangements for still larger schools, with 800 or more students, are the office-suite layouts shown as Figure 2 and Figure 3.

Notice that the desk for the secretary is placed near the receiving counter and close to the principal's office. The desk of the principal is placed away from the entrance so that the principal will have some privacy and so that it will be necessary for people who come to his office to pass by the secretary's desk and receive her permission to speak with the principal.

The receiving counter should be high enough for the average person to write on while standing up and wide enough to provide storage room in the form of drawer and cabinet space. It sets off the receiving area from the working area of the clerk or other office workers.

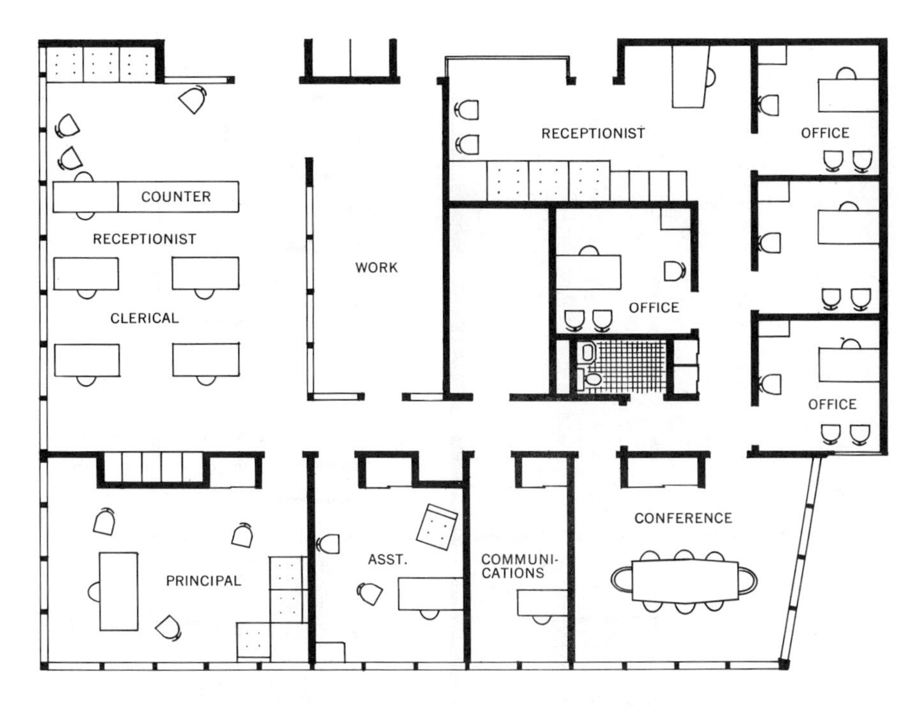

FIG. 2. *Thomas Jefferson and George Washington High Schools, Cedar Rapids, Iowa*

This sketch provides administrative facilities for principal's offices, counseling, reception, duplicating, and conferences. Health and teachers' lounges, other important facilities not included in the suite, are located convenient to instructional areas.

In offices of all sizes there will be found space with seats for receiving the public, a fireproof vault for valuable records, a lavatory, a wardrobe arrangement, filing cabinets, a bulletin board, and mailboxes for each of the teachers.

THE LARGE SCHOOL. In the large schools of more than 800 students there should be (as shown in Figure 3) additional space for an office for one or more assistant principals, for a communication system, and for one or more conference rooms. There should also be adjoining offices for counselors, school nurses, other central service people, and assistant administrators.

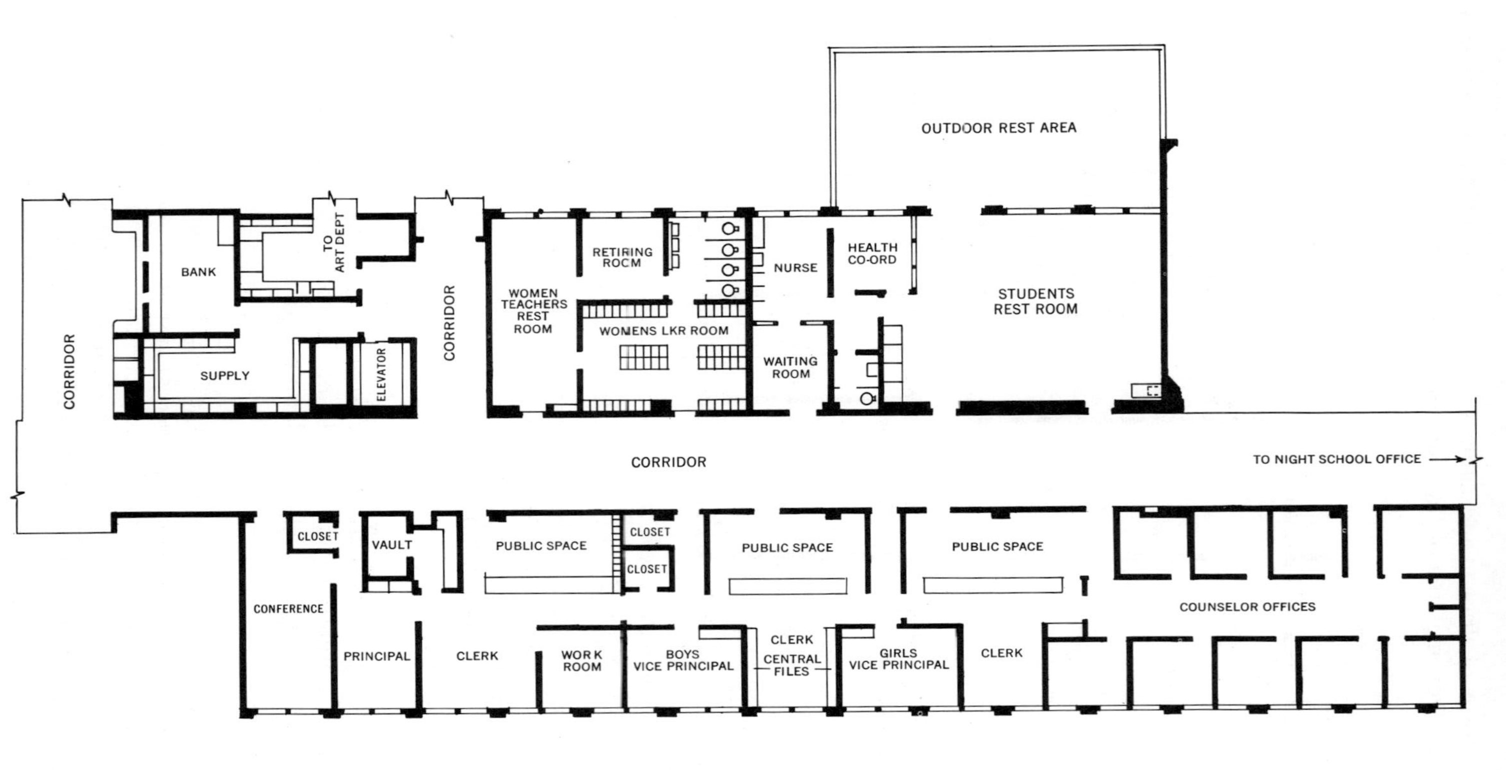

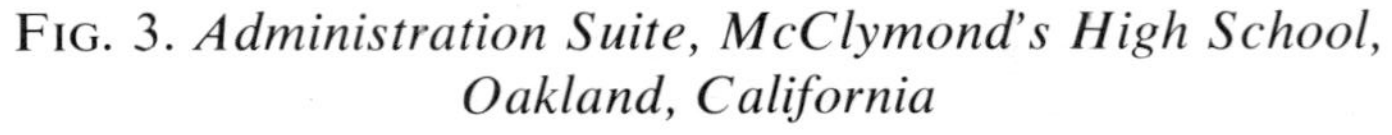

Fig. 3. *Administration Suite, McClymond's High School, Oakland, California*

IN ALL SCHOOLS. On the secretary's desk there should be a telephone with extensions to each administrator housed in the office or suite of administrative offices. In the larger schools the secretary's desk may be set well back from the receiving counter since there will be one or more secretarial assistants to serve at the counter.

In the larger schools the mimeograph and related supplies are housed in an adjoining room so as to reduce the mutual distraction of those operating the machine and others in the office. In small schools, however, such equipment should be in the main office so that the secretary does not have to leave that office.

There should be, adjacent to the office suite, one or more small, cheerful conference rooms with table and comfortable chairs for the use of student committees, teachers, transportational personnel, school-lunch personnel, custodial personnel, student aides, librarians and assistants, student class officers, special groups or committees of parents, or other laymen including alumni. One of these rooms should be large enough to seat the student council comfortably. If there are several conference rooms, they should be of different sizes.

OFFICE EQUIPMENT. Although the office furnishings need not be numerous, elaborate, or expensive, they should be suitable and sufficient to give the office dignity and cheer. They should include a respectable coat rack or closet, a floor covering of some sort (if the floors are not in excellent shape), and two or three well-chosen, large pictures in neat frames. Furniture should be substantial and of good finish. Reasonable working equipment, proportional to the services attempted and the size of the school, should be provided.

Among the items of working equipment which should be in the principal's office or office suite are the following:

1. A large flat-topped desk with drawers and a chair.
2. Chairs for visitors.
3. An auxiliary table or two.
4. A telephone located conveniently on the desk usually occupied by the principal.
5. A program clock.
6. Duplicating machine adequate to the needs of the school.
7. Stapling or clipping machine.
8. A memorandum tickler.
9. Filing cabinets sufficient to house all records, professional pamphlets, bulletins, and correspondence.
10. One or more typewriters.
11. A paper and cardboard cutter.
12. A vault or safe large enough to hold the most important records.
13. Shelves for books and journals.

In all but the smaller schools the following items should be part of the standard office equipment:

1. A dictaphone and transcribing machine.
2. An adding or calculating machine.
3. Rubber stamps as needed.
4. A numbering machine.
5. Test-scoring equipment.
6. A machine for making facsimile copies.
7. A card-punching and card-sorting machine—a less expensive type for smaller schools and the IBM type for the larger schools; related equipment.

OTHER DESIRABLE EQUIPMENT. Certain items invite brief discussion. The duplicating machine, preferably a standard mimeograph or its equivalent, is an important economy as well as a convenience. Such a machine will be very serviceable for duplicating assignment and instruction sheets and examination questions of the objective type for teachers, notices and bulletins to members of the staff, school songs and programs, instructions to students and advisers at registration and other times, notices of various sorts to parents, (including notices of meetings of parent-teacher or similar organizations), and many other types of materials.

For the housing of records, card files of a size to fit the card records kept in the school should be selected and built into a complete file unit. There should also be files for correspondence and for pamphlets, bulletins, journals, and other professional reading materials. The file of reading materials may be of three types: shelves for books, journals, and catalogues; small cardboard boxes to be labeled and placed on shelves for bulletins and pamphlets; files similar to correspondence files for notes and perhaps also for bulletins and pamphlets containing material relative to professional subject (if the box containers are not available). There should also be a card catalogue of good references on various professional subjects, kept as an index to articles in journals or other material received and read. In the correspondence file and deep-desk-drawer files there should be compartments for the filing of papers and notes relative to the various problems of administration: for example, Athletics, Activities, Committee Meetings, and Teachers' Meetings.

Important records, such as the achievement records of the present pupils and recent graduates, financial accounts, and any other records which may be impossible, difficult, or expensive to replace, should be protected by fireproof and burglar-proof housing in a safe or vault. Such space also provides for the safekeeping of valuables, such as funds from entertainments, valuable jewelry of visiting athletic teams, and unusually valuable laboratory supplies.

THE PRINCIPAL'S DESK. The most important unit of equipment in the principal's office is his desk. This desk should be of the flat-topped variety, of ample width and length to accommodate papers and materials employed for reference, as well as the desk files; it should also afford the writing space frequently needed by the principal as he works on a problem. Storage space in the drawers should be ample. The principal should not often be required to leave his desk for needed materials. Since he is not usually provided with clerks to run errands at the touch of a buzzer, he requires more storage space in his desk than the average businessman. If a deep drawer is included, it should be used as a file for materials in folders, not as a catchall. A glass desk-top does not make a satisfactory writing surface; a linoleum top is to be preferred. Drawers should be set aside for certain purposes, and the habit should be formed of using them for these purposes—for example, one (with compartments) for small items, such as clips, pencils, and rubber stamps, another for small files of 3 by 5 inches or 4 by 6 inches, and another possibly for certain flat files. There should be kept on the desk or in a drawer a "Work Organizer," a flat file consisting of from eight to ten compartments for the filing of flat papers, the compartments being so arranged that the separating walls extend each about three fourths of an inch beyond the one above, providing a place for labeling. This file should go a long way toward keeping the top of the desk clear without danger of misplacing or misfiling material which will be needed or which should be attended to in the near future. These compartments may be labeled "Letters to dictate," "Postponed correspondence," "Correspondence to be filed," "Papers for matters coming up today," "Reports from teachers," "Ideas to be thought out later," or other classifications adapted to the principal's manner of handling his office routine. A folder file established in a drawer of the desk is often used in a similar way.

Another essential is a memorandum tickler, of either the pad type or the spindle type. It is useful in calling to mind duties which otherwise would escape attention until after the desired time for attending to them had passed.

INTERCOMMUNICATION SYSTEM. In most large high schools there will be found an intercommunication system. Such systems are of various types, some of them being two-way systems for communication, from the central office to the classroom and back to the office. There has been much discussion in recent years concerning the desirability of these systems, their uses, their abuses, and their relative advantages. It has been contended by a considerable number of teachers that such systems enable the superintendent, principal, or supervisor to listen in on the activities of the classroom. This objection is rather general and positive, although it seems a little far-fetched, especially in cases where the principal or supervisor is recognized as one of a friendly nature, who visits the classroom for the purpose of being of help and of learning what is going on, rather than for the purpose of inspection. Certainly, few teachers do things in the classroom that they would be ashamed to have the principal hear or see. The intercommunication machine should not be located in the principal's office, but it should be located nearby for his convenient use and supervision.

Among the legitimate uses of an intercommunication system are the following:

1. Emergency announcements.
2. Daily routine announcements.
3. "Listening in" on class activities when approved by the teacher concerned.
4. Special radio programs channeled to all rooms or to individual rooms that request them. These include such programs as the Presidential inauguration, opening of Congress, UN conferences, and Christmas programs.
5. Recorded programs for individual rooms.
6. Music furnished to the cafeteria or recreation room for dancing.

Among the dangers and limitations of the intercommunication systems, the following were mentioned:

1. Interruption of classroom activities with announcements other than at the regular time. Teachers object very strenuously to announcements that do not come at the beginning of the class period.
2. Announcements made which concern only a few students but which all have to listen to. Such announcements encourage inattentiveness.
3. Carelessly prepared announcements.
4. Reading of long lists of names.
5. Fear on part of teachers that the principal will "listen in."
6. Overuse in advertising school events.
7. Difficulty in understanding when pupils use it, since they do not enunciate clearly enough.
8. Lack of clarity in some rooms, such as locker rooms, lunchroom, and some of the shop classes.
9. Faulty equipment or a breakdown impairing the whole system.
10. Important radio programs often coming at inconvenient times for class use.
11. Impersonality. The system cannot take the place of personal contact, assemblies, or classroom contacts.

From publications and letters received from secondary-school principals, the following suggestions have been gathered:

1. The intercommunication system may be used for daily announcements at the beginning of the school day, with only emergency announcements made at any other time. Some schools use it for announcements during the home-room period, while others make daily announcements once each morning and each afternoon. Usually from 2 to 4 minutes are employed for this purpose.
2. Apparently the great majority of principals attempt to hold the announcements on the intercommunication system to a minimum, supplementing them with mimeographed sheets of announcements and instructions distributed to each teacher with indication of what portion of the announcements should be read to classes.
3. It is the usual and probably desirable custom for all individuals wishing to use the intercommunication system to receive approval in advance from the principal.

OTHER OFFICES. If the school is large enough to have one or more assistant principals, each should have an office somewhat similar to that of the principal. The exact nature of the office, its furnishings, and its equipment will depend somewhat upon the division of duties between the principal and his assistant principal or assistant principals. If there is only one assistant principal, he may share reception space and secretarial help with the principal. If there are two or more assistant principals, it is difficult to arrange for them to share facilities with the principal; separate housing and equipment for secretaries and the receiving of visitors must be provided for.

In nearly all schools the offices of the counselors are located close to the principal's office. Such an arrangement should make it possible for the principal and the counselor to employ the same files of data about individual pupils and to consult with one another conveniently. Counseling rooms should be equipped with a counselor's desk and chair, appropriate files, and comfortable seats for at least two, and preferably three or four, other people. These seats are useful when parents or teachers are in conference with the counselor, or with the counselor and student, and when several students are in conference with the counselor at the same time. Great advances have been made in recent years in providing and furnishing guidance and counseling offices. For more details the reader is referred to a very useful publication of the U.S. Office of Education.[1]

2. *Secretarial and Clerical Assistants*

DESIRABILITY OF CLERICAL ASSISTANCE. Good business management provides clerical help to perform all such duties as may be delegated to it by members of the organization who represent a distinctly more highly paid class of worker. The schools have been tardily but surely following the example of commercial organizations in this respect. It is rare today, even in smaller schools, if there is no clerical or stenographic assistance provided. In small schools it may well consist of a common secretary for the superintendent and principal, possibly on half-time.

In all but the smallest schools there should be at least a part-time, if not a full-time, secretary for the secondary-school principal; as the secretarial and clerical work becomes greater, the secretary should have one or more assistants. These workers usually take over the tasks related to entering and filing records, correspondence, telephone communications, errands about the building, receiving visitors and providing information for them, looking after the school post office, operating duplicating machines, making tabulations for records and reports, making appointments, and other similar duties. When properly trained, they are

[1]Don D. Twiford, *Physical Facilities for School Guidance Services*, Washington, D.C., Office of Education, U.S. Department of Health, Education and Welfare, 1960. [Suggestions for office equipment and conference rooms; illustrative diagrams.]

able to render valuable service in handling the details of many phases of administration and management in connection with storage and distribution of books, materials, and supplies, management of the school calendar, operating punch-card machines, tardiness and attendance, lockers and locker keys, sale of tickets for exhibitions, entertainments, and contests, and keeping the records incidental to such problems. The wise principal will delegate to office clerks as many of his routine duties as possible and thus free himself for the better discharge of responsibilities which cannot be delegated. A good secretary will soon learn to assist the principal in remembering various little things that would otherwise escape his attention.

DUTIES OF THE SCHOOL SECRETARY. The secretary or other clerical help should relieve the teachers of as many clerical activities as possible. There is an increasing tendency in many high schools where good clerical service is available to place the clerical department at the disposal of teachers for the scoring of achievement, intelligence, and other tests which do not require much special training and the operation of data-processing machinery. There is also a growing tendency to use clerical service more and more for gathering of statistical data and for statistical computation in connection with various kinds of reports and investigations carried on by the principal, heads of departments, or committees of the faculty. It is coming to be good practice to insist that most of the work for the school secretary and her aides be approved in advance by the principal; work may be taken directly to the secretary only when the amount is very small and a precedent has been definitely set.

Among the duties given in many schools to school secretaries are the following:

Clerical Duties

- Keeping records and administering record forms relative to attendance and tardiness
- Going around to rooms to secure information for stated reports
- Checking off deliveries against office duplicates
- Keeping teachers' bulletin board up to date
- Checking out materials from office: scissors, paper-cutters, etc.
- Writing out transfer slips for pupils
- Compiling principal's annual report
- Compiling age-grade report
- Taking annual inventory of stock
- Checking intelligence-test data in special cases
- Filling teachers' requisitions for supplies
- Sending in changes of address of the teachers to the superintendent's office
- Checking teachers' attendance
- Making graphs of test results
- Taking charge of the professional library
- Writing out reports on accidents for principal's signature

Duties Relating to Dictation, Typing, and Mimeographing

Typing stencils for tests, drills, or outlines prepared by teachers and principal for pupils' use
Typing stencils
Taking dictation and typing letters
Operating and caring for duplicating machines
Typing bulletins, notices
Caring for typewriter—cleaning, dusting, and oiling
Typing stencils for bulletins, etc.

Duties Involving Meeting and Dealing with People

Answering the telephone
Meeting visitors and answering their inquiries
Managing lost-and-found articles
Delivering messages of all descriptions either to teachers or to principal
Writing out admission slips for entering pupils
Signing excuses—tardiness and absence—for principal's O.K.
Notifying teachers when they are assigned to lunchroom duty
Telephoning homes to help nurse
Selling tickets

Financial Duties

Counting and wrapping the lunchroom money
Selling car tokens
Receipting all moneys: a record of all money received is kept by the clerk
Checking bank deposits of lunchroom and other school funds
Receiving and caring for money until bank messenger arrives

Miscellaneous Duties

Keeping desks and office furniture in order
Filing records, correspondence, and other paper material
Handling United States and school mail

CORRESPONDENCE. Effective school administration requires that the principal have sufficient clerical assistance to provide for a reasonable amount of business correspondence. Such correspondence should be neatly typed in approved business form. A carbon copy of every letter issued should be filed and kept, along with selected letters received, for future reference. The need to refer to these may not be frequent; but, when occasion does arise, possession of such copies is extremely desirable. It is frequently well worth while to submit to others in the system memoranda of discussions and agreements and to file carbon copies of these.

CLERICAL ASSISTANCE. There has been in recent years a pronounced tendency to employ more clerical service in order to reduce the load of the teachers, counselors, and other members of the staff whenever possible. It seems quite foolish for busy teachers and other professional staff members to be engaged in clerical work which can be done by individuals paid less than half as much. Furthermore, it has been discovered that it is very useful to have many types of clerical work carried on in schools today. It is probably true to say that in secondary schools today there are twice as many people engaged in secretarial and clerical work as there were a quarter of a century ago.

Even though new types of work develop for the secretary and her assistants and clerical work is transferred from teachers and others to the secretary's office, the secretary should not be overburdened; one or more assistants should be employed to assist her. In some of the larger schools as many as twelve or fifteen people are employed in the administrative offices of the secondary school. In many schools student help is often employed for clerical services. Pupils in commercial curricula are assigned regular periods in the office as practical laboratory training for their future occupation and as a part of their regular courses in stenography or office management. Such assistants are useful and certainly much better than none at all; but they are distinctly inferior, on the average, to the regularly employed assistants, even if these also be pupils carrying some studies in the school. The usefulness of clerical assistants is certain to be much greater on the average if they may be held to account as a paid employee may be. The chances are not great that pupils who spend no more than an hour a day in the office will become sufficiently trained in the duties to be equal in effectiveness to the employee who gives full time or even half time to such work.

Furthermore, the administrative offices deal with affairs and data of a confidential nature with which students should not be familiar.

When student assistants are employed, it is better for the assistants and for the school to have one full-time office secretary act as supervisor and director and co-ordinate the work, train the assistants, and assume general responsibility for the activities of all. If the secretary is a mature person rather than a student, she may safely be assigned duties of management in problems of attendance and tardiness, supplies, and other matters to a much greater extent.

The principal should be careful not to exploit willing students unduly merely to save on expenses for clerks. If the student-clerks are not students in the office-training classes and are therefore not using the office for laboratory experience, they should ordinarily be paid wages, even though the wages may be only a half or less of what a trained clerk or secretary would receive. It is wise, whether the student is paid or not, to write a memorandum to his parents, outlining the arrangement and asking the parent to notify in writing whether it is satisfactory. Where this sort of agreement has not been reached, some parents have complained bitterly about the arrangement and gossiped about it in the community.

ASSISTING THE SCHOOL SECRETARY. The principal has the important responsibility of assisting the school secretary in the improvement of her service and in meeting the responsibilities of her position. The secretary depends largely upon the principal for essential information about other personnel in the school and for information about the school, its policies, and its procedures, particularly with respect to the ideas of the principal on how the office should be managed. He should, in particular, give her specific instructions and help her in dealing with teachers, students, custodial help, and the public in general. This help is very important for the secretary who is new to the school. There is no position in the business world quite like that of the school secretary.

The principal must make it clear to the school secretary that she is to be co-operative and diplomatic in dealing with members of the teaching staff but that she is not to permit overenthusiastic teachers to give her responsibilities which do not lie definitely in the categories of responsibilities which the principal has told her specifically she may accept from members of the staff. The school secretary should know what matters she should refer to the principal. There are many teachers who raise questions or suggest activities which the secretary may not know how to handle. She should be diplomatic in referrals, saying to a teacher, "I think Mr. Brown would like to have you take that up with him," rather than "You will have to see Mr. Brown about that." The secretary must be cautioned not to discuss one teacher with another or to discuss controversial aspects of school policy with teachers, their grievances against each other, or their grievances against the principal, superintendent, or supervisor.

The principal should likewise instruct the secretary relative to dealing with students. The secretary should be cheerful and at least reasonably popular with the students who meet her in the outer office. In some respects she is one of the members of the counseling staff of the school, particularly with reference to such things as attendance, tardiness, use of supplies, and so on. She must be told to take a quiet and firm but tolerant attitude toward the overbearing, officious, or rude student when he comes to the office.

In dealing with the lay public, the value of diplomacy, co-operation, and appropriate reticence about many matters must be impressed upon the school secretary, particularly if she is young and particularly if she is a local product. With respect to complaints, it is her responsibility not to attempt to explain matters to the public but to assure the complaining individual that she will report it to the appropriate person, in many instances urging the individual himself to speak to the appropriate person in the school, whether he be the principal, a particular teacher, the coach, or someone else. It should be impressed upon her that the slightest discourtesy or arguing with patrons who call in person or on the telephone is not to be tolerated. If any argument is necessary, it should be taken care of by the principal or a person designated by him.

The secretary must be briefed about many things. A number of principals prepare a mimeographed statement and supply the school secretary and each of her assistants with a copy. Such a statement may present a list of matters with which the secretary should be familiar: the dispensing of books, equipment, and supplies; the care of school records; attention to reports; clerical details of admitting and enrolling students during the year, of attendance, tardiness, and transfer of pupils to other schools; how various funds are handled and to whom funds should be delivered; receipting for, or requiring receipt for, the delivery of equipment or materials for the school; the collection of and accounting for funds from students for materials or equipment sold to them at the school; rules relating to the use of school telephones by students or by parents who wish to speak to their children or teachers; appropriate notations about articles delivered to her care and surrender of those articles to appropriate individuals, particularly lost-and-found articles; conditions under which the office will accept and handle mimeographing or other duplicating work for teachers, or the P.T.A. and other parent groups; responsibilities of the clerical staff in connection with any drives, ticket-selling, or other sales campaigns; responsibilities of the clerk for conveying to the custodian the requests of the teachers for repairs, more heat, or less heat; instructions concerning what to do with various kinds of visitors to the school; names of chairmen of faculty committees, student-carnival officers, club officers, and athletic managers; policy with respect to such matters as calling students and teachers to the telephone and use by the public of various rooms of the building, athletic fields, and playgrounds.

3. Records and Statistics Which Should be Kept in the Principal's Office

RECORDS. The principal's office should be the central bureau of records pertaining to his school. Because they allow greater flexibility in locating the records of given individuals and in withdrawing and adding records, card records are greatly to be preferred to books. Safe and convenient housing should be provided for all records in the form of card cabinets of various sizes built into units and drawers and compartments for ledgers, vouchers, and other book or noncard records. Standard card sizes which are most convenient and for which cabinets are most frequently constructed are 3 by 5 inches, 4 by 6 inches, 5 by 8 inches, and 8½ by 11 inches. As must as possible of the following data should be obtained, properly recorded, and filed:

1. Names of pupils registered: sex, age, race, date of birth, address, and the names, nativity, address, telephone number, and occupation of parents.
2. Daily schedule of each student.
3. Marks and credits of pupils by subjects and date.
4. Intelligence, achievement, and prognostic scores of pupils: name of test, date, derived ages or quotients.
5. Records of personality traits of pupils: honesty, initiative, industry, cooperation; cases of major discipline.

6. Records of vocational choice of pupils
7. Physical and health records: disease history, results of physical and medical examinations, immunization, and school accidents.
8. Attendance records showing extent, causes, and dates of absence.
9. Extracurricular activity record: participation of each pupil, membership, and adviser.
10. The social and activity calendar of the school.
11. Records of graduates: college attendance and marks, occupation, and address.
12. Data concerning the experience, preparation, appropriate personal items, and teaching assignment of each member of the staff.
13. Supervisory records of observations, interviews, minutes of teachers' meetings.
14. Teachers' summaries of instructional materials covered in each class each semester.
15. Schedule of classes with the number of pupils enrolled in each class.
16. Requisition of equipment and supplies.
17. Receipt and removal of supplies and equipment: date, description, and from whom received or to whom delivered.
18. Inventory of portable equipment, including a card catalogue of library books.
19. Accounts of all funds of the school and student-body organizations not handled by the treasurer of the board of education.
20. Records of employment service, work permits, and similar data.
21. Records of accidents to pupils and teachers.
22. Records of all inspections by fire, health, or educational authorities.

In practically all secondary schools today, except the very smallest ones, all or most of these types of records are kept; in the larger schools a number of additional types are kept. Pupil data likely to be employed by counselors should be housed in a place which is accessible to them.

PURCHASE OF RECORD AND REPORT FORMS. There are four principal sources of supply for forms of school records, administrative notes, and administrative communications:

1. Local printing firms supplying forms to order.
2. Supply houses furnishing standard forms in quantity.
3. The printing department and the duplicating machines of the school.
4. The National Association of Secondary School Principals.

In general the sources named above are in order of their relative expensiveness; however, if supplies are ordered in quantities of a thousand or more, there will ordinarily be little difference between the first two sources, especially if it is desired that the name of the school or any deviation from a standard form made up by the supply house appear on the card or form. If the quantity is small, as in the case of school-attendance registers or other record books, the necessary cost per register or per book will be so great as to make local printing prohibitive; consequently, such record books should be obtained from an educational supply house.

The principal should obtain catalogues or specimen sets of forms and records from a number of firms specializing in them. A list of such firms may be made up from the advertisements in journals intended especially for school executives, such as *The American School Board Journal, Overview, School Management, The Nation's Schools,* and the *Bulletin of the National Association of Secondary School Principals.* Publishers of the journals just mentioned will forward the names and addresses of school officials to firms distributing supplies in which the officials are interested. Excellent record forms are often suggested by the specimens submitted by the better of these concerns. Satisfactory admission slips and similar forms not to be employed as permanent records may be prepared at great saving in the school printing shop or on the school duplicating machine.

Permanent records that are not of the book type should be entered on durable cards. If card files of uniform size are employed for different purposes and are likely to be confused, different colors may be employed to advantage.

DESIRABLE STATISTICS. From his records the principal should compile, or have compiled, statistical information which he will find of service from time to time. What should be compiled will depend upon the various projects of publicity, administration, and supervision, the types of reports the principal is called upon to make, and the investigations he is making in his particular school, as well as the types of records he has at his disposal. In addition to the records previously mentioned, the following data, useful in the principal's study of his school, should be kept, computed, and recorded:

1. Age-grade table showing percentages of pupils at age, accelerated or retarded one, two, three, or more grades.
2. Mental age-grade table, the same as the age-grade table except that it employs mental ages of pupils instead of chronological ages.
3. Statistical tables showing trends in enrollments over a period of several years by subjects, by classes, and so on.
4. Statistics showing attendance and tardiness over a period of years by months.
5. Statistical tables showing the number of pupils participating in each extracurricular activity.
6. Statistical tables showing the percentages of failures over a period of years by subjects, by teachers, by grades, by ages, and by I. Q.'s.
7. Statistical tables showing the retention or withdrawal of pupils over a period of years by age at entrance, by I. Q., by average grade and by occupational and social classification.
8. Statistical analysis of schedule of classes, with tables showing the frequency of class sections of various sizes, load of the individual teacher, etc.

The preparation of such statistical computations, tables, and graphs will be serviceable in stimulating and guiding the principal's analysis of his school and its achievements and problems. It will enable him to furnish promptly upon need data regarding any one of a large number of problems that may arise in connection with faculty meetings, newspaper and other publicity opportunities, and requests from the superintendent, the board of education, or organizations. In addition to ensuring that he knows his school, its problems, the causes and sources of its problems, and its trends and tendencies in many respects, this information enables him to speak authoritatively regarding these things upon any occasion and upon a moment's notice.

4. *Office Management and Relations*

DELEGATING ROUTINE. The administrator must learn early the importance of his own time and the great desirability of effective apportioning of his time to his many duties. In addition to the desirability of economizing time in connection with visiting parents and teachers, he must acquire as soon as possible the tendency and the ability to delegate as much of his work as can be done effectively by others—assistant principals, supervisors, department heads, teachers, student officers, and clerical help—without interfering with the effective discharge of his responsibilities, directly or indirectly, and without requiring too much of his subordinates. For example, he should, whenever possible, delegate such work as recording, filing, or tabulating data, the supervision of extracurricular activities, and the handling of office routine in connection with absences, tardiness, report cards, lockers, textbooks, supplies, and standard achievement and intelligence tests. When the services of capable assistants among his lieutenants are available, he should utilize them in making investigations, in managing teachers' meetings, in classroom visitation, in managing assemblies, and in enrolling, advising, and registering students. With good organization, good secretarial and clerical help, and good advisers, he may be relieved of a great deal of administrative routine and educational, personal, and disciplinary guidance. The young principal desirous of demonstrating his versatility and ability in the activities of the school will find this extremely important lesson a very difficult one to learn.

APPORTIONING TIME. The principal must set aside some reserve time each week, if not each day, for three purposes: (1) for such unforeseen emergencies or demands on his time as are certain to arise almost daily; (2) for reflection and study of his school and its problems (as an important business executive told one of his division subordinates, he should have time to "shut his door, cock his feet upon his desk, and think out better ways of doing things"); and (3) for visiting classes as part of his supervisory responsibility. He must rarely let himself become so beset by calls upon his time that he works ineffectively and creates the atmosphere of desperate hurry and lack of organization. He must learn early not to spend valuable time in relatively unimportant or unnecessarily long conversations with pupils, patrons, and teachers. He must develop skill in being able to bring such conversations to a close pleasantly and without offense, but promptly. Suggesting that in a few minutes his presence will be needed elsewhere, making preliminary motions of rising from the chair, turning the conversation toward a rational termination, and avoiding digresssions are methods of ending conversations which in some instances may have to be supplemented by pleasantly bidding the visitor good-by, inviting him to call again, expressing pleasure at having had him come, unostentatiously leading the way to the door, or making other more impressive suggestions.

OFFICE HOURS. The principal should maintain stated office hours at which he may be found regularly. These should be such as will not interfere systematically with the visitation of classes at any one period in the daily schedule. They should include at least some time each week after the close of school for conferences with teachers who cannot conveniently come at office hours during the regular school day. The amount of time spent in regular office hours need not be great, but designated office hours should be kept conscientiously. At times when he is not in the office but elsewhere in the building, the principal should keep his clerk informed as to where he may be found and when he will be back, training her not to interrupt supervisory visits except in cases of importance. He must learn to plan his activities ahead, monthly, weekly, and daily, making and keeping notes of his plans. He must at all odds save himself from becoming so immersed in the details of his daily work that he loses perspective. He should accustom himself to look ahead and to prepare for the work of the next day, the next week, and the next year. He should constantly strive to reduce the number of situations where preparations for closing school, for board or staff meetings, for examinations, or for various other functions have been overlooked until too late or until he has been compelled to make them so hastily that he has not been able to give them sufficient thought.

THE PRINCIPAL'S CALENDAR AND OTHER TYPES OF REMINDERS. A considerable number of principals have found it very useful to develop a calendar as a reminder of various responsibilities throughout the year. Perhaps the best form is a card file, a file of cards 3 by 5 inches, divided into twelve divisions according to the months of the year and arranged within each division from the first day of the month to the last. Beginning such a file, a principal may through the summer and the early fall think of all the things that he can that are likely to need attention throughout the year and make additions as the need occurs. The file developed for one year is a good "nest egg" for the next year.

Most principals also use a special type of school calendar to alert them ahead of time to their responsibilities. Forms for school calendars are furnished by a considerable number of colleges, commercial companies, and state activity or athletic associations. A principal should have one of these in his office, where he can see it frequently and make additional notations of things to do and things that are coming up so that he can be planning ahead and be ready to meet situations that arise. Each year's calendar should be kept for the following year and used as a basis for notations on the new calendar.

Many principals also develop for themselves a weekly calendar which they keep on their desks for immediate reference. Excerpts from such a calendar, used by the principal of the Jackson High School of Miami, Florida, are included here as illustrations.

Jackson High School, Miami, Florida

WEEKLY CALENDAR OCT. 21-27

Tues.	Home Room, Club, & Honor		
Oct. 21	Societies Presidents	Aud.	1st Per.
	10th Grade Home Room Program		
	Chairmen	Cafe Annex	2nd Per.
	$8B_7$ Basic Ed.	All Apattah	
		Library	1:00 p.m.
	Monitors meeting	Cafe annex	2:45 p.m.
	9th Grade Representatives	342	5th Per.
	Sr. Tap Dance	Rec. Room	3:00 p.m.
	Operetta rehearsal	Aud.	6:30 p.m.
Wed.	Assemblies for Group A & B		9:37 &
Oct. 22			10:37 a.m.
	Student Council Meeting	Aud.	2:00 p.m.
	Cheerleader Try-outs	Aud.	3:00 p.m.
	Modern dance	Gym & Rec.	7:00 p.m.
Thurs.	Cheerleaders to Edison		8:30 -
Oct. 23			10:00 a.m.
	Color Day contestants	Aud.	1st Per.
	Pep Assembly	Gym	1:30 p.m.
	Spanish Honor Society	237	3:00 p.m.
	12A Executive Board	215	3:00 p.m.
	Red Cross Rally	Central Sch.	3:00 p.m.
	9th Grade Representatives	115	3:00 p.m.
	Jr. Tap dance	Rec. Room	3:00 p.m.
	Learn To Swim Club	Y – Pool	3:15 p.m.
	Football Jackson vs. Edison	Orange Bowl	8:15 p.m.
Fri.	Learn To Swim Club	Y – Pool	8:15 a.m.
Oct. 24	Life Saving	Y – Pool	3:00 p.m.
	$8B_8$ Party	West Patio	3:00 p.m.
	12th Grade Speakers	Aud.	3:00 p.m.
	Speakers for Tallahassee Congress	337	3:00 p.m.
Sat.	Drama Group to Key West		
Oct. 25	Horseback riding	N.W. Academy	9:00 a.m.
Mon.	Assembly – Senior High		
Oct. 27	12th Grade Speakers	147	3:00 p.m.
	N.F.L. Board	337	7:00 p.m.

Office Relations with Staff and Students. The principal must learn to maintain poise and reserve in his relations with members of the staff and pupils, even under annoying or humiliating circumstances. This does not imply that he should be austere or pompous, but he should maintain a professional attitude that is unruffled by the details of the day's work, however disconcerting they may be. He should be neither quarrelsome nor chummy, but pleasant and businesslike, at once inviting confidence, respect, and good will. He should not aggressively attempt to impress either pupil or teacher with his superior position or knowledge. If he possesses knowledge and the qualities of leadership, recognition of these will be an incidental but certain outcome of his work. Above all, he should not bluff; dignified silence is much more serviceable as well as more honorable.

The principal should not have to learn by sad experience that the office should not be a loafing place for students or members of the faculty. Work should proceed even when "company" is present if the "company" has no business to transact. Visitors should be encouraged to depart as soon as their business is finished. To attain this desired condition necessitates that the principal establish the condition without exception during the first few weeks of office. Establishing such procedure not only operates to conserve time but surrounds the office with an atmosphere of dignity which is useful upon many occasions.

The Principal and His Office Relations with Patrons. Upon all occasions the principal should be careful to avoid comments about pupils, teachers, and other people in the community. What he actually says may pass through several intermediaries and undergo an astounding transformation. Praise of pupils and teachers should be given in moderation—negative criticism rarely, even if it is no more than agreement with such criticism by a visitor. Praise given should never be such that it could be interpreted as favoritism or "politics."

The problem of the complaining or irate parent or other visitor furnishes a crucial test of the administrative ability of the principal. The most successful administrator never forgets his professional poise and balance, even in the face of angry, unfair, or personal criticism. He realizes that the complainant is very often misinformed and that, if he is properly approached, he is likely not only to be appeased but to be sorry for his mistake and respectful of the patience with which he has been received, even though his pride may prevent him from giving any indication of it upon the particular occasion. On the other hand, loss of temper and patience on the part of the principal only serves to alienate the visitor and to stimulate him to hostile activities, even though he may later learn that his original grievance was without adequate foundation.

The principal should keep before him the example of the well-poised, self-contained business head who receives angry complaints from important customers in a relatively unruffled manner and by so doing arouses feelings of respect. Consideration of the cause of complaint should always be promised and given. A noncommittal position should be taken until there is an opportunity to get all the facts in the case and the other side of the story. Complaints given in an emotional frame of mind over the telephone should be received politely and the complainant promised an investigation, given an explanation, or, perhaps better still, in all appropriate situations urged to call at the office, thus allowing time for the angry father or mother or other individual to cool off before the matter is dealt with. Only upon very rare occasions should complaints be countered with complaints about the misbehaviors of the complainants' children. Such countering should be confined to instances in which the misbehavior is a factor in, or pertinent to, the subject of complaint. Even then, the countercomplaint should be made without show of personal anger. In general, administrators, when dealing with complainants, should let them do most of the talking, especially in the first part of the interview. A little later in the interview, when the complainant has gotten things off his chest, the administrator may begin to pick up the pieces in a diplomatic way in an effort to cause the complainant to see things as they really are.

The spirit of these principles of handling official or business visitors should be instilled into the members of the staff. Certain conditions make this project one that requires skill and caution. Among high-school teachers there is a high percentage of novices who, as a class, are more than ordinarily sensitive and conscious of their intellectual training. In general, they possess a marked aversion to servility. It is difficult for them to acquire the desired professional poise and emotional control in the face of sharp or unwarranted criticism. As the professional leader of his staff, the principal should, without demanding servility or appearing to demand it, assist his teachers to see the value of, and to acquire, a calm, professional attitude.

5. *Opening and Closing of the School Year*

SUMMER AND PREOPENING PREPARATION. The principal (or superintendent in smaller schools) should in his first year make out a list of things to be attended to in the summer before school opens. He should consult his superintendent about these responsibilities. Each year he should revise and add to this list. It will probably include such things as preparing items for the first teachers' meeting or preopening bulletins to teachers; checking up on repairs, supplies, and orders; preparing items of publicity to parents and students relative to opening day; making committee assignments; arranging the school calendar of events and activities; seeing that textbooks and supplies are ordered and available; sending out notices to teachers concerning day, hour, and place of the preopening staff meeting and the meeting at the end of the first day; checking up on the football schedule.

He will want to arrange for and publicize the times when new students and parents may see him just before the opening of school. He will want to lay plans for the home rooms and assemblies for the first few weeks or see that such matters are being planned by committees.

In schools of more than 400 or 500 pupils, the principal should be available for at least a week after the close of school and two weeks before the opening, to consult with parents and social workers, to continue to work on the school schedule, to prepare transcripts for students going to college, to help graduates and other students in obtaining positions, to attend to various aspects of ordering and receiving supplies and equipment, to give guidance service to students and former students, and to consult with teachers about their work for the coming year. In a very large school, perhaps one with more than 1500 pupils, these duties will require at least half of the summer. In some schools the principal stays on during the summer session; but usually the administration of the summer session is assigned to an assistant principal or a teacher on part time after the school begins, since there are not enough important duties to require the services of the principal.

Closing the School. The last few weeks of every school year are hectic weeks, in which the beginning principal may forget many things and make many mistakes unless he plans carefully. Here is a list of some of the duties peculiar to this time of the year.

1. Getting inventories from members of the staff of library books, major pieces of equipment, textbooks, and supplies.
2. Requiring and auditing reports and accounts of all funds in the keeping of student officers or members of the staff.
3. Requiring and administering requests or requisitions for instructional supplies and equipment for the following year, especially such as should be on hand at the beginning of the school year.
4. Seeing that members of the staff check in keys and other school property lent to them for their individual use.
5. Getting from the staff requests for needed repairs and replacements.
6. Arranging for janitorial work during the summer, particularly for plants, landscaping, and aquaria.
7. Getting the summer addresses of members of the staff.
8. Getting from members of the staff names of textbooks and descriptions of supplies needed for students at the opening of school.
9. Seeing that textbooks are ordered by the bookstore or, if textbooks are furnished students, by the school.
10. Planning or supervision of planning of senior day or senior week or other senior activities.
11. Seeing that all grades and other reports are turned in by members of the staff, including brief synopses of work covered in each class for the semester or year.

12. Getting necessary data for the awarding of honors, scholarships, and prizes.
13. Planning and making arrangements for commencement and other year-closing student activities.
14. Completing the task of sending to colleges and universities data concerning students who are attempting to become accepted for college entrance.
15. Making contact with new teachers and furnishing handbooks and other appropriate information about the school, their assignments, and the community.

PRINCIPAL'S REPORT. The number of principals preparing mimeographed or printed reports of the work of the school for the year has increased greatly in recent years. These reports, addressed to the superintendent of schools, include data which vary from school to school. A principal should exchange reports with principals of other schools, preferably larger ones, in order to get ideas about the contents and the methods of presenting data in their reports. These reports usually contain data concerning the achievement of interscholastic teams, attendance of students, enrollment in each subject and department, grade distribution of students by semester, notable events of clubs and activities, student organizations, unusual programs of the year, school publications, teachers' assignments, and scholarships and other scholastic honors won by students or former students.

The principal should be selective in deciding what to include in his report, so that it will not be long, tedious, and somewhat uninteresting. Unusual care should be taken to note all important changes in curriculum and methods of teaching, addition of new important equipment, unusual achievement of honors, new members of the staff, and other new and interesting developments in the school program. Most principals include a statement of the more important needs of their schools.

COMMENCEMENT. The commencement, or closing, exercises are discussed in Chapter 11. The principal should begin early in the year to plan for the commencement exercises. He should have the help of a senior-class adviser, a faculty committee, a student committee or a joint student-teacher committee, and the superintendent. Among the committees sometimes used to advantage may be mentioned the following: program, finances, caps and gowns, invitations and tickets, line of march and seating, class day, reception, and dance or social-affairs.

At the exercise it is customary for the principal, on behalf of the faculty, to recommend the class to the superintendent, for the superintendent to present the class to the board, and for a member of the board to present the diplomas, with the principal calling each name and the student proceeding to the center of the platform and receiving his diploma from the representative of the board. The audience should be requested to withhold applause until all diplomas are awarded, especially if the class is large.

WORK PRELIMINARY TO OPENING SCHOOL. The principals of all but the smaller high schools usually spend from two to four weeks just before the opening of school in various types of duties. Among other things they check up on the physical condition of the school plant, see that all repairs have been made and that the plant is ready for operation, and also check up on receipt of materials, equipment, and supplies which were ordered in the spring and during the summer and which will be needed in the first few days or weeks of the school year.

At this time principals also maintain and advertise office hours at which they will see students, parents, and teachers, relative to problems they wish to discuss with him. New teachers especially are encouraged to call upon the principal, discuss with him their work, and learn about the school, its mode of operation, the students, and the community. New students and their parents are also encouraged to visit the principal, learn about the school, register, receive advice, and select the courses they will take the first semester. A principal may wish at this time to send communications to teachers, particularly new ones, relative to their assignments, responsibilities, and activities during the first few days of school.

It is quite common for the principal to have at least one general all-faculty meeting before the opening of school, at which detailed instructions are given relative to the first day's procedure and other points, including the following: the time teachers are expected to report for duty, special duty assignments, plans for putting the schedule into effect, blank forms to be used, questions that students are almost certain to ask the first few days, records and reports to be kept (particularly with respect to the attendance of students), the handling of textbooks and reference books, and the like.

In addition to this meeting of the teachers for purposes indicated above, many schools are operating a preschool in-service program for at least several days and sometimes for as much as a week. In many schools these days are counted as part of the year for which the teacher is employed and paid.

THE OPENING DAY. The following suggestions for principals for the first day of school were based largely upon a list prepared by Professor Edwin Brown of Santa Clara University:

First-day duties:

1. Be on hand early. Get an upperclassman for a clerk if you do not have one. Let her take care of any case she is able to handle. Many of the interruptions are trivial in importance and can be handled in this manner. Answer no phone calls this first morning.
2. If a waiting list accumulates in your outer office, or in the hallway if there is no outer office, go out and determine what cases you can handle at once with a word or two. Make quick decisions on unimportant cases—make ap-

pointments for later dates for the more difficult cases. This is your busy day—take no unnecessary load.

3. Have no chairs in your office this first day except the ones used by your aides and yourself. Meet students while seated and dispose of them quickly. Meet parents and others standing, and pleasantly and courteously, but quickly, dispose of their cases. When the person wishes to visit and the question can be postponed to a later date, make an appointment.
4. Books needed, seating difficulties, conflicts, questions which interest the entire staff, should be considered at a brief meeting for all teachers. Dismiss early and handle special cases after the meeting. This allows teachers who are having no difficulties to prepare their first-day reports and go home.
5. Meet your assistants at the close of the day to canvass any problems that may have arisen.

First-week duties other than those of the first day:

1. Organize your fire drills on the second day of school. The first day is better if it can be done. To wait is dangerous, possibly criminal.
2. Make up your first week's report for the City Superintendent's office (if you are a principal in a city system), and for the State Department of Education office, if such a report is a requirement in your state.
3. Get a final check-up on books and supplies. Find out what has been delivered, and which classes are still in need of books.
4. Get your general assembly program outlined for the year. Whatever be the agency in charge, see that it is organized for efficient work. Make the first meeting a good one. Don't talk too much yourself.
5. Get the high-school library organization to functioning. If there is a regular librarian, this is easy. If there is no official librarian, you are responsible directly.
6. Look over the town's calendar (if a small town). There is usually a "Harvest Home Festival," a "Corn Carnival," a circus, or an "Old Settlers' Reunion" early in the fall.
7. Make up the official school roll at the end of the week.

Second-week duties:

1. Make plans for the out-of-class activities of the high school if the plan is not definitely carried over from the previous year. If it is, see that it is functioning.
   a. Apportion load among teachers. Give responsibility and authority.
   b. Check the schedule of meetings—both time and place.
   c. Study the regular class schedule for the best possible utilization of time.
2. Complete the football schedule, if not already done.
   a. Consult coach or physical education director.
   b. Carefully study both school and town calendar in arranging for games. Conflicts are dangerous here as football must pay its own way—and aid other activities.
   c. Examination dates and game-scheduling must be considered together.
3. Check eligibility of football players. Interpret carefully and make clear your intention to enforce the rules.
4. Develop (with the coach) the mechanics for handling home games.

Other first-month duties:

1. Organize your personal daily working schedule.

2. Appoint an assembly committee of students and faculty.
3. Perfect the organization dealing with the school paper and the yearbook (if you have one).
4. Get your first month's report. This is frequently a State Office requirement, a City Superintendent's requirement, or a desirable offering to the Board of Education (if not required by it).
5. Check to see that the program of the Parent-Teacher Association has been or is being made.
6. Check up on the supply room and order supplies that are running low.
7. Plan carefully and co-operatively your teachers' meetings for the first semester.

Problems, Questions, and Exercises

1. Draw a plan of an administrative office or suite of offices for a school of a size to be selected by you, showing the major pieces of furniture, built-ins, and so forth. In what ways would it be different from the plan given in the book for the school most approximating the size selected by you?
2. Of the different types of small items of standard office equipment mentioned in the book, which would you think for the school of the size selected by you would be most desirable, fairly desirable, or not very desirable?
3. Be able to discuss the uses of an intercommunication system, pointing out its possible values and dangers and indicating how it might be used to greatest advantage.
4. Describe what you think of the principle duties that you could assign to office clerks or secretaries in a school of 600 students; in one of 230 students; in one of 100 students.
5. What are some of the details often handled by the principal of which the secretary might be able to relieve him?
6. Make a list of several suggestions which ought to be kept in mind when using student clerical help.
7. In the order of approximate importance, make a list of what you think are the twelve most important types of data which ought to be kept in the principal's files.
8. Discuss the matter of delegating routine and the matter of apportioning time as a good principal would do it.
9. Be able to discuss the principles of good office management in dealing with parents and other callers.
10. Make a list of specific items you think might go on the principal's calendar of activities for the two following periods: the first few days after the opening of school; the last few weeks of school.
11. For a typical week, for a school of a size selected by you, plan the distribution of a principal's time, showing the nature of activities and the probable amount of time devoted to each.
12. Can you give some examples of how a principal has violated the principles of good office management in dealing with parents?
13. What are some of the things that a principal should plan for the closing of the school year?
14. Be prepared to explain the operation of punch-card and sorting machines.

Selected Supplementary Readings

Administrative Facilities in School Buildings, Washington, D.C., Office of Education, U.S. Department of Health, Education, and Welfare, 1957. [Good modern discussion of housing equipment for administrative offices.]

Crew, A. B., "Secretarial Work Experiences Within the School," *Bulletin of the N.A.S.S.P.* (March, 1960), No. 253, pp. 142-149.

Elicker, Paul, and others, *Public Address in the Secondary School,* Washington, D.C., National Education Association, 1952.

Fitch, M., "Developing a Student Secretary Program," *Journal of Business Education* (March, 1949), Vol. 24, pp. 17-18. [Gives nine hints about introducing and developing a student secretary program in the school office.]

Fromuth, Carl L., "Please Be Seated," *Bulletin of the N.A.S.S.P.* (February, 1948), Vol. 32, p. 81. [Public relations in the office; place of the school secretary.]

Hauser, L. J., "Office Procedure—Improves After Secretaries Produce Handbook," *Nation's Schools* (July, 1951), Vol. 48, No. 7, pp. 30-32.

Planning Schools for Use of Audio-Visual Materials, Washington, D.C., Department of Audio-Visual Instruction, National Education Association, 1954. [Presents desirable performance standards for planning, designing, and operating an instructional-materials center.]

Preston, J. H., "Planning for Office Efficiency," *Catholic School Journal* (September, 1959), Vol. 59, pp. 70-71.

Walter, Ralph, "The School Secretary and the Faculty," *Education Digest* (May, 1949), Vol. 14, pp. 212-232.

Wynn, John W., "Utilization of the Central School System in the Secondary School," *Bulletin of the N.A.S.S.P.* (October, 1952), Vol. 36, No. 188, pp. 105-109. [Useful suggestions to eliminate unwelcome interruptions to classroom work.]

Yeager, William A., *Administration of the Non-instructional Personnel and Services,* New York, Harper, 1959. [Chapter 10, "The Secretarial and Clerical Services.]

22

High-School Housing and Its Care

1. Determining Housing Needs

THE PROBLEM OF PLANNING HIGH-SCHOOL HOUSING. The effective housing of a modern high school has become a complicated problem. Because of the complex nature of the program of studies offered in the high school of today, the planning of a modern high-school building presents to the principal, superintendent, and architect a task much more involved than that of a few decades ago. It is much more than a question of providing classrooms, an assembly room, a principal's office, a library, a gymnasium, and heating and toilet facilities. The modern secondary-school building includes an auditorium, a cafeteria, administrative offices, and special rooms and arrangements for instruction in science, sewing, cooking, typewriting, manual and industrial arts of various kinds, and physical education. It must also house counseling services, health services, audio-visual units, and new features such as an instruction-materials unit, a school store, language laboratories, and a common or general education room. Furthermore, there are many new ideas and plans about the shape, size, and location of various rooms and units.

The planning of these units and their location within the building so that they will conform best to the educational program and future needs of the particular school constitutes more than a problem of architecture. The cooperative services of an architect and someone in close touch with the educational program and needs of the school are required.

There are three types of situations requiring the erection of a high-school building or an addition to one already in use. They are: (1) newly organized districts with no housing for their high schools; (2) districts in which the high-school buildings have become unsafe or unfitted for high-school purposes; and (3) districts in which the high-school building is overcrowded. In each instance a careful survey of the needs for housing should be conducted.

Estimating the Prospective Secondary-School Population for Schools Just Being Established.[1] For the district in which no high school has been previously maintained, the survey is more difficult than in the second and third situations. There are less reliable data available. It must be very fairly estimated how many students will attend the new high school and how this number will increase. Three classes of students must be included in the calculation: those residing in the district who have been attending high school in other districts; those who have not been attending high school but would attend if there were one in the district; and those who would attend from neighboring districts. Ordinarily data concerning the first group are available from the records of the superintendent, the school clerk, or the county superintendent of schools. Data regarding the second group must, under any circumstances, be based merely on guesses. Estimates of numbers of pupils falling in the third group depend upon the laws and regulations obtaining in the state with respect to the tuition and transportation of nonresident students. In states where districts that do not maintain high schools contract with others that do for the tuition of those students residing within the district who wish to attend high school, estimates may be obtained from contracting boards of education of the neighboring districts. In states in which nonresident high-school students individually select the school they attend, serviceable estimates may be based upon interviews with students and school officials of the neighboring districts. Districts not previously maintaining high schools are usually units with relatively small high-school populations. Estimates of these districts may be made fairly accurately, without excessive expenditure of effort and time.

In districts where a high school has been maintained but where the building is no longer safe, is overcrowded, or cannot be adapted to the educational program (that is, where new housing is needed), a prediction of enrollment may be made with more accuracy. The enrollments of the school for years past should be available and estimates based on these may be made.

Estimating Secondary-School Enrollment. In estimating high school enrollments, the most important factors are the number now in the elementary school and the number of births in the past five years (an indication of the number of children not now in school). Using these numbers, with appropriate deductions for withdrawal of students from school on a ratio slightly less than that of past years, there may be made a fair estimate of future high-school population grade by grade.

In estimating the number of youngsters likely to be retained through the grades, a very slight increase in the percentage retained, as compared

[1]Most properly, this estimating should be done as a part of a unified building-program study for the entire school system.

to that of previous years, should be assumed in recognition of the trend toward students' remaining in school longer. In addition, of course, estimates must be made of the future population of the district on the basis of sources other than births within the district; there may be decreases or increases depending on factors such as shifts in industry, shifts in the highways and railroad transportation, and shifts in opportunities for employment.

Estimates of future population often may be obtained from the research departments of public-utility corporations, such as telephone, gas, water, light, and power companies. An estimate based upon all such data available should be utilized. The change in high-school enrollment may be calculated from the change in population by employing the ratio of high-school enrollment to population at present and allowing for a slight increase in the percentage of population attending high school in the years covered by the prediction.

The predicted future school population may be modified, as may seem necessary, to conform to influences which seem most pertinent to the community: for example, the closing of mills or industries, the recent location of new shops or industries, the imminent establishment of high schools in neighboring districts, or a change in the nature of the population.

ESTIMATING AND UTILIZING THE CAPACITY OF PRESENT HOUSING. In determining the extent of the need for additional housing, consideration must be given to the extent to which present facilities are being employed to maximum capacity with educational efficiency. The writer, together with a colleague, was once asked to make a building and financial survey of a district maintaining a high school of about 325 students. The principal and the superintendent reported the building to be crowded and exhibited such evidence as French classes being conducted in a physics laboratory and a small Latin class in the library. Upon investigation it was found that the building could house approximately 400 students with little crowding or danger to instructional efficiency. The sources of waste were found to be as follows:

1. Small classes because of semiannual promotions—midyear classes.
2. Small classes in advanced years of instruction in three foreign languages.
3. The failure to offer certain nonsequential subjects only in alternate years.
4. The use of the large cooking laboratory for only two periods during the day, for one class of seven students.
5. The use of a large sewing room for only two periods a day.
6. A short school day—one less period than other schools.
7. Failure to use the cafeteria at times other than lunch periods.

In view of the fact that housing is an important part of high-school costs, it is not only ethical but an evidence of good management to utilize available facilities to the maximum consistent with instructional efficiency before urging additional housing. Studies of building utilization have shown that the percentage of utilization of many buildings is low.

Remodeling and Adding Space. In many cases it is not practical to construct a new building; there is then the problem of remodeling the old building, planning additions to it, or both. Frequently, when a new senior high school is built, the junior high school takes over the old building of the senior high school; as a result, it is often necessary to remodel the old building. When additions are made to existing buildings, there is the danger that the additions will make the schools much larger than optimum size (which experts in secondary education have almost uniformly maintained to be about 800 students).

2. *Provisions for Instructional Space*

Location and Size of Site for Plant. The criteria which are most important in choosing the location of a high-school building are as follows:

1. Unless transportation for pupils is provided by the school, the location should be central so as to minimize the distance necessary to be traveled by students attending the school. The great majority of walking students should either live within one and a half miles of the school (one mile in icy-cold climates) or be on convenient transportation lines.
2. The school should be so located as to have from three to five acres of play space, depending upon the size of the school; in addition, there should be athletic fields of from ten to twenty acres, depending upon the size of the school.
3. In choosing a site, consideration must be given to providing parking space for faculty, other employees, and students.
4. Secondary-school buildings, especially those of junior high schools, should be located so that the dangers and difficulties of coming and going are minimized. This means that there should be a minimum of unprotected railroad crossings, "through streets," and other dangerous thoroughfares to be traversed. It means that there should be enough avenues of approach to permit transportation of pupils without congestion or danger. The building should not be located adjacent to main automobile thoroughfares or railway lines or close to buildings in which explosives or dangerous gases are stored.
5. The building should be located so as to be free from present and probable future distractions in the way of noise and odors that are likely to come from railway trains and streetcars and certain types of factories and industrial plants, such as foundries, saw and planing mills, packing houses, and gas plants.
6. Ordinarily, high-school buildings should not be located in business centers or near centers where pool halls or other breeding places of low standards of thought and conversation prevail.

NEW TYPES OF BUILDINGS.[2] In recent years very radical ideas have been developed with respect to school buildings. In planning a new building, consideration should be given to these ideas and investigation should be made of how satisfactorily these ideas have worked out in practice.

Many new buildings and many rooms within buildings are not rectangular in shape, but are circular or semicircular or have five, six, or seven sides.

Because of new ways of planning class size and teacher assignment (such as those suggested by the Trump Plan of Teacher Utilization), space units within buildings are planned and constructed for flexibility. Partitions are used to make changes in the size and indeed in the shape of rooms and units within buildings. Because of the great increase expected in secondary-school enrollments, buildings are being constructed so as to permit additions; in fact, many times potential additions are included in original building plans even though only part of the entire building may be constructed at first.

There has been a distinct trend away from multiple-story buildings and toward one-story buildings; furthermore, there has been a tendency to plan schools of several units instead of one building, in what might be called a campus form. One-story and campus-type construction provides greater safety from fire and panics and reduces the amount of space that must be given to halls and stairways. However, in cold climates this type of building involves much greater cost for heating.

Many new buildings have been and are being constructed with separate instructional units, each unit consisting of a number of classrooms in a subject field or related subjects. These units are grouped around a central unit of common housing, in which usually will be found the main library, the auditorium, the gymnasium, and administrative and service offices of various kinds. There are sometimes separate units for heating, for home-economics instruction, and for shops.

Headmaster Rowland H. Nelson of the Metarie Country Park Day School at Metarie, Louisiana, suggests that there be a unit building for each area of approximately 40,000 square feet, with about 12,300 square feet for lectures, 6200 square feet for study, 4100 square feet for library, 4100 square feet for administration, 8200 square feet for laboratories, and 4100 square feet for service and equipment. Such a unit would accommodate approximately 325 or 330 students. It might include two large

[2]When a new building is to be planned, the principal should write immediately to the Educational Facilities Laboratories, Inc., 427 Madison Avenue, New York 22, New York, and obtain copies of the small publications of a series called *Profiles of Significant Schools*. In this series are reports, with illustrations and discussions, of the plans of the new high schools at North Hagerstown, Maryland; Rich Township, Illinois; San Mateo, California; Ann Arbor, Michigan; Newton, Massachusetts; Jefferson County, Colorado; and other districts. One may also see plans of new types of buildings or buildings with new features in recent issues of *The Nation's Schools, School Management,* and *The American School Board Journal.*

lecture rooms (which might be broken up into smaller rooms by means of movable partitions), a considerable number of study carrels (which accommodate two students each), a library, administrative offices, and three or four laboratories.[3]

LITTLE SCHOOLS WITHIN LARGE SCHOOLS. Still another trend in the planning of large schools has come to be known as the "little-school" idea. Recognizing the limitations of the very large school, particularly the impersonal nature of human relations in such a school, some planners have divided large schools into separate units which are little schools within themselves, each unit housing a variety of instructional rooms and an administrative office for the principal of the little school. In Newton South High School at Newton, Massachusetts, for example, there are three separate units; each unit is a little school in itself, with academic classrooms, and is connected by outdoor corridors with central units such as the auditorium, gymnasium, administrative quarters, main library, and cafeteria.

LOCATION OF THE ROOMS WITHIN THE BUILDING. As far as possible, shops employing machinery, band and orchestra rooms, and other quarters in which noisy activities are carried on should be in detached units or in a segregated wing of the building, not immediately below classrooms, study halls, or offices. If shops must be in the basement, the laboratories or kitchens should be placed immediately above. The heating plant (if properly fireproofed), the bicycle sheds, and the storage rooms are units which may legitimately be assigned to basement space. Many modern buildings are being built today with basements, however.

For two reasons laboratories for chemistry and cooking may well be assigned to top floors or remote parts of the building. Such an assignment reduces the inconvenience likely to result from fumes and odors. In addition, since class sections are relatively small in these subjects and the rooms are often not occupied throughout the day, especially in smaller schools, overall pupil traffic, vertical and horizontal, is minimized.

Toilets should be assigned convenient but inconspicuous locations. In all but the smallest buildings, toilets for each sex should be provided on each floor; in large one-story buildings two toilet rooms for each sex should be provided on each floor. In the campus type of construction, a toilet room for each sex should be provided in each building unit. There should also be separate toilets for each sex of the faculty. There should also be toilets in the administrative offices.

The library, as the heart of the school, should be located centrally and preferably quite close to the study hall or halls. In the smallest schools a

[3]Rowland H. Nelson, "Here is How an Educator Would Put the Perception Core into Effective Use," *School Management* (March, 1960), Vol. 65, No. 3, pp. 85-90.

large room with the library at one end behind an attendant counter and the rest of the room available as a study hall is an excellent arrangement, rendering the use of the library convenient to all students in the study hall and automatically eliminating the red tape and management problems incident to checking up on the passage of students to and from the library and study halls. At the same time one person is able to supervise library and study hall simultaneously, a very desirable arrangement in small schools. In larger schools the location of one or two study halls adjacent to the library will serve much the same end. Where it is advisable or necessary to have study halls on more than one floor, locating the study hall just above the library, with provision for a built-in speaking tube and dumb-waiter, will eliminate the necessity of the traveling of many students from study hall to library for the purpose of obtaining needed reference books.

The auditorium should be located so as to be accessible from the street; if consistent with the general building plans, it should be possible to enter and leave the auditorium without passing through the rest of the building.

The administrative offices should, of course, be located centrally so that they may be readily and promptly found by visitors without the necessity of their traversing the remainder of the building.

If there is a radio workshop-studio, it should be located in a quiet area; a television workshop-studio should be located where there will be adequate space overhead to accommodate ceiling lighting facilities and enough room for two or more camera chains.

CLASSROOMS. Ordinary classrooms should not all be of the same size. There should be one or more (probably about one in five or six) capable of accommodating from 50 to 60 pupils; the typical classroom should accommodate a maximum of 35 or 36 pupils; and probably one room in four or five should be of smaller size. In schools of less than 200 pupils, classrooms may be slightly smaller. Large classrooms should have two doors, one at the front and one toward the rear. In large high schools, with staffs of selected, experienced teachers, more large rooms will be needed and fewer medium and small ones. In small schools more small rooms should be provided in order that costs may be kept in proportion to needs.

In schools following the Trump plan or a similar plan of teacher utilization, there should be one or more classrooms large enough to seat at least 70, and preferably 100, students. There should also be from six to twelve conference rooms, depending upon the size of the school and the details of the plan of teacher utilization. These rooms should be half the size of a classroom so that, if a partition is removed, the two rooms may be used for a conventional classroom. Similarly, large classrooms should be constructed so that they may be divided at times into two smaller classrooms.

Approximately one third of the rooms should be provided with chalk board on three sides; the others may have chalk board on two sides. The boards should be 36 inches in width (from 40 to 42 inches is better for the front chalk board) and should be placed 32 inches above the floor in junior high schools, about 35 inches above the floor in senior high schools, and about 34 inches above the floor in four-year high schools. In a room with chalk board on two sides, the boards should be placed in front and on the side containing no windows.

A good statement relative to high-school classrooms is quoted below:

Under this heading will be considered the high-school recitation, academic, or interchangeable room, as distinguished from the more highly specialized laboratories and shops. It should never be assumed that small, bare, boxlike rooms are sufficient for classrooms used for social studies, language arts, and mathematics. These classrooms also should be learning laboratories. Their size and equipment will depend upon class-size policy, teaching methods, programming, and whether or not they are to be used as home rooms.

For certain types of secondary-school programs, where academic classrooms were equipped with tablet-arm chairs and used only for lecture and recitation, the old standard of 18 to 20 square feet per occupant was probably adequate. The trend, however, has been to lengthen the class period and to use a portion of the period for directed study. This type of classroom procedure requires more desk space for texts, reference books, and notebooks. There is also a tendency toward more informal small-group activities within the classroom, especially in the core subjects. These modern practices require informal seating and floor areas of 22 to 25 square feet per pupil. In small high schools, with considerable variation in class size, space utilization can be increased by providing classrooms of different sizes.

High-school classrooms should be provided with adequate storage cabinets, shelves, and filing cases for teaching supplies, materials, and books. Sufficient tackboard at eye level and chalk board should be provided for the teaching program. The tackboard and chalk-board requirements will vary with subjects, but usually about 16 linear feet of each is sufficient.

Classrooms should be designed and equipped so as to reflect their use. In large secondary schools, it is desirable to plan departmental rooms *en suite,* including a conference room and a special-materials library. High-school classrooms should be furnished with movable seat-desk units or tables and posture chairs.[4]

One door to each classroom, located toward what will be the front of the room, should swing outward and should contain in the upper half translucent glass. Bulletin and exhibit boards may be placed in spaces corresponding to chalk-board space on the rear wall or on the side walls toward the front of the room. Plug-in sockets for projection machines should be placed in the middle of the rear end of the room.

---

[4]American Association of School Administrators, "Planning Instructional Features to Fit the Educational Program," *American School Buildings,* Washington, D.C., National Education Association, 1949, pp. 93-95.

STUDY HALLS AND LIBRARY. Study halls should not be too large; a maximum seating of 70 to 80 is desirable. In smaller schools of less than 125 pupils, the library should be used as a study hall and should be large enough to seat at least one third of the pupils enrolled.

The library should be of ample size, even when it is not used as a study hall also. The minimum seating capacity of the main reading room will vary with the size of the school. In schools of from 100 to 200 students, libraries should be large enough to seat from 40 to 50; in schools of from 200 to 500, they should be large enough to seat from 50 to 60; and in schools with 500 or more, they should be large enough to seat from 60 to 100. Ample stack room should be provided in larger libraries, as should a workroom and a storeroom for repairing and cataloguing. There should be either a charging counter or a charging desk, depending upon the size of the school.[5] There should also be from one to four conference rooms, depending on the size of the school.

AUDITORIUMS OR ASSEMBLY HALLS. The auditorium, or assembly hall, should be located on the main floor. In junior, senior, and four-year high schools, except those with more than 600 or 700 students, the hall should be large enough to seat the entire student body and to be serviceable for plays and entertainments open to the public.

Because of the great expense of building auditoriums and the small number of hours they are in use, they should probably be built not larger than necessary to seat 600 or 700 students, even in the larger schools. Assemblies may be held in two or more sections if the auditorium seats only part of the student body.

In all but the smaller schools the auditorium should be equipped with an adequate stage, not less than 20 feet deep by 30 feet wide and larger if possible. Stage space should not be sacrificed for dressing rooms. In many schools these small rooms, of little real value and difficult to supervise, have been torn out to provide more stage space. Gymnasium dressing rooms in which locker and lavatory facilities are available are often more satisfactory.

The auditorium should be equipped with footlights, overhead lighting, drops, flies, and other fundamental stage equipment. It should be free from posts and pillars and should be provided with facilities for motion-picture and still projection. With respect to its interior decoration, it should be one of the features of the building contributing to the development of aesthetic appreciation. Care should be taken to see that the acoustics of the room are good. The architect should be asked to consider this point carefully. If necessary, acoustic plaster should be used and there should be acoustic treatment of the ceiling.

THE COMBINATION AUDITORIUM AND GYMNASIUM. Because of the expense involved in the construction of an auditorium, many school

---

[5]For a discussion of the equipment and furnishings of the library see Chapter 20.

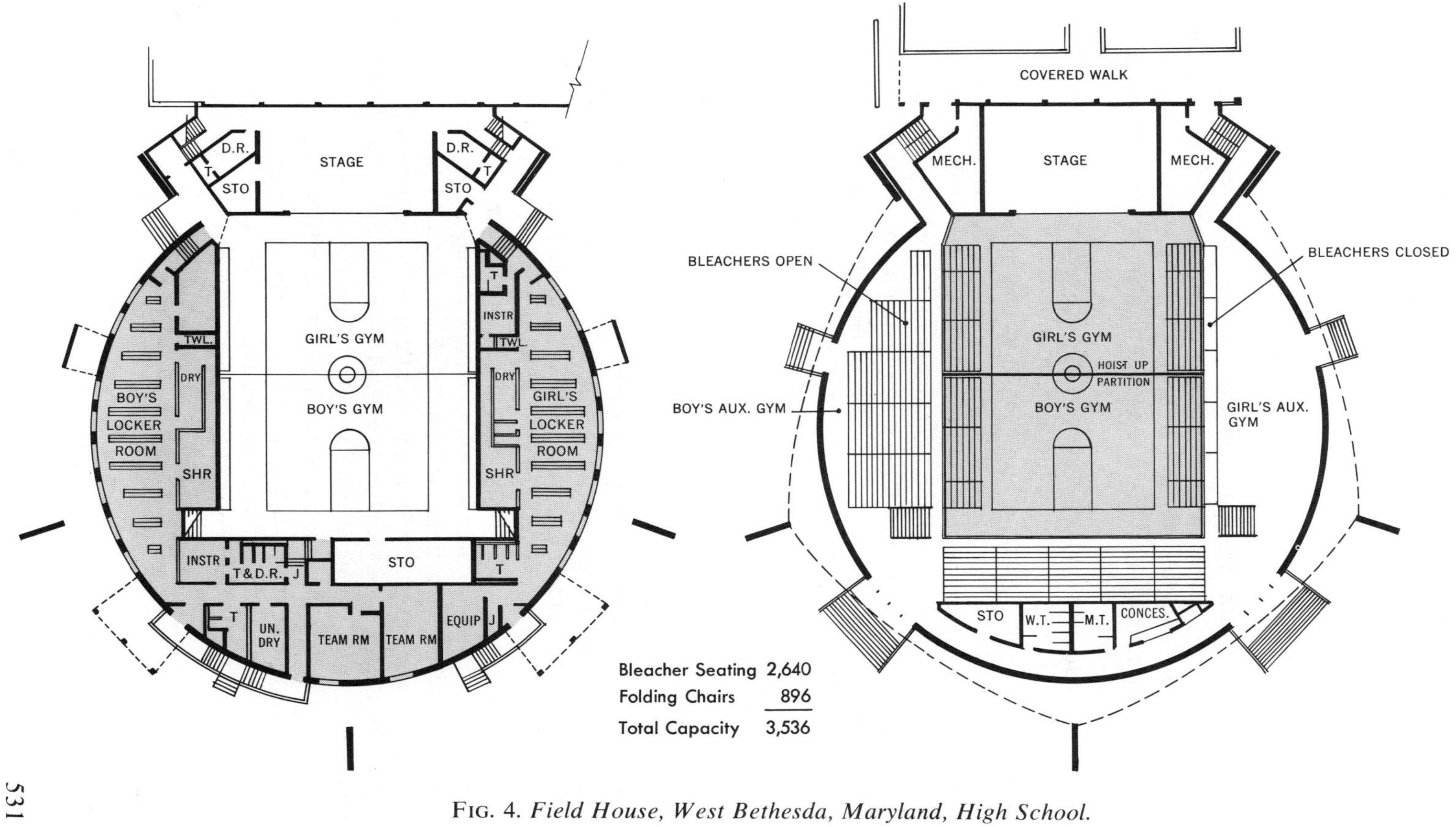

Bleacher Seating	2,640
Folding Chairs	896
Total Capacity	3,536

FIG. 4. *Field House, West Bethesda, Maryland, High School.*

buildings are planned to include a combination auditorium and gymnasium. The gymnasium is planned so that it may be divided into two smaller gymnasium floors, one for the girls' gym classes and one for the boys' classes. Undivided the area constitutes a basketball playing floor, along the sides of which may be placed roll-away bleachers to be employed when the main floor is used for basketball games with large audiences.

In planning a combination gymnasium and auditorium, not less than 18 feet should be allowed for the height of both gymnasium and auditorium; 25 feet or more should be allowed for the latter if it is to carry a balcony. From such a room there should be planned four plainly visible exits, two on each side.

In many buildings constructed recently, provision has been made for a swimming pool. Because of the large number of drownings that occur yearly, there is strong support for swimming instruction; indeed, in some high schools the ability to swim is a requirement for graduation. As a matter of fact, it probably should be required for graduation from junior high school, in order to reduce the number of senior high school youngsters who drown and to reach the many young people who do not finish senior high school. In some new schools a field-house structure has been erected to serve as auditorium and gymnasium. At West Bethesda, Maryland, the field house cost $6000 less and provided 4000 more square feet of space than the alternative plan for a gymnasium-auditorium.[6]

SPECIAL-INSTRUCTION ROOMS.[7] The effectiveness of instruction in science, household arts, industrial and manual-training subjects, commercial subjects, art, music, speech, and physical education depends somewhat upon more or less permanent equipment which should be taken into consideration when the building is being planned. In many school buildings, old and new, provision is made for foreign-language laboratories which involve: (1) a raised platform on one side, to be occupied by the instructor and his communication equipment; (2) separate receiving and study booths for each individual student. In recent years many new ideas have been developed about science laboratories and home-economics units. Built-in electrical conduits, gas and water leads, and waste channels in the floor and walls are economical and forestall unattractive installations as afterthoughts. With the value of new developments in mind, the principal should seek the advice and assistance of his department heads and teachers, who should be asked to make thorough investigations of their respective problems. Especially in the smaller schools, the principal should seek advice and suggestions, as

---

[6]*Conventional Gymnasium vs. Geodesic Field House,* New York, Educational Facilities Laboratories.

[7]See chapter bibliography for references to good treatments of housing and equipment for special-instruction rooms.

well as assistance in checking plans, for qualified teachers or experts outside his own school.

The principal should also obtain and study carefully pamphlets, bulletins, and books which contain information about types of housing units and equipment for instruction in various subject fields.

STUDENT CENTER, NORMAN HIGH SCHOOL, NORMAN, OKLAHOMA.

By courtesy of Caudill, Rowlett, and Scott, Architects, and Perkins and Will, Associate Architects, of Houston, Texas. Photography by Hedrich-Blessing, Chicago.

THE COMMON OR GENERAL EDUCATION ROOM. In many secondary-school buildings being constructed today, there is provision made for what is called a common or general education room or student center. The student-center room at Norman, Oklahoma, High School is shown above. This room makes provision for a variety of purposes, including space for a number of small student committees to work together; for reading and discussion before school, during lunch period, and after school; for plays and lectures; sometimes for dancing; and sometimes for the meeting of a large class.

There should also be provision made for display windows. These are particularly desirable in a school having a program of distributive education. Of course, there should be display windows for various kinds of exhibits which may be changed from time to time and for the trophies of the school.

THE SMALL THEATER, CHORAL ROOM, AND BAND OR ORCHESTRA ROOM. In all but the smallest schools a special room should be provided for dramatics (which special room may be little more than a wide classroom with a stage) which may also be used for forensics and other speech work.

There should also be provided a band or orchestra practice room and a choral room; properly planned, one room may serve both purposes. The room may also be used for classes at hours when not in use for music. The room (or rooms) for band, orchestra, or chorus should be located in a far corner of the building and should be well insulated to prevent sounds from disturbing classes in adjacent rooms. The room calls for special seating arrangements.

3. Provision for Noninstructional Space[8]

THE CAFETERIA OR LUNCHROOM. Recently constructed high-school buildings provide much more convenient and attractive lunchrooms than formerly were considered necessary. More and more children are eating their lunches at school, and the lunchroom or cafeteria in a high school of any size is a necessity. If planned carefully, the cafeteria room may also be used as a study hall or as a room for meetings, especially dinners or after-school meetings, if a small platform has been built in at one end or side of the cafeteria room. The cafeteria has been planned in some schools to serve also as the common or general education room.[9] In schools experimenting with the Trump plan, the cafeteria is used as a room for large classes. In some junior high schools it has been planned to be used as a library. In a few schools it is used also as an assembly room. The cafeteria in the Ferndale, Michigan, High School, for example, seats 640 students.

One or more small dining alcoves found in many school cafeterias are useful for meetings of committees of faculty and of pupils. In most schools food-vending machines are confined to those selling orange juice or milk.

For convenience, delivery of supplies, maximum safety, taking away of garbage, economy in plumbing, and accessibility to adults when

---

[8]Discussion of administrative offices and equipment is given in Chapter 21.

[9]See Robert G. Andre, "An Image of the Future Arises in Olympian Fields," *Nation's Schools* (July, 1960), Vol. 66, No. 1, pp. 56-66.

meetings are held in the cafeteria, the lunchroom may be assigned to the ground floor. Probably the best location for the cafeteria is in a separate annex or in a wing of the main building. From the standpoint of odors, it is better on a top floor. While the main floor is probably best for the cafeteria, there is a question raised by the allocation of main-floor space to a unit in use for so small a part of the time. In small schools, as a means of economizing in equipment, it may be best to have the lunchroom combined with the food laboratory or located adjacent to it. It should be so planned as to be of ample size and attractive.

The matter of noise is a real problem in the cafeteria. The floors and, in many cases, the ceilings need to have special treatment; linoleum or cork composition is excellent as floor material and as a covering for table tops. Sometimes acoustical treatment of the ceiling is very desirable. In some schools paper plates are used on trays, cutting down dishwashing expense, expense of breakage, and the amount of noise very materially.

TEACHERS' OFFICES AND LOUNGES. If boards of education and school patrons could be brought to appreciate the value of such provisions in terms of increased efficiency of the teaching staff, office space and desk and filing equipment would be provided for every teacher. Especially in schools on a seven-period or eight-period schedule, economy of building space forbids the exclusive assignment of a room to each teacher as combination office and classroom, desirable as that practice is for some reasons. In lieu of that, office space where each teacher may work effectively should be available. Since each teacher is engaged in teaching during much of the time spent in school, several teachers may be assigned to the same office and even to the same desk if adequate drawer and filing space is available. In very small schools one room may be used, but in larger schools a number of rooms should be provided, probably one for every ten or twelve teachers. A section of a teachers' workroom in the Tucson, Arizona, High School is shown on page 536.

In addition, there should be in larger schools one or more teachers' lounges for each sex; in very small schools there should be one for both sexes. A lounge provides teachers with a place for conversation and relaxation at times when they are free during the day, before school, or after school. Many schools have made provision for both offices and lounges and teachers are almost unanimous in their approval. If there are both offices and lounges, the former may be kept as places of quiet for work which demands concentration, and should be furnished with desks, filing cabinets and comfortable chairs.

THE HEATING PLANT. For purposes of safety and cleanliness, the heating plant should be housed separately from the rooms used for instruction. Since enrollments in secondary schools are certain to continue to increase for several decades yet, the heating plant should be constructed with possible building additions in mind.

The heating and ventilating systems, with their thermostatic controls, should be organized in such units that the auditorium, cafeteria, library, gymnasium, and administrative offices can be heated and ventilated independently of the rest of the building.

TEACHERS' WORKROOM, TUCSON HIGH SCHOOL, TUCSON, ARIZONA.

By courtesy of Superintendent Don Garrison. Photography by Ray Manley, Tucson.

THE CUSTODIAN'S ROOM. Every building should provide at least one room for the custodial employees, the number and size of the rooms depending upon the number of such employees. In addition to a small workshop and receiving room, there should be provided a lavatory, a convenient place for changing from street clothes to work clothes, and lockers for the safekeeping of clothes and personal effects. Since custodian's rooms are most likely to be located in the basement, an effort should be made to compensate for the location by making them otherwise attractive. Communication should be provided with at least a buzzer, but preferably a telephone or a speaking tube, connected with the administrative offices. In schools in which the custodian is expected to make repairs, his room should be equipped with a workbench, wood and metal lathes, power saw, and small tools.

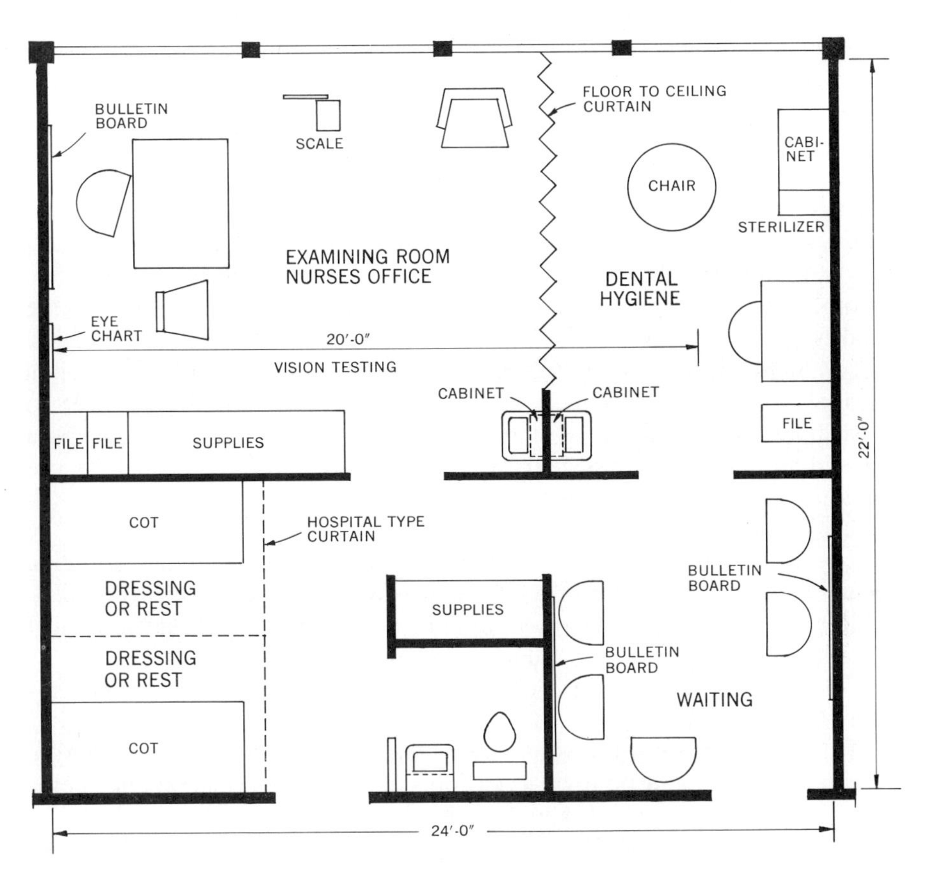

FIG. 5. *Diagram of Medical Suite.*

This layout represents functional planning for health service facilities for schools ranging in enrollments from 300 to 800. Larger schools may use a similar design but a larger area.

MEDICAL SUITES. In nearly half of the new secondary-school buildings for more than 500 students, there are medical suites which house school nurses, offer space for examinations of students, and serve other important purposes. A well-planned medical suite is shown here in diagram.

AUDIO-VISUAL EQUIPMENT AND STORAGE. In all but the smallest schools the auditorium should be equipped with a projection booth and a large screen of high quality, and all other rooms should be planned so that they may be easily darkened and furnished with portable screens. Every school should have projection equipment, including at least the following: opaque projector, preferably of the overhead type; a 16-millimeter sound film projector; a microprojector; a slide projector for 35-millimeter transparency films, a tachistoscope, and one or more tape recorders. Storage space must be provided for this equipment and for the material which is to be projected. Furthermore, some provision must be made for scheduling the use and general supervision of the equipment.

New secondary-school buildings, except smaller ones, are now being wired so that closed-circuit television may reach each room. Even though television may not be installed at once, provision should be made for it so that it may be installed later without unusually great expense. It is recommended that next to the studio there be a space for a control room, a small equipment maintenance shop, and a workroom for making and painting scenery and for storing scenery for stage props. It is further recommended that there be provision for a modern master-antenna coaxial system: (1) to pick up standard broadcasting signals; (2) to distribute these signals to classroom receivers; and (3) to distribute closed-circuit television signals originating in the studios through its use of a monitron or similar piece of equipment.

INSTRUCTIONAL-MATERIALS QUARTERS. In recent years many building plans have included one or more rooms to be used as an instructional-materials center. Such a center sometimes includes the library and most frequently includes audio-visual equipment and materials.

The center should also include a small darkroom for teachers' previewing of all films.

It naturally follows that some individual, perhaps with assistance from a committee, should be in charge of this center, supervising it and seeing that new materials are obtained for it.

Over a period of years, a large and very useful collection of locally made visual materials may be constructed and placed in the instructional-materials center.

4. *Miscellaneous Features*

STUDENT LOCKERS. The problem of the storage and safekeeping of the wraps, hats, caps, books, and supplies of high-school pupils, like many other problems of high-school management, seems never to come to a final solution. Thefts, real and imagined, cause high-school principals and parents many irritating moments.

Although some secondary-school buildings are being built today with coatrooms, most principals prefer to have a locker for each student. Measuring 12 by 12 by 72 inches, each locker may have a shelf for books and hat and may be used to store all wraps, hats, and books when they are not in use. Lockers should be built into the walls of the halls, not placed in rows in a room. Less space is thus consumed, and supervision is facilitated. Although the placing of lockers along the walls requires little more space and is slightly less expensive, it is considerably less attractive. If lockers are so placed, those with slanting tops, which make storage on top of them impossible, should be provided. Care should be taken to distribute the lockers in such a way as to avoid congestion. Double tiers of lockers are not preferable to wider distribution, even if it is necessary to place lockers on the upper floors for some pupils.

Experience has shown that the purchase of combination locks which can readily be reset (that is, the combination changed) will eliminate much waste of time on the part of both pupil and office assistants resulting from loss or misplacement of keys. If locks with keys are to be used, standard high-grade locks should be furnished by the school so that only one pupil will possess a key for each lock; there will be in the possession of the principal master keys to all lockers.

Acoustical Treatment. In buildings in which large numbers of people congregate and where clear hearing is important, acoustical treatment of ceiling and floor deadening are called for, at least in the rooms. Acoustical ceiling finish is recommended for corridors, auditorium, cafeteria, speech room, little theatre, and music rooms. Floor deadening is recommended for corridors, stairways, and library.

Classroom Seating. A problem closely associated with that of high-school housing is that of the seating in the various rooms. Various types of seating in classrooms and other units are recommended. What constitutes the most desirable seating for academic classrooms depends upon the spirit and method of classroom teaching. Socialized class discussions are best carried on in rooms furnished with movable chairs with tablet arms; laboratory and project teaching of several types places a premium upon group-work tables and movable chairs. When the traditional recitation method is employed, the fixed individual desk and seat possess the advantage of always being placed in order and of eliminating much of the "disciplining" necessary when movable chairs are employed. Perhaps, in schools of medium and larger size, two or three types of seating facilities should be provided for, thus permitting teachers and classes to be assigned to rooms in which the type of seating is adapted to the spirit and method of instruction.

Lighting. In most school buildings built today, reliance is not placed upon the light which may come through the windows; artificial light of the fluorescent type is provided in every room and in the corridors. Indeed, in some new buildings today (as the author of this volume many years ago predicted there would be) there are rooms which have no windows at all, getting light, fresh air, and heat through other channels.

Storage Space. One of the most common regrets of the principals and teachers who have planned new buildings has resulted from the failure to provide sufficient storage space. This is particularly true of storage space for supplies, for free and rental textbooks, for gymnasium and athletic equipment, for laboratory equipment and supplies (particularly for chemistry), for inactive files in connection with the offices of principals, counselors, nurses, and health officials, and for supplies and tools used in the shops and home-economics rooms. Care should be taken to canvass the needs of all the various departments and to insist that the architect provide adequate space. The school which has too much storage space seems to have been as yet undiscovered.

5. Building Supervision Related to Human Safety[10]

STAIRWAYS AND CORRIDORS. All stairways and corridors on other than the first floor should be fireproof. There should be no passageways or tunnels in the building, other than stairways and corridors, which might serve as air tunnels in case of fire. On the first floor of the central sections of a building of more than one story a corridor 12 to 15 feet wide will be necessary to provide ample room for traffic in both directions. In remote wings of the building and on upper floors, the corridors may be several feet narrower. Both ends of all corridors should have natural or artificial lighting. Each corridor should terminate at or near an exit. No corridor should extend more than 35 feet beyond exits or stairs. Stairs should be located not in corridors but at right angles to them. They should be placed near exits.

There has been in recent years a definite trend towards having a more spacious lobby at the entrance of the building.

PREVENTION OF FIRE. Because of the considerable number of young people in school buildings (most of which are rather crowded), careful attention must be given to the prevention of fire and to the safe removal of human beings in case of fire. Once a year there should be, in every home room or in the general assembly, a program related to fire prevention, fire fighting, and the evacuation of the building in case of fire.

Among things that can be done to prevent fire are the following: (1) invite representatives of the fire department to inspect the school plant and to make recommendations; (2) discuss at least once a year with the head custodian the matter of fire prevention and the storage of various kinds of materials that are likely to cause fires, such as waste paper, oily rags, cleaning materials, paint, kerosene, gasoline, films, and other readily inflammable material; (3) inspect the building and the storage closets at least twice a year to see whether or not inflammable material that has to be kept in the building is stored in fireproof containers (this includes oily rags and mops); and (4) see to it that corridors from the furnace and boiler rooms to the rest of the building are fireproof and kept closed at all times. Particular attention should be given to stairways and to closets

[10]The principal should acquaint himself with state laws and local ordinances on the subject of regulations applying to school buildings.

under stairways. They should be inspected and studied with a view to fire prevention and their use in case of a fire.

The Committee on Fire Research of the National Academy of Science of the National Research Council has published a very helpful bulletin entitled *School Fires—An Approach to Life's Safety*. Bulletins may be obtained, for $2.50 each, by writing to the Research Council at 2101 Constitution Avenue, Washington 25, D.C. Each principal should have a copy of this very helpful bulletin.

FIRE DRILLS. The attitude and the practice with respect to fire drills have changed greatly in the past few years. Formerly, there were fairly frequent fire drills, in an atmosphere of excitement, to see how rapidly a building could be cleared. Time records were kept, and pride was developed in the rapidity with which a building could be emptied. This is no longer believed to be wise procedure. Ordinarily there is plenty of time to empty a building if students in all parts of the building are notified as soon as the fire is discovered and if they behave in an orderly fashion. The principal goal is quiet and safe exit from the building—not speed. Fire drills should be conducted for the purpose of acquainting the students and the teachers in various rooms of the building with the routes to be employed from those rooms to the outside of the building. Some principals, particularly those in one-story schools, have discontinued fire drills, but authorities on fire safety strongly advise their use.

PLANS FOR EVACUATING THE BUILDING. Students and teachers in every room in the building must know not only the route to be followed in case none of the exits is endangered or shut off but also, in addition, their alternative routes, so that, if any exit from the building cannot be used, the students ordinarily going out that exit may be distributed to other exits. In some schools, near the door of every classroom, there is posted a diagram of the route to be followed by the students leaving that room. And, in some schools, there are also authoritative directions, indicating at least the general route to be followed in case Exit A, Exit B, or Exit C is cut off.

There should be special attention given to the evacuating of the auditorium at times when there is a large crowd in it; exits should be plainly marked and preferably made conspicuous by means of illuminated signs which are kept lighted at all times when the auditorium is occupied. The fire-alarm system should include alarms that will ring in shower and dressing rooms and in boys' and girls' toilets. And, actually, provisions should be made for notifying the fire department at the very instant that what seems to be an uncontrollable fire is discovered.

It is very desirable that students be told how and where to form lines and that they keep those lines until they are out of the building. Dependable leaders should be appointed in each class section in each period in the day. Ordinarily there should be only one line from a room, because that line will likely have to share the corridor and the steps with at least one other line coming from another room. At the head of each stairway there should be a designated student or instructional leader to determine the order of the groups going down the stairs and to hold back all but two lines at a time—one line on the inside of the stairway and one on the outside.

FIRE ALARMS. There should be a definite understanding as to who is to sound fire alarms and under what conditions. For example, in many schools every student is told in assembly or in roll room where and how to sound the fire alarm; that he must sound it immediately if he sees a large fire in the building; and that, if there is doubt in his mind, he must report to the nearest teacher, whether in classroom or not—or, in small schools, to the principal's office. In many schools the only place for giving a fire alarm is in the principal's office, while in other schools one or more additional places for turning in alarms are located on other floors and in the wings of the building. There is definite danger in having too many places for fire alarms, as practical jokers among the students may decide to set off false fire alarms. Where there is a good communication system between various parts of the building and the principal's office, there need not be a place to set off a fire alarm other than in the principal's office. The fire signal itself not only should be sufficiently loud to be heard throughout the building but should be sufficiently distinctive in character to be recognized unmistakably when it is sounded. The number of fire drills held per year need not be more than three or four; indeed, many schools try to get through with only one or two held at the beginning of the year.

Students should be instructed not to stop at lockers for books, wraps, or other personal property; nor should they, under any circumstances, attempt to rescue any property of the school, such as typewriters, unless they are given specific instructions to do so.

If there are crippled children attending the school, there should be appointed one or more youngsters in every class a crippled child attends to act as his escort to see that he gets out of the building safely.

Some signal which can be heard outside the building must be developed and agreed upon for the return of the students to the building after a fire drill or a fire.

FIRE EXTINGUISHERS AND HOSES. Every school should be equipped with sufficient hoses and fire extinguishers and these should be inspected and adjusted frequently. Students, as well as faculty members, should be trained in their use. What is adequate in the way of fire extinguishers and hoses that may be used in case of fire should be determined through consultation with local fire officials or the state department of education.

Accident Prevention. The following are some precautions, listed by Viles, which custodians can take to eliminate needless accidents in special rooms:

1. Watch all gas heaters for fumes. Flexible hose contacts should be permitted only between the shutoff cock and the burners. Even then, a rigid connection is preferable.
2. Watch gas for possible leakage. Gas purchased from service companies usually has in it a malodorant, so that a leak may be detected easily. All canned gas purchased in pressure tanks should also have in it a malodorant.
3. Have fixed racks for acid carboys.
4. In chemical laboratories keep a woolen blanket to use in smothering possible fires in clothing or elsewhere.
5. Treat tops of chemical laboratory tables to make them acid resisting.
6. Have all machine guards in shops fastened securely.
7. Remove rubbish from around power machines. Eliminate slick floor conditions from around power machines.
8. Keep boiler room clean. Have fire doors free acting. Do not block fire door openings.
9. Watch boiler steam pressure, also water level in boiler. Even "popping off" of the boiler has been known to give alarm to pupils in the building.
10. Pick up soap in shower rooms.
11. Remove all obstacles that might cause tripping around swimming pools.
12. Regulate hot-water flow in showers and laboratories.
13. Place handrails on ramps for swimming pool.[11]

6. *Supervision of Custodial Service*

One of the smaller but vexatious problems of the principal is the supervision of the cleaning and care of the school plant. The principal usually has to learn about such supervision on the job. In the supervision of custodial service, he often wishes for standards which he can set up for custodians with a feeling that he is not requiring too much or requiring less than the plant should receive. He also needs to be able to evaluate such service in terms of methods employed. Only in the larger city school system is a special official employed for this type of supervision.

There is considerable variation among administrators as to standards of custodial service. The standards mentioned in this section seem to represent a consensus of opinion and approved practice.

Keeping the Plant Clean. Walls, ceilings, picture frames and moldings, and window shades should be dusted or vacuum-cleaned with proper tools two or three times a year. Windows should be cleaned either with warm water containing a little ammonia or with cleaning fluid purchased for this purpose. This cleaning should be done when needed, usually

[11]N. E. Viles, *The Custodian at Work,* Lincoln, Nebraska, University Publishing Company, pp. 148-149.

every two or three months, depending on the amount of dust and soot in the neighborhood. Glass in doors should be washed more often.

In buildings heated by hot-air furnaces with registers in or close to the floor, the registers should be cleaned twice a month. Chalk boards (blackboards) should be erased daily and cleaned once a week. They should be washed with a heavy cloth or towel and immediately wiped with a dry cloth to prevent absorption of the water. The use of kerosene, except on slate boards, is not advised, owing to the danger of making the board slippery. Toilet floors, if of tile or concrete, should be flushed or mopped daily. Urinals, toilet bowls, and seats should be washed and disinfected daily. The custodian should be instructed to take care that toilet paper and towels are supplied for lavatories. Deodorants need be used sparingly, if at all; if proper care is taken of the equipment, there will be little need for them. Wash bowls, drinking fountains, and sinks should be cleaned daily. All metalwork should be polished occasionally, never being permitted to tarnish. Industrial-arts rooms should be thoroughly swept every day, and shavings, sawdust, and rubbish should be removed. The cooking room, including the pantry and the dining room, should be scrubbed once a week, and the garbage containers should be emptied and cleaned each day the room is used.

HEAT REGULATION. The principal should leave to his engineer, custodian, and teachers as much of the problem of heating and ventilating as possible, while maintaining necessary conditions of temperature and air in the building. He should see that the temperature in all classrooms and other rooms in which pupils are at work remains between 67 and 72 degrees, preferably between 68 and 70 degrees. He should impress his teaching staff with the necessity of avoiding overheated and stuffy classrooms. Especially with older teachers, who often enjoy rooms with a temperature of 75 degrees or warmer, this is difficult to do and requires firmness and persistence. He should train them in window ventilation if there is no system of artificial ventilation, urging them to allow for some fresh air at all times except when closing is necessary to prevent the temperature from falling below 68 degrees. Windows should be lowered from the top rather than raised from the bottom, as the latter practice may expose some children to drafts. Lowering several windows slightly is to be preferred to lowering one all the way. Student monitors seated close to the room thermometer may be appointed by the teacher and relied upon to look after such matters more closely than the teacher himself is likely to do.

Teachers should be trained not to tamper with the radiator or valves except as advised by the custodian or heating engineer. When insufficient heat is being supplied, the proper course is to send for the custodian and have him make adjustments. Many heating systems are so constructed that tampering with valves or steam inlets or opening windows interferes with the heating of other rooms as well. Teachers should be urged to observe correct procedures. Heat regulation is a realm in which the authority of the custodian or engineer should be respected and full responsibility placed upon him.

The relations between the custodian and the principal are more important than they would seem at first sight, for these reasons:

1. The principal has a responsibility for seeing that the custodial service of his building measures up to standard efficiency.
2. In many communities the good will of the custodian may be an important influence for good for the principal and his school.
3. Understanding co-operation between the principal and the custodian is contributory to mutual convenience, prestige, and enjoyment of professional life at the school.

Many years ago Dean Ellwood P. Cubberley, Dean of the School of Education of Stanford University, set forth in his book *The Principal and His School*[12] an excellent statement of good principles which should govern the relationship between principal and custodian. These suggestions are as sound today as when written. They are reproduced as follows:

1. Make your janitor feel that you are open to suggestions, and will welcome any ideas as to procedure that he may offer. If they are good, thank him and tell him so; if you cannot use them, explain to him why. The janitor often knows pupils and teachers well, and in addition possesses a fund of practical experience that can be made to contribute to the efficiency of the school.
2. The principal should stand ready to make the janitor's work as light as reasonably good service permits. To this end he should insist that he be provided with as good quarters and as good supplies as possible.
3. Keep in mind that his hours are long, and that he gets tired and sleepy just as other people do. Try to help him to adjust his work to a good schedule so as to lighten it when possible, and do not allow teachers to delay him unnecessarily in his work or make it difficult for him to do.
4. Protect him as far as possible from the fussy teachers of the building. Some women are never pleased with anything a man does, particularly in the line of housekeeping. Ask them not to find fault with him, especially in the presence of their pupils.
5. Do not address him as "janitor" or "George," but as "Mr. Strowbridge," and ask your teachers to do the same. When you give him instructions, do not say "Do so and so," but rather "Will you please do so and so." Don't forget to say "Good morning" to him, and if he tells you that his wife or baby is sick, ask him occasionally how they are getting along. If he works well and is attentive to little things, express appreciation from time to time. In showing visitors about the building do not ignore him, but ask him to explain things, though you might easily do it yourself.
6. Cultivate in him a feeling of ownership in the building and grounds, and occasionally take orders from him. You can afford to let him be a little important and officious provided he is rendering efficient service. Occasionally ask him if everything is all right, if he needs anything, how the furnace is working today, or how much coal was burned last month, and how that compares with a year ago. Teach him to read the meters, if he does not know

[12]Published by Houghton Mifflin Company, Boston. Passage quoted by permission of the publishers.

how, and to figure out something as to maintenance costs. Occasionally give him an article relating to his work, or show him a picture of some new school or school appliance.

7. Cultivate in him a pride in doing his work, and help him to find better and more economical ways of doing things. Sometimes the suggestion that you will furnish the paint or varnish for some little job will start a regular clean-up about the building. If he is interested in having some flowers in the yard let him put them out, and if necessary train the pupils to let them alone.

To these may be added the following:

1. As far as possible provide a convenient and cheerful office and workroom and necessary tools and supplies. When we realize how long the janitor's hours are (often from 6 to 7 in the morning until 5 or 6 at night), it does not seem unwise to provide or permit him to provide a lounge for a midday nap.
2. As far as possible prevent complaints concerning a willing and conscientious janitor from reaching the superintendent of schools or the board of education. Help him to overcome his weaknesses and solve his problems. Usually such a policy calls forth renewed efforts to make good and a spirit of gratitude on the part of the janitor.

The principal should attempt to discover what requirements and conditions of work of custodians and heating engineers obtain in other schools in the city and in other comparable cities. In many districts the board of education has printed rules and regulations regarding these matters which may be obtained for the asking.

RESPONSIBILITY OF THE PRINCIPAL. The principal should acquaint a new custodian with the school and its personnel, explaining building regulations and procedures which affect the work of the custodian. He should with the custodian occasionally inspect the building. He should co-operate with the custodian in planning ways to improve custodial service and efficiency. He should get the co-operation of teachers and pupils in keeping the plant clean and sightly. He should annually evaluate the custodial services in his building and report the findings to the custodian and to the superintendent of school.

He should ask the custodian for a daily schedule of his activities. This schedule should show where the custodian may be found at any time during the day. The principal may make suggestions for improving the schedule, improving the custodial service, or reducing the number of hours that the custodian spends at the school.

7. Repairs and Replacements

DETECTING NEED OF REPAIRS AND REPLACEMENTS. The part the principal should play in detecting the need for repairs and replacements and in requisitioning them will differ depending upon whether there is a building and grounds department for the school system. Where such a department exists, the custodian of the building and the principal will both request repairs and replacements from it. Where it does not exist, the principal may instruct the custodian, or he may go to the superintendent's office if repairs or replacements involve any considerable cost. Under any circumstances, all requests for repairs and replacements by members of the staff should be cleared through the principal's office. Instructors or heads of departments should report needs to the principal; in many instances he should utilize their services in planning the type of repair or replacement needed.

The principal, with the assistance of his staff and custodians, should make an annual survey of the plant in the late spring to decide on repairs and replacements which should be made in the summer months. Similarly, surveys for repairs should be made just before the Christmas and spring vacations. The principal should make a careful inspection of the plant, noting needed repairs and replacements and inspecting those reported to him. The custodian should occasionally accompany him on trips made for that purpose. The principal should study the relative necessity for repairs, selecting those to be recommended on the basis of relative merits and the funds thought to be available. As far as possible in his recommendations he should make detailed specifications as to exactly what is desired. By so doing he will increase the chances of obtaining approval for his recommendations, as well as of obtaining repairs and replacements of a desirable type. He should also attempt to arrange, as far as possible, for inspection of the repairs and replacements at the time that they are made either by himself, by his custodian, or by the member of the staff asking for them.

NEED OF MAKING REPAIRS IMMEDIATELY. Many repairs should be made immediately. Lack of care on the part of the school management and the existence of obviously needed repairs invite rough usage or vandalism. Pupils tend to respect well-kept buildings and equipment. The plant should be kept attractive and never be permitted to assume a run-down appearance. Not only is it bad financial policy but it also serves to complicate the problems of discipline and to create an unfavorable attitude on the part of the pupils toward the school and its administration. Pupils and their parents should be held personally accountable for all unnecessary damage occasioned by breakage or neglect.

8. Community Uses of the Building

INCREASING USE OF PLANT BY COMMUNITY GROUPS. The high-school plant of today is excellently suited for various types of community activity, with its gymnasium, dressing rooms and showers, its auditorium, little-theater room, kitchen and cafeteria, library, music room, and shops. The thinking of school people is undergoing a long overdue change to a very sensible point of view with respect to community uses of the school plant. Until recently, there has existed an unwarranted feeling that the school plant and resources were intended to be used only for "school" purposes, during the "school" day, and with "school" children. It escaped those who shared this view that the school plant belonged to the entire community and might well be employed for any purpose of the community, particularly if that purpose partook in any way of an educational or recreational nature.

With the expansion of adult education, the use of the school plant for other than classroom instruction of regularly enrolled pupils has increased greatly. Among the community uses of secondary-school buildings may be mentioned the following:

1. Forums and discussion groups.
2. Regularly organized classes in adult education.
3. Youth clubs of various kinds—Boy Scouts, 4-H Clubs, Y.M.C.A., etc.
4. Rural-life organizations—the Farmers' Union, the Grange, etc.
5. Organized adult recreation groups of various types.
6. Civic and municipal concerts, committee meetings.
7. Parent-teacher association and various community-improvement organizations.
8. Athletic organizations of out-of-school youth—basketball, softball, etc.
9. Mothers' clubs, service clubs, and various similar clubs and organizations.
10. Various occasional meetings—political meetings, lectures, addresses by representatives of state and national governments.
11. Community musical and theatrical organizations.
12. Public-library service.

FINANCIAL ARRANGEMENTS. While there is no uniform practice relative to the charges made for use of the building, in general the following practices are common:

1. To require a nominal fee to cover heat, light, and custodial service, to be paid into the general funds, from all organizations which charge no public admission. In cases where a program is entirely educational, the fee is often waived.
2. To require a very small fee or no fee from approved meetings of groups of students of the school.
3. To require a fair commercial rental from all organizations for use of the plant for occasions on which the public is charged admission.
4. To have a schedule of rental fees for each portion of the building used—for example, the auditorium, the gymnasium and showers, the library, the little theater.
5. To require all organizations to pay, over and above fees or rentals, for all damage to plant or equipment, above ordinary wear and tear, done by anyone using the building or equipment, regardless of whether he is a member of the organization or not.
6. To place the responsibility for the supervision of the building during the time of its use by an outside group upon the organization and its officers, relieving the school and its staff from extra service except custodial service.

The wider the use of the plant by the community and the greater the service rendered, the more favorable is the attitude of the community likely to be toward the financial support of the school and, indeed, toward its entire program. It is a good public-relations policy to encourage use of the building and equipment and to promote the school as a community center.

Problems, Questions, and Exercises

1. Explain how you might plan to estimate the enrollment for a high school for the next twenty years so as to have some idea of the size of building that you would need.
2. Consider that you have playing fields for football, track, and baseball taken care of; how much additional ground would you want for a junior high school of 600 students or a senior high school of the same size? What would the ground be used for?
3. What effect does climate have upon the size and shape of a building?
4. If you were a high-school principal participating in the planning of a new building for a school of 700 students, about how many rooms and what kinds of rooms would you want to see the plan include?
5. For a school of 700 students, what particular features would you like to see incorporated in a new high-school building?
6. Make a list of suggestions relative to the size and location for a high-school building.
7. Make a list of suggestions for the locations of various types of rooms and units in the high-school building.
8. For a school of about 250 students, what do you think is the best plan for providing auditorium and gymnasium space?
9. According to your particular interest, select one of the following areas and write up eight or ten pages of suggestions for housing and prividing equipment for (1) dramatics, (2) music, (3) science instruction, (4) business department, (5) home-economics courses, and (6) shop courses. Make all the suggestions you can for making the building safe.
10. What types of classroom seating would you advocate for a modern high school with 500 students?
11. Write out your suggestions for the use of a central communication system in the high school.
12. Do you believe that fire drills should be conducted in junior high schools? In senior high schools? In junior-college buildings? Be able to give the reasons for the position that you take in these matters.
13. After reading carefully the section on fire drills, draw up a plan for fire drills for a school of a size and grade levels of your own choosing.
14. What do you regard as the greatest possible dangers in case of a fire; what are the major provisions you would make for them?
15. Select a school of a given size and tell what you think the problem of supervision of student automobiles would be in a school of that size and how you would proceed to handle it.
16. How do you think the principal might go about seeing that the building and equipment are properly cleaned and otherwise taken care of?

17. In what ways do you think the principal might be active in co-ordinating relationships between the teachers and the custodians?
18. Examine the list of suggestions for the principal in dealing with the custodian. To which of these do you take exception; which do you think are the most important?
19. After reading the discussion on community use of school buildings, outline a plan for administration of a related problem.

Selected Supplementary Readings

"A School Where Walls Fall Away and Teachers Have Individual Offices," *The Nation's Schools* (November, 1961), Vol. 68, No. 5, pp. 32-35.

American Association for Health, Physical Education, and Recreation, *Planning Facilities for Health, Physical Education, and Recreation,* Washington, D.C., National Education Association, 1956.

American Association of School Administrators, *Common Sense in School Lighting,* Washington, D.C., National Education Association, 1956.

Anderson, Edward J., and Harkness, J. C., "Planned Variability," *Nation's Schools* (April, 1960), Vol. 65, No. 4, pp. 83-91.

Anderson, Robert H., and Mitchell, Donald P., "Team Teaching, New Learning Concepts Demand Changes in School Plant Design," *Nation's Schools* (June, 1960), Vol. 65, No. 6, pp. 75-82.

The Audio-Visual Equipment Directory, National Audio-Visual Association, Inc., Fairfax, Virginia. 1961, 290 pp.

"Carpeting in the School House," *Overview* (March, 1962), Vol. 3, No. 3, pp. 54-57. (Andrews, Texas, Shaker Heights, Ohio, and Newtonville, New Jersey)

Clinchy, Evans, *Profiles of Significant Schools: Wayland Senior High School, Wayland, Massachusetts,* New York, Educational Facilities Laboratories, January, 1960.

Cochran, F. L., "Significant Departures in High School Design at Keokuk," *Nation's Schools* (February, 1951), Vol. 47, No. 2, pp. 44-47.

Colbert, Charles R., "Perception Core School," *Nation's Schools* (March, 1960), Vol. 65, pp. 79-87. [Units of secondary-school buildings, diagrams, pictures.]

Committee on Fire Research, *School Fires: An Approach to Life Safety,* Washington, D.C., Building Research Board, National Academy of Sciences, and National Research Council, 1959.

Cross, A. J. Foy, and others, *Planning Schools for Use of Audio-Visual Materials* (Third Edition), Washington, D.C., Department of Audio-Visual Instruction of the National Education Association, 1958.

Design for ETV—Planning for Schools with Television, New York, Educational Facilities Laboratories, 1960.

De Barnardes, Amo, et. al., *Planning Schools for New Media,* U.S. Office of Education, 1962, 72 pp. [Housing and Equipment for Audio-Visual Education]

Educational Policies Commission, "School Building and Equipment," *Education for All American Youth,* 1952, pp. 43-44, 121-123, 159-161, 340-341.

Engelhardt, N. L., Sr., and McMillan, Doris, "Planning the Art Suite for Junior High Schools," *School Board Journal* (January, 1952), Vol. 124, No. 1, pp. 33-35.

Erickson, R. J., "Use of School Buildings for Non-school Purposes," *Bulletin of the N.A.S.S.P.* (December, 1953), No. 198, pp. 34-87.
Fabrizio, Benedetto, "The How's, Why's, and Where's of Language Laboratories," *Nation's Schools* (June, 1960), Vol. 65, No. 6, pp. 58-60.
"Five Superintendents Plan a Junior High School," *School Management* (November, 1960), Vol. 14, No. 11, pp. 88-91.
Fleming, Alfred T., "School Fire Safety," *Journal of School Health* (September, 1951), Vol. 21, pp. 245-246. [How fire spreads within the building.]
Fraser, Dorothy McClure, "The Social Studies Classroom," *The Teacher of the Rocial Studies,* Twenty-third Yearbook of the National Council for the Social Studies, George Banta, 1952, pp. 113-160.
Freeman, Herbet M., "Good Business Education Is Adequately Housed and Equipped," *Bulletin of the N.A.S.S.P.* (November, 1949), Vol. 33, pp. 35-43.
"Getting Away from the Rectangular Classroom," *School Management* (July, 1960), Vol. 8, No. 7 pp. 60-66.
Hardman, B. Reede and Lones, Philip F., "Two-Story Circular Building and Trapezoidal Classrooms," *The Nation's Schools* (July, 1960), Vol. 60, No. 1, pp. 55-56.
The High School in a Changing World, Thirty-sixth Yearbook, Washington, D.C., American Association of School Administrators, 1958. [Chapter 10, "Housing the New High School," pp. 245-296.]
Hayes, Alfred S., "Procedure for Language Laboratory Planning," *Bulletin of the N.A.S.S.P.* (March, 1962), No. 272, pp. 120-123.
Hillyard, Walter S., "Preventive Maintenance," *Catholic School Journal* (January, 1953), Vol. 53, No. 1, [Discusses how to care for and treat asphalt tile as a flooring material.]
Hocking, Elton, "Language Laboratories," *Nation's Schools* (February, 1961), Vol. 67, No. 2, pp. 83-86.
Johnson, Palmer O., Nesbitt, William O. and Felder, Dale, "Snyder High School (Texas) Redeploys Students to Improve Instruction," *Bulletin of the N.A.S.S.P.* (January, 1959), Vol. 243, pp. 161-167. [Management; list of types of expendable materials for construction of visual aids.]
"Language Laboratory," *Bulletin of the N.A.S.S.P.* (October, 1959), No. 249, pp. 159-160.
"A Language Laboratory Without Loss of a Classroom," *School Management* (August, 1959), Vol. 3, No. 8, pp. 44-46.
Mathematics and Science Teaching and Facilities, Washington, D.C., National Education Association, 1959.
Morrisett, Lloyd N., and Linn, H. H., "Planning and Maintaining the School Plant," *Bulletin of the N.A.S.S.P.* (March, 1951), No. 177, pp. 130-146.
Music Educators' National Conference, *Music Buildings, Rooms, and Equipment,* Washington, D.C., National Education Association, 1955.
National Commission of Safety Education, *Fire Safety for Junior High Schools,* Washington, D.C., National Education Association, 1950.
National Commission of Safety Education, *Fire Safety for Senior High Schools,* Washington, D.C., National Education Association, 1951.
"New Look in Language Laboratories," *School Management* (September, 1960), Vol. 4, No. 1, pp. 52-56.
Price, J. W., "More Experience with Utilizing a New School Plant at Syosset, New York, in Contributing to Staff Use and Curriculum Development," *Bulletin of the N.A.S.S.P.* (January, 1959), No. 243, pp. 167-180.

Profiles of Significant Schools—High Schools 1962, Educational Facilities Laboratories, Inc., 477 Madison Avenue, New York, N. Y.
Ryan, L. V., "Management of the School Plant," *Catholic School Journal* (January, 1956), Vol. 56, No. 1, pp. 28-30.
"School Building Costs Can Be Cut," *School Management* (August, 1959), Vol. 3, No. 2, pp. 40-43.
"School Planning Recommendations and Check Lists," *Catholic Property Administration* (October, 1959), Vol. 23, pp. 137-140.
Seagers, Paul W., "Building for Safety," *High School Journal* (March-April, 1950), Vol. 33, No. 2, pp. 86-89. [A very good collection of ideas for incorporating safety and building maintenance.]
Spiers, Edward, *The Central Catholic High School,* Washington, D.C., Catholic University of America Press, 1951. [Chapters 4 and 5.]
Stoneman, Merle A., Broady, Knute O., and Brainard, Alanson D., *Planning and Modernizing the School Plant,* University of Nebraska Press, 1949. ["The Gymnasium-Auditorium," pp. 110-114; "The Library-Study Hall," p. 116; "The Science Classroom-Laboratory," pp. 117-119; "The General Shop," pp. 120-122; "The Community Room," "The Homemaking Combination Room," pp. 122-124; "The School Office," pp. 125-126; "The Teacher and Health Room," p. 126; "Improvement of the School Plant Site," pp. 178-189.]
Taylor, Kenneth I., "Instructional Materials Center," *Nation's Schools* (December, 1960), Vol. 66, No. 6, pp. 45-51. [Combining the traditional school library with the audio-visual department into an instructional-materials center makes possible a new and broader range of services to student and teacher.]
Thompson, L. O., "'Super Vision' in Supervision of Custodians," *Bulletin of the N.A.S.S.P.* (October, 1950), No. 172, pp. 77-82.
Turille, Stephen J., "Evaluating the Physical Part of the Department of Business Education," *Balance Sheet* (October, 1951), Vol. 33, pp. 55-59.
Twiford, Don D., "Physical Facilities for Guidance," *Vocational Guidance Quarterly* (Autumn, 1957), Vol. 6, No. 1, pp. 5-16.
Twiford, Don D., *Physical Facilities for School Guidance Services,* Washington, D.C., Office of Education, U.S. Department of Health, Education and Welfare, 1960. [Suggestions for offices, equipment, and conference rooms; illustrative diagrams.]
Urtes, Nelson E., "Maintaining and Replacing Schools," *The American School Journal* (July, 1959), Vol. 139, No. 1, pp. 22-25.
Walsh, Donald D., "A Dozen Do's and Don'ts for Planning and Operating a Language Lab," *Bulletin of the N.A.S.S.P.* (March, 1962), No. 272, pp. 120-123.
Williams, Lloyd J., and others, Acoustics in the School, *Nation's Schools* (May, 1961), Vol. 7, No. 5, pp. 95-129. [A series of illustrated articles on designing and equipping schools for good hearing in classrooms, music rooms, auditoriums, etc.]
Yeager, William A., *Administration of the Non-instructional Personnel and Services,* New York, Harper, 1959. [Chapter 11, "Planning and Construction of the School Plant and Facilities"; Chapter 12, "Operation and Maintenance of the School Plant and Facilities."]

23

Community and Public Relationships

1. Fundamental Considerations

THE SPECIALIST AND THE LAYMAN. There is necessity for a balance between two points of view with respect to the public schools. One is that the teachers, supervisors, and administrators are specialists, that they know best what should be done in the schools, and that laymen should not concern themselves too much with the program of the schools. Another theory is that the children are the children of the laymen, that laymen furnish the financial support of the schools, and therefore that teachers, supervisors, and administrators should operate the schools and construct the courses of study as the parents and taxpayers think best. Serious thinking about this matter should result in the conclusion that neither of these points of view is in itself correct and that there should be a compromise. There should be leadership by those with professional training and experience; but the specialists should work with the people of the community, taking into consideration their ideas about the program and utilizing them as consultants in the development of policies, the school program, and its courses of study.

There has been in recent years a pronounced tendency in the direction of utilizing lay consultants, as members of advisory committees on both financial and educational problems, and of keeping the public much better informed about, much more interested in, and much more co-operative with the public schools.

THE NECESSITY FOR BETTER PUBLIC RELATIONS. In recent years there has been a greatly increased need for school funds, as a result of the very greatly increased number of births. Between 1943 and 1957 the annual number of births grew from less than 3,000,000 to more than 4,000,000. Consequently, there has been a necessity for spending much greater amounts of money on correspondingly greater numbers of school buildings and correspondingly increased teaching staffs. In addition, greatly increased wages and salaries in occupations other than teaching have served to attract young people into other vocations and to increase further the shortage of classroom teachers and the necessity for increasing the salaries paid to teachers. These things, together with the staggering increase in Federal taxes for past war costs and for armaments, have created a most unusual problem in obtaining funds for public education and have, as a result, created an increased need for effective public relations.

PECULIAR NEED BY THE SCHOOLS. The school is especially dependent upon public appreciation of its procedures and results; also, unlike most other social institutions for which the public provides support and which render service to the public, the direct and normal contacts of the school with the adult public are few.

The fact that the results of teaching are so much more intangible and difficult of measurement than material goods and services adds to the difficulties of the public in judging the merits of school methods and procedures; it likewise increases the necessity for special consideration of the problem of bringing the achievements of the school to the attention of the public. Schools are often judged by hearsay and rumor only slightly correlated with the truth. The work of the school is often judged by the criteria of "discipline" and the personal popularity of the principal and his staff. In the absence of the proper sort of information, the public is not in a position to pass intelligent judgment on its schools. In fact, in this connection the public must be protected from itself by the professional schoolman.

LEARNING ABOUT THE LOCAL COMMUNITY. The administrators of public schools must realize that carrying on a successful administration involves successful relations with, and leadership of, the local community; it involves a study of the local community, its needs, its possibilities, and the means by which leadership may be most effectively exercised.

Upon taking over the responsibility for a local high school, the principal should inform himself as to the assessed valuation of the district, the relation of assessed valuation to true valuation, the present tax rate, and the indebtedness of the district. These figures should be studied and interpreted in the light of similar figures for comparable districts in the state and in other states. A careful study of the state school law should be made, with a view to ascertaining the sources of school funds and the extent and conditions of state aid and funds for secondary education and for new buildings.

It is a part of professional wisdom to make a careful study of the resources of the community, interpreted in the light of comparable data, before formulating the educational program for a high school, in order to avoid the possibility of recommending or initiating a program which is not in keeping with the ability of the local district to pay.

COMMUNITY ATTITUDES. The shrewd principal also studies his community for other types of data. Realizing that he must command the support of his community for his school and his program, he is careful to avoid crucial mistakes due to his ignorance of the divisions which exist among the people in his district. In the large majority of village and town districts, one or more types of division are fairly acute. The principal or even the teacher who participates in local factional struggles assumes immediately a handicap.

The attitudes of district toward many things—religious and political beliefs and social practices, for example—vary. Although seemingly trivial, they are in reality very important in determining the success of the principal or the superintendent in the administration of a school. In the first school in which the writer taught, he and his wife were thought unsocial and "high-hat" because they failed to partake of the liquid "refreshments" served at a party given at the house of the clerk of the board, though this impression was partly offset by their participation in dancing. In the next district it would have been equivalent to professional suicide for any teacher to dance or to let it be known that he was not a teetotaler, and the blinds were always carefully drawn when friends came in to play bridge.

Discretion is often the better part of valor. To fail to know what the undercurrents of prejudice are, or not to take them into consideration, is more than likely to place the schoolman in a position in which his influence and leadership as a schoolman are seriously impaired.

SOURCES OF INFORMATION. Data will be available in varying amounts from various sources. Among the sources are the following:[1]

1. Data concerning financial aspects of the district—the state school law, the county superintendent, the county assessor, the district clerk and his records, the local chamber of commerce.
2. Data concerning the economic and social aspects of the district—publications of the local chamber of commerce, service clubs, or other promotion bodies, records of students showing occupations of fathers, conversation with business and professional men of the village or city.
3. Data concerning religious and racial composition of the population—registration cards of school pupils, city census data, conversations with business and professional men of the village or city.
4. Data regarding attitudes of the people toward things cultural and educational, lines of cleavage, key men and women and organizations—conversations, newspaper items, pointers, and information picked up on all occasions by generally keeping one's eyes and ears open.

Counselors, school nurses, and visiting teachers are also very useful as a source of information relative to community activities and needs.

[1]The principal may and should get much data from the superintendent, particularly that relating to financial matters.

2. *The Principal and His Community Affiliations*

The administrator must remember that, since the schools are open to all the children of all the people and are supported by all taxpayers, an important factor in establishing professional leadership is the character and nature of the religious, business, fraternal, and social affiliations made in the new community. Too vigorous assertion of independence or partisanship may not serve any good purpose or benefit either personal freedom or the school. The administrator should not hesitate to follow his conscience in the matter of membership in and attendance at his favorite house of worship. Beyond that point, participation in religious affairs may or may not be wise from the standpoint of professional success. At any rate, participation in any denominational strife is not only undignified but also almost certain to prove disastrous to professional leadership.

PARTICIPATION IN BUSINESS AFFAIRS. It is not suggested that the schoolman must be servile or allow himself to be victimized in his business dealings, but it is a mark of the possession of diplomatic qualities to be able to carry on one's business relations in a small community in such a way as not to arouse antagonisms which are strong enough to alienate support of the principal and his educational program.

It should go without saying that the principal should not attempt to assist in the conduct of any commercial enterprise as a side line to his profession during school months. Time and energy so spent would be better used in improving his school or his own professional knowledge, or in leisure and recreation. Neglect of the school will probably be charged to him by dissatisfied patrons and other unfriendly persons, sometimes with and sometimes without justification. Rare, indeed, are the instances of the schoolman who has forged ahead in his profession and at the same time has been actively interested in commercial enterprises.

PARTICIPATION IN POLITICAL AFFAIRS. Independence in political affairs has become so general among men of learning that, except for those who have political ambitions, party regularity and policital partisanship, particularly of an active sort, involve many dangers and promise few benefits. The role of the educational leader is hard to reconcile in the public eye with that of the party politician, and the tendency to divorce school affairs from political affairs is a desirable one which should be encouraged. The political activities of principals should probably be limited to independence and freedom of views and voting. Nothing here is meant to imply that the principal should remain mute on all political or civic matters. Certainly in those questions which relate to the health or to the civic and moral welfare of the local community he should have a citizen's interest. In those questions which affect young people particularly, he should have a leader's interest. Any restrictions on discussion should not apply to classroom teaching.

A Positive Program of Community Leadership. The study of the community should be made to reveal as accurately as possible the key men and women and the key organizations.[2] In every community there are men, women, and organizations that are outstandingly influential in determining community attitudes and actions. The principal must not neglect to know these people and to gain their confidence and good will. First among these are the members of the local board of education. These men and women are those who should be, and usually are, most influential in school affairs, being delegated by the voters as their representatives in these matters. These individuals should be studied somewhat; and their views, ways of thinking, degrees of progressive attitude, ideas regarding financial support of education and the several types of educational enterprises (physical education, school activities, vocational education and guidance, superior teachers) should be ascertained.

In many districts the board members, the voters, or both are sensitive to the influence of a few key men, women, or organizations in the community. What men, women, or organizations these are should be learned early; they should be studied and contacts with them established.

The principal must ever keep in mind that his program must be thought through not only in relation to the schools but also in relation to the community and its reactions. He must realize that in overt action he can progress only slightly in advance of his community, particularly the board of education and other influential citizens. By the very nature of the organization of public education, this is a principle which is of necessity true; to fail to observe it and take advantage of it is likely to lead to temporary successes followed by discouraging or disastrous reverses. Much time and effort must be spent in educating the community to understand, desire, and support better education.

The Principal's Relation to His Superintendent in Community Contacts. It should be noted that in the foregoing paragraph little distinction has been made between principal and superintendent, and little distinction will be made in the following paragraphs. The chief responsibility for policies related to the school's out-of-school contacts will lie with the superintendent. This does not mean that the principal should not have informal contacts with board members, with key men, and with organizations; it does mean, however, that programs, policies, new departures, or plans concerning the school that are discussed with such men or organizations should bear the approval of the superintendent. The

[2]Robert P. Bullock, "Power Elite in the Community," *School Executive* (March, 1959), pp. 59-61. [The use of influential people in good public relations.]

superintendent as chief executive officer of the school should determine, after conference with the principal or others recommended by him, what the program of public relations for the high school should be. Even in the education of the community to that program, the principal should be in close consultation with the superintendent, always obtaining his approval and working largely under his direction.

With reference to contacts with the board of education, the superintendent of schools is the official representative of the principal and the teachers; it is questionable professional ethics for the principal to appear before the board except upon invitation of the superintendent or to carry on educative activities with board members except as a part of a cooperative plan of superintendent and principal.

3. Relations With Key Community Organizations

THE PARENT-TEACHER ASSOCIATION AS A RESPONSIBILITY. The most convenient organization to employ in obtaining support for the program of the high school is the parent-teacher association. This association has already become an adjunct of a very large number of high schools, so that the high-school principal has in many instances practically no choice as to whether the organization shall be represented in his school or not. Wherever the organization exists, it may prove either a liability or an asset.

Though founded as organizations for assisting and improving the schools, such associations always run the risk of being directed by individuals who are really less interested in the school than in personal interests of various natures—individuals or organizations with special axes to grind, such as the reduction of taxes, the dismissal of the superintendent, the principal, or one or more of the teachers, the defeat of certain members of the school board, the changing of the curriculum, and the promotion of certain departments in the school in which these individuals may be interested, possibly because of personal relations or friendships with the teachers or heads of those departments.

The high-school parent-teacher association is particularly open to this danger. The genuine interest of the majority of parents wanes perceptibly after their children have passed through the first few years of the elementary school. The percentage of those attending meetings of high-school associations who are open-minded and genuinely interested in the welfare of the whole school is likely to be smaller. As a result, it is easier for those who wish to exploit the organization for personal or partisan purposes to turn out, command a majority of those attending, and thus obtain control of the chapter. For this reason if for no others, the principal must give the organization careful and constant attention.

THE PARENT-TEACHER ORGANIZATION AS AN ASSET. On the other hand, the association may be a very valuable advisory body or council, serving as a means of sampling representative thought in the community regarding the school, interpreting the community to the principal and teachers, and interpreting the school to the community of which it is representative. Some principals have been successful in instilling into the more regularly attending members of the association the idea that they are his lieutenants in educating the community to desirable innovations. Protests and reactions in the association meetings may be very valuable forewarnings of possible unfavorable community reactions to administrative devices and teaching plans and may indicate the probable wisdom of modifying the plans or of postponing their execution.

Proposed plans, innovations, or changes may be well discussed with the parents attending the meetings before their adoption is advocated or put into effect. Community attitudes favorable to proposed changes may be developed in the meetings of the chapter, the innovations being explained and justified before the group. Through the organization, pride in the school and its achievements may be developed. The meetings may be employed as opportunities to inform the public of the progress, honors, and achievements of the school, its staff, and its pupils. Through it the community may be educated to desire more effective or more modern developments: supervised study, art, music, physical education, junior high schools, provisions for guidance, and better housing and equipment.

The Guidance of Parent-Teacher Associations. If the parent-teacher association seems intent on forcing upon the board of education or the superintendent of schools improvements or changes or preventing changes authorized by the board of education, the principal must keep clear of rendering assistance or encouragement in any way, even though he may not actually attempt to dissuade the leaders. Only under extremely rare circumstances should he openly or secretly incite the association to force the board or to oppose it in matters upon which it has made definite decisions. Often, however, it may be useful to have such associations urge upon boards of education changes or improvements which will be acceptable to them rather than have the demand for changes appear to originate with the board, the principal, or the superintendent.

Under any circumstances the parent-teacher organization of whatever nature is of sufficient importance to warrant the careful attention of the principal. Care should be taken to get attendance which is representative and open-minded and to prevent the offices from falling into the hands of those with axes to grind. The program of the meetings should be utilized to contribute to the valuable functions mentioned above and to minister to the development of support for the proposed program and policies of the school. Teachers, heads of departments, and outside speakers should be utilized in presenting new ideas to the meetings and in explaining new departments, plans, devices, or proposals. At all times the work of the pupils and the teaching staff should be kept in the foreground.

The principal should be active in furnishing assistance to parents and teachers who appear upon the program for papers and addresses, helping them to obtain the most useful material from local libraries, state institutions of higher learning, and the state library. It is fortunate if he is appointed as a member of the program committee.

The principal should cause the teachers to see the importance of assisting in making the meetings profitable from the standpoint of the school, of being present, and of *meeting the parents.*

In some communities there has been operated by the local association and the administrators of the local schools a workshop for interested parents who wish to learn more about the schools and to be of service in the public relations of the schools.

Parent-Teacher-Association Programs and Meetings. The programs should be sufficiently attractive to invite attendance. In addition to the more serious discussions, there should be provided at every meeting short entertaining features such as musical numbers, dramatic skits, one-act plays, costume dances, and similar pleasing types of activities. In most large high schools there is almost always something already prepared for assembly or other purposes which may be repeated at parent-teacher meetings. If speeches are made, care should be taken to see that they are short and as interesting as possible.

Some schools provide a period just before or just after the meeting during which parents may visit teachers in their offices or classrooms and confer with them about the work of their children. The principal should also utilize the opportunities afforded by meeting of the association to meet parents and patrons and to form acquaintanceships and friendships with them, learning to call them by name and to associate them with their children who are pupils in the school.

One of the most valuable contributions of a parent-teacher association lies in its ability to stimulate parents to study information useful in enabling them to be of most service to their children in an educational way.[3] The school as the chief ally of the home should assist in every way to make the association useful.

In many cities at least some, if not all, P.T.A. meetings are held in the evening, so that fathers as well as mothers may attend. Refreshments should be served at association meetings, during which the teachers and principal should mix among the parents to greet them and to say a few words to at least several of them.

Collaboration with Other Youth-Serving Agencies. There has been in recent years a trend toward correcting an unfortunate past

[3]In the March, 1961, issue of *Coronet* there appeared an excellent and reliable article entitled "How to Raise a Teen-Ager," reprints of which may be obtained in quantities at low cost for distribution to parents.

tendency of the school to operate as a lone wolf in the matter of serving the youth in the community. Because of the lack of orientation in the matter, the failure to understand the importance of relationships between the school and other youth-serving agencies, or lack of time on the part of teachers and administrators, the schools have not brought about co-operation, collaboration, and co-ordination of youth-serving agencies in the community. In recent years there has been a tendency to set up various kinds of youth councils or committees in communities, involving representatives from the high schools and such community organizations as the Y.M.C.A., Y.W.C.A., Y.M.H.A., Boy Scouts, Girl Scouts, local recreation groups, 4-H clubs, Future Farmers of America, Future Homemakers of America, Junior Red Cross, Girls' Reserves, Junior Employment Service of the State Employment Services, Camp Fire Girls, and Junior Achievement, Inc.

While it should be clear that the schools should not attempt to dominate the youth-serving agencies of the community, it should also be clear that the schools are in perhaps the best position to act in the formation of a community youth council and to give leadership, along with others in the community, in co-ordinating and improving school services to youth in the community.

In this way it is possible to improve the services to youth and to eliminate unwise allocation of time and expense; also the school people participating are certain to acquire a better orientation toward the problems of youth and ways of dealing with them.

ALUMNI MEETINGS. One means of establishing cordial relations with a group of people in the district who are unusually interested in the school is by planning meetings of the alumni of the school. Alumni organizations already exist in many communities, though they are not always valuable in improving relations. In fact, in many instances the feeling of alumni toward more recent administrations and their ideas and policies is unsympathetic: "The good old school has gone to the dogs." Many principals believe that their experience has taught them that formal organizations of alumni do not prove to be advantageous.

On the other hand, it may be beneficial for the principal, with the help of a committee of alumni appointed by him, to plan an alumni program. Annual or semiannual alumni meetings may be held which afford opportunities for keeping former students informed about the school and its progress, educating them to the forward march of the school, its innovations and changes, promoting personal good feelings and school loyalty, and, if properly managed, imparting to the undergraduate, through the agency of the graduates of the school, such ideals and traditions as will make for progress and higher standards of conduct and scholarship in the school.

Meetings of alumni are held most often during the Christmas holidays.

Since the increasing number of high-school graduates who are going to college return to their homes for the holidays and since business is slack after Christmas, it is a favorable time of the year for meetings.

Talks by the principal, a conventional and natural part of the program, should not only include remarks about the achievements of former classes, organizations, teams, and students but also focus attention upon the achievements of the present student body and the school of today. The talks should in all cases be well prepared, interesting, and not too long or in too serious a vein and should exhibit a good sense of humor.

FOLLOW-UP OF GRADUATES. Many schools now issue every few years a survey check list to obtain opinions of recent graduates about certain aspects of the school program. This check list not only brings in information and opinions useful in improving the high-school program but generates interest and good will.

4. Commencement Exercises as Public Relations[4]

One of the most favorable times of the year to appeal to and develop pride in and good will toward the school is at commencement. At graduation time many adults of the community gather under conditions making them very receptive to efforts to put the school and its program in a good light through the medium of the loved young graduates who are the product of the school. Among the characteristics of a commencement program, from the point of view of its public-relations possibilities, may be mentioned the following:

1. Opportunities should be utilized to emphasize the achievements, honors, and evidence of high quality of the student body in general, the graduates in particular, and the faculty incidentally.
2. Praise for, or exhibition of, individual students should not be such that by comparison some pupils will be humiliated or parents disappointed.
3. Acknowledgment of the co-operation of the community should be sincere, clear, and definite.
4. Brief mention may be made in some way of the special features, philosophy, or objectives of the local school program (with special emphasis on a few of them) in the year just past and the year to come.
5. The program should not be too long, should be carefully planned, and should be devoid of dry or uninteresting features. As commencement speakers there should be chosen individuals who are known to give interesting commencement talks.
6. The costs of commencement to the individual student or family should be held to a minimum which should not embarrass any student or his parents. Most of the expense should be paid from school funds. In some schools proceeds from a class play or carnival are used for such expenses as corsages for the girls, the commencement dance, invitations, and programs.

[4] A discussion of the administration of commencements is given in Chapter 11.

7. The board of education should be given adequate recognition and opportunity for participation. The superintendent or principal should not be too conspicuous.

Good suggestions for commencement programs may be obtained from the National Education Association, 1201 Sixteenth Street, N.W., Washington, D.C., and from the files of *Extra-Curricular Activities,* a monthly professional periodical. The "vitalized" commencement idea has had much vogue in recent years and should be explored for possible suggestions.

5. Public Relations Through The Personnel of The School

THROUGH THE STUDENTS. Whether or not they will admit it, most parents form their impressions of the high school largely on the basis of the reports of their children. The high-school student is old enough to be more reliable as a source of information than the elementary-school child, and what he says about the school carries more weight. The affection of the parent for the child also injects the emotional factor into the situation, and this insures the student a sympathetic audience at home. Every student entertains opinions that are certain to crop out in his conversation about his teachers, the principal, the control of the school, the methods of teaching, the student activities, and other phases or incidents of school life.

It is wise, therefore, to give some attention to the matter of assisting high-school students to understand the school and its procedures and to induce them to take pride in its progress and achievements. It is highly desirable that there be developed in the student body good will and respect for the administration and the staff and pride in the educational side of school life and the educational achievements of the school.

Many principals, aware of the value of creating good will and confidence on the part of students, have employed various types of procedures for the realization of these ends. Among avenues for bringing to the attention of the student body the achievements and good points of the school are assemblies, roll-room meetings, exhibits, bulletin boards, contests, commencement, the school paper, and school news in the local papers.

Through these avenues such items as the following may be made the subject of announcement and congratulation: results of standard tests; victories of individuals and teams in interscholastic contests; achievements and honors of recent graduates of the school at college, in business, or in public life; favorable comment by visitors, inspectors, or other outsiders on the work of the school or the conduct of the students; and honors or special achievements of the faculty.

Frequently the students may be taken into the confidence of the administration in regard to proposed or new plans or methods, which may be explained to them and discussed as modern improvements.

In such activities emphasis should be placed upon selling the school, not any given individual, to the student body. It is bad ethics as well as bad psychology to use such activities to promote the individual interests of any particular members of the faculty or the principal or the superintendent.

Though it will have to be conceded that much mention must be made of athletic victories, special effort should be made to arouse pride in achievements in other fields of endeavor, particularly in scholastic achievement and honors.

At all times the value of maintaining good will and a good spirit on the part of the students should be appreciated. It should go without saying that good will should not be cultivated by lowering academic standards, by frequent holidays, by unusual laxity, by fanatical athletic enthusiasm, by special privileges to undeserving leaders, or by other questionable means. Among legitimate and important means may be mentioned a general attitude of dignified friendliness on the part of the administration and faculty toward the students and their activities, reasonable display of confidence in them, abstinence from petty snooping and nagging, and a co-operative attitude in many phases of the management of the school, particularly those in which very often a part in the management is given to the students. It should be taken for granted that the students are interested in the good name of the school and in its honor in all its endeavors, even though this may not always be exactly the fact.

"IT STARTS IN THE CLASSROOM."[5] In recent years there has been an increased emphasis upon, and attention to, the problem of the public-relations implications of the classroom activities of teachers and students. These include such matters as the following:

1. Having the students better understand the values of the subject matter and learning activities.
2. The use of much more learning activity having to do with the application of subject matter to problems of life by youngsters in their homes and in their communities.
3. Much greater use of audio-visual aids, field trips, and excursions.
4. Much more careful attention to seeing that the learning activities are adapted to the abilities and interests of the individual student.
5. Seeing that each youngster has a reasonable opportunity for success in the tasks assigned to him.
6. Interesting challenges to the youngster of greater abilities and background.

[5]See *It Starts in the Classroom*, published by the National School Public Relations Association, a department of the National Education Association.

7. Much more opportunity given for pupil discussions in class and in small groups into which the class may be divided.
8. Making assignments in homework which involve information gotten from parents and other people in the community.
9. Avoidance of sarcasm and of unnecessarily embarrassing pupils in class; employing of the principle of praise in public and criticism in private.
10. Greater effort to have youngsters feel that they are recognized as individuals and that they are accepted and liked by the teacher and belong to the group.
11. Improvement of the marking system so that youngsters will not develop too unfavorable attitudes toward the school.
12. Development of better means of reporting to the student and parents of the student's status and growth in the school.

THROUGH THE FACULTY. The members of the teaching staff (including substitute instructors), and indeed the custodians and clerical assistants, constitute important avenues through which the public gathers its information regarding the school. That principal is indeed fortunate, though not rare, who can achieve the feat of obtaining on the part of all teachers and other employees a spirit of good will toward the program of the school, a feeling of confidence in it, and a "booster" spirit for it. To discuss the many ways in which progress in that direction may be made would quickly carry us far afield into the realm of supervision and elsewhere. Briefly, members of the faculty should understand and believe in the undertakings in the school. Progress rarely should be forced upon them, but they should grow to or with it.

Pleasant and dignified personal relations should be preserved between the administration and the staff. Keeping informed of and expressing appreciation for work well done by members of the staff are practices which are not only fair but wise. Unnecessary heartaches and discouragements should be avoided, as should, of course, superficial flattery or misguided or extreme "good fellowship" and democratic flourishes.

The teachers should be kept informed by an enthusiastic leader of the achievements of the school, the student body, and the teachers and of the success of new ventures.

As far as possible, the personal element should be kept in the background. Invidious comparisons should be avoided. No teacher should be handicapped by being made to appear the object of favoritism. Above all, care should be taken by the administration to avoid the appearance of seeking glory for itself. The glory will follow indirectly, and any direct or obvious attempts in that direction will usually operate as boomerangs. This is especially true of schools located in villages or small cities. It may be mentioned that the principal should be constantly on the lookout for opportunities to furnish members of the staff with good contacts that will facilitate legitimate publicity: for example, arranging for public talks and demonstrations by members of the staff that will enable them to present favorably the work of the school. On every occasion the principal should keep himself more or less in the background, avoiding the appearance of taking undue credit or arousing the feeling on the part of the teacher that he is doing so.

Teachers should be encouraged to study and develop techniques of making friends with parents. Parents appreciate it when:

1. Teachers treat them with courtesy and welcome when they visit the school.
2. Teachers are sufficiently interested in knowing them as parents to take advantage of opportunities to meet and to talk with them about their children.
3. Teachers know their children well enough to appreciate their virtues as well as their faults.
4. Teachers treat their children with dignity and respect; they particularly resent the use of terms of contempt.
5. Teachers give them a reasonable amount of warning concerning any unusual expenditure of money for books, supplies, or social affairs.
6. Teachers inform them concerning any impending crisis in a pupil's school relations before the situation becomes very serious.
7. Teachers place special emphasis on instruction in matters of honesty, fairness, co-operation, respect for the rights of others, purity of speech, and other desirable qualities of conduct.
8. Teachers train their children in such a way as to enable them to make reasonable progress in their school subjects; if pupils are not successful, parents want the teachers to be able to diagnose their difficulties.
9. Teachers develop a spirit of good attitude towards themselves and their subjects so that their children will like to go to school.
10. Teachers assign homework in such a way that it will be in large part self-motivated and will not require great pressure by parents to enforce home study.
11. Teachers express a degree of confidence in their children.

In many elementary schools there has been established a practice of having office hours, usually for an hour once a week after school. This practice is spreading to secondary schools and apparently it is thought to be a valuable provision.

Principals have several responsibilities in assisting the faculty in connection with their public relations. Among the more important ones are the following:

1. To assist teachers to see the importance of public relations.
2. To assist the teachers in meeting the public and to introduce them to parents at meetings of the P.T.A., assisting them (particularly the unmarried teachers) to develop a social life in the community.
3. To assist teachers to avoid indiscretions in the community and to understand what the community expects of the teachers. This is particularly desirable in the case of beginning teachers who are likely to have problems of readjusting from a college campus life to the life of a community.
4. To assist teachers in preparing stories for the press and in understanding what kinds of things should be publicized.
5. To assist teachers in in-service study of good principles and practices in interviews with parents at the school and at the home.

THROUGH OTHER EMPLOYEES. Custodial and clerical employees should be regarded as an integral part of the staff of the school. They should be kept informed about many of the educational projects of the school, especially new ones and extracurricular activities. They should be caused to feel that they belong and are accepted. At the beginning of the year they should be introduced to all new members of the staff. They should be protected from unreasonable demands of teachers, and each one must be accorded a status of dignity and respect which teachers observe. They should be invited to attend the general assemblies when so doing will not interfere with their duties. They should be included in at least a considerable part of the staff's social activities at the school. New members of these staffs, as well as those of the teaching staff, should be presented at a school assembly early in the fall. In schools which have a visiting teacher, that individual may render valuable public-relations service in discussing with parents the work of the schools and meeting their objections and complaints. The principal should see that the visiting teacher is kept informed about the schools; the principal should be willing to discuss with the visiting teacher all the complaints which he or she wishes to make or has heard about the schools.

Counselors in the schools also play an important part in public relations. Assisting all young people to approach, if not to solve, their current pressing problems makes friends not only among the students but also among the appreciative parents of students.

In Detroit there has been tried, at first on an experimental basis, a program of public relations which is directed toward school improvement. In the Detroit "Great Cities Program for School Improvement," which was begun in 1959, the following school personnel were employed: the school-community co-ordinator, the visiting teacher, and the coaching teacher, as well as the school faculty. Teachers engaged in stepped-up community relations in connection with report cards, conferences with parents, newsletters, and personal-improvement classes for the people.

6. Exhibits as a Means of Public Information

Exhibits as a type of publicity are convincing and effective if they are well managed and if the things exhibited are really of merit. To discuss in detail the technique of producing successful exhibits of various sorts would require a volume in itself. A summary of the more important points is given here.

TYPES OF EXHIBITS. Among the types and places of exhibits are the following:

1. *Materials Placed in Halls and on Bulletin Boards of the School.* These exhibits are largely for the purpose of developing in the pupils, faculty, and visitors a knowledge and appreciation of the work and achievements of the school, its departments, students,

and faculty. Appropriate newspaper items, favorable letters about the work and achievements of the school, pictures, articles in journals, and exhibits of good work in various departments should be placed in prominent places where they may be easily seen by passers-by. An effort should be made to place on exhibit as many really creditable things as possible. A commitee of faculty and students may often be of assistance in the search for exhibit material.

2. *Contests and Entertainments.* Exhibits of talent, skill, or prowess in athletics, dramatics, debate, pageants, group dancing, and instrumental or vocal music of individuals, bands, orchestras, quartets, glee clubs, and operetta groups, are usually interesting and, when well done, create good impressions. Free entertainments in the way of assembly programs should often be made the occasion of inviting the public or selected parents and friends.

3. *Programs before Nonschool Organizations.* Various service clubs, women's clubs, church brotherhoods, and other nonschool groups are usually willing to have appropriate phases of school work presented on their programs. They particularly prefer musical numbers, speeches by members of winning teams or by pupils who have achieved unusual distinction, and "booster" talks by high-school pupils. To be effective, these should be brief, snappy, and well rehearsed. The principal should not be reluctant to suggest possibilities to chairmen and program committees of such organizations, and he should not be discouraged or hurt if occasionally no place may be found on the program of an organization approached at a particular time. In promoting such programs, as always, the principal should exercise care to give students and teachers full credit and to avoid the appearance of inserting himself unnecessarily into the limelight.

4. *The Show Windows of Business Houses.* Show windows of business houses may often be obtained for the display of trophies, awards, letters of especial commendation, or the products of shop, laboratory, kitchen, or sewing room. The business-house display is especially valuable to the school in that it reaches many people who would not or could not visit the school. The willingness of merchants to furnish valuable display space should not be abused by employing it for commonplace or uninteresting exhibits, and all exhibits should be removed after a brief display.

5. *County Fairs and Exhibits.* Schools are usually welcome to space at fairs and industrial, agricultural, and commercial exhibits, and here also many people who would otherwise not be reached may see the exhibit. Here may well be exhibited products of the manual-training and metal shops and the household-arts departments; material projects of classes in history, geography, science, literature, foreign languages, and other subjects; posters, charts, and pictures.

6. *Community Parades, Celebrations, and Entertainments.* In typical communities large enough to maintain a high school, there occurs during the year at least one general community celebration or public function in which high-school pupils may assist in a way possessing publicity value. Of this nature are historical pageants or parades, health demonstrations or parades, "old settlers" days, conventions, and home-coming parades.

Particularly in smaller communities the talents of high-school pupils may find a place in public entertainments of various sorts. Glee clubs, bands, orchestras, dramatic clubs in one-act plays, amateur magicians, readers, comedians, and speakers may participate in such entertainments. Though it is entirely proper for the principal to offer to assist in such functions, or to encourage the students and faculty to do so, it should be remembered that only good performances will reflect credit upon the school and that it is unwise to offer talent when it is reasonably certain that the only interest of the audience will be interest arising from a sense of duty to encourage the efforts of young people. Care should be taken that student participation is not overdone and that certain groups (like the school band) are not exploited and overworked.

RELATIONS WITH THE PRESS. Not only should the principal welcome friendly personal and business relations with the local press but he should also actively seek to achieve and maintain such relations. The newspaper must occasionally print news which does not reflect credit upon the school, its achievements, or its administration. Occasionally it does not agree with the administration in matters of finance or management. The newspaper reporter in his effort to get "all the news that is fit to print" appears to pry into matters which the schoolman would prefer not to have exposed to public view. Because of these things, many schoolmen develop an aversion to reporters and editors which is unwise and often costly. The reporter or editor is much more likely to be sympathetic toward the arguments for withholding from publication certain stories or phases of them if the principal has been consistently co-operative in assisting the paper to get at stories of high news value and has more or less frankly confided in and trusted the responsible representatives of the paper.

Very often the personal friendship naturally growing out of such relationships will result in attitudes on the part of newspapermen which prove fortunate in times of need. It is not at all unusual for reporters or editors, appreciating co-operation and being in a position to be especially well informed on community attitudes and opinions, to offer privately very useful advice and information, to "tip off" the principal concerning expressions of dissatisfaction heard in the community regarding policies or methods of the school in time to place the principal on his guard, and even to suggest ways and means of counteracting unfavorable publicity and of conducting publicity campaigns.

Dealing with Reporters and the Press. Among the concrete suggestions relative to establishing good working relations with the local papers should be mentioned the following:

1. Seek to know personally and to establish on your list of personal friends the editors and managers of the local paper or papers.
2. Avoid facetious remarks about any local paper, even if it is imperfect in many ways and your remarks are not intended to be unfriendly or taken seriously.
3. Avoid controversy with the editorial policy of the paper in matters that do not affect the welfare of the school or the things for which it stands. Learn to disagree with papers and people without showing annoyance, personal feeling, or other emotional instability.
4. If the local paper has a job department, do not encourage the giving of printing patronage of pupil organizations or the school to concerns outside the district. Attempt to effect an equitable division of such patronage among the newspapers in the district.
5. Make the reporters welcome in their visits to the school, and assist them to conserve time in getting at news. They will appreciate this help. Remember that the reporter's "beat," or "run," is ordinarily long in relation to the time at his disposal and that ordinarily the school is not considered one of the most fruitful sources of important news stories. Occasionally drop your work or interrupt teachers in order that reporters may get their facts with a minimum expenditure of time and effort. Remember that the school is getting valuable space at no cost.
6. Attempt to avoid favoring any one paper over any other with reference to news stories. Be actively impartial. Do not have stories "break" consistently in favor of an afternoon paper as opposed to a morning paper, or vice versa.
7. Educate reporters slowly and patiently but enthusiastically to your program and to the projects and achievements of the school.
8. Do not pester the reporter because of his failure to give school stories more space or to play up the features of the story you wish played up. A casual, good-natured expression of disappointment is much more effective than "crabbing."
9. Study the interests of the reporter and the paper until you understand their scale of values in news stories.

The Conservation of News Opportunities. Many schoolmen have neither a well-developed sense of what constitutes news nor a technique or system for realizing the possible publicity values of happenings in and concerning the school. When the reporter calls personally or by telephone and inquires for news, the principal is likely to reflect a moment and reply, "Well, I don't think of anything, Mr. Hayward," or relate some commonplace incident of doubtful news interest. Often days or weeks later the news possibility of an event or development occurs to him. By that time it is no longer news.

Many principals make a canvass of the faculty members and student officials most likely to furnish data for stories, either just before the expected call of the reporter or, more usually though not more desirably, when he calls.

Some principals have formed the useful habit of constantly thinking of all things going on in the school as news possibilities and of keeping memoranda of all that promise to be acceptable to the paper, so that when the reporter calls these will not be overlooked. Some have trained their staff to report to the office immediately data which might be useful as news, and a few have actually given attention in teachers' meetings to developing a news sense. A very effective stimulus to thinking of possible stories is a school-news calendar, such as the following:

PUBLICITY CALENDAR FOR HIGH SCHOOLS

AUGUST

General plans for the coming school year
School improvements made during the summer
Alterations and new equipment
New departments and courses offered
Fall-registration instructions
Names of faculty and departments
Staff changes or additions
Teachers' activities during the summer
High-school graduates going to college
Value of high-school education

SEPTEMBER (BEFORE OPENING OF SCHOOL)

Announcement of opening day
Prospects for football team
General procedure for registration; text-book lists
New plans of instruction: supervised study, etc.
School-attendance laws
Information about working certificates
Fall-registration announcements
Courses and curricula offered
First teachers' meeting

SEPTEMBER (AFTER OPENING OF SCHOOL)

Registration statistics
Organization of classes
Student organizations
Organization of various clubs
Football schedule
Football turnout and practice
Selection of cheerleader
"Pep" meeting to learn cheers and songs
Work of physical-education department
Parent-teacher association: first meeting
Fire drill and protection
Punctuality of pupils in the schools
First issue of school paper
Vocational-guidance program
Value and progress of health inspection
Announcement of class advisers
Boys in agricultural classes visit state fair
Organization and prospects for debate
Evening school and Americanization work
Testing program
School gardens
Rotary loan fund
Assisting pupils to find work
Teachers' institute week
Teachers' directory
Dinners and receptions for teachers

Calendar for coming school events
Staff of school paper chosen
Work of glee club gets under way
Exhibits at state fair
School orchestra
Organization of school band
School credit for private music lessons
Reception for new teachers
University-extension lecture courses
County fair, any vacation, or change of session
Arbor Day and Bird Day
Constitution Week
Freshmen boys' mix or other student social events

OCTOBER

Statistics of physical and health examinations
Enrollment statistics compared with previous years
Lyceum course this year
Outside speakers in assembly
Columbus Day activities
Publicity stories for football; results of games
New clubs started
Rallies
Progress of new departments in school
Increased enrollment
Student dance or reception
Other social activities
Serving milk to pupils
Report of convention attended by superintendent
Halloween festivities: respect for property; etc.
Comparative study of enrollments
Extension work of staff
Teachers' institutes
Issuance of reports to parents

NOVEMBER

School programs; changes
Better-English Week
National Education Week
School exhibits; open hours
Explanation of classification of students
Urge parents to visit schools
P.T.A. meeting
Net proceeds of football season
Civics class and election day
Plans for sending Thanksgiving baskets to the poor
School play
Hot lunches, cafeteria, etc.
Honor roll: six weeks' report
Radio concern given by school musical organizations
Interclass debates
Class parties
Football season: big games; season record
Letters earned
Football-team banquet
Armistice Day program
Speed contests: commercial department
Announcement of coming school carnival
Physical examinations of pupils completed
Results of physical and medical examinations
Special accomplishments of students
Thanksgiving Day: vacation and program
First basketball meeting: prospects

DECEMBER

Sale of Christmas seals opens
Football banquet and letter awards
Out-of-doors recreation
Question announced for interschool debate
Christmas program
Personals on teachers' vacations
Schools close for holidays
Unusual events
Alumni meetings and contests

Physical education for cold months
Interclass basketball games
Basketball practice and prospects
Students' health reports
Suggestions on winter diet by home-economics department
Report of Christmas-seal sales

JANUARY

New Year's resolutions
Resuming school work
Preregistration
P.T.A. activities for past half-year
Glee club and orchestra
Examinations
Student reports and elections
Child-labor week
New subjects offered for second semester
Midyear promotions to high school
Reports of basketball games
Results of first semester
Address made to high-school assembly
Epidemics of communicable diseases
Name of honor student in first semester
News from graduates in colleges and universities
Attendance record

FEBRUARY

Formation of boys' radio club (activities)
Lincoln's Birthday activities
Washington's Birthday activities
Basketball games
Tryouts for senior play
Evening school for parents
Better-English Week
Annual staff organized
Interschool debate
Operetta
Evening citizenship schools
Midyear commencement exercises

MARCH

Baseball news and schedule
Election of teachers
Typing contest
Basketball tournament
Review
Basketball season reviewed
Clean-up week
School gardening
First call for baseball and track
Senior-play practice
Parent-teacher entertainment
Debating
St. Patrick's Day program
School fair
Field trips of science class
Spring music festival
Track news and schedule
Campaign to prevent dropping out
Easter program
Vacation of teachers

APRIL

First baseball game
Local institute
Budget meeting
Arbor Day
Camp Fire Girls and Girl Scout organizations
Easter vacation
School exhibit
Boy Scout week
Plans for May Day festivities
Senior-class commencement plans
Father-and-son banquet
Annual goes to press
Agricultural Club banquet
Oratorical contest
Track practice
Preparation for class stunt night
Athletic awards: basketball
Janitor's efficiency
Style shows
Clerical assistants
Home-beautifying
Travel tips
Physical-education reports

MAY

New officers of P.T.A. and report of year's activities
May Day exercises
Mother's Day and mother-and-daughter banquet
Track meets
Baseball games
Sale of school annuals
Stunt night
Physical-efficiency tests
Athletic awards
Preregistration statistics
Financial report
Memorial Day

JUNE

Examination schedule
College plans of graduates
Summary of progress of school year
How student government worked during the year
Preparing for fair exhibit
Value of high-school and college training
Alumni who graduate from college
Teachers who are going to summer school
Commencement-plan announcements
Senior play
Junior Prom
Class Day
Senior banquet
Baccalaureate sermon
Commencement exercises
Scholarship awards
Honor students
School closes
Review of achievements of year
Needs of the school for the coming year
Attendance record

JULY AND AUGUST

Building alterations
Teachers in summer school
Improvement of grounds
Plans for coming year

THROUGHOUT THE YEAR

Election of officers
Social events
Athletic events and other contests; other public entertainments
Assembly programs
New organizations
Achievements of graduates at colleges
Programs and activities of clubs and organizations

WRITING NEWS STORIES. Particularly in small cities or villages where the reportorial staff is small and visits are not frequent, it is good policy for the principal to write the copy for news stories and take it or send it to the local papers while the stories are still news. This practice possesses the virtue of reducing to a minimum the chances of "garbling," inaccuracies, or misunderstandings likely to occur frequently in the smaller papers, where relatively inexperienced reporters are employed. It also furnishes an objective record by which to settle all arguments as to what the principal actually did say. The schoolman, like other laymen, is not well qualified by training to know what the readers of a paper desire; therefore, he should accept the editors' decision as to what shall be printed.

Among the more acceptable types of news data are the following:

1. Stories relating to contests of all sorts: athletics, debating, typing, and dramatics.
2. Unusual occurrences or situations: for example, achievements in spite of handicaps, records broken, superlatives—the youngest pupil or the tallest—queer, odd, and freakish occurrences or problems.
3. Contrasts and comparisons: past and present; the local school test scores and state or national averages or norms.
4. Human-interest stories: achievements of the blind, the crippled, the self-supporting; marriages, deaths, serious illnesses, accidents; pretty girls and athletic boys.
5. Things that appeal to community pride: results of standard tests; distinctions or honors of pupils or faculty, particularly of individuals; comments on the school and its work by people from a distance, particularly officials, eminent people, or people well known in the community.
6. Stories about individuals, pupils, or teachers related to individuals already in the public eye; stories about events related in some way to peculiar interests of the moment or of the locality: for example, relatives of famous aviators, athletes, public officials, and men or women prominent in industry, finance, or business; events related in some way to a forthcoming community celebration or to "drives."
7. Stories that permit of interesting illustration with pictures.
8. Stories that "live": that is, those that are still fresh news.
9. Stories that affect the interests of large numbers of individuals in the community: proposed changes in tax rates, new buildings, the transfer of units or grades from one building to another, changes in the time of opening or closing school, and in the school day.
10. Stories that center about and include the names of individuals are preferable, especially if individuals are prominent in the community or are related to those who are.

In short, news value is largely dependent upon the relation of the data of the story, or the turn which may be put upon them, to instincts of combat or contest, to the instinct of curiosity, to the interest in individuals as human beings (especially in aspects of sex and personal characteristics), to the interest in things affecting the reader's own routine or interests, and to the interest in the present as opposed to the past or the future.

Teachers and others in the school should clear written news stories with the high-school principal; he may be of assistance in guiding teachers relative to making strong and interesting stories and he may make suggestions for the elimination or modification of some points in the stories or for the elimination of the stories entirely. The principal, however, should be rather conservative in modifying news stories by members of his staff.

PICTURES. The reporter should be assisted in getting good pictures. Often these must be taken and furnished to the reporter, who cannot be present when the pictures must be taken at rehearsals or exercises of various sorts. Action pictures are preferable to stilted, posed pictures. Particularly desirable are pictures which depict the individual or individuals in some action relative to the principal item of the story. Pictures of pretty girls, athletic boys, and prominent persons are preferred, as are those taken of individuals in costume appropriate to the story.

UNFAVORABLE NEWS. It is desirable at times to withhold news, at least temporarily and occasionally permanently. Examples include news affecting the reputation of pupils and teachers and stories relative to expansions or changes, premature announcement of which would embarrass the administration of the school. The professional newspaperman who has absorbed the ethics of his calling is appreciative of these considerations and is quite willing to weigh the matter of publication and often to soften the story or to withhold it altogether. However, news is the paper's stock in trade, and the paper which fails to publish interesting news is like a grocer who wantonly destroys his wares. Consequently, one must not expect too great sacrifices by the local papers in the interests of mercy or of the administration of the schools.

Certain ways of approaching this problem are distinctly better than ways that are frequently employed. It is naturally more logical to request co-operation in such matters if the school has pursued a consistent policy of aiding the paper to get the news. The best approach is to present the argument for withholding the news in a calm and pleasant manner, appealing to the human and logical side of the editor or reporter. Though, of course, the principal may for various reasons wisely refuse to talk for publication, particularly if he is to be quoted, it is not wise to attempt openly to block the papers from getting at the story, except in instances where those in charge of the papers have no sense of ethics or when dealing with a paper of the sensational and scandalmongering type. In a majority of instances fair treatment of the representatives of the paper will result in at least the "toning down" of the objectionable phases of the story; frequently, complete frankness and confidence will not be abused. Editors and reporters differ greatly with respect to co-operation in such matters. Therefore, the principal may have to modify his policy and practice in dealing with them according to the degree of co-operation which he discovers they are going to give to the school.

If the story does appear in a form less desirable than is expected by the principal, little is gained by making it the occasion for bitterness or a quarrel. Such a procedure is not likely to prevent similar treatment in the future in like situations and is likely to arouse a more critical attitude toward favorable school stories of less news value. A calm, friendly expression of disappointment is more likely to achieve beneficial results.

The principal should not be too sensitive to stories that appear about him and the school. They cannot all be lavish in praise, personal or otherwise, even were that desirable. More often than not, what seems to him a doubtful compliment or a reflection upon him or his school does not appear so to the busy, casual reader.

7. *School Publications*[6]

Of not nearly so great importance for purposes of publicity as the newspaper, but fairly useful and worthy of attention, are:

1. The student publications: the school paper, the monthly, and the annual.
2. Official school reports.
3. The student handbooks.
4. Communications to parents.
5. Daily bulletins to the students.

STUDENT PUBLICATIONS. School publications are potential liabilities as well as potential assets in influencing public opinion about the school, its staff, work, and pupils. The publicity value of student publications is secondary to their educational value. Since they are little read by others, their chief value for publicity lies in the selling of the school to the pupils —arousing school spirit and pride and furnishing information and orientation with reference to the school.

The principal factor in the success of school publications is the presence on the staff of a teacher who is reasonably well trained in journalism and English, who can be relied upon to comprehend the significance of publicity to the school, who knows the values and dangers of school publications, and who is able to establish leadership with the student editors and managers.

Influence must be exercised to keep at a minimum the trivial and ultra-juvenile material and the abortive attempts at humor which give undesirable and false impressions of the life of the school; there should be an attempt to bring about the inclusion of such material as will give some idea of the character of the more important work of the school.

REPORTS TO THE PUBLIC. More and more principals are preparing annual reports to be submitted to the superintendent of schools. A great many principals also are preparing a second type of report, which is somewhat shorter and written in a more interesting fashion. This report is to be distributed to the families of children in the school and others who are interested.

In any report which goes to the public, tabular statistics should be

[6]The California Association of Secondary School Administrators, through its committee on public relations, has been attempting to improve public relations through various types of school publications.

For a report on this committee write to Dr. Roy E. Simpson, Superintendent of Public Instruction, Sacramento, California.

kept at a minimum and the really important statistics should be presented in correct and simple graphical form. The material should deal with the more important phases of the work of the school and its most important needs, noting outstanding distinctions and achievements of the year. Fairly intensive reports on a few main topics are preferable to comprehensive reports scattered over all phases of the work of the school. Many principals or superintendents employ this plan of intensive reports, alternating from topic to topic in different years. Copies of the report should be furnished to the local papers, or parts of it should be modified for a series of articles or news items.

Much more commonly than previously, these reports contain a considerable number of pictures of youngsters at work and a much smaller amount of reading material. Experience seems to show that these are more effective in communicating to the public the principal ideas intended.

COMMUNICATIONS TO PARENTS. An increasing number of schools are sending several communications each year to the parents. These are for gaining the parents' assistance in giving adequate guidance to youngsters, for developing understanding on the part of the parents as to how things are done in the school and the value of the school program, and for developing good will. Typical of such publications are the following: *An Orientation Bulletin for Parents of Freshmen,* by the Tottenville, New York, High Schools; *Let Freedom Ring,* by the Classen High School of Oklahoma City; *How Your Child's Textbooks Are Selected* by the Canton, Ohio, Public Schools.

In a rather large and rapidly increasing number of schools, printed communications are sent periodically to parents. The Evanston, Illinois, High School issues a quarterly bulletin entitled *Here's Your High School.* In one issue published in the spring, for example, there were short articles such as "P.T.A. Elections," "Spring Examinations," "The New Student Code of Conduct," "High School Budget and Tax Levy Explained," "The Evening School," "The First Year of Distributive Education," and "Magazine Articles of Interest to You" (about adolescents). The material for the publication is gathered from various members of the staff.

From some schools communications are sent at appropriate times to groups of parents. An example is entitled *Greetings from Tottenville, New York, High School to Parents of Freshmen,* with information about the school, certain rules that parents ought to know, and suggestions for school-parent co-operation.

In an increasing number of schools an appropriate handbook is prepared and students are required to take it home for the perusal of their parents, so that their parents may be informed about the way the school operates and its various services. Furthermore, many principals in schools that use the daily one-page bulletin to the students request the students to take it home to their parents.

Of course, reporting to parents about the educational progress of their sons and daughters is an important item in public relations. This has been discussed in Chapter 17.

8. Other Opportunities

EDUCATION WEEK. Each year a week in the fall is designated as American Education Week. Because of the publicity given the week and the fact that it is observed on a nationwide scale, it affords an excellent opportunity for the employment of various agencies for bringing the work and values of the school to the people through many of the channels just discussed. The National Education Association has available at low cost a large variety of valuable materials and suggestions for use in connection with Education Week. Appropriate materials include:

(1) 35-millimeter, 1-minute movie trailers.
(2) Films like the hour-long dramatic documentary entitled "Secret of Freedom," by Archibald MacLeish, and "Can America Afford Better Schools?" a 16-millimeter sound and color film which is 13½ minutes long.
(3) Public-relations idea-books of various kinds, such as *Public Relations Gold Mine,* with ideas for welcoming new teachers, piloting parent-teacher conferences, holding open house, etc., and *Let's Go to Press,* which shows how to spot newsworthy items, put them in shape for print, illustrate with newsworthy photos, and organize an efficient school-news reporting system.
(4) Various booklets, such as *The Search for Freedom* and *Talking Points,* for speakers, writers, editors, and broadcasters.
(5) Leaflets on such subjects as *What Teachers Know About Your Child* and *Learning Is Your Business.*
(6) Posters in large, attractive sizes.

Since the items vary from year to year, the principal should obtain early in the fall from the National Education Association a folder listing the various materials.

Also it is not uncommon for a school to put on a program at service clubs during this week to explain the work of the schools in a popular and interesting manner. Also used widely and effectively are very short sound movies which can be used as trailers in local movie houses.

RADIO AND TELEVISION. Many school systems have allocated to them by local radio stations certain hours in the week, or 15-minute periods every day or several times a week, in which they have interesting programs to give those who listen better information about what is going on in the schools and why. Types of programs include stories of the achievement of the schools (particularly by students) and entertainment and intellectual programs. There may be instrumental music, discussion of current questions, debates by high-school youngsters, discussion by selected teachers, supervisors, and administrative officers of current educational problems and questions (particularly as they throw light on the program of the schools), announcements about changes in the program of the schools, and various information concerning registration, selection of courses, and things of that type.

Some of the larger school systems have an educational television channel through which they produce educational television programs. Such a channel is an outlet for favorable school publicity.

SCHOOL VISITATION. Although not a new practice, it has become more common in recent years to promote better public relations and better acquaintanceship between teachers and parents by having the parents visit the school. In many schools are found such things as Dad's Day, Mother-and-Daughter Day, or Father-and-Son Night. In some schools upon these occasions programs of interest to the particular group of parents are planned. For example, on Father-and-Son Night there may be: (1) exhibitions of boxing, tumbling, wrestling, intermural basketball, or games; (2) short talks on father-son relationships, by an interesting speaker; and (3) sometimes a dinner or a banquet. Mother-and-Daughter programs may be of a correspondingly appropriate nature.

Many schools set aside a day or a week with the slogan "Visit Your School." This is not only for the purpose of having the parents see the school in operation and get some understanding but also, perhaps more important, for the purpose of bringing about an acquaintanceship between the parents and one or more teachers in the school, so as to provide the basis for easier and more friendly intercommunication later on. It is found to be true that, where parents and teacher have met and know each other, they are much more likely to communicate with each other as problems seem to develop; there is thus much less possibility of misunderstanding and hostility.

One of the more successful types of school visitation is what is sometimes called Parents' Night. At a given time, usually early in the evening, parents gather at the school following the daily school schedule, which is operated with short periods of about 10 or 12 minutes each; the parents go to the rooms where the students have their classes and meet the teachers, who give short explanations of the things emphasized in the particular classes. When the parents are not in any class, they report to the library, where refreshments are served and where they may meet the principal, the counselors, the school nurse, and other members of the school staff.

A great many secondary schools form various types of parents' organizations, such as home-room mothers or core-block parents, who act as sponsors for particular home rooms or core blocks. They have meetings several times in the year with the home-room sponsor or the core-block teacher to discuss problems of parent-teacher co-operation in promoting the all-round growth of the youngsters. Among groups of this type are the parents of members of the band, parents of members of the orchestra, and fathers of members of athletic teams.

HOME VISITATION. In recent years there has been an increased tendency to stimulate and prepare teachers for home visitation and to provide time for it. While this has been more common in the elementary schools by reason of the much smaller number of homes involved for each teacher, there has also been a tendency for high schools to develop some sort of program for home visitation. It is, of course, much simpler if there is a core program in the school, since the teacher of the core program will not handle more than two blocks of youngsters, involving perhaps 50 or 60 homes (rather than 120 or 130 homes on the average for teachers of noncore classes). Likewise, it is simpler for the homeroom sponsor to visit the homes of the youngsters in his home-room group only; by this means every home in high school is visited by one homeroom sponsor. In some schools the time has been taken in school time for home visitation. Experience has shown that teachers who have not done much home visitation need to give some time and thought to studying principles and good practices of conducting home visits. Group conferences led by the principal may be useful in this connection.

DEVELOPING PERSONAL GOOD WILL. It has become increasingly apparent that is is not safe, in view of the attacks on the schools and of increased public taxes, for schoolmen to rely upon people's faith in education and the public schools or upon the effects of merely informing people about the schools. It is obvious that a program of public relations must also include definite provisions for developing *good will.* This good will should be based at least in part upon an understanding of the program of the school and its achievements, but it must go further than that. It must also be based upon personal acquaintanceships between the parents and others in the community and the personnel of the schools—the teachers, custodians and other nonteaching employees, and supervisory and administrative personnel. This means, of course, that teachers and other personnel must develop a considerable number of acquaintanceships and friendships in the community; the school should have programs and procedures for assisting in this development. Teachers and administrators should assist each other in developing opportunities for contacts and for more social life. It is particularly important to assist the unmarried teacher, since so much social life is based upon married couples as units.

There is an increasing tendency for public high schools to develop placement bureaus, which assist in finding positions not only for the graduates but also for those who are dropping out before graduation. They assist youngsters to find summer work or part-time employment during the school year, keep in touch with them after they have severed their connection with school, obtain for them counsel and advice, and assist them in advancing vocationally. This service pays big dividends in developing appreciation and good will on the part of all former students and members of their families.

THE STUDY OF DROP-OUTS. In an increasing number of schools there has been conducted in recent years a study of the students who dropped out from school, in an effort to discover why they dropped out and what type of career they follow and to throw light upon the program of the school. A few careful studies of the drop-outs indicate that the major reason is not that they have to go to work but that they are dissatisfied with the program of the school, have lost confidence in its usefulness, and are not happy in their relationships in the school, for one of the following reasons:

1. They cannot do the work of the school.
2. They are antagonized by the teachers.
3. They do not have sufficient funds to dress as other youngsters do and to finance participation in activities requiring funds.
4. The parents have scolded and antagonized them by reason of the low grades on their report cards.
5. They feel that they are not accepted by the other youngsters of the school, this reason being given more largely by youngsters of the minority ethnic groups and the lowest economic status.
6. They have not been members of clubs or other student organizations.

These reasons offer clues and suggestions for improving pupil attitudes and public relations.

THE USE OF OPINIONAIRES.[7] In recent years, stimulated by the use of poll techniques in other fields and by the work of Professor Harold Hand of the University of Illinois, there has been an increased tendency to study the opinions held by people of the community about the schools —the opinions of students, former students, parents, and other people of the community. A great many schools have used for the community-opinion study a form devised by Professor Hand, or modifications of it.[8]

The use of these opinionaires serves a number of purposes, including the following:

1. To stimulate interest on the part of the public in the schools.
2. To bring into relief the dissatisfactions of the people of the community so that there may be *(a)* improvement of the school program and procedures and *(b)* better information for the parents so that the dissatisfactions may tend to disappear.

[7]An excellent form for this purpose, *How Would You Answer This? What Would You Do if You Were in Charge of the Public Schools?* has been prepared by the Department of Public Instruction of the State of Michigan, Lansing, Michigan.

[8]A questionnaire form prepared by Professor Hand is published as the Illinois Inventory by the World Book Company.

3. To draw statistical conclusions which may be published, showing the people of the community the satisfaction of the great majority and uncovering the efforts of the organized attackers of the school, the emotionally unstable, or those with axes to grind.
4. To contribute to in-service growth of the teachers by showing them community attitudes and areas of the school programs toward which community attitudes may not be entirely favorable.

SERVING COMMUNITY NEEDS THROUGH THE USE OF THE SCHOOL PLANT. One of the ways of gaining and inspiring friends for the school is by making the plant available to adults in the community and by encouraging their use of it—having them come to the school, be reminded of it, meet representatives of the school, and feel that it is hospitable to them and their needs. The school cafeteria, the auditorium, the gymnasium, the library, the homemaking department, the industrial-arts workshop, the argicultural shop, the school movie projector, and the school athletic field are units which may be utilized by various groups in the community for educational and recreational purposes.

THE NATIONAL ASSOCIATION OF PUBLIC RELATIONS. As a division of the National Education Association, the National Association of Public Relations operates with headquarters at 1201 Sixteenth Street, N.W., Washington, D.C. The high-school principal who has not done so should write to this association and obtain from it a list of helps and publications which he may wish to purchase and employ.

Problems, Questions, and Answers

1. Outline plans of procedure for a high-school principal in a new community in which he has just begun his work as principal.
2. What should a principal know about his community? (Make a list.)
3. After reading the section in the textbook, formulate your own position and be able to give it as to the principal's participation in various activities in the community, including religious, fraternal, business, and political affairs.
4. Contrast a parent-teacher association that does not operate effectively and one that does, describing how each of them operates and tell, if you can, how a principal might be active in assuring a better type of P.T.A. program and activity.
5. Be able to discuss the place of alumni meetings in a program.
6. Be able to discuss in class "The High School and Community Youth-Serving Agencies."
7. Be able to discuss a follow-up study of drop-outs and former students, indicating what types of data you would want to gather and how you would go about gathering them.
8. Be able to discuss commencement programs as a means of public relations.
9. What do you think is the effect of scholastic athletics upon the general public's attitude toward the school? Do you think, for example, that the athletic fans are likely to prove mainstays in support of the school? Do you

think that reducing the emphasis upon interscholastic athletics is likely to affect the attitudes of the bulk of the community toward the school's financial and other needs?

10. Why is a continuous program of publicity better than a campaign?
11. Do you believe that the surest way to develop favorable attitudes on the part of the parents is through the children? Be able to explain specifically why this might be true.
12. Make a list of things that teachers could do in the classroom to promote better attitudes toward the school and a list of things that some teachers do in the classroom that are likely to develop bad attitudes. Take into consideration the attitudes of both students and parents.
13. Be able to discuss further publicity through the faculty and the faculty as public-relations agents outside the school.
14. Be able to discuss fully publicity through the custodian and the custodian as public-relations agent outside the school.
15. Be able to discuss fully publicity through the clerical employees and clerical employees as public-relations agents outside the school.
16. Make a list of at least seven or eight different kinds of stories about school affairs that might appear in the press almost any year; give at least one example of each type of story.
17. What do you think of the value for public-relations purposes of each of the types of school publications mentioned in this chapter? How large should a school be before it should have a school annual? A weekly school paper?
18. Mention the various different kinds of groups of parents that might be formed for good public relations.
19. What are the advantages of home visiting, and who should do it?
20. Discuss lay participation in planning in connection with the work of a high school.

Selected Supplementary Readings

Aderhold, O. C., and Williams, Joe A., "Use of the School Plant by the Adults of the Community," *School Executive* (June, 1948), Vol. 67, pp. 49-50.[A description of one community's plan for wide use of school facilities by community groups in a typical rural county. Good concrete suggestions for using the school facilities in community projects.]

Ames, Dora A., "A Community Occupational Survey as a Public Relations Instrument," *School Review* (January, 1953), Vol. 61, pp. 30-33.

Anderson, W. P., "The High School and the Community," *Teachers College Record* (April, 1955), Vol. 56, pp. 377-383.

Bakkegard, B. M., "Public School Music as a Public Relations Agent," *Music Educators Journal* (September, 1952), Vol. 39, No. 1, pp. 61-63.

Blalock, H. M., and Blalock, Ann B., "Situational Factors and Negro Leadership Activity in a Medium Sized Community," *Journal of Negro Education* (Winter, 1960), Vol. 29, pp. 85.

Brewer, A. L., "Orientation at Pattengill Junior High School," *Bulletin of the N.A.S.S.P.* (November, 1960), No. 259, pp. 106-110. [Orientation of parents to the junior high school.]

Brindel, P., "What Public Relations? What Catholic Image?" *Catholic School*

Journal (November, 1960), Vol. 60, No. 3, pp. 53-55.
Bryan, R. C., and Beisel, Mildred, "Vitalize Your High School PTA," *Bulletin of the N.A.S.S.P.* (May, 1956), No. 220, pp. 139-145.
Bullock, Robert P., "Power Elite in the Community," *School Executive* (March, 1959), Vol. 78, No. 7, pp. 59-61. [The use of influential people in good public relations.]
Ceirnick, Sylvia, and others, "Public Relations for the American High School," *Bulletin of the N.A.S.S.P.* (September, 1960), No. 257, pp. 1-137.
"Check Points for Principals," *Bulletin of the N.A.S.S.P.* (September, 1960), No. 257, pp. 37-38.
Cole, Eleanor, "Results Citizens Committees Have Secured," *School Executive* (January, 1952), Vol. 71, No. 5, pp. 61-62.
Conant, James B., *Slums and Suburbs,* New York, McGraw-Hill Book Company, 1961, 116 pp.
Cozzo, Joyce R., "Evaluation of Parent Group Meetings," *Bulletin of the N.A.S.S.P.* (April, 1962), No. 273, pp. 205-209.
Cuony, Edward R., "Student-Parent-Teacher Conferences," *Bulletin of the N.A.S.S.P.* (February, 1957), No. 226, pp. 180-187. [Techniques and results.]
Dorff, Joseph A., and Peters, Kenneth L., "How Can the School Develop Good School-Community Relations?" *Bulletin of the N.A.S.S.P.* (April, 1956), No. 219, pp. 277-281.
Dresden, Katherine W., and Stegeman, William H., "When School and Community Get Together," *Clearing House* (September, 1950), Vol. 25, No. 1, pp. 22-25. [How in four California towns laymen played a great part in improving education.]
Education Policies Commission, *Education for All American Youth,* 1952, pp. 87-93, 152-154, 198-202, 243-252; "Public and Community School Relations," pp. 369-371; "Out of School Youth," pp. 334-337, 364-368; "Study of the Community," pp. 78-95, 111-126.
Feel Their Pulse: Guide to Opinion Polling, Washington, D.C., National Education Association, 1956.
Fish, K. L., "Group Dynamics, Parents' Nights, and Consequences," *Bulletin of the N.A.S.S.P.* (March, 1954), No. 201, pp. 62-64.
Fly, Homer F., "18 Points on School Public Relations," *Clearing House* (November, 1950), Vol. 25, No. 3, p. 161, [Report of a survey made in Tazewell County, Illinois; eighteen recommendations grew out of the survey.]
Frederick, Robert W., *The Third Curriculum,* New York, Appleton-Century-Crofts, 1959. [Chapter 21, "Community School Interaction"; Chapter 22, "Public Relations and Public Information."]
Gallen, John J., "A Parent Speaks to the Teacher," *Proceedings and Addresses,* 46th Annual Meeting, National Catholic Educational Association, 1949. [What the author believes parents expect from teachers.]
Grinnell, J. E., Youth, Raymond, and others, *School and Community, Educational and Public Relations,* New York, Ronald, 1954.
Hand, Harold C., *What People Think about Their Schools,* New York, World Book, 1949, pp. 153-219.
Hines, Vynce A., and Growman, Hulda, "What Parents Think of Their Schools, and What They Know About Them," *Bulletin of the N.A.S.S.P.* (February, 1957), No. 226, pp. 15-25.
It's High Time: Guide for Parents of High School Students, Washington, D.C.,

National Association of Secondary School Principals, 1955.
Knowles, Malcolm S., "Adult Education—No Longer a Stepchild," *Nation's Schools* (January, 1953), Vol. 51, pp. 67-68. [Views adult education as an essential instrument of public relations.]
Lee, Thomas L., "They Came Back to Help Us Plan," *School Executive* (October, 1954), Vol. 74, No. 2, pp. 58-59. [Assistance from alumni.]
Let's Go to Press: The Classroom Teacher's Guide to School News Reporting, Washington, D.C., National Education Association, 1956.
Lieberman, Myron, "Parochial Schools and Public Leadership," *National Catholic Educational Association Bulletin* (August, 1960), Vol. 58, pp. 239-248.
MacDonald, Dora Mary, "A Public Relations Workshop That Works," *Bulletin of the N.A.S.S.P.* (September, 1960), No. 257, pp. 81-84.
McKeough, Reverend Michael, *The Administration of the Catholic Secondary School,* Washington, D.C., Catholic University of American Press, 1948. [Chapter 1.]
National School Public Relations Association, Action and Reaction, Washington, D.C., National Education Association, 1957. [Public relations for educational secretaries.]
Patterson, N. S., "School Yearbooks as Public Relations for Education and Training Media for Youth," *School and Society* (October, 1951), Vol. 74, No. 1923, pp. 296-298.
Print It Right: How to Plan, Write and Design School Public Relations Materials, Washington, D.C., National Education Association, 1953.
Public Relations Gold Mine, Number One, Washington, D.C., National Education Association, 1957. [Roundup of tested public-relations ideas.]
Reinert, Paul C. (S.J.), "Catholic Educators and Public Education," *Association of American Colleges Bulletin* (October, 1952), Vol. 38, No. 3, [A president of a Catholic university expresses his respect for the work of the public schools, and suggests that private education and public education can be mutually helpful.]
Rice, Arthur H., "Planned Propaganda," *Nation's Schools* (October, 1957), Vol. 60, No. 4. pp. 98-102, 150-152.
Ryan, L. V., "The Project Technique in Consumer Education," *Catholic Educational Review* (March, 1952), Vol. 50, No. 3. [Suggests ways and means of tying the school into the community.]
Ryan, Calvin T., "Service Clubs and Public Relations," *School Activities* (April, 1951), Vol. 22, No. 8, pp. 248-250.
School Photojournalism—Telling Your School Story in Pictures. Washington, D.C., National Society for Public Relations, 1958. [Heavily illustrated and bristling with successful word and picture techniques. An unusual pictorial manual.]
Scott, Walter L., "Community Use of School Facilities in Long Beach," *California Journal of Secondary Education* (April, 1952), Vol. 27, pp. 226-228.
"Ten Criticisms of Public Education," *National Education Association Research Bulletin* (December, 1957), Vol. 35, No. 4.
Toy, Henry, Jr., "How to Organize Local Citizens Committees," *Nation's Schools* (July, 1950), Vol. 46, pp. 26-28. [Pointers in organizing local committees.]

Watson, Norman E., "Why Do Our Schools Cost So Much?" *School Management* (November, 1960), Vol. 4, No. 11, pp. 67-84. [How to explain the costliness of a new high-school plant.]

Xavier, Sister Mary (O.P.), "Relationships of the (Catholic) Secondary Schools with the Community and with the Public Schools," *Proceedings and Addresses,* 46th Annual Meeting, Catholic Educational Association, 1949. [A well-stated summary which cites the common problem of the two organizations and the need for a thoroughly co-operative effort.]

24

Types of Secondary-School Organization

1. Types of Secondary Schools Today

While approximately one third of our secondary schools today, enrolling approximately one fourth of the students in grades 9 through 12, are four-year high schools based upon eight-year elementary schools, there are many other types of secondary-school organization, including the following more common ones: a five-year high school based upon a seven-year elementary school, a three-year high school based upon a three-year junior high school, a three-year junior high school based upon a six-year elementary school, a four-year junior college, including grades 11 and 12, based upon a four-year junior high school. There will probably never be in this country, at least for many years, any one type of organization which is standard throughout the country. The trend towards the 6-3-3 and the 6-6 type of organization continues and will probably accelerate in the late 1960's and 1970's. As enrollments in secondary schools increase and new buildings have to be built, administrators have more choice and are not bound by the types of buildings already available. The larger 8-4 school systems will probably change to 6-3-3 organization; smaller 8-4 systems will change to 6-6; and larger 6-6 systems will change to 6-3-3. In a carefully conducted nationwide study by W. C. Wood, the opinions of 66 recognized authorities on secondary education favored the 6-3-3 and 6-4-4 plans decidedly in comparison with all other plans of organization, the 6-6 plan being third (Table 10).

THE REORGANIZATION MOVEMENT. Throughout the nineteenth century and in the first decade of the twentieth century, practically all secondary schools were four-year secondary schools based upon a seven-year elementary school (in the South), a nine-year elementary school (in some places in New England), or an eight-year elementary school (in the rest of the country). There were several major criticisms of the 8-4 plan as far back as 1885. The objections were that too much time was given to elementary education, that teachers in the upper grades of elementary school were not properly prepared, and that departmentalization should be begun earlier. By 1910 there was a trend toward the 6-3-3 plan of organization. The spread of this type of organization has continued steadily since that time.

TABLE 10. *Number and Percentage of Types of Organization, Ranked by Authorities in Order of Preference*

Types of Schools	First		Second		Third		Weighted Total
	No.	Per Cent	No.	Per Cent	No.	Per Cent	
6-3-3	25	38	24	39	5	9	128
6-4-4	32	48	11	18	6	10	142
6-6	3	4	13	21	22	38	57
5-7	—	—	—	—	2	3	2
8-4	—	—	3	5	7	12	13
4-4-4	—	—	4	6	4	7	12
9-3	2	3	1	2	3	5	11
7-5	—	—	2	3	7	12	11
Miscellaneous	4	7	3	6	2	4	20

By 1962, less than 30 per cent of the school systems in the United States were organized on the 8-4 plane, 42 per cent on the 6-6 plan, and approximately 28 per cent on the 6-3-3 plan. With respect to enrollments, about 37 per cent of the boys and girls in schools beyond the eighth grade were in junior or senior high schools; approximately 30 per cent were in six-year secondary schools; and only 28 per cent were in conventional four-year secondary schools. A considerable number of four-year high schools exists in Illinois, California, and Arizona, where districts are organized as special secondary-school districts; in the same areas there are separate eight-year elementary school districts.

ADVANTAGES OF THE JUNIOR HIGH SCHOOL PLAN. The following conclusions may be drawn with reasonable validity relative to the advantages and disadvantages of the junior high school plan:

I. Conclusions relative to instruction
   1. The curriculum of the junior high school is broader and provides for more enriched learning experiences than does the 8-4 system, especially for pupils in grades seven and eight.
   2. It is easier to introduce changes in the curriculum especially when the junior high school is first introduced.
   3. A broader program of extraclass activities can be provided. This is possible for ninth-grade pupils as well as those in grades seven and eight.
   4. Teachers with better preparation, particularly in the special subject fields, can be attracted.
   5. It is easier to attract men teachers than in grades seven and eight of the elementary school.
   6. The supply of well-qualified administrators, supervisors, and teachers for the junior high school has been increasing in recent years.

II. Conclusions relative to pupil achievement

7. Pupils in junior high schools do as well in the fundamentals as pupils in schools under the 8-4 plan, even though they spend less time on these subjects because they take a number of new subjects and participate in extraclass activities.
8. Pupils from junior high schools do as well as those from other schools when they enter the senior high school.

III. Conclusions relative to guidance, meeting pupil needs, and retention of pupils

9. Better guidance personnel, facilities, and activities in grades seven and eight are provided.
10. It is easier to make provision for individual differences in the junior high school because the number of pupils in grades seven and eight is larger than in an elementary school.
11. There are usually more opportunities in both the curricular and the extraclass programs for pupils to explore their interests, abilities, and talents.
12. Pupils tend to remain in school longer, usually through the ninth grade.
13. There are fewer failures and less retardation in the junior high school, especially in the ninth grade.
14. Articulation between the elementary and the secondary school has improved in most communities where the junior high school has been introduced. However, much still needs to be done to achieve satisfactory articulation.
15. Although evidence is lacking on this point, many educators believe that the disciplinary situation, both in the elementary school and in grades seven and eight of the junior high school, is better when the older pupils are separated from the younger ones.
16. Ninth-grade pupils are less likely to develop early sophistication because they do not have contact with older high school pupils. Furthermore, they can usually participate more fully in pupil activities in the junior high school than in the four-year high school.

IV. Conclusions relative to housing and costs

17. Better building facilities, equipment, and athletic fields can be provided, especially for seventh- and eighth-grade pupils.
18. The cost of providing an adequate educational program for young adolescents is less in the junior high school. If comparable facilities were provided for grades seven and eight in the elementary school they would need to be duplicated in every school.[1]

Co-operative Study of Reorganization by the Staff. Those of the staff who will constitute the faculty of the new junior unit should be familiar with the theory, underlying principles, and details of practice involved. They should be encouraged to attend summer school or extension courses relating to the junior high school. Committees should be appointed to investigate different aspects of reorganization: for example, articulation with the senior high school and with the elementary school; junior high school student organizations and activities; educational and

[1]William T. Gruhn and Harl R. Douglass, *The Modern Junior High School* (Second Edition), New York, Ronald, 1956.

vocational guidance; provisions for individual differences; means of effecting gradual transition; and the reorganization of subject matter in the various departments of instruction. A series of meetings and conferences should be held during the year preceding the establishment of the school, for the complete orientation of the faculty and administration in junior high school purposes and practices. In such a series of meetings, lectures and discussions on the junior high school movement should precede reports of the various committees just mentioned.

In selecting the principal of the junior high school, care should be taken that he possess appropriate academic and professional training and a personality suitable for working with youngsters of junior high school age and with members of the junior high school staff; he should also be in full sympathy with the philosophy of the junior high school and cognizant of its objectives. In some school districts the principal is employed a year before the school is opened and he spends the year in working and planning for the new school: assisting in the planning of the building and the selection of equipment; working with teachers and others in planning curriculum, guidance service, and other specialized services; and employing people for these services.

In selecting the faculty for the new type of unit, more than ordinary care should be exercised. In addition to the conventional qualifications, special fitness, training, and experience for the junior high school procedure should be emphasized. The success of the school reorganization will depend largely upon getting a favorable start. The precedents set in the beginning years are likely to determine in great measure the procedures in a particular school and the concepts of junior high school education held by the staff and the community.

2. *The Six-Year Secondary School*

The very large majority of districts maintaining high schools, being small communities of less than 5000 people, should not establish separate junior and senior high schools. If reorganization is contemplated in these districts, it is most probable that a combined junior-senior high school should be established. At first the movement for reorganization promoted the 6-6 plan; only later was the 6-3-3 plan developed. In 1961 approximately two thirds of the more than 14,000 reorganized schools were organized as six-year schools, principally in small districts not large enough to have separate junior and senior high schools.

There is a definite tendency, when enrollments become large enough, for six-year schools to shift to the 6-3-3 plan.

Advantages and Disadvantages of the Six-Year School. The six-year school is without doubt more advantageous for the smaller system. Schools enrolling fewer than 400 pupils above grade 6 are not likely to find the 6-3-3 plan best adapted. The combination junior-senior high school plan of organization permits the following material economies:

1. The common use of equipment of special departments which would be in use only a portion of the day if separate schools were maintained: household-arts rooms and related equipment; rooms and equipment for instruction in music, art, and science.
2. The common use of certain expensive rooms and equipment: the gymnasium, the swimming pool, the auditorium, the library, and the administrative offices.
3. The economy realized in the construction of one large building instead of two smaller ones.

In addition, there are many important educational advantages, among them being the following:

1. The employment of one highly paid and well-trained high-school principal who will be able to devote all his time or a very large part of it to administrative and supervisory duties, rather than two less well-paid officials who spend a major share of their day in instructional duties.
2. The more complete departmentalization of the teaching staff, the members of which, if separate schools were established, would be required to teach two or more subjects.
3. Better articulation between the two schools:
   a. A more complete articulation of the subject matter in the two divisions, owing to the fact that members of the teaching staff of the various departments serve in both divisions.
   b. Easier arrangements for students who are ready for some tenth-grade subjects to go ahead with them while carrying ninth-grade subjects. This problem has proved an annoying one in schools organized on the 6-3-3 plan.
   c. Better articulation and more adequate provision for guidance service as a result of more continuous close contact with students by the staff.
4. The elimination of the necessity for transfer from one school to another at the end of the ninth grade; consequent encouragement for students to continue in high school after the completion of the junior division.
5. The possibility of promoting ninth-graders who are failing in one or more subjects.

The six-year school is open to certain dangers. One of these is the temptation to emphasize the student activities of the upper three or four grades and to neglect those of the lower grades. Another danger is the possibility that the staff will have a philosophy of education which is more suitable to the upper grades than it is to the junior high school level; furthermore, they may give more attention and effort to the teaching of the older students and neglect, at least slightly, the younger ones.

Administrative Practices. In 1958 a very thorough study was made of the practices of organization and administration in six-year schools.[2]

[2]Committee on Junior High-School Education, *The Junior High-School Grades in the Six-Year High School,* Washington, D.C., National Association of Secondary School Principals, 1958.

Questionnaires were filled out and returned by 2120 six-year schools. In addition, many of the questions in the check-list were asked of chosen specialists in secondary education – state department officers, professors of education, and directors of secondary schools in school systems. The following are the results of that study as reported:

> In 30 per cent of the schools there was no separation between the junior and senior high schools units; they were administered as one school. This arrangement was found predominantly in small schools. In the large majority of schools, however, there was separation of some of the activities of the junior high school and the senior high school units. Of the principals 39 per cent preferrèd to administer the school with separate junior and senior high school units. Specialists in secondary education were practically unaminous in believing that schools should be administered as far as possible as a unit.
>
> In 35 per cent of the schools the two units were assigned separate parts of the building; 57 per cent of the principals preferred that arrangement, as did the majority of the specialists.
>
> In practically all the schools the same administrative staff was responsible for both units. In the larger schools, however, it was fairly common to have an assistant principal for the junior high school or to have one for the junior high school unit and one for the senior high school unit. The latter practice was preferred by the principals and by 60 per cent of the specialists, although 18 per cent of the specialists favored having all of the administrative staff responsible for both junior and senior high schools.
>
> In all but the largest schools there was only one suite of administration offices used by both units. In a few of the larger schools there were separate administrative offices. Only 30 per cent of the principals indicated that they preferred the arrangement of separate offices and the specialists were almost equally divided on this point.
>
> In a great majority of the schools one bell schedule served both units; the use of the same schedule by both units was found particularly in the larger schools. However, only 50 per cent of the principals preferred the practice of using a common bell and common schedule. It is likely that a number of the junior high school principals wanted to go on the seven-period schedule, while the senior high school principals wanted a six-year schedule. About one fourth of the principals were undecided, while the secondary-school education specialists split almost evenly on this point.
>
> With respect to the student personnel records, a prevailing practice was to have one set of accumulative records for all students; this practice was recommended by a great majority of the principals and specialists.
>
> Although in a great majority of the schools teachers were assigned specifically to either the junior or the senior unit, in a great many of the smaller schools the majority of the teachers were assigned to a subject in both the junior and senior units. A great majority of the principals and three fourths of the specialists preferred to have teachers assigned specifically to one unit only. The prevailing practice is either to have department heads assigned to both units or to have no department heads at all. Only a few schools have separate department heads. A substantial minority of the principals preferred to have separate department heads; one fourth of the specialists recommended no department heads, but

the other specialists preferred the same department heads for both units.

It was almost a universal practice for the school nurse to be assigned to both units; this practice was preferred by the great majority of principals and specialists.

The prevailing practice was to have one coaching staff for both units, but a considerable number of schools had one director of athletics for the entire school and separate coaching staffs. This latter practice was used particularly in the larger schools. The principals preferred to have one director of athletics and separate coaching staffs, as did two thirds of the specialists.

A large majority of the schools had the same guidance staff, although in some of the larger schools there was a director of guidance with different counselors for the two units. This latter practice was strongly preferred by the principals and the specialists.

The usual policy was to have meetings of the entire faculty; however, a considerable number of the principals indicated a preference for both separate and joint meetings, as did the great majority of the specialists.

In practically all of the schools the salary schedule was the same for both units; this practice was preferred by the great majority of the principals and practically all of the specialists.

In a great majority of the schools the teachers in both units had similar class leads; most of the principals and practically all of the specialists preferred such a distribution.

The average class size in the junior high school unit was a little larger than that in the senior unit. The principals strongly preferred having the class size the same for both units, as did four fifths of the specialists.

While elective offerings in the academic subjects were usually given in grades 9 through 12, in one third of the schools they were given in only grades 10 through 12. The principals preferred to offer electives in all grades of both units and the specialists were divided on the point.

In a majority of the schools there was the same number of study periods weekly in both units, although in a substantial minority of the schools there were more study periods in the senior unit. This latter practice was preferred by most of the principals, although quite a few of them preferred to have no study periods at all. The specialists were almost equally divided between having no study periods in either unit, having more study periods in the senior unit, and having approximately the same number of study periods in both units. In practically all of the schools students were expected to do homework in all grades. The most common practice was to increase homework gradually from the seventh grade on up. In a considerable minority of the schools, however, the approximate amount of homework was the same for both units. Principals preferred a gradual increase in homework, as did the specialists.

In practically all of the schools the two units had equal access to the library, an arrangement preferred by a majority of the responding principals; a considerable minority preferred to have separate libraries, as did the specialists.

In all but a few schools the same marking system was used in both units; the principals preferred this practice, as did three fourths of the specialists.

Most schools provided separate junior and senior high school interscholastic athletic teams, although a few schools limited interscholastic competition to senior high school grades. Principals preferred separate teams, although quite a few principals preferred to have only a senior high school team; a slight majority of the specialists favored teams for the senior unit only. Basketball was by far the most popular sport for interscholastic competition in the junior schools; football, baseball, and track were also offered in quite a few schools; and a small number had touch football, swimming, tennis, and wrestling.

About half the principals believed that there should not be interscholastic junior teams of any kind; of those who believed in having them, about 30 per cent preferred basketball and track teams and about 20 per cent preferred baseball teams. Only a very few mentioned teams in regular football, golf, and wrestling. The usual practice was to permit participation of pupils in grades 9 through 12 on the senior high school interscholastic teams, although in about one fifth of the schools participation was limited to pupils in grades 10 through 12. This latter arrangement was found principally in the larger schools. The majority of the principals preferred to limit participation to grades 10 through 12, although more than one third of them favored participation in grades 9 through 12. Slightly more than one half of the specialists would limit participation to grades 10 through 12. In a majority of the schools, provision was made for the intramural athletics were separate teams for the junior and the senior high school units. However, in more than one fourth of the schools there was no planned program for intramural athletics at either level. Principals indicated clearly that they were in favor of intramural athletics with separate junior and senior high school teams, as did all but a few of the specialists.

There was apparently considerable conflict between preferred and actual practices in the use of gymnasiums and athletic fields. Although principals in general felt that the teams of both units should have equal access, almost one half of the principals reported that the senior high school unit was given the preference. More than half of the specialists believed in equal access, although a considerable number of them indicated the belief that each unit should have its own gymnasium and athletic field.

The prevailing practice was to have both units attend assemblies together, although in one fourth of the schools the policy was to have separate assemblies. The majority of principals, particularly those in charge of larger schools, believed in separate assemblies. An overwhelming majority of the specialists recommended separate assemblies.

In most schools there were separate clubs for the two units; the great majority of the principals and the specialists preferred this plan.

With respect to the student council, the most common practice was to have one council with equal representation from each unit. However, a considerable number of the schools had larger representation from the senior unit. About one half of the principals indicated a preference for one council for the entire school, but these principals were divided in their opinion concerning the amount of representation the junior high school should have. A great many principals preferred separate councils, as did one half of the specialists. Only a few of the specialists favored more representation for the senior unit.

There was usually only one school newspaper for both units; this plan was preferred by the great majority of the principals and the specialists. The same plan applied to the yearbook.

With respect to attendance at school social functions, the practice in 38 per cent of the schools was to have some social functions attended by pupils from both units but to schedule others separately. In almost as many schools students in both units attended the same social functions. Two thirds of the principals preferred either some or complete separation, as did all but a very few of the specialists.

Other Types of Organization. There is a small and decreasing number of schools in which elementary grades are housed with all six secondary grades, sometimes under a single principal. Since there are so few of these schools, they will not be considered in this volume.

There was a movement for a time towards the 6-4-4 organization, with a four-year junior high school and a four-year combined senior high school and junior college. Only a few schools, principally in California, adopted this type of organization, which was strongly recommended by a majority of the leading professors of secondary education. In recent years the trend has been away from this type of organization; except in a very few schools, it has disappeared. The 6-4-4 type of organization was opposed vigorously by sport fans and coaches, who found it difficult to organize interscholastic teams and develop schedules under the plan. It was also opposed by teachers in grades 13 and 14, who preferred to be considered as faculty members of a junior college.

3. *Small and Large Schools*

More than a fourth of all high schools enroll fewer than 85 pupils. The median enrollment is slightly less than 160 pupils. The great number of small schools is not the result of a conviction that small schools are more desirable; rather, it is a result of small high schools being preferable to no high schools in those sections of the country where larger high schools are impossible, owing to the sparseness of population and the lack of good roads which can be kept open the year round.

In addition, the continuance of many small schools may be attributed to certain other causes. Local pride often stands in the way of closing a small, inefficient, unattractive high school and providing transportation of pupils to a large school with better plant, staff, equipment, curriculum offerings, and social opportunities. Board members, merchants, and some parents may oppose the closing of the local school.

Limitations of the Small School. There are many reasons why it is logical to conclude that the small high school is less effective than the larger school. Chief among these are the following:

1. The period of training of the teaching staff is on the average slightly less than that of the teachers in larger schools. There are fewer teachers with substantial graduate training.
2. Teachers in the smaller schools are less experienced, include a very small percentage of men teachers, and are not likely to remain for more than two or three years.
3. The teaching load of teachers in small schools is usually greater than that of teachers in larger schools, as judged by *(a)* the number of classes taught daily, *(b)* the number of different daily preparations, *(c)* the number of different subjects taught, and *(d)* the number of subjects taught in fields in which the teacher is poorly trained.

4. The plant and equipment are inferior, in that *(a)* gymnasiums and auditoriums are inadequate or lacking and *(b)* science, shop, and library equipment is inadequate.
5. The curricular offerings are meager and afford less opportunity for exploration and for satisfying different pupil needs and interests, being confined often to a nucleus of academic, college-preparatory subjects.
6. The opportunities for extracurricular activities and for good guidance service are more limited, owing to a lack of pupils and an inadequacy of financial support.
7. The cost of instruction per pupil is greater than in larger schools.
8. Departmentalization of staff is difficult.
9. It is more difficult to provide good supervision, since the principal is apt to be engaged in teaching and administrative work and the superintendent is apt to be engaged in administrative work and supervision in the elementary school.

In addition to these items, there is the fact that the general tone and dignity of the larger school are usually more desirable, as are the opportunities for contacts which stimulate personal and social development. There are, nevertheless, important advantages in the small school, chief of which is the fact that the relationships between the students, the teachers, and the principal, as well as those among the students, are much more personal. The teachers and the principal know each student individually and are, therefore, able to teach and counsel him more effectively.

Scores on state and national achievement tests almost invariably show that students from smaller schools do not do as well on the average as those from larger schools. This fact, however, may not be entirely or even partly attributable to the conditions that exist in the smaller schools, since the intelligence or academic-ability test scores of students in smaller schools run on the average slightly below those of students from larger schools.

THE CONSOLIDATED SCHOOL. Because of the recognition of the limitations of the smaller school, a very steady swing toward replacing small schools with larger consolidated schools has been noticeable during the past three decades. With the continued and unprecedented development of good roads, which has resulted from the almost universal use of the automobile, the opportunities for consolidation have increased markedly.

It is impossible to operate a really good secondary school with less than 300 students, especially if the students differ greatly as to academic ability, college-going intentions, and vocational and other interests.[3] Every principal or superintendent of schools in a district maintaining a

[3]Dr. James B. Conant (in *The American High School Today*, New York, McGraw-Hill, 1959) strongly advises eliminating as many as possible of the senior and four-year schools which do not have at least 100 students in the twelfth grade, so that ability grouping may be put into effect.

high school of less than 200 students should carefully survey the possibilities of improving secondary education for the boys and girls of his district by means of consolidation with neighboring districts or high schools. To effect consolidation requires a very high type of leadership, since it runs so quickly afoul of local pride, intercommunity jealousies, and noneducational interests. Certainly no worthy administrator can discourage, much less oppose, a practical proposal for consolidation because of the possibility of his losing his position.

In recent years there has been a steady trend toward consolidation; before many years have passed, the very small high school will be a rare thing except in areas where the population is quite sparse and transportation in the winter quite difficult.

In many small districts it is quite probable that the best interests of the pupils would be served by transporting them for one or more years to larger schools close by. They may thus receive instruction in subjects which may not be economically offered in the local school.

SPECIAL AIDS FOR SMALL SCHOOLS. As a means of improving the quality of the educational program in very small high schools, a number of procedures have been followed, including: *(a)* provision for supervision of students carrying correspondence courses in some nearby college or university; *(b)* the common use of specialists in music, art, health education, guidance, and other fields by several small high schools in the same area, these specialists usually spending one or two days each week in each school they serve;[4] and *(c)* extension libraries of state departments of education which are circulated among the smaller schools in the state. Even where the devices for improving educational facilities of small schools are used, the small school still provides an educational opportunity which is inferior to that offered by a larger school.

THE OPTIMUM SIZE OF A HIGH SCHOOL. For many years there has been a tendency in cities to build large high-school buildings. To offer a rich program of secondary education economically, a secondary school must not be too small. In his doctoral study Mennozi gather opinions from 10 prominent recognized authorities and specialists in the area of schoolhouse planning and construction and school administration. The planners favored schools large enough to accommodate 750 to 1400 students, while the administrators preferred that schools be not quite so large.[5] As the enrollment and size of the building increases beyond 800 students, little of value may be added to the offerings. Indeed, certain disadvantages begin to accrue: teachers and pupils know each other as individuals less

[4]Information about the districts for such co-operative services that are organized in New York may be obtained from the Board of Co-operative Services, Chappaqua, New York.

[5]John C. Mennozi, *An Attempt to Determine the Optimum Size of Public Secondary Schools,* Doctor of Education dissertation, University of Denver, 1959.

well; students and teachers have farther to walk; more automobiles are used by students; and students have fewer opportunities to participate in extracurricular activities.

Oliver reported that his jury of experts, including 37 outstanding writers on secondary education and 72 outstanding principals, favored secondary schools of from 500 to 750 students as the optimum size (see Table 11). Junior high schools should probably be smaller, with an enrollment of 400 to 500 students. Administrators should urge boards of education to avoid the construction of buildings of larger size, and principles should restrain their ambitions to preside over schools too large to be most effective educationally.[6]

TABLE 11. *Opinions as to Most Desirable High-School Size*

OPINIONS OF	NUMBER OF PUPILS DESIRED IN A HIGH SCHOOL						
	200	300	400	500	750	1000	1500
Expert jury......	1	2	1	16	10	6	1
Field jury	2	4	5	16	8	6	0
Totals	3	6	6	32	18	12	1
Per cent	4.1	8	8	41	23	15.2	1

Oliver also recorded the opinions of his authorities as to what obstacles stand in the way of improvement in the small schools, as shown in Table 12.

TABLE 12. *Opinions as to Obstacles to Small-School Improvement*[7]

OBSTACLE	COMBINED JURY (EXPERT AND FIELD)	
	Weight*	Rank
Inadequate library	89	1
Lack of equipment	87	2.5
Teacher turnover	87	2.5
Low salaries	83	4
Inadequate health services	82	5
Inexperienced teachers	72	6.5
Inadequate supervision	72	6.5
Restricted extracurricular program	70	8
Inexperienced administrators	67	9
Community pressure for "old way"	66	10
Little chance for educational research	51	11
Too few teachers	50	12

*The weight was determined by giving two points for each single check, denoting "inherent," and one point for each double check, which denoted "very serious obstacle."

[6]Albert I. Oliver, Jr., "How Big Should the Small School Be?" *School and Society* (Feb. 19, 1949), Vol. 69, pp. 127-128.
[7]*Ibid,* pp. 122-123.

THE LARGE HIGH SCHOOL. In many densely populated cities high schools with large enrollments are to be found, many enrolling more than 1000 students and some enrolling more than 5000. Proponents of large secondary schools claim that:

1. Better libraries may be made available.
2. A greater variety of courses and curricula may be provided.
3. More specialized staff members may be provided, such as directors of health education, of guidance, of curriculum, and of extracurricular activities.

Opponents of large high schools argue that:

1. The relationship between pupil and teacher is too impersonal.
2. Interpupil acquaintances and relationships are less personal.
3. Many students are "lost" in big schools and do not feel that they belong.
4. Distances between home and school are too great.
5. Opportunities to participate in extracurricular activities are not as numerous.
6. A school need not enroll more than 700 or 800 students *(a)* to provide all the desirable courses and curricula and *(b)* to justify specialized staff members, though maybe some may have to teach a class or two.

THE SCHOOL-WITHIN-A-SCHOOL PLAN. In a number of communities (including Newton, Massachusetts; Fairfield, Connecticut; Highland Park, Michigan; and Atlanta, Georgia) large schools have been divided into three or more smaller autonomous divisions. Each of these divisions has its own student body, its own faculty of teachers and counselors (to a very large extent), and an administrator to act as principal under the general supervision of the principal of all of the small schools within the larger school. Although each of the smaller schools maintains a considerable amount of separateness and autonomy, there are general plans and regulations of administration, especially with respect to what courses are offered, what subjects are required for graduation, attendance regulations and procedures, the marking system, the nature of the reports to parents, and the record system.

Although assemblies are held for each small school, there are occasionally all-school assemblies. Also, although there are various types of teams and organizations such as bands, orchestras, and glee clubs in each school, there are usually all-school organizations such as the varsity athletic team, the school orchestra, and the all-school glee club. The obvious purpose of the school-within-a-school type of organization is to take advantage of the more personal relationships that exist in small schools and to avoid the extremely impersonal situation that exists in large schools.

4. Specialized and Comprehensive High Schools

DEVELOPMENT OF SPECIALIZED HIGH SCHOOLS. With the development of large city school systems (especially as the great tide of increasing high-school enrollments set in after 1890) many city school systems, finding it necessary to maintain not one or two but several high schools, thought it desirable to designate one or more of these as special types of schools, emphasizing certain types of curricula and catering to the needs of specialized groups of students. Though the most prominent of the early specialized institutions was the manual-training high school, others which came to be equally or more numerous were the high school of commerce, the high school of industrial arts for boys, the polytechnic high school, and the girls' high school, in which household arts and commercial courses were emphasized. In only the very large school districts is it practical to establish such specialized high schools. Until 1950 the high schools in New York City were chiefly specialized vocational or academic high schools. Since that time most of the new high schools built have with few exceptions been comprehensive institutions.[8]

ARGUMENTS AGAINST THE SPECIALIZED HIGH SCHOOL. The tendency to establish specialized high schools has met with vigorous opposition. It is maintained that the establishment of these schools:

1. Tends to break down the spirit and practice of democracy and the melting-pot function in American secondary education.
2. Tends to lessen the value of cultural training by concentrating on narrow, technical, bread-and-butter types of training.
3. Does not serve the needs of pupils as represented, because students usually attend the nearest high school without reference to its adaptability to their needs.
4. Develops economic class consciousness.
5. Emphasizes vocational education disproportionately and prepares more workers in certain vocational pursuits than industry and commerce will absorb.
6. Hastens a premature choice of vocation and the decision as to education beyond the high school.
7. Weakens the vocational departments in the comprehensive, general, or academic high schools.

CLAIMS MADE IN FAVOR OF THE SPECIALIZED HIGH SCHOOL. Very plausible arguments in favor of the specialized vocational high school have been advanced. Among them are the following:

1. Students electing vocational curricula in the comprehensive high schools become class conscious and are often discriminated against socially by students electing college-preparatory curricula.
2. Because the foregoing is true, many students elect general or college-preparatory curricula, though their real interests and needs demand vocational curricula.
3. The administration of most comprehensive schools is neither sympathetic toward programs of vocational education nor informed concerning them; as

[8]Dr. James B. Conant, in *The American High School Today,* strongly recommended the comprehensive high school.

a result, the realization of the most effective programs of vocational education is extremely difficult to achieve.

4. It is much easier to develop a desirable vocational morale in the specialized high school.
5. By concentrating vocational preparation for a city in specialized high schools, it is possible to provide adequate, if not exceptional, equipment and instruction, with less duplication and at not excessive cost.

In recent years many intellectuals and some ambitious parents have advocated a specialized academic high school to which only students with definitely superior scholastic ability would be admitted; the school would be concerned largely with preparation for college. In 1960 Robert J. Havighurst, Professor of Education at the University of Chicago, advocated specialized secondary schools in large cities, in order to promote "drastic changes to save the public schools from further severe deterioration in the nation's great cities." He urged the establishment of a set of academic high schools, which would serve the abler students in a large district, and a group of vocational high schools, which would admit boys and girls with average or better than average school records and interest in vocational work.[9]

School officials should give the matter most careful study before committing themselves to a specialized high school. Such a school may be of doubtful value; and, even if it is desirable, the location of the specialized high school and the selection of the vocation in which instruction is to be given in the light of the probable absorption of those trained are problems which demand a most careful and painstaking survey by people well trained in the technique of that type of activity.

5. *Nonpublic Schools*

TYPES. Nearly 15 per cent of the secondary-school students in the United States attend schools that are not financed by public taxation or controlled by any branch of the government. Enrollments in these schools have materially increased in recent years. With greater prosperity, parents have been able to pay the cost of their children's attending parochial schools and other nonpublic schools which specialize in preparation for college or boarding school. There are many types of nonpublic secondary schools and there is great variety in their quality and in the quality of achievement and academic status of their students and graduates. The following general classifications may be mentioned: (1) parochial schools (principally Catholic) which enroll more than one half of the students attending nonpublic schools; (2) preparatory secondary schools which have as their principal aim the preparation of students for colleges, particularly colleges which have higher standards of admissions

[9] "A Program to Save City Schools from Deterioration," *Phi Delta Kappan* (June, 1960), Vol. 32, p. 407.

and require college-entrance examinations; (3) boarding schools and country-day schools which have as a major purpose the preparation of students for college but also maintain social and moral education as an important objective; and (4) commercialized vocational schools for students of high-school age who are preparing for special occupations such as the repairing of automobiles and secretarial, clerical, and sales work.

FUNCTIONS OF NONPUBLIC SCHOOLS. Most nonpublic schools are somewhat more specialized than public schools in their function, aims, and values. This is particularly true of the schools operated by religious organizations which wish very much to imbue their students with a religious faith of a particular denomination. Some schools are primarily for the purpose of preparing students for college and give no courses in vocational education; in such schools general education for life is an incidental contribution. Some other schools exist primarily for the socialization of boys and girls, other aims being considered secondary. There are also boarding schools for boys or girls who may have become problem cases.

Some nonpublic schools are established in order to experiment with, to demonstrate, or to follow a progressive or otherwise specialized philosophy of education. They have proven very valuable in their work with various curricula and various methods of directing learning. Some schools offer to parents the satisfaction of having their boys and girls attend a school in which they will have as fellow students boys and girls of upper economic and social levels.

DIFFERENCES IN ADMINISTRATION. While in general the problems and techniques of administration of nonpublic schools are the same as or quite similar to those of public schools, they do differ, sometimes greatly, in certain respects. For example, there are important differences in the planning of housing and equipment between those schools which have no programs of vocational education and those schools which do. In schools in which all or practically all of the students enrolled are of superior scholastic ability, there is little or no need for ability grouping and the problem of the adaptation of learning activities to the individual is not so great. The teachers in nonpublic schools are not required to hold state certificates or to have professional training for their positions. While many of them do have such certificates and training, a great many of them do not. Tenure does not exist in any legal form in a majority of nonpublic schools. In contrast to the administration of public relations in public schools, the public-relations activity of nonpublic schools concentrates almost entirely upon the parents of students and little, if any, upon other taxpayers and citizens.

Salaries vary greatly in nonpublic schools. In some of these schools salaries are very high, much higher than those in public schools; however, in some nonpublic schools salaries are definitely below those in public secondary schools outside of some southern states. In some nonpublic schools teachers receive no definite salary since they are members of religious orders whose economic needs are taken care or by those orders.

In recent years the general level of nonpublic secondary schools has been raised. A great many of these schools have adopted ideas developed in the public schools. The amount of money available to nonpublic educational institutions has been greatly increased as a result of the much larger number of families in the United States who have a very greatly increased annual income. There have been in recent years much more co-operation and much greater interchange of ideas between teachers and administrators of public and nonpublic schools.

A number of studies have indicated that, on the whole, a student's attendance at a nonpublic preparatory school does not increase greatly the probability of his making high grades in college. It may, however, increase his chances of passing college-entrance board examinations and getting into college, particularly if he has definitely limited academic ability. Studies made of the relative academic achievement of graduates of public and nonpublic secondary schools in Yale, Princeton, Cornell, Amherst, and other colleges and universities have indicated that, although those coming from preparatory schools average a little better in the first semester, after the first year those from the public schools do better, a larger number of them being elected to honorary societies such as Phi Beta Kappa. Of course, the students attending such colleges and universities represent a much smaller percentage of all public-school graduates than of all nonpublic-school graduates. Perhaps what is indicated by the studies is that a student with good academic interest and ability is little penalized, if at all, by having attended a good public secondary school.

SUMMER SCHOOLS. In the great majority of the public secondary schools in the United States (in fact, in practically all except the smaller schools) there is a summer session of from six to ten weeks.

Characteristics of summer sessions that are of interest to the administrator are the following:

1. The large majority of the staff members are members of the regular school-year staff.
2. They are usually paid an additional salary, the ratio of which to the school-year salary is a little less than the ratio of the length of the summer session to the length of the regular session.
3. Students receive credits at about the rate of one unit for each six weeks or one and one-half units for eight or nine weeks, if they carry a full and intensive program.
4. The classes usually meet in the morning, beginning not later than 8:00 and sometimes as early as 7:30.
5. There are courses offered which carry no credit and are largely of a recreational or general-interest type. These include some adult-education courses.

6. There is a trend towards giving driver training during the summer session; apparently it can be given more cheaply then and without interfering with other subjects.
7. Class periods are usually two hours in length with a 5-minute break between classes.

The length of the summer term is almost always between six and ten weeks, usually about eight weeks. Usually no tuition is charged, but in some instances there is a small tuition, usually $15. Various kinds of classes are offered in summer schools, including the following: (1) make-up classes for students whose work was failing or at least highly unsatisfactory in one class during the previous semester or year; (2) classes for bright students who wish to graduate from high school in three years by carrying courses during the summertime; and (3) courses which are taken not primarily for credit but for recreation and interesting summer activities.

In the last group of summer-school classes will be found vocational agriculture projects; programs of distributive occupations; reading in the school library; musical groups practicing in the music studios for orchestras, bands, and concerts; swimming in the swimming pool; and games in the gymnasium and on the playgrounds. Also, in many places during the summer there are day camps organized for boys and girls, so that they may camp out during the day and return to their homes at night; also there are plans by which boys and girls may live at nearby recreational centers. In some schools during the summer experimental work is done by teachers with volunteer students.

Problems, Questions, and Exercises

1. How do you account for the fact that, although the 6-4-4 organization is highly recommended by authorities, it exists rarely in actual practice?
2. What claims made for the junior high school do you think are most clearly justified, which ones do you think are not justified or least well justified?
3. How small do you think a school ought to be to have a six-year plan? Do you believe that for a small school a 6-6 plan is better than 8-4? For what reasons?
4. How large ought a community be to support a good junior college? How would you go about studying a community to see if it was large enough to support a good community college?
5. What do you think are the principal purposes and functions of a community college?
6. What advantages are there to the small school?
7. What problems are special to the consolidated high school?
8. What do you think is the optimum size of the traditional four-year high school; the three-year junior high school; the three-year senior high school; the six-year secondary school?
9. Which of the arguments against and the claims in favor of the specialized high school do you think are most clearly valid?

10. Do you believe that we shall ever come to year-round secondary schools? What do you think the future has in store in that area?
11. Be able to discuss the place and administration of summer high-school programs.

Selected Supplementary References

Campbell, W. H., "Summer High School Survey," *Bulletin of the N.A.S.S.P.* (March, 1960), No. 254, pp. 44-49.

Condon, J. J., Gibbs, E. F., Perry, O. M., Tibbet, W. E., "How Can Summer Schools Enrich or Accelerate the Educational Program of Capable Students?" *Bulletin of the N.A.S.S.P.* (April, 1960), No. 255, pp. 121-129. [Practices at Porter Junior High School, Syracuse, New York; San Bernardino, California, High School; and William Penn Senior High School, York, Pennsylvania.]

Dorn, A. H., "Administrative Patterns in the Coinstitutional High Schools," *Catholic School Journal* (November, 1960), Vol. 60, pp. 37-41.

Douglass, Harl R., "The Role of the Junior High School," *Bulletin of the N.A.-S.S.P.* (April, 1952), Vol. 36, pp. 303-310. [Calls for recognition of the importance of social and emotional adjustment of youth and argues that the major role of the junior high school lies in providing continuity of such adjustment.]

Educational Policies Commission, "Community Colleges," *Education for All American Youth,* 1952, pp. 230-240, 305-307.

Fitzpatrick, E. A., "Reconstruction of Catholic Education," *Catholic School Journal* (November, 1960), Vol. 60, pp. 40-41.

Gaumnitz, Walter H., and Hull, J. Dan, "Junior High Schools Versus the Traditional (8-4) High School Organization," *Bulletin of the N.A.S.S.P.* (March, 1954), No. 201, pp. 112-121.

Gaumnitz, Walter H., and Langfett, R. Emerson, "How Can We Meet the Administrative Problems of the Small High School?" *Bulletin of the N.A.S.S.P.* (May, 1949), No. 163, pp. 173-184.

Gold, Milton J., and Robertson, Harley L., "'Classroom' in the Cascades," *Clearing House* (October, 1950), Vol. 25, No. 2, pp. 80-84. [Description of an outdoor education program for secondary youth in the State of Washington.]

Gruhn, William T., and Douglass, Harl R., *The Modern Junior High School* (Second Edition), New York, Ronald, 1956. [Chapter 1, "Growth of the Junior High School"; Chapter 2, "Philosophy of the Junior High School"; Chapter 3, "Advantages and Limitations of the Junior High School"; and Chapter 15, "Organization and Articulation."]

Gruhn, W. T., Tompkins, Ellsworth, Trump, J. L., and Roe, Virginia, "The Junior High-School Grades in the Six-Year High School," *Bulletin of the N.A.S.S.P.* (November, 1960), No. 259, pp. 46-78. [Report of the study referred to in this chapter.]

Hatch, Terrance E., "State Standards for Summer Programs in Secondary Schools," *Bulletin of the NASSP* (April, 1962), No. 273, pp. 72-82.

Heely, Allan V., *Why the Private School?* New York, Harper, 1951. [The headmaster of Lawrenceville School (New Jersey) tells what he thinks the private schools can contribute to American education.]

Herriott, M. E., "Organizing the Junior High School," *Bulletin of the N.A.S.S.P.* (December, 1951), Vol. 35, pp. 156-157. [Considers organization and administrative factors, suggests ways and means of improvement, and indicates some prevailing influences which are likely to produce transitions.]

The High School in a Changing World, Washington, D.C., American Association of School Administrators, 1958. [Chapter 7, "The Organization of the Secondary School."]

Jenkins, Albert O., "Administrative-Problems of Consolidated Schools with Grades One to Twelve," *Bulletin of the N.A.S.S.P.* (April, 1952), Vol. 36, pp. 143-146. [The difficulties and problems involved in consolidating small schools; the role of the new board of education; the new staff; tenure problems; curriculum, pupil adjustment, transportation, school lunch, and public relations; pitfalls and how to cope with them.]

The Junior High-School Grades in the Six Year High School, Washington, D.C., National Association of Secondary School Principals. [A project of the Committee on Junior High-School Education.]

McComb, Stuart F., "Why Pasadena Dropped 6-4-4 Plan," *Nation's Schools* (November, 1954), Vol. 54, No. 5, pp. 60-61. [Arguments for and against the 6-4-4 plan and reasons for shifting to 6-3-3-2 plan at Pasadena.]

"Middle School for Tomorrow; Successor to the Junior High School," *School Management* (November, 1960), Vol. 4, No. 11, p. 101.

Oliver, A. I., "How Big Should the Small School Be?" *School and Society* (February 19, 1949), Vol. 69, No. 1782, pp. 127-128. [A summary of opinions of leaders in secondary education.]

Phelps, Seth P., "A Community Looks at a High School Work Camp," *The School Review* (April, 1948), Vol. LVI, pp. 202-209.

"Place of the Private and Church Related Schools in American Education," *Progressive Education* (September, 1956), Vol. 33, pp. 152-154.

Quensel, Raymond H., "Staff Utilization with Talented Students in a Small High School During the Summer Months," *Bulletin of the N.A.S.S.P.* (January, 1959), No. 243, pp. 240-242.

Romney, Miles C., "Issues Challenging Educators and Citizens," *Bulletin of the N.A.S.S.P.* (September, 1960), No. 257, pp. 129-134. [Description of the "school-within-a-school" plan.]

Ryan, L. V., "Teachers and Administrators of Our Central Catholic High Schools," *Catholic School Journal* (November, 1958), Vol. 58, pp. 21-22.

Sales, M. V., "Some Legal Aspects of Public Summer High Schools," *Bulletin of the N.A.S.S.P.* (February, 1961), No. 262, pp. 62-66.

"San Diego's Year-Round School Camps," *School Management* (September, 1949), Vol. 19, pp. 6, 10-11.

Schmidt, C. D., "Administrative Practices in Large Six-Year High Schools," *Bulletin of the N.A.S.S.P.* (December, 1953), No. 198, pp. 82-86.

Shaw, Archibald B., "The Eight-Four Type of Organization," *School Executive* (October, 1948), Vol. 68, pp. 67-70. [Arguments for the eight-four plan: allows for fuller utilization of gymnasiums, auditoriums, workshops, home-economics department, etc.; allows children to enter high school before they are old enough to quit.]

Shuey, Audrey M., "Academic Success of Public and Private School Students in Randolph-Macon Women's College: I. The Freshman Year." *Journal of Educational Research* (March, 1956), Vol. 49, No. 7, pp. 481-492.

"Small Schools Needn't Be Weak Schools," *School Management* (March, 1960), Vol. 4, No. 3, pp. 64-66. [Tape-recorded interview.]

Ward, R. A., *Patterns of Administration in Diocesan School Systems,* Washington, D.C., Catholic University Press, 1957.
Whitcomb, Mildred, "A Living Laboratory for Improving Small High Schools," *Nation's Schools* (March, 1959), Vol. 63, No. 3, pp. 50-53.
"Work Experience Through Work Camps," *School Review* (October, 1949), Vol. 57, No. 8, pp. 391-396.
Wright, Grace S., and others, *Education Unlimited: A Community High School in Action,* Bulletin No. 5, Washington, D.C., Office of Education, 1951. [Shows how one small high school was able to overcome limitations of financial resources, inadequate plant and equipment, small enrollments, and restricted curriculum offerings.]

25

Evaluation of the Secondary School

1. Who Evaluates?

OUTSIDE AGENCIES AND INDIVIDUALS. Since about 1870 there have been in different sections of the United States organizations and institutions which have undertaken to evaluate secondary schools. In 1871 the University of Michigan became dissatisfied with the practice of selecting its students by means of entrance examinations and provided instead for the entrance to the university of students who had graduated from a selected group of schools which had been inspected and placed on a list of approved or accredited secondary schools. The University of Chicago developed a similar procedure in the 1890's and referred to certain schools as being "affliated with" the University of Chicago. Through this period a considerable number of universities developed lists of "accredited" schools within states, and, in the case of nonstate universities, within regions. In recent decades the state departments of education have taken over the accrediting of high schools within states.

In the early part of this century there was a development of regional accrediting associations; the North Central Association was established in 1905 and was followed by the Southern Association, the Middle States Association, and the Northwest Association of Colleges and Secondary Schools. The regional association would inspect schools upon invitation; those meeting the standards set up by the association would be placed on an accredited list. Graduates from these schools who had earned credits in the subjects required by a given college or university might be admitted to that institution without examination. The accrediting association set up standards upon the basis of which the schools would be selected and provided for visitors to inspect the schools and report the degree to which the schools met the standards.

The standards set by the accrediting associations and by the state departments of education were in the main stated in objective terms, so as not to leave too much to the discretion of the inspectors. Areas for inspection included such things as the school plant, the library, the laboratory and equipment, the school records, preparation of the staff, teaching load, pupil load, and the subjects offered.

STATE DEPARTMENTS OF EDUCATION. Since the accrediting associations did not provide for the accrediting of schools of less than four or five teachers, state departments became the sole accrediting agencies for the smaller schools, which in some states constituted the majority of the schools.

The state departments of education had unusual power, although they did not usually exercise it with great vigor; they distributed funds to the high schools of the state and could withhold state aid from a school in case the state standards were not met by the school.

LOCAL SUPERVISORS AND ADMINISTRATORS. Supervision and evaluation are carried on in most communities where high schools exist by supervisors and administrators, including the high-school principal and superintendent. The procedures of the supervisors and administrators have been various and have been far more subjective and subject to bias and guesswork than those of the accrediting associations. On the other hand, in recent years there has been an effort to make supervision and evaluation by administrators and supervisors more objective through the use of various kinds of objective tests and other measures of the growth and status of pupils. In fact, in many places far too much emphasis has been placed on subject-matter tests in the evaluation of the work of schools, departments, and teachers. Rating scales for evaluating teachers, plant, and other aspects of the school have been used widely.

EVALUATION BY TEACHERS. Particularly in recent years there has been much more dependence upon teachers themselves. Teachers have been encouraged to rate themselves and self-rating scales have been developed for the purpose.

For the purpose of gathering opinions of teachers a check list has been developed by Professor Harold Hand of the University of Illinois.[1] The teachers are asked to give their sex, their age group, the school in which they teach, and then their opinions on some seventy questions, including those which follow:

In general are you satisfied or dissatisfied with the school in which you teach? (Check one.)

_____ (1) Very well satisfied.
_____ (2) Satisfied.
_____ (3) About half and half.
_____ (4) Dissatisfied.
_____ (5) Very much dissatisfied.
_____ (6) I have no opinion.

Do differences in discipline among the teachers in your school (some too strict, others not strict enough) keep the pupils from getting as much as they could from their school work? (Check one.)

[1] Illinois Inventory of Teacher Opinion, from *What People Think about Their Schools*, New York, World Book, 1948, p. 195. This form is also published separately.

_____ (1) Yes.
_____ (2) Uncertain.
_____ (3) No.

How many of the teachers in your school seem to care about each pupil as a person who needs sympathetic understanding and attention? (Check one.)

_____ (1) All or almost all.
_____ (2) Most.
_____ (3) About half.
_____ (4) Few.
_____ (5) None or almost none.
_____ (6) I have no opinion.

Do you feel that the school does a good job or a poor job of telling the parents about the work of the school? (Check one.)

_____ (1) Very good.
_____ (2) Good.
_____ (3) Fair.
_____ (4) Poor.
_____ (5) Very poor.
_____ (6) I have no opinion.

All things considered, are you satisfied or dissatisfied with the way you are treated in the school in which you teach? (Check one.)

_____ (1) Very well satisfied.
_____ (2) Satisfied.
_____ (3) About half and half.
_____ (4) Dissatisfied.
_____ (5) Very much dissatisfied.

How often can you find enough time to prepare adequately for your teaching? (Check one.)

_____ (1) Always or almost always.
_____ (2) Usually.
_____ (3) About half the time.
_____ (4) Seldom.
_____ (5) Never or almost never.

All things considered, how good a job do you think the school in which you teach is doing? (Check one.)

_____ (1) Very good.
_____ (2) Good.
_____ (3) Fair.
_____ (4) Poor.
_____ (5) Very poor.

In general, how much help do you get from the administration with your discipline problems? (Check one.)

_____ (1) All or almost all of the help I need.
_____ (2) Most of the help I need.
_____ (3) Some of the help I need.
_____ (4) Very little of the help I need.
_____ (5) None or almost none of the help I need.

If you are not getting all the help you need with your discipline problems, what king of help do you need, and from whom? _____________________

What is the *one* thing you *like* most about your school? _____________________

What is the *one* think you *most dislike* about your school? _____________________

2. *What Should Be Evaluated?*

The most important thing to be evaluated is the progress that is being made towards the various aims and objectives of secondary education. Although such an evaluation is quite difficult to make, some effort must be spent in attempting to make it. Some good may result from an evaluation of the means by which a school is attempting to achieve it objectives of education—the qualifications of its staff, the school plant and equipment, for example.

It became obvious in the early history of accrediting that, if inspection and rating were to be done by outside agencies, it would be very desirable and most satisfactory to those rating to have standards set up in objective terms, so that there would be little room for opinion, bias, prejudice, or guesswork on the part of the inspector or rating individual or agency. Naturally, standards tended to be set up in terms of physical equipment. Laboratories were required to have certain standards with respect to tables, utilities, and equipment, such as one microscope to so many students, equipment for performing specific experiments in physics or chemistry, tools for students to use in the biological laboratory, a certain number of Bunsen burners, and so on.

Another objective and fairly easily checked type of standard was that which measured the preparation and load of the staff and the pupil load. Definite training standards were set for high-school teachers, including, usually, graduation from a college (in early years some states required only two years of college training), at least a modicum of training (set forth in terms of a certain number of semester hours in the subject taught), and a modicum of professional training (usually twelve to fifteen semester hours, although more has been required in recent decades).

EDUCATIONAL PROCEDURES. Used for evaluation by representatives of state departments of education and accrediting associations, as well as by supervisors, administrators, and others, have been the educational procedures employed in the schools. As means of evaluation these are employed more in surveys conducted by outside people who are attempting not to accredit but to assist the schools in improving organization, equipment, staff, and services.

The attempt to evaluate educational procedures results neither in an accurate measurement of the degree to which a school has attained the aims and functions of secondary education nor in an accurate picture of the quality of its services. It is quite difficult to arrive at any objective evaluation of procedures.

The procedures which are evaluated usually include such matters as methods of instruction, methods in discipline, and procedures in guidance and in work with extracurricular activities. The evaluation usually consists of observation of class instruction, counseling, and management of extracurricular activity.

The Pupil Product. One of the measures of the effectiveness of the school is the degree to which it retains its students through to the twelfth grade and graduation. Its success in this area, however, must be assessed in the light of the percentage of the youngsters who are of average or superior intelligence and the percentage of those who are of inferior intelligence. It also must be assessed in terms of financial and cultural background of the parents of the students. Naturally, the most logical approach to evaluation through the most valid type of data involves the obtaining of measures of the influence of educational experiences upon the all-round growth, the physical growth, the social growth, and the emotional growth of the pupil. Naturally, this type of data is difficult to get; in order to measure influence upon growth and behavior, it is necessary to follow the student out of school for a considerable number of years. In addition, it is extremely difficult to separate the influence of school-related experience upon growth and behavior from the influence of experience which is not school-related but received before, after, and during the student's attendance at school.

A way to measure the pupil product is to follow up the students who have left the school and get data which are indicative of the degree of success they have had in life, including their experience in the vocations for which they made special preparation and their experience in college. Use should be made of the records of students who went to college, including data on how they succeeded in the courses which they took there, how many graduated from college, and how many went on to graduate work.

Another means of measuring the product of the schools is the use of subject-matter tests in the various subjects of instruction. Most of these tests do not measure the progress toward all the objectives of the subject; rather, they concentrate almost exclusively upon the acquisition of information and subject-matter skills. They do not measure applications to life; they usually do not measure, except in a very minor way, growth or status in attitudes, interests, ideals, emotional balance, social adjustment, and other very important types of educational outcomes. They rarely measure understandings and the ability to apply to problems in life has been learned in school.

The use of test results as means of evaluating the school is not to be condemned entirely; but certainly it is only one of a considerable number of approaches to evaluation and, if employed alone or highly emphasized, will do much to cause teachers to select course-of-study materials and learning activities which are not at all to be recommended as means of assisting young people to grow toward the stated objectives of secondary education.

It is desirable to continue the progress that has been made in the direction of attempting to measure the effect of schooling upon the growth of high-school students, particularly in their participation in life activities.

EVALUATION ON THE BASIS OF PUPIL NEEDS. A considerable number of high-school principals and others concerned professionally with secondary education have in recent years attached great significance to the consideration of pupil needs as a means of setting up the objectives of the secondary-school program and of providing standards by which the quality of the program may be judged. The Educational Policies Commission and the National Association of Secondary School Principals set up a list of ten important educational needs of youth, which they termed the imperative needs of youth. William L. Ransom prepared a check list of characteristics by which may be indicated the degree to which a secondary school contributes to the imperative needs of youth.[2] Copies of this check list may be obtained from the National Association of Secondary School Principals, 1201 Sixteenth Street, N.W., Washington, D.C., for $.20 each, with discounts on quantity orders.

The ten needs are as follows:

1. All youth need to develop salable skills and those understandings and attitudes that make the worker an intelligent and productive participant in economic life. To this end, most youth need supervised work experience as well as education in the skills and knowledge of their occupations.
2. All youth need to develop and maintain good health and physical fitness.
3. All youth need to understand the rights and duties of a citizen of a democratic society, and to be diligent and competent in the performance of their obligations as members of the community and citizens of the state and nation, and of the world.
4. All youth need to understand the significance of the family for the individual and society and the conditions conducive to successful family life.
5. All youth need to know how to purchase and use goods and services intelligently, understanding both the values received by the consumer and the economic consequences of their acts.
6. All youth need to understand the methods of science, the influence of science on human life, and the main scientific facts concerning the nature of the world and of man.
7. All youth need opportunities to develop their capacities to appreciate beauty in literature, art, music, and nature.
8. All youth need to be able to use their leisure time well and to budget it wisely, balancing activities that yield satisfaction to the individual with those that are socially useful.
9. All youth need to develop respect for other persons, to grow in their insight into ethical values and principles, and to be able to live and work co-operatively with others.

[2]William L. Ransom, "How Well Does Your High School Rate on the Ten Imperative Needs of Youth?" *Bulletin of the N.A.S.S.P.* (October, 1949), Vol. 33, No. 164. pp. 8-46.

10. All youth need to grow in their ability to think rationally, to express their thoughts clearly, and to read and listen with understanding.[3]

Check lists are provided for each of the ten imperative needs. In a considerable number of secondary schools, committees of teachers and other members of the staff have employed these check lists to review and evaluate the program of their schools as it contributes to important objectives of modern secondary education. Following are representative excerpts from the check list for Imperative Need Number 2:

IMPERATIVE NEED NUMBER 2*

All Youth Need to Develop and Maintain Good Health and Physical Fitness.

	N	1	2	3	4	5
1. The school provides for varied physical activities and encourages students to participate, not only for the physical exercise but also to provide for active social life and satisfying leisure-time activities	☐	☐	☐	☐	☐	☐
2. The school provides for periodic physical examinations covering all students and leading to corrective action as needed	☐	☐	☐	☐	☐	☐
3. Health records of individuals are complete and up-to-date, and pertinent facts are made known to those responsible for any pupil's guidance	☐	☐	☐	☐	☐	☐
4. The school approaches the problem of the unadjusted youth as it does the physically ill, seeking causes and making provisions leading to satisfactory adjustments	☐	☐	☐	☐	☐	☐
5. The school designs its health program to stimulate and supplement home health care – not to supplant it	☐	☐	☐	☐	☐	☐
6. Courses entitled "Health" may be offered for all, but health instruction pervades the school program and is continuous, directly or indirectly, throughout the pupil's school life	☐	☐	☐	☐	☐	☐
7. The school, recognizing the importance of mental health, supports student activities of a nonphysical recreation type if they answer social and/or emotional needs of pupils	☐	☐	☐	☐	☐	☐

**Key:* N. This characteristic does not apply in this situation; 1. Very inferior in this characteristic; 2. Inferior in this characteristic; 3. Average in this characteristic; 4. Superior in this characteristic; 5. Very superior in this characteristic.

3. The Evaluative Criteria and Their Use

THE CO-OPERATIVE DEVELOPMENT OF EVALUATIVE CRITERIA. In the late 1930's various regional associations made a co-operative study of

[3]See Will French and William L. Ransom, "Evaluating the Curriculum for Provision for the Imperative Needs of the Youth," *Bulletin of the N.A.S.S.P.* (April, 1948), No. 144, pp. 48-69.

standards that might be used for accrediting the schools.[4] This study showed a definite tendency to get away from the objective criteria which measure such things as staff preparation and equipment and neglect the functioning of the school. In 1940, 1950, and 1960 there was published, as a result of the co-operative study of secondary school standards, a manual containing procedures, forms, and instructions for gathering data and opinions necessary to any evaluation.[5] The manual contains descriptions of procedures for self-evaluation and evaluation by visiting committees, suggestions for reports on evaluation, and suggested activities to follow evaluation. It contains schedules for evaluation of such things as pupil population of the school community, educational needs of youth, program of studies in each subject field (including pupil-activity program), library services, guidance services, school plant, school staff and administration, and schedules for each individual staff member; there is also a statistical summary of evaluation. Following is a statement of the scope of the criteria employed:

THE SCOPE OF THE CRITERIA

Philosophy and Objectives
1. Statement of Philosophy and Objectives
2. Procedures Followed in Development of Philosophy and Objectives
3. Comments on the School's Statements of Philosophy and Objectives

School and Community
1. Basic Data Regarding Pupils
    A. Enrolled Pupils and Graduates
    B. Age-Grade Distribution
    C. Mental Ability
    D. Stability
    E. Withdrawals
    F. Educational Intentions
    G. Occupational Intentions
    H. Follow-up Data of Graduates (Class of 19____)
2. Basic Data Regarding the Community
    A. Population Data for the School Community
    B. Occupational Status of Adults
    C. Educational Status of Adults
    D. Financial Resources – Public Schools
    E. Financial Resources – Nonpublic Schools
    F. Rural Pupils
    G. Composition of the Community
3. Community Agencies Affecting Education
    A. Educational Agencies
    B. Recreational Opportunities
    C. Civic Organizations
    D. Health and Sanitation Facilities

[4]The study was made by the Northwest, North Central, Southern, and Middle States Associations of Colleges and Secondary Schools. Membership in these associations is voluntary and selective.

[5]*Evaluative Criteria,* Washington, D.C., National Study of Secondary School Evaluation, 1960.

4. Procedures

Program of Studies

1. Organization
2. Curriculum Development Procedures
3. Subject Offerings
   A. Extent of Subject Offerings
   B. General Characteristics of Program
   C. Instructional Activities
   D. Methods of Evaluation
4. General Outcomes of the Program of Studies
5. Special Characteristics of the Program of Studies
6. General Evaluation of Program of Studies[6]

There is for each of the subject divisions in the school a check list similar to that shown for Mathematics:

MATHEMATICS

1. Organization.
   A. Courses in mathematics are required of all students in grades 7, 8, and 9.
   B. Courses in mathematics are provided for all students in grades 10, 11, and 12.
   C. Courses are available throughout the secondary school program to suit the student's ability and to meet his academic and vocational needs.
   D. The mathematics teacher advises students about mathematics and assists them in the selection of the proper courses.
   E. Each mathematics course is based upon instruction which has preceded it and is preparation for courses that follow.
   F. Provision is made for students to prepare for advanced standing in mathematics.
   G. Provision is made for the transfer of students from one mathematics sequence to another.
   H. Courses are organized to recognize the related areas in which the student may be enrolled, such as science, business, shop, and agriculture.
2. Nature of Offerings
3. Physical Facilities
4. Direction of Learning
   A. Instructional Staff
   B. Instructional Activities
   C. Instructional Materials
   D. Methods of Evaluation
5. Outcomes
6. Special Characteristics of Mathematics
7. General Evaluation of Instruction in Mathematics[7]

In addition to the sections for the various subject fields, there are sections such as "Health Education," "Driver Education," "Religion," and "The Core Program." In the blank to the left of each of the items in the check list, one making an evaluation places the number 1, 3, or 5: 5 indi-

[6]*Ibid.*, pp. 25-59.
[7]*Ibid.*, pp. 167-176.

cates that this criterion is met splendidly; 3 indicates that it is met tolerably well; and 1 indicates that it is met not well at all. This evaluation is done first by the local committees; then the visiting committee reviews these ratings, perhaps drawing a line through a rating made by a local committee and placing its own rating at the left of it.

OTHER AREAS. In addition to sections on the curricular part of the school program, *Evaluative Criteria* includes sections such as "Student Activity Program," "Instructional Materials Services—Library and Audio-Visual," "Guidance Services," "Health Services," "School Plant," and "School Staff and Administration."

Evaluative Criteria may be employed for self-evaluation without the visitation of a committee from the regional association. Of course, self-evaluation alone is not likely to be so fruitful or useful as the evaluation of outside people.

PROCEDURE IN EVALUATION. Since procedure is described rather clearly in *Evaluative Criteria,* the reader is referred to that manual for details; in general, however, the following points summarize the basic procedure for evaluation:

1. A school wishing to be evaluated applies to a state committee of the regional association.
2. The committee sets a tentative date for the evaluation, usually almost two years from the time the application is made.
3. To the staff of the school wishing evaluation there are delivered forms and instructions for preparing a statement of the objectives and philosophy of the school; also a group may prepare a statement on the school and the community, on the basis of data which will be submitted to the evaluating committee. Forms are also sent for self-evaluation by each member of the staff of the local school and by the various committees concerned with student-activity programs, instructional-materials service (library and audio-visual), guidance services, health service, school plant, and staff administration.
4. After the staff subcommittees have done all the work on self-evaluation sheets (which should be delivered to the regional association to allow ample time for study), a date is set for a visiting committee. The visiting committee will be composed of from nine to sixteen members, depending upon the size of the school, and will be made up of representatives of the regional accrediting association and the state department of education, appropriate faculty members of colleges and universities, and carefully selected members of the administrative, library, guidance, health, and teaching staffs of good secondary schools in the state.
5. The chairman of the visiting committee should visit the school prior to the date of the visit of the evaluating committee and go over the self-evaluation work to see that it has been done in such a manner as to make the visit of the entire committee fruitful and practical.
6. The chairman requests the members of the visiting committee that he has chosen to express their preference in assignments of responsibility when the school is visited. Committee members may indicate their first, second,

and third choices. The chairman of the committee works out the appointments co-operatively with the head of the school.

7. The head of the school to be visited sends a complete list of visitors who have accepted to each member of the visiting committee so that plans for sharing transportation can be made. At the same time he inquires from each visitor what and when sleeping accommodations will be required.
8. The head of the school to be visited should send materials about the school to be visited to each member of the committee as soon as is convenient, at least a week before the date of the visit.
9. A school making preparations for entertaining a visiting committee should keep in mind the time-consuming tasks which the committee faces and their desire to do a superior job. Arrangements should not be made for sightseeing or other "extracurricular activities" during the visitation; if possible, arrangements should be made for meals in the building.

During the visitation, the various members of the committee, in accord with the arrangements which have been made in advance, will concentrate upon different parts of the school, although there will no doubt be some discussion among committee members across the somewhat artificial lines of division. Included in this chapter is a suggested schedule for a visiting committee.

While most visits last for three days, some last for four or even five days. The entire committee usually comes together for introductions and organizational formation on the evening before the first day of visitation. Conferences may be made which do not appear on the schedule shown here; for example, a conference about health services may be arranged with school nurses and other health officers. Members of some committees may wish to talk with individual teachers at the end of the first day; they may want to visit them in departmental groups.

As may be noted in the schedule shown here, the various subcommittees report to the whole committee on each of the three visitation days; these reports are combined by the chairman of the visiting committee into a total report on the whole school and submitted with a letter of transmission. Frequently, the oral report is omitted so that the members of the staff of the local school may recover from their excitement before detailed reports are made to them.

SUGGESTED VISITING-COMMITTEE SCHEDULE

First Day		*Room Number*
8:00 – 8:20	Introduction of visitors to high school staff	____________
8:30 – 9:00	Organization meeting	
9:00 – 9:15	Report by chairman of high school's self-evaluation committee on Section B (Report may be made by the principal or headmaster.)	
9:15 – 9:30	Report by chairman of high school's self-evaluation committee on Section C (This report may be made	

	by the principal or headmaster.)	
9:30 – 2:30	Visiting classes, lunch at _____ (hour) in ______________________	
2:30	Tour of plant by I Subcommittee with staff member as guide	
2:40	Student activity conference: E Subcommittee with student representatives of all or selected activity groups	____________
2:40	Library conference: F Subcommittee with high school's library staff, including student assistants and representatives of the English and social studies department	____________
2:40	Guidance conference: G Subcommittee with counselors and other high school staff members connected with guidance department	____________
4:00 – 6:00	Subcommittee meetings and review of appropriate blanks	
6:00	Dinner	
7:00	Final report of I Subcommittee	
8:30	Final report of F Subcommittee	
Second Day		
8:30 – 2:30	Continue visiting classes; lunch at _________ (hour)	
2:40	Curriculum conference: D Subcommittee with heads of departments	____________
2:40	Student activity conference: E Subcommittee with faculty sponsors of all or selected student activities	____________
2:40	Guidance conference: G Subcommittee with a group of students (6-10) selected at random by visiting committee	____________
2:40	J Subcommittee with principal and administrative assistants	____________
4:00 – 6:00	Subcommittee meetings and review of their blanks	
6:00	Dinner	
7:00	Final report of E Subcommittee	
8:30	Final report of G and H Subcommittees	
Third Day		
8:30 – 10:30	Continue visiting classes	
10:30	All written reports on curricular areas (D-1 – D-19) submitted to chairman	
10:30	Final report of J Subcommittee	
_____	Lunch	
12:45	Final report of D Subcommittee and brief reports from all subject area	

(D-1 – D-19) subcommittees
3:45 Oral report, all staff members of the high school invited[8] ____________

THE FOLLOW-UP. Since several days of a considerable number of busy people are involved in a survey of a school, it would be unfortunate if some use were not made of a visiting committee's suggestions.

In *Evaluative Criteria* the following recommendations are made for a follow-up.[9]

1. The principal should become familiar with the information contained in the written report and pass on to appropriate members of his staff, according to his discretion in the matter, the parts of the report in which they would be interested.
2. The staff should study the graphic summary of the evaluation, checking the high and the low points and comments in the written report.
3. Committees that were appointed to carry on the original evaluation, or other committees appointed by the principal, should follow up the report with recommendations for improving the work of the school in their particular phase of interest.
4. There should be faculty meetings and group discussions in which questions such as the following will be considered.
   A. What desirable element makes these areas good?
   B. How can we go about seeing that this same success is carried into other fields?
   C. Is the difficulty due to administration? Student reactions? Lack of teacher interest? Lack of finances? Or simply oversight?
   D. Have we perhaps made no one definitely responsible for the items listed?
   E. Would a change in sponsors help the situation?
   F. Who will be responsible for improving the program from now on?
   G. Why should they be done in this school?
   H. Who should do them?
   I. How and when do we plan to start?
   J. How can we determine the success of our efforts?
   K. Why are they not applicable to this school?
   L. If changes could be made to bring about conditions where they might be possible, would such changes be worth the effort?
   M. Will the students suffer if these conditions are neglected?

EVALUATIVE CRITERIA FOR JUNIOR HIGH SCHOOLS. Although the manual *Evaluative Criteria* may be used for junior high schools, many junior high school principals do not believe that it is quite suitable for use in the evaluation of junior high schools. In recent years there has been developed in several states (notably Utah, Connecticut, Oklahoma, California, and Texas) a set of evaluative criteria especially adapted to

[8]*Ibid.*, p. 12.
[9]*Ibid.*, p. 17.

junior high schools.[10] Each junior high school principal should obtain copies of at least one publication which presents evaluative criteria for junior high schools; he should use these criteria in evaluating and thinking about his school and the various aspects of its program.

The results of a study of possible accreditation of junior high schools by the North Central Association of Secondary Schools were reported by Stephen A. Romine, Dean of the School of Education of the University of Colorado. In 1960 the answers indicated on questionnaires showed that, of the administrators questioned, 66 per cent of the junior high school principals were in favor of accreditation, 62 per cent of the superintendents of districts having junior high schools also favored it, 20 per cent of each group were in opposition, and 14 per cent of the principals and 18 per cent of the superintendents were uncertain.

Although these responses indicated general approval of accreditation, further study will be made of the organizational patterns of junior high schools, the purposes for which they may be accredited, some of the processes which may be utilized, and the names of resource personnel in the states in the area of the North Central Association.

LOCALLY CONSTRUCTED CRITERIA. There is nothing particularly magic in the standards presented by *Evaluative Criteria*. They constitute criteria and procedures which have grown out of the experiences of hundreds of people who have been concerned with the evaluation of secondary schools; they are thus of great value in the evaluation of schools. A local school faculty may well prepare its own criteria. People particularly interested in various aspects of the school—such as staff preparation and load, extracurricular activities, guidance, English in the schools, program of studies, and so forth—may develop a set of criteria for judging the school and its product. To be sure of the development of good criteria there should be a considerable length of time spent in examining the best books that have been written on the various subjects and in organizing and revising the first draft of criteria.

In addition, it must be remembered that the use of evaluative criteria should not preclude studies of the former students of the school or of the opinions of teachers, parents, or students, as indicated in the earlier sections of this chapter.

In evaluating and comparing teaching loads, *Evaluative Criteria* has failed to provide means for very careful assessment of the loads of different teachers; the omission is apparently based on the assumption that the nature of the subject taught and the size of the class have no important bearing upon the load of any given teacher. Formulas are evidently considered to be too complicated for practical school administrators.

---

[10]Information about publications containing these criteria may be obtained from the state departments of education in the states mentioned.

Interpreting Data Relative to Any Criteria. It is obvious that the interpretation of data gathered in evaluation is the critical part of the whole procedure. Any interpretation of the efforts of a school to provide a superior educational program should be made in the light of particular community needs and the resources of the community (financial and otherwise) for developing a plant, staff, and procedures of the ideal or desired type, it being quite obvious that there is among districts great variation in the ability to support a program. Some districts maintaining high schools possess ten times the per-capita wealth and per-capita income of others in the same state; it is not at all uncommon for some high schools to be three or four times as wealthy as others in the same county.

In addition, it is clear that an educational program should be adapted somewhat to local community needs: what might pass as unimportant in one community might be regarded as definitely important in another because of the peculiar community needs.

Originally, inspections by state committees using evaluative criteria were for the purpose of selecting schools which produced graduates who could be expected to do satisfactory work in college and could, therefore, safely be admitted without examinations, as long as they had studied the subjects required for admission. However, evaluations by local staffs and visiting committees are very valuable in stimulating thought in the field of improving the school—its facilities, staff, and procedures. Indeed, as time goes on, evaluative criteria may be more used for purposes other than accreditation, particularly since many colleges and universities now are requiring that all students take entrance examinations.

According to Ely and others, the great majority of teachers in schools that have been evaluated by outside committees have agreed that the evaluation was a useful experience and that the evaluating-committee members were adequately qualified. Ely urges that teachers should be well oriented and acquainted with the problems and procedures of the evaluation before it begins. Self-evaluation should be carried out without tension and under leadership which will prevent undue apprehension on the part of teachers.[11]

Problems, Questions, and Exercises

1. Do you believe that the accrediting system by state or regional accrediting associations should be continued much longer? If so, by which or by both?
2. What do you think is the best method or combination of methods by which to evaluate a secondary school?
3. Describe the part you think parents ought to play in the evaluation of

[11]Laurence E. Ely, "Teachers' Reactions to School Evaluations Using Evaluative Criteria," *Bulletin of the N.A.S.S.P.* (December, 1959), Vol. 43, pp. 38-43.

school and how the principal might employ their assistance.

4. Do you believe that in the evaluation of secondary schools much attention should be given to the physical side—for example, plant, library, and so forth?
5. How would you go about using the "Ten Imperative Needs"; to what extent do you think they constitute a complete basis for the evaluation of a secondary school?
6. Be prepared to give a complete description of how to organize and operate a co-operative survey of the school employing evaluating criteria.
7. To what extent and in what way do you think the students themselves could be employed in evaluation? The former students? The teaching staff?
8. Draw up plans and criteria for evaluating one of the following: the library and its operation, the cafeteria, the guidance program, the extracurricular program, interscholastic athletics, the health program, the transportation program, the test and record system, marking and reporting to parents.
9. In what ways do you think evaluative criteria for junior high schools should be different from evaluative criteria for four-year schools?
10. Do you believe that the use of evaluative criteria for junior high schools might lead to the unfortunate practice of accrediting junior high schools for the purpose of college admissions.
11. Do you think that evaluative criteria and procedures should be used by visiting committees to identify superior junior high schools and thus encourage other junior high schools to improve their facilities or program?
12. How do you think a board of education might evaluate its local school or schools? Should the board avoid evaluation and rely on reports from the superintendent and the principal?

Selected Supplementary Readings

Aikin, Wilford, *The Story of the Eight-Year Study,* New York, Harper, 1942. [A report of the results of the experiment in thirty secondary schools, with abundant data for evaluation of the results of progressive practices.]

"Check Points for Principals," *Bulletin of the N.A.S.S.P.* (September, 1960), No. 257, pp. 37-38. [A check list by which principals may evaluate themselves as leaders in public relations.]

Educational Policies Commission, "Evaluation of Schools," *Education for All American Youth,* 1952, pp. 360-380.

French, Will, *Adapting the Secondary-School Program to the Needs of Youth,* Fifty-second Yearbook, Part I, National Society for the Study of Education, University of Chicago Press, 1953. [Chapter 16 presents bases for deciding what characteristics secondary schools should have; characteristics of a youth-oriented school.]

Hand, Harold C., *Prospectus of the Local Area Consensus Studies,* Circular Series A, No. 51, Illinois Secondary-School Curriculum Program, Bulletin No. 15, Springfield, Illinois, Office of the Superintendent of Public Instruction, March, 1951.

Hodge, Leslie W., "The Effect of Evaluation: Accreditation at Bakersfield," *California Journal of Secondary Education* (November, 1959), Vol. 34, pp. 433-436.

Lane, Robert J., *An Assessment Guide for Use in Junior High Schools,* Hartford, Connecticut, State Department of Education, 1960.
Reinert, P. C., "Administrative Self-Appraisal," *Catholic School Journal* (March, 1959), Vol. 59, pp. 65-67.
Romine, Stephen, "Opinions about North Central Association Accreditation of Junior High Schools," *The North Central Association Quarterly* (Fall, 1961), Vol. XXXVI, No. 2, pp. 193-200.
Texas Junior High School Criteria Study, Austin, Texas, University of Texas Press, 1954. [Criteria for evaluating junior high schools.]
Trump, J. L., "Two Instruments for Evaluating Junior High Schools," *Bulletin of the N.A.S.S.P.* (November, 1960), No. 259, pp. 130-135. [Brief description of the Utah criteria and the Anderson criteria for self-evaluation.]
Unruh, Adolph, "Improvement Program for Nine High Schools," *Nation's Schools* (October, 1954), Vol. 54, No. 2, pp. 55-58.
Winget, Lerue, and others, *Junior High School Evaluative Criteria,* Salt Lake City, Utah, State Department of Public Instruction, 1960.

Topic Index

Author Index

*—Bibliographical Reference

B C D E F G H I J 7 0 6 9 8 7 6 5 4
PRINTED IN THE UNITED STATES OF AMERICA